Kylie Crabbe
**Luke/Acts and the End of History**

Beihefte zur Zeitschrift
für die neutestamentliche
Wissenschaft

Edited by
Matthias Konradt, Judith Lieu, Laura Nasrallah,
Jens Schröter and Gregory E. Sterling

Volume 238

Kylie Crabbe

# Luke/Acts and the End of History

DE GRUYTER

ISBN 978-3-11-076331-7
e-ISBN (PDF) 978-3-11-061519-7
e-ISBN (EPUB) 978-3-11-061475-6
ISSN 0171-6441

**Library of Congress Control Number:** 2019944332

**Bibliographic information published by the Deutsche Nationalbibliothek**
The Deutsche Nationalbibliothek lists this publication in the Deutsche Nationalbibliografie; detailed bibliographic data are available on the Internet at http://dnb.dnb.de.

© 2021 Walter de Gruyter GmbH, Berlin/Boston
This volume is text- and page-identical with the hardback published in 2019.
Printing and binding: CPI books GmbH, Leck

www.degruyter.com

*To*
*Merrilyn, Peter,*
*Delia, Maree, and Narelle Crabbe*

# Preface

This book began as a nagging question, posed well before I began my doctoral work: how do ancient writers make sense of experience, especially negative experience? For reasons that I hope will become obvious, this became a set of questions about how texts portray the structure of time, what they say about divine and human agency in history, and why Luke/Acts in particular has been at the centre of controversy over just these questions. I became fascinated by the ways the post-war context had shaped the most influential of modern Lukan scholars and their concepts of delayed parousia, *theologia gloria*, and salvation-historical paradigms. When I found these same ideas embedded deep within the assumptions and footnotes of contemporary commentaries and introductory textbooks, this book—or, more precisely, the 2017 Oxford doctoral dissertation on which it is based—started to take shape.

By examining Luke/Acts alongside ten contemporaneous texts, I hope to illuminate these themes of history, time, and divine and human agency. These are themes which, in turn, are essential for understanding other matters—like how ancient writers explain experience, including negative experience, and their approaches to hope, politics, and divine justice. As well as having something helpful to say about these themes in Luke/Acts, my hope is that this study is a way of hosting a conversation about these big ideas, and about how we go about doing Lukan studies when it comes to these kinds of questions.

This book is itself the product of many earlier conversations. It is also the product of the support and care of a great number of people, to whom I owe much more than these notes of thanks can say.

To my doctoral supervisors, Christopher Rowland and Markus Bockmuehl, I owe a great debt of thanks. They were ideal supervisors, excellent individually and formidable in combination. Chris's careful questioning in the early stages of my project sharpened my questions; Markus's insightful suggestions for further reading likewise shaped my thinking and research. They both have a deep familiarity with an extraordinary range of primary texts, and discussions with them helped me to identify the scholarly patterns and assumptions that lay behind so much of what I was wanting to question about Luke/Acts. Emails and conversations with Chris retain his characteristic mix of intellectual insight and pastoral depth. I'm similarly appreciative of Markus's consistent work with me in the years following Chris's retirement, for his absolute commitment to supporting my professional development as well as my doctoral project, and for his kindness.

Given the breadth of my project, I have boldly enlisted the expertise of scholars from diverse areas, and I am very grateful for the good humour and excellent advice particularly of Barnaby Taylor, Tristan Franklinos, and Tessa Rajak. Loren Stuckenbruck offered enthusiastic support of my project and a prepublication copy of his recent work on time in Second Temple Judaism and the New Testament, and John Barclay generously engaged with me about his work on 4 Ezra. Martin Bauspieß and Michael Tilley happily made themselves available to discuss Lukan eschatology in and around Tübingen, and Michael Wolter has been a great encouragement ever since he gave the response to a related paper I presented in Bonn. I'm also much obliged to the classicists who welcomed me into the Princeton-Oxford Classics conference and gave me helpful feedback, as well as to the communities of biblical scholars who gave me feedback on papers related to parts of this work, including the British New Testament Society Acts session, the Society of Biblical Literature Acts session, the New Testament graduate and senior seminars at Oxford, and the members of the Texts, Traditions, and Early Christian Identities team at Australian Catholic University.

I am grateful to my examiners, Loveday Alexander and Teresa Morgan, as well as to those who gave feedback on my doctoral project at the earlier internal stages of assessment: David Lincicum, Mary Marshall, and Christopher Tuckett. I also welcomed comments from two anonymous reviewers on behalf of the BZNW series editors. Together they have all helped to strengthen, refine, and correct my work; any remaining weaknesses are all my own doing. I have been privileged with an amazing team of proof-readers, both for the thesis and the finished book. Thanks go to the marvellous Nicholas Moore (who read and commented on a considerable proportion of the thesis manuscript), Christine Joynes, Jenny Crane, Sarah Leeser, Roosmarijn de Geus, Sarah Apetrei, and Sam Kiss. And my sincere thanks to Martin Wright, who was not daunted by the book's longer manuscript, producing indexes and identifying errors with characteristic efficiency, accuracy, and good humour. I am also grateful for the care and efficient work of the de Gruyter editorial team and the BZNW series editors.

Over the course of this project, I have been the grateful recipient of generous financial support from the Clarendon fund, the Keble Association, Ivens-Franklin Travel Fund, Alan Stockbridge Award, Squire and Marriott Bursaries, Crewdson Fund, and a bursary from Gladstone's library. Academic communities have supported me in manifold ways; I'm grateful for the communities at Keble and Trinity Colleges and ACU, and the extraordinary hospitality of Jenny Read-Heimerdinger, who welcomed me into her research house in Wales for an intense week of writing.

Thanks are due to those who supported my academic work in earlier stages, particularly Brendan Byrne, who taught me to read Luke in new ways and supervised my Masters thesis, and Dorothy Lee, who taught me many things, not least the surprising reality that NT Greek reading could be a good class with which to ease back into study after a bereavement! And thanks to Sean Winter, who encouraged me to consider the outlandish possibility of undertaking doctoral work in the UK.

Finally, to the communities who have supported me through this time of research and the long road that led to it: thank you. For all those who have shared meals over the years, exchanged tense messages over particularly frustrating chapters, or discussed the frivolous and the divine, shared joy and profound grief, and politics and faith and theodicy—thank you, and may the conversation (and meals) continue! Whether in Oxford or in Melbourne I have been so fortunate to have extraordinary friends around me, and—conscious of the inadequacy of any list of names—I would like particularly to thank: Sam Kiss, Roosmarijn de Geus, Jenny Crane, Robbie Davies, David Bowkett, Ellie Healey, Liam Gannon, Alma Brodersen, Jennifer Strawbridge, Sarah Apetrei, Christine Joynes, Mary Marshall, Jonathan Downing, Donovan Schaefer, Megan Dent, Anik Laferriere, Sarah Leeser, Kirk Robson, Mavis Robson, Peter Robson, Nicole Batch, Joel Townsend, Annie Quail, Naomi Flanagan, Tara Shackell, Melina Shackell, Anita Major, Martin Wright, Sally Douglas, Andy Hamilton, Alistair Macrae, Clare Boyd Macrae, Robyn Whitaker, Sharon Hollis, and so many others I could name but "I suppose the world itself could not contain the books that would be written" if I were to do so. I will simply hope that you really do all know, whether named or not, what a very great deal you mean to me.

And it is with deep appreciation that I thank those to whom I dedicate this work: my parents, Merrilyn and Peter, and my sisters, Delia, Maree, and Narelle Crabbe. You have been there through thick and thin, and I'm so grateful.

# Contents

**Abbreviations —— XV**

**Translations —— XVII**

**Chapter 1: Introduction —— 1**
1      A note on nomenclature —— 2
2      Hans Conzelmann and post-war debates about uneschatological Luke —— 3
2.1    The reception of Conzelmann's work —— 6
2.2    Oscar Cullmann and a linear schema of history and its end —— 9
3      Genre, rhetoric, and Graeco-Roman comparisons —— 14
4      This study —— 19

**Chapter 2: Genre, themes that transcend genre, and the approach of this study —— 21**
1      The importance and limits of genre —— 21
1.1    Ancient and contemporary genre theory and practice —— 23
1.2    Maintaining precision regarding genre —— 28
1.3    Views shared across ancient texts of different genres —— 29
2      This study's approach to examining Luke's conception of history —— 32
2.1    Mapping understandings of history in Luke's context —— 32
2.2    Building a series of detailed case studies —— 33
2.3    Expanding the scope of texts relevant to Luke's cultural context —— 35
3      The case study texts —— 37
3.1    Texts chosen for analysis —— 40
3.2    Texts omitted from detailed discussion —— 51
3.3    General approach to Luke/Acts —— 54
4      The aspects of history discussed in the following chapters —— 56

**Chapter 3: The direction and shape of history —— 57**
1      Introduction: the importance of schemas of history —— 57
2      Texts without a sense of an endpoint to history —— 63
2.1    Hints of positive progress in history —— 63
2.2    Steady continuation of history —— 73
2.3    Decline in history —— 76

| 3 | Periodised history with an end —— 80 |
|---|---|
| 3.1 | Progress to the end of history —— 82 |
| 3.2 | Steady continuation of history with an end —— 87 |
| 3.3 | Decline in teleological history —— 107 |
| 4 | Periodised and teleological history in Luke/Acts —— 113 |
| 4.1 | Times and periods in Luke/Acts —— 115 |
| 4.2 | Teleological history in Luke/Acts —— 129 |
| 4.3 | The direction of history in Luke/Acts —— 132 |
| 5 | Conclusion —— 133 |

## Chapter 4: Determinism and divine guidance of history —— 135

| 1 | Introduction —— 135 |
|---|---|
| 2 | The forces in history —— 138 |
| 2.1 | τύχη/*fortuna* —— 140 |
| 2.2 | πρόνοια/*providentia* —— 146 |
| 2.3 | εἱμαρμένη/*fatum* —— 149 |
| 2.4 | ἀνάγκη/*necessitas* —— 154 |
| 2.5 | δεῖ —— 157 |
| 2.6 | Summary: personal and impersonal forces in history —— 164 |
| 3 | Prophetic insights into the future —— 166 |
| 3.1 | Prophetic insights according to Polybius, Diodorus, Valerius, and Tacitus —— 166 |
| 3.2 | Prophecy in Virgil's *Aeneid* —— 170 |
| 3.3 | Prophecy, determinism, and divine guidance in the study's remaining texts —— 172 |
| 3.4 | Summary: prophetic signs and determinism —— 183 |
| 4 | Prophetic insight and the divine plan in Luke/Acts —— 184 |
| 4.1 | Prophecy in Luke/Acts: interpreting the past and assuring for the future —— 185 |
| 4.2 | Assurance of the divine βουλή in Luke/Acts —— 192 |
| 5 | Conclusion —— 203 |

## Chapter 5: Human responsibility and freedom —— 205

| 1 | Introduction —— 205 |
|---|---|
| 2 | Interactions of, or conflicts between, divine and human agency —— 208 |
| 3 | Engaging with Deuteronomistic approaches to divine and human agency —— 212 |
| 3.1 | Deuteronomistic approaches —— 213 |

| 3.2 | Extensions of Deuteronomistic themes in late Second Temple texts —— 217 |
|---|---|
| 3.3 | Other spiritual forces in late Second Temple texts —— 229 |
| 3.4 | Θεομάχοι —— 231 |
| 4 | Divine and human responsibility in other texts —— 235 |
| 4.1 | Human responsibility and divine action —— 235 |
| 4.2 | The divine *as* the opponent —— 239 |
| 5 | Summary: divine and human agency in the key texts —— 241 |
| 6 | Interactions between divine and human agency in Luke/Acts —— 242 |
| 6.1 | Attributions of responsibility in explanations of the past —— 243 |
| 6.2 | Θεομάχοι in Luke/Acts —— 246 |
| 6.3 | Human response and reversal in Luke/Acts —— 251 |
| 7 | Conclusion: human response in Luke/Acts —— 266 |

**Chapter 6: The present and the end of history —— 269**

| 1 | Introduction —— 269 |
|---|---|
| 2 | The present and the future in non-teleological texts —— 272 |
| 3 | The historical present *is* the *telos*: Virgil's *Aeneid* —— 276 |
| 3.1 | Virgil's portrait of the end —— 276 |
| 3.2 | The significance of the "now" in the *Aeneid* —— 278 |
| 3.3 | The consequences of aligning the present with the end —— 281 |
| 4 | The present and the end of history in late Second Temple texts —— 283 |
| 4.1 | The relationship between the present and the end —— 283 |
| 4.2 | Consequences of the dynamic relationship between the present and the end —— 296 |
| 5 | The present and the end of history in Luke/Acts —— 301 |
| 5.1 | The events of the end in Luke/Acts —— 301 |
| 5.2 | The placement of the present in Luke's schema of history —— 303 |
| 5.3 | The character of life in the present according to Luke —— 309 |
| 6 | Conclusion: hope, politics, and invitation at the end of history —— 330 |

**Chapter 7: Conclusion —— 336**

| 1 | Luke's eschatology and its effects —— 336 |
|---|---|
| 2 | Assessment of method —— 339 |
| 3 | Salvation history and post-war concerns —— 342 |

**Appendices —— 345**
Appendix 1: ὁ αἰών in the Gospels and Acts —— **345**
Appendix 2: ὁ καιρός in the Gospels and Acts —— **346**
Appendix 3: ὁ χρόνος in the Gospels and Acts —— **347**
Appendix 4: ἡ ὥρα in the Gospels and Acts —— **348**
Appendix 5: ἡ ἡμέρα in the Gospels and Acts —— **349**

**Bibliography —— 353**

**Index of ancient sources —— 380**

**Index of modern authors —— 408**

**Index of subjects —— 414**

# Abbreviations

Abbreviations used in this monograph are in keeping with *The SBL Handbook of Style*, 2nd ed. (Atlanta: Society of Biblical Literature, 2014). The following specifies abbreviations for items that this style guide does not include.

    I use English titles for Classical texts, in keeping with the Loeb Classical Library.

### Abbreviations for ancient sources

| | |
|---|---|
| Diod. *Library* | Diodorus Siculus, *Library of History* |
| Polyb. *Hist.* | Polybius, *The Histories* |
| *Doings* | Valerius Maximus, *Memorable Doings and Sayings* |

### Other abbreviations

| | |
|---|---|
| *OED* | *Oxford English Dictionary*, Oxford University Press |

# Translations

Unless otherwise specified, the New Revised Standard Version is used for biblical citations throughout, and the Loeb Classical Library wherever relevant for other texts. The key texts of the study are quoted from the following translations (full details in the bibliography).

Loeb Classical Library editions:
Diodorus Siculus, *The Library of History*, trans. C. H. Oldfather.
Josephus, trans. H. St. J. Thackeray.
Polybius, *The Histories*, trans. W. R. Paton, F. A. Walbank, and Christian Habicht.
Tacitus, *The Histories and Annals*, trans. Clifford H. Moore and John Jackson.
Valerius Maximus, *Memorable Doings and Sayings*, trans. D. R. Shackleton Bailey.
Virgil, trans. H. R. Fairclough and G. P. Goold.

The New Revised Standard Version:
2 Maccabees
4 Ezra
Luke/Acts

Other texts:
The Dead Sea Scrolls, trans. Florentino García Martínez and Eibert J. C. Tigchelaar.
2 Baruch, trans. A. F. J. Klijn.

# Chapter 1:
# Introduction

"Everything began with history and eschatology."[1] So François Bovon commences his authoritative summary of fifty-five years of Lukan studies. On the subsequent pages he evokes the tightly-wound series of problems through which interpreters have troubled over, and even reprimanded, Luke.[2] Bovon deftly captures a core issue: divergent views of Luke's purpose and the major themes of his *Doppelwerk*, such as his portrayal of the plan of God, are bound up in assessments of Luke's eschatological consciousness (or alleged lack thereof).[3] In this monograph I argue that Luke's eschatology—that is, his understanding of the end of history—is indeed central to this whole suite of issues, as Luke explains the past, offers assurance for the future, and exhorts appropriate human response in the present. Furthermore, by setting Luke/Acts[4] alongside a broad range of ancient sources, I demonstrate that separating history from eschatology in Luke/Acts is a false distinction.

Two broad strands of Lukan scholarship have contributed to common misrepresentations of Lukan eschatology. Influential mid-twentieth-century scholarship placed Luke within a presumed trajectory of decreasing eschatological interest and increasing focus on the day-to-day matters of the church over the generations following the first disciples.[5] Drawing on polemical contrasts between Paul and Luke and accentuating synoptic differences, these studies portrayed Luke as distinctively uneschatological within the NT.[6] More recent studies have particularly considered the genre of Luke/Acts instead, tending to empha-

---

[1] François Bovon, *Luke the Theologian: Fifty-Five Years of Research*, 2nd ed. (Waco, TX: Baylor University Press, 2006), 11. That these words appear under the heading "the Plan of God" is also pertinent.
[2] The title of Kümmel's article, "Current Theological Accusations against Luke," exemplifies this attitude towards Luke (Werner Georg Kümmel, "Current Theological Accusations against Luke," *ANQ* 16 (1975): 131–45).
[3] Bovon describes conflicting assessments, according to which interpreters variously claim that Luke suggests humans are left to their own devices by an absent (ascended) Christ, or portrays people as "puppets" to an all-encompassing divine plan (Bovon, *Luke the Theologian*, 12).
[4] On my use of Luke/Acts, rather than Luke-Acts, see below pp. 54–55.
[5] Although avoiding the label *Frühkatholizismus*, Conzelmann even uses his assessment of Luke's position on this trajectory to date Luke/Acts (Hans Conzelmann, "Luke's Place in the Development of Early Christianity," in *Studies in Luke-Acts: Essays Presented in Honor of Paul Schubert*, ed. Leander E. Keck and J. Louis Martyn (Nashville: Abingdon Press, 1966), 302–7).
[6] See §2 below.

sise certain similarities to non-Jewish Graeco-Roman texts, while overlooking themes (such as those of an eschatological character) that these texts do not share.[7] In different ways, each of these two strands has influenced an enduring tendency to underestimate the centrality of eschatology for understanding Luke/Acts.

Expanding the range of ancient sources suitable for pertinent comparison, this study investigates how understandings of history in the Graeco-Roman period illuminate Lukan eschatology. The analysis underscores Luke's periodised and teleological schema of history, the important continuities and differences in Luke's portrayal of divine and human agency in history, and how all of these features are shaped by Luke's understanding of the relationship between the end of history and the present time. I argue that the resultant insight into history in Luke/Acts clarifies not only Lukan eschatology, but related concerns or *effects* of his eschatology: Luke's politics and approach to suffering.

## 1 A note on nomenclature

Throughout this study I use "history" in its philosophical sense to denote understandings of the whole "course of human affairs,"[8] also encompassing elements of a writer's understanding of time that may extend beyond affairs in which humans are involved. A schema of history can include a conception not only of the beginning and the end of history, but also, for instance, events *beyond* the end of history. Additionally, throughout the discussion I reserve the term "historiography" for a literary genre of texts that give an account of events.[9] This definition does not challenge the legitimacy of the other dictionary meanings for "historiography" (in addition to "written history" the OED includes "the writing of history" and "the study of history-writing").[10] Neither does my limited use of "history" undermine other meanings of the term. I am simply attempting a measure of clarity in a work that will make considerable use of so many related terms by excluding these other meanings from the present discussion. I use "end" to mean the "termination, conclusion,"[11] while recognising that this can be portrayed in diverse ways when related to history, some of which also include a

---

7 See §3 below.
8 *OED* definition II 7b.
9 On definitions of literary genre, see Chapter 2, §1.1.
10 *OED* definitions 1 and 2.
11 *OED* definition II 7a.

sense of "goal"; on the varied ways in which ancient writers portray the "end" of history, see Chapter 3.

## 2 Hans Conzelmann and post-war debates about uneschatological Luke

Shortly following the Second World War, in which he himself was injured, Hans Conzelmann (1915–1989) published a work which would profoundly shape the conversation within, and assumptions of, Lukan studies.[12] In *Die Mitte der Zeit*, Conzelmann argued that Luke responded to a crisis caused by the parousia's delay[13] by distancing his narrative from imminent eschatological expectation and focusing instead on the time of the early church as a new salvation-historical period. For Conzelmann, this separation of history from eschatology reflected the evangelist's distortion of the primitive kerygma.[14] It is important

---

[12] Conzelmann's doctorate on geographical features of Luke was completed in 1951; his habilitation was then published in 1954, as *Die Mitte der Zeit: Studien zur Theologie des Lukas* (BHT 17 (Tübingen: Mohr Siebeck, 1954)), which incorporated the geographical themes but became particularly renowned for the later parts of the argument, which dealt with Luke's eschatology and understanding of salvation history. (The book was translated into English as *The Theology of St Luke* in 1960, trans. Geoffrey Buswell (London: Faber, 1960)). See also Conzelmann, "Zur Lukasanalyse," *ZTK* 49 (1952): 16–33, which introduced key themes.
[13] Kim rightly points out that imminent expectation of the parousia (*Naherwartung*) and delay of the parousia are scholarly, not ancient, terms (Young Ho Kim, *Die Parusie bei Lukas: Eine literarisch-exegetische Untersuchung zu den Parusieaussagen im lukanischen Doppelwerk*, BZNW 217 (Berlin: de Gruyter, 2016), 49), and that Lukan eschatology cannot be reduced to this kind of dichotomy (pp. 50–51).
[14] Disdain for Luke's perceived compromise of the radical message of the early discipleship movement is shared by numerous contemporaneous scholars, including Philipp Vielhauer, "Zum 'Paulinismus' der Apostelgeschichte," *EvT* 10 (1950–1951): 14–15; Rudolf Bultmann, *Theology of the New Testament*, trans. Kendrick Grobel (London: SCM, 1952–1955), 2:116–18; Bultmann, *History and Eschatology*, The Gifford Lectures 1955 (Edinburgh: Edinburgh University Press, 1957), 38–39; Ernst Käsemann, "Das Problem des historischen Jesus," *ZTK* 51 (1954): 136–38, 141; Käsemann, "Neutestamentliche Fragen von Heute," *ZTK* 54 (1957): 20–21; Erich Grässer, "Das Problem der Parusieverzögerung in den synoptischen Evangelien und in der Apostelgeschichte," in *Les Actes des Apôtres: Traditions, Rédaction, Théologie*, ed. Jacob Kremer, BETL 48 (Gembloux: Duculot; Leuven: Leuven University Press, 1979), 125–27; Ernst Haenchen, *The Acts of the Apostles: A Commentary*, trans. Bernard Noble, Gerald Shinn, and R. McL. Wilson (Oxford: Blackwell, 1971), 116; Günter Klein, "Lukas, 1, 1–4 als theologisches Programm," in *Zeit und Geschichte: Dankesgabe an Rudolf Bultmann zum 80. Geburtstag*, ed. E. Dinkler (Tübingen: Mohr, 1964), 214–15; and John Drury, *Tradition and Design in Luke's Gospel: A Study in Early Christian Historiography* (London: Darton, Longman & Todd, 1976), 12. Conzelmann notes the importance

that Conzelmann's work is understood in its own historical context: this was not an endorsement of Lukan theology, but reflected Conzelmann's grave concerns about what he perceived as Luke's project of identifying the divine purpose with the events of history. Concomitantly, Conzelmann posited that the shift from eschatological expectation to salvation history had steered Luke's politics and understanding of suffering.[15]

The claims put forward in *Die Mitte der Zeit* were not new in every respect.[16] Scholars such as Albert Schweitzer[17] and one of Conzelmann's great influences, Rudolf Bultmann,[18] had already advanced theories about the delayed parousia and its consequences for early Christian communities and NT texts. Likewise,

---

of comparison with the Pastoral epistles (Conzelmann, *Luke's Place*, 303). Bultmann judges that Luke represents a developing "Christian-bourgeois piety" (Bultmann, *Theology of the New Testament*, 2:114). As Drury aptly summarises, "Luke has drawn upon himself the hatred of some modern theologians who have good reason to suspect such a marriage of God's will with history" (Drury, *Tradition and Design*, 12).

**15** Conzelmann discusses the role of salvation history in Luke's "political apologetic" towards Rome (Conzelmann, *Theology of St Luke*, 137–49) and, although classifying the change as "unconscious modification rather than … conscious alteration (*unbewußte Erweichung als eine bewußte Gestaltung*)," he interprets, for instance, θλῖψις in Luke/Acts, as an uneschatological and extended experience of suffering for believers, rather than the sign of the end as in Matthew and Mark (pp. 98–99; 3rd German edition, *Die Mitte der Zeit* (1960), 89). Throughout, life in this extended period is explained by a divine plan to history—even the suffering which Conzelmann attributes to necessity through his interpretation of ἀνάγκη (p. 98). Barrett notes precursors to the view that Luke does not feature *theologia crucis* (C. K. Barrett, "Theologia Crucis—In Acts?", in *Theologia Crucis—Signum Crucis: Festschrift für Erich Dinkler zum 70. Geburtstag*, ed. Carl Andresen and Günter Klein (Tübingen: Mohr Siebeck, 1979), 73–75), though he concludes himself that Luke does not engage with such themes particularly theologically (p. 84).
**16** This study only considers Conzelmann and his reception in order to highlight the initial debate about history and eschatology and the assumptions which endure in contemporary commentaries and studies. For detailed accounts of this period of scholarship, see Bovon, *Luke the Theologian*, 11–85; Joel B. Green and Michael C. McKeever, *Luke-Acts and New Testament Historiography*, IBR Bibliographies 8 (Grand Rapids: Baker, 1994), 35–45, 71–78; Robert Maddox, *The Purpose of Luke-Acts*, SNTW (Edinburgh: T&T Clark, 1982), 100–102; John T. Carroll, *Response to the End of History: Eschatology and Situation in Luke-Acts*, SBLDS 92 (Atlanta: Scholars Press, 1988), 1–30; Scott Shauf, *Theology as History, History as Theology: Paul in Ephesus in Acts 19*, BZNW 133 (Berlin: de Gruyter, 2005), 4–84. Note, however, that each of these helpful summaries remains shaped by its own framework—for instance, even Bovon's magisterial annotated bibliography criticises studies that do not have a strong redaction-critical focus and maintains that Luke anticipated an extended delay of the parousia (p. 58).
**17** Albert Schweitzer, *The Quest of the Historical Jesus: A Critical Study of Its Progress from Reimarus to Wrede*, trans. William Montgomery (London: Black, 1910), 358; Schweitzer, *The Mysticism of Paul the Apostle*, trans. William Montgomery (London: Black, 1931), 334–39.
**18** Bultmann, *Theology of the New Testament*, 2:111–18.

## §2 Hans Conzelmann and post-war debates about uneschatological Luke — 5

as Conzelmann theorised about Luke's reasons for focusing on a historical account (especially in narrating the life of the early church in Acts), he cited Philipp Vielhauer's earlier argument: that simply by *writing* a narrative of the early church in Acts, Luke demonstrated a turn to focus on history instead of eschatology.[19] But Conzelmann was responsible for at least two significant developments. Giving prominence to his new redaction-critical method, he claimed to have demonstrated Luke's systematic tendency to remove expectation of the imminent parousia from his sources.[20] And he developed a detailed account of Luke's schema of salvation history, which he identified as Luke's "solution" to this delay:

> If Luke has definitely abandoned belief in the early expectation, what does he offer on the positive side as an adequate solution of the problem? An outline of the successive stages in redemptive history (*der gegliederten Kontinuität der Heilsgeschichte*) according to God's plan.[21]

Conzelmann thus proposed a threefold structure of history (the times of Israel, Jesus, and the church), arguing Luke has moved the time of Jesus from the end of history to "*die Mitte*."[22]

---

[19] In an early footnote, Conzelmann cites Vielhauer appreciatively: "How uneschatological Luke's thinking is is proved not only by the contents, but by the very fact of the Acts of the Apostles" (Conzelmann, *Theology of St Luke*, 14 n. 1; Vielhauer, "Zum 'Paulinismus,'" 14). See Käsemann, "Neutestamentliche Fragen," 20–21; Bultmann, *Theology of the New Testament*, 2:117; Siegfried Schulz, *Die Stunde der Botschaft: Einführung in die Theologie der vier Evangelisten*, (Hamburg: Furche, 1967), 293; Haenchen, *The Acts of the Apostles*, 94. Such comparisons of Luke and Paul go back to Baur (see discussion in Haenchen, *The Acts of the Apostles*, 16–17) and are already embedded in these treatments, cf. Vielhauer, "Zum 'Paulinismus,'" 1–15; Ulrich Wilckens, "Interpreting Luke-Acts in a Period of Existentialist Theology," in Keck and Martyn, *Studies in Luke-Acts*, 67–69; Conzelmann, *Luke's Place*, 307–9. They also feature in later work (Joel B. Green, *The Theology of the Gospel of Luke*, New Testament Theology (Cambridge: Cambridge University Press, 1995), 126–27). Bultmann distinguishes between Luke and the other synoptic evangelists, whom he describes as "preachers and teachers" in their presentation of the good news, while Luke is a "historian" (Bultmann, *History and Eschatology*, 38).

[20] Conzelmann reverses Bultmann's interest in peeling back the evangelists' additions to reveal the historical Jesus, instead accenting *alterations* to highlight Luke's beliefs, thus contributing to the development of redaction criticism (Charles H. Talbert, "Conzelmann, Hans Georg (1915–1989)," *DMBI* 325).

[21] Conzelmann, *Theology of St Luke*, 135 (3rd German edition, *Die Mitte der Zeit* (1960), 127).

[22] He further divides Jesus' life into three periods (Conzelmann, *Theology of St Luke*, 17). This aspect of Conzelmann's theory has not endured (Joseph A. Fitzmyer, *The Gospel according to Luke: A New Translation with Introduction and Commentary*, AB 28 & 28 A (New York: Doubleday, 1981–1985), 1:183); it conflates Luke's narrative structure with salvation-historical periodisation.

Conzelmann rightly identified the importance of both periodisation and the divine plan to Luke's understanding of history. However, in light of his assumptions about Luke's situation and his negative assessment of what he perceived to be Luke's project, he overlooked continuities between Luke's understanding of history and other contemporaneous writers,[23] with serious ramifications for his influential representation of Lukan eschatology and its effects. For instance, Conzelmann took periodisation to be a characteristically Lukan modification, whereas this feature is shared by texts from Jewish apocalypses to Diodorus's historiography.[24] Moreover, historical apocalypses demonstrate that expectations of an imminent end are not mutually exclusive with a periodised schema of history overseen by a divine plan. When Luke's portrayal of history is placed within a broader context, I suggest, a quite different view of Lukan eschatology emerges.

## 2.1 The reception of Conzelmann's work

The significance of Conzelmann's contribution was immediately recognised, though his work was not received uncritically. Henry Cadbury referenced pre-publication summaries from Conzelmann in support of his delayed parousia hypothesis,[25] and C. H. Dodd purportedly commented, "I suspect we shall have to

---

[23] Conzelmann also overlooked key sections of Luke/Acts. While centring his thesis on texts such as Luke 16.16, he excluded the infancy narratives from discussion, which later studies have emphasised as central to any interpretation of key themes in Luke/Acts (Paul S. Minear, "Luke's Use of the Birth Stories," in Keck and Martyn, *Studies in Luke-Acts*, 118–25; Charles H. Talbert, "Shifting Sands: The Recent Study of the Gospel of Luke," *Interpretation* 30 (1976): 385; Fitzmyer, *The Gospel according to Luke*, 184). See also discussion in Kim, *Die Parusie bei Lukas*, 51.

[24] See Chapter 3. Conzelmann argues that, in light of the distance of the parousia, "a more reflective attitude emerges" and as a result Luke has separated out events of history from those leading up to the end (see, for instance, Conzelmann, *Theology of St Luke*, 132). This he sees as supporting his claim that Luke has created a separate time of the church in between the time of God's activity in Jesus and the parousia. However, he does not note the ways that other writers also picture the unfolding of end-time events, without reducing their claims to eschatological imminence. Given Conzelmann's personal focus on the decisive irruption of God in a singular Christ event, it is also not clear whether he would in any case be satisfied by the unfolding of end-time events as presented in historical apocalypses, even though he critically characterises Luke's "struggle" as "essentially an anti-apocalyptic one" (p. 123).

[25] Henry J. Cadbury, "Acts and Eschatology," in *The Background of the New Testament and Its Eschatology: Studies in Honour of C. H. Dodd*, ed. W. D. Davies and D. Daube (Cambridge: Cambridge University Press, 1956), 320. Cadbury later revised his view to focus on the salvific nature

give (the Lukan writings) over, so to speak, to Conzelmann."[26] Several studies built on Conzelmann's methodology and findings. For instance, Erich Grässer extended the approach into a more detailed assessment of Acts as well as Mark and Matthew[27] and Günter Klein applied Conzelmann's model to Luke's prefaces.[28] Ernst Käsemann embraced the salvation-historical framework with some venom at Luke's endeavour and employed labels that would become key criticisms: Luke was a representative of *Frühkatholizismus* and proponent of *theologia gloriae*.[29]

Not all scholars who supported Conzelmann's conclusions, however, took as negative a view as the Bultmann school. Ulrich Wilckens affirmed the framework of salvation history, relegation of imminent eschatological expectation, and the assessment that Luke was early catholic, without judging any of these features to be negative[30]—a position with which many contemporary treatments of Lukan eschatology show considerable sympathy.[31]

---

of events already realised in Luke's narrative (see Maddox, who also shares this view of Lukan eschatology (Maddox, *The Purpose*, 145 n. 4; cf. pp. 116–17)).

**26** Talbert, "Shifting Sands," 383–84. See also H. D. F. Sparks, review of *Die Mitte der Zeit: Studien zur Theologie des Lukas* (3rd ed.), by Hans Conzelmann, *JTS* 14 (1963): 454.

**27** Grässer, "Das Problem der Parusieverzögerung," 99–127.

**28** Klein, "Lukas, 1, 1–4," 183–216. Klein discusses the role of tradition (including predecessors) in carrying on during the extended period of delay. He argues Luke makes a distinction between the first apostles of the "tradition" and Luke's generation, in light of the Jerusalem council (see esp. pp. 214–16). See also Schulz, *Die Stunde der Botschaft*, 275–76. Schulz adds that Luke's divine plan reflects Graeco-Roman understandings of εἱμαρμένη/*fatum*; few contemporaneous studies relate to this non-Jewish Graeco-Roman literature (Siegfried Schulz, "Gottes Vorsehung bei Lukas," *ZNW* 54 (1963): 108–9). See my Chapter 4 below.

**29** Käsemann, "Das Problem," 143; Käsemann, "Neutestamentliche Fragen," 21.

**30** Wilckens, "Interpreting Luke-Acts," 66–67; cf. Kümmel, "Current Theological Accusations," 131–45. Wilckens also offers incisive assessments of the theological and ideological influences in the Bultmann school and in the legacy of Karl Barth, which contribute to the negative attitudes towards "history" (as diametrically opposed, in the latter, to "revelation"; pp. 69–77). This also relates to the question I raised above (n. 24) about whether Conzelmann would find the eschatological hopes of historical apocalypses sufficient as decisive, singular irruptions of divine activity, a question which can be expanded to other members of the Bultmann school. The social and intellectual context profoundly directed these attitudes in post-war NT scholarship. See my Chapter 7.

**31** See Bovon's appreciation for Wilckens's positive approach, in keeping with his broad affirmation of other elements such as the role of the delayed parousia for Luke (Bovon, *Luke the Theologian*, 39); elsewhere Bovon emphasises a twofold division between the periods of promise and fulfilment, while still further dividing the period of the church (François Bovon, *Luke: Commentary on the Gospel of Luke*, trans. Christine M. Thomas, Donald S. Deer, and James Crouch, Hermeneia (Minneapolis: Fortress, 2002–2013), 1:10–11). Gunkel also retains the threefold divi-

Numerous studies accepted the broad strokes of Conzelmann's historical schema, but suggested amendments to particular elements. For instance, some debated the exact points of transition between historical periods.[32] By contrast, for writers like E. Earle Ellis, Luke's account reflects a balance between *both* the imminent and future aspects of eschatology, as Luke seeks to counter not the crisis of the parousia's delay, but the problem of disciples who were *too* focused on "apocalyptic" expectation. In notable distinction from Conzelmann, Ellis emphasises a two-age schema of history, though he divides this timing into two further stages for Jesus and his followers. For Ellis, Luke's concern lies in correcting ethical practice, hence Luke emphasises the unknown timing but instantaneous nature of the parousia *whenever* it arrives.[33]

Some studies responded to concerns about history similar to those evident in Conzelmann's work, but attempted to defend Luke from the Bultmann school's criticisms by focusing on spatial rather than temporal considerations. Helmut Flender expressed a deep concern about "the false sacralisation of history," from which he distanced Luke by emphasising the ascension, which in a sense

---

sion (Heidrun Gunkel, *Der Heilige Geist bei Lukas: Theologisches Profil, Grund und Intention der lukanischen Pneumatologie*, WUNT 2/389 (Tübingen: Mohr Siebeck, 2015), 266–69). Similarly, see also Darrell L. Bock, *A Theology of Luke and Acts: God's Promised Program, Realized for All Nations*, Biblical Theology of the New Testament (Grand Rapids: Zondervan, 2011), 389–405; Drury, *Tradition and Design*, 9.

[32] William Childs Robinson, "Theological Context for Interpreting Luke's Travel Narrative," *JBL* 79 (1960): 27; Fitzmyer, *The Gospel according to Luke*, 1:185–87.

[33] E. Earle Ellis, "Eschatology in Luke," in *Eschatology in Luke*, FBBS 30 (Philadelphia: Fortress, 1972), 118; Ellis, "Present and Future Eschatology in Luke," in *Eschatology in Luke*, 146; Ellis, *The Gospel of Luke*, rev. ed., NCB (London: Oliphants, 1974), 49. See also Wilson, who claims there is a difference between Luke and Acts on this measure (S. G. Wilson, "Lukan Eschatology," *NTS* 16 (1970): 336–47; cf. Beverly Roberts Gaventa, "The Eschatology of Luke-Acts Revisited," *Encounter* 43 (1982): 27–42), and extended discussion of this double-edged perspective in Carroll, *Response to the End*. Carroll is particularly interested in aligning questions of Luke's setting with the eschatological perspective suggested by his text, and concludes similarly to Ellis that Luke is concerned with ethics and the kind of lived responses that will emerge from recognising the unknown nature of the timing of the end (rather than the overconfidence of banking on extended delay or disregard of responsibilities that might emerge from imminent eschatological expectation). Green likewise emphasises the ethical purpose to which Luke puts the extended present period (Green, *The Theology*, 126–27). Farrell, while maintaining a similar two-edged perspective, ties a separation of history from eschatology to the fulfilment of the apostles' mission and arriving in Rome, as the "ends of the earth" in Acts 1.8 (Hobert Kenneth Farrell, "The Eschatological Perspective of Luke-Acts" (PhD diss., Boston University Graduate School, 1972), 266–79). Tannehill emphasises expectations of suddenness, which may indicate suddenness at either the individual's death or the parousia (Robert C. Tannehill, *The Narrative Unity of Luke-Acts: A Literary Interpretation*, FF (Philadelphia: Fortress, 1986–1990), 1:249).

he equated with the parousia.³⁴ Keeping Jesus at one remove from the events of history, Flender pointed to a lordship that has already been inaugurated in the heavenly sphere and exists concurrently.³⁵ Conversely, writers like Charles Talbert and Günter Klein saw Luke's emphasis on grounding the story of Jesus in historical events and attending to the bodily realities of Jesus' resurrection as a response to so-called Gnosticism.³⁶

Although interacting in different ways with the themes Conzelmann highlighted, by and large these studies maintain the basic premise that Luke divorces history from eschatology.³⁷ However, there was also a different approach to salvation history which kept history and eschatology together.

## 2.2 Oscar Cullmann and a linear schema of history and its end

Publishing prior to Conzelmann, Oscar Cullmann argued that like the texts of the HB, NT texts present a linear schema of history (what he termed "the continuous redemptive line"),³⁸ in which human history exists in continuity with the events of the end.³⁹ The key difference in NT texts, however, is that rather than antici-

---

**34** Helmut Flender, *St Luke: Theologian of Redemptive History*, trans. Reginald H. Fuller and Ilse Fuller (London: SPCK, 1967), 106, cf. 91–94, 139–40. Flender also warns against a danger of falling "into historical pantheism" and argues that Luke saw that he must keep history and eschatology separate, fighting a "danger of a confusion between salvation and history" (pp. 5, 140).
**35** This is notwithstanding the deputising function Flender attributes to the Spirit during the time of the church (Flender, *St Luke*, 145–46). See also Eric Franklin, "The Ascension and the Eschatology of Luke-Acts," *SJT* 23 (1970): 191–200.
**36** For Talbert, Luke's point is to champion history over against myth, rather than history over eschatology (Charles H. Talbert, *Luke and the Gnostics: An Examination of the Lucan Purpose*, (Nashville: Abingdon, 1966), 111–12); Klein, "Lukas, 1, 1–4," 183–216. See also C. K. Barrett, *Luke the Historian in Recent Study*, A. S. Peake Memorial Lecture 6 (London: Epworth, 1961), 63–64; Werner Georg Kümmel, *Introduction to the New Testament*, trans. A. J. Mattill., rev. ed., NTL (London: SCM, 1975), 146–47, and the emphasis on salvation in I. Howard Marshall, *Luke: Historian and Theologian* (Exeter: Paternoster, 1970), 20–24 (though Marshall argues against the view that Luke sought to counter Gnosticism, p. 22).
**37** Kümmel offers a slightly more nuanced view, but retains this division (Kümmel, *Introduction*, 144).
**38** Oscar Cullmann, *Christ and Time: The Primitive Christian Conception of Time and History*, trans. Floyd V. Filson, rev. ed. (London: SCM, 1962), 35; Cullmann's original publication was *Christus und die Zeit: Die urchristliche Zeit- und Geschichtsauffassung*, Zollikon-Zürich: Evangelischer Verlag, 1946.
**39** Cullmann, *Christ and Time*, 53–54, 79–80, 83; Cullmann, *Salvation in History*, trans. Sidney G. Sowers (London: SCM, 1967), 122–27, 169.

pating God's action at the end of history, the entire historical schema is characterised by God's decisive action in Jesus' death and resurrection at its "midpoint." Stressing the significance of the past decisive event, Cullmann likened the relationship between Jesus' resurrection and the parousia to that between D-Day and V-Day—that is, in Cullmann's view, the decisive battle that determines the outcome of the war has already taken place and only the armistice documents remain to be signed.[40]

Cullmann's forceful critique of the Bultmann school,[41] particularly Conzelmann, in the introduction to his revised edition of *Christus und die Zeit* in 1962, led him to focus on Luke/Acts.[42] Though his analysis was offered largely without reference to non-biblical texts, Cullmann represents a valuable approach within post-war scholarship, which used comparisons with other biblical texts to challenge approaches to Luke/Acts that severed eschatology from history or caricatured differences between Luke/Acts and other NT texts.[43]

Some other scholars also challenged uneschatological readings of Luke's history. Although simplifying "apocalyptic" perspectives into a "two-aeon" framework, A. J. Mattill Jr. helpfully emphasised that Luke's understanding of the "Last Things" is in keeping with apocalypses including Daniel and Revelation,[44] while F. O. Francis focused on Acts 2.17 in arguing that Luke believed

---

**40** Cullmann, *Christ and Time*, xix, 84. The salience of imagery related to World War Two is of note; see discussion of the impact of the social context on these mid-twentieth-century interpreters in Chapter 7 below.
**41** He also responds to criticism from the Barthian school (Cullmann, *Christ and Time*, xxv).
**42** Conzelmann makes only passing reference to Cullmann, though suggesting his "discussion of 'consistent eschatology' also of course deserves our close attention" (Conzelmann, *Theology of St Luke*, 95 n. 1; cf. Cullmann's critique of "consistent eschatology," however (Cullmann, *Christ and Time*, 85–86)). For his part, Cullmann claims Conzelmann depends upon his own work, arguing even Conzelmann's title is derivative of his concept of the "mid-point in time" (Cullmann, *Christ and Time*, xxiii). (Though the two scholars understand this middle in relation to the end of history in very different ways!)
**43** Schlaudraff concludes that the enduring contribution of Cullmann's work lies in this insight: "Kerygma und Geschichte sind nicht gegeneinander auszuspielen, sondern gehören im Blick auf die göttliche Offenbarung zusammen" (Karl-Heinz Schlaudraff, *"Heil als Geschichte?" Die Frage nach dem heilsgeschichtlichen Denken, dargestellt anhand der Konzeption Oscar Cullmanns* (Tübingen: Mohr Siebeck, 1988), 253).
**44** Mattill rightly asserts that Luke's understanding of history and its end is less original among NT writers than Conzelmann suggested. His diagrams on the structure of history are helpful (Andrew J. Mattill, *Luke and the Last Things: A Perspective for the Understanding of Lukan Thought* (Dillsboro, NC: Western North Carolina Press, 1979), 12), although his characterisation of apocalypses and identification of seven "miniapocalypses" in Luke is not convincing (pp. 6–8).

the last days had already begun, lending an eschatological character to all of history.⁴⁵

In some important recent studies, focusing particularly on illuminating Pauline literature, interpreters have engaged in detailed examinations of themes related to the understanding of history in Second Temple Jewish texts. For instance, Loren Stuckenbruck's analysis of the structure of time and overlapping ages in Second Temple Judaism has offered a welcome challenge to some simplistic characterisations of "apocalyptic" in Pauline studies.⁴⁶ Other studies, drawing on the work of John Barclay, have sought to clarify understandings of divine and human agency in Second Temple Judaism and Paul.⁴⁷

---

Luke's Gospel does not need to be "an apocalypse" in order to share elements of this view of history. It is perhaps surprising that Mattill makes no reference to Cullmann.

**45** Fred O. Francis, "Eschatology and History in Luke-Acts," *JAAR* 37 (1969): 51–59. So also Panagopoulos, who sees history divided into two eras, the second of which is already inaugurated by the Spirit and centred on the presence of the risen Jesus in the church's midst (Johannes Panagopoulos, "Zur Theologie der Apostelgeschichte," *NovT* 14 (1972): 149–59). The extent to which Panagopoulos retains a future temporal sense in his understanding of Luke's eschatology, rather than purely realised in the present, is less clear. Smith's concept of salvation history explains previous delay in terms of the salvation-historical significance of the universal mission, while arguing that history and eschatology are inherently connected (Robert H. Smith, "History and Eschatology in Luke-Acts," *CTM* 29 (1958): 888–94, 901). Rasco likewise strongly criticises Conzelmann's hypothesis, attributing it partly to Conzelmann's Lutheran doctrine (Emilio Rasco, "Hans Conzelmann y la 'Historia Salutis': A Propósito de 'Die Mitte der Zeit' y 'Die Apostelgeschichte,'" *Gregorianum* 46 (1965): 318).

**46** Loren T. Stuckenbruck, "Overlapping Ages at Qumran and 'Apocalyptic' in Pauline Theology," in *The Dead Sea Scrolls and Pauline Literature*, ed. Jean-Sébastien Rey, STDJ 102 (Leiden: Brill, 2014), 309–26; Stuckenbruck, "Posturing 'Apocalyptic' in Pauline Theology: How Much Contrast with Jewish Tradition?", in *The Myth of Rebellious Angels: Studies in Second Temple Judaism and New Testament Texts*, WUNT 335 (Tübingen: Mohr Siebeck, 2014), 240–56. In addition to a critique of scholarship of Pauline literature, in a later work Stuckenbruck also incorporates analysis of historical Jesus research (Stuckenbruck, "How Much Evil Does the Christ Event Solve? Jesus and Paul in Relation to Jewish 'Apocalyptic' Thought," in *Evil in Second Temple Judaism and Early Christianity*, ed. Chris Keith and Loren T. Stuckenbruck, WUNT 2/417 (Tübingen: Mohr Siebeck, 2016), 142–52). For other helpful discussions of the structuring of time and history in Second Temple Judaism, see also Ari Mermelstein, *Creation, Covenant, and the Beginnings of Judaism: Reconceiving Historical Time in the Second Temple Period*, Supplements to the Journal for the Study of Judaism 168 (Leiden: Brill, 2014); Hindy Najman, *Losing the Temple and Recovering the Future: An Analysis of 4 Ezra* (Cambridge: Cambridge University Press, 2014). And see my Chapters 3 and 6 below.

**47** See especially John M. G. Barclay, "Introduction," in *Divine and Human Agency in Paul and His Cultural Environment*, ed. John M. G. Barclay and Simon J. Gathercole, T&T Clark Biblical Studies (London: T&T Clark, 2008), 1–8; Barclay, *Paul and the Gift* (Grand Rapids: Eerdmans, 2015), 309–28; Jason Maston, *Divine and Human Agency in Second Temple Judaism and Paul:*

These recent directions in Pauline scholarship highlight important areas for exploration in relation to other NT texts and, given the enduring questions on these themes in Lukan studies, particularly in relation to Luke/Acts. Despite the numerous strengths in Cullmann's approach to salvation history, his understanding, for instance, of decisive divine action in the past, obscured for him the features of Luke's portrayal of divine and human agency in the *present*, especially as they relate to Luke's explanation of suffering.[48] Considering Luke/Acts within a broader range of texts helps to clarify these important features of Luke's text.

Despite these shortcomings, studies like that of Cullmann provide an important corrective for assumptions that lay at the heart of Conzelmann's hypothesis. However, Cullmann is rarely cited in recent studies.[49] The basic tenets of Conzelmann's view have been challenged from a number of angles, such as Robert

---

*A Comparative Study*, WUNT 2/297 (Tübingen: Mohr Siebeck, 2010); Kyle B. Wells, *Grace and Agency in Paul and Second Temple Judaism: Interpreting the Transformation of the Heart*, NovTSup 157 (Leiden: Brill, 2014); and my Chapter 5 below.

[48] Cullmann encountered difficulty in explaining how evil was constrained in the present, given the decisive event had already taken place (Cullmann, *Christ and Time*, 198). He introduced a better appreciation for historical contingency in his later *Heil als Geschichte*, ascribed to insights from reading Gerhard von Rad (Cullmann, *Salvation in History*, 122–27; see also debate between Conzelmann and von Rad on these questions in a series of articles addressed to each other in *Evangelische Theologie* (Hans Conzelmann, "Fragen an Gerhard von Rad," *EvT* 24 (1964): 113–125; Gerhard von Rad, "Antwort auf Conzelmanns Fragen," *EvT* 24 (1964): 388–94)). Diminishing the role of human agency emerges also in some studies of "apocalyptic" Paul (see J. Louis Martyn, *Theological Issues in the Letters of Paul* (London: Continuum, 1997), 111–13, 120–22, 143–47, and analysis in Douglas A. Campbell, *The Deliverance of God: An Apocalyptic Rereading of Justification in Paul* (Grand Rapids: Eerdmans, 2009), 191–92), as was also the case in Mattill's more "apocalyptic" treatment of Luke/Acts (Mattill, *Luke and the Last Things*). See my Chapter 5 below.

[49] Bauspieß supplies a notable exception (Martin Bauspieß, *Geschichte und Erkenntnis im lukanischen Doppelwerk: Eine exegetische Untersuchung zu einer christlichen Perspektive auf Geschichte*, Arbeiten zur Bibel und ihrer Geschichte 42 (Leipzig: Evangelische Verlagsanstalt, 2012), 137–45; cf. also an article by Moessner specifically dedicated to Cullmann's work, written ten years after his death (though Moessner does not refer to Cullmann in his other analysis of Luke/Acts), David P. Moessner, "Das Doppelwerk des Lukas und Heil als Geschichte: Oscar Cullmanns auffälliges Schweigen bezüglich des stärksten Befürworters seiner Konzeption der Heilsgeschichte im neuen Testament," in *Luke the Historian of Israel's Legacy, Theologian of Israel's "Christ": A New Reading of the "Gospel Acts" of Luke*, BZNW 182 (Berlin: de Gruyter, 2016), 302–14). Cullmann does not appear in the annotated bibliography by Green and McKeever, *Luke-Acts and New Testament Historiography*, and is listed only in a footnote among other theologies of history in Shauf, *Theology as History*, 325 n. 2.

§2 Hans Conzelmann and post-war debates about uneschatological Luke — 13

Maddox's thorough redaction-critical reappraisal of Conzelmann's exegesis.⁵⁰ However, the understanding, for instance, that eschatology "is not a prominent topic in Acts" remains surprisingly enduring.⁵¹ This is particularly evident in introductory textbooks and commentaries.⁵² Even commentators who name a mild-

---

**50** Maddox, *The Purpose*, 100–57. See also Carroll, *Response to the End*.
**51** Richard I. Pervo, *Acts: A Commentary*, Hermeneia (Minneapolis: Fortress, 2009), 25; similarly, cf. Craig S. Keener, *Acts: An Exegetical Commentary* (Grand Rapids: Baker Academic, 2012–2015), 1:518–19; Carl R. Holladay, *Acts: A Commentary*, NTL (Louisville: Westminster John Knox, 2016), 76. In work published up until the turn of the twenty-first century, François Bovon maintained the view that the delay of the parousia was so central to Luke's setting that, for instance, layers of redaction in the parable of the widow and the unjust judge (Luke 18.1–8) could be discerned through removing such interests (François Bovon, "Apocalyptic Traditions in the Lukan Special Material: Reading Luke 18.1–8," in *Studies in Early Christianity* (Grand Rapids: Baker Academic, 2003), 51–58). Bovon even notes language which was consistent with other Lukan passages, but attributes this to the writer of Luke's special material and *not* to Luke on the grounds that fervent apocalyptic expectation must relate to an earlier layer of text and to have been written by Luke's source, whom he also argues was a superior writer to Luke (p. 53). It is a consistent habit in Lukan studies to start with these assumptions about Luke's delayed parousia setting and salvation-historical response, and then to peel off any textual elements that do not seem to fit the hypothesis and attribute these to others.
**52** Introductory texts consistently rely on these assumptions: see V. George Shillington, *An Introduction to the Study of Luke-Acts*, T&T Clark Approaches to Biblical Studies (London: Bloomsbury, 2015), 20–21; Bock, *A Theology* (though Bock attempts to distinguish his view from Conzelmann regarding the parousia's delay (p. 399), his schematisation of Luke's history is strongly influenced by Conzelmann). See also Ulrich Busse, "Eschatologie in der Apostelgeschichte," in *Eschatology of the New Testament and Some Related Documents*, ed. Jan G. van der Watt, WUNT 2/315 (Tübingen: Mohr Siebeck, 2011), 163–66, 171–75. Commentaries similarly follow key elements of Conzelmann's approach to salvation history: Fitzmyer, *The Gospel according to Luke*, 1:182–87, 2:1115; Holladay's 2016 commentary simply cites Conzelmann for reference to "sequential and even progressive stages" of history unfolding in accordance with the divine purpose (Holladay, *Acts*, 48). Cf. Jacob Jervell, "The Future of the Past: Luke's Vision of Salvation History and Its Bearing on His Writing of History," in *History, Literature, and Society in the Book of Acts*, ed. Ben Witherington III (Cambridge: Cambridge University Press, 1996), 106 on Luke's emphasis on history over eschatology, though contrast Jervell, *The Unknown Paul: Essays on Luke-Acts and Early Christian History* (Minneapolis: Augsburg, 1984), 25, on living in the last days though the end has not come. No themes related to eschatology are included in the list of key themes in Johnson's introductions to his commentaries on either Luke or Acts (Luke Timothy Johnson, *The Gospel of Luke*, SP 3 (Collegeville: Liturgical Press, 1991), 21–24; Johnson, *The Acts of the Apostles*, SP 5 (Collegeville: Liturgical Press, 1992), 14–18). For Tannehill, the parousia's delay is tied to misunderstandings about the tragic necessity for Israel's rejection to play out (Tannehill, *Narrative Unity*, 1:258–61). John T. Carroll, *Luke: A Commentary*, NTL (Louisville: Westminster John Knox, 2012) offers a helpful exception to this tendency among commentators, which is perhaps not surprising given the focus of his doctoral dissertation (cf. Carroll, *Response to the End*).

er approach in their introductions can go on to make scarce further references to eschatology in the body of their commentaries, as they engage with others' habitually uneschatological readings of passages throughout.[53]

Thus, although recent studies may seek to project more moderate views about Luke's understanding of history, the assumption that Luke has in some sense traded a reduced emphasis on eschatological expectation for a focus on the life of the church and the presence of the Spirit emerges frequently in contemporary writing on Luke and Acts. For many interpreters, these background assumptions endure predominantly because their areas of interest have largely moved away from these more theological or philosophical questions of the nature of history.

## 3 Genre, rhetoric, and Graeco-Roman comparisons

Much recent Lukan scholarship has centred instead on the genre of Luke/Acts (or on distinct genres of Luke and Acts). Luke's linguistic and rhetorical skills, often identified as superior among NT texts,[54] have led to studying Luke/Acts in the context of Graeco-Roman literary conventions. Many recent studies have focused on assessing the genre(s) of the Lukan writings and then considering Luke/Acts predominantly in relation to ancient texts of the same genre(s). Drawing on dominant views of Luke/Acts as historiography since Martin Dibelius and Henry Cadbury,[55] various recent interpreters identify Luke/Acts with a sub-type of histori-

---

[53] For example, see Beverly Roberts Gaventa, *Acts*, ANTC (Nashville: Abingdon, 2003), 67; Mikeal C. Parsons, *Acts*, Paideia (Grand Rapids: Baker Academic, 2008), 7, 58, 123–4; Eduard Schweizer, *The Good News according to Luke*, trans. David E. Green (Atlanta: John Knox, 1984), 328 (Schweizer argues Luke does not have a schema of salvation history; pp. 92, 326); cf. also David Lyle Jeffrey, *Luke*, Brazos Theological Commentary on the Bible (Grand Rapids: Brazos, 2012), 243–51. Holladay includes eschatological claims as the final point in his nine-step outline of the Lukan kerygma (Holladay, *Acts*, 53), but makes few further references to end-time events and does not discuss any sense Luke presents of their imminence; of the parousia he says: "in any event, Jesus's role as eschatological deliverer receives scant attention in Luke-Acts (cf. 3.20–21)" (p. 76).

[54] Note, however, Alexander's important delineation between everyday language (evident in some other NT texts, such as Mark), higher literature, and Luke's language—which falls into neither category. Alexander emphasises that Luke's language is competent, but Luke/Acts does not display the stylistic and rhetorical features of literary texts (Loveday Alexander, *The Preface to Luke's Gospel: Literary Convention and Social Context in Luke 1:1–4 and Acts 1:1*, SNTSMS 78 (Cambridge: Cambridge University Press, 1993), 170–71).

[55] See the helpful overview in Clare K. Rothschild, *Luke-Acts and the Rhetoric of History: An Investigation of Early Christian Historiography*, WUNT 2/175 (Tübingen: Mohr Siebeck, 2004),

ography, such as "institutional"[56] or "apologetic" historiography (the latter making a clear link between genre and purpose).[57] Another significant perspective extends work by Charles Talbert to argue that Luke wrote a form of biography. Beyond more general studies of the Gospels as biographies,[58] Talbert identified Luke/Acts as a two-volume form, encompassing the life of a movement's leader followed by an account of the leader's followers.[59] Other literary genres also fea-

---

32–59. See also Keener, *Acts*, 1:90–115, and Daniel Marguerat, *The First Christian Historian: Writing the "Acts of the Apostles,"* trans. Ken McKinney, Gregory J. Laughery, and Richard Bauckham, SNTSMS 121 (Cambridge: Cambridge University Press, 2002), 1–34, though Marguerat assesses that Luke/Acts contains elements of other literary traditions while most closely reflecting historiography with an apologetic purpose. Moessner similarly discusses historiography in relation to Luke's genre, though with a strong sense of Luke's Jewish heritage, not simply Graeco-Roman historiographical traditions (David P. Moessner, *Luke the Historian of Israel's Legacy*, 33–38, 315–39).

**56** From a slightly different angle, Cancik offers a renewed version of the argument about Luke's "catholicising" tendencies (Hubert Cancik, "The History of Culture, Religion, and Institutions in Ancient Historiography: Philological Observations Concerning Luke's History," *JBL* 116 (1997): 673–95). See, for example, his discussion of increasingly rigorous rules for membership and developing internal structures for the "Christian *ekklesia*" (pp. 678–79). The features Cancik notices in Acts relate to his parallels with non-Jewish historiographies; his portrait of Acts and its purpose makes no reference to eschatological expectations or the relevance of beliefs about divine guidance.

**57** Gregory E. Sterling, *Historiography and Self-Definition: Josephos, Luke-Acts, and Apologetic Historiography*, NovTSup 64 (Leiden: Brill, 1991), 349–69. Lee considers the relevance of "'tragic' history" for Luke/Acts, without specifying a new "genre" (DooHee Lee, *Luke-Acts and "Tragic History": Communicating Gospel with the World*, WUNT 2/346 (Tübingen: Mohr Siebeck, 2013)). See also Susanne Luther, "'Jesus Was a Man, … but Christ Was a Fiction': Authentizitätskonstruktion in der antiken narrativen Historiographie am Beispiel lukanischer Gleichniserzählungen," in *Wie Geschichten Geschichte schreiben: Frühchristliche Literatur zwischen Faktualität und Fiktionalität*, ed. Susanne Luther, Jörg Röder, and Eckart D. Schmidt, WUNT 2/395 (Tübingen: Mohr Siebeck, 2015), 181–208; Darryl W. Palmer, "Acts and the Ancient Historical Monograph," in *The Book of Acts in Its Ancient Literary Setting*, ed. Bruce W. Winter and Andrew D. Clarke, BAFCS 1 (Grand Rapids: Eerdmans, 1993), 1–29. By contrast, Alexander's detailed examination of the Lukan prefaces, which are frequently appealed to as evidence in support of the genre designation "historiography," finds instead that they share more with the prefaces of scientific and technical texts (Alexander, *The Preface*, 147–48, 164–67, 187; though for other views on genre and the prefaces, see Sean A. Adams, "Luke's Preface and Its Relationship to Greek Historiography: A Response to Loveday Alexander," *JGRChJ* 3 (2006): 177–91; Moessner, *Luke the Historian*, 68–107).

**58** Richard Burridge, *What Are the Gospels? A Comparison with Graeco-Roman Biography*, SNTSMS 70 (Cambridge: Cambridge University Press, 1992), 185–212.

**59** Charles H. Talbert, *Literary Patterns, Theological Themes, and the Genre of Luke-Acts*, SBLMS 20 (Missoula: Society of Biblical Literature and Scholars Press, 1974). For collected biography,

ture in discussions, including the ancient novel[60] and epic,[61] while some argue Luke/Acts displays elements of multiple genres.[62]

Building on the conclusions of such studies, further research addresses other interpretative questions through the lens of a particular ancient genre. Here scholars move from appreciating the importance of genre for correctly interpreting texts, to limiting discussion of other themes—including Luke's theology—to a set of texts *determined by genre*. For instance, John Squires considers Luke's divine plan alongside providence, fate, and fortune in Hellenistic historiographies.[63] Scott Shauf's portrait of "the divine in Acts" likewise is tied to historiography.[64] Historiography and its generic features also occupy the focus for Daniel Marguerat,[65] Clare Rothschild,[66] Samson Uytanlet,[67] and Eve-Marie Becker,[68]

---

see Sean A. Adams, *The Genre of Acts and Collected Biography*, SNTSMS 156 (Cambridge: Cambridge University Press, 2013).

[60] Richard I. Pervo, *Profit with Delight: The Literary Genre of the Acts of the Apostles* (Philadelphia: Fortress, 1987).

[61] Marianne Palmer Bonz, *The Past as Legacy: Luke-Acts and Ancient Epic* (Minneapolis: Augsburg Fortress, 2000). MacDonald argues that Mark and Luke imitated Homeric models in their storytelling (Dennis R. MacDonald, *The Gospels and Homer: Imitations of Greek Epic in Mark and Luke-Acts*, New Testament and Greek Literature 1 (Lanham: Rowman & Littlefield, 2015), 28–29), and in particular that Luke also imitated Virgil's *Aeneid* not only in the broader structure of stories, but in Virgil's reception of Homeric themes and even (unconvincingly) on topics crucial to Luke's theology (MacDonald, *Luke and Vergil: Imitations of Classical Greek Literature*, New Testament and Greek Literature 2 (Lanham: Rowman & Littlefield, 2015), 112–77). On these questions, see Krauter's excellent response to Bonz, dismissing claims of Lukan literary dependence on the *Aeneid* or the genre designation "epic," but providing a nuanced reflection upon themes in each (Stefan Krauter, "Vergils Evangelium und das lukanische Epos? Überlegungen zu Gattung und Theologie des lukanischen Doppelwerkes," in *Die Apostelgeschichte im Kontext antiker und frühchristlicher Historiographie*, ed. Jörg Frey, Clare K. Rothschild, and Jens Schröter, BZNW 162 (Berlin: de Gruyter, 2009), 214–43).

[62] Daniel L. Smith and Zachary L. Kostopoulos, "Biography, History and the Genre of Luke-Acts," *NTS* 63 (2017): 390–410; Parsons, *Acts*, 4; Thomas E. Phillips, "The Genre of Acts: Moving toward a Consensus?", *CurBR* 4 (2006): 365–96; David Peterson, *The Acts of the Apostles*, Pillar New Testament Commentary (Grand Rapids: Eerdmans 2009), 15. Alexander provides a list of texts treated in earlier studies as parallels for Luke's literary style (Alexander, *The Preface*, 10 n. 18).

[63] John T. Squires, *The Plan of God in Luke-Acts*, SNTSMS 76 (Cambridge: Cambridge University Press, 1993). Squires diminishes the importance of eschatology in relation to the divine plan (cf. pp. 8–9, 187).

[64] Scott Shauf, *The Divine in Acts and Ancient Historiography* (Minneapolis: Fortress, 2015).

[65] Marguerat, *The First Christian Historian*. Marguerat also emphasises the influence of both Graeco-Roman and Jewish historiography (p. 25).

among many others. This focus on the genre(s) of Luke/Acts has also resulted in a separation of non-Jewish from Jewish texts. Todd Penner's 2004 analysis of studies in Acts over the previous fifteen years observes that studies compared Acts to Jewish texts when addressing theological questions and non-Jewish texts for rhetorical matters.[69] Although some more recent studies have incorporated Jewish historiographies, the continued dominance of genre studies has generally confirmed the prominence of non-Jewish Graeco-Roman texts in Lukan studies.[70] Moreover, particularly through the emphasis on rhetoric, non-Jewish Graeco-Roman texts have also become the focus of studies of theological themes within Luke/Acts.[71]

---

[66] Rothschild, *Luke-Acts and the Rhetoric*, though Rothschild also observes historiography's connections to biography and epic in its development (pp. 8–9), while focusing on historians' rhetorical techniques.

[67] Samson Uytanlet, *Luke-Acts and Jewish Historiography: A Study on the Theology, Literature, and Ideology of Luke-Acts*, WUNT 2/366 (Tübingen: Mohr Siebeck, 2014). Cf. David P. Moessner, "'Completed End(s)ings' of Historiographical Narrative: Diodorus Siculus and the End(ing) of Acts," in *Die Apostelgeschichte und die hellenistische Geschichtsschreibung: Festschrift für Eckhard Plümacher zu seinem 65. Geburtstag*, ed. Cilliers Breytenbach and Jens Schröter, AGJU 57 (Leiden: Brill, 2004). However, Molthagen emphasises differences between Luke/Acts and Herodotus, Thucydides, and Polybius (Joachim Molthagen, "Geschichtsschreibung und Geschichtsverständnis in der Apostelgeschichte im Vergleich mit Herodot, Thukydides und Polybios," in Frey, Rothschild, and Schröter, *Die Apostelgeschichte*, 181).

[68] Eve-Marie Becker, *The Birth of Christian History: Memory and Time from Mark to Luke-Acts*, AYRL (New Haven: Yale University Press, 2017). Becker distinguishes between "micro-" and "macro-historiography," whereby the former refers to texts exhibiting key features shared with the generic archetypes of Thucydides, Polybius, Sallust, and Tacitus, and the latter is an umbrella term which incorporates various narratives about the past, including biography, micro-historiography, gospels, etc. (cf. p. 69).

[69] Todd Penner, "Madness in the Method? The Acts of the Apostles in Current Study," *CurBR* 2 (2004): 232.

[70] Most recently, Becker did not include Jewish sources for her study of both Mark and Luke/Acts (Becker, *The Birth of Christian History*). Reviews of studies like Squires, *The Plan of God* have emphasised the need for engagement with Jewish ideas (e.g. Robert C. Tannehill, review of *The Plan of God in Luke-Acts*, by John T. Squires, *Biblica* 75 (1994): 425–28). Some recent studies have incorporated Jewish comparison texts, although generally these have also continued to restrict the analysis to genre categories (e.g. Uytanlet, *Luke-Acts and Jewish Historiography*; cf. Brian S. Rosner, "Acts and Biblical History," in Winter and Clarke, *The Book of Acts in Its Ancient Literary Setting*, 65–82; James D. G. Dunn, "The Book of Acts as Salvation History," in *Heil und Geschichte: Die Geschichtsbezogenheit des Heils und das Problem der Heilsgeschichte in der biblischen Tradition und in der theologischen Deutung*, ed. Jörg Frey, Stefan Krauter, and Hermann Lichtenberger, WUNT 248 (Tübingen: Mohr Siebeck, 2009), 385–401).

[71] Shauf, *The Divine*; Rothschild, *Luke-Acts and the Rhetoric*, 185–212; Bonz, *The Past as Legacy*, 56–57.

However, although an awareness of the rhetorical features of its genre will be important for correctly interpreting any given text, I argue that many elements of a writer's beliefs transcend genre. Indeed, ancient texts of all genres are shaped by their writers' underlying conceptions of, for instance, divine and human agency in history or the end of history.[72] Further, as the analysis in this study demonstrates, those texts with which Luke/Acts shares greatest *generic* similarity are not always those most closely aligned with Luke's conception of history. Tying the conversation to historiographies, or biographies, has limited discussion of some key features of Luke's text relevant to longstanding debates in Lukan studies, such as the impact of Luke's eschatology on his presentation of human history. In an important contribution, C. Kavin Rowe identifies Luke as "apocalyptic."[73] This label should invite interpreters to consider the relevance of apocalypses as texts that might provide illuminating comparison with Luke/Acts.[74] But Rowe himself makes this claim without reference to any apocalypses (indeed, he makes minimal use of any Second Temple Jewish texts). In this discussion, I suggest that greater precision is required in the way in which generic categories are employed in the methodologies of Lukan studies. In order to address the kinds of themes upon which this study centres, the scope of texts with which Luke/Acts is compared must be expanded.

---

[72] See Chapter 2 for detailed discussion, including criticism of the idea of "mere" rhetoric.
[73] C. Kavin Rowe, *World Upside Down: Reading Acts in the Graeco-Roman Age* (Oxford: Oxford University Press, 2009), 137. Kim also represents an important exception, paying attention to apocalypses and other non-historiographical texts in his analysis of Luke's understanding of the parousia (Kim, *Die Parusie bei Lukas*, 55–140).
[74] The relationship between "apocalyptic" and "apocalypses" (both contemporary scholarly terms seeking to make sense of ancient texts) in definitions has been the subject of longstanding debate (cf. John J. Collins, "Apocalypse: The Morphology of a Genre," *Semeia* 14 (1979): 1–19; Benjamin Reynolds, "John and the Jewish Apocalypses: Rethinking the Genre of John's Gospel," in *John's Gospel and Intimations of Apocalyptic*, ed. Christopher Rowland and Catrin H. Williams (London: Bloomsbury, 2013), 36–57; G. I. Davies, "Apocalyptic and Historiography," *JSOT* 5 (1978): 15–28; Michael E. Stone, *Ancient Judaism: New Visions and Views* (Grand Rapids: Eerdmans, 2011), 59–89; Todd R. Hanneken, *The Subversion of the Apocalypses in the Book of Jubilees*, EJL (Atlanta: Society of Biblical Literature, 2012), 1–26). I take the view that apocalypses provide a key insight into any content interpreters might attribute to the adjective "apocalyptic" (such as beliefs about revealed insights into the world as it really is, including its spatial structure and temporal plan of history), though a text of a different genre may also share such characteristically "apocalyptic" views.

# 4 This study

This monograph seeks to illuminate Lukan eschatology by considering the conception of history in Luke/Acts alongside a wide range of texts of the Graeco-Roman period, including Greek and Latin historiography, popular exempla, Latin epic, Jewish Hellenistic historiography, Dead Sea Scrolls, and Jewish apocalypses. In doing so, it builds upon Cullmann's insights as noted above,[75] by expanding the focus to texts beyond the NT, and responds to the criticism I highlighted from Penner, by incorporating both Jewish and non-Jewish texts.[76] Despite the number of studies that have dealt with history and Luke/Acts previously, I am not aware of any that has offered a systematic treatment of these questions among a fuller spectrum of the texts of Luke's setting.

In Chapter 2, I set out the study's methodology. Clarifying the importance and limits of genre, I illustrate that conceptions of history—such as beliefs about the end of history, or divine and human agency in history—transcend genre. I argue that the possibility of shared views about these topics in texts of different genres justifies—or, indeed, *necessitates*—the cross-genre comparisons in this study. I describe key elements of the study's approach and introduce the ten texts which will be Luke's conversation partners.

Chapters 3 to 6 then consider each key text and Luke/Acts in relation to a different aspect of their writers' conceptions of history. Chapter 3 asks: how do the direction and shape of history in these texts illuminate the schema of history in Luke/Acts? I note that in the vast majority of texts, the writers present history as periodised—that is, comprised of ages or epochs, and that Virgil's *Aeneid* and the Jewish texts portray history as teleological—that is, history follows a linear shape that draws to some sort of culmination at its end. Concluding that these are the texts to which Luke's periodised and teleological conception of history is most similar, I note that Luke/Acts differs from most of the texts with which it shares generic features, and thus those with which it is most likely to be compared in current scholarship.

In Chapter 4, I analyse evidence of the writers' attitudes to determinism and divine guidance of history. The texts treated reveal diverse views: determinism can confirm hope for the future, endorse existing authorities, or underscore the futility of human resistance. Moreover, in some texts divine personal or impersonal forces drive the course of history as part of a larger plan; in others they simply react in the moment. Again, Luke displays strikingly little use of the char-

---

75 Cullmann, *Christ and Time*; Cullmann, *Salvation in History*.
76 Penner, "Madness in the Method?", 232.

acteristic language or concepts employed by Graeco-Roman writers in how he portrays divine guidance of history (even in comparison to Josephus). Nonetheless, divine guidance over the whole course of history and its end remains central to the assurance Luke provides: the βουλή τοῦ θεοῦ can be opposed, but it cannot be stopped.

Chapter 5 considers how the writers portray interactions between divine and human agency, in order to illuminate the ways Luke apportions *human* responsibility—both for the events of the past and for action in the present and future. Through analysing treatments of "opponents," I demonstrate that temporal concerns draw out apparent inconsistencies—that is, for many writers, explanations of the negative events of the past centre on human culpability or divine punishment, while prospective reflections affirm divine sovereignty as assurance for the future. Human agency is particularly important for Luke. He explains past negative events as the result of tragic opposition to the divine purpose, while an (urgent) universal invitation confirms the human freedom to respond positively in the present.

Finally, Chapter 6 examines characterisations of the present and the end of history, and the relationship between the two. Like contemporaneous Jewish writers, Luke draws on past events to provide assurance of God's faithful action in the future. However, for Luke, the key event of the past—namely Jesus' resurrection—constitutes a unique and decisive transition to the final period of history. Luke's understanding of the relationship between the end of history and the present thus shares features with Virgil's *Aeneid*. But I argue that both the *placement of the end of history in relation to the present* and the dynamic *character of the present* crucially affect the ways in which the writers portray hope, suffering, and political structures, revealing important differences in the ways eschatology functions in each of the *Aeneid* and Luke/Acts.

In Chapter 7, in addition to summarising the study's findings, I assess the methodology and consider further implications for understandings of history and eschatology in texts across the NT. I conclude that Luke's understanding of the end, far from being severed from his understanding of history, is integral to each of the other aspects of history examined in this study. And I maintain that in each aspect of history discussed, Luke/Acts shares significant features with the texts of different genres with which it is rarely compared. In each of these areas across Luke/Acts, Luke's understanding of the end of history plays a key and shaping role, as he explains past experience, provides assurance for the future, and exhorts appropriate human response in the present.

# Chapter 2:
# Genre, themes that transcend genre, and the approach of this study

As set out in Chapter 1, much recent scholarship of Luke/Acts has focused on genre, including studies which have tied their methodologies to genre-related decisions.[1] But in describing the method I use in this study, this chapter demonstrates that ancient texts of different genres can reflect the same beliefs about the nature of the world. That is, a text of one genre can be compared to a text of another genre with respect to elements such as their writers' portrayals of the shape and end of history and the divine forces and human agents who act in history. As a result, comparing texts of diverse genres is not only possible, but necessary, when dealing with the kinds of questions this study seeks to address.

After an overview of ancient and contemporary genre theory and practice, I highlight classical and biblical texts which confirm that the same underlying assumptions can be reflected in texts of different genres. I then set out this study's approach. Finally, I provide general information about each key text used as a case study in this monograph, as background for the analysis which follows.

## 1 The importance and limits of genre

Although this study is not *about* genre, it recognises that genre is important. This will become evident in a range of ways. But the prominent position genre occupies in the history of biblical scholarship, particularly in relation to theological interests in interpretation, warrants a brief note.[2] For instance, an appreciation for genre has played a key role in modern interpretations of mythological texts such as Gen 1–11, which scholars frequently contrast with literalist approaches.[3]

---

[1] For instance, see Shauf, *The Divine*; Uytanlet, *Luke-Acts and Jewish Historiography*; Squires, *The Plan of God*.

[2] See, for instance, genre divisions in John Barton, ed., *The Biblical World*, 2 vols. (London: Routledge, 2002). Conversely, Alter argues biblical narrative represents a unique category unlike genres represented elsewhere (Robert Alter, *The Art of Biblical Narrative*, rev. ed. (New York: Basic Books, 2011), 221–22).

[3] See John Van Seters, *Prologue to History: The Yahwist as Historian in Genesis* (Louisville: Westminster John Knox, 1992), 8–23; Gerhard von Rad, *Genesis: A Commentary*, trans. John H. Marks, rev. ed., OTL (London: SCM, 1972), 31–43; cf. William G. Doty, "The Concept of Genre in Literary

In earlier eras, theological interests similarly energised form-critical studies which analysed units of tradition for insights into the historical Jesus.[4] And theological concerns were embedded in debates about the genre "historiography" as it was conflated with claims about historicity, which has been significant for Acts scholarship especially.[5] Therefore, as biblical scholars stress the importance of genre, they highlight a methodological issue which connects to significant theological convictions (and conflicts).

Attending to a text's genre remains important in biblical research—as a tool which clarifies features of the text, but not a prescriptive means of determining the boundaries of discussion.[6] Some treatments of genre have become unduly rigid,[7] and even attribute the theological claims in a text to generic convention

---

Analysis," in *Seminar Papers: The Society of Biblical Literature, 108th Annual Meeting*, ed. Lane C. McGaughy (Missoula: SBL Press, 1972), 432.

**4** Aune traces the origins of genre criticism in biblical studies back to late nineteenth-century interests in form criticism, which considered strands of oral tradition within *sui generis* "Gospel" texts (David E. Aune, "Genre Theory and the Genre-Function of Mark and Matthew," in *Jesus, Gospel Tradition and Paul in the Context of Jewish and Greco-Roman Antiquity: Collected Essays II*, WUNT 303 (Tübingen: Mohr Siebeck, 2013), 27–29).

**5** See discussion of this tension in Acts scholarship in Alexander, *The Preface*, 3; Sterling, *Historiography and Self-Definition*, 2; Penner, "Madness in the Method?", 224–25, 229, 234. Penner also distinguishes between the "historicity" (of particular events) and the "historical world" (that is, the historical plausibility of such events in context, e.g. trial scenes; pp. 251–60).

**6** Sterling rightly argues genre is for "clarification not classification" (Sterling, *Historiography and Self-Definition*, 16).

**7** Grethlein reflects a strong tradition in Classics when he notes the ways ancient writers recognise overlap between historiography and biography (Jonas Grethlein, *Experience and Teleology in Ancient Historiography: "Futures Past" from Herodotus to Augustine* (Cambridge: Cambridge University Press, 2013), 22–23); also recognised by Adams, *The Genre of Acts*; cf. Joseph Farrell, "Classical Genre in Theory and Practice," *New Literary History* 34 (2003): 383. Becker conceptualises biography as a sub-genre of a larger category, "macro-historiography," and names "gospel," as well as "micro-historiography" and so on, as subsets of the larger category in a similar way (Becker, *The Birth of Christian History*; note that at times Becker begins to refer even to the writers of epic, like Virgil and Ovid, as "historians," which introduces a somewhat obscure element at points, cf. pp. 54, 60–61). Though helpfully clarifying, studies such as Talbert, *Literary Patterns*, Burridge, *What Are the Gospels?*, and Adams, *The Genre of Acts* (biography); Pervo, *Profit with Delight* (ancient novel); Sterling, *Historiography and Self-Definition* (apologetic historiography); and Cancik, "The History" (institutional historiography), also run the risk of overlooking distinctive features of these NT texts (see especially Burridge, *What Are the Gospels?*, 255–56), and overstating the distinctions between sub-genres. Aune argues that biblical research has often overlooked insights from contemporary genre theory (Aune, "Genre Theory and the Genre-Function," 54).

alone.⁸ Importantly, as Paul Hernadi rightly asserts, texts share a range of things in common with one another, not all of which will relate to genre.⁹ Interpreters who exclude from their analysis all texts which have been designated a different genre inevitably exclude texts which would illuminate these other features. I suggest it is helpful to be more precise about how and why interpreters make genre distinctions, as part of clarifying how we might examine textual features that transcend genre.

## 1.1 Ancient and contemporary genre theory and practice

The tensions between the stipulations of ancient genre theory and the practices employed by ancient writers are well documented. Plato's distinction between different forms of poetry (*Republic* Book 3), which Aristotle consolidated into his renowned framework of tragedy, comedy, and epic (*Poetics* 1447a),¹⁰ do not map directly onto actual texts.¹¹ When writers such as Polybius set out methodo-

---

**8** See, for instance, Rothschild's explanation of some theological themes as rhetorical devices employed by historians (Rothschild, *Luke-Acts and the Rhetoric*, and discussion at §1.2 below).
**9** Paul Hernadi, *Beyond Genre: New Directions in Literary Classification* (Ithaca: Cornell University Press, 1972), 7, 153. Cohen distinguishes between shared features that tie texts together and strengthen their generic relationship, and those features which weaken the generic relationships (Ralph Cohen, "Introduction," *New Literary History* 34 (2003): vi). However, my argument, as also Hernadi's, is that texts can share various other features that do not relate to genre. See further below.
**10** Heather Dubrow, *Genre*, The Critical Idiom 42 (London: Methuen, 1982), 46–49. Najman stresses that Jewish texts supply no equivalent explication of their use of genres (Hindy Najman, "The Idea of Biblical Genre: From Discourse to Constellation," in *Prayer and Poetry in the Dead Sea Scrolls and Related Literature: Essays in Honor of Eileen Schuller on the Occasion of Her 65th Birthday*, ed. Eileen M. Schuller, Jeremy Penner, Ken M. Penner, and Cecilia Wassen (Leiden: Brill, 2012), 311).
**11** Farrell, "Classical Genre," 395–96. Najman demonstrates that some traditions rely on awareness of generic rules, such as theatres which required that tragedies submitted for performance meet certain criteria (Najman, "The Idea of Biblical Genre," 309–10). Hellenistic-period texts provide few examples of formal genre theory (S. J. Harrison, *Generic Enrichment in Vergil and Horace* (Oxford: Oxford University Press, 2011), 3), though they can still indicate "implicit theory" in how they apply conventions (Farrell, "Classical Genre," 386–87, 403). Lucian's satirical account of contemporaneous historiographical practice in *How To Write History* also indicates formal generic understanding. Contemporary scholars variously characterise tensions in defining genres through contrasts between the emic and etic (Adena Rosmarin, *The Power of Genre* (Minneapolis: University of Minnesota Press, 1985), 7, 50–51; cf. Najman, "The Idea of Biblical Genre," 309), theory and history (Hayden White, "Anomalies of Genre: The Utility of Theory and History for the Study of Literary Genres," *New Literary History* 34 (2003): 597–615), or pre-

logical commitments related to generic convention (cf. Polyb. *Hist.* 2.56.7–12), they can fail to realise them in their own writing—as in Polybius's famed denunciation of tragic features in historiography and his own apparent use of dramatic and tragic features.[12] Moreover, in some cases texts appear to draw on features from other genres in order to "enrich"[13] or undermine formal generic claims or expectations in the text. Although some Graeco-Roman writers' renowned generic playfulness may seem to devalue generic conventions, in fact the opposite is true: this playfulness relies on readers' awareness of distinctions between genres.[14]

Defining genre is notoriously difficult. My purpose here is not to become embroiled in what Daniel Chandler describes as the "theoretical minefield" of genre theory,[15] but to set out some key points that will help to clarify textual features that *transcend* genre. A literary genre can be defined as "a type of text recognised by particular conventions of form and content which are shared by other texts of that type."[16] As "competent" readers[17] recognise them, these conventions shape

---

scriptive and descriptive approaches (Rosmarin, *The Power of Genre*, 7, 50–51; cf. Mark Edwards, "Gospel and Genre: Some Reservations," in *The Limits of Ancient Biography*, ed. Brian McGing and Judith Mossman (Swansea: Classical Press of Wales, 2006), 52).

**12** Frank Walbank, "History and Tragedy," *Historia* 9 (1960): 216, 234; Walbank, *A Historical Commentary on Polybius* (Oxford: Clarendon, 1957), 1:15; Kenneth S. Sacks, *Polybius on the Writing of History* (Berkeley: University of California Press, 1981), 144–70.

**13** Harrison's term (Harrison, *Generic Enrichment*, 14). Harrison's helpful description of "genre enrichment" highlights how a primary ("host") genre may exhibit features of a secondary ("guest") genre, through which a reader's expectations may be challenged or extended ("enriched"). Harrison also suggests that the primary genre might best be expressed as a noun, with the secondary, as a "mode," expressed in terms of an adjective (p. 14).

**14** A text's form and content can act in creative tension, as Farrell illustrates with an example from Horace. Observing the importance of meter in ancient genre distinctions, Farrell demonstrates that Horace playfully undermines his own content (namely: "directives regarding generic purity") by employing the incorrect meter for his text type (Farrell, "Classical Genre," 394). As in the "enriched" texts Harrison discusses (see previous note), the irony of Horace's generic playfulness relies on a firm grasp of the generic conventions elicited (and disrupted). See further discussion in Farrell, "Classical Genre," 386, 389–91. By contrast, some less-refined texts may also mimic formal conventions without following them completely, perhaps simply to evoke the general mood of a formal style. In the latter case, the intended generic features may not be salient or consistent enough to shape readers' interpretation.

**15** Daniel Chandler, "An Introduction to Genre Theory," rev. ed., 2000 (https://www.researchgate.net/publication/242253420_An_Introduction_to_Genre_Theory), 2. Dubrow likewise notes that, "though the effects of genre are manifest and manifold," defining genre is difficult (Dubrow, *Genre*, 4).

**16** Daniel Chandler and Rod Munday, "Genre," in *A Dictionary of Media and Communication* (Oxford: Oxford University Press, 2011), 173.

the readers' expectations and interpretations.[18] Five elements of this understanding of literary genre warrant further comment.

(1) Genres are by definition about groups of texts, not individual texts, given the focus on shared features.[19] Where claims are made that a text is *sui generis*, this reflects an assessment that any sharing of formal features between that text and extant others is so weak that it cannot be interpreted in light of expectations raised by shared features.[20] (2) Genres are about real texts, not imagined texts that might be designed as members of a generic category.[21] These groupings of real texts are best conceptualised as a constellation of examples gathered around prototypical texts,[22] with which they exhibit greater or lesser degrees of similarity.[23]

---

**17** This is a concept Harrison draws from Culler (Harrison, *Generic Enrichment*, 14; cf. Jonathan D. Culler, *Structuralist Poetics: Structuralism, Linguistics and the Study of Literature* (London: Routledge & Kegan Paul, 1975), 140–41).
**18** Contemporary genre theory goes beyond texts; Seitel speaks about genres as "*tools* for living in society" (Peter Seitel, "Theorizing Genres: Interpreting Works," *New Literary History* 34 (2003): 277). Notwithstanding any overlap between the functions of such genres, it is not my intention to ensure the discussion here is applicable beyond ancient literary texts.
**19** Cohen, "Introduction," vi.
**20** Edwards cites Xenophon's *Reminiscences of Socrates*, as the only example of its genre, to demonstrate the possibility of *sui generis* texts, and therefore this possibility for the Gospels (Edwards, "Gospel and Genre," 53–54). However, this conceptualises genre from the wrong direction. Other texts with shared features may simply have been lost. All that can be claimed is that, on the basis of extant texts, such unique works would not appear to raise expectations in competent contemporaneous readers. Also contra Burridge, who argues that texts *must* have genres (Burridge, *What Are the Gospels?*, 53, 255–56).
**21** This highlights again the tension between descriptive and prescriptive or emic and etic understanding of genre distinctions. See n. 11 above.
**22** For instance, in the case of Graeco-Roman historiography, Becker lists the prototypical exemplars as Thucydides, Polybius, Sallust, and Tacitus (Becker, *The Birth of Christian History*, 69). Note that this is what Becker describes as historiography in the narrow ("micro-") sense, as opposed to her umbrella category "macro-historiography," which describes all prose accounts of the past including the sub-types biography, micro-historiography, and also gospels (pp. 69–76).
**23** Aune suggests genres reflect a "core of prototypical members" and "fuzzy boundaries" (Aune, "Genre Theory and the Genre-Function," 54; also Chandler, *An Introduction to Genre Theory*, 3). Najman uses a "constellation" image to describe "classes" of texts (though she avoids equating this with classical understandings of the term "genre" (Najman, "The Idea of Biblical Genre," 316)). She notes that using a classification system to imagine a further "star" into the constellation "is to imagine another constellation altogether" (p. 317). Though valuably observing that texts may share diverse features (p. 312), Najman does not take her discussion further to consider how other shared features may cut across generic or other "type" divisions.

(3) Genres are based on shared features related to the texts' form and content. Such features may be described as a "generic repertoire," where this includes external (e.g. metre, literary structure) and internal (subject, tone) features.[24] Texts may share many different kinds of things: a given group may all be written by British authors or Roman citizens, printed in Times New Roman or written on papyrus, or published in 1983 or under the reign of Tiberius. One could rightly argue that such attributes might be more common in texts of one genre or another. However, they are not directly indicative of genre. The importance of these perhaps obvious kinds of distinctions will become clear below. Internal features such as subject must be weighted appropriately with other external features.[25] Certainly some thematic considerations are significant for genre: biographies narrate the life of a particular individual,[26] and apocalypses reveal information through a vision or otherworldly journey, often mediated by the explanations of an angelic guide.[27] However, if an emphasis on theme is taken to an extreme and at the expense of external features, any genre differentiation becomes meaningless[28]—on some readings, all biblical texts, whether prose or poetry, that describe divine faithfulness would converge to the same "genre"; likewise would letters, legal documents, and unauthorised biographies pertaining to the same key political figure.

(4) In the words of William Hanks, genre creates "orientating frameworks" and "sets of expectations,"[29] thus performing a function in communication. In order for generic features to raise such expectations, therefore, readers must have reasonable levels of what Stephen Harrison, following Jonathan Culler, calls "literary competence" or David Aune describes as "literary socialisation."[30]

---

**24** Alastair Fowler, *Kinds of Literature: An Introduction to the Theory of Genres and Modes* (Oxford: Clarendon, 1982), 55–56. See also Harrison, *Generic Enrichment*, 11.
**25** Aune supports a threefold division of form, function, and theme, but emphasises the need to balance their importance. He also notes that some features may be more important than others in some genres (Aune, "Genre Theory and the Genre-Function," 30–31).
**26** Burridge, *What Are the Gospels?*, 61–63.
**27** Cf. Collins, "Apocalypse," 9.
**28** Cf. Chandler, *An Introduction to Genre Theory*, 1.
**29** William F. Hanks, "Discourse Genres in a Theory of Practice," *American Ethnologist* 14 (1987): 670. See also Seitel, "Theorizing Genres," 277. Such expectations may then be met or disrupted (see n. 14 above on Horace).
**30** Harrison, *Generic Enrichment*, 14; Aune, "Genre Theory and the Genre-Function," 33. Todorov recognises that readers may be affected by generic features unconsciously (Tzvetan Todorov, *Genres in Discourse*, trans. Catherine Porter (Cambridge: Cambridge University Press, 1990), 19).

Naturally, this immediately raises difficulties inherent in literary interpretation: the impasse between writer, text, and reader.[31] Following Harrison, I suggest it is most helpful to approach the text from the perspective of an ideal, contemporaneous, "competent" reader.[32] Harrison is cognisant of the dangers intrinsic to such a conceptualisation, but compellingly argues for this approach, "believing as I do that it is an easier task to attempt the reconstruction of the cultural horizons of the collective model readership of a classical text than of the mental processes of its single historical author."[33] This approach remains vulnerable to the possibility that writers may have articulated what they mean in such a way that their intended audiences could not understand—like teachers who fail to pitch their lectures to their student audiences and whose lecture notes would not illuminate the recipients' experience. However, coupled with further knowledge about the historical setting, on balance the model reflects the best approach to an insoluble tension, avoiding the greater pitfall of suggesting that texts have intentions severed from their writers and readers.

(5) Finally, genres can evolve over time.[34] As soon as Virgil's *Aeneid* evoked the expectations of epic for his readers, but then adapted these conventions, the genre "epic" had shifted. Later readers bring slightly different expectations to "epic" texts, which in turn shape their interpretations.[35] Over time, genres may be stretched or divided[36] and new genres may emerge.[37]

Thus, the ways that shared features set frameworks for expectation and shape interpretation for competent readers in their socio-historical context justify—and exhaust—the purpose of identifying a particular text's genre.[38] Genre is not "an end in itself."[39]

---

**31** Rosmarin critiques the "explanatory power" of the increasingly detailed theory addressing the tension between text and reader as ultimately "self-exhausting" (Rosmarin, *The Power of Genre*, 3).
**32** "Reader" here need not be taken literally; an audience in any form will require competence for generic conventions.
**33** Harrison, *Generic Enrichment*, 14.
**34** Fowler, *Kinds of Literature*, 23, 45–48.
**35** Farrell, "Classical Genre," 395, 400.
**36** Farrell, "Classical Genre," 400.
**37** Fowler, *Kinds of Literature*, 23; Fowler, "The Formation of Genres," 187.
**38** Fowler asserts: "there is no doubt that genre primarily has to do with communication. It is an instrument not of classification or prescription, but of meaning" (Fowler, *Kinds of Literature*, 22; cf. Seitel, "Theorizing Genres," 292).
**39** Hernadi, *Beyond Genre*, 7. Cf. Edwards, "Gospel and Genre," 61; Sterling, *Historiography and Self-Definition*, 1; Chandler, *An Introduction to Genre Theory*, 10.

## 1.2 Maintaining precision regarding genre

The above discussion about genre is important because it attempts to set out which textual features rightly belong to genre and which reflect something else, to avoid attributing *all* features of a text to a loose notion of its "genre" or suggesting that all beliefs a writer conveys through a text will fit within parameters inherent to its genre (a tendency that has been particularly limiting in recent Lukan studies). Indeed, I suggest quite the opposite is true: numerous elements of a text transcend genre.[40] A particular theme, such as belief in divine guidance, may be present in an apocalypse and a historiography, although not present in all historiographies.[41]

Conflating content claims with genre can create the problematic assumption that content reflects generic convention alone. For instance, Clare Rothschild contends that Luke makes use of the rhetorical techniques of recurrence, prediction, divine guidance, and eyewitnesses as common methods for establishing a historian's authority and credibility,[42] and that, even where these techniques explicitly bear on theological issues, Luke does so without affirming the theological implications.[43] I understand "rhetoric" as "the art of using language effectively so as to persuade or influence others."[44] The *OED* also countenances more negative uses of the term, as for an overblown style, but does not include linguistic forms that simply contradict their content. By contrast, Rothschild's approach to rhetoric as "any means available"[45] leads her to divorce the rhetoric from sub-

---

[40] Clarke observes the methodological difficulties posed by blurred genres and different scholarly traditions regarding local historiographies and calendar documents, though both kinds of texts reflect interests in the "structures of time" (Katherine Clarke, *Making Time for the Past: Local History and the Polis* (Oxford: Oxford University Press, 2008), 51).

[41] Distinctions between genre and beliefs about the world that transcend genre may also illuminate other contentious discussions of genre in biblical studies, such as those related to apocalypse/apocalyptic/apocalypticism (see, for instance, John Ashton, "Intimations of Apocalyptic: Looking Back and Looking Forward," in Rowland and Williams, *John's Gospel and Intimations of Apocalyptic*, 3–35; Reynolds, "John and the Jewish Apocalypses"; Stuckenbruck, "Posturing 'Apocalyptic'"). See also p. 18 n. 74, and p. 180 n. 205.

[42] Rothschild argues that in a "competitive climate," as the profession of historian burgeoned in the Hellenistic period, writers employed "any means available" to them in order to establish their authority and credibility (Rothschild, *Luke-Acts and the Rhetoric*, 95). She argues, for instance, that in passages where it is clear that something of divine action is at work in Luke's narrative, δεῖ is "conspicuous by its absence" (Rothschild, *Luke-Acts and the Rhetoric*, 212). See my Chapter 4 below.

[43] Rothschild, *Luke-Acts and the Rhetoric*, 7.

[44] *OED* definition 1 A.

[45] Rothschild, *Luke-Acts and the Rhetoric*, 95.

stance. The texts I discuss in this study challenge the notion of "mere" rhetoric. The writers employ rhetorical devices in support of, not counter to, their conceptions of history and, in the case of late Second Temple Jewish texts, to maintain a characterisation of the divine in keeping with Jewish antecedents.⁴⁶

As part of his critique of recent methodological "madness" in Acts scholarship, Todd Penner observes that theological themes often reduced to rhetoric, such as "retribution and providence," are not limited to historiography, and thus require a "cross-generic comparison."⁴⁷ The presence of these themes in epic texts, to which the evidence of the current study could add apocalypses, confirms that these ideas cannot be dismissed as rhetoric tied to generic convention, even if presented in characteristic ways in particular kinds of texts. Rather, these themes evoke features of the underlying beliefs portrayed by the writers.⁴⁸

## 1.3 Views shared across ancient texts of different genres

A writer does not have to produce historiography to present a view about the nature of history and its end, or divine and human agency over the events of history. Such beliefs show through in diverse texts—from apocalypses like 2 Baruch to the historiography of Diodorus Siculus or Virgil's epic. Importantly, as noted

---

**46** Chapter 4 demonstrates this point, for instance, in relation to Josephus's adaptation of τύχη. Similarly, Walbank asserts Polybius uses rhetoric to highlight elements he believes are "objectively present in the fabric of events, and necessarily to be stressed if the historian is to fulfil his [or her] true function as a moral historian" (Walbank, *A Historical Commentary*, 1:15). Likewise, Luke does not use terms such as δεῖ independently of his theological claims—in the imagery of Walbank, like embroidery detached from fabric—but rather to reinforce them. Similarly, on rhetoric in apocalypses, see Carol A. Newsom, "The Rhetoric of Jewish Apocalyptic Literature," in *The Oxford Handbook of Apocalyptic Literature*, ed. John J. Collins (Oxford: Oxford Unviersity Press, 2014), 202–3.
**47** Penner, "Madness in the Method?", 240. Note, however, that Penner still leans towards identifying these as literary *topoi* which are shared across texts of different genres (illustrated with Marguerat's comparison of sea voyages in epic and historiography), rather than exploring the extent to which themes such as providence, retribution, and so on may represent shared understandings of the world. Rothschild includes epic among the exemplars drawn upon by Hellenistic historians (Rothschild, *Luke-Acts and the Rhetoric*, 95), though her focus remains on rhetoric.
**48** In *Beyond Genre*, Hernadi refers to a text's "evoked world" (Hernadi, *Beyond Genre*, 7), but does not clearly develop it. At points he seems to equate "evoked world" with attributes of genre (as also do Farrell, "Classical Genre," and Seitel, "Theorizing Genres," when drawing on similar ideas), but elsewhere Hernadi discusses a feature of the world evoked as a kind of "principle of reality" (p. 182). This, I suggest, is a feature that transcends genre.

above, various perspectives may be shared by the writers of texts of different genres without being shared by others who write in the same genre—as this study demonstrates is true of Luke/Acts and the other (non-Jewish) Greek and Latin historiographies in almost every aspect of history discussed.

Ancient texts of different genres written by the same author illustrate that conceptions of history transcend genre. Seneca produced a generically broad corpus, from manuals and epigrams to letters and tragedies.[49] But his Stoic commitments are in evidence to one degree or another across his collection. For instance, Thomas Rosenmeyer stresses continuity in the portrayal of the nature of the gods, determinism, and a Stoic emphasis on the control of nature even in Seneca's tragedies.[50] Similarly, Ovid's *Fasti* and *Metamorphoses* share some key perspectives about the world, despite their different genres.[51] Such examples of ancient authors who work in multiple genres, but communicate the same underlying beliefs about the world—including claims about the shape and end of history, or divine and human agency in history—demonstrate that it *is* possible for texts of different genres to reflect the same beliefs about such topics.

Biblical texts also provide explicit evidence of shared understandings of the world across diverse genres. For instance, the poetry of Psalm 1 sets out the theology of divine reward and punishment within the events of history for the right-

---

[49] This is despite the presuppositions of ancient theorists like Plato and Aristotle (who suggested that writers will work in a particular genre, arising from their temperaments). Such assumptions here relate to the hierarchy of genres; writers of more serious character were believed to be drawn to a more serious genre and vice versa (Farrell, "Classical Genre," 384). The early suggestion of "multiple Senecas" may simply reflect this assumption that authors wrote in one characteristic genre, rather than a suggestion that his works reflected diverse beliefs (James Ker, "Seneca, Man of Many Genres," in *Seeing Seneca Whole: Perspectives on Philosophy, Poetry and Politics*, ed. Katharina Volk and Gareth D. Williams, Columbia Studies in the Classical Tradition 28 (Leiden: Brill, 2006), 19–41).

[50] Seneca's tragedies have traditionally been regarded differently, but contemporary studies affirm continuity in these underlying views (cf. Thomas G. Rosenmeyer, *Senecan Drama and Stoic Cosmology* (Berkeley: University of California Press, 1989), 63–90).

[51] Virgil represents another good example of generic diversity by the same writer (see Farrell, "Classical Genre," 392–93), though the perspectives reflected in the *Eclogues*, *Georgics*, and *Aeneid* famously differ (see Chapter 3 §3.1 on the golden age). Demonstrating that comparing features between the texts remains possible, critics identify a development in Virgil's perspective itself, extending to intertextuality between the works (Elena Theodorakopoulos, "Closure: The Book of Virgil," in *The Cambridge Companion to Virgil*, ed. Charles Martindale (Cambridge: Cambridge University Press, 1997), 157). That these features can be compared across Virgil's generically diverse corpus nonetheless supports my point.

eous and wicked.⁵² These beliefs also appear in historiographical texts such as the explanation of the fall of the northern kingdom in 2 Kings: "This occurred because the people of Israel had sinned against the Lord their God" (2 Kgs 17.7a, cf. vv. 7–23).⁵³ Both texts imply features of the same understanding of the world in relation to divine involvement in history, specifically God's use of the events of history as a punishment for sin. Not all biblical writers present exactly the same views, for instance, when identifying causes of suffering in the past, but the particular views they do present *are not determined by the genre of their texts*. Therefore, whichever *particular* beliefs are present, it is nonetheless possible to compare these features across different texts.

Some generic features do seem to lend themselves to the articulation of particular beliefs more readily. For instance, the device of *vaticinia ex eventu* (presenting inspired "predictions" of historical events by a character set in the past) is particularly common in historical apocalypses and portrays a sense of determinism over history. However, such views are not simply equated with this genre, but can be communicated through other texts and forms (see, for example, the discussion of Josephus's *Ant.* 10 and Luke 21 in Chapters 4 and 6 below). Moreover, divergent explanations of divine and human responsibility emerge from the differences between, for instance, 4 Ezra and 2 Baruch, despite their great many similarities—including that of genre. As a result, it is too simplistic to conclude that there is simply "a" view of history which is characteristic of all apocalypses, and different from texts of other genres.

It remains important to take due account of a text's genre as it provides readers with a framework of expectations that will shape interpretation, including any rhetorical or other conventions that frame how such underlying beliefs are communicated. However, undue concentration on genre has bred unhelpfully narrow methodology in some biblical research. These methodologies have featured particularly in studies of Luke/Acts, excluding from the field of vision key elements of Luke's writings that transcend genre.

---

52 The focus in Psalm 1 remains on the blessing of the way of the righteous during earthly life and its opposite for the wicked (Hans-Joachim Kraus, *Psalms 1–59*, trans. Hilton C. Oswald (Minneapolis: Augsburg, 1988), 115–22).
53 See Chapter 5 on Deuteronomistic theology.

## 2 This study's approach to examining Luke's conception of history

In order to investigate how the understandings of history in diverse texts of the Graeco-Roman period illuminate Lukan eschatology, this study examines key texts to build up a picture of the variety of views that are evident in Luke's context. I argue that approaching each text as a detailed case study provides the best data for assembling this picture, and that Greek and Latin non-Jewish texts and diverse late Second Temple Jewish texts are all relevant as part of Luke's first-century setting. Each of these claims requires some justification.

### 2.1 Mapping understandings of history in Luke's context

The usefulness of the comparisons undertaken in this study does not lie in any claim to Luke's literary dependence upon these texts. Other studies have explored Graeco-Roman historiographies in order to determine Luke's use of rhetoric without claiming direct dependence. Likewise, there is widespread agreement that cultural influences have mediated the effect of, for instance, formal Stoic or Epicurean philosophies upon diverse texts. Evidence of these philosophical frameworks can be found in Paul's letters, Josephus's works, or Acts, even where the writers display limited evidence of any direct engagement with philosophical texts.[54] Similarly, I suggest that mapping the conceptions of history underlying a range of texts of the Graeco-Roman period illuminates Luke/Acts without requiring Luke's familiarity with those particular texts.[55]

This method draws on concepts developed in cultural history, particularly among the proponents of the history of *mentalité*. Introduced by mid-twenti-

---

[54] E. P. Sanders, "God Gave the Law to Condemn: Providence in Paul and Josephus," in *The Impartial God: Essays in Biblical Studies in Honor of Jouette M. Bassler*, ed. Calvin J. Roetzel and Robert L. Foster, New Testament Monographs 22 (Sheffield: Sheffield Phoenix, 2007), 90; Pervo, *Acts*, 431; Keener, *Acts*, 2:2614–17. Similarly, see Tov on possible benefits of studying scribal practices in diverse texts, including older texts, without requiring literary dependence, in his study of scribal practices in the Dead Sea Scrolls (Emanuel Tov, *Scribal Practices and Approaches Reflected in the Texts Found in the Judean Desert*, Studies on the Texts of the Desert of Judah 54 (Leiden: Brill, 2004), 4).

[55] Likewise, this exercise of mapping the conceptions of history in Luke's literary setting does not require that Luke is familiar with all of the languages in which such texts are written. See §2.3 below.

eth-century historians Lucien Febvre and Marc Bloch,[56] this approach considers the ideas and *ways* of thinking—what Febvre termed the *outillage mental* ("mental tools")—in evidence in a given cultural setting.[57] From this developed the idea of mapping the diversity of ways of thinking, or the set of "mental tools" available, in a given context.[58] This approach has been applied helpfully to the ways ancient writers employed terms and concepts in their cultural setting.[59] In this study, I work with diverse texts to consider the ways of thinking about history that were in evidence in Luke's broader context,[60] so that comparisons might illuminate Luke's particular emphases and assumptions as they fit within that pattern of views.

## 2.2 Building a series of detailed case studies

I deal with comparison texts as a series of detailed case studies that together build up the picture of the ways of thinking about history that were present in Luke's wider setting. Not only Luke/Acts, but each text must be read as far as

---

**56** Cf. Lucien Febvre, *The Problem of Unbelief in the Sixteenth Century: The Religion of Rabelais*, trans. Beatrice Gottlieb (Cambridge: Harvard University Press, 1982). For further discussion of this movement, see Anna Green, *Cultural History*, Theory and History (Basingstoke: Palgrave Macmillan, 2007), 29–34; Roger Chartier, *Cultural History: Between Practices and Representations*, trans. Lydia G. Cochrane (Cambridge: Polity, 1988), 21–37.

**57** Febvre, *The Problem of Unbelief*, 355–79, esp. pp. 355–63. Febvre's objective was to assess the plausibility of particular views in his chosen setting, given the "mental tools" available. He has been criticised for prescribing what is possible, thereby ruling out any radical thought and creating difficulties in understanding how change might take place, rather than describing the diversity evident in a given setting (see critiques in Chartier, *Cultural History*, 24–35; Green, *Cultural History*, 33–34; Peter Burke, "Strengths and Weaknesses of the History of Mentalities," in *The Annales School: Critical Assessments*, ed. Stuart Clark (London: Routledge, 1999), 2:442–56). My emphasis is not on constraining what is possible in a context, but illustrating the range of approaches employed. Perhaps the image of a paint palette, which encompasses all the colours in evidence in a historical and cultural setting, is helpful. Writers draw on ideas, perhaps as painters choose from a palette. Some colours come up in a given context; others do not seem to be present. Sometimes one might show creativity and mix a couple of colours or add another new discovery, to produce some variation. Some draw particularly on one part of the colour spectrum; others tend to focus on other shades.

**58** Chartier also uses the phrase "modes of thought" (Chartier, *Cultural History*, 25).

**59** See, for instance, Teresa Morgan, *Roman Faith and Christian Faith: Pistis and Fides in the Early Roman Empire and Early Churches* (Oxford: Oxford University Press, 2015), 10–11, 24–27.

**60** In doing so I seek to reflect the diversity evident in the context, rather than the all-encompassing kind of implications inherent in claims about the "worldview" of a particular group or time.

possible in light of its own set of complex relationships with other literary and cultural traditions.⁶¹ For instance, it is not enough to observe the number of texts in a given period that use a term like τύχη ("chance" or "Fortune"), if the interpreter does not also attend to whether or not, say, writers like Polybius and Josephus seem to mean the same thing when they use it.⁶² Making this assessment will include considering how the concept functions in each text as a whole, relates to the writers' rhetorical purposes, and might be shaped by the cultural expectations, for instance, of a Jewish or non-Jewish audience.

Set out in this form these claims may be obvious to students of ancient texts. However, various practical constraints inevitably press interpreters into choosing between areas of compromise.⁶³ Historians of *mentalité* seek to collate vast data banks of information in which patterns across a given period may then be discerned. Notwithstanding its particular strengths, this approach encounters practical problems of analysing large volumes of texts at sufficient depth for accurate interpretation.⁶⁴ Whereas some kinds of texts may be well suited to this type of analysis,⁶⁵ other texts in which ideas about the nature of the world are embedded in long narratives of causation will be better suited to a more detailed, case study approach. Case studies allow for appreciating the particularity of a given text as its various features interact, while also facilitating a richer comparison between texts.

---

**61** This naturally creates an elusive conundrum between reading the part in light of the whole, and the whole in light of its parts. On this tension, Hernadi follows Müller's observation about the interdependence of definitions: before determining if any individual text is "tragedy" one needs a set of texts already defined as "tragedy" with which to compare it (see Hernadi, *Beyond Genre*, 2–3).
**62** Polybius and Josephus do use τύχη differently. See Chapter 4.
**63** See, for instance, Vovelle's discussion of serial and case study approaches to the history of *mentalité* (Michel Vovelle, *Ideologies and Mentalities*, trans. Eamon O'Flaherty (Cambridge: Polity, 1990), 232–45).
**64** Green, *Cultural History*, 56–58; see also discussion of this difficulty in Morgan, *Roman Faith and Christian Faith*, 38–39. Some of this work also raises the related issue of how interpreters can apply quantitative measures effectively across diverse texts where, for example, "one" instance of a given idea within a sample may differ in significance depending on how central this idea is to the text's scheme or purpose.
**65** Proverbs or sayings that are readily separable from their immediate context and frequently used in this way even within the ancient sources provide ideal material for this approach. Morgan demonstrates the usefulness of large databases of proverbs, fables, *gnomai*, and exempla, for building up a picture of popular morality (Teresa Morgan, *Popular Morality in the Early Roman Empire* (Cambridge: Cambridge University Press, 2007)). See also discussion of the value of large samples of data in Morgan, *Roman Faith and Christian Faith*, 38–39.

Inevitably, case studies are limited. The ideal would be to incorporate very large numbers of detailed case studies, to map the elements of understandings of history evident in the setting as completely as possible. Nonetheless, recognising inevitable practical constraints, the key texts discussed throughout this study encompass appropriate diversity and have been carefully chosen. They are not eccentric and in most cases can be seen to be somewhat exemplary, reflecting the interests of some other texts within this diverse setting. But, having identified each for its value in filling out the range of perspectives, I then treat it in detail as an individual example, not a representative of a wider class.

## 2.3 Expanding the scope of texts relevant to Luke's cultural context

Finally, given this approach to mapping the understandings of history evident in Luke's setting, the scope of texts to be included must be considered to contribute to the same, broad cultural context. Teresa Morgan convincingly demonstrates the interpenetration between Greek and Latin worlds during this time, evident not only in the geographical spread of inscriptions in each language and cultural parallels, but even Latinisms in the Greek NT (cf. δηνάριον, Mark 6.37; πραιτώριον, Mark 15.16).[66] Roman linguistic and cultural influences were present across the Roman empire, and the NT as well as related archaeological evidence demonstrates that members of the messianic movement following Jesus, whether in Rome, Jerusalem, or the communities of Paul's mission like Corinth, were in contact with ideas present in Latin texts. My approach therefore does not rely upon, for instance, assumptions about a common location for the intended audience of each of the texts discussed.[67] Nor does it require evidence that Luke himself read texts in every language represented by these case study texts, but simply that there is some commerce in ideas across these linguistic divides.

---

**66** Morgan, *Roman Faith and Christian Faith*, 26–27, 36–38.
**67** Contrary to the claims of studies that presume Latinisms in Mark's Gospel suggest a Roman provenance or intended audience (cf. Robert H. Gundry, *Mark: A Commentary on His Apology for the Cross* (Grand Rapids: Eerdmans, 1993), 1043–45; Ben Witherington III, *The Gospel of Mark: A Socio-Rhetorical Commentary* (Grand Rapids: Eerdmans, 2001), 20–28), the cultural and linguistic cross-fertilisation across the region in this period precludes drawing such conclusions from only this evidence.

Diverse late Second Temple Jewish[68] texts necessarily also fit within the scope of the cultural world within which the NT emerged. Jewish texts remain relevant conversation partners for Luke/Acts because of both the strong connections to themes and traditions from Jewish texts in Luke's narrative[69] and the well-documented influence of Hellenism on Second Temple Judaism.[70] Writers like Luke, as well as Josephus or Philo, make use of themes, terms, and genres from the Graeco-Roman setting because this is also naturally their *own* context.[71] These interconnections similarly also exist across linguistic divides. The diverse engagements between the themes and concepts of Hebrew, Aramaic, and Greek texts confirm that an ongoing, complex relationship existed between Jewish traditions articulated in these languages. This is evident not only in the very existence of the Septuagint,[72] but in diverse influences across other texts and traditions. Some recent studies illustrate such interconnections, for instance, by

---

**68** I use "late Second Temple Judaism" given the broad timespan covered by "Second Temple Judaism." This study's key texts fall in the latter part of that period (or, technically, just beyond the time of the temple in the case of Josephus's *Jewish War*, 4 Ezra, and 2 Baruch).

**69** Gregory E. Sterling, "'Opening the Scriptures': The Legitimation of the Jewish Diaspora and Early Christian Mission," in *Jesus and the Heritage of Israel: Luke's Narrative Claim upon Israel's Legacy*, ed. David P. Moessner, Luke the Interpreter of Israel 1 (Harrisburg: Trinity, 1999), 199–225; Sterling, *Historiography and Self-Definition*, 358–59; David P. Moessner, "Luke's 'Plan of God' from the Greek Psalter: The Rhetorical Thrust of 'The Prophets and the Psalms' in Peter's Speech at Pentecost," in *Scripture and Traditions: Essays on Early Judaism and Christianity in Honor of Carl R. Holladay*, ed. Patrick Gray and Gail R. O'Day, NovTSup 129 (Leiden: Brill, 2008), 223–38; Moessner, "The 'Script' of the Scriptures in Acts: Suffering as God's 'Plan' (βουλή) for the World for the 'Release of Sins,'" in Witherington, *History, Literature, and Society in the Book of Acts*, 218–50.

**70** Significant studies that reshaped understandings of Second Temple Judaism, its diversity, and its relationship to Hellenism, include: Martin Hengel, *Judaism and Hellenism: Studies in Their Encounter in Palestine during the Early Hellenistic Period*, trans. John Bowden, 2 vols. (London: SCM, 1974); E. P. Sanders, *Paul and Palestinian Judaism: A Comparison of Patterns of Religion* (London: SCM, 1977); Martin Hengel and Christoph Markschies, *The "Hellenization" of Judea in the First Century after Christ*, trans. John Bowden (London: SCM; Philadelphia: Trinity, 1989); Gabriele Boccaccini, *Middle Judaism: Jewish Thought, 300 BCE to 200 CE* (Minneapolis: Fortress, 1991); John M. G. Barclay, *Jews in the Mediterranean Diaspora: From Alexander to Trajan (323 BCE–117 CE)* (Edinburgh: T&T Clark, 1996). It is clear that Judaism exhibited extensive interaction with Hellenism before the messianic sect that would become Christianity emerged—Hellenisation was already part of its late Second Temple Jewish context.

**71** Earlier readings that presumed Luke must be gentile because of his use of Graeco-Roman tradition would similarly ensure (nonsensically) that Josephus and Philo could not meet the criteria for "Jewish writers" (cf. Sterling, *Historiography and Self-Definition*, 327).

**72** See, for instance, James Aitken, "The Language of the Septuagint and Jewish-Greek Identity," in *The Jewish-Greek Tradition in Antiquity and the Byzantine Empire*, ed. James Aitken and James Carleton Paget (Cambridge: Cambridge University Press, 2014), 120–34.

illuminating the often-neglected place of influences of Greek literature and philosophy in shaping the language of later rabbinic texts which connect back to traditions of early Judaism, as well as archaeological evidence, for example in funerary inscriptions.[73]

Luke/Acts therefore is situated on the same spectrum of interrelationship between Graeco-Roman and Jewish literary and cultural conventions as other late Second Temple writers, recognising that the ways in which these writers incorporate such traditions are themselves diverse (illustrated by the differences between, for instance, the level of Hellenistic influence that might be gleaned from the texts of Maccabean literature, the Dead Sea Scrolls, or Philo).

Thus, this study's cross-genre method seeks to map aspects of the understandings of history present in Luke's cultural context, using case studies for detailed treatment of key texts and a wide scope of texts. It recognises that Greek, Latin, and late Second Temple Jewish texts can all contribute to the understandings of history that are relevant to Luke/Acts. In addition to offering conclusions about the ways diverse understandings of history illuminate Lukan eschatology, I return to assess the usefulness of this cross-genre methodology at the conclusion of the study.

## 3 The case study texts

The key texts selected all date within an approximate range of the second century BCE to the early second century CE. In order to build up the understandings of history present in Luke's cultural context, and given diachronic changes, for instance in the way Graeco-Roman texts portray divine involvement in human history, these parameters are appropriate. At the earliest boundary, the period I consider includes the Hellenistic historiographical perspective of Polybius, with his focus on the rise of Rome, and the reflections on the Seleucid empire provided by 2 Maccabees. At the later end, Tacitus's perspective on earlier Roman politics from his early second-century vantage point is included, as well as various responses to the fall of Jerusalem, but material beyond the Bar Kokhba revolt is excluded.

---

[73] See discussion in: Günter Stemberger, "Jews and Graeco-Roman Culture: From Alexander to Theodosius II," in Aitken and Paget, *The Jewish-Greek Tradition*, (Cambridge: Cambridge University Press, 2014), 15–36; T. M. Law and A. Salvesen, *Greek Scripture and the Rabbis*, Contributions to Biblical Exegesis and Theology 66 (Leuven: Peeters, 2012); Philip S. Alexander, "The Rabbis, the Greek Bible and Hellenism," in Aitken and Paget, *The Jewish-Greek Tradition*, 229–46.

Notably, while the texts for discussion have been chosen carefully, any feasible selection will be limited. Inevitably readers will notice texts omitted, including perhaps texts they should like to have seen included—no doubt for good reasons. Thus although my comparisons are not exhaustive, they are sufficient to illustrate the key concerns of the study, and to host a conversation about these important methodological and thematic issues in Lukan studies. As set out in Chapter 1, I have deliberately steered away from including other NT texts as case studies in the analysis, particularly given that earlier work has already taken this as a key focus[74] and my intention is to expand the breadth of texts considered alongside Luke/Acts—though I recognise that there may be scope for revising such earlier studies and I do at points note connections to the treatment of other NT texts.

Finally, it is worth briefly noting further elements of Luke/Acts' position in relation to other Jewish and non-Jewish texts of the Graeco-Roman period. Throughout this work I treat Luke/Acts as Graeco-Roman historiography,[75] though such a designation is not as straightforward as the archetypes of the genre like Thucydides, Polybius, or Tacitus[76] (as confirmed also by the extent of ongoing contention about Lukan genre). In offering his extended narrative of the causation of events—a core attribute of ancient historiography[77]—Luke follows various common historiographical conventions, for instance incorporating speeches (a key feature of Acts),[78] and presenting his narrative as a continuation of an earlier text, here that of the earlier biblical account of God's dealing with

---

[74] Cullmann, *Christ and Time*; Cullmann, *Salvation in History*; Maddox, *The Purpose of Luke-Acts*; Carroll, *Response to the End*.

[75] There is not space here to rehearse the debates on the genre of Luke/Acts. I am persuaded that the two-part work exhibits the features of historiography (for a summary, see Keener, *Acts*, 1:90–115) and would raise expectations associated with historiography in first-century readers, though this is more pronounced in the second volume with the extended focus on speeches. In the Gospel, Luke clearly responds to the sources shared with the synoptics, which affects the episodic nature of the narrative.

[76] See Becker, *The Beginning of Christian History*, 69.

[77] This key element of the definition of Graeco-Roman historiography is core to the designation of historiography over biography here, despite the ways in which Luke incorporates narrative accounts of the lives of individuals within his account. Most importantly, even in the ancient world, these genres were not starkly separated and so, given the understanding of genre as setting expectations for competent readers argued for above, rigid distinctions between ancient historiography and βίοι in contemporary scholarship are something of a red herring. See n. 7 above.

[78] On the centrality of this feature in historiography, see John Marincola, "Speeches in Classical Historiography," in *A Companion to Greek and Roman Historiography*, ed. John Marincola, Blackwell Companions to the Ancient World 1 (Malden, MA: Blackwell, 2007), 118–32.

God's people in the Septuagint.[79] Here Luke shows important similarities to other Hellenistic Jewish historiographies, of which Josephus's are the prototypical examples.[80] As Josephus adapts Graeco-Roman literary conventions, he produces an extended narrative of historical causation which draws on Jewish tradition. Nonetheless, Josephus is closer to such Graeco-Roman historiographical convention than Luke. Despite Luke's linguistic skills, which set him somewhat apart from many other NT writers, Luke/Acts is not an upper register literary text such as we might find in Thucydides or Tacitus.[81] Moreover Luke's literary conventions are also derived from Jewish literary conventions. In particular, as he presents his story as a continuation of the Septuagint, he not only presents the events of his account as the fulfilment of earlier prophecy or a continuation of the pattern of divine involvement with God's people, but employs patterns of word choice (such as the characteristic καὶ ἐγένετο) and themes (for instance, of women who are eventually made able to conceive children when all hope had seemed lost) which mimic the literary style of the Septuagint.[82]

Like other writers of the late Second Temple period, Luke engages in various ways with themes from the biblical text, and in doing so incorporates elements which, as I've argued above, transcend genre. One among many possible examples arises from texts' various engagements with the visions in Daniel. The eagle vision in 4 Ezra 11–12 draws on Daniel 2 and 7, adapting the application of the vision to a new historical context, but retaining the apocalypse genre, whereas Josephus applies interpretation of Daniel 2 to philosophical groups in his own context in a historiographical text (*Ant.* 10), and the Qumran War Scroll reflects a different engagement again with Daniel. Similarly, imagery used to describe eschatological anticipation in many Second Temple texts, despite the frequent

---

**79** For tables outlining Greek and Roman historiographies which present continuations of earlier historiographies, such as Polybius's portrayal of his historiography as a continuation of those by Aratus and Timaeus, see John Marincola, *Authority and Tradition in Ancient Historiography* (Cambridge: Cambridge University Press, 1997), 289–92, as well as discussion of the nuances between polemic and praise in the portrait of a predecessor in pp. 217–57.
**80** As noted further below, Rajak views Josephus as the peak of this tradition of Hellenistic Jewish historiography. See Tessa Rajak, "The Sense of History in Jewish Intertestamental Writing," in *Crises and Perspectives: Studies in Ancient Near Eastern Polytheism, Biblical Theology, Palestinian Archaeology, and Intertestamental Literature*, ed. Johannes C. de Moor, OtSt 24 (Leiden: Brill, 1986), 124–45.
**81** See Alexander, *The Preface to Luke's Gospel*, 170–171, and p. 14 n. 54 above.
**82** See further discussion in Chapter 3 §4.2 below.

short-hand of "apocalyptic eschatology," is not limited to apocalypses, and is also taken up in Luke.[83]

Thus, like many contemporaneous texts, Luke/Acts is situated both in relation to various non-Jewish Graeco-Roman literary traditions, and also within a strain of tradition that, to a greater or lesser degree, applies these to the themes and literary conventions of Jewish literature.

## 3.1 Texts chosen for analysis

The five non-Jewish key texts are introduced below in chronological order, followed by the five Jewish texts. Some (historiographical) texts have frequently featured in studies of Luke/Acts.[84] The others extend comparisons into texts such as popular exempla, Latin epic, and apocalypses.

**Polybius's *Histories*** — Written in the second century BCE, Polybius's historiography of 40 volumes, of which about a third remain extant, traces events initially from 220–167, though he later extends his account until the mid-140s BCE.[85] The Greek-language historiography recounts events from the time the Republic annexed territories to become provinces and continues up to the destruction of Carthage and Corinth. Polybius was well connected as the tutor for a leading family in Rome.[86] His social and political situation seems to influence his

---

[83] In some ways, this offers a response to a suggestion put forward by Adela Yarbro Collins, who designates Mark "historiography in the apocalyptic mode" (Adela Yarbro Collins, "Apocalypses and Apocalypticism: Early Christian," *ABD* 1:289), and the earlier work of G. I. Davies who describes "apocalyptic historiography" (Davies, "Apocalyptic and Historiography," 16–19). Though each of these scholars rightly recognises significant elements of the historiographical texts with which they are engaging, my suggestion is that texts like Mark, Luke, and Josephus's historiographies reflect some relationship with the themes of particular Jewish apocalypses because they share some beliefs which transcend genre, not because they are writing a particular form of the genre "historiography" which needs to be specified as in some sense "apocalyptic."
[84] Though also historiography, 2 Maccabees has not been studied alongside Luke/Acts as frequently as historiographies by Josephus, Polybius, or Diodorus Siculus (though, as an exception, see Daniel R. Schwartz, "Circular or Teleological, Universal or Particular, with God or Without? On 1–2 Maccabees and Acts," in Frey, Rothschild, and Schröter, *Die Apostelgeschichte*, 119–29).
[85] The first five books survive fully. Books 17 and 40 are entirely lost, while only one fragment from Book 37 is extant. Fragments of each of the other books remain. Livy's almost "word for word" Latin translation is an important source for the material he covers in his *History of Rome*, Books 31–45 (see Habicht's introduction to the LCL edition of Polybius, *The Histories*, 1:xv–xvi).
[86] Boris Dreyer, "Polybius," *BNP* 11:495.

account, as well as providing his privileged access to events.[87] Polybius's historiography focuses on Rome's rise as a unique military and political feat. His focus on historical causes, the rise of Rome and "universal" historiography, and important (if varied) references to the role of τύχη, as well as scholars' frequent use of his historiography as a conversation partner for Luke (and Josephus),[88] makes this text an illuminating contributor.

**Diodorus Siculus's *Library of History*** —Diodorus advocates extending historiography both temporally and geographically. His 40-volume Greek-language *Library* (of which Books 1–5 and 11–20 remain, with some further fragments from most of the books extant)[89] includes primeval myths and stories from both eastern and western sources, tracing "the accounts which each people records of its earliest times" (1.4.5) up until the mid-to-late 50s BCE.[90] Originally from Sicily (Agyrium), Diodorus then lived in Egypt (c. 60–56 BCE) and Rome (at least 56–30).[91] He claims to have worked on his *Library* for over 30 years, and to have gone to great pains to provide this compilation (1.4.1) for those who hadn't time to read all the sources individually (1.3.5–8). Though often dis-

---

[87] As discussed in later chapters, Polybius may incorporate some subtle resistance to Rome (see Erich S. Gruen, "Polybius and Josephus on Rome," in *Flavius Josephus: Interpretation and History*, ed. Jack Pastor, Pnina Stern and Menahem Mor, Supplements to the Journal for the Study of Judaism 146 (Leiden: Brill, 2011), 153).
[88] Cf. Molthagen, "Geschichtsschreibung und Geschichtsverständnis"; Shaye J. D. Cohen, "Polybius, Jeremiah, and Josephus," *History and Theory* 21 (1982): 366–81; Miriam Pucci ben Zeev, "Polybius, Josephus, and the Capitol in Rome," *JSJ* 27 (1996): 21–30; David P. Moessner, "'Managing the Audience': The Rhetoric of Authorial Intent and Audience Comprehension in the Narrative Epistemology of Polybius of Megalopolis, Diodorus Siculus, and Luke the Evangelist," in *The Word Leaps the Gap: Essays on Scripture and Theology in Honor of Richard B. Hays*, ed. J. Ross Wagner, C. Kavin Rowe, and A. Katherine Grieb (Grand Rapids: Eerdmans, 2008), 179–97; Gruen, "Polybius and Josephus."
[89] Kenneth S. Sacks, *Diodorus Siculus and the First Century* (Princeton: Princeton University Press, 1990), 3. The fragmentary sections of the work create some difficulties. For instance, Book 7 derives almost exclusively from Eusebius, whose understandings of history might significantly interfere (see Clarke, *Making Time*, 127). On the various sources Diodorus has used for his text, and a traditional argument about Diodorus's (lack of) skill and independence, see P. J. Stylianou, *A Historical Commentary on Diodorus Siculus Book 15*, OCM (Oxford: Clarendon, 1998), 8–10.
[90] Klaus Meister, "Diodorus Siculus," *BNP* 2:444. Diodorus gives his own structure in 1.4.6–1.5.1, though he is thought to have adjusted the finishing point, perhaps for political reasons as the content approached his own time (Sacks, *Diodorus Siculus*, 160–61), or due to age (C. H. Oldfather, Introduction to *Diodorus of Sicily: The Library of History*, LCL (Cambridge: Harvard University Press, 1933–1967), 1:xix).
[91] Meister, "Diodorus Siculus," 444.

missed as a compiler of earlier sources,⁹² several recent studies have asserted Diodorus's role in shaping his text, particularly highlighting his creativity in his prefaces.⁹³ As an "outsider," his portrayal of Rome is not always positive. Diodorus's focus on morality is evident throughout, including in his understanding of the historian's purpose, which he also relates to divine πρόνοια. Together with his approach to "universal" historiography, these themes in his *Library* reveal important features of Diodorus's conception of history, which, in addition to its frequent use as a comparison to Luke/Acts,⁹⁴ make Diodorus's *Library* a helpful inclusion in this study.

**Virgil's *Aeneid*—**Virgil worked on his epic poem of Roman origins from the battle of Actium in 30–31 BCE until his death in 19 BCE.⁹⁵ The 12-volume Latin epic plays on inherited themes, particularly as found in Homer.⁹⁶ This is evident even in the overall structure of the epic, in which the first six books recreate and allude to themes from Homer's *Odyssey*, and Books 7–12 to the *Iliad*.⁹⁷ Virgil presents Rome as the *telos* of history achieved in the reign of Augustus—although this presentation also displays elements of ambiguity.⁹⁸ The plot covers mythic events following exile from Troy and a search to found a new city, and

---

**92** Stylianou maintains Diodorus is not only a compiler but that he *mishandles* earlier sources (Stylianou, *A Historical Commentary*, 1–3, 15–17, 21; cf. P. J. Stylianou, review of *Diodorus Siculus and the First Century*, by Kenneth S. Sacks, *Bryn Mawr Classical Review* 2 (1991): 388). By contrast, Sacks, *Diodorus Siculus*, 3–4; Lisa Irene Hau, "The Burden of Good Fortune in Diodorus of Sicily: A Case for Originality?", *Historia* 58 (2009): 172.
**93** This is the central argument of Sacks, *Diodorus Siculus*, 5–6.
**94** Cf. Squires, *The Plan of God*; Moessner, "'Completed End(s)ings'"; Moessner, "'Managing the Audience'"; Rothschild, *Luke-Acts and the Rhetoric*.
**95** Elaine Fantham, "Introduction," in *Virgil, Aeneid: A New Translation*, ed. Frederick Ahl (Oxford: Oxford University Press, 2007), xvii. Disagreement exists over whether some inconsistencies in the finished text indicate sections Virgil intended to alter but left incomplete when he died; the subtlety at work elsewhere suggests that these types of explanations are not necessary (James J. O'Hara, *Inconsistency in Roman Epic: Studies in Catullus, Lucretius, Vergil, Ovid and Lucan*, Roman Literature and Its Contexts (Cambridge: Cambridge University Press, 2007), 77–78).
**96** R. D. Williams, "The Sixth Book of the *Aeneid*," in *Oxford Readings in Vergil's Aeneid*, ed. S. J. Harrison (Oxford: Oxford University Press, 1990), 194–96; G. N. Knauer, "Vergil's *Aeneid* and Homer," in Harrison, *Oxford Readings in Vergil's Aeneid*, 390–412; David Quint, "Repetition and Ideology in the *Aeneid*," *Materiali e discussioni per l'analisi dei testi classici* 23 (1989): 9; on effects of other intertextual links, see O'Hara, *Inconsistency in Roman Epic*, 90–91.
**97** Quint, "Repetition and Ideology," 9.
**98** See Karl Galinsky, *Augustan Culture: An Interpretive Introduction* (Princeton: Princeton University Press, 1996); Philip Hardie, *Virgil's Aeneid: Cosmos and Imperium* (Oxford: Oxford University Press, 1986); D. C. Feeney, "History and Revelation in Vergil's Underworld," *Proceedings of the Classical Philological Society* 32 (1986): 1–24.

concludes with the figurative founding of Rome as Aeneas kills Turnus.[99] The *Aeneid*'s portrayal of deterministic prophecy and the nature of the end of history, which the reader is invited to see as realised in the historical present, ensures that the *Aeneid* represents an illuminating comparison text, often overlooked in NT studies.[100] Virgil's epic fills out the diverse understandings of history in evidence in Luke's broader context, and makes a particularly valuable contribution because it is a non-Jewish text that presents a teleological view of history.[101]

**Valerius Maximus's *Memorable Doings and Sayings*** — Valerius's Latin compilation of exempla provides significant insights into popular views of history. The nine books of anecdotes,[102] produced in approximately 30 CE during Tiberius's reign,[103] are collected under thematic headings to assist the ancient rhetorician in need of an illustration (cf. 1.praef), on topics ranging from "ancient institutions" (2.1) and "rashness" (9.8), to "those who degenerated from famous parents" (3.5).[104] Under each heading, Valerius divides the material into Roman and non-Roman stories. Not much is known about Valerius himself, and his text has often been dismissed as merely derivative of its sources and popular in register.[105] However, its "middle-brow," popular nature indicates one of Valerius's

---

[99] R. O. A. M. Lyne, "Vergil and the Politics of War," in Harrison, *Oxford Readings in Vergil's Aeneid*, 338.

[100] Previous discussions of the *Aeneid* in Lukan studies have generally focused on genre and a minority view that Luke/Acts is an epic and/or on Luke's imitation of Virgilian literary structures (Bonz, *The Past as Legacy*; MacDonald, *Luke and Vergil*, 112–77). This is not my intention here; as argued above, an author's portrait of the nature of the world, such as in relation to the shape and end of history, or divine and human agency in history, can share elements with another writer's portrait, without the text exhibiting the same generic conventions.

[101] Although I will at times refer to the *Eclogues* and *Georgics*, the focus will remain on the *Aeneid*.

[102] Wardle argues that the original end is likely lost (D. Wardle, ed. and trans., *Valerius Maximus: Memorable Deeds and Sayings, Book 1*, Clarendon Ancient History (Oxford: Clarendon, 1998), 6; cf. C. J. Carter, "Valerius Maximus," in *Empire and Aftermath: Silver Latin II*, ed. T. A. Dorey, Greek and Latin Studies, Classical Literature and Its Influence (London: Routledge & Kegan Paul, 1975), 29).

[103] D. R. Shackleton Bailey, Introduction to *Valerius Maximus: Memorable Doings and Sayings*, LCL (Cambridge: Harvard University Press, 2000), 2–3.

[104] Valerius claims to have undertaken the labour of compiling the anecdotes across scattered sources so that "those wishing to take examples may be spared the labour of lengthy search" (1.praef). See discussion of the development of collections of exempla for declamation in W. Martin Bloomer, *Valerius Maximus and the Rhetoric of the New Nobility* (London: Duckworth, 1992), 8.

[105] Bloomer, *Valerius Maximus and the Rhetoric*, and Clive Skidmore, *Practical Ethics for Roman Gentlemen: The Work of Valerius Maximus* (Exeter: University of Exeter Press, 1996), reignited in-

great contributions to study of the first century.[106] Moreover, he leaves his mark by redacting particular anecdotes and through the selections themselves.[107] Significantly, rather than the irony and scepticism of some first-century literary works,[108] Valerius affirms the assumptions of Roman religion and the place of the *princeps* in it,[109] alongside everyday anecdotal reflections on virtue and fortune. This renders his text a valuable addition to these case studies.

**Tacitus's *Histories*** —Like Diodorus Siculus, Tacitus focuses on moral order and moral explanations for historical events. This fits with his political preference for governance by an elite, asserting that without such controls the people will descend into licentiousness.[110] Tacitus lived from approximately 55–120 CE and was a senator during the Flavian period (70–96).[111] The *Histories*, a Latin historiography believed to have comprised either 12 or 14 books (of which Books 1–4 and sections of Book 5 remain), dates to 105–109 CE.[112] It describes the period of Flavian rule and the events that immediately preceded it, beginning from 1 January 69 CE and recounting the tumultuous year of the four emperors, with the extant sections concluding in the summer of 70 CE.[113] Given the period with which it deals, I have chosen the *Histories* as the case study text, but the *Annals* will occasionally feature as it helps to interpret Tacitus's

---

terest in the text in the 1990s. See also Wardle, *Valerius Maximus*, v. Conversely, see Carter on Valerius's "supreme mediocrity of talent" (Carter, "Valerius Maximus," 30; cf. p. 51).

**106** Hans-Friedrich Mueller, *Roman Religion in Valerius Maximus*, Routledge Classical Monographs (London: Routledge, 2002), 3. Mueller asserts, "Valerius Maximus was no theologian, even less a philosopher, and his work, no *De natura deorum*, is consequently most useful. Valerius is middle-brow, and thus likely represents attitudes more commonly diffused—attitudes not necessarily strictly logical or without internal contradictions, but so much the better for approaching a living system of belief" (p. 3).

**107** See discussion in Mueller, *Roman Religion in Valerius*, 118–21; Wardle, *Valerius Maximus*, 16–17.

**108** Ovid's *Metamorphoses*, for instance, is contemporaneous and sceptical. For Ovid's relevance to the period, with reference to Valerius, see Fergus Millar, "Ovid and the Domus Augusta: Rome Seen from Tomoi," *The Journal of Roman Studies* 83 (1993): 2–4.

**109** In his preface to Book 1, Valerius provides a glowing dedication to the Caesars. The text is frequently taken to indicate a popular attitude towards the principate. Mueller describes Valerius's "nationalistically narrow and chauvinist religiosity," and observes, "Valerius was obviously both educated enough to compose the *Facta et dicta memorabilia* and conventional enough to support the contemporary regime with enthusiasm" (Mueller, *Roman Religion in Valerius*, 178).

**110** Ronald Syme, *Tacitus* (Oxford: Clarendon, 1958), 1:169.

**111** Thomas Franke and Egon Flaig, "Tacitus," *BNP* 1:63–70.

**112** Franke and Flaig, "Tacitus," 106.

**113** Miriam T. Griffin, "Tacitus as a Historian," in *The Cambridge Companion to Tacitus*, ed. A. J. Woodman (Cambridge: Cambridge University Press, 2009), 183.

conception of history in the *Histories*. Through his focus on morality and scepticism about the involvement of divine forces in history, Tacitus contributes helpfully to this study.

**Second Maccabees**—Written in Greek,[114] 2 Maccabees offers a valuable perspective within Second Temple Judaism, reflecting support of the revolutionary activities of Judas Maccabeus.[115] The text comprises two letters (1.1–2.18), and a historiographical narrative recounting the events related to Judas (chps 3–15), incorporating both a preface (2.19–32)[116] and an epilogue (15.37–9). It records an anonymous epitomiser's claim to have condensed the historiographical sections from a (no longer extant) five-volume account by Jason of Cyrene (2.23).[117] While recounting the situation in Judea under the Seleucid empire, 2 Maccabees indicates a more positive attitude towards Rome, which most scholars suggest indicates a dating in the late second century BCE, after initial Roman victories over the Seleucids but before the Roman general Pompey's action against the Hasmoneans in 63 BCE.[118] Its presentation of the role of humans in enacting divine will, as well as the understanding of reward and punishment within history, make 2 Maccabees a worthy contribution to the range of views within which to situate Luke/Acts.

---

**114** The Greek is original, not translated from Hebrew or Aramaic as other LXX texts (Schwartz, "Circular or Teleological," 199; Daniel J. Harrington, *The Maccabean Revolt: Anatomy of a Biblical Revolution*, OTS 1 (Wilmington, DE: Glazier, 1988), 103).
**115** On the relationships between the Maccabean literature and historical considerations, see Harrington, *The Maccabean Revolt*, and on theological and ideological differences between 1 and 2 Maccabees see Schwartz, "Circular or Teleological"; Robert Doran, "Independence or Co-Existence: The Responses of 1 and 2 Maccabees to Seleucid Hegemony," in *Society of Biblical Literature, 1999 Seminar Papers*, SBLSPS 38 (Atlanta: Society of Biblical Literature, 1999), 94–103; and Katell Berthelot, "Philo's Perception of the Roman Empire," *JSJ* 42 (2007): 166–87.
**116** See Doran on the possible relationships between the historiographical summary and the letters (Robert Doran, *2 Maccabees: A Critical Commentary*, Hermeneia (Minneapolis: Fortress, 2012), 14–15). The letters appear to reflect the diaspora situation and traditions of sending letters with other texts. The first letter is commonly considered authentic; the second is not. Dates provided in the letters are also used in dating the narrative; see below.
**117** The epitomiser justifies his digest version as enabling ease of reading (2 Macc 2.24–32), which is reminiscent of some of Valerius Maximus's claims about the simpler and more user-friendly product he offers his reader (1.praef). Similarly, see Diod. *Library* 1.3.5–8.
**118** Second Maccabees is generally placed between 124/5 and 63 BCE (Doran, "Independence or Co-Existence"; Harold W. Attridge, "Jewish Historiography," in *Early Judaism and Its Modern Interpreters*, ed. Robert A. Kraft and George W. E. Nickelsburg, BMI 2 (Philadelphia: Fortress, 1986), 318–20). Schwartz provides an earlier date, based on a different reading of dates provided in the letters in manuscripts (Daniel R. Schwartz, *2 Maccabees*, CEJL (Berlin: de Gruyter, 2008), 14–15).

**Qumran War Scroll**—Written in Hebrew, the War Scroll sets out the events of an eschatological battle to take place between the sons of light and the sons of darkness, in highly choreographed, even liturgical, terms. It incorporates thanksgiving hymns, prophetic claims about the outcomes of seven phases of battle, and the final victory. Although not a manual the community intended to implement in real life battles,[119] details about battle formation and weapons indicate Roman military strategies[120] and suggest conflict with Roman forces as the setting that gave rise to the text. This would indicate the text should be dated to the mid-first century BCE.[121] 1QM provides the most detailed text. There is disagreement about which other fragments are to be attributed to the War Scroll, though certainly texts from Cave 4 confirm the presence of different recensions of the text (cf. 4Q491–96).[122] This study will focus particularly on 1QM as a single detailed manuscript,[123] with occasional references to other fragments—although apparent seams exist even within 1QM, between the overview of column 1, and

---

**119** Sharon Lea Mattila, "Two Contrasting Eschatologies at Qumran (4Q246 vs 1QM)," *Biblica* 75 (1994): 530–31; contra Phillip Alexander, "The Evil Empire: The Qumran Eschatological War Cycle and the Origins of Jewish Opposition to Rome," in *Emmanuel: Studies in Hebrew Bible, Septuagint, and Dead Sea Scrolls in Honor of Emanuel Tov*, ed. Shalom M. Paul et al., VTSup 94 (Leiden: Brill, 2003), 28.
**120** Geza Vermes, *The Complete Dead Sea Scrolls in English* (London: Penguin, 1997), 163. Cf. the battle formations and weapons (2.1–4; 5.3–6.16) and titles to be provided on standards (columns 3–4).
**121** Schultz argues the events of 63 BCE catalysed the later editions of the War Scroll and their further criticism of Rome and the Kittim (Brian Schultz, *Conquering the World: The War Scroll (1QM) Reconsidered*, STDJ (Leiden: Brill, 2009)). Davies dates the text to the late first century BCE/early first century CE, though he has been criticised for such a late dating (Philip R. Davies, "War of the Sons of Light against the Sons of Darkness," in *Encyclopedia of the Dead Sea Scrolls*, ed. Lawrence H. Schiffman and James C. VanderKam (New York: Oxford University Press, 2000), 2:965–68; cf. Adam S. van der Woude, "Fifty Years of Qumran Research," in *The Dead Sea Scrolls after Fifty Years: A Comprehensive Assessment*, ed. Peter W. Flint and James C. VanderKam (Leiden, Boston, and Köln: Brill, 1998), 1:12). Davies notes his dating would also fit with the Herodian script of the 1QM manuscript, though he recognises the possibility for error in dating scripts (Davies, "War of the Sons of Light"); there is also the obvious possibility of earlier manuscripts.
**122** Numerous studies debate which of the texts should be included as versions of the same text. See Alexander, "The Evil Empire," 19–20, 29–30; Schultz, *Conquering the World*; Vermes, *The Complete Dead Sea Scrolls*, 162, 184–86.
**123** Davies argues that, given the unclear relationships with the seven other texts sometimes attributed to the War Scroll, the designation should be reserved for 1QM (Davies, "War of the Sons of Light," 365).

then significant repetition in columns 2–14 and 15–19 suggesting two strands of tradition.¹²⁴

The Dead Sea Scrolls contribute important information about Second Temple Judaism. The particular circumstances of their preservation and discovery do not of themselves indicate an eccentric perspective uncharacteristic within the diversity of Judaism. Recent research into the Qumran site's archaeology, as well as the observation that many of the scrolls appear to predate the settlement and therefore to originate elsewhere,¹²⁵ suggest a community at Qumran may not have been as isolated as some scholarship has presumed.¹²⁶ The texts included in the Dead Sea Scrolls collection are diverse. Although I draw occasionally on other texts (particularly Pesher Habakkuk and the Rule of the Congregation), the focus will remain on the War Scroll. The War Scroll's longer treatment, explicit references to history from the distant past to the future, and focus on divine and human activity portrayed as part of the events of the end, provide a valuable case study to fill out the picture of understandings of history.

**Josephus's *Jewish War*—**Josephus witnesses to the adaption of Hellenistic literary convention for communicating Jewish theological ideas, thereby offering a helpful reminder of the immersion of first-century Judaism in Hellenism. Josephus wrote his seven-volume¹²⁷ Greek historiography in the late 70s CE, tracing

---

**124** Vermes, *The Complete Dead Sea Scrolls*, 162, 184–86. See Schultz, *Conquering the World*. While some have maintained that the final form of the text is original (Alexander, "The Evil Empire," 28), others have presented various hypotheses as to the history of the text's redaction. For source-critical solutions to these problems, see John J. Collins, *The Scepter and the Star: The Messiahs of the Dead Sea Scrolls and Other Ancient Literature*, ABRL (New York: Doubleday, 1995). Davies' doctoral dissertation provides a detailed hypothesis about stages of 1QM's development, though see criticism in van der Woude, "Fifty Years of Qumran Research," 12. Also see van der Woude for the history of scholarship on this and other points in relation to the War Scroll.
**125** Suggestions that the scrolls were brought from the temple for protection would indicate a high degree of interaction with other Jewish groups. See discussion in Eric M. Meyers, "Khirbet Qumran and Its Enrivons," in *The Oxford Handbook of the Dead Sea Scrolls*, ed. Timothy Lim and John J. Collins (New York: Oxford University Press, 2010), 22–23. On older views of the texts as libraries, particularly those found in Caves 1 and 4, and an argument against these conclusions, see Tov, *Scribal Practices*, 2–5.
**126** Meyers, "Khirbet Qumran," 32. This is also supported by the Cairo Geniza manuscript of the Damascus document.
**127** Some suggest the seventh book, or some sections of it, may have been written later (Daniel R. Schwartz, "Josephus, Catullus, and the Date of the Judean War," in Pastor, Stern, and Mor, *Flavius Josephus*, 344). Josephus's works were preserved by Christian groups. The reception of Josephus and its somewhat precarious manuscript history have recently gained particular prominence. See discussion regarding manuscripts and recent work on reception in Tommaso Leoni, "The Text of the Josephan Corpus: Principal Greek Manuscripts, Ancient Latin Translations, and

the events from the time of Antiochus Epiphanes, leading up to the destruction of Jerusalem and its temple and Titus's victory. Some elements indicate a non-Jewish intended audience, such as descriptions of Jewish practices.[128] But Josephus's explanations of the recent disasters as punishment, laying blame predominantly on the Jewish revolutionaries, but also on the people as a whole for being swayed by the revolutionaries, and his emphasis on the people's need to repent to God and Rome, demonstrates an interest in persuading a Jewish audience as well. Josephus's apology in the *Jewish War* thus operates in both directions and indicates a dual focus for his audience.[129]

Josephus presents his own religious and military experience as evidence of his authority in the text—an authority which extends to his account of his own defection, leading to later service to Vespasian.[130] He writes under Roman benefaction, and the positive portrayal of Rome linked to some subtle hints of resistance is perhaps reminiscent of Polybius.[131] I have selected the *Jewish War* as the case study text because of the rhetorical and pastoral focus of Josephus's explanation of the war, his account of prophecy, determinism, and human responsibility, and the central role he attributes to his own character. However, I will make some reference to his other works, especially the *Jewish Antiquities*, as helpful in illuminating the *Jewish War*. Similarities between Josephus's and

---

the Indirect Tradition," in *A Companion to Josephus in His World*, ed. Honora Howell Chapman and Zuleika Rodgers (Chichester: Wiley, 2016), 307–21. In this study I use the LCL text.

**128** See Sterling, *Historiography and Self-Definition*, 241, 302.

**129** In the words of Sterling: "it is a mistake to think that the *Jewish War* should be read either as Roman propaganda or as Jewish propaganda: it was not one or the other; it was both by design" (Gregory E. Sterling, "Explaining Defeat: Polybius and Josephus on the Wars with Rome," in *Internationales Josephus-Kolloquium Aarthus 1999*, ed. J. U. Kalms, Münsteraner Judaistische Studien 6 (Münster: Institutum Judaicum Delitzschianum, 2000), 149). Sterling notes important similarities between Josephus's and Polybius's apologies, as they each offer an explanation which provides solace in the face of otherwise "inexplicable" events (p. 139; see n. 131 below, and further discussion in Chapter 4).

**130** See Rebecca Gray, *Prophetic Figures in Late Second Temple Jewish Palestine: The Evidence from Josephus* (Oxford: Oxford University Press, 1993), 37.

**131** Gruen, "Polybius and Josephus," 153. Sterling highlights the similarly "complex stances" each of Polybius and Josephus took in relation to Rome (Sterling, "Explaining Defeat," 136). He concludes that Josephus must, either through direct literary dependence or via another source, have known Polybius's *Histories* when writing the *Jewish War*, which he bases particularly on the alignment of "explaining defeat" through the actions of a troublesome minority (which he concedes was not an unusual strategy) and the role of τύχη (pp. 150–151).

Luke's projects are frequently noted.¹³² As borne out by the following chapters, Josephus's combination of (Deuteronomistic) explanations for the past, hope for the (perhaps distant) future, and encouragement of certain attitudes in the present make him an important conversation partner for Luke.

**Fourth Ezra**—Like 2 Baruch (below), 4 Ezra is an apocalypse which offers theological reflection on the destruction of Jerusalem. The writers of both texts spell out their conceptions of history explicitly in *vaticinia ex eventu* historical reviews. Although set in a literary present of the period following the first destruction of the temple in 586 BCE, the historical setting for both texts is patently the period following the destruction of Jerusalem and the second temple in 70 CE. There is a general consensus that the texts come before the Bar Kokhba uprising;¹³³ 4 Ezra is normally dated approximately 100 CE¹³⁴ and 2 Baruch shortly after.¹³⁵

Fourth Ezra was most likely first written in Hebrew, though it is extant only in secondary and tertiary translations.¹³⁶ It comprises seven episodes. Although a Jewish text, it has been preserved through Christian traditions, most obviously affecting the text through explicitly Christian additions at the beginning and end (5 and 6 Ezra respectively).¹³⁷ The first three episodes are dialogues between the pseudonymous legal scribe, Ezra, and an angelic interpreter, Uriel, and the remaining four are visions, all but the last of which are also interpreted by Uriel. The final episode describes an encounter with a voice from a bush, and Ezra's instruction direct from the Lord. The history of interpretation of 4 Ezra is divided over the relationship between the voices of each of Ezra and Uriel,

---

**132** Cf. Kylie Crabbe, "Being Found Fighting against God: Luke's Gamaliel and Josephus on Human Responses to Divine Providence," *ZNW* 106 (2015): 21–39; Sterling, *Historiography and Self-Definition*; Squires, *The Plan of God*.
**133** Matthias Henze, "Torah and Eschatology in the Syriac Apocalypse of Baruch," in *The Significance of Sinai: Traditions about Sinai and Divine Revelation in Judaism and Christianity*, ed. George J. Brooke, Hindy Najman, and Loren T. Stuckenbruck, TBN 12 (Leiden: Brill, 2008), 206.
**134** Bruce M. Metzger, ed. and trans., "The Fourth Book of Ezra," in *Apocalyptic Literature and Testaments*, vol. 1 of *The Old Testament Pseudepigrapha*, ed. James H. Charlesworth, ABRL (Garden City, NY: Doubleday, 1983), 520.
**135** A. F. J. Klijn, "2 (Syriac Apocalypse of) Baruch," in Charlesworth, *Apocalyptic Literature*, 617.
**136** Michael E. Stone, *Fourth Ezra: A Commentary on the Book of Fourth Ezra*, Hermeneia (Minneapolis: Fortress, 1990), 10. Occasionally I draw on one of these languages where it will illuminate discussion.
**137** Exercising caution about other possible Christian interpolations is necessary; for instance, see questionable references to the messianic figure as "my son" (4 Ezra 13.32, 37). On the impact of Christian transmission of 4 Ezra, see Theodore A. Bergren, "Christian Influence on the Transmission History of 4, 5, and 6 Ezra," in *The Jewish Apocalyptic Heritage in Early Christianity*, ed. James C. VanderKam and William Adler, CRINT 4 (Minneapolis: Fortress, 1996), 102–13.

and the view affirmed by the writer, as well as the relationship between the perspectives described in each episode.[138] I take the view that Ezra's grief is transformed as he comes to see the present from the view of the future,[139] but his lament across the episodes contributes in important ways to the perspective affirmed by the writer. Although overlooked in treatments of Luke/Acts due to genre differences, 4 Ezra provides a crucial conversation partner, given the writer's teleological view of history and sustained engagement with questions of divine and human agency in explaining the events of the past and portrayal of hope for the future.

**Second Baruch**—A relationship between 4 Ezra and 2 Baruch clearly exists, whether direct dependence or mediated via a shared source.[140] Second Baruch offers a more conservative interpretation of Jerusalem's destruction, in which Deuteronomistic understandings of the disaster as just divine punishment for sin, within a deterministic eschatological framework, both justify God's action and affirm restoration in an eschatological future for a privileged elect.[141] The most likely explanation is that 2 Baruch was written to counter 4 Ezra or the

---

[138] Since works by Brandenburger and Harnisch, interpreters have questioned where the author's voice is found in 4 Ezra (Egon Brandenburger, *Die Verborgenheit Gottes im Weltgeschehen: Das literarische und theologische Problem des 4. Esrabuches*, ATANT 68 (Zürich: TVZ, 1981); Wolfgang Harnisch, *Verhängnis und Verheißung der Geschichte: Untersuchungen zum Zeit- und Geschichtsverständnis im 4. Buch Esra und in der syr. Baruchapokalypse*, FRLANT 97 (Göttingen: Vandenhoeck & Ruprecht, 1969)). Possibilities considered include Ezra, Uriel, or some merging of the two, whether as two sides of an individual's concerns (Hermann Gunkel, "Das vierte Buch Esra," in *Die Apokryphen und Pseudepigraphen des alten Testaments*, ed. E. Kautzsch (Tübingen: Mohr, 1990), 2:331–402), dialectical tensions resolved through differences of temporal perspective (Barclay, *Paul and the Gift*, 280–308), or airing the theological questions of a community (Karina Martin Hogan, *Theologies in Conflict in 4 Ezra: Wisdom Debate and Apocalyptic Solution*, Supplements to the Journal for the Study of Judaism 130 (Boston: Brill, 2008), 4). Hogan argues that the views represent dialogue with sages from the wisdom traditions, specifically that expounded in 4QInstruction (p. 36). In addition, interpreters frequently note a turning point in Ezra's perspective as the episodes progress, normally associated with the fourth episode (Najman, *Losing the Temple*, 136).

[139] See also Barclay, *Paul and the Gift*, 302–3, though in Barclay's account of this future, the justice of God can no longer accommodate mercy for the unrighteous (opponents) (pp. 307–8).

[140] Note, for instance, cross-references in standard editions of 2 Baruch, such as Klijn, "2 (Syriac Apocalypse of) Baruch," or Michael E. Stone and Matthias Henze, eds. and trans., *4 Ezra and 2 Baruch* (Minneapolis: Fortress, 2013). Sparks also notes similarities in Ps-Philo's *Biblical Antiquities*, which he suggests supports the possibility of another source or theological approach upon which they both draw (H. D. F. Sparks, "The Syriac Apocalypse of Baruch," in *The Apocryphal Old Testament*, ed. H. D. F. Sparks (Oxford: Clarendon 1984), 838).

[141] Henze, "Torah and Eschatology," 201–15.

type of views presented in 4 Ezra.[142] Second Baruch also describes a pseudonymous scribe, here Jeremiah's scribe, Baruch, experiencing visions which are interpreted variously by the Lord or by an angel, Ramael. The fully extant Syriac manuscript claims to be a translation from a Greek text; a Greek fragment found at Oxyrhynchus supports this claim.[143] Second Baruch comprises chapters recounting Jerusalem's destruction (1–8), Baruch's lament (9.1–12.4), and a series of dialogues and visions Baruch experiences (12.5–20.4, 20.5–30; 35–43; 47–52; 53–76) and their interpretations (31–34; 44–46), with Baruch's address to the people (77) and an attached letter to the "nine and a half tribes of the dispersion" (78–87). Second Baruch makes an important contribution to this study through its portrayal of the shape of history, shared explicitly with 4 Ezra, coupled with its contrasting approach to divine and human agency as it draws differently on earlier traditions.

## 3.2 Texts omitted from detailed discussion

By necessity, many texts are not included in this study. Some earlier works fall outside the timeframe of texts for detailed treatment but will still be addressed at times due to their influence on the later texts under discussion. Such texts fall into three categories. First, work by earlier Greek writers such as Homer, Hesiod, and Thucydides will occasionally be relevant given later writers deliberately evoke these texts.[144] Secondly, Hebrew Bible/Septuagint texts provide important background, given their crucial contributions to later texts that emerge from Jewish traditions. And similarly, earlier (canonical and non-canonical) apocalypses with historical reviews, namely Daniel and 1 Enoch's *Apocalypse of Weeks* and *Animal Apocalypse*, will be discussed at times; the reception and reinterpretation

---

142 Klijn argues the differences suggest a common source is more likely than direct rebuttal of 4 Ezra (Klijn, "2 (Syriac Apocalypse of) Baruch," 620), though the differing theological explanations of events would still indicate an element of adjustment in order to counter the kinds of views reflected in sources, whether one or both of the writers of 2 Baruch and 4 Ezra adjusted the theological perspective of their common source, or the writer of 2 Baruch altered the theology of 4 Ezra if they consulted it directly.
143 Klijn, "2 (Syriac Apocalypse of) Baruch," 616. See also *Oxyrhynchus Papyri*, 3 (1903) §403, 3–7. A fully extant Arabic manuscript also depends on the Syriac (Klijn, "2 (Syriac Apocalypse of) Baruch," 616).
144 Although illuminating background, it is important to view these earlier texts separately, particularly given significant shifts away from portraying the gods' involvement in history in later texts. These changes render the synchronic treatment of texts spanning a very broad time period, seen in studies such as Uytanlet, *Luke-Acts and Jewish Historiography*, less effective.

of these apocalypses is important not only in 4 Ezra and 2 Baruch, but also for writers of texts of other genres, like Josephus.

Some other texts would also fill out the variety of conceptions of history evidenced in the chosen period, but unfortunately there is not space in this study for their inclusion as case studies, though many are mentioned briefly at points in the study where this illuminates the case study texts. I initially sampled a much larger collection of texts before selecting the key texts above.

A number of non-Jewish Graeco-Roman texts would have provided further insights into conceptions of history in this period, including Strabo's *Geography* and Pliny's *Natural History*, both wide-ranging texts reflecting Stoic interests,[145] the former with an explicit interest in writing for an "educated," non-specialist audience.[146] The more sceptical views of Ovid's *Metamorphoses* or Lucan's *Civil War* would have provided additional insights, as also would Lucian's satirical treatment *How to Write History*, although much of the latter criticises historians' approaches to the writing of historiography itself and thus focuses on generic concerns. Other historiographies, such as those by Livy or Dionysius of Halicarnassus frequently feature as comparisons in Lukan studies. A historian such as Sallust would likewise offer helpful insights, with his nostalgic approach to the past, using his historical account to emphasise morality and virtue, all within a framework of decline and fall. However, in selecting non-Jewish texts frequently compared to Luke/Acts, I have chosen Diodorus Siculus over other, in some ways similar, texts like that by Dionysius, as well as Polybius's (Greek) and Tacitus's (Latin) *Histories*. Similarly, Diodorus and Tacitus are included over Sallust as texts which give a central role to concerns of morality in their histories, and likewise I have selected Tacitus's account, with its focus on nostalgia and decline, over his earlier Latin model in Sallust.[147]

Biographies, such as the *Lives* by Plutarch or Suetonius, would offer an interesting counter and I will refer to these texts at some points in the discussion. However, although biographies occasionally receive attention in some studies of Luke and Acts, this is almost exclusively in relation to generic attributes and as part of claims that Luke/Acts exhibits features of ancient βίοι.[148] These studies

---

[145] Karl-Ludwig Elvers, "Strabo," *BNP* 13:865; Klaus Sallmann, "Pliny (the Elder)," *BNP* 11:387.
[146] Elvers, "Strabo," 866.
[147] Tacitus's first line in the *Annals* alludes to Sallust's words in the *Catiline War* (6.1), through which Tacitus signals that he is writing in Sallust's pessimistic tradition of decline, which Sallust had in turn developed through adapting the style of Thucydides (see discussion in C. S. Kraus, "Sallust," in *Latin Historians*, ed. C. S. Kraus and A. J. Woodman (Oxford: Oxford University Press, 1997), 11–12).
[148] See Burridge, *What Are the Gospels?*; Adams, *The Genre of Acts*; Talbert, *Literary Patterns*.

do not tend to raise the same kinds of comparative theological or content questions based on studies of βιοί and Luke/Acts as those found in discussions of historiographies. In selecting texts as case studies for this monograph I have deliberately included some texts with which Luke/Acts is frequently compared, as something of a control, as well as other less common comparanda. Given the different ways in which historiographies and biographies feature in Lukan studies, I have chosen common historiographies as the case study texts (though occasionally I will draw in biographies as they illuminate beliefs about history and divine and human agency), leaving space to focus on the other selected case study texts which are those less commonly addressed in Lukan studies.

For a more popular perspective, I have chosen Valerius Maximus for the reasons described above over a writer like Strabo. And I have chosen Virgil's *Aeneid* as an example of epic, because of the important insights Virgil's teleological view of history provides alongside teleological Jewish texts. I have also deliberately excluded formal philosophical texts due to a preference for texts which indicate their conceptions of history in less systematic ways in the course of other narratives or purposes.

Likewise within the variety of Judaism in this period, a number of further valuable contributions could have been included to good effect. Philo of Alexandria represents a rather unique voice among Jewish writers of the period and his philosophical approach to biblical interpretation and political aspects of his life experience would illuminate contemporaneous understandings of history, as would the theological approaches to history and providence taken in his so-called historical treatises, *Against Flaccus* and its sequel *On the Embassy to Gaius*.[149] Similarly, canonical and non-canonical wisdom texts would provide further insights, as would the fragmentary Jewish Hellenistic historians such as Demetrius and Eupolemus. However, within the constraints of this study, I have prioritised Josephus's contribution to Jewish Hellenistic traditions over both Philo and the fragmentary historians, because of important similarities to and differences from Luke in his conception of history, frequent engagement with his work in Lukan studies, and the common assertion that he represents the peak of this tradition of Jewish Hellenistic historiography.[150] For some balance with a different historiographical perspective, I have chosen 2 Maccabees. For the reasons stated above I have chosen the War Scroll as the case study from the Dead Sea Scrolls, and prioritised 4 Ezra and 2 Baruch because their historical

---

**149** See discussion in van der Horst's introduction to his translation and commentary on *Flaccus* (*Philo: Flaccus: The First Pogrom*, ed. and trans. Pieter W. van der Horst, PACS 2 (Leiden: Brill, 2003), 1–3, 16–18).
**150** Rajak, "The Sense of History," 124–45.

reviews provide important and contrasting insights into conceptions of history for Luke's setting.

Thus, the texts that have been chosen for detailed discussion represent a range of views of history from among the broader collection of texts initially sampled. They include texts frequently cited in connection to Luke/Acts and some unusual in NT studies. And, as they fill out the range of understandings of history in Luke's broader context, they each contribute in different ways to illuminating eschatology in Luke/Acts.

## 3.3 General approach to Luke/Acts

Finally, a few further comments about my approach to Luke/Acts are warranted. Throughout this study I deal with Luke/Acts as a literary unity. Despite recent challenges prompted by the absence of material unity of Luke and Acts in manuscript evidence[151] and some studies querying unity based on stylistic analysis,[152] I consider the continuity in narrative, prefaces, parallel themes, and so on, too great to suggest the texts should be viewed separately.[153] Reading Luke and Acts together will illuminate both.[154] I do however use the designation Luke/

---

[151] C. Kavin Rowe, "Literary Unity and Reception History: Reading Luke-Acts as Luke and Acts," *JSNT* 29 (2007): 449–57; Andrew Gregory and C. Kavin Rowe, eds., *Rethinking the Unity and Reception of Luke and Acts* (Columbia: University of South Carolina Press, 2010), 43–49. See also the earlier challenge posed by Mikeal C. Parsons and Richard I. Pervo, *Rethinking the Unity of Luke and Acts* (Minneapolis: Fortress, 1993).

[152] See for instance Patricia Walters, *The Assumed Authorial Unity of Luke and Acts: A Reassessment of the Evidence*, SNTSMS 145 (Cambridge: Cambridge University Press, 2009). While an important area of exploration in terms of unity, Walters's study relies heavily on statistical methods that her sample size cannot support (namely examples of the "summaries and seams" passages, which she considers without attention to control samples from other collections of texts which are known to have been written by the same author). There is also an important difference between attempting to prove (or disprove) "authorial unity" and discussions of "literary unity"—for instance, Acts may be intended as a continuation of the gospel (or the gospel as a prequel to Acts) irrespective of authorship.

[153] Johnson puts this argument compellingly (Luke Timothy Johnson, "Literary Criticism of Luke-Acts: Is Reception History Pertinent?", in Gregory and Rowe, eds., *Rethinking the Unity*, 66–69).

[154] Bockmuehl suggests an illuminating dialectic emerges from attending to both the place of Luke and Acts in their reception(s) in the church, and their literary relationships to each other (Markus N. A. Bockmuehl, "Why Not Let Acts Be Acts? In Conversation with C. Kavin Rowe," in Gregory and Rowe, eds., *Rethinking the Unity*, 72). Moessner supports literary unity, including a prospective unity introduced in the Gospel as Luke anticipated writing Acts, with the result that

Acts (rather than Henry Cadbury's emphatic Luke-Acts)[155] in recognition that, at least on the basis of extant manuscripts, the earliest readers do not appear to have received the text as a contiguous whole.[156]

In terms of synoptic relationships, I presume Markan priority, and take care with material shared by Matthew and Luke over Mark—though I do not rely heavily on conclusions arising from claims to redaction from either a Q-source or Luke's editing of Matthew.[157] Indeed, Conzelmann's focus on redaction criticism was one of the difficulties with his analysis, as he problematically presumed that redaction indicated material about which Luke felt more strongly.[158] This fallacy overlooks the core material shared between the synoptics, and downplays continuity between them. I therefore focus on reading Luke as a narrative, with due attention to synoptic parallels, but without allowing these parallels to overshadow the way passages function in Luke's account.

I date Luke in the decades after 70 CE and Acts shortly following, both before the turn of the century[159] and, as noted above, I treat both parts of the work as historiography, though aware of some difficulties with this designation. In general I use the Nestle-Aland 28 composite text, though I recognise certain criticisms of this text, particularly given the different manuscript traditions of Acts, and occasionally refer, for instance, to the text from Codex Bezae where this is illuminating.[160] Finally, I refer to the authorial voice "Luke" without making particular claims about the historical author (as I do also in relation to the authors of the other texts treated). Rather, I use the name to indicate the author implied by the text, seeking to read from the perspective of an ideal, "competent," first-century reader, as discussed above.

---

Luke also must be understood in light of the full two-volume work (Moessner, *Luke the Historian*, 38).
**155** Henry J. Cadbury, *The Making of Luke-Acts*, 2nd ed. (London: SPCK, 1958), 10–11; original edition 1927.
**156** Rowe, "Literary Unity and Reception History," 450; cf. Andrew Gregory, "The Reception of Luke and Acts and the Unity of Luke-Acts," *JSNT* 29 (2007): 459–72.
**157** I prefer the latter explanation of synoptic relationships, but in this study do not rely on it.
**158** See discussion in Ellis, "Eschatology in Luke," 106; Maddox, *The Purpose*, 100–57; cf. Conzelmann, *Theology of St Luke*; and criticism in Minear, "Luke's Use," 121.
**159** Contra those who support a second-century date for Acts (cf. Richard I. Pervo, *Dating Acts: Between the Evangelists and the Apologists* (Santa Rosa, CA: Polebridge, 2006)).
**160** See Josep Rius-Camps and Jenny Read-Heimerdinger, *The Message of Acts in Codex Bezae: A Comparison with the Alexandrian Tradition*, 4 vols. (London: T&T Clark, 2004–2009). Also discussion in Penner, "Madness in the Method?", 242–43.

## 4 The aspects of history discussed in the following chapters

Therefore, I argue that texts share a range of features in common, not all of which should be attributed to genre. In particular, features such as portrayals of the shape and end of history, and divine and human agency in history, transcend genre. Texts of different genres can evoke the same underlying beliefs about history, while texts of the same genre may not, making the cross-genre approach of this study not only possible but necessary, given the themes with which it is concerned.

Chapters 3 to 6 address different elements of the understanding of history portrayed in the case study texts and Luke/Acts, namely: Chapter 3, the direction and shape of history; Chapter 4, determinism and divine guidance of history; Chapter 5, human responsibility and freedom; and Chapter 6, the present and the end of history. The diverse interactions between these varied themes across the texts illuminate Luke's explanation of the events of the past, hope for the future, and call for response in the present—clarifying Lukan eschatology and its effects.

# Chapter 3:
# The direction and shape of history

> *It is impossible to get from writers who deal with particular episodes a general view of the whole process of history. For how by the bare reading of events in Sicily or in Spain can we hope to learn and understand either the magnitude of the occurrences or the thing of greatest moment...*
>
> —Polybius, *The Histories*, 8.2.2–3

## 1 Introduction: the importance of schemas of history

As he begins his description of the siege of Syracuse in Book 8, Polybius takes the time to tell his reader (again!) about the superiority of his own *Histories*.[1] His narrative takes due account not only of all the moving parts in the strategies played out by Rome and Carthage across a wide geographical spread,[2] but also the overarching trajectory of these events (8.2.2–11; cf. 1.4.3). And this is important, he says, because the significance of any individual incident can only be discerned in light of the bigger picture (8.2.3, 7). Polybius's words point to an element of truth not only for his narrative, but for all the texts discussed below: the framework in which a writer imagines history affects their claims about the significance of particular moments and hope for the future. Later in his narrative, Polybius will reveal a further pattern of change which will frame how even Rome's ascendency should be understood. For some other writers, important consequences arise from a schema of history which spans the rise and fall of empires since the beginning of human communities, or indeed from the beginning of the universe until its projected end.

This chapter begins the investigation into how understandings of history in diverse texts of the Graeco-Roman period illuminate Lukan eschatology. It asks how the direction and shape of history in the study's texts clarify the schema of

---

[1] As noted in Chapter 2, of Polybius's 40 books, only the first five are fully extant. Book 8 has survived in fragmentary sections. See Habicht's introduction to the LCL edition of Polybius, *The Histories*, 1:xv–xvi.

[2] Polybius marvels at the "vast scope of operations," which had Rome and Carthage not only fighting out for possession of Italy and Spain, but initiating battles in various other locations such as Sardinia and Sicily, which, he says, also need to be included in the historiography, in order to explain the attempts at "conquest all the world over" (8.2.1).

history in Luke/Acts.³ And in doing so it focuses on three key elements: whether and how each writer depicts an end to history, historical periodisation, or a sense of progress or decline. Firstly, by considering the relationship between history and its end in writers' schemas of history, the chapter addresses a crucial controversy in Lukan studies. As set out in detail in Chapter 1, Hans Conzelmann influentially argued that Luke's concern at the parousia's delay led him to focus on salvation history *instead of* eschatology.⁴ In a move that would shape Lukan studies and reflect conflict in other areas of NT interpretation,⁵ he claimed that texts could not deal with both history and eschatology but rather a focus on one precluded the other.⁶

The following treatment of key texts demonstrates that this is a false dichotomy. The writers of several of the study's texts hold history and eschatology together in a *teleological* schema of history, that is, a view that history follows a linear shape and draws to some sort of conclusion at its end.⁷ These writers

---

**3** On the definitions of "history" and "historiography" used throughout this study, see Chapter 1 §1.
**4** Conzelmann, *Theology of St Luke*, 14, 131–32; Hans Conzelmann, *Acts of the Apostles*, trans. James Limburg, A. Thomas Kraabel, and Donald H. Juel, Hermeneia (Philadelphia: Fortress, 1987), xlv.
**5** On studies that set "apocalyptic" Paul against an understanding of salvation history, see below.
**6** By the time of writing his commentary on Acts, in which he argues the "view of history" from the Gospel is "presupposed," Conzelmann also identifies this shift as one of ecclesiology: "the polity of the earliest Christian community cannot be retained." He summarises that in Acts, "The presupposition is that the church is a historical entity which has its own particular time; in other words, that *the imminent end of history has been transformed into a portrait of history*" (Conzelmann, *Acts of the Apostles*, xlv; my emphasis). As noted in Chapter 1, for Conzelmann, following Bultmann, "eschatology" was itself a radical irruption of divine action and therefore any sense that divine action could be plotted according to historical time reflected a kind of domestication of the divine or sacralisation of human historical events. However, importantly, the kind of "imminent end of history" that Conzelmann prefers in the quotation above still suggests some temporal consciousness. As demonstrated by the discussion below, a range of texts maintain a sense in which radical divine otherness is confirmed in decisive divine action which can be expected imminently, as communicated, for instance, by *vaticinia ex eventu* historical reviews.
**7** This monograph discusses the end or *telos* of history in the sense of an *endpoint* to history, and teleological in terms of a *linear trajectory that leads to an end*. However, even texts which are non-teleological in this sense can display a sense of *purpose* to history. The OED defines "telos" in English as "the end, purpose, ultimate object or aim." A similar range of meanings emerges from the use of τέλος in Greek texts (see the extensive study of meanings and etymology by F. M. J. Waanders, *The History of ΤΕΛΟΣ and ΤΕΛΕΩ in Ancient Greek* (Amsterdam: Grüner, 1983), 232–39, especially the diagram on p. 239). The semantic field of the Greek term, which includes the temporal point "marking the end of a duration," the last stage of a process (con-

are interested in *both* the nature of history and its periods over time *and* the events of the end, and portray these as related in essential ways. In particular, many ground their claims about the events to take place at the end of history in their assertions about divine guidance over time.[8] For example, the writers of *Urzeit zu Endzeit* apocalypses such as 2 Bar 53–76 display an almost scientific interest[9] in the periods of history since creation, while simultaneously asserting that the determinism that has structured the course of history in the past guarantees the promised culmination of history and vindication of the righteous which is imminently anticipated.

From the outset, it is worth noting some caricatures of the distinctions between Graeco-Roman and Jewish texts on these questions, which careful readings of particular texts dispel. Considerable controversy has arisen as a result of past scholarship in which labels such as "cyclical" and "linear" were associated with implicit judgements about "primitive" or "sophisticated" views of history. Not only Oscar Cullmann[10] but also writers such as Jacob Taubes, Karl Löwith, and Mircea Eliade[11] frequently made a blanket division between Graeco-Roman conceptions of time as circular and Jewish and Christian as linear.[12] More recent scholarship has criticised these treatments as simplistic readings of the Graeco-Roman texts; see for instance the summary of eschatologies pro-

---

clusion), or the goal or outcome to which a process is pointed (BDAG, 998), raises potentially significant implications for instance in 2 Macc 6.15, where the writer could mean the fullness of sin, the end of a person's lifetime, or the end of history (see below). Furthermore, in some Greek texts τέλος may indicate the end of a historiographical work, or of history itself, or the fulfilment of some purpose. See below for discussion on this point in Polybius.
**8** Attributions of divine and human agency in history are explored in Chapters 4 and 5.
**9** Cf. also 4 Ezra 7.78–101. This interest is particularly pronounced in 1 Enoch's historical apocalypses (the *Apocalypse of Weeks* (1 Enoch 93.1–10, 91.12–17) and *Animal Apocalypse* (85–90)).
**10** Cullmann, *Christ and Time*, 57–58.
**11** Jacob Taubes, *Occidental Eschatology*, trans. David Ratmoko, Cultural Memory in the Present (1947; Stanford: Stanford University Press, 2009), 20–23; Karl Löwith, *Meaning in History*, Phoenix Books (Chicago: University of Chicago Press, 1949), 188–89; Mircea Eliade, *The Myth of the Eternal Return: Cosmos and History*, trans. Willard R. Trask, Bollingen Series 46 (1949; Princeton: Princeton University Press, 2005), 104.
**12** See discussion in Ludwig Edelstein, *The Idea of Progress in Classical Antiquity* (Baltimore, MD: Johns Hopkins Press, 1967), xxi; Clarke, *Making Time*, 14–17. Criticising the simplistic dichotomy, Momigliano calls attention to cyclical elements in Judeo-Christian festivals (Arnaldo Momigliano, "Time in Ancient Historiography," in *Essays in Ancient and Modern Historiography*, Blackwell's Classical Studies (Oxford: Blackwell, 1977), 184), and Barr similarly highlights Qohelet and some other Hebrew texts (James Barr, *Biblical Words for Time*, 2nd rev. ed., SBT 33 (London: SCM, 1969), 143–58).

vided by Hubert Cancik in the *Encyclopedia of Apocalypticism*.[13] He attributes the earlier reductive views to post-war reactions,[14] and examines a range of non-Jewish texts that he claims provide a teleological sense of "the end of the world, of history, and of the individual."[15]

Similarly, this chapter confirms that circular and linear features can interact in important ways in *both* Jewish and non-Jewish texts, one of the many indications of diversity across the range of comparison texts. For instance, many Dead Sea Scrolls texts have sharpened awareness of the importance of cyclical patterns in accounts of both past divine saving acts and practices of piety in the present, which are still portrayed within a linear progression to a final *telos*.[16] The discussion of Virgil's *Aeneid* below also demonstrates circular patterns of recurrence within Virgil's ultimately teleological view of historical progress. An appreciation for all of these features serves to clarify the implications of writers' schemas of history and the traditions to which they relate,[17] without reducing texts to simplistic categories.

The second key element, the periodisation of history, addresses another aspect of Conzelmann's hypothesis. Not only the writers of historical apocalypses, but writers across the texts in this study likewise envisage history as divided into periods or epochs. But the writers do attach varying degrees of significance to this periodisation, from simply practical divisions between different eras or political administrations to cataclysmic transitions in history. But in contrast to Conzelmann's claims, periodisation does not reflect any lack of interest in the

---

[13] Hubert Cancik, "The End of the World, of History, and of the Individual in Greek and Roman Antiquity," in *The Origins of Apocalypticism in Judaism and Christianity*, vol. 1 of *The Encyclopedia of Apocalypticism*, ed. John J. Collins (New York: Continuum, 1998), 89–90.
[14] Cancik, "The End of the World," 90.
[15] Cancik, "The End of the World," 84.
[16] Particular attention has been devoted to Pesher Habakkuk on these temporal questions; see for instance Loren T. Stuckenbruck, "Temporal Shifts from Text to Interpretation: Concerning the Use of the Perfect and Imperfect in the *Habakkuk Pesher* (1QpHab)," in *Qumran Studies: New Approaches, New Questions*, ed. Michael Thomas Davis and Brent A. Strawn (Grand Rapids: Eerdmans, 2007), 124–49. On the end of days in the Dead Sea Scrolls, see John J. Collins, "Expectations of the End in the Dead Sea Scrolls," in *Eschatology, Messianism, and the Dead Sea Scrolls*, ed. Craig A. Evans and Peter W. Flint, Studies in the Dead Sea Scrolls and Related Literature 1 (Grand Rapids: Eerdmans, 1997), 80. Schwartz argues that 2 Maccabees offers a circular view of history (Schwartz, "Circular or Teleological," 119–20), but I suggest below that, despite the strong sense of continuity and return to divine favour at the end of the narrative of 2 Maccabees, the writer does hint at an eventual end to history. See §3.2 below.
[17] For instance, see the reference to traditions of decline in Roman historiography in §2.3 below.

end for those who portray a teleological view of history or diminished expectation of its imminence (the latter is the topic of Chapter 6).[18]

In this way, writers often balance concerns about *rupture* and *continuity* in history.[19] Arguably, it is this feature that has animated the dichotomy between history and eschatology in NT studies. For instance, studies of Pauline literature have often reduced apocalypses to a "two-age" model, overlooking any interest in earlier periods of history in Jewish apocalypses and importing an "apocalyptic eschatology" based entirely on rupture into their interpretation of Paul.[20] Conzelmann brought the opposite emphasis to Lukan studies, stressing continuity across Luke's history and identifying periodisation as Luke's method of extending "history," while postponing the disruption of the end to an irrelevant future.[21] This study shows that periodisation in not only apocalypses, but also texts like Polybius's *Histories* and even Luke/Acts, is more complex than this.

---

[18] Chapter 6 discusses the timing of the end in relation to the present in these texts, building on the current chapter's analysis of the overall shape of each text's schema of history.

[19] In an important study among several recent investigations into understandings of time and the structuring of history in Second Temple Judaism, Mermelstein offers a compelling analysis of remedies for the sense of rupture in history employed by post-exilic writers. He particularly highlights an emphasis on tracing Israel's history from creation rather than from Sinai, so as to stress continuity in divine faithfulness and address the fear that exile might mark the end of the covenant (Mermelstein, *Creation, Covenant*, 11–13).

[20] These themes also link to Conzelmann's personal perspective on the decisive irruption of divine action in the Christ event (see Chapter 1), and run throughout key strands of Pauline scholarship. See, for instance, discussion in Ernst Käsemann, "Justification and Salvation History in the Epistle to the Romans," in *Perspectives on Paul*, trans. Margaret Kohl, NTL (London: SCM, 1971), 60–78 (though, see Käsemann's critical engagement with Conzelmann on pp. 76–78); Martyn, *Theological Issues*; N. T. Wright, *Paul and the Faithfulness of God* (London: SPCK, 2013), 1034–96. Beverley Roberts Gaventa, ed., *Apocalyptic Paul: Cosmos and Anthropos in Romans 5–8* (Waco, TX: Baylor University Press, 2013) offers a compilation of recent views. Important responses to these themes may be found in Stuckenbruck, "Overlapping Ages"; Stuckenbruck, "How Much Evil?" Stuckenbruck, "Posturing 'Apocalyptic,'" particularly critiques the simplification of the schema of history in apocalypses into a "two-age" model. See also discussion in J. P. Davies, *Paul Among the Apocalypses? An Evaluation of the "Apocalyptic Paul" in the Context of Jewish and Christian Apocalyptic Literature*, LNTS 562 (London: T&T Clark, 2016), 72–112. Even Stone in his commentary on 4 Ezra reduces the writer's framework to that of "two ages" (Stone, *Fourth Ezra*, 92–93; see discussion in §3.3 below). Longstanding debates about the central concerns of apocalypses have led to a general consensus that exclusive focus on "apocalyptic eschatology" overlooks other essential interests, such as history over time, the dimensions of the world and other worlds, and theodicy. See Davies, "Apocalyptic and Historiography, 16–19; Collins, "Apocalypse," 1–19.

[21] Conzelmann, *Theology of St Luke*, 97 and passim. This is partly also the concern behind Wolter's recent claim that Conzelmann's error was periodisation itself, as Luke envisages history as

Finally, schemas of history may also be characterised by assumptions about the *direction* of history. For some writers, for instance, history progresses—that is, things improve over time—as the needs humans encounter prompt the development of new skills or people learn from the mistakes of the past.[22] For others, nostalgia[23] or suffering[24] signal history's decline, or, alternatively, beliefs about the universality of human traits and situations suggest that, though history continues, things remain essentially the same.[25] These elements affect the texts in fundamental ways. Writers who portray improvement in history elicit particular assumptions about the people of the past and hope for the future, while descriptions of history in decline can approach nihilism,[26] or—where such decline fits within a schema of history in which an endpoint is anticipated—the decline itself can constitute the precursor to divine action that will bring about a final end.[27]

Therefore, this chapter explores the schemas of history reflected in each of the key texts of the study, first considering texts which do not indicate an endpoint to history before turning to those which do. For each category, I consider texts which suggest history is generally progressing positively, remaining constant, or declining. The discussion highlights the diversity of understandings across the texts of the study, both among Jewish and non-Jewish texts, not only in relation to which ideas are present in each text but also where each writer places emphasis. The varied perspectives enable a comparison to Luke/Acts, to which I turn in the final section of the chapter. This analysis highlights that, as in the vast majority of texts, history in Luke/Acts is *periodised*—that is, comprised of ages or epochs. Further, in keeping with a subset of both Jewish and non-Jewish texts of the Graeco-Roman period, it is also *teleological*—that is, it follows a linear shape that draws to some sort of conclusion at its end. Thus

---

"one single overall history," not three, or even two, parts (Michael Wolter, "Eschatology in the Gospel according to Luke," in van der Watt, *Eschatology of the New Testament*, 98).

22 See discussion of Polybius and Diodorus Siculus (§2.1).

23 Nostalgia is evident in Tacitus's understanding of decline (see §2.3), though it can also be present in different ways—see Josephus (§3.2) and Virgil (§3.1).

24 This features in Second Temple texts such as apocalypses (§3.3).

25 See discussion of Valerius Maximus (§2.2).

26 Ovid's cynical presentation of the continued decline of history, in which ironically only the writer endures (*Metam.* 15.871–79), offers an interesting parallel to the decline in teleological texts such as Jewish apocalypses, in which the *telos* reflects an inversion of decline through divine vindication. Ovid's account is also illuminating when considered as a response to Virgil's account of progress (Julia Dyson Hejduk, "Ovid and Religion," in *A Companion to Ovid*, ed. Peter E. Knox, Blackwell Companions to the Ancient World (Chichester: Wiley-Blackwell, 2009), 52; E. J. Kenney, "The *Metamorphoses*: A Poet's Poem," in Knox, *A Companion to Ovid*, 144).

27 See §3.3.

the chapter demonstrates the essential connection between history and eschatology for writers who draw on teleological understandings of history, including Luke.

## 2 Texts without a sense of an endpoint to history

Several of this study's key texts indicate expectations that history will continue without an end. Although the vast majority still describe some sense of historical periodisation, they reflect diversity in the significance they attribute to particular periods. Other features of their schemas of history are likewise diverse, from the scope of history imagined by the writer, to beliefs about progress or moral decline, or the continuity of human conditions in all times and places.

### 2.1 Hints of positive progress in history

Polybius and Diodorus Siculus provide historiographies frequently considered in relation to Luke/Acts, normally with a focus on rhetorical or generic features. For both, though for different reasons, history progresses over time,[28] even though empires rise and fall.[29] However, whereas Polybius stresses the significance of Rome's moment, Diodorus maintains a broader scope over the course of history.

---

[28] For general discussion of historical progress in classical texts, particularly in accounts of scientific advance, contrasted with traditional portrayals of decline, see Edelstein, *The Idea of Progress*, xxxiii and passim; E. R. Dodds, *The Ancient Concept of Progress and Other Essays* (Oxford: Clarendon, 1973), 1–25.

[29] Momigliano outlines ancient writers, such as Seneca and Florus, who illustrate the stages of an empire's reign with the human life cycle. Although observing that attributing a political moment to a regime's "childhood, youth, maturity, or old age" may seem to imply an overall ageing of history, he does not find this idea in the ancient sources. Rather, he says the imagery underscores the rise, fall, and transition to the next regime as a natural process (Arnaldo Momigliano, "The Origins of Universal History," in *The Poet and the Historian: Essays in Literary and Historical Biblical Criticism*, ed. Richard Elliott Friedman, HSS (Chico, CA: Scholars Press, 1983), 136). Diodorus Siculus suggests Pythagoreans used the stages of human life as an analogy for seasons, but not history (10.9.5; cf. Clarke, *Making Time*, 16).

**Polybius's *Histories***
Written in the second century BCE,[30] Polybius's *Histories* focus on the rise of Rome. Polybius measures time in terms of Olympiads and the successive reigns of political rulers (1.5.1; cf. 11.1.1; 39.8.6).[31] Katherine Clarke argues that the extant fragments from Timaeus (one of two historians Polybius presents his work as continuing),[32] demonstrate that Olympiads provided "the first coherent, universal, and continuous dating device" and that this is "vividly exemplified for the first time in Polybius' *Histories*."[33] Olympiads supply the general structure of Polybius's divisions between the events he says he will cover in each of the individual books of his historiography (9.1.1; cf. 14.1.5).[34] And they attain particular significance in his description of his official starting point: the 140th Olympiad (1.3.1). This is a key turning point in history for him, which reveals the superiority of the Romans, who he says have "subjected to their rule not portions, but nearly the whole of the world, and possess an empire which is not only immeasurably greater than any which preceded it, but need not fear rivalry in the future" (1.2.1, 7–8).[35]

---

**30** See Chapter 2 §3.1 for further background information on each text.
**31** Clarke, *Making Time*, 114–15.
**32** Marincola discusses the wider tradition of continuations of earlier histories, suggesting that the tradition involves balancing criticism of earlier historians in order both to justify the new work, and to identify it with exemplary earlier writers. So in some cases a writer might present the work in continuity with an earlier positive example, and in polemical contrast with others (Marincola, *Authority and Tradition*, 218). He notes that of the two historians Polybius claims to extend, Aratus and Timaeus, the first he treats as a positive exemplar, while the second he treats very critically (pp. 231–32, 238–39). Marincola asserts: "In no other surviving historian is polemic so widespread or so important a method of self-definition as in Polybius" (p. 229). For discussion of these themes of continuity and contrast, see pp. 217–57. For tables on continuation relationships between Greek and Roman historiographies, see Marincola's appendices 6 and 7 (pp. 289–92).
**33** Clarke, *Making Time*, 110. Despite Polybius's polemic against Timaeus, among the ways in which he follows him is in periodising by Olympiad (see discussion on pp. 109–21).
**34** Clarke, *Making Time*, 113.
**35** This is as reconstructed by W. R. Paton, F. A. Walbank, and Christian Habicht in the LCL edition of the *Histories*. Dionysius of Halicarnassus likewise praises Rome's achievement. Balch argues Dionysius complies with rules for encomia, as set out by Menander of Laodicea, as he praises the city Rome. Notably, Balch stresses, Dionysius offers a "definitive apologetic," for instance in Book 1, defending Rome against those who claimed it was founded by "immoral barbarians and slaves," and achieved greatness only through the role of τύχη (David L. Balch, "Two Apologetic Encomia: Dionysius on Rome and Josephus on the Jews," *JSJ* 13 (1982): 114). By contrast, Polybius is very happy to involve τύχη in his praise of Rome here, though elsewhere he prioritises the merits of human skill (see further discussion in Chapters 4 and 5 below).

For Polybius, with the rise of Rome under the guidance of τύχη ("fortune" or "chance," a notoriously varied force in Polybius, as discussed in Chapter 4), history itself has been unified as a single body:[36]

> Previously the doings of the world had been, so to say, dispersed, as they were held together by no unity of initiative, results, or locality; but ever since this date (ἀπὸ δὲ τούτων τῶν καιρῶν) history (ἱστορίαν) has been an organic whole (σωματοειδῆ), and the affairs (πρᾶξις) of Italy and Africa have been interlinked with those of Greece and Asia, all leading up to one end (τέλος). (1.3.3–4)

Given his stated scope and the importance of this historical moment, it is interesting that Polybius's first move is immediately to recount events from an *earlier* period, back to the 124th Olympiad (Books 1–2),[37] which he presents as background to the events upon which he wishes to focus (cf. 1.4.4; 1.12.6–9; 2.71.1–10). These earlier stories describe disparate, localised events (which he notes are all other historians have attended to, 1.2.1–6), making the transition to the single, universal narrative from the 140th Olympiad all the more pronounced. Rome's comprehensive dominance has made universal or "general" historiography not only possible, but necessary (8.2.2–3).

Polybius also makes use of other terms for time, like καιρός.[38] This is often simply a narrative marker for the time during which events took place (e.g. 1.29.8; 1.32.1; 1.88.8; 2.11.1; 2.26.1; 2.27.1; 2.37.1; 2.55.1) or the right moment or opportunity for military action (1.45.5; 2.67.1), but sometimes Polybius uses καιρός to indicate a particular moment of significance, which can also reflect his perio-

---

[36] Frank Walbank argues that Polybius had inherited the idea of a historiographical work as a σῶμα, but that "the novelty in P. is that, facilitated by his conception of the role of *Tyche*, he projects the notion of the unity of an historical work upon the objective course of historical events" (Walbank, *A Historical Commentary*, 1:43). For a focus on the importance of building unity at milestone moments, see also Plutarch's account of Theseus's role in "making one people of one city out of those who up to that time had been scattered about and were not easily called together for the common interests of all, nay, they sometimes actually quarrelled and fought with each other" (Plu. *Thes*. 24.1).

[37] Although Polybius still measures time in the first two books according to Olympiads, note the debate in R. M. Errington, "The Chronology of Polybius' Histories, Books I and II," *The Journal of Roman Studies* 57 (1967): 96–108, about whether Books 1 and 2 reflect any attempt by Polybius at accurate and consistent ordering of Olympiads or a looser chronology derived from his disparate sources (cf. 39.8.4–6).

[38] Polybius also uses χρόνος, describing previous times (1.3.3), a long duration of time (1.66.10) and so on.

dised view of history.[39] This is especially apparent when he speaks about the present times (e.g. ἀπὸ δὲ τούτων τῶν καιρῶν, (1.3.4); καθ' ἡμᾶς καιρῶν, (1.4.1)).[40] Elsewhere he describes "those times," for instance, in which the Carthaginians faced conflict with mercenaries (1.65.89; cf. 2.39.5; 2.71.2), which he contrasts with "our times" ἐν τοῖς καθ' ἡμας καιροῖς (2.15.1).[41]

Polybius's use of καιρός, as it underscores the significance of the present moment and of the transition to the time in which Rome dominates, goes hand in hand with his portrait of the successions of political leaders, as they align also with the movement through Olympiads.[42] He uses all of these ideas together to denote the periods into which history is divided, seen for instance in his summary of the first two books (which features καιρός, Olympiads, and an overview of political successions, with parallels drawn between the deaths of three kings in each of the 124th and the 139th Olympiads, 2.71.1–10),[43] before he turns to the events from the Social War onwards, as he had promised, in Book 3.

---

[39] For discussion of Polybius's use of καιρός in the context of developments in the range of meanings for the term in the Hellenistic period, and in particular the movement from "exact, right, critical time" or "opportunity" to a sense of a "period" of time, see Barr, *Biblical Words for Time*, 33–35. Polybius also refers to τύχη in the same setting as καιρός, though again this is mixed and can refer to a less intense sense of periodisation (cf. 2.20.7).

[40] Polybius's focus on the present time expressed, for instance, as "these times" or the "now," is discussed in further detail in Chapter 6 §2.

[41] Note that this can be in relation to quite mundane matters, as here in 2.15.1, where Polybius is discussing the price of wheat in "our times" as opposed to earlier periods.

[42] Clarke helpfully highlights the importance of the Olympiadic temporal structure for Polybius's account of this turning point, as well as synchronisms in which Polybius aligns other temporal markers such as the succession of political rulers within this overall Olympiadic framework (Clarke, *Making Time*, 115–16). Clarke notes that "The succession of rulers in different parts of the Mediterranean world seems to have been the single most important factor determining Polybius' sense of periodisation" (pp. 114–15), but goes on to demonstrate how this also relates to the Olympiadic structure, aligning political changes with particular Olympiads.

[43] These successions feed into Polybius's portrait of events that bring together unified Roman domination. He justifies giving an account of a period earlier than that originally promised, claiming it was "necessary for me, to make clearly known to everyone the state of affairs in Macedonia and Greece at this time. Just about the same time Ptolemy Euergetes fell sick and died, being succeeded by Ptolemy surnamed Philopater. Seleucus, the son of the Seleucus surnamed Callinicus or Pogon, also died at this time, his brother Antiochus succeeding him in the kingdom of Syria. The same thing in fact occurred in the case of these three kings, as in that of the first successors of Alexander in the three kingdoms, Seleucus, Ptolemy, and Lysimachus, who all, as I stated above, died in the 124th Olympiad, while these kings died in the 139th.... I must now bring this Book to its close, which coincides with the final events preceding these wars and the death of the three kings who had up to now directed affairs" (2.71.2–6, 10).

For Polybius, the momentous current historical period confirms that history has advanced. History's progress is manifest not only in the unprecedented achievements of Rome's rise, drawing together different parts into a whole, but in the historian's work of facilitating readers' learning from the past to avoid future error.[44] Polybius sees this as intrinsic to the historian's role and his own project.[45] He claims to write "for the sake of the improvement of the readers of this history" (1.35.6),[46] with a particular focus on political and military strategies and their outcomes,[47] affirming that insights provided by comprehensive accounts of the past are widely generalizable (1.35.6–10).

However, despite presenting Rome's rise as an unprecedented culmination of past regimes and progress, even for Polybius, Rome takes its place in the succession of empires.[48] His account of periods prior to Rome establishes the pattern (1.2.1–6, noted above). He goes on to hint at Rome's fall both through the analogy of decline of seemingly-invincible past regimes, and by explicit reference to a premonition about Rome's demise. For instance, he recalls an earlier prophecy by Demetrius of Phalerum, providing a none too subtle clue that, even at the height of an empire when it seems most unlikely, one may still be assured that this empire too will fall:

> Do you think that fifty years ago either the Persians and the Persian king or the Macedonians and the king of Macedon, if some god (τις θεῶν) had foretold the future (προύλεγε τὸ μέλλον) to them, would ever have believed that at the time when we live (τοῦτον τὸν καιρόν), the very name of the Persians would have perished utterly—the Persians who were masters of almost the whole world—and that the Macedonians, whose name was formerly most unknown, would now be the lords of it all? (29.21.4)[49]

---

**44** Marincola, "Speeches in Classical Historiography," 123; Dodds, *The Ancient Concept of Progress*, 1–25.
**45** Dodds, *The Ancient Concept of Progress*, 18.
**46** Polybius goes on to assert: "We should regard as the best discipline for actual life the experience that accrues from serious history (ἱστορίας); for this alone makes us, without inflicting any harm on us, the most competent judges of what is best at every time and in every circumstance" (1.35.6–10).
**47** Frank W. Walbank, "Fortune (*Tychē*) in Polybius," in Marincola, *A Companion to Greek and Roman Historiography*, 2:350–51. Polybius considers τύχη an explanation of last resort (2.38.5) and asserts the superiority of achievement through human skill (10.9.2–3; cf. 10.2.6; 10.5.8–10). See Chapters 4 and 5.
**48** Momigliano, "The Origins of Universal History," 139–41.
**49** This material from Polybius is reproduced by Diodorus Siculus at 31.10, whose very minor changes to the passage include describing the fulfilment of the prophesied events during the current period he discusses (κατὰ τοὺς νῦν χρόνους, 31.10.2).

Thus Polybius hints that the current empire will likewise come to an end.[50] His account of Scipio's sombre observation at the fall of Carthage, as preserved in fragments given in Book 38, provides even more explicit allusion to future transitions:[51]

> Turning round to me at once and grasping my hand Scipio said, "A glorious moment (καλὸν μέν), Polybius; but I have a dread foreboding (ἐγὼ δέδια καὶ προορῶμαι) that some day the same doom will be pronounced upon my own country (περὶ τῆς ἡμετέρας πατρίδος)." (38.21.1–2; cf. 38.22.2)[52]

Polybius's understanding of both the uniqueness of Rome and the ongoing succession of empires highlights the importance of the scale of history envisioned by a writer. As in this chapter's opening quotation, Polybius criticises historians who limit attention to particular episodes or places (8.2.2–3; cf. 1.4.6–10).[53] But his own account focuses on one empire (however grand), whereas, for instance, the "universal" scope of Diodorus Siculus's historiography or the *Urzeit zu Endzeit* overview of 2 Bar 53–76, expands well beyond Polybius's limits.[54] Nonetheless, even within these limits, Polybius retains the sense that history itself continues before and after the period of his focus.[55] The events he relates may lead up to "one end (τέλος)" (1.3.4), but this is the conclusion of the significant events he has claimed need to be included in his account (cf. 1.4.2–3; 1.14.1), not the

---

[50] Gruen argues that this is part of a subtle resistance from Polybius, who began by admiring the feats of Rome until his homeland fell (Gruen, "Polybius and Josephus," 153). He makes parallel observations of Polybius and Josephus in this respect, as recipients of Rome's benefaction who at the same time wrote historiographies with subtle hints of an end to Rome's dominance, concluding: "How many Roman readers would pick up on these subversive sentiments—or would care—we cannot know. But acute Greek readers of Polybius would understand and appreciate—as would the discerning Jewish audiences of Josephus" (pp. 160–61).
[51] Gruen, "Polybius and Josephus," 159.
[52] The second account, preserved in Appian's *Punica* 132, also explicitly refers to the succession of the four empires between Assyria, Media, Persia, and Macedonia (Polyb. *Hist.* 38.22.2). On comparisons between the different extant versions of this story and manuscript conditions, see Walbank, *A Historical Commentary*, 3:722–25 (though note also Walbank's particular interest in the historicity of the incident).
[53] In 1.4.6–10, Polybius applies the image of someone viewing parts of a deceased animal being similarly mistaken in claiming to have as good an idea of the living creature as an eye-witness, upon which he bases his claims for the need for the synoptic view supplied by universal historiography.
[54] On the development of universal historiographies from Ephorus of Cyme, see Clarke, *Making Time*, 96–109, 130. Hernadi includes the "scope" or horizon of the writer's imagination in his account of the "world evoked" by the text (Hernadi, *Beyond Genre*, 171–72).
[55] See Grethlein, *Experience and Teleology*, 227.

terminus of history itself. Polybius is clear that he continues the work of other historians, as he may expect others to carry on after him.[56]

Thus, Polybius shares the common expectation that different regimes will rise and fall while offering no indication that such a pattern is itself expected to reach an end. Through the work of τύχη and the historian, history progresses, epitomised by the present time's achievement of unity under Rome. But unlike some others who write in praise of Rome (see the discussion of Virgil below), for Polybius: Rome too will fall.[57] Although Rome's period constitutes the focus of Polybius's own work, and even if a rival to Rome is not yet imminent (1.2.8) and Rome's grand achievement is unparalleled to date (1.4.1–5), Rome itself is not the end of history.[58] As exemplified by Scipio's comment and the account of Demetrius's prophecy, Polybius anticipates a continuation of the pattern of new dominant regimes, each replaced in turn by the next.

### Diodorus Siculus's *Library of History*

Although likewise presenting a schema in which history progresses positively but does not anticipate an endpoint, Diodorus Siculus means something quite different by "universal" historiography. As Anne Burton observes, Diodorus would dismiss Polybius's claims that historiography generally limited to one em-

---

**56** Walbank, *A Historical Commentary*, 1:43. See n. 32 above regarding continuations of earlier historiographies.
**57** There are other important differences between Polybius and Virgil in the sense that Polybius writes as an outsider from Rome (see n. 50 above), while Virgil is an insider. As discussed below, although Virgil incorporates some sense of ambiguity about Rome, he ultimately affirms *imperium sine fine*, which is quite different from Polybius's expectations about a future fall for Rome.
**58** Grethlein argues the endpoint to Polybius's story dominates his account. This kind of "teleology" is a retrospective narrative technique, which ensures that readers interpret all of the events recounted in light of the end to which they will lead (arguably best illustrated by a film which begins by showing the final climax of the plot, before taking the viewer, for instance, "six months earlier," to trace the events that led to that final moment, through which all the earlier events will thus be assessed by the viewer). While noting Polybius's emphasis on this type of teleology, a category with which he also identifies Herodotus, Grethlein contrasts this approach with other ancient historians who focus on communicating the experience of the moment to their readers, without colouring it with too much information from the end of the account, such as Tacitus (see outline in Grethlein, *Experience and Teleology*, 8). But Grethlein does not suggest that Polybius is "teleological" in the sense that he believes Rome is the end of history (p. 225). See Grethlein also for a helpful discussion on the consequences for Polybius's presentation of the *telos* of his account by his use of delay, his decision to continue the narrative further than originally indicated, and even the uncertain beginning, when Polybius spends the first two books recounting events prior to his official starting point (pp. 234–37).

pire could meet the definition.⁵⁹ By contrast, written during the Late Republican period, Diodorus's *Library* extends from mythological narratives about the origins of the world until the mid- to late 50s BCE,⁶⁰ claiming to incorporate "all events that have taken place in the known parts of the inhabited world (οἰκουμένης)" (1.6.2; cf. 19.1.10).

For Diodorus, as for other writers of this study's key texts, history is periodised. He marks time in terms of Olympiads and periods of rule by named magistrates (see key passages, for example, in Book 11 (11.1.1; 11.38.1; 11.48.1)),⁶¹ and uses καιρός and χρόνος to designate durations of time (cf. 1.5.1; 11.49.4; 12.10.2; 12.26.1).⁶² For instance, his introductory overview divides his account into periods from before Troy (Books 1–6), then Troy until Alexander's death (Books 7–17), followed by the events of the expansion of Rome into Britain (Books 18–40; cf. 1.4.6–7),⁶³ which he also calculates in terms of Olympiads and years for the periods following the Trojan War (1.5.1; cf. 13.1.2–3).⁶⁴ Diodorus notes, however, that one cannot "fix with any strictness" the boundaries of the periods (χρόνοι) before the Trojan War, due to lack of a "trustworthy chronological table" (1.5.1).⁶⁵

Diodorus shapes his narrative particularly through his interest in the moral utility of historiography. On this basis he claims for historians the role of "ministers of divine providence (ὑπουργοὶ τῆς θείας προνοίας)" (1.1.3).⁶⁶ As divine providence has set and guided the universe and human nature, so historians bring together events into one narrative of the past, and thereby facilitate

---

59 Anne Burton, *Diodorus Siculus, Book I: A Commentary* (Leiden: Brill, 1972), 38.
60 Diodorus gives his own structure to the history in 1.4.6–1.5.1. See Chapter 2 §3.1.
61 Clarke, *Making Time*, discusses these chronological systems in detail on pp. 130–31; cf. pp. 109–21.
62 As in Polybius's *Histories*, καιρός and χρόνος appear in Diodorus Siculus's work with a range of meanings, many quite domestic, and sometimes to indicate a particular moment in time (13.24.6), or opportunity (14.45.5), as well as other uses that designate a duration or period, such as Diodorus's reference to the periods (χρόνοι) covered by his history, including those before the Trojan War, in 1.5.1.
63 Cf. also 1.3.3–6.
64 On counting time from Troy, see Clarke, *Making Time*, 124–25.
65 Diodorus explicitly recognises the different demands for dealing with mythological material (1.5.1; 1.6.1). In his treatment of Dionysius of Halicarnassus, Luce notes that, though similar in many ways to Diodorus, Dionysius takes the opposite approach to the distant past, seeking to present his narrative as though containing precise historical detail, whereas Livy emphasises the legendary nature of these stories (T. J. Luce, "Livy and Dionysius," *Papers of the Leeds International Latin Seminar* 8 (1995): 229).
66 See also Chapter 4. Likewise, historians are tasked with explaining "the changes in τύχη" (18.59.6) (see Sacks, *Diodorus Siculus*, 41).

human progress. Here progress is made not through anecdotes to improve military strategy (a key area of interest for Polybius),[67] but through the benefit of moral guidance from the past. According to Diodorus, the greatest benefit is thus derived from exemplars (both those to emulate and to avoid, cf. 37.4)[68] from the broadest range of times and geographical settings, for:

> a knowledge of history is of the greatest utility for every conceivable circumstance of life. For it endows the young with the wisdom of the aged, while for the old it multiplies the experience which they already possess. (1.1.4–5)

As for Polybius, for Diodorus universal historiography enables readers to see as a whole rather than unnaturally divided parts.[69]

According to Diodorus, questions of moral utility also account for the transitions within history.[70] The cause of regime change lies in consistent human failings; an empire's downfall reliably ensues when, having become accustomed to power, its rulers become complacent and treat their subjects harshly (cf. 19.1.1–8; 37.29.5–37.30.2).[71] As he follows Polybius as his source in Books 28–32,[72] Diodorus adds escalating Roman "greed" (31.26.2; cf. Polyb. *Hist.* 31.22). In the fragmentary later sections, Diodorus traces the tendency to immoderation through Persian, Macedonian, and Roman dominance (37.1.1–6). Having identified the pattern of rise and fall, Diodorus simply observes new phases of Roman tyranny (37.2.12–14; 37.3.1–4). He explains:

> In days of old the Romans, by adhering to the best laws and customs, little by little became so powerful that they acquired the greatest and most splendid empire known to history. But in more recent times, when most nations had already been subjugated in war and there was

---

**67** Though frequently characterised by his interest in military strategies, Polybius is also interested in morality; see Chapter 5.
**68** Sacks, *Diodorus Siculus*, 24–25. Contrast Dionysius of Halicarnassus, who only narrates positive examples (cf. 1.6.5); see Luce, "Livy and Dionysius," 230. Also see Sacks for further discussion of the different views in antiquity on including negative as well as positive examples (Sacks, *Diodorus Siculus*, 28–29).
**69** But, as Sacks observes, for Diodorus it also demonstrates "the universality of certain moral values" (Sacks, *Diodorus Siculus*, 82). Diodorus's example of seeing the full living creature rather than unrelated parts (1.3.8), is similar to Polybius's example at 1.4.6–10, though their historiographies reflect different scales for determining the "whole."
**70** Sacks, *Diodorus Siculus*, 54. Τύχη also plays a complementary role in regime change (see Chapter 4).
**71** Sacks argues Diodorus applies this to myth, transitions between the Egyptian and Median empires, and "in nearly two dozen other circumstances spread throughout the *Bibliotheke*" (Sacks, *Diodorus Siculus*, 43).
**72** Sacks, *Diodorus Siculus*, 8.

a long period of peace, the ancient practices gave way at Rome to pernicious tendencies. (37.3.1)

Diodorus then leaves the reader to consider whether Rome seems inevitably likely to suffer the same fate as earlier regimes of immoderation (cf. 37.4).[73]

For Diodorus, human history also progresses[74] through necessity (ὠφέλεια, 1.8.1–9),[75] where skills (for example, speech) are developed as the need arises (in this case, humans working together in groups as defence against wild animals; 1.8.1–4).[76] This accounts for human developments since a more "primitive" origin. When he describes the world's origins, Diodorus notes two alternate theoretical approaches: some believe the world had a point of origin and will lead to decay, and others that it is constant with no beginning or end (1.6.3).[77] But he endorses neither view explicitly and especially avoids any claim that the universe is moving toward decay.[78]

Kenneth Sacks observes that this cosmogony and anthropology puts Diodorus at odds with contemporaneous writers who present narratives of a golden age and the decay of empires. He argues that Diodorus deliberately avoids such views: "though the *Bibliotheke* is the greatest repository of utopian litera-

---

[73] Sacks also argues: "Diodorus was a provincial, with strong allegiance to Sicily; he was less concerned with what occurred within Roman society than with how Rome treated its subjects" (Sacks, *Diodorus Siculus*, 52). Diodorus was "ambivalent" about "imperial power" but believed Rome had "reached the point of terrorising its subjects" (p. 52). Though it likely does not counteract this approach, it is worth bearing in mind that the portion of the *Library* that covers the latter part of the Republic is fragmentary (cf. Sacks, *Diodorus Siculus*, 47).

[74] Clarke suggests Diodorus sees history in decline, but she only cites passages about the loss of Roman virtue or decline of the Senate since the second century BCE (cf. 30.8; 37.3–8; Clarke, *Making Time*, 132–33) in support of this assessment, overlooking the broader picture, in which moral decline in one regime leads to the rise of a new regime. Conversely, Burton rightly emphasises the importance of progress for Diodorus, despite the rise and fall of empires (Burton, *Diodorus Siculus*, 48–49, 55–82).

[75] Sacks argues that: "Three important forces or historical patterns help to shape Diodorus's narrative: benefit, chance, and the decline of empires" (Sacks, *Diodorus Siculus*, 23). Stylianou claims that Diodorus's emphasis on "chance and utility" is derived from his sources, though recognising that Diodorus nonetheless supports the view (Stylianou, *A Historical Commentary*, 3–5).

[76] Sacks, *Diodorus Siculus*, 57–58; Burton, *Diodorus Siculus*, 48–49.

[77] Dodds, *The Ancient Concept of Progress*, 10–11; Edelstein, *The Idea of Progress*, 140.

[78] The philosophical background on Diodorus's cosmogony is unclear (Burton, *Diodorus Siculus*, 44–46). Oldfather labels Diodorus's philosophy "eclectic" (Oldfather, *Diodorus of Sicily*, 1:28–29 n. 2).

ture from antiquity, none of it is set in a Golden Age of the past."⁷⁹ Rather, in Diodorus's *Library* "utopias" are simply located elsewhere during the same period, such as on an island, and actually remain imperfect (5.41.4, 42.4, 45.3, 46.1), or he hints that utopias are fictitious (2.55.1; 3.53.4–5).⁸⁰ Crucially, Sacks rightly claims that Diodorus "refuses to equate the material destiny of Rome in any way with the future well-being of civilisation."⁸¹

Thus, while for Diodorus history progresses, neither Rome nor any other moment realised or anticipated represents its end. Rather, divine providence (πρόνοια) "continually directs their [stars' and humans'] courses through all eternity (ἅπαντα τὸν αἰῶνα)" (1.1.3), with no further change anticipated. The *Library* leaves the reader with an impression of continuous progress in history, alongside exhortation to further moral improvement. Indeed, Diodorus argues history itself offers the motivation for upright life; heroic acts are exhorted on the basis of the fame accorded by history and public honour after death ("immortality of glory" (τῷ διὰ τῆς δόξης ἀθανατισμῷ), 1.1.5), in contrast to those who are immediately forgotten upon perishing (1.2.3; cf. 1.1.praef.), while making no claims about postmortem rewards of any other kind.⁸²

Though Diodorus's schema of history is characterised by an overarching pattern of progress, it contains repeated elements in the constant rise and fall of political regimes. History is periodised, but he does not stress a particular period as seen above in Polybius. In Diodorus's broader scope, history progresses through necessity, and the historian plays a key role in supplying exemplars for moral improvement. But, while moral progress and more sophisticated responses to human need give history purpose, this process does not lead to any endpoint.⁸³

## 2.2 Steady continuation of history

### Valerius Maximus's *Memorable Doings and Sayings*
Valerius Maximus simply implies that history continues in a constant fashion, without decline, progress, or anticipated end. Whereas traditions such as the *saeculum* festival presume a sense of continuity, even where history is clearly de-

---

79 Sacks, *Diodorus Siculus*, 69.
80 Sacks, *Diodorus Siculus*, 69 n. 69.
81 Sacks, *Diodorus Siculus*, 82.
82 See also, for instance, 2 Macc 6.44, which demonstrates a similar emphasis on good name and memory to exhort courage.
83 Sacks asserts: "Rome is only 'the factual endpoint' of his history" (Sacks, *Diodorus Siculus*, 157).

lineated into periods,[84] for Valerius, continuity in history stems from his implicit claim that people function in characteristic ways in all settings.[85] Produced during Tiberius's reign, Valerius's compilation of exempla affirms: models of human valour or failings, institutional errors, or vulnerability to fortune are relevant in any setting. Unlike that of Polybius or Diodorus Siculus, Valerius's treatment of the past is not an explanatory narrative of historical causes but a popular collection of Roman and non-Roman anecdotes arranged first by category, and then chronology. He makes no attempt to delineate broad movements of history.[86] As W. Martin Bloomer rightly notes, Valerius's purpose and form themselves reflect his static view of history.[87] I argue that Valerius indicates his schema of history through three related features: recognition of stories and characters from the past; the application of diverse anecdotes as exempla; and the decision to detach anecdotes from their original settings in his sources. Each of these contributes to

---

**84** In the popular views underlying the *saeculum* festival, history is comprised of successive periods or *saeculae* based on the natural lifespan of a city. The periods are generally viewed in cycles of ten, in keeping with Etruscan traditions (Susanna Morton Braund, "Virgil and the Cosmos: Religious and Philosophical Ideas," in Martindale, *The Cambridge Companion to Virgil*, 208–9), though in some cases in cycles of four, which Galinsky suggests indicates that conflation with Hesiod's generations, or traditions based on this, has taken place (Galinsky, *Augustan Culture*, 101). They are often also associated with the idea of "the Great Year," which denotes a full cycle of the stars back into their original position from the beginning of the universe (Braund, "Virgil and the Cosmos," 209). In the *saeculum* festival, it was believed that by careful ritual observance at the right moment, the city's lifespan could be extended (Cancik, "The End of the World," 99–101). This is not a teleology as such, but a means by which the rotation through regimes can be maintained in the current position for a further period. The festival's necessity indicates an implicit threat: failure to celebrate properly will surely result, not in decline in history or its end, but in transition to the next empire in line.

**85** In her work on popular morality, Morgan observes that ethical material deals with individuals without expanding to a view with corporate implications or a sense of change over time (Morgan, *Popular Morality*, 242). Though Morgan notes Publilius's pessimistic saying, "Every day is worse than the last," and suggests this sentiment may also be relevant to Valerius's *Doings* 2.1–6, she goes on to summarise helpfully, "The concept of progress over generations has been identified elsewhere in Greek and Roman thought, but in popular ethical thinking there is little or no sign of it" (p. 242).

**86** In describing the ways Valerius expands upon his sources, Mueller identifies a tendency to focus on "personal conduct" with the result that the reader "views neither the sweep of history nor the character of the individual. Rather, one views the building blocks of human character" (Mueller, *Roman Religion in Valerius*, 176–77).

**87** Bloomer argues that Valerius's own narrative intrusions confirm this view of history, thus reflecting not simply his chosen form but also his view (Bloomer, *Valerius Maximus and the Rhetoric*, 25).

the presentation of history as consistent, without decline, progress, or anticipated end.

First, Valerius's anecdotes deal with the past, both as commemoration[88] and as moral lesson for the present (1.1.11; 3.4.praef; 3.7.praef; 3.8.6). His stories go back to earlier times, tracing for instance the actions of Romulus and Remus (1.4.praef; 3.2.praef; 3.2.3). But within his anecdotes he provides no sense of a development or decline in society, or in human behaviour. Unlike writers like Diodorus, Valerius chooses to keep his focus narrow, dismissing the impossible task of encompassing all of history and targeting his own work towards rather less demanding aims. He declares he is not "seized with ambition to be all-embracing," for "who should comprise the transactions of all time in a moderate number of volumes?" (1.praef). In limited ways, some of Valerius's anecdotes incorporate a description over time, such as his treatment of social institutions in Book 2.[89] However, this does not contribute to any larger view of history and, though he recognises that particular changes take place, such as the loss of elections or battles (cf. 7.5), there is no pattern to this beyond human character.

Indeed, secondly, Valerius's approach to exempla in itself *relies* upon a certain stability of human experience in any context. He applies diverse stories as exempla, creating what Hans-Friedrich Mueller describes as "a realm of universally and eternally valid paradigms."[90] As Bloomer observes:

> Some continuity of past with present is essential for a historical exemplum to remain a valid means of argument: the reader or audience must have enough in common with the example so that the precedent still offers a basis for behaviour, for thought, or for action. Valerius' seamless vision of Roman history ensures the connection of past with present as his chapters' chronologically ordered series of exempla sweep the reader from distant times to the present while his rhetorical techniques, such as apostrophe, involve the audience, anachronistically, in the actions of the past.[91]

Finally, Valerius intensifies the timeless applicability of his anecdotes by generally removing any further detail which provided the context for his exempla in his sources. Naturally, he is aware of ideas of periodisation. Sometimes he refers to duration of time, such as "for many centuries (*saecula*)" (2.5.2; cf. 2.2.1a), people of "that epoch (*saeculi*)" (9.1.3), or events which take place in a particular "period (*temporis*)" (3.2.11). But his purpose obscures any clear affirmation of

---

**88** Bloomer, *Valerius Maximus and the Rhetoric*, 146.
**89** For instance, Valerius on the development of the secular games in 2.4.6, or material on trends in the senate in 2.2.6.
**90** Mueller, *Roman Religion in Valerius*, 176. See also Morgan, *Popular Morality*, 244.
**91** Bloomer, *Valerius Maximus and the Rhetoric*, 205.

a periodised view of history. Occasionally, he frames his stories in a specific historical setting, such as "when Rome was captured by the Gauls" (1.1.10) or "in the Second Punic War" (1.4.3). But, as Mueller notes, frequently he removes additional detail that ties a story to its historical particularity, in the apparent interest of increasing its generalisability.[92]

Similarly, Valerius's approach also excludes any endpoint to history. Despite his glowing dedication to the Caesars (1.praef), Valerius's understanding of history excludes a teleological view of the Roman empire[93]—in fact he treats stories from the time of the Republic and imperial Rome uniformly, to the consternation of some interpreters.[94] Rather, having removed the context and generalised the details, he forces his anecdotes into a static view of human history. Indeed, Bloomer asserts that Valerius's portrayal of "seamless" history is "similarly manipulative" to the representation of progress found in the statues of Augustus's forum.[95] He argues that Valerius's omission of a sense of causation or general movement of history must be deliberate, given the "historical self-consciousness" of Rome in this period, as evident in Valerius's sources such as Livy.[96] Rather, excising his anecdotes from the narratives of his sources, Valerius presents a picture of continuous human triumph and strife.

## 2.3 Decline in history

### Tacitus's *Histories*

By contrast, as Tacitus reflects back on the civil strife of 69 CE and the reigns of the Flavian emperors with several decades' hindsight, he suggests these events demonstrate the decline of the Roman empire since the Republic. This is at base a moral failure, manifest in the corruption, violence, and lack of liberty facilitated by the principate system, which may have been a necessary compromise to bring an end to civil war[97] but is far from the republican ideals about which Tacitus expresses nostalgia as one of the Roman elite.[98]

---

92 Mueller, *Roman Religion in Valerius*, 176.
93 Bloomer, *Valerius Maximus and the Rhetoric*, 185.
94 Cf. Bloomer, *Valerius Maximus and the Rhetoric*, 206.
95 Bloomer, *Valerius Maximus and the Rhetoric*, 258.
96 Bloomer, *Valerius Maximus and the Rhetoric*, 258. Lucian's satirical critique of the fashion of writing historiography in *How to Write History* confirms this historical consciousness. Not only Valerius's choice of form, but his selection of material confirms his focus (Bloomer, *Valerius Maximus and the Rhetoric*, 146).
97 Syme, *Tacitus*, 1:206.

Like Polybius, Tacitus offers a deeply political historiography with an evident Roman focus, though for Polybius this consists in focusing on Rome's rise to dominance over other empires, whereas in Tacitus the Roman focus reflects a preoccupation with the events and individual characters *within* the empire, even where foreign wars are discussed.[99] Like Diodorus Siculus, Tacitus emphasises virtue. But, rather than Diodorus's way of attributing transitions between empires to moral failure, again Tacitus's picture of decline maintains a specifically Roman scope. On the other hand, unlike Virgil's *Aeneid*, which is discussed below, Tacitus's concentration on Rome does not evoke triumphant *imperium sine fine*. Rather, his pessimistic assessment of human nature and the apparent decline of virtue—both among political leaders and disordered *plebes*—suggests a continuing pattern of Roman regimes under the tyranny of various *principes*, without anticipating an endpoint or goal.[100]

Tacitus points to an underlying view of history as periodised, delineating epochs within Roman history such as the transition from the Republic to the principate.[101] And he affirms general assumptions about periodisation in statements such as: "Italy was distressed by disasters unknown (*novis cladibus*) before or returning after the lapse of ages (*saeculorum seriem*)" (1.2.2).

This periodised pattern fits within an overarching trajectory of decline, which emerges from the beginning of the *Histories*. Tacitus introduces the years recounted as "rich in disasters, terrible with battles, torn by civil struggles, horrible even in peace (*etiam pace saevum*)" (1.2.1). The reader is then thrown into an account whose focus on the key characters exemplifies the decay.[102] While Galba strives for noble service (1.13.2), his age and weakness (1.12, 16) complement attention to virtues that are outdated (though valued by Tacitus) and certain to be unsuccessful in the new climate (1.18). Otho in turn is drawn in continuity with Nero, the "monstrous character (*immanitas*)" (1.16.2).[103] Tacitus par-

---

**98** See discussion in Dylan Sailor, *Writing and Empire in Tacitus* (Cambridge: Cambridge University Press, 2008), 208, 213.
**99** Tacitus also draws out characters' psychological motivations and the levers of power (Syme, *Tacitus*, 1:157).
**100** Quint considers Tacitus's (plainly negative) attitude to Augustus and his "blood-stained peace" (*Ann.* 1.10) in the reflections on Augustus's funeral, as a comparison to the seemingly more positive, even if sometimes ambiguous, view put forward in Virgil's *Aeneid* (Quint, "Repetition and Ideology," 51–53).
**101** Sailor, *Writing and Empire*, 123.
**102** Tacitus attempts to establish his independence, despite his senior position within Flavian regimes, claiming to transcend all of the regimes which he will treat in turn (*Hist.* 1.1).
**103** The description is taken from Galba's speech to Piso, but Tacitus appears to support the assessment he attributes to Galba.

allels Otho and Nero in licentiousness (1.13, 22) and lack of discipline in the military (cf. 1.83–84).[104]

While the corruption of the *princeps* and military exemplifies the decline, Tacitus also blames the people.[105] He has Galba advise Piso, "Nero will always be missed by the worst citizens" (1.16.3). This, as in many of Tacitus's narrative asides (cf. 4.1), supplies a general, pessimistic assessment of human nature.[106] The narrative continues as it has begun.[107] The first three books describe decline as they report the events of 69 CE,[108] and even Vitellius's death is described as "rather the end of war than the beginning of peace" (4.1.1; cf. 4.1.3). At the beginning of Vespasian's rule, Tacitus becomes more positive, though indications are that the consecutive Flavians will bring about further decline.[109]

In the *Annals* (Tacitus's last work, in which he treats the earlier period from 14 to 68 CE), Tacitus places the beginning of historical decline even earlier.[110] Drawing on imagery of a primordial golden age, he offers a striking account of decay in an excursus on the development of legislation (*Ann.* 3.26–28). In primeval times (*vetustissimi mortalium*), Tacitus claims, people were without wrongdoing and so laws were unnecessary. The ensuing decline of morality brought the need for legislation:

---

[104] This is evident not only in mixing the proper ranks, with each soldier acting as his own commander (1.28), but in a whole system based on bribery and flattery (1.12, 18). All of these actors attract Tacitus's condemnation for motivations that do not include "real patriotism" (1.12) or because they "cared nothing for the state" (1.19; cf. 1.26). Contrast Tacitus's different assessment of Galba in 1.13, 14–16; cf. 1.18. Syme provides further examples (Syme, *Tacitus*, 1:175).
[105] On Tacitus's understanding of historians' role in this decline see Sailor, *Writing and Empire*, 123; cf. Gordon Williams, *Change and Decline: Roman Literature in the Early Empire*, Sather Classical Lectures 45 (Berkeley: University of California Press, 1978), 49, 283.
[106] See Chapter 5 on the role of human freedom and responsibility in explaining the events of history.
[107] Indeed, for Tacitus the principate system is itself corrupt (Syme, *Tacitus*, 1:208; Sailor, *Writing and Empire*, 191).
[108] Russell T. Scott, *Religion and Philosophy in the Histories of Tacitus*, Papers and Monographs of the American Academy in Rome 22 (Rome: American Academy, 1968), 52–53.
[109] Syme reconstructs missing portions of the *Histories* to suggest, on the basis of a parallel in earlier sections, that decline continues under Domitian (Syme, *Tacitus*, 1:209–10). Without relying on reconstructions, others find hints of continuing decline elsewhere, such as *Ann.* 4.32–33 (Scott, *Religion and Philosophy*, 50 n. 16), or by reading the treatment of the past as commentary on the present (Sailor, *Writing and Empire*, 225; Williams, *Change and Decline*, 294–95).
[110] Griffin, "Tacitus as a Historian," 173. Scott notes the different starting points to this decline suggested by different sections of Tacitus's work, from the beginning of the principate (*Hist.* 1.1), to the Punic wars (*Hist.* 2), and the introduction of legal codes (*Ann.* 3, see below; Scott, *Religion and Philosophy*, 48–49). In the *Agricola*, historiographical writing itself declines from Actium (Sailor, *Writing and Empire*, 153).

when equality began to be outworn, and ambition and violence gained ground in place of modesty and self-effacement, there came a crop of despotisms, which with many nations has remained perennial. (*Ann.* 3.26)

The laws follow moral decay, as "when the state was more corrupt, laws were most abundant" (3.27). Indeed, under Pompey's third consulate his "remedies" were "more disastrous than the abuses" (3.28); the laws themselves were no longer kept, resulting in an unjust reversal in which "villainy was immune, decency not rarely a sentence of death" (3.28). Finally, however, the "peace" instituted by Caesar Augustus is more chilling, as the civil war is drawn to a close by trading liberty for a hyper-vigilant state, such that under Tiberius "a reign of terror was threatened (*terror omnibus intentabatur*)" (3.28).

Tacitus exploits a well-worn trope in his narrative of decline, including in the image of a primordial golden age,[111] but he also uses the themes to serve both his narrative purpose and historical schema.[112] His is a character study of the faults of leaders who are given autocratic rule, and the consequences for the liberty of the elite and Roman institutions.[113] Symbols of decline suit his pessimism.

As in the above comparison of Polybius and Diodorus Siculus, Tacitus's schema of history is also affected in important ways by its scale: Tacitus limits his scope of interest to Rome.[114] Neither the *Histories* nor the *Annals* indicate that Tacitus anticipated an endpoint to history.[115] As Syme observes, Tacitus avoids the term *aeternitas*.[116] Despite his negative assessments, Tacitus does

---

**111** Similar decline is found in Livy and Sallust; Sallust is an important model for Tacitus (Scott, *Religion and Philosophy*, 51; Griffin, "Tacitus as a Historian," 172–73). See Chapter 2 §3.2.
**112** Griffin's suggestion that Tacitus uses whatever tools will support his mood (though in reference to his approach to divine guidance of history) is also pertinent here. She notes that for Tacitus "mood prevails over analysis" (Griffin, "Tacitus as a Historian," 172), and that he normally seeks a "gloomy" mood (p. 171).
**113** Sailor, *Writing and Empire*, 188.
**114** In *Hist.* 1.1 Tacitus goes back to Rome's founding, though he immediately disregards further events until 69 CE, claiming the intervening 820 years have been recorded appropriately already. Whereas Sailor argues Tacitus seeks the broadest scope, as befits Rome's grandeur (Sailor, *Writing and Empire*, 123), again comparison to the breadth portrayed by Diodorus Siculus or 2 Baruch illustrates Tacitus's limits.
**115** Although conclusions about themes that are absent from the *Histories* are inevitably provisional, given the text from the middle of Book 5 is no longer extant, a non-teleological view of history is entirely consistent with the extant material.
**116** Syme argues that, compared to other writers and the cultural emphasis on *aeternitas*, Tacitus clearly does not like the term and avoids it. It appears only once in the *Agricola* and once in reported speech in *Ann.* 9.71 (Syme, *Tacitus*, 1:208 n. 1).

not suggest that a regime will come to supersede Rome.[117] His vision simply does not extend beyond Roman limits. The empire might be in crisis, but it is a crisis about how to live as Rome, not about the end of Rome itself.[118] Indeed, although acknowledging prophetic claims that associate the end of the empire with the burning of the Capitol, he refutes these as "empty superstition" (4.54.2).[119] And yet, unlike Virgil's *Aeneid*, his *Histories* does not attribute to Rome any grand position as the end or goal of history. Neither does he suggest a return to an earlier golden age, whether the primeval time of equality (cf. *Ann.* 3), or the days of the Republic. As Tacitus presents it, Rome continues, imperfectly, injured by the corruption that can only be expected of the principate system. Within the general decline, some *principes* may be better or worse than others, and Roman regimes will come and go. But the process is not expected to reach an end.

In summary, Polybius, Diodorus Siculus, and Tacitus all communicate some sense of a historical schema and change over time, which Valerius Maximus in turn minimises, even seemingly removing this sense from his more literary sources when creating his popular exempla. The significance Polybius attributes to the transition of the 140th Olympiad suggests a strong sense of historical periodisation, while Diodorus's emphasis on drawing together a universal account across times and places underscores continuity with a more limited significance to historical periods, as likewise does Tacitus's emphasis on moral decay and decline since the end of the Republic. Polybius, in many ways, comes closest to the teleological texts. His accent on Rome's period and the events leading up to it which create unprecedented unity across the region offers a linear progression over the events contained within the scope of his narrative, but not a teleological schema of history. He confirms directly and indirectly: Rome too will fall.

## 3 Periodised history with an end

In some texts the schema of history does incorporate an end. The above discussion demonstrates the significance of portrayals of the periods, scope, and direc-

---

117 See Sailor for extensive discussion of the Capitoline fire (cf. 3.71–2; Sailor, *Writing and Empire*, 209). Although the fire is disastrous, the Romans destroy the Capitol themselves. When they rebuild it, they remain superior—indeed, they build using "the spoils of Jerusalem" (Sailor, *Writing and Empire*, pp. 243–44).
118 Sailor, *Writing and Empire*, 231.
119 Sailor, *Writing and Empire*, 231. See Chapter 4.

tion of history. Teleology introduces new consequences of such claims. For several writers, the periods of history still represent a succession of empires, but the end constitutes the definitive transition to a final, unending empire.[120] The "end" itself might also be envisaged differently.[121] Late Second Temple writers frequently describe expectations about a pattern of end-time events, inherently connected to a final culmination. This is generally also understood as marking the beginning of idyllic *ongoing* life. In the *Aeneid*, also, Virgil portrays the end as ongoing. These texts are also diverse with regard to the portion of their schemas of history upon which they primarily focus, whether a limited period of recent historical events, an account of end-time events, or time spanning from creation until the end.[122] In each case, however, the end of history is understood as a qualitative change; regardless of important continuities with the history that has gone before, this end-time existence will not return to features of the past, whether war, perishability, or the presence of evil.

---

**120** Wright argues that Jewish thought at the time of the NT did not incorporate beliefs about the end of history ("this makes no sense either of the basic Jewish worldview or of the texts in which the Jewish hope is expressed," N. T. Wright, *The New Testament and the People of God* (London: SPCK, 1992), 299). He argues, rather, that Jewish texts frequently used metaphors to refer to significant changes (particularly in relation to political transitions) *within* history. Wright's interest in part lies in defending against claims that Jesus' prophecy in Mark 13 has not been fulfilled; in the process he overlooks key elements of both NT and other Jewish texts. See the compelling critique in Edward Adams, *The Stars Will Fall from Heaven: Cosmic Catastrophe in the New Testament and Its World*, LNTS 347 (London: T&T Clark, 2007), 5–16.
**121** At one extreme, for instance, the end of history may emerge as the goal of a process of advancement leading to a particular political regime. By contrast, the end may comprise a reversal, terminating current experiences of suffering and decline. Rajak considers whether Hellenistic Jewish Millenarian expectations describe: "the beginning of the End? Or the end of the beginning?" (Tessa Rajak, "Jewish Millenarian Expectations," in *The First Jewish Revolt: Archaeology, History, and Ideology*, ed. Andrea M. Berlin and J. Andrew Overman (London: Routledge, 2002), 165). She rightly recognises the diverse understandings of end-time events as they unfold, which also interact with understandings of a human role in prompting the end through revolution. The end can involve joyful "weeks without number" (cf. *Apocalypse of Weeks* 1 Enoch 93.17; cf. 2 Bar 74.2–4). John Collins paints this as a "series of 'ends'" (Collins, "Expectations of the End," 79). The claim that writers envisaged idyllic life continuing afterward is not mutually exclusive with the concept of the end of history in terms of a definitive transition brought about by a final defeat of evil (see Christopher Rowland, *The Open Heaven: A Study of Apocalyptic in Judaism and Early Christianity* (Eugene, OR: Wipf & Stock, 2002), 188–89).
**122** As noted above, this chapter sets out these diverse schemas for each of the study's texts, before considering further issues such as portrayals of divine guidance of the transitions across history and the crucial question of the imminence of a writer's portrait of the end in later chapters.

## 3.1 Progress to the end of history

### Virgil's *Aeneid*

In the *Aeneid*, Virgil's epic poem of Roman origins written in the Augustan period,[123] Virgil offers a complex picture of history. He plays with time, creating patterns within history through themes of recurrence. These circular elements in Virgil's portrayal of time interact in significant ways with key themes, such as delay, and create a sense of ambiguity which is important for the political questions the *Aeneid* raises for the reader. But Virgil also addresses these questions by clarifying that these cyclical patterns of events ultimately fit within a linear progression, which advances to its goal and end in Rome.[124]

Virgil's patterns of recurrence are formed both by linking events back to earlier events within the plot[125] and by alluding to literary forerunners, especially Homer.[126] In doing so, not only does Virgil circle back between earlier and later events in the world of the text, but he invites readers to compare events of the mythic past with their own present. For instance, both Troy and Carthage function as literary types foreshadowing Rome, but they are also contrasted with it.[127] The typologies suggest both cyclical and linear trajectories of history: Rome in some ways is the completion of the search to replace Troy following exile, after failed earlier attempts to recreate it in other cities, and at the same time represents something entirely new.

Virgil makes frequent use of language denoting periodisation. He refers to time in terms of *saecula*. Jupiter promises in Book 1, "wars will cease and savage ages soften" (1.291) and in the final book, Juno asks Jupiter to "let Alban kings endure through the ages" (12.826; cf. 1.445, 606; 6.235). *Saecula* are also directly connected to golden ages—both the golden ages of the past under Saturn and the

---

[123] Fantham, "Introduction," xvii.
[124] The end in the *Aeneid* is also depicted as ongoing existence (of Rome, not of individuals), which Virgil depicts as a static *continuation of the present*. See Chapter 6 below.
[125] Quint, "Repetition and Ideology," 50.
[126] Williams, "The Sixth Book," 194–96; Knauer, "Vergil's *Aeneid* and Homer." Note that intertextual (and intratextual) links create not only recurrence, but inversion, cf. *Aen.* 6 and *Od.* 11 (Williams, "The Sixth Book," 207). Quint notes that the two halves of the epic, as they link first to Homer's *Odyssey* (Books 1–6) and then the *Iliad* (Books 7–12), also create two different types of repetition, repeating the difficulties of the past but eventually emerging victorious (Quint, "Repetition and Ideology," 9–10).
[127] Quint, "Repetition and Ideology," 10.

golden ages under Jupiter. Virgil evokes the nostalgia of the earlier golden age.[128] In Book 8, King Evander takes Aeneas and his son through woods, describing to them an unruly (if innocent) population that once reigned there, before Saturn arrived and provided laws. The king goes on, "under his reign were the golden ages men tell of" (8.324–25). From this "perfect peace," however, things fell apart. By contrast, the golden ages of Jupiter, which the reader has already encountered in a historical review in Book 6 (6.793), constitute something different. Rather than the idyllic scenario of agricultural harmony Virgil presented as already having been inaugurated in his earlier *4 Eclogue*,[129] in the *Aeneid* Jupiter's *aurea saecula* are no longer part of nostalgic longing for effortless life in Troy, but reflect hard-won progress as the culmination of Aeneas's journey, fulfilled in Rome.[130] This is a movement from laziness, ease, and luxury in the golden ages of Saturn, to Jupiter's golden ages, in which human progress is central.[131] Rather than the symbol's traditional position in a narrative of decline,[132] here Virgil employs the concept of a regained (and, indeed, *revised*) golden age, as an image of resurgence and renewal.

Thus, while Virgil's play with time creates some cyclical sense, in three exemplary passages of historical review, in Books 1, 6, and 8 (1.262–304; 6.752–892; 8.624–728), he clarifies that the underlying schema is a linear progression.

The historical review in Book 6 depicts heroes parading before Aeneas in the underworld, with commentary by his father Anchises. This is the scene in which the prophecy of the golden ages is disclosed. Unlike a similar scene by Lucre-

---

[128] Although the idea of the golden age retained currency, not all writers subscribed to it. For some writers the idea of a golden age is problematic (e.g. Diodorus Siculus, see above), and even those who use it, use it differently. See Chapter 6.
[129] Cf. *Ecl.* 4.4–10. Albeit, in Virgil's account, this age is embodied in a child whose identity has been much debated. The prophetic style of *4 Eclogue* prompted its use for divination, and some ancient Christian interpretation associated the birth of the child that inaugurates the golden age with Jesus. Some have found indications that Virgil drew on the Sibylline Oracles for this text (Braund, "Virgil and the Cosmos," 209); others find reference to expectation for a child of Octavia and Mark Antony (on this question see D. A. Slater, "Was the Fourth Eclogue Written to Celebrate the Marriage of Octavia to Mark Antony? A Literary Parallel," *Classical Review* 26 (1912): 114–19, and H. R. Fairclough and G. P. Goold in the LCL *Virgil*, 1:2).
[130] Galinsky, *Augustan Culture*, 123–24.
[131] Here, need and suffering, which are Jupiter's gift and not punishment (unlike in Hesiod's *Works and Days*), create the environment for progress through motivation to strive for improvement. Galinsky identifies this perspective on effort for progress as central in Augustan culture, and already present in *Georgics* 1.121–28 (Galinsky, *Augustan Culture*, 93–97, 121–25).
[132] As in Hesiod *Works* 106–201, Ovid *Metam.* 1.89–150, and Tacitus *Ann.* 3.26–28.

tius,[133] the passage assumes a *vaticinium ex eventu* structure: that is, in Virgil's version the heroes belong to the *literary future*, though the reader's *historical past*. Virgil further plays with time by interrupting the chronology of the parade, unexpectedly jumping forward to Augustus (6.792),[134] with a hint of the glory ahead that constitutes the *telos* of this process, and thereby relativising other characters.[135]

A similar historical review is provided in the *ekphrasis*, or graphic description, of Aeneas's shield, which he receives in Book 8 from Venus (his mother), as a gift forged by Vulcan.[136] Again, the shield functions as a *vaticinium ex eventu*, describing events beyond Aeneas's time but familiar to his readers. After referencing some earlier events, the scenes depicted on the shield then jump forward to those contemporaneous to the reader, bypassing significant moments of Roman history.[137] Again, Caesar Augustus is at the centre (8.678–79, 714–28).[138] The description functions like an excursus that also gives shape to the surrounding story.[139] Indeed, Philip Hardie argues the *ekphrasis* of the shield is the pinnacle of the *Aeneid*, in which both the "universalist themes" of Achilles's shield in Homer's *Iliad* and Virgil's broader "nationalist concerns" are held together to encapsulate Virgil's joint thrust of "*cosmos* and *imperium*."[140] The shield provides a picture of Augustus and his historical moment at the centre of a *cosmic* picture of history. But Aeneas remains unaware of the deeper meaning of the scenes set out on his new shield (8.730);[141] Book 8 ends with Aeneas

---

**133** Hardie, *Virgil's Aeneid*. Homeric associations shape the meaning of this passage (Williams, "The Sixth Book"; O'Hara, *Inconsistency in Roman Epic*, 91–95).
**134** R. G. Austin, *P. Vergili Maronis, Aeneidos: Liber Sextus* (Oxford: Clarendon, 1977), 242.
**135** The metaphysical assumptions behind this passage, namely the cyclic experience of individuals returning to earthly life from the underworld, are less Virgil's emphasis than the opportunity they supply for a prospective encounter with these heroes and emphasis on both explaining the "tragic past" and patriotic hope for the future (Williams, "The Sixth Book," 194). Note that these cycles within an individual's life, as set out in this underworld review, are not the same as a cyclic view of history itself, despite the reference to "when the circle of time is complete" (6.745). This "completion" for Virgil is a terminus, not the beginning of a new cycle.
**136** This episode and the *ekphrasis* allude to Achilles's shield in the *Iliad* Book 18 (Hardie, *Virgil's Aeneid*, 337).
**137** For instance, particularly excluding the Punic Wars (Hardie, *Virgil's Aeneid*, 350–51).
**138** See Hardie's detailed treatment of the ways the shield depicts the world and Augustus as its centre (Hardie, *Virgil's Aeneid*, 346–58).
**139** Alessandro Barchiesi, "Virgilian Narrative: Ecphrasis," in Martindale, *The Cambridge Companion to Virgil*, 278.
**140** Hardie, *Virgil's Aeneid*, 339, 362.
**141** In the unfolding story, the scene makes sense as a divine gift to assure Aeneas of his certain military victory, contra those who claim, against Homer's parallel scene, that Virgil's passage

simply shouldering the shield, awestruck by the artwork of the gift (8.730 – 31),[142] as he travels on. But the reader has again received a prospective review of the periods of history that will culminate in triumph in Rome.

All of this takes place in light of the review in Book 1, which establishes Virgil's teleological sense of history in the *Aeneid*. Here the reader is privy to a conversation between Venus and Jupiter, in which Jupiter provides an account of future events, which is to some extent performative, "further unrolling," as he says, "the scroll of fate [he] will disclose its secrets" (1.262).[143] Venus, and thereby also the reader, is told about the events through which Aeneas will provide both city walls and civilisation (*mores*; 1.263 – 64, cf. 1.7), and thus the space in which Romulus will eventually found a city (1.276). Jupiter declares of the thus-named Romans:

> For these I set not bounds in space or time (*tempora*);
> But have given empire without end (*imperium sine fine*). (1.278 – 79)

Furthermore, an age will dawn in which Aeneas's line (renamed "Iulus" (1.277– 78, 288)) will produce "Caesar, a Trojan ... Julius" (1.286, 8).[144] His boundless reign will encompass oceans and the stars. Ultimately he will be elevated to the heavens to become a focus of prayer himself (1.289 – 90). Jupiter's promise governs the whole of the story. Unknown to Aeneas at this stage, who of course fails to understand even after he receives the shield in Book 8 (8.730), the *telos* of his story is determined.

There are, however, delays in the prophecy's fulfilment. Some recent studies have problematised the prophecy; James O'Hara even claims that Jupiter is shown to be deceiving Venus.[145] And certainly, as the epic proceeds, from the Odyssean wandering of the first half to the Iliadic struggle of the second,[146] it

---

incorporates the shield without fitting it into any narrative purpose (see discussion in D. A. West, "Cernere erat: The Shield of Aeneas," in Harrison, *Oxford Readings in Vergil's Aeneid*, 295–96).
**142** The text reads: "though he knows not the events, he rejoices in their representation, raising up on his shoulder the fame and fortunes of his children's children" 8.730 – 31. See discussion of Aeneas's lack of understanding in West, "Cernere erat," 304.
**143** Here Virgil makes a self-conscious play on the etymology of *fatum* (cf. 1.258, 261– 62), indicating inevitability. This episode is discussed further in the introduction to Chapter 4.
**144** The identification is assiduously vague, but most interpreters see Virgil referring here to Augustus, though simultaneously exploiting his connections to Julius Caesar (Galinsky, *Augustan Culture*, 251).
**145** O'Hara, *Inconsistency in Roman Epic*, 78–81; James J. O'Hara, *Death and the Optimistic Prophecy in Vergil's Aeneid* (Princeton: Princeton University Press), 1990. This is an important and nuanced area in recent study; see further discussion in Chapters 4 and 6 below.
**146** Quint, "Repetition and Ideology," 9.

is clear that the *telos* is achieved at a cost. But the delays serve to heighten the reader's experience.[147] Contrary to some recent explorations of subtle, anti-imperial tendencies in Virgil,[148] the numerous delays do not undermine Virgil's teleology, though the struggle may suggest some ambivalence on Virgil's behalf *about* this inevitable trajectory.[149] The *Aeneid*'s version of history confirms the end has already been achieved, even where it is clear that there are problematic issues in the historical events to which the *vaticinia ex eventu* refer.[150] From the chronological vantage point of reader and writer, Augustus can be highlighted by appearing in the wrong place chronologically in the parade of Book 6 and the centre of the shield in Book 8. The narrative takes place in the space between the exile from Troy and the establishment of Rome and its unending dominion. But this is all in the past for the reader. While delay adds to the drama, the reader's vantage point of life under Augustus, alongside the dramatic irony of having

---

[147] Horsfall notes characteristic terminology for delay in the Trojans reaching their goal, for instance at 3.131, 205, 278; 6.2 (Nicholas Horsfall, *Virgil, "Aeneid" 6: A Commentary* (Berlin: de Gruyter, 2013), 2:66). It is notable even here that the powers of Juno—the *Aeneid*'s goddess of Carthage and force for delay—are noted, but Jupiter promises she will come to benefit Rome (1.279–82), as also Dido, patron of Carthage, is kept ignorant of the future in the service of its fulfilment (1.299–300).

[148] Galinsky's introduction supplies an insightful discussion of the impact of pre- and post-World War Two contexts in interpretation of Virgil (Galinsky, *Augustan Culture*, 3–9; cf. S. J. Harrison, "Some Views of the *Aeneid* in the Twentieth Century," in Harrison, *Oxford Readings in Vergil's Aeneid*, 1–20). See further discussion of the political implications of Virgil's teleological view of history in Chapter 6. Krauter also refers to the pessimistic and optimistic schools (which he identifies with American and German Virgilian scholarship respectively), and argues that the latter features more often in theological discussions which seek to draw the *Aeneid* in as a comparison text (Krauter, "Vergils Evangelium und das lukanische Epos?", 240–42). Krauter's discussion is helpful, including his attention to the stress on suffering in the *Aeneid*, although there is an important temporal distinction in which this suffering is emphatically placed in the past, while the reader lives in the celebrated time of Augustus to which the historical reviews in the epic point.

[149] Theodorakopoulos, "Closure," 157. O'Hara notes "doubt" and "regret," and considers how they relate to the Augustan teleological elements, which he nonetheless recognises in the text (O'Hara, *Inconsistency in Roman Epic*, 102). Quint argues Virgil portrays the glorious Augustan ideal he hopes for, tinged with a darker fear, but that ultimately Virgil still affirms the former. By contrast, Quint argues a "worst case" interpretation of the teleology to Rome is portrayed, not in the *Aeneid*, but in Ovid's reception of the *Aeneid* in the *Metamorphoses*, in which these themes turn to despair (Quint, "Repetition and Ideology," 53–54).

[150] See Feeney, "History and Revelation," 5, 7; Elaine Fantham, ed., *Virgil: Aeneid*, trans. Frederick Ahl, Oxford World's Classics (Oxford: Oxford University Press, 2007), 376. See also Chapter 6 below.

access to Jupiter's speech to Venus, underscores the certainty of success[151] and even that the end itself has been achieved.[152]

Thus, in the *Aeneid*, Virgil not only presents a teleological view of history but, as I will further argue in Chapter 6, identifies the end of history with Rome itself.[153] Through gruelling labours, history has progressed to this *telos*. The delay, strife, and effort described as part of Aeneas's journey, involving failed attempts to re-create Troy elsewhere and traversing even the underworld, is all chronologically prior to the foretold events contemporary to the reader: the culmination of history in the foretold *imperium sine fine* of the Roman empire.

## 3.2 Steady continuation of history with an end

Although all of the Jewish texts of this study reflect some kind of teleological schema, there is great diversity among them in terms of which kinds of eschatological expectations feature and where across the historical schema the writers focus their attention.[154] These differences are perhaps most evident in the examples of texts which do not present history within a particular paradigm of either progress or decline.

Each text discussed in this section has its own preoccupations reflected in the choice of narrative focus. For instance, 2 Maccabees focuses on recounting recent historical events, as also does Josephus's *Jewish War*, while the War Scroll is set in the events of an end-time war. Thus the frame of events described are importantly different. However, while these provide the setting, each text nonetheless indicates to its readers an understanding of history that reaches outside the frame of the events narrated. For the writer of the War Scroll, divine action in creation and covenant warrants frequent mention as part of recounting the past and characterising the divine behaviour which undergirds expectations about these end-time events. In 2 Maccabees, the narrative of events includes frequent

---

151 See Chapter 4 on assurance of this end in relation to the role of fate and the gods.
152 See Chapter 6.
153 As in texts like 4 Ezra and 2 Baruch (§3.3), which invite readers to identify their own present by placing contemporary events in a prophetic account of the past, the effect of Virgil's play with time is a focus on the historical present.
154 The texts also differ in how imminent they consider such an end to be; as noted above, I return to this question in Chapter 6. The focus of the current chapter is on the broader sense of whether writers suggest a teleological framework and, if so, in what sense. An appreciation for the diverse ways in which these views are presented across the texts of the study provides the necessary background for the later consideration of the level of urgency to which each writer attributes this eschatological expectation.

references to belief in resurrection to eternal life, while Josephus's narrative incorporates claims about both individual eschatology and a larger pattern of periodic changes in the cycle of ages and future succession of empires. For each of these texts (as, indeed, for all of the texts of the study at some level), despite the frame of events upon which the narrative focuses, the writing is itself targeted towards addressing an element of experience in the intended readers' present time.[155]

## Second Maccabees

Of the Jewish texts of this study, 2 Maccabees is the most understated in its indications of the end of history. The text concentrates for the most part on divine justice *within* the events of history. Key elements of eschatological expectation found in later texts are not present, including messianic expectation,[156] eschatological woes, or graphic descriptions of final judgement scenes or of a heavenly Jerusalem. What is present, however, is a strong sense of post-mortem realities and consequences, expressed in temporal language, for instance, with *eternal* (ongoing) life. There is an end to earthly life and transition to eternal life, certainly for individuals or communities of individuals,[157] which is the main focus in this text centred on military battles and gruesome martyrdoms (or, alternatively, grizzly downfalls for opponents). Although the end of an individual's earthly life is not the same as the end of history itself, and nor is it unique to Jewish literature of this time,[158] in some key passages, this individual eschatology interacts with a broader teleological view.

Importantly, hints of any end-time expectations require looking beyond the narrative frame, which I noted above is significant for each of the texts discussed

---

[155] Collins helpfully recognises this dynamic in relation to the end-time focus in apocalypses, which he rightly notes ultimately serves the writers' interests in addressing the circumstances of their own time (Collins, "Temporality and Politics," 40–41). See further discussion below in Chapter 6.

[156] John J. Collins, "Messianism in the Maccabean Period," in *Judaisms and Their Messiahs at the Turn of the Christian Era*, ed. Jacob Neusner, William Scott Green, and Ernest Frerichs (Cambridge: Cambridge University Press, 1987), 97–109. See further discussion in my Chapter 6.

[157] The martyrdom stories demonstrate a particular emphasis on the communal benefit of individuals maintaining piety (cf. 2 Macc 6.31), and the group found with amulets in 2 Macc 12.39–45 are likewise treated corporately in some sense.

[158] The idea of individual eschatology is present, for instance, in influential Graeco-Roman philosophical literature. For discussion of non-Jewish Graeco-Roman texts which presume the end of individuals and how this interacts with what might broadly be understood as eschatological expectation and teleological schemas, see Cancik, "The End of the World," 96–98.

in this section. In his comparison of 1 and 2 Maccabees and Acts, Daniel Schwartz characterises 2 Maccabees as portraying a circular narrative,[159] and in doing so also implies elements of a circular view of history. Schwartz rightly notes that this late second-century BCE narrative[160] begins and ends in a stable situation. The Jewish protagonist groups are free to practice their faith without interference from political rulers.[161] Schwartz argues this is characteristic of diaspora historiography (exemplified by Esther), in which a crisis emerges but is resolved within the course of the narrative.[162] There is a sense that things return to "normal" at the conclusion of these narratives. However, despite the clear emphasis on divine rescue *within* the events of history, the writer of 2 Maccabees does give some sense of future events imagined beyond the close of the narrative. This is encapsulated in claims about storing up sin (or treasure), resurrection of the righteous,[163] eternal life, and the possibility of post-mortem adjustments to eschatological status before the resurrection.

---

**159** Schwartz also points to 3 Maccabees and Philo's *In Flaccum* (Schwartz, "Circular or Teleological," 124). Schwartz uses the language of "circular" or "teleological" history in his discussion of 1 and 2 Maccabees and Acts in a slightly different sense from me. He focuses only on the trajectory of the narrative itself, equating teleology for instance with 1 Macc's transition to Hasmonean leadership and the narrative trajectory he identifies in Acts from the kingdom of Israel (1.6) to the kingdom of God (28.31, and from Israel to Rome; pp. 128–29).
**160** Second Maccabees is generally placed between 124/5 and 63 BCE (Doran, "Independence or Co-Existence"; Attridge, "Jewish Historiography," 318–20). Schwartz provides an earlier date, based on a different reading of dates provided in the letters in manuscripts (Schwartz, *2 Maccabees*, 14–15). See Chapter 2 §3.1.
**161** In doing so, Schwartz also downplays the significance of the threat represented by opponents such as Antiochus IV. According to Schwartz, in these historiographies secular rulers are essentially positive: a crisis emerges through a misunderstanding, is ultimately resolved, and things return to normal (Schwartz, "Circular or Teleological"). His perspective, not only on 2 Maccabees but also on Acts, emphasises a quietism that, I suggest, is not present in the text. Antiochus IV is not portrayed as a well-meaning political ruler who persecutes as a consequence of misinterpreting a Jewish custom, but an archetypal θεομάχος, who is justly punished in the narrative. See Chapter 5.
**162** Schwartz, "Circular or Teleological," 124.
**163** Goldstein argues that the writer goes to considerable effort to present Judas Maccabeus as believing in the resurrection of the dead, asserting "we can be quite certain that he misunderstood his source," in contrast to other sections which he claims are "unadulterated by Jason's theories" (Jonathan A. Goldstein, *II Maccabees*, AB 41 A (Garden City, NY: Doubleday, 1983), 449). This illustrates a type of scholarship which is optimistic about our ability to distinguish the text from historical realities behind the text, and sees this as a primary task of interpretation of a historiographical narrative such as 2 Maccabees.

The martyrdom stories of 2 Macc 6–7 function as a "key turning point" in the narrative.[164] A narrative aside in 6.12–17 provides the interpretative lens for the stories which follow, namely the martyrdom of Eleazer (6.18–31), and of seven brothers and their mother (7.1–41), which are followed by a final closing statement (7.42). The narrative aside exhorts: "Now I urge those who read this book not to be depressed by such calamities, but to recognise that these punishments were designed not to destroy but to discipline our people" (6.12). It goes on to explain the benevolence of "immediate" punishment in terms of divine action to punish before the people's sins have reached completion ("πρὸς τέλος"; 6.15; cf. 7.38; Ps 93.12–13 LXX; Isa 54.7–8; Wis 16.11), unlike the other nations who are allowed to continue accruing sins: "the Lord waits patiently to punish them until they have reached the full measure of their sins" (6.14).[165] The use of πρὸς τέλος enjoys an interesting parallel in 1 Thess 2.16, which describes the gentiles as having "constantly been filling up the measure of their sins," while God's wrath reaches them εἰς τέλος. Gordon Fee suggests that the 1 Thessalonians passage is "more distantly echoed" in 2 Macc 6.14–15,[166] and he takes the Greek to mean "at the end" (rather than something like fullness or to the uttermost).[167]

In 2 Maccabees, the potential benefits of suffering as discipline are not understood as an ascetic or Stoic virtue in assenting to suffering itself. Rather the benefit lies in satisfying the need for punishment, and reforming before it is too late. The sense of sins filling up across a period that leads to an end suggests an eschatological extension of Deuteronomistic theology,[168] in which post-mortem reward for the protagonists, and ultimately punishment for the (not-so-passive) divine instruments of the people's punishment, will resolve remaining tensions. Although many injustices are resolved within history in 2 Maccabees, this under-

---

164 George W. E. Nickelsburg, "1 and 2 Maccabees: Same Story, Different Meaning," *Concordia Theological Monthly* 42 (1971): 522.
165 Doran, *2 Maccabees*, 150. Second Maccabees likewise emphasises the piety of the women who have circumcised their sons and those observing Sabbath in 6.10–11, which leads into the narrative aside about discipline through calamity meaning those favoured by God are not storing up punishment for sin.
166 Gordon D. Fee, *The First and Second Letters to the Thessalonians*, NICNT (Grand Rapids: Eerdmans, 2009), 100–1 n. 47.
167 This contrasting view is suggested by Bruce (F. F. Bruce, *1 & 2 Thessalonians*, WBC (Waco, TX: Word, 1982), 48). Even if the sense in 2 Macc 6.14–15 is that gentiles will be punished when their sins have reached their fullness, this still implies some kind of end for judgement, at the point of an individual's death or the end of history.
168 See further discussion in Chapter 5 below.

standing of an end hints at eschatological elements and a hope beyond the end of the narrative, which is also borne out in the ensuing martyrdom accounts.

In the following incident, Eleazer endures his suffering with the rationale that he fears God (6.30)—though here it is not explicit that it is the torture and death itself that Eleazer considers divine action, but perhaps rather that his fear of God ensures he would not give in to the demand to eat the pork, which Antiochus has used as the pretext for the torture. Nonetheless, Eleazer is clear: "even if for the present I would avoid the punishment of mortals, yet whether I live or die I will not escape the hands of the Almighty" (6.26).

The responses of the seven sons in the following passage outline eschatological expectations, with further elements filled out as each son faces death.[169] Resurrection to "ever-flowing life" (ἀενάου ζωῆς: 7.36) is presented as the promise for those who die for keeping the law (vv. 23, 29; cf. *Ag. Ap.* 2.218 and below).[170] Throughout, the hopes are described through a contrast between Antiochus and God. The second son's emphatic use of pronouns initially establishes the comparison,[171] as he addresses the earthly king: "you accursed wretch" who may "dismiss us from this present life," juxtaposing "the King of the universe [who] will raise us up to an everlasting renewal of life" (v. 9).[172] The fourth son informs Antiochus that "there will be no resurrection to life" for the king (v. 14).[173] The seventh son offers the longest speech as he draws all of the elements identified by each brother together, not only affirming belief in the resurrection but repeating the narrator's sentiment about benevolent, immediate pun-

---

**169** Although these passages describe the martyrdoms dramatically, Doran rightly cautions against labelling the narrative "tragic history" (Robert Doran, "2 Maccabees and 'Tragic History,'" *HUCA* 50 (1979): 114).
**170** Notably, belief in resurrection does not feature in 1 Maccabees (Harrington, *The Maccabean Revolt*, 47).
**171** Doran, *2 Maccabees*, 157.
**172** Doran suggests the grammar is reminiscent of Dan 12.1, rather than offering a direct quotation (Doran, *2 Maccabees*, 158). See discussion at n. 175 below.
**173** The narrative simultaneously underscores the punishment that will also rightly come the way of Antiochus (7.19; cf. 4.17; 8.11). Nicklas notes elements of irony in how characters like Antiochus and Nicanor are treated, despite the serious subject matter (Tobias Nicklas, "Irony in 2 Maccabees?", in *The Books of the Maccabees: History, Theology, Ideology*, ed. Géza G. Xeravits and József Zsengellér, Supplements to the Journal for the Study of Judaism 118 (Leiden: Brill, 2007), 111). See also discussion of the contrasting positions between Antiochus and the martyrs in 2 Macc 7, in Jan Willem van Henten, *The Maccabean Martyrs as Saviours of the Jewish People: A Study of 2 and 4 Maccabees*, Supplements to the Journal for the Study of Judaism 57 (Leiden: Brill, 1997), 172–82.

ishment (vv. 31–38; cf. 6.12–16).[174] Robert Doran notes that the passage shares interesting overtones with Daniel, mirroring grammatical features which likewise emphasise the passing nature of the earthly king's power and stressing resurrection "to everlasting life" as in Dan 12.2.[175]

The mother of these seven sons links her trust in post-mortem restoration with the mysterious divine activity of creation in the womb, concluding as she addresses the seventh son before his martyrdom: "therefore the Creator of the world, who shaped the beginning of humankind and devised the origin of all things, will in his mercy give life and breath back to you" (7.23, 28–29; cf. 7.9, 14). The divine ability to create in the past is the basis for hope in *re*creation. And yet the restored creation will not be the same as the first. Only the righteous are restored, while there is no post-mortem possibility for opponents like Antiochus or, in later chapters, Nicanor.[176]

An intriguing incident later in 2 Macc 12 likewise emphasises resurrection, but here more clearly within a framework of a future time of judgement. Judas initiates a collection for an offering, to atone for soldiers whose deaths during battle are attributed to their sinful recourse to amulets (12.43). Here the narrator praises the offering, as it demonstrates Judas's confidence in the resurrection:

> In doing this he [Judas] acted very well and honourably, taking account of the resurrection. For if he were not expecting that those who had fallen would rise again, it would have been superfluous and foolish to pray for the dead. But if he was looking to the splendid reward that is laid up for those who fall asleep in godliness, it was a holy and pious thought. Therefore he made atonement for the dead, so that they might be delivered from their sin. (12.43–45)[177]

---

**174** Nickelsburg notes the paradox that the sons recognise the torment as divine discipline for transgressing the law, and yet it comes as a result of *refusal* to transgress the law (Nickelsburg, "1 and 2 Maccabees," 522).
**175** See Doran's observations about the similarities between Dan 12.2 and 2 Macc 7.9 (Doran, *2 Maccabees*, 157), and similarities between 2 Macc 7.15 and Dan 8.4 and 11.3, as well as the effect of "the asyndetic grouping of participles ("having ... being")" in 2 Macc 7.15 (p. 158). While it may be unhelpful to read too much into these similarities, they do at least suggest a similar anticipation of resurrection of the righteous and the passing reign of kings, even if they do not necessarily indicate that 2 Macc shares the broader eschatological expectations found in Daniel.
**176** Despite a possible hint of post-mortem punishment in Eleazer's speech at 2 Macc 6.26, the explicit rejection of the possibility of post-mortem existence for Antiochus in 7.14 suggests this is the more probable view for the writer of 2 Maccabees. This contrasts with developments in 4 Maccabees, which describes both earthly and post-mortem punishments (4 Macc 12.18; cf. 18.5; van Henten, *The Maccabean Martyrs*, 172). On the relationship between 2 and 4 Maccabees, see van Henten's pp. 58–82.
**177** See Chapter 5 for discussion of the different ways that 2 Maccabees portrays opponent and protagonist characters whose deaths are attributed to divine punishment.

This passage, which has influenced later theology about purgatory,[178] not only continues the text's interest in resurrection of the righteous, but introduces the idea of a separation between the time of death and a future time of judgement, as well as the possibility of not only sins stored up for later punishment as in 6.12–17, but also treasure stored up for the pious. Although evidently not immediate, the text is not clear when the ultimate judgement that Judas is concerned to influence will take place for the individuals; Jan Willem van Henten suggests "the resurrection at the end of time may well be meant in this passage."[179] While this seems likely, whether or not the episode in 2 Macc 12.42–45 does indicate belief in a judgement and end-time general resurrection as found across many other late Second Temple texts, it clearly introduces themes of judgement and reward to be implemented at a point in the future, with the possibility that the eschatological status of these dead soldiers may be altered in the interim. This is certainly an end, but it is the least detailed approach to end-time expectations across the teleological texts of this study.

Other temporal language appears throughout 2 Maccabees, with a sense of particular times and periods. This terminology functions as a way of demarcating events in the narrative, or at times labelling particular times of hardship within the historical events described. The letters with which 2 Maccabees begins set out history in terms of years and the period of reign under Demetrius (1.7). Throughout, the writer uses temporal language to denote periods of the past, such as the "former times (χρόνοις, 14.38)," "time of separation (χρόνοις, 14.3),"[180] and even looking back to the "times of Joshua (τοὺς Ἰησοῦ χρόνους, 12.15)"—the last of which to an extent provides a "type" for the time of Judas Maccabeus.[181] The terminology extends also to times of hardship in a more general sense, as "in times of evil (ἐν καιρῷ πονηρῷ)" (1.5). But the sense of these particular "times" does not lead the writer to set out a structured schema of history. In this sense, though demonstrating a temporal sensitivity and periodisation found across the texts of this study, rather than the kind of periodisation found in motifs like the five-kingdom paradigm of Daniel discussed below, 2 Maccabees reflects periodisation more akin to that described by Diodorus Siculus and Tacitus.

---

178 Goldstein, *II Maccabees*, 450.
179 Van Henten, *The Maccabean Martyrs*, 182.
180 Doran translates "in the times of chaos (ἀμειξίας)," observing this is literally "in the times of unmixedness" and, though he discusses various views of which specific historical events the author wishes to allude to, he notes that the text here is primarily concerned with the portrait of Alcimus (Doran, *2 Maccabees*, 263, 267).
181 Χρόνος and καιρός also have domestic or colloquial meanings (2 Macc 1.22; 3.5; 4.23; 5.1; 9.1; 10.3), including denoting opportunity (4.32; 9.25; 14.5). See discussion at §4.1.2.

Schwartz is right to emphasise the writer's focus on justice within history and the return to normal programming evident at the end of the narrative. The epitomiser's ambiguous comments about where he chooses to end the account (15.37–39), perhaps indicating some further material available to him beyond Jason of Cyrene's narrative, implies that there is more to tell; perhaps he is aware that already the peace described has started to fracture.[182] An earlier prayer in which Judas and his followers ask that God again punish them, should it become necessary for their discipline (10.4; cf. 6.16; 7.33), reveals a general possibility of further cycles of divine punishment and rescue.

However, the martyrdom accounts, as also the prayers for post-mortem redemption for the dead soldiers, give a hint of a teleological perspective which stretches beyond the end of the narrative and even a separation between the time of death and a future time of judgement or adjustment to the group's eschatological status. Linked back to creation, the possibility of future resurrection is confirmed. Such a trajectory does not fit into a pattern of decline or progress, and nor does it lead to further detail about eschatological expectations found in some other texts. But it does describe a future, heavenly reality, grounded in claims about divine activity in the past, and a clear transition from current experience—the forces opposed to the protagonist characters cannot participate in this eternal reality and will be brought to an end.

### The Qumran War Scroll

The War Scroll[183] focuses on events from the beginning of the eschatological war until the end of history, as noted above. The events narrated depict the seven phases of the war to be waged between the sons of darkness and the sons of light (1QM 1.1–2), which will lead to the complete and eternal destruction of the sons of darkness (1.5; 9.5–6; 15.2, 12; 18.1)[184] on a divinely-appointed day (1.10; 13.14, 18; 14.13; 17.5–6; 18.10), and eternal rejoicing for the sons of light (1.8–9; 15.1; 18.11–12).

---

[182] On the difficulties of dating Judas's death in relation to the time of writing for each of Jason of Cyrene and the epitomiser, see Harrington, *The Maccabean Revolt*, 37.
[183] See Chapter 2 §3.1 for discussion of the various manuscripts associated with Qumran's War Scroll and my approach to these textual issues, primarily focusing on 1QM in this analysis.
[184] Mattila notes a conflict between complete destruction of the enemy here and the traditional imagery of enemies being made subject to Israel at 19.2b–8 (Mattila, "Two Contrasting Eschatologies," 534).

The War Scroll's author shows great attention to questions of time, in keeping with preoccupations evident in other texts found at Qumran. The writer presumes time is divided into periods or seasons, with appointed moments for particular acts. So the war and its effects constitute "a time (עת) of salvation for the nation of God and a period (קץ) of rule[185] for all the men of his lot" (1QM 1.5). Indeed, following the defeat of the Kittim:

> [the sons of jus]tice shall shine to all the edges of the earth, they shall go on shining, up to the end of all the periods (מועדי) of darkness; and in the time (ובמועד) of God, his exalted greatness will shine for all the et[ernal] times. (1QM 1.8)

Thus, the writer uses temporal language in various places to describe the sense of an appointed moment or durations of time, which in turn can denote a succession of periods or seasons. In some cases the same term is used for both ideas. This is found also in Daniel,[186] where the term מועד, translated by Florentino García Martínez and Eibert Tigchelaar in 1QM 1.8 as "period"[187] and Geza Vermes as "season,"[188] is also used to indicate an appointed moment in addition to this sense of a period of time.[189] For instance, in Dan 11.27, למועד takes the sense of a given moment ("for the end is yet to be at the time appointed"; cf. vv. 29, 35),[190] whereas in Dan 12.7 the same term clearly takes the meaning of units of duration in the terms translated "a time, times, and half a time": למועד מועדים וחצי.[191]

Several passages of historical review in the War Scroll, normally presented in the context of speeches or hymns of praise, likewise portray an overarching

---

**185** Vermes translates: an "age of dominion" (Vermes, *The Complete Dead Sea Scrolls*, 163). See Barr on the increasing use of the term to mean periods in the sense of "divine periodisation of historical epochs" (Barr, *Biblical Words for Time*, 124).
**186** The eschatological war itself is reminiscent of 1 Enoch's *Apocalypse of Weeks* and *Animal Apocalypse*, as well as the Book of Daniel. See Chapter 6 below.
**187** Florentino García Martínez and Eibert J. C. Tigchelaar, *The Dead Sea Scrolls Study Edition* (Leiden: Brill, 1997). So also Delling on עת in 1QM 1.8, in the *TDNT* entry for χρόνος (9:588).
**188** Vermes, *The Complete Dead Sea Scrolls*, 163.
**189** See Barr, who traces the use of מועד as "appointed time," indicating this is "especially in theological passages about allotted times fixed by God" (Barr, *Biblical Words for Time*, 124). In later use the term maintains aspects of cyclical time as festival seasons, as in the use of Moed as "set feasts" in the Second Division of the Mishnah.
**190** ESV translation.
**191** The Aramaic of Dan 7.25, where the English translation is identical, uses עדן. The LXX renders the terms in both Dan 7.25 and 12.7 as καιρός (cf. also Rev 12.14), which fits with some uses of καιρός as a period of time in Luke/Acts. See Barr, *Biblical Words for Time*, 37 and further discussion below.

sense of periodisation. Such historical reflections do not take the form of the detailed, frequently numbered, periodisation found in historical reviews in apocalypses (see discussion below). However, these passages praise God as having established the covenant and as Creator in terms that presume both a succession of ages and seasons of pious practices and festivals, unlike the narrower focus on creation as evidence of the possibility of *recreation* in 2 Maccabees. Thus, the Priest's speech prior to the battle begins in 1QM 10.3 by encouraging the soldiers with words from Deut 20.2–5 and Num 10.9, before turning to address God directly—first by remembering the covenant and then acts of creation, which includes attention, among elements of Israel's story,[192] to divine establishment "of the sacred seasons (מועדי), of the cycle of the years (ותקופות שנים) and the ages of eternity (וקצי עד)..." (10.15).

Similarly, the ongoing cycle of ages is evident in the words to be spoken by all those on the side of the light following their victory. Having washed themselves from their bloody battle and returned to sing from their positions in battle formation (14.2–4), they are to assert that God has established the covenant made with their fathers, throughout the eternal ages (למוע[ד]י עולמים, 1QM 13.7–8, cf. 14.8–9), and to identify themselves as the surviving remnant of that covenant (14.8).[193] The hymnic praise that follows fits within an account of God's faithful acts that are grounded in both covenant and creation, building to the affirmation:

> for your mighty deeds we will extol [your] spl[endour, at every] moment and at the times indicated by your eternal edicts (*literally: in all ages and ordained times/seasons of eternity*, בכול עתים ומועדי תעודות עולמים), at the on[se]t of day and at night at the fall of evening and at dawn. For great is the p[lan of] your [glo]ry and your marvellous mysteries in [your] heights.... (14.13–14)

These periods characterise the War Scroll's picture of the past and present, and also the writer's expectations of life at the end of history. Following the eschatological war, the righteous will enjoy "peace, blessing, glory and joy, and length of days" (1.9).[194] This end-time portrait however does not include any explicit ref-

---

[192] These references include the story of Babel, the division of nations, and inheritance of the land (10.14–15).
[193] In the latter passage the covenant with the ancestors endures rather through generations (דורותינו).
[194] Here, the righteous are depicted enjoying *long* life, rather than eternal life (1.9). Much in 1QM supports a view of *communal* continuity through all the ages of eternity, but the writer's view on *individual* immortality is at best unclear (in contrast, for instance, to the focus on post-mortem reward in 2 Maccabees, as discussed above). Although, elsewhere 1QM refers to

erences to resurrection.[195] They shall offer praise, and Zion is instructed to rejoice (19.5). Part of the celebration at the end of the eschatological war includes bringing in the spoils of other nations and humiliating the enemy (19.6–7). Then pious life at the end of history is expected to unfold in continuity with the practices of the faithful prior to eschatological victory,[196] as also the periods and seasons of piety continue.

Although the patterns and cycles of piety are in continuity with the past, the definitive defeat of evil for all time is unlike anything experienced in the past and will not be repeated (1.5; 9.5–6; 15.2, 12; 18.1). It shall arrive suddenly and conclude with eternal redemption (1.13). The defeat is expressed in terms of a reversal of fortunes: God has acted "to open the mouth of the dumb to sing [God's] marv[els], and to train feeble [hands] in warfare." Turning to direct address, the praise continues, "You raised the fallen with your strength, but those high in

---

the "book of the names ... the number of the just" (12.2), suggesting a Danielic-style ledger of those predetermined for salvation (cf. Dan 12), which may indicate some ambiguity about the writer's beliefs about eternal life for individuals. See also references to "eternal redemption" (1.12), and the claim that "all the sons of his truth will have enjoyment in everlasting knowledge" (17.8), though here it seems the *knowledge* of truth is everlasting, not any individual's celebration of it.

**195** Although there are several references to "raising up" they relate almost always to God rising up in judgement. In 14.14, the reference to raising people from the dust and bringing others down could be a more obscure allusion to resurrection, but more likely a reference to reversal, perhaps alluding to soldiers standing up after falling. On the longstanding debate about resurrection in the Dead Sea Scrolls (inevitably also constrained by the difficulties of identifying the relationships between the texts, the nature of the collection, and to what extent the texts provide an insight into a shared community) see Philip R. Davies, "Death, Resurrection, and Life after Death in the Qumran Scrolls," in *Death, Life after Death, Resurrection and the World-to-Come in the Judaisms of Late Antiquity*, ed. Alan J. Avery-Peck and Jacob Neusner, Judaism in Late Antiquity 4 (Leiden: Brill, 2000), 189–232; Emile Puech, "Messianism, Resurrection, and Eschatology at Qumran and in the New Testament," in *The Community of the Renewed Covenant: The Notre Dame Symposium on the Dead Sea Scrolls*, ed. E. C. Ulrich and James C. VanderKam (Notre Dame: University of Notre Dame Press, 1994), 235–56; John F. Hobbins, "Resurrection in the Daniel Tradition and Other Writings at Qumran," in *The Book of Daniel: Composition and Reception*, ed. John J. Collins and Peter W. Flint, VTSup 83 (Leiden: Brill, 2001), 2:395–420; George W. E. Nickelsburg, *Resurrection, Immortality, and Eternal Life in Intertestamental Judaism and Early Christianity*, rev. ed. (Cambridge: Harvard University Press, 2006); N. T. Wright, *The Resurrection of the Son of God* (London: SPCK, 2003), 238–42 (though note that Wright's earlier pages under the heading "Resurrection at Qumran" deal instead with information about the Essenes from sources such as Josephus's *Antiquities*).

**196** Davies highlights differences between the eschatological views in various Dead Sea Scroll texts (Philip R. Davies, "Eschatology at Qumran," *JBL* 104 (1985): 39). See further discussion in Chapter 6 of the ways in which present practices mimic expectations of the end in Qumran texts.

stature, you cut down" (14.6, 10 – 11; cf. 5 – 12).[197] This comes with a time of special insight for those who understand what God is doing (17.7), a unique period of afflictions just prior to the victory,[198] and the newfound peace, joy, and long life[199] following (1.9; 17.9).

Thus, for the War Scroll's writer time comes divided into periods,[200] marked by repeated patterns of piety but also anticipating events that signal a definitive transition into a new epoch of history. The appeals to God's faithfulness in the past and absolute control over history's unfolding assert that the action foretold for the defeat of evil reflects a steady plan from a God with continuous oversight of history,[201] not a sense of rupture or a sudden move to act. Given the scope of events described in the text, it is not clear whether a sense of decline over time is to be presumed.[202] The events set out in the War Scroll constitute the moment for the final battle in which the groups that have been equally matched[203] finally meet to bring victory to those in the company of God. In the War Scroll, history follows a teleological path to an end in the definitive defeat of evil, while simultaneously, *all* time—including that beyond the end brought about by the war—is envisaged as an ongoing succession of "eternal ages" (1QM 1.8; cf. *Apocalypse of Weeks*, 1 Enoch 93.17; 2 Bar 74.2 – 4).

---

**197** This forms part of the victory hymn. There are some striking similarities here to the language of Hannah's song (1 Sam 2.1 – 10) and the Magnificat (Luke 1.46 – 55). See also alternate themes in 1QSa 2.7 – 8, where the tottering are those explicitly excluded from the messianic meal and assembly.
**198** Rather than unnatural cosmic events (cf. 4 Ezra 6.21 – 24), these afflictions indicate the military combat itself, though heightened by the supernatural elements of the enemy.
**199** See n. 194 above.
**200** Stuckenbruck notes the Damascus Document also refers to "divisions of times in their Jubilees and in their weeks" (CD 16.3 – 4; Loren T. Stuckenbruck, "The Formation and Re-Formation of Daniel in the Dead Sea Scrolls," in *Scripture and the Scrolls*, vol. 1 of *The Bible and the Dead Sea Scrolls*, ed. James H. Charlesworth, Princeton Symposium on Judaism and Christian Origins 2 (Waco, TX: Baylor University Press, 2006), 125; cf. also Jub 50.4; Nicholas J. Moore, *Repetition in Hebrews: Plurality and Singularity in the Letter to the Hebrews, Its Ancient Context, and the Early Church*, WUNT 2/388 (Tübingen: Mohr Siebeck, 2015), 42).
**201** See Chapter 5.
**202** The claim that God has created Belial, and even a reference to the empire of Belial (which seems to imply a rule and also a period of reign, 13.4) may suggest that all history prior to the events of the eschatological war has been equally marked by evil, without specifying any explicit sense of historical progress or decline.
**203** Vermes, *The Complete Dead Sea Scrolls*, 163.

### Josephus's *Jewish War*

Writing shortly after the Jewish war with Rome, in the late 70s CE, motivated at least in part by a desire to redirect blame for Jerusalem's destruction away from Rome and onto the Jewish revolutionaries (cf. *J.W.* 2.352–55, 390–91; 6.249–53),[204] Josephus tempers his account with a sense that life under Rome is not without its advantages or divine purpose.[205] Similarly to Polybius, Josephus stresses the importance of Rome's achievement while presuming Rome will nevertheless eventually fall; for both, their political vulnerabilities allow for only subtle references to a future change of regime.[206] However, unlike Polybius, Josephus not only hints at a *change* of empire, but an *end* to the further pattern of the rise and fall of empires. In contrast to Virgil, for Josephus the end is not Rome itself but, however subtly he alludes to it, the installation of an unending divine reign after Rome's fall.[207]

Significantly, Josephus's *Jewish War* is the only text of this study from among those I suggest reflect a teleological sense of history that is frequently compared to Luke/Acts. This heightens Josephus's importance for this investigation. Nonetheless, studies that examine Josephus primarily to illuminate NT texts tend to focus on different aspects of his texts. Josephus scholars such as Per Bilde[208] and Harold Attridge[209] recognise a kind of eschatology reminiscent of apocalypses in Josephus, drawing attention to his understanding of the periodisation of

---

[204] See Chapter 2, §3.1.
[205] Tessa Rajak, *Josephus: The Historian and His Society*, 2nd ed. (London: Duckworth, 2002), 89, 99.
[206] See extended comparison in Cohen, "Polybius, Jeremiah, and Josephus," 374; Gruen, "Polybius and Josephus," 159–61; and Sterling, "Explaining Defeat," 143–48.
[207] Berthelot argues that Philo shares a similar view of Rome's eventual replacement by an unending rule of Israel (Berthelot, "Philo's Perception of the Roman Empire").
[208] Per Bilde, "Josephus and Jewish Apocalypticism," in *Understanding Josephus: Seven Perspectives*, ed. Steve Mason, JSPSup 32 (Sheffield: Sheffield Academic, 1998), 55–56 and Per Bilde, *Flavius Josephus, between Jerusalem and Rome: His Life, His Works, and Their Importance*, JSPSup 2 (Sheffield: JSOT Press, 1988), 188.
[209] Harold W. Attridge, *The Interpretation of Biblical History in the Antiquitates Judaicae of Flavius Josephus*, HDR 7 (Missoula, MT: Scholars Press, 1976), 176–78. See also Lester L. Grabbe, "Eschatology in Philo and Josephus," in *Judaism in Late Antiquity, Part Four: Death, Life-after-Death, Resurrection and the World-to-Come in the Judaisms of Antiquity*, ed. Alan J. Avery-Peck and Jacob Neusner, HdO (Leiden: Brill, 2000), 163–85; R. G. Hall, *Revealed Histories: Techniques for Ancient Jewish and Christian Historiography*, JSPSup 6 (Sheffield: JSOT Press, 1991), 22–30; Bilde, "Josephus and Jewish Apocalypticism," 48–49; and Geza Vermes, "Josephus' Treatment of the Book of Daniel," *JJS* 42 (1991): 149–66.

history and providence.²¹⁰ Rebecca Gray also emphasises the significance of prophecy in Josephus, especially in his self-presentation, dovetailing with apocalyptic themes such as visions and determinism.²¹¹ G. I. Davies even begins a discussion of the nature of "apocalyptic historiography" with an extended treatment of Josephus as an exemplary introduction to the theme, before turning to historical reviews in Jewish apocalypses.²¹² However, these elements of Josephus's text rarely feature in Lukan studies, in which, instead, a focus on shared or divergent features of genre or rhetoric remains central.²¹³ Approaching the question from the opposite angle, Joseph Sievers observes that the many scholarly treatments of themes such as individual eschatology in late Second Temple Judaism treat various pseudepigraphal texts in detail but rarely consider Josephus.²¹⁴ Thus, while recognising that Josephus remains an important conversation partner for Luke, given significant similarities in the nature of their projects and form, I suggest attention to Josephus's schema of history—including his eschatology—also illuminates Luke/Acts in important ways.

Josephus presents history as periodised. In a weaker sense, he follows the pattern of political leaders and military defeats as he describes the events from Antiochus Epiphanes to Titus's "return to Italy and triumph" in his *Jewish*

---

210 Note also that not all scholars of Josephus support claims that he holds an "apocalyptic" or "eschatological" view. See for instance Tessa Rajak, "Friends, Romans, Subjects: Agrippa II's Speech in Josepshus's *Jewish War*," in *Images of Empire*, ed. Loveday Alexander, JSOTSup 122 (Sheffield: JSOT Press, 1991), 133; Rajak, *Josephus*, 89, though Rajak is less definitive in her exclusion of eschatological themes in Josephus's text in some other works and expresses some openness to reconsidering these themes (cf. Rajak, "Jewish Millenarian Expectations," 64–88).
211 Gray, *Prophetic Figures*, 35–79.
212 Davies, "Apocalyptic and Historiography," 16–19.
213 For instance, see Rothschild's discussion of rhetoric (Rothschild, *Luke-Acts and the Rhetoric*, 216, 220, 223–4, 232). So also Lee, *Luke-Acts and "Tragic History,"* 27–33; Steve Mason, *Josephus and the New Testament* (Peabody, MA: Hendrickson, 1992). Squires discusses features of Josephus and Luke's underlying understanding of history in relation to the divine plan and providence, but this does not extend to a discussion of divine guidance over end-time events within the scope of his otherwise helpful study (Squires, *The Plan of God*). Likewise, Shauf deals with Josephus's portrayal of God and divine forces in history, but not his treatments of the end of history (Shauf, *The Divine*, 134–70). See also Manuel Vogel, "Traumdarstellungen bei Josephus und Lukas," in Frey, Rothschild, and Schröter, *Die Apostelgeschichte*, 130–56.
214 The examples Sievers provides from Josephus's works demonstrate the relevance of his corpus on these types of questions, particularly in seeking to fill out the range of views across late Second Temple Judaism. See Joseph Sievers, "Josephus and the Afterlife," in Mason, *Understanding Josephus*, 20. Similarly, see the review of scholarship of both Josephus studies with reference to apocalypticism, and of Jewish apocalypticism with reference to Josephus in Bilde, "Josephus and Jewish Apocalypticism," 36–39.

*War* (cf. 1.19, 29),²¹⁵ and divides his account accordingly. He also makes frequent use of terms like καιρός.²¹⁶ However, here καιρός is not applied in the full range of its meanings. As a particular moment, καιρός describes the time when, for instance, Antiochus Epiphanes was in conflict with Ptolemy VI (1.31) or when the "great war of the Romans broke out" (1.218). It also designates moments of opportunity for revenge (1.62) or attack (1.117, 127). But Josephus does not use καιρός to denote a period of time.

He reveals a stronger sense of periodisation, however, in references to the revolution of the ages and the succession of empires. These ideas are included in speeches Josephus attributes to his own character in the *Jewish War*; while some concepts in Josephus's writing may reflect a more ambiguous relationship to his own views, those placed in his own character's mouth may be more confidently aligned with the perspective he wishes to promote.²¹⁷

For example, in a key interaction, as Josephus exhorts his colleagues against suicide, while they are holed up at Jotapata (just before his own famed defection), he includes a reference to the cycle of ages. Those whose souls (ψυχαί) remain "spotless and obedient (καθαραὶ δὲ καὶ ἐπήκοοι)" (in the context of the concerns of Josephus's speech here, this means dying at the time initiated by God and not through suicide), "are allotted the most holy place in heaven, whence, in the revolution of the ages (ἔνθεν ἐκ περιτροπῆς αἰώνων), they return to find in chaste bodies a new habitation (ἀντενοικίζονται σώμασιν)" (3.374). This passage is fraught with Josephus's apologetic attempt to present his defection in a positive light, casting himself as a prophet with insight to intuit correctly that God is working through Vespasian. For all these reasons it is a key turning point in the narrative of the *Jewish War*. However, none of these rhetorical features of the setting need undermine the portrait itself of the cycle of the ages; indeed, a close parallel in *Against Apion* 2.218²¹⁸ confirms Josephus broadly as-

---

**215** Josephus similarly demarcates time according to different political periods and the reigns of various rulers in other texts, including *Against Apion* (see, for example, *Ag. Ap.* 1.156, 159).
**216** Josephus uses καιρός 296 times in total across his works: 57 occurrences in the *Jewish War*, and 216 in the *Antiquities* alone.
**217** Sievers criticises Mason for keeping his examples of those passages which reflect Josephus's own views too narrow, but at the same time affirms that the passages discussed here from Josephus's speeches are the strongest examples, even if Sievers himself would also like to add further references to individual eschatology (Sievers, "Josephus and the Afterlife," 22–23).
**218** The parallel in *Ag. Ap.* 2.218, coming at the end of a section on those who keep and even die for the law, says for those "God has granted a renewed existence and in the revolution (of the ages) (ἐκ περιτροπῆς) the gift of a better life." Note that this reference does not include the phrase "of the ages" found in *J.W.* 3.374, though commentators and translators, such as Thack-

sumed this kind of account of history. In *J.W.* 3.374 as also in the reference in *Ag. Ap.* 2.218, the transition in history does not simply reflect a shift to the next period, as found in several of the texts discussed above, and as a background assumption also, for instance, to the *saeculum* festival. Rather, it comes with further eschatological claims for the individual. In *J.W.* 3.374, there is a distinction in time specified between the death of the spotless person, and the time of the revolution of ages during which some kind of renewal of life takes place. Similarly, in *Ag. Ap.* 2.218, the revolution is explicitly associated with "renewed existence (γενέσθαι τε πάλιν)" and "the gift of a better life" (βίον ἀμείνω) for those who observe the law.[219]

In a later speech in Book 5 of the *Jewish War* (*J.W.* 5.362–419),[220] Josephus's character again exhorts his compatriots, in this case to turn away from the continued military conflict with Rome. He explains Rome's dominance (those "to whom all things are subject," ὑποχείρια τὰ πάντα, 5.366) in terms of the succession of empires:

> For fortune (τύχη) has moved over to them from all sides, and God, bringing about rule (ἐμπεριάγοντα τὴν ἀρχήν) nation by nation (κατὰ ἔθνος), now (νῦν) is upon Italy.[221] (5.367; cf. 3.354; 5.2; *Life* 17–18)

Here Josephus describes a process in which God determines the reign of political empires.[222] Josephus's social position and political perspective are commonly cited as complicating factors in his portrait of historical events, his attitude towards Rome, and his relationship to Jewish communities.[223] As Gregory Sterling

---

eray here in the LCL and Barclay in the newer Brill series, take this to be presumed (John M. G. Barclay, ed. and trans., *Flavius Josephus: Against Apion*, Flavius Josephus: Translation and Commentary 10 (Boston: Brill, 2006), 296).

219 See Barclay's helpful discussion, in which he asserts that Josephus most likely presumes a decisive turning point in history here, and the broader assumption of a distinction between the present and coming age (*Against Apion*, 296 n. 891).

220 This scene is discussed further in the introduction to Chapter 5. Many of the themes in Josephus's speech here are paralleled in Agrippa's speech in *J.W.* 2.345–401 (cf. Rajak, "Friends, Romans, Subjects," 122–34). See also Acts 7.2–53.

221 My translation.

222 On divine guidance, including Josephus's use of τύχη and θεός, see Chapter 4.

223 Diverse approaches to Josephus's political perspective have also sparked different accounts of his views over his lifetime, and whether changes in fortunes over the years of different political regimes may have affected his writing. See discussion by Bilde, who rightly observes the different rhetorical purposes of each work which explain differences, while affirming considerable continuity between the works (he also observes that several theories of significant change in Jo-

notes, both Josephus and Polybius took "complex stances" in relation to Rome.²²⁴ And certainly Josephus's privileged position affects his account in his interpretation of events in many ways, as a moderate, pragmatically advocating positive relationships with Rome, but it does not entirely displace his account of the powers behind worldly empires—both their establishment and their removal. As observed by Per Bilde, the difference between Josephus and the proponents of more radical views is not *whether* they hold a future hope for Israel, but the mechanism of its realisation.²²⁵ The citation from Josephus's speech here in *J.W.* 5 suggests an underlying movement through empires, which is guided by God. In the same speech Josephus argues for the rule of the stronger (5.367), that is, that Rome's dominance should in the first place be recognised as evidence of divine support (see also *J.W.* 2.390).²²⁶ Nonetheless, any such dominance remains provisional and, having been divinely appointed, it will in turn be divinely removed. Significantly, despite his generally positive treatment of Rome, as he asserts that God rests upon Italy *now* (5.367), Josephus reveals that Rome will also come to an end.²²⁷

For late Second Temple Jewish writers like Josephus, a model of transition between regimes may be found not only in writers who presume a succession of empires, as discussed above in relation to Polybius and Diodorus Siculus, but the four kingdoms succeeded by a fifth divine kingdom portrayed in Dan 2 and 7, and taken up in other texts such as 4 Ezra 11–12.²²⁸ In these Jewish

---

sephus's politics are predicated on assumptions about Josephus's changes in standing for which there is no direct evidence (Bilde, *Flavius Josephus*, 173–81)).
**224** Sterling, "Explaining Defeat," 136.
**225** Bilde, *Flavius Josephus*, 187.
**226** See also Thuc. 1.76.2, and discussion in Kinch Hoekstra and Mark Fisher, "Thucydides and the Politics of Necessity," in *The Oxford Handbook of Thucydides*, ed. Sara Forsdyke, Edith Foster, and Ryan Balot (New York: Oxford, 2017), 382–83.
**227** See Crabbe, "Being Found Fighting against God," 24.
**228** Bilde argues that "Despite the Hellenistic colouring of the sentence" (that is, the reference to τύχη), "it is a genuine expression of the apocalyptic worldview which we find in Dan 2 and 7" (Bilde, "Josephus and Jewish Apocalypticism," 54). This paradigm is arguably also evident in 1 Enoch's *Animal Apocalypse*, in the four periods governed by untrustworthy shepherds following the exile (1 Enoch 89.65–90.19). See Daniel C. Olson, *A New Reading of the Animal Apocalypse of 1 Enoch: "All Nations Shall Be Blessed"* (Boston: Brill, 2013), 190. Note that some similarities between Dan 2 and 7 are sometimes overlooked because the passages are not identified as the same genre and tend to be grouped separately into Books 1–6 and 7–12. Davies' claim, that there is a difference of paradigm between Dan 2's diminishing empires and Dan 7's increasing violence between regimes, also misses the essential continuity between these portraits of five kingdoms (e.g. Philip R. Davies, "Daniel in the Lion's Den," in Alexander, *Images of Empire*, 165).

texts, the four worldly kingdoms are installed in turn, but finally replaced by an unending divine reign, which ensures vindication of the righteous and punishment of the wicked.[229]

Josephus's understanding of the succession of ages is more explicit in the *Antiquities*,[230] where he offers an interpretation of the Book of Daniel including this five-kingdom paradigm, participating in what would become a long tradition of applying Daniel's visions to the writer's own setting. As he describes the statue from Nebuchadnezzar's dream and its explanation in Dan. 2.34–45, in which the various sections of the statue are said to represent the four regimes, Josephus chooses not to specify events associated with a key element of Nebuchadnezzar's dream that he also does not identify: the stone "not made from human hands" which will destroy the entire statue of past empires in the biblical account. Instead, conspicuously circumspect, Josephus directs the inquiring reader who "wishes to learn about the hidden things that are to come" to "take the trouble" to consult the Book of Daniel itself (*Ant.* 10.210).[231] However, later, when he sets out Daniel's vision in Dan 8.3–14 and its interpretation, he asserts, "And these misfortunes our nation did in fact come to experience under Antiochus Epiphanes, just as Daniel many years before saw and wrote that they would happen"

---

[229] Contra Hall, who refers to the paradigm as it is taken up in these Jewish texts as a four-kingdom paradigm (Hall, *Revealed Histories*, 83), rather than noting the distinctive difference of the fifth unending age in these texts.

[230] In discussing Lindner's identification of Josephus as a "priestly apocalyptist" (Attridge, *The Interpretation of Biblical History*, 176), Attridge attributes to "apocalypticism" both an eschatological outlook and a view of history as periodised. He argues that though the *Antiquities* displays an interest in the future that may be considered eschatological, "there is none of the apocalyptic structuring of history into distinct periods subject to divine determination as there had been in the *Bellum*" (p. 177–78). However, Josephus's treatment of Daniel in the *Antiquities* challenges this view.

[231] Bilde rightly sees this passage as crucial for understanding Josephus's eschatology and his thought more broadly (Bilde, *Flavius Josephus*, 187–88). Begg and Spilsbury suggest that Josephus's reservations about identifying the stone in Daniel 2 may likewise be the reason he entirely omits Daniel 7 from his account. Noting that Josephus also omits the visions from Dan 9–12 (though occasionally importing some of their details into other sections of his manuscript), they go on: "Josephus may simply have felt that his summary of chapter 8 already said as much as he wanted to, and that he had by this time already given Daniel more than his fair share of space in the *Antiquities*" (Christopher T. Begg and Paul Spilsbury, eds. and trans., *Flavius Josephus: Judean Antiquities 8–10*, Flavius Josephus: Translation and Commentary 5 (Leiden: Brill, 2005), 306 n. 1110). Certainly, Josephus's extended attention to the Book of Daniel suggests this was an important text for him, and supports a decision, as argued by Bilde, to see the view of history that emerges from these passages as central to Josephus's thought (Bilde, "Josephus and Jewish Apocalypticism," 47).

(*Ant.* 10.276; cf. 12.322).²³² He then claims: "And in the same way Daniel also wrote about the empire of the Romans, and that it would be laid waste by them."²³³ Despite his reluctance to specify Rome's identity when describing the method of the regime's foretold destruction, his interpretation here clarifies the implication of the earlier passage, and is widely taken to confirm that Josephus identified the fourth kingdom in Dan 2 with Rome.²³⁴ Following the interpretation of Dan 8, Josephus moves immediately into praise for Daniel's reliability (10.277–80), as he also does elsewhere (cf. 12.322),²³⁵ further underscoring his support of the historical paradigm found in Daniel, with periods of political regimes and a divinely appointed end.

Finally, Josephus portrays the direction of history leading up to the end differently in varied contexts. Particularly in the *Antiquities*, he exhibits the nostalgia associated with traditional views of the golden age discussed above. Employing what Louis Feldman identifies as a "Greek framework,"²³⁶ Josephus portrays creation as an idyllic age, in which the animals all spoke a common language (*Ant.* 1.41), and from which, after enjoying an initial period of bliss, humanity then brought about a decline (*Ant.* 1.46).²³⁷ Even beyond this initial period, Re-

---

**232** When Josephus narrates the events associated with Antiochus Epiphanes in *Ant.* 12, he likewise refers to Daniel's prophecy about them, which he sees as having been fulfilled (see Begg and Spilsbury, *Judean Antiquities 8–10*, 306).
**233** This is Begg and Spilsbury's translation, which retains some ambiguity in the meaning of "it" and "them" here, whether the Jewish people are to be destroyed by Rome, or the reverse (see Begg and Spilsbury, *Judean Antiquities 8–10*, 306). In the LCL Thackeray adds a further detail: "...and that Jerusalem would be taken by them and the temple laid waste." This comes from a variation found in Chrysostom, which Thackeray justifies including by noting rabbinic writing roughly contemporary to Josephus also made this connection between Daniel's prophecy and Jerusalem's destruction (p. 311).
**234** In the words of Begg and Spilsbury, "Josephus' statement in the present context also confirms our suspicion that for him the 4th kingdom of Nebuchadnezzar's statue vision represented Rome" (Begg and Spilsbury, *Judean Antiquities 8–10*, 306). Begg and Spilsbury also note that the LXX of Dan 9 identifies the Kittim as Rome, and that Josephus appears to read other Danielic passages through the lens of Dan 9. Such an identification of Rome in Daniel's visions, which Josephus takes to be authoritative, therefore makes considerable sense (see p. 306). See also Bilde, *Flavius Josephus*, 188.
**235** Josephus is deeply invested in Daniel's reliability, not only because of the way he enlists it in his polemic against the Epicureans (*Ant.* 10.277–80), but because of his own self-presentation as a reliable prophet in this type (see Gray, *Prophetic Figures*, 35–79).
**236** Louis H. Feldman, *Studies in Josephus' Rewritten Bible*, Supplements to the Journal for the Study of Judaism 58 (Leiden: Brill, 1998), 1.
**237** Feldman analyses Josephus's depiction of a golden age at the beginning of his biblical account (Feldman, *Studies in Josephus' Rewritten Bible*, 3–8). Decline is also evident in Josephus's treatment of the five kingdom paradigm in Daniel, cf. *Ant.* 10.244. This also includes an interest-

becca Gray argues, Josephus displays a sense of nostalgia that people of an earlier time were closer to God.[238] As he seeks to present the ancient roots of Judaism positively to an external audience, he couches his description of the patriarchs in glowing terms.[239]

By contrast, in the *Jewish War* Josephus appears more concerned to emphasise the positives of the present. As he recounts biblical and post-biblical history in his own speech in 5.376–94, he focuses on God's faithfulness over time, as support for his exhortation to repent not only to God (5.415–16) but also to Rome, the instruments of God's punishment (5.372), and to live peaceably under Roman rule until God brings about the final reign. Despite the behaviour of the revolutionaries, and those they beguiled (*J.W.* 5.407; 6.285), leading to the destruction of Jerusalem as punishment (5.412),[240] there is no indication in the *Jewish War* that current life is in decline. Indeed the Romans are benevolent to those who repent (5.372–73) and more pious than those who failed to keep the Jerusalem temple holy (5.402).[241]

For Josephus, history follows a linear trajectory to a final end. His focus may be on trusting Rome now and criticising revolutionary activity, but this does not entirely obscure his underlying assumption, shared with much contemporaneous Jewish literature, that God will in due course bring a conclusion to current circumstances. This is not the "end" (of Rome only) about which Polybius attributes insight to Scipio, in which the period of the next regime simply follows in due course, or the similar kind of end which the *saeculum* festival sought to delay for a further period. But this is the installation of a permanent divine reign that brings a halt to the entire process (*J.W.* 5.367; cf. *Ant.* 10.210, 276), or a decisive transition following which some will lead a kind of renewed life (*J.W.* 3.374; cf. *Ag. Ap.* 2.218). Nonetheless, this divine reign will be installed in God's own time. How imminent or otherwise Josephus takes it to be is a separate question (addressed below in Chapter 6) from establishing that there are hints of eschatological expectation in Josephus's text. In the interim, Josephus indicates life continues satisfactorily under Rome's rule.

---

ing reference to God "having weighed the time"; see reference in Begg and Spilsbury, *Judean Antiquities 8–10*, 300.
**238** Gray, *Prophetic Figures*, 34.
**239** Gray suggests that this nostalgia extends in the *Antiquities* from the patriarchs even until John Hyrcanus (Gray, *Prophetic Figures*, 34).
**240** Josephus structures this historical review to convince his reader that the destruction of Jerusalem was a result of taking matters into their own hands. See Chapter 5.
**241** Eyal Regev, "Josephus, the Temple, and the Jewish War," in Pastor, Stern, and Mor, *Flavius Josephus*, 280–83.

## 3.3 Decline in teleological history

**Fourth Ezra and 2 Baruch**
Fourth Ezra and 2 Baruch each represent late first-century or early second-century CE responses to the fall of Jerusalem, couched in apocalyptic visions involving *vaticinia ex eventu* and angelic dialogues.[242] Although there are significant differences between the texts in terms of their theological reflections on these events, with respect to their schemas of history they are very similar.[243] The historical reviews in 4 Ezra and 2 Baruch portray history in a strongly periodised, teleological schema of decline. As the divine or angelic characters reveal that the world is ageing and approaching its nadir, they assert the imminence of divine intervention to bring about the end of history, including the vindication of the righteous and punishment of the wicked.

The nature of history's periodisation is part of the content of the revelation these apocalypses purport to supply. They each refer frequently to historical periods, which can even be numbered (cf. 4 Ezra 12.11; 2 Bar 23–30; 53–76).[244] Fourth Ezra 6.7–28 sets out the explanation of Ezra's concerns in the dialogue with Uriel as a discussion of "the dividing of the times" (6.7).[245] And 2 Baruch borders on a riddle with its picture of compounding "times" that "will inherit times, and periods periods," leading to "the length of periods and the hours of periods" (2 Bar 42.6; cf. 48.38).

Although the various visions and dialogues focus on different aspects of history and theological concerns, all portray history as teleological. Indeed, Baruch prays, "for if an end of all things had not been prepared, their beginning would have been senseless" (2 Bar 21.17). And the divine voice responds:

---

[242] By setting the events in the context of the first destruction of the temple (see Chapter 2), Mermelstein notes, 4 Ezra confirms that the current crisis does not represent a "temporal rupture" (Mermelstein, *Creation, Covenant*, 177) but a continuation in a series of transitions in history—though this time the restoration will be definitive and final, incorporating judgement of the unrighteous and vindication of the remnant.

[243] Similarities between the texts suggest some kind of dependence. In Chapter 2 I suggested the most likely explanation is that 2 Baruch is a response either directly to 4 Ezra or more generally to the kind of theological perspective it represents.

[244] Cf. 1 Enoch 89.65–90.19; 93.1–10; 91.12–17.

[245] Dimant emphasises the writer of 4 Ezra envisages time in "specific, measurable segments" (Devorah Dimant, "4 Ezra and 2 Baruch in Light of Qumran Literature," in *Fourth Ezra and Second Baruch: Reconstruction after the Fall*, ed. Matthias Henze, Gabriele Boccaccini and Jason M. Zurawski, Supplements to the Journal for the Study of Judaism 164 (Leiden: Brill, 2013), 37), as also does 2 Baruch (p. 47).

Baruch, Baruch, why are you disturbed? Who starts on a journey and does not complete it? Or who will be comforted making a sea voyage unless he can reach a harbour? Or he who promises to give a present to somebody—is it not a theft unless it is fulfilled?" (22.2–4; cf. 85.10)

The speech continues with further examples of situations in which the beginning requires the end.

This emphasis on the need for an end, however, does not eliminate the writers' interest in all of history, or what 2 Baruch describes as "the course of times" (20.6). Across both 4 Ezra and 2 Baruch, passages of historical review vary with respect to the scope of history they include in the revelation. In some cases the review extends from creation to the culmination of history. For instance, 2 Bar 53–76 divides all of history from creation into twelve periods of alternating positive and negative events ("bright" and "dark" waters) plus two further periods of greatest darkness and light.[246] The periods set out in the vision follow Israel's biblical past quite clearly, without the type of cryptic allegory often found in apocalypses. Likewise, the angelic interpreter in 4 Ezra, Uriel, outlines events from creation to the end in the third dialogue (7.10–44). In 2 Bar 57.1–3, the review extends back to Abraham, as the beginning of the covenant.[247]

Other prophecies within these texts limit the scope to events identified, for instance, with the fourth empire and its promised end from the paradigm in Dan 2 and 7, such as the eagle vision (4 Ezra's fifth episode) in 4 Ezra 11–12 (see also the vision of the cedar, vine, and forest in 2 Bar 39.1–8).[248] In 4 Ezra's eagle vision, the activities of multiple wings and heads on the eagle depict different historical events in Rome, enabling readers particularly to identify recent events under Flavian emperors.[249] This framework, frequently taken up in apocalypses

---

**246** Second Baruch 53–76 is reminiscent of the *Apocalypse of Weeks* (1 Enoch 93.1–10, 91.12–17) in its scope and inclusion of the watchers, though the 1 Enoch apocalypse does not share the oscillating pattern of 2 Bar 53–76. The *Apocalypse of Weeks* identifies two particular times of decline and restoration: the corruption through the fallen watchers leading to the events of the flood, and the current experience of corruption and God's action for permanent restoration in week nine (somewhat similarly, cf. 1 Enoch 85–90).
**247** As noted above, Mermelstein identifies a transition in post-exilic texts to tracing history back to creation, rather than the beginning of the covenant at Sinai (Mermelstein, *Creation, Covenant*). Here the connection back to Abraham decouples the covenant relationship from Sinai.
**248** In 2 Bar 23–30 the writer also divides time into twelve periods, however, these periods demarcate times of atrocities prior to the revelation of the Messiah.
**249** For detailed discussion of the historical referents for features and activities of the eagle, see Laura Bizzarro, "The 'Meaning of History' in the Fifth Vision of *4 Ezra*," in *Interpreting 4 Ezra and 2 Baruch: International Studies*, ed. Gabriele Boccaccini and Jason M. Zurawski, LSTS 87 (London: Bloomsbury, 2014), 34.

(and as discussed also in relation to Josephus's treatment above), bears similarity to the metal generations of Hesiod's *Works and Days* (106–201), especially as it appears in Dan 2 where the epochs relate to metals.[250] In Hesiod's version, a generation of heroes (156–173) is inserted between the bronze and iron generations, interrupting the decline which nonetheless remains evident in Hesiod's portrayal of the present (174–76).[251] Ovid also adapts Hesiod's model[252] into a series of gold, silver, bronze, and iron ages, continuing the decline across the four ages in his *Metamorphoses* (1.89–150).[253] In stark contrast, at the end of 4 Ezra's eagle vision, a lion, which Uriel identifies as the Messiah, destroys the eagle and saves the faithful remnant, who then exist joyfully in anticipation of a final judgement (12.31–34). As noted above in relation to Josephus, texts based on Daniel's paradigm envisage a final divine reign, whose inauguration brings an end to all previous political powers and suffering.

---

**250** James C. VanderKam, *Enoch and the Growth of an Apocalyptic Tradition*, CBQMS 16 (Washington, DC: Catholic Biblical Association of America, 1984), 142.

**251** Note that there are therefore actually five generations in Hesiod's model (the present being identified with the fifth and worst), though only four are assigned metals, and it is these four that are used in other texts. Importantly, the ages described by Ovid come at the beginning of primordial history, and lead into a decline that prompts the gods to bring an end to the iron age (1.177–252) with a flood (1.262–347). There is therefore no sense of foretelling the future with this paradigm in Ovid, as in the use of this imagery in Jewish apocalypses (VanderKam, *Enoch and the Growth*, 142), or identification of any of these world ages with the historical present.

**252** On possible adaptation in local historiographies, see Clarke, *Making Time*, 16; on the use of this paradigm in other Greek and Latin sources, see Momigliano, "The Origins of Universal History," 134–35.

**253** In marked contrast to 4 Ezra 11–12 and similar schemas of history, Ovid's adaptation of the picture of decline is self-consciously *anti*-teleological. His poem ends with a reference to Augustus, relativised in turn by his epilogue, which seems to underscore ironically the absence of any meaningful *telos* to history, perhaps explicitly to contradict the teleological claims of others such as Virgil. In 15.870, Ovid states that Augustus will listen to prayers from heaven when he dies. But the poem concludes with the epilogue, in which Ovid reveals the true power behind his poem: his written work will ensure that he alone is remembered and thereby achieves immortality (15.871–79). Hejduk notes that Ovid himself is thus supplied as a unique example of a "mortal whose triumph over the wrath of Jupiter, and over death itself, rises above the pettiness of Olympian squabbles" (Hejduk, "Ovid and Religion," 52). Similarly, on the epilogue, Kenney notes that Ovid presents even Jupiter as unable to compete with the ultimate power "over the fate of the poem and of its creator" (Kenney, "The *Metamorphoses*," 144). See Thomas for discussion of Ovid's allusions to Virgil in the *Metamorphoses* (Richard F. Thomas, "Ovid's Reception of Virgil," in Knox, *A Companion to Ovid*, 294–307, esp. 296–303).

Although the different episodes in 4 Ezra present slightly different structures to end-time events,[254] focusing on different issues,[255] both 4 Ezra and 2 Baruch feature elements such as: messianic woes (4 Ezra 5.1–12; 6.21–24; 2 Bar 26–28; 70.7), a period of insight for a privileged group (4 Ezra 6.20; 12.36–38; 13.53–56; 14.26, 45–47; 2 Bar 27.15; 48.3, 33),[256] revelation of a pre-existent Messiah (4 Ezra 7.28; 12.32; 13.26, 52; 2 Bar 30.1) or glorious Zion (4 Ezra 7.26; 13.35–36), judgement of the wicked (4 Ezra 7.70; 9.18; 12.34; 13.58; 2 Bar 44.15), and vindication for the righteous (cf. 2 Bar 15.2; 51.11–13; 54.15–16; 73.1–74.2), including "eternal peace" and "joy" (2 Bar 73.1).[257]

But the writers' interests do not lie only in the revelation of the events of the end.[258] They maintain an emphasis on explaining the *past*, with accounts of cre-

---

**254** Fourth Ezra's third dialogue appears to conflict with the account of God's direct involvement and the immediate culmination of history in the second. For instance, the third dialogue describes a messianic golden age of 400 years, the death of the Messiah (7.29), and a seven-day period in which all will be dead prior to a general resurrection (7.31; cf. 2 Bar 30.1; 50.2–4; 52.2–3), in contrast to the immediate culmination in the second dialogue (4 Ezra 6.18–28). Stone claims such a reference to the death of the Messiah is "almost unparalleled," suggesting only 2 Bar 30.1 could be similar (Michael E. Stone, "The Question of the Messiah in 4 Ezra," in Neusner, Green, and Frerichs, *Judaisms and Their Messiahs*, 210). See Hill on the inclusion of a chiliastic period in 4 Ezra, 2 Baruch, and the Book of Revelation, which he claims is unique to these texts in this period (Charles E. Hill, *Regnum Caelorum: Patterns of Millennial Thought in Early Christianity*, 2nd ed. (Grand Rapids: Eerdmans, 2001), 45).
**255** As Stone notes, the focus of 4 Ezra is not to provide a systematic account of the course of history but rather to answer the challenges of theodicy posed by the situation of the writer, for which an account of history is a helpful tool (Michael E. Stone, "The Concept of the Messiah in IV Ezra," in *Religions in Antiquity: Essays in Memory of Erwin Ramsdell Goodenough*, ed. Jacob Neusner, SHR 14 (Leiden: Brill, 1968), 295–312). He argues that, rather than smoothing the differences between episodes, "the end" should be understood as the "decisive turning point in history" in the context of a pericope, and the "eschatological sequence" set out in that passage (Stone, "Coherence and Inconsistency in the Apocalypses: The Case of 'The End' in 4 Ezra," *JBL* 102 (1983): 239, 241). See also Stone, *Fourth Ezra*, 103–5, including discussion of the related Latin, Syriac, Armenian, and Hebrew terms on pp. 104–5.
**256** See also Chapter 4 on the role of privileged insight in *vaticinia ex eventu* in 4 Ezra and 2 Baruch.
**257** See further discussion in Chapter 6. According to 2 Baruch, at this time wild beasts will serve children, women will no longer experience pain during labour, and harvesters will not tire. Ramael declares: "For that time is the end of that which is corruptible and the beginning of that which is incorruptible" (74.2). On 2 Baruch's eschatological rewards, see Daniel M. Gurtner, "Eschatological Rewards for the Righteous in 2 Baruch," in Boccaccini and Zurawski, *Interpreting 4 Ezra and 2 Baruch*, 110–13.
**258** Rowland helpfully observes of Daniel: "The focus of the book is not so much on the future as on the divine control of the totality of human history" (Rowland, *The Open Heaven*, 139). He

ation and the introduction of evil or periods of corruption, seen for instance in 2 Bar 53–76's account of creation, the watchers, and the ensuing alternating times of faithfulness and sin in the vision of alternating light and dark waters. The reviews also focus on the *present*, in placing current experience within one of a succession of periods, though the deeper suffering in the present confirms that a change of periods is imminent.[259] And it is this concern with the present that leads to depictions of the *future*.[260] This point perhaps cannot be made strongly enough, in light of scholarship that has focused on the eschatological elements of apocalypses as reflecting interest in the events of the end of history only.[261]

The succession of periods and teleological structure confirm a linear conception of time throughout 4 Ezra and 2 Baruch. Reviews such as 4 Ezra 11–12 (the eagle vision) that are based on a Danielic succession of empires demonstrate this clearly, as the anticipated state unveiled in the final, fifth kingdom describes an entirely new situation. However, this is also true of *Urzeit zu Endzeit* reviews such as 2 Bar 53–76 (the vision of dark and light waters), where the final state in some way mirrors the beginning (cf. also 2 Bar 29.8)—even here, the end is not the same as the beginning, but a period of *greatest* brightness, which leads into eternal ages of this type (74.2–4).[262] And, following the description

---

also suggests 2 Bar 53–74 appears to demonstrate "an interest in history in its own right" (p. 142).
**259** See Chapter 6.
**260** As Collins rightly notes, despite any ostensible focus on the future in apocalypses, "The main political impact of the apocalyptic literature lies not in any program it may imply for the future but in its rejection and condemnation of the present order" (John J. Collins, "Temporality and Politics in Jewish Apocalyptic Literature," in *Apocalyptic in History and Tradition*, ed. Christopher Rowland and John Barton, JSPSup 43 (Sheffield: Sheffield Academic, 2002), 40–41).
**261** See §1 above. Nickelsburg even summarises 4 Ezra and 2 Baruch as sharing a two-age understanding of history, going on to suggest somewhat abstrusely that the four-kingdom paradigm represents one "period" (George W. E. Nickelsburg, *Jewish Literature between the Bible and the Mishnah: A Historical and Literary Introduction* (Philadelphia: Fortress, 1981), 283), though I suggest each text reflects a much stronger sense of multiple periods across the course of history. In his commentary on 4 Ezra, Stone reduces the writer's framework to that of "two ages," despite the many places where the past "ages" of the Lord are discussed, which he also notes are plural—e.g. 4.26–27; 6.20, 25; 14.9 (Stone, *Fourth Ezra*, 92–93). The renewed world referred to when Uriel says "the Most High has made not one world but two" (7.50) is different from the understanding of periodisation of history, and closer to the idea reflected in the eschatologically renewed Jerusalem.
**262** Even in the *Animal Apocalypse*, despite its symmetry, the end is different because the final state will not be compromised again (1 Enoch 90.38). Scott identifies an ultimate return to an original state in the schema of history in Jubilees, asserting that the end exactly mirrors the be-

of the general resurrection in 2 Bar 30.3, the Lord says those restored to life will "know that the time has come of which it is said that it is the end of times."

Finally, the writers of these texts consistently present history in decline,[263] especially in the period of the historical present.[264] Baruch laments, "for now, therefore, everything is in a state of dying" (2 Bar 21.11). Similarly, 4 Ezra exhibits a persistent emphasis on the ageing and deterioration of the world. The voice from the bush in the seventh vision says: "for the age has lost its youth, and the times begin to grow old" (4 Ezra 14.11, cf. 5.54–55; 2 Bar 85.10). The calculations of the periods which then follow lead into Uriel's claim:

> For the weaker the world becomes through old age, the more shall evils be multiplied among its inhabitants. For truth shall go farther away, and falsehood shall come near. For the eagle you saw in the vision is already hastening to come. (14.18)

Similarly, 2 Bar 23–30 (the twelve periods of calamities) outlines signs to the wise that the end is imminent (28.1), and Baruch is told: "It will happen when they lose hope, that the time will awake" (25.4). In this way, the writers profess that the historical present is approaching the nadir of human history, which itself indicates the planned moment of decisive divine action.[265]

In summary, historical reviews in 4 Ezra and 2 Baruch reveal history's periodisation, decline, and end. Rather than the irony and possible despair of de-

---

ginning (James M. Scott, *On Earth as in Heaven: The Restoration of Sacred Time and Sacred Space in the Book of Jubilees*, Supplements to the Journal for the Study of Judaism 91 (Leiden: Brill, 2005), 8). Nonetheless, in any such eschatological hope, the parallel with the perfection of the beginning is held together with a new element: that this will continue indefinitely without further corruption.

**263** In his discussion of the succession of empires theme in Graeco-Roman and Ancient Near Eastern texts, Momigliano argues that Daniel's model does not imply decline (Momigliano, "The Origins of Universal History"). Rather, he suggests the focus lies on the stone that destroys the entire statue at once, indicating divine destruction of all of history simultaneously in the inauguration of the divine reign. Clearly this is an argument relevant to Dan 2 and not Dan 7, although emphasising the uniqueness of the fifth empire remains helpful. Nonetheless, the surrounding narrative in Dan 2 does imply decline, as in Daniel's affirmation of Nebuchadnezzar as the ruler of the golden—implied superior—empire, and his identification of subsequent empires as inferior (Dan 2.37–43).

**264** Flannery Dailey presents history in 4 Ezra and 2 Baruch in an "ascending" spiral model rather than a linear, to demonstrate connections between points in history (Frances Flannery Dailey, "Non-Linear Time in Apocalyptic Texts: The Spiral Model," in *Society of Biblical Literature, 1999 Seminar Papers*, 241). While some periods in the historical reviews in these apocalypses do incorporate shared patterns or repetition within the overall teleological shape, both texts are very clear that the direction of history is decline.

**265** See Chapter 6.

cline without an end, as in Ovid's *Metamorphoses*, or even Tacitus's portrait, here the decline offers a particular kind of hope: things are so bad that the time for God to bring an end to history and vindicate the righteous is imminent.

## 4 Periodised and teleological history in Luke/Acts

The above discussion demonstrates the considerable diversity among the texts of this study, both Jewish and non-Jewish, and a broad spectrum of ways in which writers' temporal conceptions play out in their texts. A number of elements emerge which will be important when considering Luke/Acts alongside these comparison texts.

First, the discussion above demonstrates that periodisation is extremely common. In many texts a sense of periodisation allows for change within history—even very decisive and cataclysmic change—without forcing a complete rupture. However, the writers balance the concerns of continuity and rupture in different ways. For Diodorus Siculus, universal historiography comprises a unifying narrative of progress across the events of every time and place and, although this is comprised of periods, these units do not necessarily equate with moments of any particular significance. Whereas, beyond even Polybius's stress on Rome's extraordinary period,[266] for those who draw on Daniel's pattern of a succession of empires, such as the writer of 4 Ezra in the eagle vision (4 Ezra 11–12), history's periods are profound epochal shifts. In the five-kingdom paradigm the preceding three empires establish the pattern of regime change—indeed, part of the revelation *itself* involves being given a correct understanding of past transitions between empires, and how they fit within the broader pattern of history. But the movement from the fourth and most harrowing empire to the final,[267] unending divine reign, though in some ways similar, ensures that the end of history is nonetheless a meaningfully different transition. Thus, periodisation is common,[268] but it can function in different ways. In what follows, I suggest that Luke/Acts also displays an understanding of periodisation, in which the central

---

[266] Chapter 6 also highlights the ways different writers stress the significance of the present, such as Polybius's focus on the "now" of Rome's moment.
[267] Regarding the pattern of identifying the historical present with the nadir of history, see VanderKam, *Enoch and the Growth*, 142; Collins, "Temporality and Politics," 26–43; and Chapter 6 below. Although tapping into the five-kingdom paradigm, 4 Ezra only begins with the fourth kingdom (12.11), accentuating the focus on the impending end to the present regime.
[268] Dodds also notes periodisation in Stoic perspectives on history (Dodds, *The Ancient Concept of Progress*, 18).

concern lies in divine control over the transitions throughout history, including the events of the end. Some of Luke's temporal references simply indicate key moments, or even the cycle of the seasons. But, without incorporating the explicit, numbered historical reviews of some reinterpretations of Dan 2 or the twelve periods plus two final periods in 2 Bar 53–76, at key points Luke uses language that is reminiscent of the kind of periodisation revealed to seers in texts like Daniel, confirming an underlying conception of history shared with these traditions. Luke's periodised schema similarly accommodates the possibility of monumental changes held together with an affirmation that God remains in charge.

Secondly, in several of the texts discussed above, history and eschatology are not only held together in a teleological schema of history but, importantly, the writers' assertions about continuity across the course of history serve to support their claims about the events of the end.[269] For instance, while the War Scroll focuses on describing events anticipated as part of an eschatological war at the end of history, these descriptions incorporate hymnic reviews of God's faithful action in creation and covenant which assert an explicit continuity with the faithful divine action that will vindicate the sons of light at the end of history. Similarly, as the *vaticinia ex eventu* in 4 Ezra and 2 Baruch set out the events and periods of all of history, they likewise confirm the promised events of the end. I argue that Luke's teleological schema of history demonstrates a similar interest in the past as it also confirms continuity with, and assurance of, the events of the end.

Thirdly, the direction of history constitutes a significant preoccupation in a number of the texts discussed above. For some, this connects to other important literary traditions, such as in Tacitus's narrative of decline, or Diodorus Siculus's self-conscious refutation of tropes of decline from a golden age through his narrative of progress and development through necessity. Similarly, for the writers of 4 Ezra and 2 Baruch, the sense of decline reflects not only interpretations of the present time but theological affirmations about the signs of imminent divine vindication. But in several cases, the direction is less crucial to the schema portrayed. Similarly, I suggest history in Luke/Acts is not driven by a focus on any particular decline or progress, though a life of discipleship in any time, as a response to continuous divine faithfulness, will likely be marked by tribulation caused by others.

---

[269] Such claims to continuity frequently interact with the sense of periodisation, so that the past action is not simply continuous activity, but decisive (normally divine) action that prompted earlier transitions and is of the type also anticipated at the end.

In what follows I discuss the features of Luke/Acts that indicate Luke's schema of history is both periodised and teleological, before discussing the direction of history in Luke/Acts.

## 4.1 Times and periods in Luke/Acts

As discussed above, Conzelmann saw in Luke/Acts a periodised, three-stage model of salvation history (the periods of Israel, Jesus, and the church),[270] which he argued Luke employed in order to *distance* his narrative from eschatological claims.[271] In more recent work, Gregory Sterling creates a similar model when he divides Lukan history by asserting: "the period of promise is the LXX; the period of fulfilment is Luke-Acts subdivided into the age of Jesus (Luke) and the church (Acts). The key to the division of the last two is the coming of the Spirit."[272] Numerous others have proposed similar adaptations of Conzelmann's schema.[273] Conversely, reluctance about Conzelmann's three-stage view of salvation history has led some recent interpreters to assume that periodisation itself does not feature in Luke/Acts—frequently while maintaining the hypothe-

---

**270** Conzelmann, *Acts of the Apostles*, xlv.
**271** Conzelmann notes Mussner's claim that Jesus' response to the disciples' question in Acts 1.7 does not directly refute this kind of "apocalyptic expectation," only the expectation of its imminence, implicitly associating χρόνοι and καιροί with "apocalyptic" views of history (Conzelmann, *Acts of the Apostles*, 7).
**272** Sterling argues for a two-age model of promise and fulfilment, with the major transition at the time of Jesus, but his division of the second period into two further periods, though more nuanced than Conzelmann's earlier model, inadvertently recreates something close to Conzelmann's middle of time because it does not retain decisive urgency in his account of the turn of the ages (Sterling, *Historiography and Self-Definition*, 361–62; see also his detailed account of his two-stage schema with the second part divided into two, alongside Conzelmann's schema, in Gregory E. Sterling, "'Do You Understand What You Are Reading?' The Understanding of the LXX in Luke-Acts," in Frey, Rothschild, and Schröter, *Die Apostelgeschichte*, 112–14). Adams also attempts to span a two- and three-part schema, though without subscribing to the delay hypothesis (Adams, *The Stars Will Fall*, 172–73 n. 198). An alternate schema of periods within Luke's account, which is not more convincing though it includes an explicit disagreement with Conzelmann's model, is provided by M. D. Goulder, *Type and History in Acts* (London: SPCK, 1964), 111–42 (for his appendix responding to Conzelmann, see pp. 142–44). Gunkel maintains the three-stage schema of salvation history especially strongly in his 2015 discussion of the role of the Spirit in each of these salvation-historical periods (Gunkel, *Der Heilige Geist bei Lukas*, 266–69).
**273** See Chapter 1.

sis that Luke/Acts does not reflect eschatological interest.²⁷⁴ However, the above analysis of this study's key texts demonstrates a widespread belief in the periodisation of history, but diverse views about its significance. Affirming that Luke understands history to be divided into periods does not of itself require assent to Conzelmann's model or assumptions.

Conzelmann built his three-stage model on a particular verse from the Gospel, Luke 16.16, which it will be helpful to consider in its own setting before discussing the diverse terms for temporal periods in Luke/Acts.

### 4.1.1 Luke 16.16 in context

Conzelmann centred his claims about Luke's periodisation of salvation history on: "the law and the prophets were in effect until John came (Ὁ νόμος καὶ οἱ προφῆται μέχρι Ἰωάννου); since then (ἀπὸ τότε) the good news of the kingdom of God is proclaimed, and everyone tries to enter it by force" (Luke 16.16). The verse, and Conzelmann's application of it, has created considerable debate, including important criticism from Paul Minear for placing so much weight on such an uncertain, single verse,²⁷⁵ with limited reference to its context or other key passages in Luke/Acts.²⁷⁶ Indeed, the verse must be read in light of its posi-

---

**274** Pervo, *Acts*, 25.
**275** More recently, Kim is similarly sceptical about focusing on individual texts rather than the whole narrative to analyse Lukan eschatology, in relation to both Conzelmann's treatment of Luke 16.16 and also recent attention to Luke 22 and Acts 20 (Kim, *Die Parusie bei Lukas*, 51–52).
**276** Minear was particularly concerned about Conzelmann's omission of the infancy narratives (Minear, "Luke's Use," 122–23). The extensive debate on the eschatological status of John the Baptist in Luke's schema is less illuminating. See overviews of interpretations of Luke 16.16 (including the difficult saying about entering the kingdom by force), in Carroll, *Luke*, 332–33 and Fitzmyer, *The Gospel according to Luke*, 1:182–87, 2:1115–16. Bovon agrees this verse is central to Luke's schema of history, but argues it moves the position of the kingdom from the parousia (Bovon, *Luke: Commentary*, 2:466, 469). Kümmel discusses Matt 11.12 and Luke 16.16 as part of an attempt to uncover the historical Jesus' eschatological understanding (Werner Georg Kümmel, *Promise and Fulfilment: The Eschatological Message of Jesus*, trans. Dorothea M. Barton, 3rd rev. ed., SBT 23 (London: SCM, 1957), 122–24). Knight argues the focus of the passage is the relationship between Judaism and Christianity (Jonathan Knight, *Luke's Gospel*, New Testament Readings (London: Routledge, 1998), 76–77), which is arguably similar to the somewhat problematic periodisation Wright attributes to NT salvation history, as a play in multiple "acts" in which the time of Israel is the precursor to the time of the church (N. T. Wright, "How Can the Bible Be Authoritative? (The Laing Lecture for 1989)," *VE* 21 (1991): 7–32). Conversely, Luke's emphasis on the continuity of the law and the unfolding of prophecy in Luke 16.16 disproves this type of distinction.

tion within a pericope concerned with the *continuing* validity of the law (the Matthean parallel has a different setting; Matt 11.12–13).²⁷⁷

Luke 16 begins with the parable of the dishonest manager (vv. 1–13), which Luke has Jesus interpret in light of the urgency of acting against one's own interests in the service of a more important consequence. This elicits particular criticism from nearby Pharisees, whom the narration then denounces as "lovers of money" (v. 14). It is the related sin of self-justification that prompts Jesus to go on to assert the ongoing importance of the law (including the statement about the law and the prophets in v. 16), giving the concrete example of divorce law (v. 18), before moving to another parable that focuses on tragic distraction from the call to live by the values of the kingdom of God, in the Rich man and Lazarus (vv. 19–31).²⁷⁸ Luke seems clear in this passage that the contrast with the past lies not in any diminution of the importance of the law nor, as Luke/Acts elsewhere demonstrates (Luke 21.5–36; Acts 21.6–10), the end of prophecy from the time of John.²⁷⁹ Rather, Luke 16.16 confirms the significance of the proclamation of the kingdom of God as part of the pattern of end-time events which are already unfolding in continuity with the events of the past and are reflected in further events such as Jesus' resurrection, highlighting the dire consequences of failure to respond positively to this proclamation.²⁸⁰ Rightly

---

**277** Fitzmyer points out the reverse ordering of the ideas in Matt 11.12–13 (Fitzmyer, *The Gospel according to Luke*, 2:1114).
**278** Fitzmyer aligns this parable with the parable of the lost sons, as "exempla" and as stories which have two main characters who are contrasted (in addition, for instance, to the same terminology used for Lazarus and the younger brother's longing for food; Fitzmyer, *The Gospel according to Luke*, 2:1126, 1131). Byrne's model of Lukan triangles makes a similar point, but notes the importance of third characters in these, and other, stories (here, Abraham, or the father of the lost sons) and incorporates a challenging barb which the reader experiences alongside the challenged character(s) (Brendan Byrne, *The Hospitality of God: A Reading of Luke's Gospel* (Strathfield: St Pauls, 2000), 4–5).
**279** By contrast, Acts 13.39 appears more ambiguous in its presentation of the law. In his speech at Antioch, the Lukan Paul describes the proclamation of release from sin (ἄφεσις ἁμαρτιῶν), extrapolating with the claim "by this Jesus everyone who believes is set free from all those sins from which you could not be freed by the law of Moses (ἀπὸ πάντων ὧν οὐκ ἠδυνήθητε ἐν νόμῳ Μωϋσέως δικαιωθῆναι, ἐν τούτῳ πᾶς ὁ πιστεύων δικαιοῦται)." The sentence is distinctive in Acts for its use of language found in Pauline letters, such as δικαιόω alongside discussion of the law's efficacy. Having noted similarities particularly with Colossians and Ephesians, Sterling explains the language as most likely a result of Luke combining a phrase typical of the "Pauline mission" for this section of the narrative with another phrase more common in Luke's narrative (ἄφεσις ἁμαρτιῶν) (Sterling, "'Do You Understand?'", 110).
**280** Sterling argues that the structure of Paul's speech in Acts 13 also supports the salvation-historical stages he finds in Luke 16.16 (Sterling, "'Do You Understand?'", 112–13). Certainly one of

viewing this passage in its literary setting, Joel Green discerns that the issue at hand is the "coming of the kingdom of God to displace other world systems. Not least of these is the rule of Wealth (v. 13)."[281] Thus, Luke 16.16 does not supply the division into three salvation-historical periods that Conzelmann built upon it—indeed there is no sense here of distinct periods of Jesus and the church.[282] But it does suggest a contrast of allegiances within which is contained an eschatological urgency.

### 4.1.2 Periodisation with αἰών, καιρός, and χρόνος

Nonetheless, as evidenced elsewhere and similarly to the other ancient writers discussed above, Luke does presume that history is divided into periods.[283] At the most basic level, and in parallel with the treatment in the other Gospels, Luke shares an understanding of "the age" (ὁ αἰών, see Appendix 1)[284] also evi-

---

Sterling's key claims, that Luke seeks to present the story of Jesus in continuity with the story of Israel (here structuring Israel's story in order to conclude with David and to show Jesus as the messianic fulfilment of the Davidic tradition, pp. 107, 114–15), is well supported by both Paul's speech in Acts 13 and the similar historical review in Stephen's speech in Acts 7, as also Peter's speech in Acts 2. However, in reflecting on this continuity and the shape of the Acts 13 speech itself (divided into three sections by verses of direct address to the audience, vv. 16, 26, 38, cf. pp. 102–3), Sterling's emphasis on finding a salvation-historical period up until John the Baptist, followed by the next section about Jesus, obscures the rhetorical thrust of the second section: this is not only about Jesus' death, but about the failure to understand the prophecies which led, ironically, to their fulfilment by those who took Jesus's life (vv. 27–28; see Chapter 4 below). As in Peter's speech at Pentecost, the accent returns again to divine action: God has raised him from the dead. And again it is the resurrection that prompts the further opportunity for salvation. For further discussion of the role of the resurrection as a transition point in history for Luke, and the cascading further end-time events which follow, see Chapter 6 below.

281 Joel B. Green, *The Gospel of Luke*, NICNT (Grand Rapids: Eerdmans, 1997), 603.
282 Given his support for Conzelmann's three-stage schema of salvation history and, noting that Luke 16.16 actually outlines only two of Conzelmann's epochs, Fitzmyer argues: "Acts 1.6b has to be related to this verse in order to understand it properly" (p. 2:1115).
283 Cullmann, *Christ and Time*, 45–46. Barr's important study, *Biblical Words for Time*, responds to problematic lexical claims by Cullmann. Barr concludes that the overlap in meanings for καιρός, αἰών, and χρόνος in both the LXX and NT precludes the distinctions Cullmann made (Barr, *Biblical Words for Time*, 84–85). Barr's second edition makes a further response, rightly recognising that Cullmann's other arguments did not all rely on his incorrect claims about the terms (pp. 179–80). The revised edition offers a very helpful overview of related publications (pp. 175–84).
284 Αἰών appears a total of 34 times in the Gospels and Acts, 7 and 2 of which are in Luke and Acts respectively. Appendix 1 provides a table indicating all the uses of ὁ αἰών in the Gospels and Acts. Although in any attempt to map the uses of a word, strictly allocating each use to

dent in other late Second Temple Jewish literature.²⁸⁵ Here the αἰών is a duration of time, employed particularly in contrasts between the period of the present time and the coming (eschatological) period.

Following the account of the dishonest manager's action, the Lukan Jesus observes that the children of light fall short of the shrewdness of the children of this age (οἱ υἱοὶ τοῦ αἰῶνος τούτου Luke 16.8). It is worth noting that standard translations such as the NRSV and ESV translate τοῦ αἰῶνος τούτου here as "of this world," losing the temporal element inherent in Luke's phrasing (cf. also Matt 13.22; Mark 4.19).²⁸⁶ Elsewhere Luke compares the children of this age (οἱ υἱοὶ τοῦ αἰῶνος τούτου) who marry—here the NRSV and ESV do translate the same phrase "of this age," rather than "world," no doubt helped by the following contrast—with those who attain that age (τοῦ αἰῶνος ἐκείνου) and the resurrection of the dead, who do not (Luke 20.34–35).²⁸⁷ Indeed, the current time (τῷ **καιρῷ** τούτῳ) promises more than the disciples have given up, alongside eternal life in the age to come (τῷ **αἰῶνι** τῷ ἐρχομένῳ, Luke 18.30; cf. Mark 10.30).²⁸⁸ Thus Luke establishes a contrast between periods, not only using the term αἰών for both the present and future ages (Luke 20.34–35; cf. also 16.8–9; Matt 12.32), but καιρός and αἰών (Luke 18.30).

Luke uses καιρός often, both to denote periods of duration and significant, punctiliar moments (see Appendix 2).²⁸⁹ Moreover, his frequent use of χρόνος

---

one category or another can be difficult, the table does nonetheless give a sense of the range of the semantic field as used in these texts.

**285** See Christopher Rowland, *Christian Origins: An Account of the Setting and Character of the Most Important Messianic Sect of Judaism* (London: SPCK, 1985), 88–89.

**286** Green retains "the age" in his ET, and explores the implications for the parable in thinking about this as a contrast between two aeons (Green, *The Gospel of Luke*, 588, 593). After a discussion about Lukan dualisms and possible parallels in his historical setting (including Philo and a type of Platonism), he asserts that "The duality Luke sets up in vv. 8–9 continues to shape the meaning of this text (vv. 10–13), and it is eschatological, not cosmological, in orientation" (p. 596).

**287** This sentence is not included in the synoptic parallels for this story in Matt 22.23–46 or Mark 12.18–34.

**288** Note that in Mark the contrast is between **νῦν** ἐν τῷ καιρῷ τούτῳ and ἐν τῷ αἰῶνι τῷ ἐρχομένῳ.

**289** Καιρός appears 13 and 9 times respectively in Luke and Acts, compared to 10, 5, and 3 in Matthew, Mark, and John. Luke/Acts also makes greater use of χρόνος (7 and 17 uses, compared to 3, 2, and 4), however some uses are more mundane, such as the times of a person to indicate age. See Appendix 2 and Appendix 3 for a table outlining all uses in the Gospels and Acts of καιρός and χρόνος respectively. For a full study of the semantic fields in classical texts, LXX, and NT, see Barr, *Biblical Words for Time*. *TDNT* emphasises the sense of "fateful" or "specific and decisive" point for καιρός, to which are attributed texts that are better suited to a "duration"

(see Appendix 3) exhibits considerable interchangeability with καιρός, as also reflected in the LXX and other NT usage, as James Barr has shown in his detailed study of words for time in this material.[290]

Where καιρός takes the meaning of a duration of time, rather than simply a moment or opportunity,[291] it sometimes denotes a season rather than a historical period. For instance, the adjective καρποφόροι with καιροί makes it clear that Acts 14.17 describes seasons, and here the Lukan Paul discusses the divine benevolence in providing rain and "fruitful seasons." But other uses of καιρός as a duration reiterate the periodised schema I have suggested above is also indicated by Luke's use of αἰών.

Luke's underlying periodised schema of history is made particularly plain in Acts 1.7, by the use of both καιρός and χρόνος together in plural form. Prior to Jesus' ascension, the disciples ask whether now is the time (χρόνῳ τούτῳ) when the kingdom will be restored to Israel (v. 6).[292] Jesus responds: "it is not for you to know the times or periods (χρόνους ἢ καιρούς) that the father has set by his own authority" (v. 7). While traditional interpretation has focused on the epistemological claim in the statement,[293] and rallied this text as evidence that Luke has distanced his account from eschatological claims,[294] the more

---

meaning (e.g. Dan 2.21 LXX; Acts 1.7), though Dan 7.25 LXX is rightly included among a list of rare uses with the sense of "duration."

**290** As found by Barr, *Biblical Words for Time*, 84–85 and Delling's *TDNT* entry for χρόνος, 9:585.

**291** This use is common in Luke as also in Josephus or Polybius, as discussed above.

**292** Keener explores other texts' expectations of the restoration of Israel (Keener, *Acts*, 1:687–88). Peterson uses Acts 1.8 to structure the periods of history in terms of the geographical spread of the mission (Peterson, *The Acts of the Apostles*, 112–13). Interpreters frequently employ verse 1.8 as a literary structure for Acts (Gaventa, *Acts*, 65; Sterling, "Do You Understand?", 112–13), though Tannehill demonstrates that it does not really map onto the narrative (Tannehill, *Narrative Unity*, 2:17), and Ellis rightly shows the inappropriateness of designating Rome the "end of the earth" (E. Earle Ellis, "The End of the Earth (Acts 1:8)," in *History and Interpretation in New Testament Perspective*, BibInt 54 (Leiden: Brill, 2001), 58; cf. Eric D. Barreto, *Ethnic Negotiations: The Function of Race and Ethnicity in Acts 16*, WUNT 2/294 (Tübingen: Mohr Siebeck, 2010), 120); contra Fitzmyer, who does equate Rome with the end of the earth (Joseph A. Fitzmyer, *The Acts of the Apostles*, AB 31 (New York: Doubleday, 1998), 201). See further discussion of this passage in Chapter 6 §5.3.1.

**293** See discussion in Rius-Camps and Read-Heimerdinger, *The Message of Acts*, 1:74–75. This verse does connect to the tradition of the "unknown hour" of Jesus' return.

**294** Conzelmann, *Acts of the Apostles*, 6; Haenchen, *The Acts of the Apostles*, 143; Keener, *Acts*, 1:686–87. Fitzmyer interprets this episode in light of his overall affirmation of Conzelmann's salvation-historical schema, but with minor amendments (Fitzmyer, *The Acts of the Apostles*, 201). See more detailed discussion of this passage in relation to questions of the imminence or otherwise of Luke's eschatological expectation in Chapter 6, §5.3.1.

basic assumption the statement reveals has been overlooked. By Luke's understanding, authoritatively announced in words attributed to Jesus, history comes divided into times and periods, which have been set by divine authority.[295]

Luke's use of χρόνοι and καιροί in Acts 1.7 is reminiscent of the only appearances[296] of the two terms in parallel in this way in the LXX: Dan 2.21 and 4.37. These verses elicit a sense of the divinely determined succession of ages. In Dan 2, in response to his insight about Nebuchadnezzar's dream, Daniel praises that God changes (ἀλλοιοῖ) the καιροὺς καί χρόνους and, interestingly, removes and establishes kings. The Greek text of 4.37[297] reports Nebuchadnezzar's praise at his own healing and restoration of his reign, but his words almost directly echo Daniel's at Dan 2.21. In 4.37 Nebuchadnezzar praises God as: αὐτὸς ποιεῖ σημεῖα καὶ τέρατα καὶ ἀλλοιοῖ καιροὺς καὶ χρόνους ἀφαιρῶν βασιλείαν βασιλέων καὶ καθιστῶν ἑτέρους ἀντ' αὐτῶν.

The combination of terms in parallel in Acts 1.7 underscores the relevance of these ideas from Daniel,[298] as does the context of the disciples' inquiry about restoration of the kingdom to Israel (see also the sense of duration with καιρός in Dan 7.25, a verse noted above in relation to the War Scroll, and the eschatological anticipation of that setting).[299] Moreover, the only other NT use of the combined terms supports this interpretation: in 1 Thess 5.1, Περὶ δὲ τῶν χρόνων καὶ τῶν

---

[295] Barr cites Acts 1.7 as a "critical" NT example of temporal terminology in biblical texts, suggesting here the terms should be translated "epoch" or "period" (Barr, *Biblical Words for Time*, 105–6). Barrett rightly notes that one cannot distinguish between the meanings of χρόνοι and καιροί here, observing the difficulties of translations and citing examples from Latin texts (C. K. Barrett, *A Critical and Exegetical Commentary on the Acts of the Apostles*, ICC (Edinburgh: T&T Clark, 1994–1998), 1:78). This interpretation is also contra those who assume Luke uses the plural to denote a *single extended* period (Bock, *A Theology*, 393; I. Howard Marshall, *The Acts of the Apostles: An Introduction and Commentary* (Leicester: InterVarsity Press, 1980), 93–94).

[296] The only other uses of the two terms together in the LXX come from Nehemiah 10.35 and 13.31, where the situation is quite different. The terms do not form a pair, but "seasons *by times* year by year," which are explicitly connected to annual celebrations: εἰς καιροὺς ἀπὸ χρόνων ἐνιαυτὸν κατ' ἐνιαυτόν (10.35, cf. the same construction at 13.31). See Fitzmyer for some other limited examples of this terminology outside the biblical text, namely examples from Demosthenes and Strato of Lampsacus (Fitzmyer, *The Acts of the Apostles*, 205).

[297] The Greek text in 2.21 parallels the MT, but in Dan 4 the Greek and MT vary widely from each other in the section including 4.37. Here I have used the numbering in Rahlfs, who numbers the subsequent verses also 37a–c. Collins numbers this verse 4.34 (Old Greek), in John J. Collins, *Daniel: A Commentary on the Book of Daniel*, Hermeneia (Minneapolis: Fortress, 1993), 213.

[298] Also in contrast to interpreting the καιροί and χρόνοι as cyclical seasons. See discussion below.

[299] See above in relation to the War Scroll.

καιρῶν introduces instruction on the day of the Lord and messianic woes.³⁰⁰ Therefore, while periodisation can be diverse and present in a great range of texts (as shown above), the χρόνοι and καιροί in Acts 1.7 reflect the kind of explicitly eschatological framework found in other NT texts such as 1 Thess 5.1, and imply a schema reminiscent of Daniel and discussed above as a feature of Josephus's *Jewish War*, 4 Ezra, and 2 Baruch.

Such an understanding of divinely determined periods is also evident in the Lukan Paul's speech to the Athenians at the Areopagus in Acts 17.22–31, where καιροί and χρόνοι are also both used, though not directly next to each other (vv. 26 and 30). Here Paul contrasts the "objects of your [the Athenians'] worship" (v. 23) with the God he proclaims: "who made the world and everything in it … the Lord of Heaven and Earth" (v. 24). In developing this contrast, Paul first sets out the credentials of his God (vv. 24–26) and then the details of God's relationship with humanity (vv. 27–28), which in turn underscores God's radical difference from idols (v. 29). This leads to a call for a response from his audience (v. 30), in light of a powerful affirmation of significant transition in history (identified in Jesus' resurrection), which foreshadows a final judgement (v. 31).³⁰¹

Here καιροί appears in the context of describing divine activity. Having affirmed God's sovereignty as Creator,³⁰² Luke's Paul asserts:

> From one ancestor he made all nations to inhabit the whole earth, and he allotted the times of their existence (καιρούς) and the boundaries of the places where they would live (τὰς ὁροθεσίας τῆς κατοικίας αὐτῶν). (Acts 17.26)

Martin Dibelius argues that καιροί here refers to the gift of seasons, inspired by Greek philosophical traditions (and noting the other connections to Greek philosophy evident in Paul's speech, cf. 17.18, 28).³⁰³ Although I have suggested

---

300 Conzelmann cites 1 Thess 5.1 as evidence that the terms together "(in itself an innocent enough expression), became a topic in elementary Christian instruction" (Conzelmann, *Acts of the Apostles*, 7). The connections to Daniel suggest that this set phrase may have a longer history of association with the succession of empires.
301 This passage is discussed further in Chapter 6, when considering questions of imminence in Luke's eschatological expectation.
302 See discussion below at §4.2.
303 Dibelius argues this as part of a so-called "philosophical" interpretation (Martin Dibelius, *Studies in the Acts of the Apostles* (London: SCM, 1956), 29–34). So also Haenchen, who interprets 17.26 as seasons in light of Acts 14.17, rather than associating the verse with 1.7 or 17.30 (Haenchen, *The Acts of the Apostles*, 523; Tannehill, *Narrative Unity*, 2:212). Gaventa leaves the interpretation as "uncertain" (Gaventa, *Acts*, 251). Johnson attempts a third approach, neither

this is the sense of καιροὶ καρποφόροι in Acts 14.17, the broad scope of history which underpins the Areopagus speech throughout suggests that the use in Acts 17.26 is reminiscent rather of the traditions found in Acts 1.7, and other texts such as 1QM 10.15, discussed above.[304] As C. Kavin Rowe observes, Luke frames Paul's Areopagus speech between the poles of "creation (17.24, 26) and consummation (17.30 – 31)."[305] Rowe rightly discerns that, between these bounds, the speech sets out the call to turn from ignorance and "to locate the decisive event of human history in the resurrection of Jesus."[306] The creation of humanity, like the governance of human history, includes demarcations of dominion in time and space (v. 26), as well as oversight of the events of the end (vv. 30 – 31).[307] As he outlines these claims, Paul also includes a reference to historical periods (χρόνοι) that he asserts have now passed: the times of ignorance (χρόνους τῆς ἀγνοίας, v. 30).

### 4.1.3 Other temporal terminology

Some uses of "beginning" (ἀρχή; ἄρχομαι) in Luke/Acts also communicate a sense of significant transition. Although Conzelmann argues that Luke uses ἀρχή in "a technical sense," in the several places in which he makes this obser-

---

the seasons of Greek philosophy nor periods of Jewish apocalypticism, but "a standard statement of God's creative power" (Johnson, *The Acts of the Apostles*, 315). Although the imagery of separation is reminiscent of creation accounts, I suggest this does not account for the ways it is used in this passage.

**304** By contrast, Johnson uses the χρόνοι at Acts 17.30 to caution against supplying "apocalyptic" overtones to καιροί in 17.26 (Johnson, *The Acts of the Apostles*, 317). This distinguishes the meaning of the two terms too strongly (see Barr, *Biblical Words for Time*, 84 – 85), and overlooks the understanding of periods of history since creation and until final judgement that is evident throughout this speech.

**305** Rowe, *World Upside Down*, 40.

**306** Rowe identifies this as a passage which, rather than affirming the pagan philosophical models, refutes them for a call to embrace a Christian understanding of history and engage in repentance (Rowe, *World Upside Down*, 40 – 41).

**307** Notably, divine sovereignty in establishing political boundaries and governing the transitions through different empires is evident not only in Jewish texts like apocalypses and Josephus's *Jewish War*, but the Graeco-Roman texts discussed above, from Polybius's *Histories* and Diodorus Siculus's *Library* to Virgil's *Aeneid*. Cf. Virgil's portrayal of Jupiter's divine gift of rule without limits in time or space in the specific case of Rome (1.279). Ways in which the transition between empires is attributed to personal or impersonal forces are discussed in Chapter 4 below.

vation he does not explain any further.[308] By contrast, David Moessner suggests that Luke's use of "beginning" takes its meaning more from its historiographical style, identifying the scope of events to be included within a work, for which he finds further evidence in roughly contemporaneous Graeco-Roman literature.[309] This is probably the best interpretation of the "beginning" in Luke 1.2.

But in a key example in Acts 11.15, as Peter recounts the story of Cornelius and his household becoming Jesus believers, he says "And as I began to speak (τῷ ἄρξασθαί με λαλεῖν), the Holy Spirit fell upon them just as it had upon us at the beginning (ἐν ἀρχῇ)." The verse links back to Pentecost in Acts 2, an event identified within the narrative as the fulfilment of what was prophesied to take place "in the last days" (2.17), and part of the series of end-time events Luke shows to be cascading into the discipleship community (discussed further in Chapter 6). In Acts 11.15 the connection to Pentecost is also emphatic for a different reason: to show that the pneumatic experience of the gentile household was the same as the experience of the Jerusalem community earli-

---

[308] In his commentary on Acts, Conzelmann makes this claim of Acts 11.15 (Conzelmann, *Acts of the Apostles*, 86), but refers only to a lengthy footnote in his article: "Was von Anfang war," in *Neutestamentliche Studien für Rudolf Bultmann, zu seinem siebzigsten Geburtstag am 20. August 1954*, ed. Walther Eltester, BZNW 21 (Berlin: Töpelmann, 1954), 199–200 n. 20. This article in turn references a footnote in *Die Mitte der Zeit*. He does not offer much to support the idea of a "technical sense" to the term, though he does associate the claim with ideas of the church as a "new creation," which he argues are not yet present in Luke (*Theology of St Luke*, 211 n. 1). Sterling likewise sees Luke as paralleling two different types of "beginning," the first in Jesus' baptism and the second in the beginning of apostolic ministry at Pentecost, supporting his overall framework of salvation history in which the period of fulfilment is further divided into two periods: that of Jesus' ministry and the church (Sterling, "Do You Understand?", 113).

[309] Moessner finds Luke's use of "beginnings" to be a way of dividing up a historiographical narrative (Moessner, *Luke the Historian*, 334–38), and shows through the example of Paul's description of his pious life "from the beginning" (Acts 26.4–5) how the same language can be used for the span of Paul's life, as a period of focus for narration (p. 103). In addition to establishing the rhetorical role of ἀρχή in Luke 1.2, Moessner suggests the term functions to link Luke and Acts, by the reference to ἀρχή in Luke 1.2 and ὧν ἤρξατο in Acts 1.1 (p. 169; cf. pp. 122–23). See the examples from other Graeco-Roman texts that Moessner gives on pp. 99–105, 139–41, 182–85. Affirming the ultimately eschatological orientation of Luke/Acts, with obvious reference to and yet distinction from Conzelmann, Moessner concludes that Luke's way of dividing up the narrative supports his overall story: "The period of Jesus and the time of the church are narrated as one era, as one new reality; the Messianic activity of Jesus (Gospel) and that of Messiah through his disciples (Acts) must be grasped as *the one new reign and realm of God*" (p. 185, italics original).

er.³¹⁰ In the process, it likewise confirms the "beginning" associated with the events of the last days which reflects a fundamental shift in history.

Luke uses other temporal terms, such as ἡ ὥρα (the hour) and ἡ ἡμέρα (the day), which denote both mundane and (occasionally) eschatologically significant meanings (see Appendices 4 and 5). In the vast majority of cases, these words simply appear in the narrative detail of the account ("about the ninth hour" (Acts 10.3), or "about eight days after" (Luke 9.28)). In Luke's parables of crisis in Luke 12, "the hour" is the unexpected moment at which the Son of Man is coming (Luke 12.39–40, cf. v. 46).³¹¹ At some points, Luke uses ἡμέρα in the plural as a way of denoting a duration of time or political period, such as in the days of King Herod of Judea (Luke 1.5; cf. 4.25; Acts 5.37; 7.45); similar wording also expresses a contrast, for instance, between "the days of Noah" and "the days of the Son of Man" (Luke 17.26–29), the latter denoting a period of eschatological activity. In the plural, "those days" can refer to an anticipated period of suffering, whether eschatological woes or other times of war and suffering, seen particularly in Jesus' so-called eschatological speeches in Luke 17 and 21 (Luke 17.22; 21.6, 22–23),³¹² and also in Jesus' lament over Jerusalem and on the way to the cross (19.43; 23.29).³¹³

Apart from these uses as a duration of time or period, ἡμέρα also appears in the singular and as a punctiliar moment, describing a final judgement in keeping with the established eschatological tones of the LXX concept of the Day of the Lord.³¹⁴ In Luke/Acts, sometimes "the day" is specified through terms like "the day of the Son of Man," or "on the last day," but other times the reference to this final day is presumed simply by "a day" (Acts 17.31) or "that day" (Luke 10.12). In a complex series of sayings, Luke 17 describes both "the days of the Son of Man" and "the day of the Son of Man" (vv. 22, 24, 26, 30–31). As a speech from the Lukan Jesus to the disciples, the passage parallels the days of Noah and Lot with the days of the Son of Man in terms of a time of sudden judgement, while also talking about "his day," which will be sudden and illuminating like

---

**310** Johnson notes the way ὥσπερ functions to establish this emphatic parallel (Johnson, *Acts of the Apostles*, 201).
**311** In Luke, the term does not achieve the particularly Johannine use of "the Hour" or Jesus' Hour (John 2.4; 7.30; 8.20; 12.23, 27; 13.31; though cf. Luke 22.53). A full table of uses of ὥρα in the Gospels and Acts is provided in Appendix 4.
**312** Chapter 6 below includes a longer treatment of Jesus' speeches in Luke 17 and 21, including discussion of the eschatological elements of the prophecy in chapter 21 and those which relate to events from the reader's own time, such as the destruction of Jerusalem.
**313** Most uses of ἡμέρα in Luke/Acts appear simply in narrative description, references to day time (as opposed to night), constant practice, or festival days.
**314** See discussion in Barr, *Biblical Words for Time*, 60.

lightning. While here it seems to indicate the day of judgement, Jesus' declaration a few verses earlier that "the days are coming when you will long to see *one of* the days of the Son of Man" (v. 22, emphasis added), seems to use the singular and plural differently. The obscure phrasing appears to describe a desire to experience even just a part of that time of eschatological vindication.[315]

### 4.1.4 Temporal periods qualified by additional terms

Occasionally these times or days are qualified by additional terms. As already noted above, the Lukan Paul describes **the times (χρόνοι) of ignorance** (Acts 17.30), which he already places in the past, having been brought to an end by Jesus' resurrection.[316] Turning from ignorance to insight is reminiscent of themes in apocalypses, such as 1 Enoch's *Animal Apocalypse*, where the moment of insight through revelation lies at the cusp of God's decisive divine action at the end of history (1 Enoch 90.6, 9; and, as discussed above, 1QM 17.7; 4 Ezra 6.20; 12.36 – 38; 13.53 – 56; 14.26, 45 – 47; 2 Bar 27.15; 48.3, 33). Elements of this tradition also complement the importance Luke gives the phrase.[317] In Luke/Acts, the capacity for enlightenment now, through attending to the proclamation of the resurrection, confirms that ignorance is no longer an option. Rather, the audience is faced only with a choice between positive or negative response to their newfound knowledge, leading to the call to repentance which features in speeches about the resurrection throughout Acts (cf. 2.38; 3.19; 5.31; 11.18; 17.30; 20.21; 26.20).[318]

---

[315] Carroll suggests that the plural "the days of the Son of Man" in 17.22 and 17.26 reflects a different use, in which v. 26 refers to the period leading up to the end, while the longing in v. 22 describes days that are a part of the final judgement (Carroll, *Response to the End*, 93 n. 211). As Carroll notes, the longing described in v. 22 is not for simply one of the days in the period of struggle leading to the end, but "just one of the days of bliss" (p. 93 n. 211). By contrast, Bovon suggests that there is an "enigmatic" logic behind the convoluted passage: "The Son of Man has his days and his day; he will come and he has come" (Bovon, *Luke: Commentary*, 2:512). For a fuller discussion of this passage, see Chapter 6 §5.3.1.

[316] Peter also refers to past ignorance in his speech in Acts 3.17, though here the context indicates this is a particular instance of ignorance: the unknowing role played by those who facilitated the death of Jesus and thus the fulfilment of what had been foretold by the prophets.

[317] Themes of ignorance and knowledge are important to apocalypses and shine through also in their treatments of the ordering of time at the cusp of end-time events, as in the way that the sheep's eyes are opened in the *Animal Apocalypse* at key moments, especially at the point just prior to God's decisive action at the end of history (1 Enoch 90.6, 9).

[318] See Chapter 6 for further discussion of repentance as a response to the proclamation of the resurrection.

§4 Periodised and teleological history in Luke/Acts — 127

Jesus laments that Jerusalem did not recognise **"the time of your visitation** (τὸν καιρὸν τῆς ἐπισκοπῆς σου)" (Luke 19.44; cf. Jer. 6.15 LXX;[319] cf. Luke 12.56; 20.10).[320] Here the lack of recognition lends an additional note of tragedy to ignorance. Luke draws on images of divine visitation for judgement or saving intervention in the HB,[321] applying the phrase to denote the time of *Jesus'* presence. The right time (καιρός) for harvest in the following parable of the wicked tenants (Luke 20.10) similarly illustrates moments of (rejected) divine initiative.

In Jesus' prophecy in Luke 21, the reader is introduced to the concepts of **the days (ἡμέραι) of vengeance** (Luke 21.22) and **the times (καιροί) of the gentiles** (a period to be "fulfilled," Luke 21.24). These phrases play a role in longstanding debates about the extent to which Jesus' prophecy here focuses on historical events (such as the destruction of Jerusalem) or eschatological events.[322] Each of these particular temporal phrases draws on other biblical images of judgement. Notably the passage from Isa 61.2 from which Jesus announces the "year of the Lord's favour" in Nazareth (Luke 4.19) includes a second line, proclaiming "the day of vengeance of our God." At Nazareth this line is cut off, keeping the focus on acceptance, but by the time of Jesus' prophecy in Luke 21 such days are announced among the trials to be endured[323] before the end of history.

Similarly the phrase the "times of the gentiles" relates to a broader tradition of the gentiles trampling the rebellious city for a (limited) period, as part of eschatological woes. This tradition, drawn originally from Ezek 8.5–18, appears in Revelation 11.1–2 as an association between the gentiles and the Roman em-

---

319 Fitzmyer, *The Gospel according to Luke*, 2:1259.
320 Bovon interprets καιρός in Luke 20.10 in the sense of "opportunity," given the associated eschatological pressure in the stories (Bovon, *Luke: Commentary*, 2:255, 3:19 n. 43); Johnson suggests it indicates a moment of eschatological significance (Johnson, *The Gospel of Luke*, 299, 305).
321 See discussion in Johnson, *The Gospel of Luke*, 299. The alignment of the "visitation" with Jesus' presence is also supported by related LXX connections pointed out by Johnson, including references to visitation for punishment (Jer 6.15; 10.15) or a more general sense of saving intervention (Gen 50.24–25; Exod 3.16; 13.19; see Johnson's further discussion and examples on p. 299).
322 The speech is discussed in greater detail in Chapter 6 §5.3.1, which analyses Luke 21 as a *vaticinium ex eventu* as part of considering elements of imminent eschatological expectation in Luke/Acts.
323 Byrne equates these days of vengeance with the times that prompt Jesus' lament in Luke 13.34–35 and 19.41–44, as well as the days he warns about just prior to his crucifixion in Luke 23.27–31 (Byrne, *The Hospitality of God*, 166–67).

pire.³²⁴ This is not a period of gentile priority reflected perhaps in the gentile mission in Acts,³²⁵ nor targeted criticism of gentiles as such. In the context of Luke 21.24, the phrase denotes a period of suffering among the events recounted in the prophecy, with overtones of Roman oppression, which nonetheless will come to an assured end.

Finally, Luke has Peter exhort repentance so that **the καιροί of refreshing** may come (Acts 3.20), and Peter goes on to assert that the appointed Christ, Jesus, will remain in heaven until **the times (ἄχρι χρόνων)³²⁶ for restoring all things** (Acts 3.21).³²⁷ These times refer to the promise of ongoing restoration at the culmination of history.

Thus Luke uses varied temporal language, but at numerous points his use of terms like αἰών, καιρός, and χρόνος reveals an underlying sense of historical periodisation of a kind found in texts which reflect Danielic traditions, like 4 Ezra and 2 Baruch, and other NT passages such as 1 Thess 5.1. When Luke introduces additional phrases, creating something almost like proper names for temporal periods, he incorporates ideas seen in earlier Jewish literature about eschatological expectation or judgement, such as turning from ignorance, or the prophecies about times of vengeance or trampling by the gentiles. Many of these phrases will come up again in this study, particularly in the discussion of the relationship between the present time and the end of history in Chapter 6. These phrases are not set out in an itemised chronological framework in a particular Lukan passage and then applied consistently across Luke's narrative. But, as they indicate Luke's recourse to the language of periods and times, and as they relate to passages with an explicitly eschatological focus (such as Jesus' speech in Luke 21 and Peter's speeches in Acts 2 and 3), I suggest they reflect an underlying sense of periodisation within an eschatological framework.

---

324 The association is often also identified in overlaps between the oracle of Jerusalem's destruction recorded by Josephus and the account in Rev 11 (Judith Kovacs and Christopher Rowland, *Revelation: The Apocalypse of Jesus Christ*, Wiley Blackwell Bible Commentaries (Oxford: Blackwell, 2004), 123).
325 Cf. Adams, *The Stars Will Fall*, 176.
326 English translations such as NRSV and ESV render this as singular.
327 Indeed, in this instance, Luke uses three temporal terms within two verses (the καιροί of refreshing, leads to sending Jesus who is in heaven until the χρόνοι for restoring, as foretold by prophets ἀπ' αἰῶνος), and it may simply be a stylistic preference that led him to do so.

## 4.2 Teleological history in Luke/Acts

For Luke, as for Josephus and the writers of Qumran's War Scroll, 4 Ezra, and 2 Baruch, history is conceptualised as a movement that stretches from creation to the events of the end. Likewise in the *Aeneid*, history extends to its end and goal, which Virgil identifies with the Roman empire. Though depicted in various ways, in each of these cases the events of the past are important for the writer's portrayal of the end; that is, history and eschatology are not falsely severed, but intimately connected in a teleological schema of history. Luke demonstrates this teleological approach through his own attention to the events of the past, emphasis on the continuity of God's faithfulness throughout the periods of history, and range of assumptions about the events of the end.

Firstly, Luke's teleological schema of history can be seen in an interest in the past which extends back to creation. In the genealogy he traces the connection from Jesus back to "son of Adam, son of God" (Luke 3.38), underscoring not only the cosmic significance of Jesus' anointed ministry, death, resurrection, and ascension,[328] but the continuity of divine guidance over this great expanse of time. As in the War Scroll and 4 Ezra, divine action in creation establishes God's identity and characteristic behaviour throughout the whole schema of history.[329] At the Areopagus, as noted above, the Lukan Paul grounds his claims about the certainty of the judgement which God has set at the end of history (Acts 17.31) in the divine sovereignty and power of the Creator: "The God who made the world and everything in it, he who is Lord of heaven and earth" (17.24).[330]

The past also meaningfully grounds Luke's narrative through his emphasis on prophecy and its fulfilment, which reflects divine faithfulness across the periods of history—a second element of Luke's teleological schema. As discussed in more detail in Chapter 4, by presenting his account's events as the fulfilment of biblical promises (cf. Luke 4.18–19; Acts 2.14–36)[331] and of prophecies made

---

[328] Charles H. Talbert, *Reading Luke: A Literary and Theological Commentary on the Third Gospel* (New York: Crossroad, 1982), 46–47. Luke's version of the genealogy also emphasises universality, over against Matthew's account which goes back to Abraham (Johnson, *The Gospel of Luke*, 72).
[329] This is consistent also with the analysis Mermelstein offers of the ways in which post-exilic writers trace their historical origin and identity back to creation, rather than to Sinai (Mermelstein, *Creation and Covenant*).
[330] The immediate context for this characterisation is demonstrating the uselessness of idols (Haenchen, *The Acts of the Apostles*, 520), though the affirmation of God's character as Creator remains important through the speech. See Rowe, *World Upside Down*, 40, and §4.1.2 above.
[331] Mroczek has helpfully highlighted the difficulty of presuming a "biblical" or even book-based literary imagination for first-century writers in their use of earlier authoritative texts

within his narrative (Luke 1.17, 33; 2.34–5; Acts 9.11–12, 15–16; 27.24), Luke provides assurance that prophesied events yet to be fulfilled beyond the end of the narrative will also take place (Luke 17.24, 26–37; 20.42–44; 21.25–28; Acts 3.21; 17.31). Importantly, this approach to prophecy establishes continuity with the events of the past as well as using authoritative earlier texts to interpret the significance of the events unfolding within Luke/Acts. For instance, Acts uses the language of Pss 16, 110, and 118 to describe the eschatological significance of Jesus' resurrection (Acts 2.25–28, 31, 34–35; 3.11–12), and in so doing makes a claim to a divinely-appointed *telos* of history, to which the past points.[332]

Sterling rightly observes that Luke sees his work as a "*continuation* of the LXX,"[333] similar to other extensions of earlier historiographies[334] and reflected also in Josephus's treatment of post-biblical history in the second half of the *Antiquities*. Such a continuation is not only stylistic, but appeals to organic connections between the past, present, and, indeed, the future. From the infancy narratives' Septuagintal style onwards, Luke grounds his story in a broader narrative seen as having begun already in the account of God's interaction with God's people throughout the history of Israel.

Finally, Luke's references to events at the end of history confirm his teleological schema. Here Luke/Acts likewise shares many of the expectations spelt out in 4 Ezra, 2 Baruch, and the War Scroll, and shared across many texts of Second Temple Judaism. While Luke's characterisation of these end-time events and their imminence is discussed in detail in Chapter 6, for now the important

---

(Eva Mroczek, *The Literary Imagination in Jewish Antiquity* (New York: Oxford University Press, 2016), 4–9). While aware of this difficulty, here I use "biblical" in an attempt to communicate some sense that the earlier texts were cited as authoritative, without making claims about the formation of the canon by this time.

**332** Prophecies made within Luke's narrative include descriptions of end-time events, some of which are also *fulfilled* within Luke's narrative, such as Stephen's vision of Jesus already at the right hand of God (Acts 7.55–56), as prophesied earlier (Luke 22.69).

**333** Sterling, *Historiography and Self-Definition*, 363. The importance of Israel's past and an extension of the style and themes of the LXX to Luke/Acts is widely accepted in studies of Luke/Acts and the arguments need not be rehearsed here. For a range of views see Sterling, "'Opening the Scriptures,'" 199–225; Rothschild, *Luke-Acts and the Rhetoric*, 158–84; Michael A. Fishbane, *Biblical Interpretation in Ancient Israel* (Oxford: Oxford University Press, 1985); and, though now rather dated, Goulder, *Type and History*, 145–78; Drury, *Tradition and Design*, 46–66. For prophecy and suffering see Moessner, "The 'Script,'" 249. See n. 331 above about the work of Mroczek, however; the concept of continuing earlier traditions does not imply that the LXX must be viewed as a closed canon, but rather a collection of texts treated as authoritative and a source of inspiration in interpreting the present time. In this regard, Mroczek's imagery of a database rather than closed book is helpful (Mroczek, *The Literary Imagination*, 40–41).

**334** See above, p. 64 n. 32.

point is that Luke, like his fellow synoptic evangelists, continues to describe traditional expectations about the end of history, which are embedded in Jesus' parables, predictions about the future difficulties to be faced by his followers, and also the speeches of the apostles in Acts.[335] In addition to messianic claims, further expectations include a period of afflictions (Luke 21.9 – 26; 23.28 – 31; Acts 14.22),[336] resurrection (Luke 11.31; 14.14; 20.27 – 38; Acts 24.15; 26.23),[337] judgement (Luke 10.13; 11.31 – 32; 17.26 – 37; 21.34 – 36; 22.30; Acts 10.42; 17.31),[338] vindication of the righteous (Luke 14.14; 18.28 – 30; 21.19),[339] and restoration (Luke 18.29 – 30; 21.28; 22.28 – 30; 24.21; Acts 1.6 – 7).[340]

Thus, Luke depicts continuity across the events of the past and maintains that all of history is overseen by the sovereign Creator. Indeed, as discussed in Chapter 4 below, Luke asserts that the events of his narrative, including the events of the end, are unfolding according to an unstoppable divine βουλή.[341] In all of this he affirms a teleological schema of history.

But the striking events of the end represent a decisive new transition, even some *dis*continuity. Already, as noted above, Paul announces in Athens, the times of ignorance are over (Acts 17.30; cf. 3.17). The rejection of Jesus, though similar to the rejection of the prophets, brings new consequences (Acts 7.52; cf. 2.36),[342] and Jesus has become the first to rise from the dead (26.23).[343] Indeed, as I argue in Chapter 6, key events in Luke's narrative, namely the resurrection and ascension, mark the movement to the final period of history. An apprecia-

---

**335** For comparisons between the eschatological elements of synoptic parallels, see Maddox, *The Purpose*, who highlights the great continuity between the synoptic approaches in the pericopae in which Conzelmann, by contrast, suggested there was great disparity.
**336** Cf. 4 Ezra 5.1 – 12; 6.21 – 24; 2 Bar 26 – 28; 70.7; Matt 24.21 – 22, 19; Mark 13.19 – 20, 24.
**337** Cf. 2 Macc 7.9, 23, 29, 36; 12.43 – 45; *J.W.* 3.374; 2 Bar 30.3; Matt 12.41 – 42; 22.29 – 33; Mark 12.24 – 27.
**338** Cf. 1QM 1.5; 9.5 – 6; 15.2; 18.1; 4 Ezra 7.70; 9.18; 12.34; 13.58; 2 Bar 44.15; Matt 10.15; 11.22 – 24; 12.36 – 37, 41 – 42; 19.28.
**339** Cf. 2 Macc 7.14; 1QM 1.8; 2 Bar 15.2; 51.11 – 13; 54.15 – 16; 73.1 – 74.21; Matt 10.21 – 23; 19.28 – 29; 24.13 – 14; Mark 10.29 – 30; 13.12 – 13.
**340** Cf. 1QM 1.8 – 9; 15.1; 18.11 – 12; *Ant.* 10.210; 2 Bar 73.1; Matt 2.6; 10.6; 19.28 – 29; Mark 10.29 – 30.
**341** See Crabbe, "Being Found Fighting against God," 34; John A. Darr, "Irenic or Ironic? Another Look at Gamaliel before the Sanhedrin (Acts 5:33 – 42)," in *Literary Studies in Luke-Acts: Essays in Honor of Joseph B. Tyson*, ed. Richard P. Thompson and Thomas E. Phillips (Macon, GA: Mercer University Press, 1998), 139.
**342** Note that, although there are strong parallels between Stephen's speech and Paul's speech in Athens, the times of ignorance to which Paul refers are not directly analogous to the faults of which Stephen accuses his Jewish hearers. Neither is the specific form of ignorance in Acts 3.17 the same; see p. 126 n. 316.
**343** See further discussion in Chapter 6.

tion for Luke's sense of historical periodisation, as for texts like 4 Ezra and 2 Baruch, clarifies the importance of this transition (simultaneously challenging the approaches taken by both Conzelmann and Dibelius), while recognising its place within Luke's teleological schema.

## 4.3 The direction of history in Luke/Acts

Finally, for several writers of the key texts of this study, the direction of history is an essential part of how it is conceptualised, and intrinsically related to their explanations of the past, present, and future. But Luke is less concerned with such patterns. Certainly the events of the end brought about by Jesus' resurrection represent a cataclysmic shift. But according to Luke's rendering, in the time leading to this end, history neither improves steadily to achieve its *telos*, nor does it sharply decline as sign and catalyst of the end—although, as discussed in greater detail in Chapter 4, God's action in Jesus does draw out opposition that leads to affliction (Luke 16.29–31; 23.28–31; Acts 5.41; 9.16; 14.22).

Thus, the characteristic behaviour of humans can lead to opposition and suffering at any point throughout history. As for Diodorus Siculus, Luke's schema of history is shaped by an appreciation for consistent human failings, seen in Jesus' sayings and, for instance, in Stephen's historical review just prior to his martyrdom (cf. Luke 8.11–15; 13.1–5, 33–35; 20.9–19; Acts 7.2–53).[344] Rather than the type of continuous decline throughout history seen in 4 Ezra and 2 Baruch, with the historical present forming a nadir that will prompt the events of the end, Luke describes a past characterised by disobedience (Acts 7.2–53) and ignorance (Acts 17.30), arguably somewhat uniformly. Luke's schema affirms divine action across history and at its end, navigating a course between the teleological approaches of 4 Ezra and 2 Baruch, and Josephus, in which the stress falls respectively on history's nadir or on the positives of the (ultimately provisional) present.[345]

---

[344] See Chapter 5.
[345] This contrast between Luke/Acts and the *Jewish War* is seen also in the sense of urgency in Luke/Acts, which places greater emphasis on the affliction in current experience (Luke 12.11; 21.6, 12–24; Acts 14.22) and God's faithful action in intervening (Luke 2.68–79, 29–32; 12.32, cf. Matt 6.33; Luke 21.27–8; Acts 2.17–21, 32–39) than Josephus's relatively positive approach to the present (possibly affected by his political circumstances) and resultant lesser emphasis upon the events of the end (Crabbe, "Being Found Fighting against God," 39).

# 5 Conclusion

These comparisons of a range of texts of the Graeco-Roman period reveal the shared and distinctive elements of Luke's schema of history. Firstly, the discussion has highlighted that, as writers demonstrate an interest in events of the past and the end of history, they establish some continuities across all of history, including its end. In this way, in contrast to Conzelmann's influential hypothesis, writers demonstrate a clear capacity to hold together history and eschatology in teleological schemas. Moreover, writers from Diodorus Siculus to the writer of 2 Baruch depict periodisation in history, though the effects of such periodisation differ among texts. Some writers, such as Diodorus, Tacitus, or the writer of 2 Maccabees, may not attribute particular significance to the transitions between periods, whereas those like Polybius and the writers of 4 Ezra and 2 Baruch do. In many late Second Temple texts, periodisation enables writers to balance continuity across the course of history with significant transitions at key moments, without risking a sense of rupture in history.

Luke likewise maintains an interest in the course of history over time, from creation to the end of history. The connections of prophecy and fulfilment, between the events of Luke's narrative and the prophecies and events of the past, establish a continuity which also incorporates the events of the end. Thus, Luke's understanding is explicitly teleological. In this sense it is unlike anything hinted at by Diodorus Siculus, Valerius Maximus, or Tacitus. Similarly, though Polybius builds to a type of culmination across the region in Rome, unlike Virgil, he still foretells Rome's end.

However, as in many other late Second Temple texts, the events of the end also represent significant differences from earlier times—oppression will finally be brought to an end, with related cataclysmic changes to the current worldly order. Luke's understanding of the χρόνοι and καιροί of history draws on the type of periodised view of history set out in Daniel 2, balancing continuity with significant transitions and ultimately the unique achievement of the final transition to divine reign.

This chapter highlights a number of further points of interest for this study as a whole. If, as I have argued, Luke presents a view that history is periodised and teleological, then the types of comparisons with other texts from Luke's literary environment which scholars frequently undertake do not lend themselves to drawing out the significant eschatological implications of Luke's understanding of history. For instance, of those texts discussed, teleology is a feature of: Virgil's *Aeneid*, the War Scroll, Josephus's *Jewish War*, 4 Ezra, 2 Baruch, and, to a more limited extent, 2 Maccabees. These texts are also diverse in terms of where the writers place their emphasis or their treatment of end-time expectations. For instance, the key end-time event noted in 2 Maccabees is resurrection to eternal life for those judged righteous, while 4 Ezra and 2 Baruch refer to a full set of end-time events—notably events which Luke/Acts also explicitly affirms.

Crucially, aside from the *Jewish War*, the texts found to reflect a schema of history which is in some sense teleological are not those with which recent scholarship has generally put Luke/Acts in conversation—and as I have suggested, even then, comparisons to the *Jewish War* tend to be put to a different purpose. Significantly, where an examination is determined by questions of genre, and thus the key features of texts such as Polybius's *Histories* and Diodorus Siculus's *Library* become the focus, any teleological elements are likely to fall outside scholarly consideration.

Finally, from the discussion above it is already clear that a writer's schema of history relates inseparably to other claims, such as assertions of divine intervention in the events of 2 Maccabees or human responsibility for the decline of empires in Diodorus Siculus's *Library*. The following two chapters address questions about the processes that govern the course of history in the key texts: divine and human agency.

# Chapter 4:
# Determinism and divine guidance of history

*Spare your fears, Lady of Cythera; your children's fates abide unmoved. You will see Lavinium's city and its promised walls; and great-souled Aeneas you will raise on high to the starry heaven. No thought has turned me ... I will speak and, further unrolling the scroll of fate, will disclose its secrets ... Thus it is decreed.*

—Jupiter to Venus: Virgil, *Aeneid* 1.257–62, 283.

## 1 Introduction

In a dramatic scene in the *Aeneid*'s first book, Venus—grief-stricken at the repeated hardships endured by her son, Aeneas—confronts Jupiter (1.229–53). His response reveals the events to take place. Framing both the journey Aeneas will undertake across the epic and Virgil's interpretation of later Roman history, it sets out the mechanisms that ensure this path. Both god and fate determine the course. The certainty they represent shapes not only the reader's experience of the struggle that unfolds throughout the epic, but places Virgil's portrait of the sweep of history in the context of a divine declaration about the position of Rome and its *imperium sine fine*.

Such depictions of determinism—that is, the view that the events of history are fixed[1]—and divine guidance are important for writers' portrayals of history and its end. In exploring whether and how the study's key texts portray determinism and divine guidance, this chapter highlights further implications of how eschatology functions, with a bearing on related issues which have a similarly fraught legacy in Lukan studies—such as ancient writers' politics, explanations of suffering, and basis for hope.[2] The treatment here responds to two types

---

[1] Popović notes diverse conventions between disciplines in terminology related to "determinism." He contrasts philosophical approaches based on "a necessary chain of causation," with the type of historical determinism seen in apocalyptic texts, which relates to periodisation of history and its end (Mladen Popović, "Apocalyptic Determinism," in Collins, *The Oxford Handbook of Apocalyptic Literature*, 255; see full discussion pp. 255–70, esp. 255–58). Given my focus in this book, I consider determinism related to the structuring of history and ways writers portray the course of history as set—whether by divine forces like fate, or by personified gods.

[2] Representations of divine and human action significantly affect how a text's eschatology functions. For instance, if history is in decline, is that perceived as a result of divine failure to oversee events properly, divine punishment, inexorable fate, or human culpability? Alternatively, if history is understood to be continuing steadily, is that because the gods maintain an excellent balance or because they are not in any way involved with the human sphere? These

of scholarly approaches to Luke's account of the plan of God, exemplified in the work of Hans Conzelmann and John Squires. As noted in Chapter 1, for Conzelmann Luke's divine plan was part of his "solution" to the delayed parousia. By this understanding, the plan represented a kind of trade off—Luke sought to reassure his readers by affirming divine providential care over the events of history, as consolation for the loss of hope in imminent eschatological vindication.[3] By contrast, John Squires sought to set Luke's understanding of the divine plan in the context of Hellenistic historiographies, in which he recognised a "programmatic role" played by divine providence.[4]

Both Conzelmann and Squires are right to note the centrality of the divine plan in Luke/Acts. But in different ways, their analyses are shaped by assumptions that would be called into question by attending to a broader range of contemporaneous texts. Contrary to Conzelmann's theory, the texts of this study show that affirming belief in a divine plan does not mean a writer has equated God's purpose with historical (as opposed to eschatological) events. Rather, texts like the War Scroll, 4 Ezra, and 2 Baruch affirm that divine guidance governs the entire "course of times" (2 Bar 20.6). In such cases, divine oversight of the whole of history, including its end, provides confidence about the certainty of future events yet to be fulfilled.

Squires's treatment, on the other hand, helpfully illuminates some understandings Luke shares with other Hellenistic historiographies,[5] chiefly in relation to human response to divine providence. However, by tying his analysis to these historiographies only, he similarly overlooks the eschatological elements of the divine plan in Luke/Acts. Squires rightly recognises that Luke's approach to the plan of God relates to divine guidance of history, but the portrait of history he considers very rarely extends to the events of the end, which is perhaps unsurprising given most of his comparanda also do not reflect beliefs about the end of history.[6] Luke not only uses different terminology from the texts considered by

---

are the questions that animate the next two chapters' treatments of key texts, responding in particular in this chapter to Lukan scholarship that has considered divine agency within an emphatically uneschatological framework.

**3** Conzelmann, *Theology of St Luke*, 135. Key to Conzelmann's concerns here were the political consequences of identifying the divine purpose with historical events. See Chapter 1 above, which sets out the enduring influence of Conzelmann's hypothesis; scholars continue to build implicitly or explicitly on the theory that was guided by these assumptions.

**4** Squires, *The Plan of God*, 15, cf. 10–14.

**5** The key texts Squires considers across his study are Diodorus Siculus's *Library*, Dionysius of Halicarnassus's *Roman Antiquities*, and Josephus's *Antiquities*.

**6** Squires argues that the "logic" that holds together the "various strands of the Plan of God" in Luke's narrative lies in Luke's apologetic explanation on two key issues: Jesus' death and the

Squires and others who follow his lead, but his divine plan functions differently when it is understood not simply, for instance, as a mechanism for moral accountability, as is often the role of τύχη or πρόνοια in Diodorus Siculus, but as the basis for assurance about the events of the end of history.

Therefore, in examining evidence of determinism and divine guidance of history in these texts,[7] this chapter first analyses writers' depictions of the personal and impersonal forces which attract frequent attention in studies of Graeco-Roman texts, such as τύχη/*fortuna*, πρόνοια/*providentia*, and εἱμαρμένη/*fatum*. This includes attention to any ways in which these terms are relevant for Luke/Acts. I then consider how the writers present their views about determinism and divine guidance in their narratives, using their treatments of prophecies as the lens through which to illustrate these themes. Finally, I consider prophecy and the divine plan as they support Luke's portrayal of divine guidance of history.

This discussion highlights three features of divine guidance of the course of history in Luke/Acts. (1) Despite the numerous studies of the impact of genre and rhetoric on Luke/Acts, Luke makes strikingly little use of the characteristic language of Graeco-Roman historiographies on these themes, and nor can his portrayal be reduced to "mere" rhetoric.[8] (2) Luke's emphasis on the divine plan is

---

gentile mission (Squires, *The Plan of God*, 188–89, 190–94). Squires refers to the final judgement (p. 2), but eschatological events and future hope are not central to his understanding of Luke's divine plan (or of Josephus's *Antiquities*). Schulz's earlier examination of Graeco-Roman terminology and Luke's divine plan forcefully separates the plan from eschatological elements (Schulz, "Gottes Vorsehung," 105–6).

**7** Rather than a comprehensive study of all aspects of divine guidance in each text, the chapter focuses on those elements that will illuminate the implications for Luke's eschatology. For detailed treatments of a wider range of questions, see Susanne Bobzien, *Determinism and Freedom in Stoic Philosophy* (Oxford: Clarendon, 1998) (on philosophical texts); D. C. Feeney, *The Gods in Epic: Poets and Critics of the Classical Tradition* (Oxford: Clarendon, 1991), Braund, "Virgil and the Cosmos," and Galinsky, *Augustan Culture* (on Virgil); Mueller, *Roman Religion in Valerius* (on Valerius Maximus); and, for more general treatments, Gabriele Boccaccini, "Inner-Jewish Debate on the Tension between Divine and Human Agency in Second Temple Judaism," in Barclay and Gathercole, *Divine and Human Agency*, 9–26, and Arnaldo Momigliano, "Popular Religious Beliefs and the Late Roman Historians," in *Essays in Ancient and Modern Historiography*, 141–59.
**8** See studies such as Rothschild, *Luke-Acts and the Rhetoric*, Squires, *The Plan of God*, Cancik, "The History," 679–95, and Sterling, *Historiography and Self-Definition*. See also criticism of Rothschild in Uytanlet, *Luke-Acts and Jewish Historiography*, 78–79 and Bauspieß, *Geschichte und Erkenntnis*, 277, and of Squires in Tannehill, review of *The Plan of God* (by Squires), 428 and John A. Darr, review of *The Plan of God in Luke-Acts*, by John T. Squires, *CBQ* 57 (1995): 191–92, where reviewers saw a need for greater engagement with Jewish texts.

not about a "false sacralisation"[9] of events in history at the expense of eschatology, but, as for writers like that of 2 Baruch or the War Scroll, part of his broader view that the entire teleological schema of history is overseen by the biblical God, whose faithfulness assures the future. (3) And yet, rather than being grounded in a view that history is pre-programmed, Luke's portrait of divine guidance leaves space for human participation or opposition—to which, Luke's reader should nonetheless be assured, the divine plan can inexorably adapt. Thus, Luke's account of a definite, unfolding divine plan serves his explanation of past events and assurance for the future.

## 2 The forces in history

In the classic epics of Homer, Herodotus's historiography, and other earlier Greek texts, the gods are characters in the plot and essential to its unfolding. Writers of the Hellenistic period[10] have typically moved away from these traditions.[11] How-

---

[9] Flender's terminology (Flender, *St Luke*, 106), although, as noted in Chapter 1, this reflects a concern shared by many post-war biblical scholars.

[10] This tendency appears earlier in Thucydides, who sets out a rigorous, even scientific, method for his historiography. However, even he includes an appreciation for the role of τύχη in influencing events. Francis MacDonald Cornford, writing in 1907, influentially emphasised the need to set aside what he described as "the Modernist Fallacy"—that is, the assumption that because Thucydides shared some views with contemporary historical approaches about providing accounts of events, that he also presumed an underlying natural law of cause and effect behind these events thereby making any reference to τύχη incongruous (Francis MacDonald Cornford, *Thucydides Mythistoricus* (London: Arnold, 1907), 103–4). Cornford initially gives a detailed discussion of a key example, the occupation of Pylos in Book 4, to illustrate (82–109). While suggesting on the basis of small details in the account that Thucydides has overlooked or downplayed some elements of "what really happened" (simultaneously also exposing the preoccupations of his own intellectual setting), Cornford notes the key role played by τύχη in Thucydides's account, from the initial storm which contrives to place the soldiers in the right place at the right time, to the inversion (a characteristic effect of τύχη) that results in land soldiers fighting at sea and sailors on land. He rightly concludes that Thucydides's conception of history leads him to attribute particular actions to τύχη as a non-human agent in interpreting the events in his narrative, and that this "metaphysical belief" (p. 108) is in keeping with his other focus on explanations through human foresight. Such views in Thucydides are reflected in later, Hellenistic and Roman historians.

[11] Bernard F. Dick, "*Fatum* and *Fortuna* in Lucan's *Bellum Civile*," *Classical Philology* 62 (1967): 240; S. H. Braund, ed. and trans., *Lucan: Civil War* (Oxford: Clarendon, 1992), xxii, xxviii; Walbank, "Fortune (*Tychē*) in Polybius," 353. As background to his discussion of Diodorus Siculus, Sacks notes Aristotle's "four types of forces at work in the world: human agency (τὸ δι' ἀνθρώπου), divine intellect (νοῦς), nature (φύσις), and fortune or chance (τύχη)" (Sacks, *Diodo-

ever, as noted by Samson Uytanlet, even where writers claim to limit the role of gods in their texts, their narratives remain "*theological* in nature."[12] These writers attribute influence to forces such as τύχη/*fortuna* and εἱμαρμένη/*fatum*; as, for instance, Bernard Dick asserts of Lucan's *Civil War*: "If we must have a substitute for the absent deities of the *Bellum Civile*, then it would be more correct to say *Fortuna* and *fatum* fill the void left by the discarded divine machinery."[13] This is true also for several texts of this study. Moreover, Jewish Hellenistic writers that invoke these new traditions, such as Josephus's appropriation of τύχη, also apply them in their own ways. Perhaps paradoxically, Josephus adapts characteristic terms from non-Jewish Hellenistic texts, which in part function in those texts to draw attention *away* from a divine role in history,[14] in order to assert God's action.[15]

It is important, therefore, to consider these texts in light of the diverse ways in which writers adapt these terms[16]—although it is impossible in the space here to offer an exhaustive analysis. I focus on those aspects that illustrate representations of determinism or divine guidance of history, rather than, for instance, extended questions about divine character or related archaeological evidence for forms of cultic piety associated with the divine forces. Portrayals of divine action in Graeco-Roman historiographies constitute a significant area of interest in Lukan studies. This discussion demonstrates both the different ways writers use key terms and, crucially, that Luke makes very limited use of any of the technical language for forces within history—though the term δεῖ represents an important exception.

---

*rus Siculus*, 36). Sacks also adds ἀνάγκη in his discussion of Diodrous (p. 36 n. 53), which is a force discussed further below.

**12** Uytanlet, *Luke-Acts and Jewish Historiography*, 33. Uytanlet criticises Marguerat for arguing the reverse (p. 33 n. 32).

**13** Dick, "*Fatum* and *Fortuna*," 240. In comparing *fatum* and *fortuna* in Lucan, Dick argues that Lucan uses the terms at times apparently interchangeably, although he does at specific points demonstrate that they can be distinguished (for example, as in the proem to Book 2). At such points, he argues Lucan indicates: "Fate is inexorable, fortune uncertain and erratic" (Dick, "*Fatum* and *Fortuna*," 236, cf. also pp. 238, 240–41).

**14** Braund, *Lucan*, xxiii.

**15** I therefore discuss Josephus alongside non-Jewish Graeco-Roman texts, given some similarities in lexicon, while distinguishing the differences in the ways he uses the terms. There are also differences of meaning across non-Jewish texts.

**16** Though he makes some helpful observations, Uytanlet's synchronic approach (cf. Uytanlet, *Luke-Acts and Jewish Historiography*, 33) unhelpfully intermingles references from Herodotus to Tacitus, and thus elides some important distinctions, including limited attention to differences between personified deities and the different uses of terms such as τύχη or πρόνοια within and across his texts.

## 2.1 τύχη/fortuna

Τύχη/*fortuna* appears extensively in many of the texts under discussion though, even within the same texts, the term can be used diversely. **Polybius** uses τύχη in notoriously varied ways.[17] Given his stated interest in teaching future leaders how to avoid the pitfalls into which characters in his historiography stumble, he focuses on describing events in human terms,[18] whereas τύχη, as "fortune" or "chance," generally becomes a catchall term for the agent or cause of those events over which humans have no control and an explanation of last resort (cf. 36.17.2–4).[19] Polybius sets human action within the parameters of the power of τύχη, which can be characterised, for instance, as acting "like a good umpire" (1.58.1), as in a narrated battle between the Romans and Carthaginians under the leadership of Hamilcar. Here the fight (which Polybius initially describes with the image of "a boxing match between two champions" (1.57.1)), was evenly matched and neither side was able to defeat the other, until τύχη "shifted the scene in a remarkable manner and changed the nature of the contest, confining both in a narrower field, where the struggle grew even more desperate" (1.58.1). The battle continues until both parties are exhausted, and eventually Rome is the winner (1.63.4) by returning instead to a sea battle under a rigorous new training discipline (1.59.4–12, cf. 1.60.4–6). Thus, according to Polybius here, τύχη alters the conditions under which a battle is conducted, but the human agents continue to strive for victory under their own efforts.[20]

Importantly, for Polybius τύχη plays a crucial role in influencing the transitions between political regimes. In the case of Demetrius's prophecy about the fall of Persia and rise of Macedon discussed in Chapter 3 (29.21), which estab-

---

[17] At times τύχη in Polybius approaches a personified deity, whereas elsewhere it can signify "pure chance," or even function as a metaphor (Walbank, "Fortune (*Tychē*) in Polybius," 351, 354).

[18] Walbank, "Fortune (*Tychē*) in Polybius," 350–1. Eckstein also emphasises Polybius's interest in ethical instruction, not simply strategic military or political learning (Arthur M. Eckstein, *Moral Vision in the Histories of Polybius*, Hellenistic Culture and Society 16 (London: University of California Press, 1995), 281–82).

[19] Walbank, "Fortune (*Tychē*) in Polybius," 354. Although see, for instance, 1.35.2 and 1.35.5, where Polybius identifies τύχη *and* practical reasons as causes for the same event (cf. Walbank, "Fortune (*Tychē*) in Polybius," 352). For discussion of the ways Thucydides balances τύχη and human foresight (γνώμη), so that for instance τύχη can create the conditions for the Athenians' positive military outcome while a failure of human judgement at the same time causes the Spartans to lose, see Cornford, *Thucydides Mythistoricus*, 108.

[20] See discussion of the setting here in Robin Waterfield and Brian McGing, eds. and trans., *Polybius: The Histories* (Oxford: Oxford University Press, 2010), 451.

lishes a pattern of regime changes, the theme Polybius draws out is that τύχη lends "blessings" to enable the rule "until she decides to deal differently with them (ἄλλο τι βουλεύσηται περὶ αὐτῶν)" (29.21.6–7).²¹ Beyond simply effecting change through occasional changes of favour, Polybius also presents τύχη as a force which *drives* the course of history; τύχη is intimately involved in Rome's rise.²² Polybius opines that the current time is "the finest and most beneficent of the performances of τύχη ... she has not in a single instance ever accomplished such a work, ever achieved such a triumph, as in our own times (οἷον τὸ καθ' ἡμᾶς)" (1.4.1–5).²³ Although Polybius applies τύχη in diverse ways, when it comes to big movements of history, τύχη constitutes the underlying force.²⁴

**Diodorus Siculus** also links τύχη to his key themes. Kenneth Sacks observes, "although it occurs 'only' about two hundred fifty times, τύχη is the most prevalent and variable force found in the *Bibliotheke*. It plays so many different roles in the narrative that, as in Polybius's history, it ranges from a rhetorical device to a true goddess."²⁵

Diodorus describes the "incredible fickleness" of τύχη. He reflects, "for who, taking thought of the inconsistencies of human life would not be astonished at the ebb and flow of τύχη?" (18.59.4–5). However, characteristically, Diodorus also connects changes of fortune to moral lessons. Even τύχη's unpredictability provides lessons in virtue, about bearing changes of fortune well. But τύχη acts

---

**21** Diodorus also includes this episode (*Library* 31.10). See below.
**22** Plutarch makes similar attributions about the role of τύχη in supporting the founding of Rome, going on to explain that "the Roman state would not have attained to its present power, had it not been of a divine origin" (Plu. *Rom.* 8.7).
**23** Walbank captures Polybius's sense of τύχη as an overarching force of history as he summarises Polybius's understanding: "history is the work of *Tyche*, just as his πραγματεία is the work of P." (Walbank, *A Historical Commentary*, 43). Indeed, as discussed in Chapter 3 above, the breadth of τύχη's programmatic influence and the uniqueness of her achievement in the Roman empire ground Polybius's claims about the need for "universal" historiography.
**24** In a later work, Walbank suggests Polybius sometimes comes near to Stoic Providence in portrayals of τύχη, perhaps unaware he is mixing them, venturing also that Polybius's "constant use of the word with various shades of meaning may indicate that he was not alert to all its ambiguities" (Frank W. Walbank, "The Idea of Decline in Polybius," in *Polybius, Rome and the Hellenistic World: Essays and Reflections* (Cambridge: Cambridge University Press, 2002), 211).
**25** Sacks, *Diodorus Siculus*, 38. Sacks notes that Diodorus also uses θεός more frequently (approximately a thousand times) but not in a way that is generally causative. He goes on to note: "if book 16 has a greater concentration, several of the references are to the Phocian sack of Delphi in the Third Sacred War, for which divine vengeance as a theme would be expected" (pp. 36–37 n. 56; see also §3.1 below). As always with Diodorus, sections which exhibit slightly different emphases, such as in Book 16, prompt discussion about whether this arises primarily from his sources.

especially as a force of accountability for immoderation and arrogance—as, for example, for the Carthaginians:

> with such swiftness did τύχη work a change in the affairs of the Carthaginians, and point out to all ἄνθρωποι that those who become elated above due measure quickly give proof of their own weakness. (14.76.1–4)

In the fragmentary later sections, as he recounts examples of good and bad conduct in earlier regimes, Diodorus summarises, "τύχη is wont to veer towards what is morally fitting, and to involve those who have contrived some injustice against others in the same difficulties themselves" (37.17). He continues with a further warning, reflecting on the consequences of immoderate behaviour: "perhaps in the present (κατὰ τὸ παρόν) they exercise tyrannical power, but later (ὕστερον) they will have to render an accounting for their tyrannical crimes" (37.17). According to Diodorus, it is τύχη which will act to right the balance.

Thus, for Diodorus, τύχη's favour plays a particular role in political success and, as noted in Chapter 3, explains the transition between empires in moral terms.[26] But Diodorus does not present this as part of any master plan.[27] When he incorporates Polybius's account of Demetrius's prophecy about Persia and Macedon (31.10; cf. Polyb. *Hist.* 29.21), he does so in the context of gathering together stories to emphasise the power and unpredictability of τύχη[28] and inserts comments to stress that no one could have predicted these transitions in advance, underscoring the need for humility in the face of potential changes of fortune. Moreover, a fall from favour with τύχη, though inscrutable,[29] may itself derive from her revised assessment of the current regime's virtue (cf. 14.76.1;

---

[26] Τύχη reverses the fortunes of Greece (Diod. *Library* 12.1.2–4; for further examples, Sacks, *Diodorus Siculus*, 38 n. 68).

[27] Comparing Diodorus and Polybius, Sacks argues that for Diodorus τύχη never achieves the sense of a driving force of history. However, he also observes that, in any case, Diodorus's "approach to political and military actions is far less synthetic" (Sacks, *Diodorus Siculus*, 38), and "Diodorus rarely accounts for long-term causes and developments" (p. 39). On Polybius, see Sacks, *Polybius*, 123.

[28] Walbank, *A Historical Commentary*, 3:393.

[29] Translators appear to take a broader picture into account in these treatments of τύχη; in the LCL editions, the same term is translated the "cruelty of fortune" in Polybius, but the "inscrutability of fortune" in Diodorus Siculus (τὸ τῆς τύχης χαλεπόν; Polyb. *Hist.* 29.21.4; Diod. *Library* 31.10.1).

31.10.2). Diodorus simply emphasises the consequences of immoderate behaviour and the constant vulnerability to changes of fortune.[30]

Similarly to Polybius, **Josephus** also draws on the idea of τύχη lending favour to the Romans (having "moved over to them from all sides," *J.W.* 5.367; cf. 3.354), as noted in Chapter 3. But for Josephus, τύχη works in tandem with θεός.[31] Τύχη lends favour, but θεός determines the rule of each regime in turn (5.367) and thus fulfils the broader role of guiding history in an overarching sense that is missing from Diodorus's account but attributed to τύχη by Polybius. Τύχη is not an explanation of last resort for Josephus, but something essential to his understanding of the way history unfolds.[32] Josephus may flag his connections to Graeco-Roman traditions by employing the technical term, but as he attributes to τύχη a sense of divine agency and uses it in tandem with explicitly theistic words, he presents a picture of regime changes overseen by God which is consistent with his Jewish tradition (cf. *Ant.* 10.210, 277–80).[33]

The Roman understanding of *fortuna* extends elements of these images of τύχη, though Russell Scott argues that depictions of *fortuna* by writers like **Tacitus** are "demonstrably Roman," not merely re-presentations of τύχη,[34] and tied to Roman religion as a "real causal factor acting in history."[35] Tacitus subscribes to the notion of fortune's favour of a given regime, associating *fortuna* with the

---

**30** Sacks identifies a range of further examples: 9.2.2; 12.1.2; 14.46.4; 17.20.1; 17.101.2; 18.8.7; 19.42.5; 19.108.2; 20.99.1; 21.11; 22.13.6; 26.24.2; 31.12; 32.10.5; 34/35.28.2–3, 30c; 36.5.3; 36.7.2 (Sacks, *Diodorus Siculus*, 38 n. 68).
**31** Josephus commonly refers to θεός in relation to πρόνοια and τύχη in a surrounding sentence (Schwartz, "Josephus, Catullus, and the Date," 339). Vespasian's rule is attributed to τύχη (and πρόνοια) in *J.W.* 4.622, but in 3.6 and 5.2 to θεός. The close association between τύχη and θεός is exemplified in *J.W.* 5.367 (Gray, *Prophetic Figures*, 40).
**32** Rajak, *Josephus*, 101.
**33** Although Hellenistic traditions never function merely as a container for Jewish ideas in Josephus's writings (contra Bilde, *Flavius Josephus*, 205), he does use terms like τύχη, alongside θεός and πρόνοια, to recount a thoroughly Jewish story about God and God's people (Cohen, "Polybius, Jeremiah, and Josephus," 369). Attridge emphasises rightly that form and content cannot be easily separated (Attridge, *The Interpretation of Biblical History*, 182) and, suggesting that Josephus tells a Jewish story, Rajak notes he incorporates stylistic elements of each (Rajak, *Josephus*, 102). Ultimately Josephus's style is also indicative not only of a use of multiple traditions but the broader Hellenisation of Jewish communities themselves, which renders attempts to separate Hellenistic from Jewish elements inappropriate (see Hengel, *Judaism and Hellenism*, 1:103–6; and for discussion of acculturation in diverse diaspora communities see Barclay, *Jews in the Mediterranean Diaspora*, 399–400).
**34** Scott, *Religion and Philosophy*, 71.
**35** Scott, *Religion and Philosophy*, 84.

empire.³⁶ In his *Histories,* from Book 2 onwards he emphasises the *fortuna Flaviana,* and particularly of Vespasian (*Hist.* 2.1; cf. 3.1).³⁷ As Tacitus describes those who strategically (and rather opportunistically) begin to address Vespasian as emperor, he claims "their minds suddenly turned from fears to confidence in fortune's favour" (2.80). And he has Vocula passionately defend Rome's resilience in the face of civil war, saying "there are still left faithful provinces ... there still remain victorious armies, the fortune of the empire (*fortunam imperii*), and the avenging gods (*ultores deos*)" (4.57). Vocula goes on to assert that punishment by fates and gods will still be exacted for "those who break treaties" (4.57).

For **Valerius Maximus** everyday mishaps or calamities are attributed to *fortuna.* The anecdotes frequently illustrate reversals of fortune with a didactic or entertaining barb (cf. 6.9; 7.1). According to Valerius, observing the effects of *fortuna* on others "can add much confidence to our minds and take away much anxiety, whether we look at our own situations or those of our neighbours" (6.9.praef). *Fortuna* or its absence can also explain characters' actions, or even capacities, as in the case of Alexander, to whom Valerius claims *fortuna* had not supplied the necessary prudence for him to act on the warning provided by a prophetic dream (1.7.ext2). The greater bulk of examples reflect *fortuna*'s "volatility." Valerius surmises, "she loves to inflict adversity but only grudgingly vouchsafes prosperity" (7.1.praef). But he then introduces examples of good fortune with the claim that, once *fortuna* has "commanded herself to forget her malignity, she heaps blessings not only many and great but also enduring" (7.1.praef).³⁸

Importantly, in Rome *fortuna* becomes entwined with imperial office. Lydia Matthews's study of *fortuna* in Roman religious settings, literary texts, coins, and philosophy demonstrates that the negative portrayals of *fortuna* as capricious are only evident in literary texts, while inscriptions, coins, and other sources are

---

**36** See below on this relationship.
**37** Scott, *Religion and Philosophy,* 70. Scott emphasises the interaction between *fortuna* and responsibility for Tacitus, in keeping with his contemporaries (p. 70). He asserts, "They are important principles for Tacitus as he writes: the pessimism dictated by the events of the times and by the view that Roman society held of itself in any age, the *fortuna* of Vespasian, the wrath of the gods and the faults of men [sic]. They all have their basis in Roman religious ethical concepts and can be shown, I think, to have had no less importance for Tacitus than for other Roman writers" (pp. 52–53).
**38** On Valerius Maximus and other popular understandings of τύχη/*fortuna*, including the belief that fortune balances things out (and the hope that, if one must gain attention from *fortuna,* it may at least not be all *bad* fortune), see Morgan, *Popular Morality,* 242–43.

consistently positive.³⁹ Popular piety reveals a devotion to *fortuna* that connects significantly with beliefs about maintaining the empire. Here *fortuna*, once connected to a particular person, Matthews argues, became associated instead with an office, allowing continuous attributions of favour through "de-personalised Imperial *fortunae*."⁴⁰ The close relationship between imperial power and *fortuna* in turn gave rise to the kind of sceptical treatments of *fortuna* offered by Ovid and Lucan; by criticising *fortuna* the writers were able subtly to criticise the imperial powers.⁴¹

Thus, τύχη/*fortuna* takes on a wide range of meanings and purposes for these writers, even within the same text. Τύχη/*fortuna* can explain individual mishaps, particular καιροί of advantage for certain groups or leaders, drive the course of history, or confirm imperial power over time. As a random force, it can prompt virtue and humility or enable the kind of flexibility that gives readers hope that the future might be more positive—or it can become uncomfortably unpredictable when compared to the justice and reliability attributed instead to *fatum*. I return to the theme of ancient comparisons of *fortuna* and *fatum* below.

Finally, given its importance to popular piety and a broad range of texts discussed here, it is salutary to note texts in which τύχη does not appear. Although **2 Maccabees** makes considerable use of the related verb, τυγχάνω,⁴² this underscores the significance of the omission of the noun τύχη itself,⁴³ especially given its Hellenistic style.⁴⁴ In one use of the verb in 2 Macc 6.22, in the third person singular active aorist subjunctive, (τύχῃ), it is possible that some indirect allusion to the idea of the divine force is in fact intended, but the connotations are negative. It comes in the context of "friends" attempting to persuade Eleazar to feign compliance with Antiochus's dietary stipulations (to "attain" kindness), and is possibly reminiscent of another meal setting in which libations to τύχη set up a contrast between curses and blessings in Isa 65.11 LXX.⁴⁵

---

**39** Lydia Matthews, "Roman Constructions of Fortuna" (DPhil diss., University of Oxford, 2012), 100. Matthews observes the prevalence of *fortuna* in the public sphere, including, for instance: "between AD 68 and 235 there are very few years in which coins showing *fortuna* were not minted" (p. 5).
**40** Matthews, "Roman Constructions of Fortuna," 4; cf. Scott, *Religion and Philosophy*, 76.
**41** Matthews, "Roman Constructions of Fortuna," 4; Dick, "*Fatum* and *Fortuna*," 238.
**42** 2 Macc 3.9; 4.6, 32; 5.8–9; 6.2, 22; 9.1; 13.7; 14.6, 10; 15.7. Note also the use of μόρῳ (from μόρος, one's "appointed doom" or "fate") alongside τυχόντα in 13.7, referring to the death of Menelaus.
**43** Codex A includes τύχην as a variant reading for ψυχήν in 2 Macc 7.37, but Bauernfeind rightly notes in *TDNT* (8:240 n. 18) that this must be secondary.
**44** Bauernfeind, *TDNT* 8:240.
**45** Childs sees in Isa 65.11 a reference to some form of "sacred meal" (Brevard S. Childs, *Isaiah*, OTL (Louisville: Westminster John Knox, 2001), 536–37). Similarly, see Gad/τύχη in Gen 30.11.

**Fourth Ezra**'s Latin text does not mention *fortuna* and, though the languages are clearly different, nothing approaching the idea appears in the **War Scroll** or **2 Baruch**. These were prevalent ideas, and the signs of Hellenism within Second Temple Judaism are well documented.⁴⁶ But only Josephus from among the Jewish authors discussed sees fit to incorporate τύχη into his account in a positive sense,⁴⁷ and even then he does so in order to draw attention to divine involvement in history that is consistent with his heritage.⁴⁸

The only use of τύχη in the NT is found in Codex Bezae in **Luke**'s parable of the Good Samaritan, in the "chance" arrival of the priest on the same road as the beaten person (Luke 10.31). In this variant reading κατὰ τύχα replaces κατὰ συγκυρίαν,⁴⁹ though the passage does not give any other indication that the term should be read with the stronger sense of a personal divine force having acted to bring the priest into the area. Nothing in Luke's narrative suggests a sense of a personal or impersonal divine force like chance or fortune,⁵⁰ even though, as discussed in Chapter 5 below, Luke does make use of themes of reversal. So often associated with τύχη/*fortuna* in Graeco-Roman texts, reversal in Luke/Acts comes about not through the unpredictable whims of τύχη, but as a direct result of negative responses to the Lord's favour.⁵¹

### 2.2 πρόνοια/*providentia*

Some writers imply considerable overlap between τύχη and πρόνοια ("providence," or "foresight"). Although Frank Walbank suggests that when **Polybius** portrays τύχη in the manner of the driving force of history, he approaches the

---

46 See p. 36 n. 70.
47 This is particularly true of the *Jewish War*. By the time he writes the *Antiquities*, Josephus has shifted his preferences to πρόνοια τοῦ θεοῦ, especially in the first half (Cohen, "Polybius, Jeremiah, and Josephus," 374).
48 Rajak, *Josephus*. As discussed further in Chapter 5, this adaptation to Jewish tradition includes both Deuteronomistic explanations of the past and deterministic expectations for the future akin to those set out in apocalypses (see also Crabbe, "Being Found Fighting against God," 23–26).
49 This is a *hapax legomenon* in the NT. P⁷⁵ᶜ uses συντυχία, with the same meaning (cf. Fitzmyer, *The Gospel according to Luke*, 2:887). These are all simply variants for "chance" or "coincidence."
50 In *TDNT*, Bauernfiend notes the significance of the (surely deliberate) absence of the noun from the NT, despite uses of τυγχάνω (8:242).
51 These themes are also evident in HB texts (1 Sam 2.1–10; cf. Luke 1.46–55), and other Second Temple texts (cf. 1QM 14.6, 10–11).

Stoic understanding of Providence,⁵² Polybius does not use πρόνοια itself in this sense. Instead, he uses πρόνοια in the sense of human foresight, except in a couple of instances when describing popular assumptions about divine πρόνοια. For instance, Polybius praises Scipio's strategy for inspiring his soldiers prior to battle by claiming that Neptune appeared to him in a dream, supplying the battle plan and promises of assistance (θεοῦ πρόνοια, 10.11.8; cf. 23.17.10).⁵³ Elsewhere, Polybius parallels Scipio with Lycurgus, claiming that the latter was not superstitious (Polybius disparages superstition), but sought Pythian confirmation of his own excellent instincts to make his course of action publicly acceptable (10.2.12). Thus he says, Scipio "similarly made the men under his command more sanguine and more ready to face perilous enterprises by instilling into them the belief that his projects were divinely inspired" (10.2.12).⁵⁴ Thus, even when revered military figures refer to divine guidance, the focus for Polybius remains on their skill in exploiting the religious beliefs of others for pragmatic advantage.

For **Diodorus Siculus**, πρόνοια interacts importantly with human action—indeed, right human action can support the work of divine πρόνοια.⁵⁵ As noted in Chapter 3, Diodorus believes that because of the benefits of learning from past events, by compiling their accounts historians become "as it were, ministers of Divine Providence (ὑπουργοὶ τῆς θείας προνοίας)" (1.1.3).⁵⁶ He goes on to describe his understanding of πρόνοια:

> Providence, having brought the orderly arrangement of the visible stars and the natures of ἄνθρωποι together into one common relationship, continually directs their courses through

---

**52** Walbank, "The Idea of Decline," 211. These views of πρόνοια are evident in philosophical works by Seneca and Cicero. There is some evidence of personification of *Providentia* as a deity (including *Providentia Augusta* and *Providentia Deorum*), but this survives only on coins (Karin Schlapbach, "Providentia," *BNP* 12:82).
**53** Polybius goes on: "The combination in this speech of accurate calculation, of the promise of gold crowns, and therewithal of confidence in the help of θεοῦ πρόνοια created great enthusiasm and ardour among the soldiers" (10.11.8; cf. 10.2.12; 23.17.10). See also Chapter 5 §4.1.
**54** Polybius also praises Scipio for "relying (πιστεύω) not on τύχη but on inference from the facts (συλλογισμός)" (10.7.4). Though without any of the same sense of scepticism, 2 Macc 15.11 offers a similar incident in which Judas Maccabeus strengthens the soldiers for battle by recounting a dream that is presented as a divinely inspired insight.
**55** Sacks, *Diodorus Siculus*, 36, 64. On Stoic influence, see Burton, *Diodorus Siculus*, 36.
**56** Burton suggests that Diodorus's understanding of πρόνοια may arise from his sources, particularly Posidonius, though he uses a different lexical style (Burton, *Diodorus Siculus*, 36).

all eternity, apportioning to each that which falls to it by the direction of fate (τὸ ἐπιβάλλον ἑκάστοις ἐκ τῆς πεπρωμένης μερίζουσα).⁵⁷ (1.1.3)

Here Diodorus's explicit association between divine πρόνοια and the role of historians highlights his sense that the purpose of universal historiography is to support the work of πρόνοια in facilitating benefit and progress in history.[58]

**Valerius Maximus** uses divine *providentia* rarely,[59] though he does, for instance, conjecture, "but divine providence, I think, (*sed, credo, deorum providentia*)" ensured two characters received "the outcome they deserved," as he recounts a narrative which ends with poetic justice (7.6.3). Elsewhere Valerius muses, if (only) it had been possible to rectify a situation by divine *providentia*, but it wasn't (5.3.ext3f). But there is no sense that *providentia* directs history.

By contrast, **Josephus** uses τύχη and divine πρόνοια in interesting and perhaps parallel ways.[60] Though both terms appear in the *Jewish War* and *Antiquities*,[61] after extensive uses of τύχη in the former, it is almost absent from the first half of the *Antiquities* (five appearances in Books 1–10). It seems, rather, that Josephus prefers πρόνοια τοῦ θεοῦ to describe divine activity in the biblical narratives. Importantly, as with τύχη, Josephus maintains connections with the God of his tradition,[62] of which πρόνοια becomes an attribute or function. In a particularly potent image, Josephus presents divine πρόνοια at the helm of the ship of history, as he defends belief in the biblical God with polemic against what he characterises as an Epicurean disregard for divine guidance of history (*Ant.* 10.277–80).[63] Given this appears in his interpretation of Daniel's visions,[64]

---

**57** Note that this is a different form of the "fate" lexeme. There are lexical connections between these ideas (μερίζω and μείρομαι, from which εἱμαρμένη is derived) but, as I note below, the standard form (εἱμαρμένη) does not appear in Diodorus. The noun μοῖρα appears four times: 1.73; 5.28; 9.20; 15.64. Squires includes μοῖρα more broadly in his understanding of fate (Squires, *The Plan of God*, 159), though in practice the "divisions" Diodorus refers to can be very domestic, such as to do with the division of land.
**58** Sacks observes that Diodorus does not make a connection between πρόνοια and history akin to Polybius's association of Rome and τύχη (Sacks, *Diodorus Siculus*, 120).
**59** *Providentia* appears in twenty passages across the nine books.
**60** For instance, in *J.W.* 3.391, Josephus says his insight and survival at Jotapata was "by τύχη, or really by πρόνοια τοῦ θεοῦ" (see discussion in Schwartz, "Josephus, Catullus, and the Date," 338).
**61** See also, for instance, *Life* 15; 425.
**62** He also frequently uses δαιμονίου πρόνοια, including in the *Jewish War* (e.g. 1.82; 2.457; 4.622; 7.82, 318) and πρόνοια τοῦ θεοῦ (*J.W.* 3.28, 144, 391 (as above); 4.219, 366; 7.453).
**63** See discussion in W. C. van Unnik, "An Attack on the Epicureans by Flavius Josephus," in *Romanitas et Christianitas: Studia Iano Henrico Waszink A. D. VI Kal. Nov. A. MCMLXXIII XIII lus-*

vehemently asserting their accuracy, it also incorporates a sense that πρόνοια's navigation through history extends to the final events of the installation of a divine reign, to which the visions point.

Where πρόνοια appears in the **LXX** and **NT**, it relates only to human foresight (cf. 2 Macc 4.6; Rom 13.14). In Acts 24.2, Paul opens his speech before Felix by complimenting the governor's πρόνοια; no use of πρόνοια τοῦ θεοῦ appears in Luke/Acts. However, Squires argues for a programmatic role for providence across Hellenistic historiographies, and suggests that without using the term πρόνοια itself, Luke's portrayal of a divine plan nonetheless displays a similar understanding.[65] The discussion below demonstrates that the divine plan relates in important ways to Luke's understanding of divine guidance of the past, present, and *end* of history, indicating some important differences from other uses of πρόνοια or *providentia* as divine foresight or guidance over particular events within a more limited scope (as, for example, for Valerius Maximus or even Diodorus Siculus). Nonetheless, depictions of divine guidance *interacting* with human participation, such as in Diodorus's portrait of divine πρόνοια and the role of the historian, do reflect interests in Luke/Acts, as discussed in relation to human participation and the βουλὴ τοῦ θεοῦ at §4.2 below. This dynamic contrasts strongly with the inflexibility of εἱμαρμένη/*fatum*.[66]

## 2.3 εἱμαρμένη/*fatum*

Fate enters into texts as both a force in the narrative and a signpost of philosophical debates. With the literal sense of having been apportioned (the perfect passive participle of μείρομαι, "receive as one's portion"), εἱμαρμένη indicates outcomes that are both unalterable and predetermined.[67] *Fatum*'s origin in the verb

---

*tra complenti oblata*, ed. W. den Boer et al. (Amsterdam: North-Holland Publishing, 1973), 344–45, and at §3.3.2 below.
64 Josephus's other treatment of Daniel in the *Antiquities* is discussed in more detail in Chapters 3 and 6.
65 Squires, *The Plan of God*, 20.
66 Some Stoic texts do associate πρόνοια with causal determinism. See Bobzien, *Determinism and Freedom*, 46–47; on Stoic views of causal determinism and necessity, see also discussion at §2.4.
67 There are a number of other related Greek terms translated "fate," though they do not always have this particular meaning. The focus here remains on the key term εἱμαρμένη, rather than attempting an exhaustive concordance of terms which can take diverse meanings. However, it is particularly worth noting, as discussed above in n. 57, that μοῖρα is etymologically related to μείρομαι, from which εἱμαρμένη is derived. Μοῖρα is used twice in the extant text of Polybius,

to speak (*for*), similarly underscores its sense of having been set in advance; though Ronald Martin argues that *fatum* reflects a stronger association with *divine* guidance than the Greek εἱμαρμένη.[68] For some writers, the inflexibility of εἱμαρμένη/*fatum* problematises human responsibility, leading to a preference for τύχη/*fortuna*, whereas for others *fatum* represents the reliability and justice that is missing from the fickleness of *fortuna*.

In Jupiter's introduction to his prophecy in Book 1 of the *Aeneid*, with which this chapter began, **Virgil** plays on the certainty of *fatum*, both for the *vaticinium ex eventu* that follows and the remainder of the epic to which it leads. Jupiter's words pun with *fatum* and its etymology—Jupiter speaks (*for*), and as he does, he expounds the Trojans' fates (*fata*, 1.262), and declares they have been decreed (1.283). Here the agency of gods and other forces are also set in relationship, which serves to expose further nuances to Virgil's portrait of *fatum* and its inflexibility: once declared, even the gods are bound by the fates they have spoken.[69]

In **Valerius**'s anecdotes, *fatum* appears unquestioned among the forces presumed to undergird history, though it is mentioned less frequently than *fortuna*.[70] Hannibal's dream about a monstrous reptile, spouting thunderstorms and destroying everything in its path, denotes a destruction of Italy that is both inevitable and independent of human aid, as Hannibal is instructed by his guide in light of the revelation, "so hold your peace and leave the rest to the silent fates (*tacitis permitte fatis*)" (1.7.ext1).

By contrast, Squires suggests **Diodorus Siculus** is uncomfortable with the inflexibility of the concept of "fate."[71] Εἱμαρμένη does not appear in the extant

---

four times in Diodorus Siculus (see n. 57 above), and 81 times across Josephus's works. However, the vast bulk of these references do not relate to fate; one reference in Josephus concerns a sign to foretell the future (*Ant.* 1.333), all remaining uses refer to a division (for instance, of armies), a party, or some other portion. The term does not appear in the LXX or NT. In addition, χρεών means necessity, but comes to be associated with fate or destiny as a result (Uytanlet, *Luke-Acts and Jewish Historiography*, 29). It does not appear in the NT or LXX. There are 12 instances across Josephus's corpus, as discussed below.

68 Martin particularly associates this with Livy (Ronald Martin, *Tacitus: Annals V & VI* (Warminster: Aris & Phillips, 2001), 147).
69 Cf. Dionysius of Halicarnassus *Rom. Ant.* 6.54.2 (Squires, *The Plan of God*, 157).
70 *Fortuna* appears in 56 passages; *fatum* in 35.
71 Squires argues that Diodorus Siculus shares with Dionysius of Halicarnassus a discomfort with the idea of fate, and that Diodorus introduces parallel terminology when using words related to "fate" to allow for elements of human responsibility. However, most of the references Squires attributes to fate are actually uses of ἀνάγκη, which, although in some forms of Stoicism ἀνάγκη and εἱμαρμένη can be used somewhat interchangeably, is better translated "necessity" (see below); his *Library* thus seems to make even less use of these ideas than Squires suggests. Squires's overall helpful study creates some difficulties by using English terms. For instance, he

sections of Diodorus's *Library*. Similarly, **Polybius** uses the term only three times, generally to denote a character's death (16.32; 18.54; 36.17).

**Josephus** likewise makes minimal use of εἱμαρμένη, also often reserving the term as a euphemism for death (e. g. *J.W.* 1.662).[72] In a scene that is exceptional in many ways, he uses εἱμαρμένη when describing Vespasian surmising that "some just destiny (δικαία τις εἱμαρμένη)" had placed leadership in his hands (*J.W.* 4.622). The passage is ripe with related terms—τύχη, δαιμόνια πρόνοια (4.622), and σημεῖα (4.623)—leading to Josephus's account, steeped in his personal investment in the matter, of Vespasian realising that Josephus's declaration at Jotapata had truly been divine (θεῖος), and thus Josephus should be released from imprisonment (4.625).[73]

Χρεών, although a term for necessity, comes to be associated with fate as "that which must be,"[74] and Josephus makes use of the term in this stronger sense, in addition to as a euphemism for death.[75] In the *Jewish War*, he makes several references to the revolutionaries being at fault because, for instance, "they were blinded by Fate (χρεών), which, alike for the city and for themselves, was now imminent (ἤδη παρῆν)" (*J.W.* 5.572).[76] In this way he describes events within this framework of what must take place, and at the same time still reserves blame for the human actors.[77]

Finally, however, in his philosophical school passages (*J.W.* 2.119–66; cf. *Ant.* 13.171–73; 18.12–22), Josephus uses εἱμαρμένη repeatedly, suggesting that here he is deliberately signalling the traditional patterns of philosophical debate with the technical term.[78] Josephus's formulaic excursuses include loose affilia-

---

describes δεῖ as fate in some places, but then claims that fate "is almost completely absent" from *Ant.* 1–11 (Squires, *The Plan of God*, 165), although the word δεῖ appears 94 times in *Ant.* 1–10; Squires has assessed that none of the uses have this meaning. Similarly, he makes mixed use of ἀνάγκη, μοῖρα, δαιμόνιον, χρέων, and so on, under a limited set of English headings. See nn. 57 and 67 above.
72 Though cf. *J.W.* 4.297 and discussion below at §3.3.2.
73 For further information on the content of Josephus's revelation at Jotapata, see discussion below at §3.3.2.
74 LSJ meaning A.
75 The term appears 12 times across Josephus's corpus, though this includes as a euphemism for death, for instance at *Ant.* 7.383; 8.307.
76 This is the summary statement with which Josephus concludes Book 5.
77 See further discussion of this dynamic in Josephus in Chapter 5.
78 Mason argues that the differences between the treatments of these groups in each excursus and the formulaic nature of these passages caution against drawing conclusions about their historicity (Steve Mason, "Josephus's Pharisees: The Philosophy," in *In Quest of the Historical Pharisees*, ed. Jacob Neusner and Bruce D. Chilton (Waco, TX: Baylor University Press, 2007), 65–66; cf. Gunnar Haaland, "What Difference Does Philosophy Make? The Three Schools as a Rhetorical

tions between the Jewish groups and Stoicism and Epicureanism (though scholarly consensus maintains that Josephus does not base this on direct engagement with relevant philosophical texts).⁷⁹ But, even here, Josephus introduces θεός. He criticises the Sadducees, who remove θεός from all events, while noting that the Pharisees and Essenes attribute events to εἱμαρμένη and to θεός, thus connecting the two. As discussed more fully in Chapter 5, Josephus's portrayal of the Pharisees as they attribute events to εἱμαρμένη and the cooperation of ἄνθρωποι is consistent with his presentation of both divine determination *and* human responsibility.⁸⁰ Hence, even when Josephus uses the more technical terminology, and in the type of passages that signal a philosophical treatment, he still adapts εἱμαρμένη in ways that will serve his portrayal of divine guidance of history.

Although writers like Josephus introduce elements of flexibility to εἱμαρμένη, others affirm εἱμαρμένη/*fatum* over τύχη/*fortuna*, precisely because of its lack of flexibility. Matthews observes the ways in which conflicts between fortune and fate are drawn down (at times, caricatured) philosophical party lines in the imperial period:

> For many of our philosophically literate sources, a belief in the supremacy of *fatum* and *deus* is presented as the defining character of Stoic thought. In contrast, these sources present Epicurean philosophy as positing a belief in the supremacy of *fortuna*. Writers hostile to the Epicurean school represent this philosophy as replacing the moral and predictable

---

Device in Josephus," in *Making History: Josephus and Historical Method*, ed. Zuleika Rodgers, Supplements to the Journal for the Study of Judaism 110 (Leiden: Brill, 2007), 267; for a contrasting view, Jonathan Klawans, *Josephus and the Theologies of Ancient Judaism* (Oxford: Oxford University Press, 2012), 8–9). Setting aside these historical questions, Josephus's philosophical schools passages illuminate his attitude to particular views, based on his description of groups he consistently presents negatively (the Sadducees). Maston notes that the different presentation of the Pharisees in *J.W.* 2 and *Ant.* 13 reflect "rhetorical pressures" arising from this desire to contrast with the negative presentation of the Sadducees (Maston, *Divine and Human Agency*, 14). Klawans argues that the philosophical categories Josephus deals with here, particularly in relation to the Pharisees' position, relate to Jewish not Stoic philosophies, such as that of Chrysippus (Jonathan Klawans, "Josephus on Fate, Free Will, and Ancient Jewish Types of Compatibilism," *Numen* 56 (2009): 76–81; Klawans, *Josephus and the Theologies*, 49–91).

**79** Sanders, "God Gave the Law," 91. In *Ant.* 10.276–81, Josephus criticises Epicureanism for what he claims is its disregard for a guide directing the course of history, for which he uses the reliability of Daniel's prophecy as evidence (see Unnik, "An Attack on the Epicureans," 343; Vermes, "Josephus' Treatment of the Book of Daniel"; and below §3.3.2). Note, though, that in his discussion of categories here, Josephus refers positively to πρόνοια and θεός, but does not make use of the term εἱμαρμένη in his criticism of the Epicureans. On the role of fate trumping fortune in such philosophical comparisons in more literary sources, see below.
**80** See further discussion of this dynamic in Chapter 5.

forces of god and fate with capricious and amoral *fortuna*, a force over which human *uirtus* is powerless.[81]

In particular, the conflict between *fortuna* and *fatum* emerges in these texts from the association between *fortuna* and the empire discussed above.[82] Responding to the disempowerment of Roman elites at the end of the Republic and building on the association of *fortuna* with the emperor, "Seneca developed a Roman brand of Stoicism that posited as the defining battle of the philosopher's life the struggle against the supremacy of *fortuna*."[83] The political consequences of such claims thus become clear.

For most texts discussed here, however, as noted in relation to Josephus above, the discussion does not presume the technical arguments of philosophical texts, even where writers employ the technical terminology.[84] **Tacitus** offers an excursus on *fatum* and *fortuna* in *Ann.* 5.22, which Miriam Griffin suggests indicates he may not have understood the related philosophical debate.[85] Martin, however, rightly stresses Tacitus's deliberate vagueness and hesitation on these matters. Tacitus begins the excursus:

> for myself, when I listen to this and similar narratives, my judgement wavers. Is the revolution of human things governed by *fatum* and changeless necessity (*necessitas immutabilis*), or by accident (*forte volvantur*)? (5.22)[86]

After canvassing various views, but before assessing them, Tacitus draws an abrupt halt: "at present I do not care to stray too far from my theme" (5.22). The narrative turns to the next anecdote.

In whichever ways these writers portray the role of fate, often constrained by polemic either against divine involvement in history or another philosophical group, this was an idea with considerable currency. The tensions which emerge

---

**81** Matthews, "Roman Constructions of Fortuna," 6.
**82** Dick argues that Lucan's contrast between Caesar and Cato (who rejects *fortuna*) cautions against placing trust in fortune (Dick, "*Fatum* and *Fortuna*," 240–41).
**83** Matthews, "Roman Constructions of Fortuna," 6.
**84** Burton posits Diodorus is likely "unconsciously influenced by Stoic doctrine" (Burton, *Diodorus Siculus*, 37).
**85** Griffin, "Tacitus as a Historian," 168 n. 2. Griffin also notes Tacitus's inconsistency, for instance using *fatum* as "chance" in 6.46.3 (p. 168 n. 2).
**86** Martin, *Tacitus*, 149. On the question addressed by this excursus, the reliability of astrology, Tacitus indicates that accuracy is possible but misinterpretation can take place. Difficulty lies not in practitioners being intentionally deceptive but because interpretations are difficult and partial (Martin, *Tacitus*, p. 149).

from writers focusing on the reliability and fairness of fate over the fickleness of fortune, or those who prioritise the flexibility of fortune over uncompromising fate, also demonstrate important distinctions in the ways that writers engaged with these ideas. Nonetheless, again, εἱμαρμένη does not feature in Luke/Acts, 2 Maccabees, or any of the other Jewish Hellenistic texts of this study aside from Josephus's writings.[87] However, where it relates to the idea of *necessity* more overlap emerges.

### 2.4 ἀνάγκη/*necessitas*

The concept of necessity, or ἀνάγκη, has a long history in Greek philosophy and can also be attributed status as a personal deity.[88] With Stoicism, ἀνάγκη became connected to a type of appreciation for causes that leads to a deterministic natural law—things happen in a necessary and inevitable sequence of causes.[89] This facilitates the Stoic association between ἀνάγκη and εἱμαρμένη.[90] For **Valerius Maximus**, at points the ideas of fate and necessity are entwined. For instance, the elder Cyrus becomes an example of "the unconquerable necessity of fate (*invictae fatorum necessitatis*)" through a disaster foretold in a dream (1.7.ext5).

**Diodorus Siculus** uses ἀνάγκη with τύχη in ways that allow for human responsibility alongside necessity (cf. 15.63.2).[91] Squires observes that Diodorus "diminishes the power" of ἀνάγκη by equating it with τύχη.[92] The way that Diodorus tempers the inflexibility of ἀνάγκη with other forces thus complements his emphasis on virtue and benefit, preferring human cooperation with divine providence over behaviour that is simply *constrained* by fate.

---

[87] Note that fate is by contrast quite important for later Christian groups, such as the Valentinians. See for example the Nag Hammadi text *Apocryphon of John* 25.16–30.11.
[88] Development in the uses of ἀνάγκη spans from pre-Socratic conflation of physical and logical necessity to the later separation of these ideas in Plato. According to Aristotle, necessity is understood as "that which cannot be otherwise (Aristot. *Metaph.* 5.5.1015a 33f)" (cited Paul Dräger, "Ananke," *BNP* 1:642).
[89] Bobzien, *Determinism and Freedom*, 33–44.
[90] In Parmenides and Empedocles, Ἀνάγκη is portrayed as a personalised force. Philosophies such as Hermeticism distinguished the two terms, associating ἀνάγκη with astral fatalism (Dräger, "Ananke," 642). Despite this relationship between ἀνάγκη and εἱμαρμένη in Stoicism, none of the key texts of this study, including Diodorus Siculus who uses the former but not the latter, appear to be drawing on philosophical texts (cf. Burton, *Diodorus Siculus*, 36–37).
[91] In LCL, Oldfather translates ἀνάγκης καὶ τύχης here as "necessity and fate" (15.63.2).
[92] Squires, *The Plan of God*, 160.

**Josephus** sets out a relationship between various forces in the *Antiquities*, as he reflects upon whether blame for Herod murdering his own sons ought to be laid with his sons for angering him, Herod himself, or τύχη, "who has a power greater than all prudent reflection" (16.397). Josephus goes on to offer a formula which may obscure as much as it clarifies:

> we are persuaded that human actions are dedicated by her [τύχη] beforehand to the necessity of taking place inevitably (ἀνάγκη), and we call her Fate (εἱμαρμένην) on the ground that there is nothing that is not brought about by her. (*Ant.* 16.397)[93]

Returning to his question of responsibility, Josephus states that this model of recognising the influence of such forces (his mix of τύχη, ἀνάγκη, and εἱμαρμένη), "has been philosophically discussed before our time in the Law" (16.399). Having thus equated the forces of his discussion here with the divine actor of the Jewish law, he turns to explain the culpability of *both* Herod and his sons in their own ways (16.399–404).

This exemplifies Josephus's treatment of these questions: he uses Hellenistic terminology to denote the divine in his tradition, and he draws on the concepts about divine control of history principally in order to explain the responsibility of particular human characters.[94] This is true in his description of individual situations, such as Herod murdering his sons, or the Jewish people as a group, for being persuaded by the revolutionaries in the war against the Romans (*J.W.* 5.377–8, cf. 401–3, 407; 6.285).[95]

Thus, although ἀνάγκη may have been used somewhat interchangeably with εἱμαρμένη in more formal Stoic circles, it is at least interesting that Diodorus Siculus and Josephus make fairly frequent use of ἀνάγκη, but Josephus uses εἱμαρμένη only sparingly and it does not appear in the extant sections of Diodorus's *Library*.[96] Moreover, as they surround ἀνάγκη with other terms and apply it in different contexts, they subtly adapt its meaning to their broader purposes, un-

---

[93] Squires also notes this passage, but claims that Josephus uses the statement to "repudiate the power of both Fate and Fortune" (Squires, *The Plan of God*, 161). I suggest, rather, that Josephus appropriates these terms for his own context, enlisting the terminology for his characterisation of the God of Israel.
[94] See further discussion in Chapter 5.
[95] Gray argues Josephus only attributes responsibility to the revolutionaries (Gray, *Prophetic Figures*, 38). But Josephus does sometimes extend blame to the people as a whole (cf. *J.W.* 6.285).
[96] Other terms frequently translated "fate" (when used in this sense rather than, for instance, the far more common mundane uses for μοῖρα in Josephus), are not as common in Diodorus or Josephus as terms denoting more flexible forces, including τύχη and πρόνοια. On other terms that can be translated "fate," see nn. 57 and 67 above.

derscoring the sense of human responsibility. For Diodorus, this facilitates the moral programme of his historiography; for Josephus, it allows the forces which represent God to be reliable, while blame remains with the human actors.[97]

Similarly, although εἱμαρμένη does not appear in the NT, ἀνάγκη is used 17 times. Five of these refer to need or distress; 12 to something being necessary (or *not* necessary, 1 Cor 7.37; 2 Cor 9.7; Heb 7.27; Phlm 14).[98] Ἀνάγκη is only used as necessity once in **Luke/Acts**: in the mundane claims of the parable's character who declines the invitation to the great banquet because they "must" inspect a recently purchased field (Luke 14.18).[99] Notably, Luke does not use ἀνάγκη in Luke 17.1 about woe to the one who causes little ones to stumble, although Matthew does in the parallel passage (Matt 18.7).[100] Unlike Matthew's "temptations must come," Luke's parallel assessment is articulated instead by ἀνένδεκτόν ἐστιν τοῦ τὰ σκάνδαλα μὴ ἐλθεῖν, (literally, "it is impossible for stumbling blocks not to come"), making it clear that stumbling blocks are inevitable, rather than that they might be "necessary" or in any way divinely determined.[101]

Luke also uses the adjectival form, however, in a significant passage.[102] Paul and Barnabas declare to a hostile Jewish crowd in Pisidian Antioch:

> it was necessary (ἦν ἀναγκαῖον) that the word of God be spoken first to you. Since you thrust it aside (ἐπειδὴ ἀπωθεῖσθε αὐτόν) and judge yourselves unworthy of eternal life,[103] behold, we are turning to the Gentiles. (Acts 13.46)

---

97 See Chapter 5.
98 See Heb 9.23 for a positive use of ἀνάγκη.
99 In the parable this "need" is demonstrated to be quite the opposite; the character is shown to have made the wrong choice. The other use of ἀνάγκη is as distress in Luke 21.23.
100 The saying appears in a series of four sayings which are only loosely related to one another, if at all (see Fitzmyer, *The Gospel according to Luke*, 2:1136).
101 Green similarly associates the "inevitability of occasions for stumbling" with "the Lukan motif of hostility and opposition to the plan of God: All do not identify with and orient themselves around God's purpose" (Green, *The Gospel of Luke*, 612). Note also Green's helpful point that Luke has transformed sayings that address Pharisees into sayings directed to disciples but with a second tier of audience, the Pharisees, also subtly addressed in the background (p. 612).
102 The other use of the adjective, Acts 10.24, simply denotes Cornelius's intimate circle. See also the requirements (ἐπάναγκες) determined by the Jerusalem council (Acts 15.28).
103 Consistent with the way he dismisses eschatological themes, Pervo says of the reference to eternal life in Acts 13.46, the "eschatological phrase comes as a surprise" (Pervo, *Acts*, 343). Barrett notes the irony of the people's arrogance and the comment about believing themselves "unworthy" (Barrett, *A Critical and Exegetical Commentary*, 1:656).

Here Luke does employ a strong sense of necessity, though distinguished from any idea of ἀνάγκη as a personified deity, as might potentially be implied by the noun.[104] Importantly, the element declared necessary is the *proclamation*— the rejection of the good news is entirely the domain of human response.[105] This is important for Luke's treatment of divine control of history throughout, demonstrated by the following discussion of δεῖ, and of the divine βουλή below.

Aside from this passage, Luke makes surprisingly little use of the key terms for divine guidance of history common in Graeco-Roman texts. Εἱμαρμένη is absent. Τύχη appears only in a variant in Codex Bezae (Luke 10.31 D). Luke uses πρόνοια only in the introductory niceties of Paul's speech as deference to Felix's foresight and care, and as a noun denoting necessity, ἀνάγκη appears only in the setting of a claim to domestic obligation, which the wider context undermines. However, he does make frequent use of one technical term related to necessity: δεῖ.

## 2.5 δεῖ

Luke's use of δεῖ is frequently discussed in the context of a divine plan in Luke/Acts. However, the term functions differently from others that denote necessity, fate, or fortune.[106] Despite Charles Cosgrove's warning that δεῖ cannot be used as a *"terminus technicus* for divine necessity,"[107] Lukan studies frequently slide into exactly this kind of shorthand.[108]

---

104 Bovon, *Luke: Commentary*, 1:363.
105 So also Barrett, *A Critical and Exegetical Commentary*, 1:656. See below regarding a similar sense of testing and then rejecting, in Luke 9.22.
106 Impersonal verb from δέω, "I bind," "it is bound."
107 Charles H. Cosgrove, "The Divine ΔΕΙ in Luke-Acts: Investigations into the Lukan Understanding of God's Providence," *NovT* 26 (1984): 173.
108 This kind of terminology appears in Robert L. Mowery, "The Divine Hand and the Divine Plan," in *Society of Biblical Literature, 1991 Seminar Papers*, ed. Eugene H. Lovering, Jr., SBLSPS 30 (Atlanta: Society of Biblical Literature, 1991), 558–75; Brian Rapske, "Opposition to the Plan of God and Persecution," in *Witness to the Gospel: The Theology of Acts*, ed. I. Howard Marshall and David Peterson (Grand Rapids: Eerdmans, 1998), 235–56; Alan J. Thompson, *The Acts of the Risen Lord Jesus: Luke's Account of God's Unfolding Plan*, New Studies in Biblical Theology 27 (Downers Grove: InterVarsity Press, 2011); Squires, *The Plan of God*, 169–70; Tannehill, *Narrative Unity*, 1:54, 193. Conzelmann attributes to δεῖ a central role in Luke's understanding of the plan of God, connected to the passion and "the saving events as a whole" (Conzelmann, *Theology of St Luke*, 153–54). Fitzmyer discusses δεῖ in his introduction on Lukan theology, but focuses instead on fulfilment language in Luke/Acts (Fitzmyer, *The Gospel according to Luke*, 1:180). Johnson discusses δεῖ in relation to Luke 24.26, but centres on interpretation in the Jewish scriptures (John-

Moreover, as noted in Chapter 2, Clare Rothschild argues that Luke uses δεῖ as a rhetorical device, employed in reports of the least probable events as a way of emphasising a story's authority[109] and that such rhetoric is "independent of an individual author's theological beliefs."[110] Although I argue δεῖ functions differently from Rothschild's proposal,[111] it still does not denote an inflexible necessity or fate in Luke/Acts.

BDAG judges in relation to δεῖ that "strict classification of usage is not possible because of the multifunctional adaptability of this verb, especially in colloquial discourse."[112] Yet, none of the eight variations of meanings catalogued list *divine* necessity or fate.[113] Often the term takes ordinary meanings to do with practices or traditions that "must" be followed, for example, because of religious obligation,[114] or other things that "ought" to be done—including the sense that something ought to have been done but was not (often communicated with the

---

son, *The Gospel of Luke*, 395–96), and makes no mention of it in earlier passages using δεῖ, such as Luke 2.49 and 9.22. Bovon claims that Luke uses δεῖ to indicate the salvation-historical significance of an event/issue—e.g. in relation to Luke 2.49 and 4.43 (Bovon, *Luke: Commentary*, 1:164). Haenchen, however, associates δεῖ with divine will and, unlike these other commentators, recognises the conflicts that arise as a result of this understanding, though he observes that Luke himself is not concerned about these conflicts. Rather, Luke's focus is on confidence in divine control of history (Haenchen, *The Acts of the Apostles*, 159 n. 8). While I agree that there are points at which divine sovereignty trumps other concerns (see discussion of Acts 4.28 or, in some readings, Acts 2.23), these passages do not employ the term δεῖ. Haenchen elevates δεῖ with claims such as: "in Luke, δεῖ implies that God wills something and that it therefore must happen" (p. 159 n. 8). Rather, I suggest that the logic is: *God can foresee something, and thus it must happen.* That God's will ensures that all things will ultimately be turned to furthering God's plan is certainly a theme of Luke/Acts, but it is not part of Luke's use of δεῖ.
**109** Rothschild, *Luke-Acts and the Rhetoric*, 194.
**110** Rothschild, *Luke-Acts and the Rhetoric*, 7. Rothschild consistently imports a purpose to Luke/Acts that is not always convincing: "viewed, rather, in terms of the author's goal of competitive historiography, LXX citations in Luke-Acts are less concerned with literal realisation of an old promise than verification of the present account" (p. 169). If Luke's purpose is to "commend [his] version of what took place" (p. 182), this is not so much about Luke's competition with others in the historiographical marketplace, but his interpretation of the events themselves (closer to the view argued by Squires, *The Plan of God*, 125).
**111** For criticism of Rothschild's conflation of rhetoric and content, see Chapter 2 above.
**112** Grundmann's entry in *TDNT* likewise confirms the source of necessity is not intrinsic to the verb, and that in philosophical use it means "logical or scientific necessities" (*TDNT* 2:22). Unfortunately, when suggesting δεῖ does display elements of divine necessity (p. 22), Grundmann cites Acts 5.39 in support (which does not use δεῖ but only βουλὴ τοῦ θεοῦ).
**113** BDAG, 214. For earlier material, LSJ does give an association with fate as one of many meanings, citing Herodotus 2.161; cf. also *TDNT* 2:22 regarding Herodotus 8.53.
**114** Similar use in Diod. *Library* 10.9.7.

imperfect). Δεῖ appears 40 times in Luke/Acts, and many of the occurrences relate to these kinds of ordinary meanings: the disciples "need" to pray and not lose heart (Luke 18.1), the Passover lamb "had to be" sacrificed (22.7), and the Pharisees "ought" to have practiced justice (11.42; cf. Acts 20.35).[115]

For other uses, BDAG enumerates meanings related to an "internal necessity" that arises out of a "given situation," events that "take place because of circumstances ... with the context determining cause," or "compulsion caused by the necessity of attaining a certain result."[116] Though these meanings may still lend themselves to a divine cause of the necessity if the context suggests it, the term by itself does not convey divine action.

Importantly, Luke's use of δεῖ is not equivalent to his understanding of the divine βουλή; divine guidance of history in Luke/Acts is not reduced to a kind of fate or pre-programmed plan in which each character simply plays her or his predetermined part.[117] Where Luke employs δεῖ as a form of internal necessity,[118] it relates to one or both of (a) the necessity of foretold events taking place, and (b) an inherent necessity arising from the context in which characters find them-

---

**115** Δεῖ also denotes practices or fitting responses in Acts 15.15; 16.30; 26.9, and things that "ought" to be done at Luke 13.14, 16; 15.32; Acts 19.36; 24.19; 25.24; 27.21. Cf. Lev 5.17; 2 Macc 6.20; 3 Macc 1.12; Wis 12.19; 16.28; 1 Thess 4.1; 2 Thess 3.7; Rom 8.26; 12.3; Col 4.6; 2 Tim 2.6; 2.24.
**116** This is in keeping with the "practical necessity" found in Thucydides, as distinct from a "hard necessity" (Hoekstra and Fisher, "Thucydides and the Politics of Necessity," 375), which Hoekstra and Fisher, drawing on Otswald, argue is absent from Thucydides (though note: Thucydides still recognises one thing may cause another, such as an earthquake causing a tidal wave (3.89.5), but he does not use "the language of necessity" to describe such phenomena, p. 376). Here practical necessity is described as "a claim about what must be done in the circumstances one is in, given one's commitments and character" (p. 375). Hoekstra and Fisher argue that practical necessity in Thucydides may in part function to draw the readers' attention to the greater personal agency they have in how they choose to respond (p. 389).
**117** Cosgrove, "The Divine ΔΕΙ," 173. Contra Squires, Luke's approach to necessity does not "come very close to the hellenistic idea of Fate" (Squires, *The Plan of God*, 167). By contrast, Conzelmann claims that Luke/Acts contains "no reflection on fate and free will" (Conzelmann, *Acts of the Apostles*, xlvii). Holladay defines the divine βουλή with overlap with δεῖ, as "distinctively Lukan language for a divine intentionality that is comprehensive in scope but realised in particular events seen to have an element of predetermined necessity" (Holladay, *Acts*, 398). He does elsewhere note, though, that the divine purpose frequently encounters resistance (implicitly against the divine will), before it is then vindicated (p. 52).
**118** Others that might be put in this category can be discounted: Luke 2.49, when Jesus as a boy "must" be in his father's house, more easily reflects an obligation of his piety; it is not a bigger-picture assertion that his whereabouts had been predetermined. Luke 12.12, which claims that the Spirit will provide what the disciples "ought" to say in fearless defence of their faith, again indicates what they should do for faithful practice as they are assured of divine care; it is not a predetermined obligation. And Acts 19.36 indicates right practice.

selves as they seek faithfully to proclaim the gospel and fulfil their mission.[119] In the latter use, suffering often comes about because the context of proclamation leads to opposition—that is, short of denying the gospel, suffering cannot be avoided. Therefore, crucially, though δεῖ is frequently associated with suffering, it is not the suffering itself which embodies the divine βουλή, but participating in the divine βουλή elicits opposition which tragically leads to unavoidable suffering.

Although there is considerable overlap between these two applications of δεῖ in Luke's text, it will help to discuss them separately. Seven times in Luke/Acts, δεῖ is explicitly related to biblical prophecy.[120] For instance, as frequently in discussing his own suffering, Jesus claims:

> For I tell you, this scripture must be fulfilled in me (δεῖ τελεσθῆναι ἐν ἐμοί), "And he was counted among the lawless (μετὰ ἀνόμων)";[121] and indeed what is written about me (γὰρ τὸ περὶ ἐμοῦ) is being fulfilled (τέλος ἔχει)." (Luke 22.37; cf. 24.26, 44; Acts 1.16; 3.21; 4.12; 17.3)[122]

Similarly, as Peter addresses the remaining apostles, he asserts, "the scripture had to be fulfilled (ἔδει πληρωθῆναι),[123] which the Holy Spirit through David foretold concerning Judas" (Acts 1.16).[124]

---

[119] Thus this also meets the final BDAG definition above, in which something is necessary in order to achieve a desired result: faithful proclamation of the gospel and fulfilment of Jesus' and the apostles' mission. Cosgrove argues Luke's δεῖ highlights human interaction with necessity through obedience (Cosgrove, "The Divine ΔΕΙ," 176). Miller discusses it in terms of the difficulties of human interpretation of divine disclosures (John B. F. Miller, *Convinced That God Had Called Us: Dreams, Visions and the Perception of God's Will in Luke-Acts*, BibInt 85 (Leiden: Brill, 2007), 234).

[120] Cosgrove, "The Divine ΔΕΙ," 173–74. See also Holladay, who aligns δεῖ with Luke's "prophecy-fulfilment" model (Holladay, *Acts*, 49).

[121] See below in relation to Acts 2.23.

[122] A key verse that might be associated with this tradition of apparent "necessity" of Jesus' suffering, in accordance with biblical prophecy, is Paul's claim before Agrippa that the prophets and Moses said that "the Messiah must suffer" (ESV/NRSV, Acts 26.22). Importantly, however, this is not a δεῖ clause, despite this traditional translation, and reflects instead the use of εἰ and παθητός, meaning something more like "being capable of or subject to suffering" (F. F. Bruce, *The Book of Acts*, rev. ed., NICNT (Grand Rapids: Eerdmans, 1988), 390). This is better translated that the prophets and Moses said "the Messiah would suffer" or "the Messiah would be capable of suffering," rather than that he "must suffer." See further discussion in the fuller treatment of Paul's speech in Acts 26 in Chapter 6 §5.2.1.

[123] Conzelmann notes Codex Bezae attaches δεῖ instead to the selection of the replacement in Acts 1.16 (Conzelmann, *Acts of the Apostles*, 10–11). Following Rothschild's understanding of

This use of δεῖ reflects the use in Dan 2 LXX.¹²⁵ As Daniel begins his interpretation of Nebuchadnezzar's dream, he says:

> But there is a God in heaven revealing mysteries (ἀνακαλύπτων μυστήρια), who has disclosed to king Nebuchadnezzar the things which must happen (ἃ δεῖ γενέσθαι) on the last days. (Dan 2.28, LXX)¹²⁶

Here the necessity relates to a logical requirement that, if something has been reliably foretold, it is bound (the literal meaning of δεῖ, from δέω) to happen.¹²⁷ Thus, although some particular events Luke claims had been prophesied might be difficult to locate in actual scripture passages,¹²⁸ his use of δεῖ nonetheless reflects this reasoning: prophesied events *must* happen (Luke 24.26; cf. Acts 3.21).¹²⁹ Similarly, the necessity of Paul's journey to Rome centres around prophetic revelations that this will take place, and thus therefore that it must (Acts 23.11; 27.24).¹³⁰ Even the shipwreck is described as "necessary," once it has been revealed to Paul that it will take place (Acts 27.26).

---

rhetorical purpose, Keener argues Luke uses δεῖ here to combat the public embarrassment of Judas's betrayal (Keener, *Acts*, 2:1756–57).
**124** Judas was "allotted" (ἔλαχεν) his place in the ministry, but then this led to wickedness. The sense of having been allotted his place links to the processes of appointing his successor which will follow (Acts 1.26). The method of discerning the new apostle is certainly portrayed with a sense of oversight by God in the text, but it does not imply the associations of other terms such as εἱμαμένη.
**125** Fascher claimed that Luke's δεῖ reflected LXX usage rather than Graeco-Roman (Erich Fascher, "Theologische Beobachtungen zu δεῖ," in Eltester, *Neutestamentliche Studien für Rudolf Bultmann*, 228, 245–47, 254), although Dan 2 is the only place in which δεῖ takes on a meaning related to this type of necessity (though here it is used three times in two verses!). Fascher's claims about the LXX raise important considerations, but most of the LXX uses of the term fall into the more ordinary categories, such as Lev 4.2; 5.17; Esth 1.15; 2 Macc 11.18. By contrast, on associations with Graeco-Roman concepts, see Schulz, "Gottes Vorsehung," 108–9.
**126** My translation. See also Wis 16.4; 1 Cor 11.19; 15.25; 15.53; 2 Cor 5.10; Eph 6.20; Rev 1.1; 4.1; 17.10; 20.3; 22.6.
**127** The LXX introduces necessity into the passage; it is not present in the MT. See the comparison of texts in Collins, *Daniel*, 150–51.
**128** For instance, the Lukan Paul claims that Moses and the prophets prophesied that the Messiah would be subject to suffering (Acts 26.22–23; see Chapter 6), although no clear passages are cited (Johnson considers possibilities in the HB; Johnson, *The Gospel of Luke*, 395–96).
**129** Bauspieß attributes a "theologishes Sinn 'notwendig'" to δεῖ here, contrasting with both a rigid sense of fate and Rothschild's rhetorical device (Bauspieß, *Geschichte und Erkenntnis*, 277). For Bauspieß this theological sense connects to Luke's soteriology and approach to knowledge or insight (*Erkenntnis*; pp. 277–85).
**130** Uses of δεῖ regarding Paul's travel to Rome also appear at Acts 19.21 and 25.10. In the latter, the setting confirms he is asserting that he "ought" to be tried before Caesar. In 19.21 it is less

The second, but often related, application of δεῖ as an internal necessity emerges from events that must take place if characters are to fulfil their mission within their particular context.¹³¹ Thus, in order for Jesus to fulfil his mission, he must proclaim the gospel in other places (Luke 4.43; cf. 19.5).¹³² Likewise, Paul must testify in Rome (Acts 23.11; 27.24).¹³³ And as they fortify disciples with confidence in the message of the gospel, despite inevitable opposition and persecution, Paul and Barnabas assert, "it is through many persecutions (θλίψεων) that we must (δεῖ) enter the kingdom of God" (14.22).¹³⁴ Although sometimes interpreted as a claim that suffering is a "prerequisite" for the kingdom,¹³⁵ here as elsewhere, the necessity arises from the setting: in order to attain a given result—that is, steadfast proclamation of the gospel—enduring persecution will be necessary. This is confirmed by the discussion two chapters later, in which the troubled jailor asks Paul and Silas, "what must (δεῖ) I do to be saved (ἵνα σωθῶ)?" They provide the foundational response: "believe on (πίστευσον ἐπί) the Lord Jesus, and you will be saved, you and your household" (16.30; cf. Luke 10.25–37; 18.18–30; Acts 4.12).¹³⁶ Suffering is not a prerequisite for God's saving action in Luke/Acts. But a life of discipleship in a context in which others reject the good news may well make suffering necessary.¹³⁷

---

clear (see Rius-Camps and Read-Heimerdinger, *The Message of Acts*, 4:152; Kylie Crabbe, "Accepting Prophecy: Paul's Response to Agabus with Insights from Valerius Maximus and Josephus," *JSNT* 39 (2016): 188–208; and Chapter 5 §6.3.2).
131 Cosgrove, "The Divine ΔΕΙ," 175.
132 Similarly, in 2 Maccabees, Eleazer's approach to his martyrdom is fitting (6.20). So also Diod. *Library* 11.91.1.
133 Given Paul's prophetic dreams on this subject, this theme reflects both types of necessity.
134 Gaventa distinguishes suffering as "an entrance requirement" for the kingdom from suffering according to a divine plan, but says Luke still affirms the latter (Gaventa, *Acts*, 209). See also Scott Cunningham, *"Through Many Tribulations": The Theology of Persecution in Luke-Acts*, JSNTSup 142 (Sheffield: Sheffield Academic, 1997), 14.
135 Cf. Holladay, *Acts*, 398 n. 317.
136 Cf. Acts 4.12. I recognise that aligning Acts 14.22 and 16.30 as I have done here equates "salvation" with "entering the kingdom of God," but I believe this is justified in the broader literary context (cf. Luke 4.43; 7.50–8.1).
137 Contra Squires's loose connection between Stoic views of the merit of suffering and Jesus' experience at the Mount of Olives (Squires, *The Plan of God*, 171). Suffering in Luke/Acts does not have this "character forming" sense, but an entirely different element of necessity (δεῖ) is evident here, which relates to following through with proclamation leading to rejection of the prophet (Johnson, *The Gospel of Luke*, 16–17). This is also consistent with Bovon's understanding of God recasting Jesus' murder (Bovon, *Luke: Commentary*, 1:383), as discussed in relation to Luke 9.22 below.

Paul's Damascus experience incorporates both of these senses of δεῖ: what Paul must do to fulfil his mission is revealed to him (Acts 9.6), and Ananias receives a vision about "how much [Paul] must (δεῖ) suffer" in fulfilling this mission (Acts 9.16).[138] Luke includes a nice play on words in the dialogue between Ananias and God, in which Ananias objects that Paul has the chief priests' authority "to bind (δῆσαι) all who invoke your name" (9.14), but God's response outlines the necessity (δεῖ) that will unfold in suffering, as Paul himself acts "for the sake of my name" (9.16).

In the example key to Luke's narrative, Jesus' suffering is described both as a necessary fulfilment of what has been foretold and a necessity that arises as a consequence of the opposition his mission receives. In his first passion prediction, Jesus declares:

> The Son of Man must (δεῖ) undergo great suffering (πολλὰ παθεῖν), and be rejected (ἀποδοκιμασθῆναι) by the elders, chief priests, and scribes, and be killed, and on the third day be raised. (Luke 9.22)

François Bovon observes that the term used for the rejection by the elders indicates a period of testing followed by rejection: ἀποδοκιμάζω.[139] Jesus must suffer, not only because this was foretold by the prophets, but in order to fulfil his mission (cf. Luke 17.25). This is not divine necessity, but feeds into key Lukan themes throughout, such as the tragedy of the rejected prophet[140] and the tragic reversal brought about by some people rejecting his proclamation (Luke 13.33–4; cf. 4.16–30; 7.30).[141]

However, while using δεῖ to indicate that suffering becomes necessary through the circumstances of opposition, Luke still asserts that the divine

---

**138** Gaventa notes the unique wording used in describing Paul's call here, as a "chosen instrument (σκεῦος ἐκλογῆς)" (9.15) (Gaventa, *Acts*, 151). Johnson suggests that suffering "for Jesus' name" indicates suffering "as Jesus' representative" (Johnson, *The Acts of the Apostles*, 165). Johnson (perhaps rightly) focuses more on the emphasis on suffering in this passage, as opposed to Luke's supposed *theologia gloriae*, than on the mechanism of the necessity indicated, though he does argue this puts Paul in the line of the prophets (p. 165), whose suffering emerges from their mission, not the reverse. Pervo implies suffering constitutes a literary feature of the presentation of protagonists in ancient texts ("In short, if you want to be a narrative hero, be prepared to suffer") and cites the example of Heracles from Sophocles's *Philosophy* (Pervo, *Acts*, 244). While it may be true that noble suffering characterises protagonists in numerous sources, this does not exhaust the role of Paul's suffering in Luke's account.
**139** Bovon, *Luke: Commentary*, 1:383.
**140** Johnson, *The Gospel of Luke*, 16–17.
**141** Matthew includes only the lament for Jerusalem, in the verses which follow (Matt 23.37–39). See discussion of reversal in Chapter 5 §6.3.1.

βουλή is at work through Jesus' death and his vindication in resurrection and ascension (Acts 4.24–30).[142] Although he unhelpfully introduces the language of fate, which is not present in the verse, Bovon's commentary on Luke 9.22 otherwise captures the crucial element of this theme. Jesus' suffering is necessary because it is foreseen and a result of human action, but in turn even this is nonetheless incorporated into the divine plan:

> Luke adopts two theological points from Mark with special avidity: δεῖ ("it is necessary") and παθεῖν ("to suffer"). God has a plan (cf. Acts 2:23). Between divine fate and human freedom runs the path of the living God, who foresees the suffering of the Son of Man and integrates it.[143]

Bovon observes that the opposition to Jesus as it unfolds across the Gospel leads to his murder. But God responds in a way which gives Jesus' murder "an entirely new meaning."[144] Luke is clear that, as suffering is associated with δεῖ, it reflects a necessity brought about not by God, but by those who reject God's invitation, even as God enabled the prophets to foresee that they would.

## 2.6 Summary: personal and impersonal forces in history

The writers of this study's key texts use terms like τύχη/*fortuna*, πρόνοια/*providentia*, εἱμαρμένη/*fatum*, and ἀνάγκη/*necessitas* diversely, even within the same text. At times they attribute a strong sense akin to a personal deity, whereas elsewhere they supply more vague notions of impersonal forces and even ironic attributions.[145] As they participate in traditions prevalent in the Hellenistic period,

---

142 Notably, Luke does *not* use δεῖ in this key verse (cf. also 3.18).
143 Bovon, *Luke: Commentary*, 1:363.
144 Bovon, *Luke: Commentary*, 1:363.
145 The emperor's *apotheosis* also receives a mixed (sometimes ironic) treatment—such as in Ovid's epilogue in which he contrasts Augustus's *apotheosis* with his own enduring notoriety as the poet (see p. 62 n. 26 above). But even Valerius Maximus, who affirms the divine status of the emperor ("other gods we have received (*accepimus*), the Caesars we have bestowed (*dedimus*)" (1.praef)), does not attribute supernatural characteristics and guidance of history to Caesar. On Valerius's panegyric at key positions in his work, see D. Wardle, "Valerius Maximus on the Domus Augusta, Augustus, and Tiberius," *The Classical Quarterly* 50 (2000): 479, 492–93. Tacitus offers a deeply ironic account of Vespasian feigning supernatural healing powers under the rationale, "if a cure were obtained, the glory would be Caesar's, but in the event of failure, ridicule would fall only on the poor supplicants" (*Hist.* 4.81; see discussion in Syme, *Tacitus*, 1:206). Regardless, no such reticence or irony features in Luke/Acts. The only ambiguity about God's activity lies in statements such as that from the "we-group," following Paul's

these writers not only attribute activity to divine forces rather than personalised gods,¹⁴⁶ but they can also vary in how confidently they attribute the actions to those forces. Polybius, Diodorus Siculus, Valerius Maximus, Tacitus, and even Josephus at times, describe an event as taking place "as if" by divine providence.¹⁴⁷ Or they describe *others'* beliefs that fortune was the cause of particular events, distancing the narrator from these claims.¹⁴⁸ However, each writer who uses these terms nonetheless also supplies examples in which the attribution to the divine force is explicit and affirmed by the narrative.¹⁴⁹

That these writers can apply the same terms to different characterisations of these forces highlights the importance of looking beyond this terminology. The underlying concepts remain significant, as even in, for instance, comparing the uses of τύχη/*fortuna* as a driving force of history at times for Polybius, a moral force responding to human immoderation for Diodorus, or a catalyst for capricious change in the moment for Valerius. Moreover, the above analysis demonstrates that for a Jewish Hellenistic writer like Josephus, even where he uses these terms, he applies them to his own characterisation of the divine. Finally, this discussion has also demonstrated that the other Jewish texts of this study make very minimal use of this kind of terminology, and that, despite the focus on Luke's Graeco-Roman attributes in much contemporary Lukan scholarship, this is true for Luke/Acts too. Moreover, the concept of δεῖ as Luke uses it is not an equivalent idea to divine planning. Moving beyond a study of key terms, therefore, I suggest it is helpful to consider more narrative ways in which writers

---

dream of the Macedonian man, which describes "being convinced that God had called us to proclaim the good news to them" (Acts 16.10). However, this is akin to the detailed discussion of *interpretation* of accurate signs below, not a question about divine guidance itself.

**146** Various gods do nonetheless still feature in texts of this period, playing varying roles in the unfolding plot. Plutarch explains the superiority of Remus as a child, "chiefly, as it would seem, because a divinity was aiding and assisting in the inauguration of great events" (Plu. *Rom.* 7.4).

**147** See discussion of this in Josephus, with the example of *Ant.* 11.237, in Louis H. Feldman, *Josephus's Interpretation of the Bible*, Hellenistic Culture and Society (Berkeley: University of California Press, 1998), 209.

**148** Cf. *Doings* 1.5.praef; 1.6.1; *J.W.* 1.593; 3.28, 144, 391; 4.366; 6.252, 266. See Walbank's discussion of Polybius in Walbank, "Fortune (*Tychē*) in Polybius," 353. Valerius's section on "false practice of religion" (1.2) also demonstrates concern about the misuse of religious claims for political purposes. See further discussion in Wardle, *Valerius Maximus*, 24. On divine favour and kingship, including "deified rulers" and the geographical extensions of divine kingdoms on earth through kings, see Uytanlet, *Luke-Acts and Jewish Historiography*, 31–34.

**149** Cf. *Doings* 1.5.ext1; 1.6.6; Tacitus *Hist.* 5.13. Schwartz notes that Josephus confirms God is the one "pulling the strings," *J.W.* 6.250 and 7.319 (Schwartz, "Josephus, Catullus, and the Date," 339).

communicate a sense of determinism or divine guidance of history. Their treatments of prophecies are illustrative.[150]

## 3 Prophetic insights into the future

The key texts of this study depict characters gaining insights into the future through a range of means, from portents and prodigies to dreams, oracles, and revelatory encounters with angels. As the writers affirm the accuracy of these insights, they also affirm that the course of history is to some extent set. At times, they also make claims about divine guidance of these predetermined events. The following outlines prophetic insights described by writers such as Diodorus Siculus and Valerius Maximus, and the *vaticinia ex eventu* in Virgil's *Aeneid*, as they indicate views about determinism and divine guidance, before turning to prophecy in the remaining texts.

### 3.1 Prophetic insights according to Polybius, Diodorus, Valerius, and Tacitus

Writers such as Diodorus Siculus, Valerius Maximus, and even occasionally Polybius and Tacitus affirm that insights into the future provided by portents, dreams, and oracles can be truthful, even if the writers also sceptically note examples in which people wrongly took a natural event to be a portent. In these texts, accurate prophetic insights enable writers to communicate a sense of inevitability about an outcome after the fact[151] or to attribute human responsibility for failing to respond to a prophetic warning—or both!

In Book 1, **Valerius Maximus** devotes sections to numerous types of prophetic insights, including: augury (1.4), omens (1.5), prodigies (1.6),[152] dreams

---

[150] It is not possible to give a comprehensive analysis of all narrative indications of determinism and divine guidance, but prophecy offers a good example across the study's key texts.
[151] Two types of retrospect affect writers' depictions of determinism and divine involvement: the extent to which a writer allows the end of the narrative they plan to tell to intrude into their account of earlier events (see Grethlein, *Experience and Teleology*, 8); and the consequences of the writer's later historical setting. The first is a literary technique, illustrated by narrative asides like, "it is no light thing to show irreverence to the divine laws—a fact that later events will make clear" (2 Macc 4.17; cf. 8.11; *Ant*. 16.404). The second concerns information the writer and reader know, but the characters do not, and constitutes an essential element in *vaticinia ex eventu*, as discussed below and in Chapter 6.
[152] Following Bailey's translation (Bailey, *Valerius Maximus*), I retain the somewhat antiquated term "prodigy" (Latin: *prodigium*) in part because it differentiates between the categories of pro-

(1.7), and wonders (1.8). In the world of his narratives, the insights provided by these events are proved to be true. So Consul L. Sulla's experience with a snake emerging from an altar during the Social War is interpreted as encouragement to take immediate military action, which is then successful (1.6.4). Signs can be misinterpreted, but still fulfilled in unexpected ways. Valerius describes Hamilcar's dream about dining in Syracuse, which Hamilcar interprets as a sign of victory over the town, only to discover that he would dine there as a captive (1.7.ext8, cf. 1.5.4; 1.7.8).[153]

Valerius includes anecdotes in which characters go to extreme lengths in unsuccessful attempts to evade a predicted calamity (cf. 1.6.7).[154] This frequently plays on irony. Here the effect of the irony is not only, as defined by the *OED*, a situation that "seems deliberately contrary to what was or might be expected; an outcome cruelly, humorously, or strangely at odds with assumptions or expectations,"[155] but, to enlist John Lyons's helpful definition of the effect of irony in texts, it also produces layers of meaning running against one another in a text to create "insiders" and "'fall guy(s),' the person(s) who do(es) not or should not get 'it.'"[156] Readers of Valerius's anecdotes recognise the signs and know that a character attempting to thwart a portended disaster by extravagant means is set up to fail.[157] But, as the stories gel with the claims inherent in ma-

---

phetic insights Valerius discusses in Book 1. Under this category Valerius describes anomalous or unnatural occurrences that are interpreted as portents, such as a mare giving birth to a hare (1.6.ext1a) or wine poured into a bowl turning into blood (1.6.ext1b).
**153** Dreams in particular coincide with events Valerius presents as inevitable, such as Gracchus's dream of his own death (1.7.6) or Calpurnia's dream of Caesar's death (1.7.2; cf. 1.7.ext8). Josephus likewise relates prophetic insights provided by dreams as inescapable (2.114; 3.354).
**154** C. Hostilius Mancinus's response to prodigies demonstrates, Valerius suggests, "insane obstinacy (*vesana perseverantia*)." Mancinus undertakes various journeys, though changing his course does not avert the foreshadowed disaster but rather results in a continued series of prodigies as "he equalled the number of portents with the number of his disasters" (1.6.7). Valerius reflects popular views about portents and omens when he announces that Consul Octavius "feared a dire omen but could not avoid it" (1.6.10).
**155** *OED*, meaning 3.
**156** William John Lyons, "The Words of Gamaliel (Acts 5.38–39) and the Irony of Indeterminacy," *JSNT* 68 (1997): 29. Lyons introduces this definition in his discussion of Gamaliel in Acts 5. See §4.2.4.
**157** Here Valerius's genre and purpose naturally play a part; he compiles anecdotes for declamation that will entertain and provide moral instructions.

terial elsewhere (e. g. 3.7.ext6),[158] his exempla affirm the underlying assumptions about the accuracy of such prophetic insights.

Valerius's account of King Croesus's tragic attempts to escape predicted events demonstrates the effect. Following a "sleep-vision (*quietis imago*)" which disclosed that his son was destined to be taken "by steel," Croesus took extreme measures to keep his son from harm. But in an ironic tragedy, which Valerius introduces with the words "necessity opens the way to mourning (*necessitas tamen aditum luctui dedit*)," the son was eventually killed while dealing with a boar, by the sword of the guardian employed for his safety (1.7.ext4). Here Valerius reflects the popular view that the future is inescapably determined (cf. 1.6.10; 1.7.6; 1.7.2; 1.7.ext8), while providing an anecdote that will entertain the hearer, who can both appreciate the irony and be pleased to have avoided similar tragedy at the hands of *necessitas*.[159]

In some cases, however, Valerius recounts prophetic insights that he suggests ought to have functioned as a warning. As Mueller observes, Valerius "accepts fortune, fate, necessity, and nature as an integral part of divine law. He does not bother with philosophical complications arising from simultaneous belief in fate and divination."[160] Despite the sense of inevitability he portrays elsewhere, Valerius frequently (and quite passionately) bemoans characters' failures to heed prophetic warnings by acting to *avert* the portended tragedy (1.4.2; 1.6.6; 1.6.11; 1.6.ext1b). Although, in one interesting example, Ti. Gracchus accurately understands a prodigy, which warns him that his friend intends to betray him. But Gracchus then allows the events to unfold anyway; Valerius affirms his virtue in assenting to the portended future (1.6.8).

**Diodorus Siculus** describes Philip the Macedonian interpreting an oracle as part of his plans for victory over the Persian king, involving misinterpretations that lead to an ironic twist. The reader is aware of Philip's mistake from the outset. He interpreted the oracle "in a sense favourable to himself," while the reader is told, "actually, however, it was not so, and it meant (ἐσήμαινεν) that Philip himself in the midst of a festival and holy sacrifices, like the bull, would be stabbed to death while decked with a garland" (16.91.3). Diodorus continues the narrative in what becomes an ironic description of Philip's planning for the festival, punctuated by other portentous elements (16.92.2–3). Philip's death in 16.94 con-

---

**158** Exemplified by comparison between Cicero and Valerius in relation to haruspicy, which shows Valerius altering the story he shares with Cicero to safeguard claims about the accuracy of haruspicy (3.7.ext6). See Mueller's comparison (Mueller, *Roman Religion in Valerius*, 118–21).
**159** On this technical term see §2.4.
**160** Mueller, *Roman Religion in Valerius*, 188–89. See Chapter 5 on the ways this tension emerges in texts in terms of human responsibility for what takes place.

firms the oracle's accuracy, as the reader has known throughout would inevitably ensue.[161]

As noted above in relation to πρόνοια, **Polybius** recounts characters making claims to prophetic insight simply in order to persuade their audiences (10.2.12; 10.11.8; 23.17.10). Although generally more sceptical about these things, he does for instance indicate that Demetrius's prophecy about Persia and Macedonia was accurate (29.21).[162] **Tacitus** is also generally more sceptical about prophetic insights into the future. He considers techniques such as astrological divination to be open to misunderstanding, suggesting that interpreters are unable to distinguish between true and false signs.[163] Moreover, very human conditions can lead characters to make inappropriate attributions about portents and prodigies. This is shown, for instance, in the events surrounding the terror of Otho's campaign. Tacitus suggests that heightened anxiety led to incorrect interpretations following the disastrous flooding of the Tiber.[164] When Otho's military advance is then impeded by the flood, Tacitus says this "was interpreted as a prodigy and an omen of impending disaster rather than as the result of change or natural causes (*a fortuitis vel naturalibus causis*)" (*Hist.* 1.86). As Miriam Griffin summarises:

> Tacitus believed that people, when in an overwrought state, interpret natural or chance events as portents indicative of fate or the wrath of the gods (*Hist.* 4.26.1–2, cf. *Ann.* 4.64.1; 12.43.1).[165]

---

**161** On Diodorus's references to fulfilment of the oracle, see Squires, *The Plan of God*, 124–25 nn. 20–21.
**162** See also Frank W. Walbank, "Supernatural Paraphernalia in Polybius' *Histories*," in *Polybius, Rome and the Hellenistic World*, 256–57.
**163** Griffin, "Tacitus as a Historian," 170. Tacitus criticises superstition and astrology even in the practices of Vespasian: "Nor indeed was he [Vespasian] wholly free from such superstitious belief, as was evident later when he had obtained supreme power, for he openly kept at court an astrologer named Seleucus, whom he regarded as his guide and oracle" (*Hist.* 2.78). On Tacitus's reasons for countering superstitions, see discussion in J. H. W. G. Liebeschuetz, *Continuity and Change in Roman Religion* (Oxford: Clarendon, 1989), 194–96.
**164** In this situation, other prodigies identified range from "a superhuman form" exiting Juno's chapel, to an ox having "spoken in Etruria" and "many other things … which in barbarous ages (*rudibus saeculis*) used to be noticed even during peace, but which now are only heard of in seasons of terror" (*Hist.* 1.86).
**165** Griffin, "Tacitus as a Historian," 171.

But importantly, despite Tacitus's scepticism, he does present some events as genuine portents.[166] The key example lies in those that signified Vespasian's rise, involving "a favourable omen of great significance, as the haruspices all agreed" (2.78)[167]—though even here, awareness of the meaning of these signs unfolds gradually and through struggle.[168] Ultimately, the omens which foreshadow Vespasian's rule gain Tacitus's unequivocal support. He declares, "prodigies had indeed occurred" (*Hist.* 5.13).[169] This confirms that for Tacitus, as in the case of the other writers, prophetic signs *can* be accurate (though less frequently than popularly claimed);[170] his reserve stems rather from his assessment of any given case.[171]

### 3.2 Prophecy in Virgil's *Aeneid*

Prophecy takes a different form in Virgil's *Aeneid*, though themes shared with the texts above still emerge. For instance, the events prophesied are certain to unfold

---

[166] Cf. *Hist.* 2.4. According to Roman religion, failure to consult haruspices appropriately could lead to disaster through divine punishment (Mueller, *Roman Religion in Valerius*, 9).
[167] Liebeschuetz, *Continuity and Change*, 192–93.
[168] The "development" in Vespasian's understanding of his portended status suggests an element of parody. Tacitus relates, "At first, however, the insignia of a triumph, his consulship, and his victory over Judea appeared to have fulfilled the promise given by the omen (*decus implesse fidem ominis videbatur*); yet after he had gained these honours, he began to think that it was the imperial throne that was foretold (*portendi sibi imperium credebat*)" (2.78). Tacitus nonetheless seems ultimately to affirm the oracle's accuracy (cf. 5.13), as also Vespasian's divine favour (4.81).
[169] Sailor labels this declaration "striking," given it is so uncharacteristic (Sailor, *Writing and Empire*, 245). Sailor also argues Tacitus deliberately evokes here Aeneas's correct interpretation of signs in *Aen.* 8.520–29 (pp. 244–45).
[170] In polemic against the people of Judea, Tacitus asserts the error of their interpretations and the correct meaning of prodigies: "Few interpreted these omens as fearful; the majority firmly believed that their ancient priestly writings contained the prophecy that this was the very time when the East should grow strong and that people starting from Judea should possess the world (*profectique Iudaea rerum potirentur*). This mysterious prophecy had in reality pointed to Vespasian and Titus, but the common people, as is the way of human ambition, interpreted these great destinies (*tantam fatorum magnitudinem interpretati*) in their own favour (*sibi*), and could not be turned to the truth (*ad vera mutabantur*) even by adversity (*adversis*)" (*Hist.* 5.13). Moreover, when Vespasian attempts to clarify the omen by consulting the god at Carmel, Tacitus observes that the meaning of the resultant "obscure oracle" becomes a topic of much popular speculation (2.78).
[171] See also Titus's accurate use of haruspices according to Tacitus in *Hist.* 2.4.2; cf. divination which indicates an unfavourable outcome for Otho in 1.27.1.

—though, as characters can also misunderstand or receive only part of the prophecy, fulfilment of prophecies can involve an unexpected twist, as for Valerius or Diodorus. As noted in the previous chapter, the historical reviews in 4 Ezra, 2 Baruch, and the *Aeneid* set out history in structured terms. In each case, prophecies couched as *vaticinia ex eventu* are inherently deterministic. In the *Aeneid*, these passages, in which past historical events are "predicted" by a character set in an earlier time (1.262–304; 6.752–892; 8.624–728), serve to confirm that all of the events of history have been accurately foretold in advance. This form of the prophecy allows Virgil to interpret the significance of the events of past and present, and to use the "prediction" of past events to establish trustworthiness in prediction beyond the present time: the endless continuation of Rome's present rule.[172]

James O'Hara connects interpretation of prophecies in the *Aeneid* with the stunning irony with which Aeneas misinterprets Dido's mural depicting the Trojan War (1.450–90).[173] What Aeneas takes as a sensitive acknowledgement of the Trojans' suffering, the story reveals to be a glorification of victory. Indeed, Aeneas is the butt of misunderstanding on numerous occasions. He remains oblivious to the significance of the shield in Book 8 and, following his underworld tour, when he comes to the "two gates of sleep (*Somni portae*)," he exits through the ivory gate (6.893). This is the gate, the reader is told, through which "delusive dreams (*falsa insomnia*) issue upward from the world below" (6.896),[174] a device through which Virgil seems to indicate Aeneas will not remember the revelations of his underworld experience.[175] And, far from being privy to the conversation between Jupiter and Venus in the review in Book 1, he fails initially even to recognise Venus, let alone her cryptic hints about the future, in the following incident in the forest (1.321–411).

However, although O'Hara uses the image of the mural in Book 1 to suggest prophecy is untrustworthy in the *Aeneid*, the ambiguity resulting from these prophecies pertains only to *interpretation*, not *accuracy*. Prophecies throughout the *Aeneid* are proved to be truthful, though they can at times mislead characters

---

172 See further Chapter 6.
173 O'Hara, *Death and the Optimistic Prophecy*, 183.
174 Contrast Homer, *Od.* 19.562–67.
175 This reference remains more in question (Horsfall acknowledges the gates of sleep as one of very few places where he has "not been able to find a coherent explanation of V.'s meaning" (Horsfall, *Virgil, "Aeneid" 6*, 1:xxi; cf. also O'Hara, *Inconsistency in Roman Epic*, 95)). I follow Goold's suggestion that the ambiguity of the gate functions to explain how Aeneas forgets the insights from the underworld in Books 7–12 (in Fairclough and Goold, *Virgil*, 1:597), but recognise that it is an ambiguous image.

by providing only a partial insight into the future (see, for instance, 6.343–46, or prophecies which mislead through semantic ambiguity, such as 3.94–98, 255, cf. 7.116).[176] As the discussion above demonstrates, Virgil is not alone in reserving a twist in the plot, in which a character's misinterpretation of prophecy is eventually exposed in the course of the prophecy's inevitable, if unexpected, fulfilment. In all of these cases, however, the literary technique *relies* on the reader being able to recognise the foretold events in the outcome as it is recounted. Whatever ambiguity this introduces for Aeneas as a character, the dramatic irony on which the plot rests serves to confirm the accuracy of the prophecies. Virgil's *vaticinia ex eventu* underscore that the course of events is set, even if not all the characters realise, and, as noted above, once it is spoken, even Jupiter is bound by what has been fated.[177]

### 3.3 Prophecy, determinism, and divine guidance in the study's remaining texts

The writers of the study's remaining texts all present divine guidance of some kind, or a sense that events have been set in advance, which can be illustrated through their use of prophecy. At one end of the spectrum, while focusing on direct divine intervention in particular events as they unfold, 2 Maccabees gives three examples of oracles or prophetic dreams, which generally also relate to immediate events. By contrast, Josephus's treatment of prophecy, *vaticinia ex eventu* in 4 Ezra and 2 Baruch, and the War Scroll's views of the future provide a bigger picture of history, which interprets the past and provides assurance for future events yet to be fulfilled.

---

[176] O'Hara claims Jupiter's prophecy in Book 1 is false because it prioritises comforting Venus over disclosing the future (O'Hara, *Death and the Optimistic Prophecy*, 3). By contrast, however, Jupiter is a trustworthy character in the text. See further discussion in Chapter 6. Interestingly, although O'Hara acknowledges the *ekphrasis* form in Book 8 eliminates ambiguities associated with disclosure and interpretation, creating a direct connection in the text between Vulcan and the reader, he also wishes to exclude the Book 8 prophecy on the basis that all prophecy in the *Aeneid* is unreliable (p. 173).

[177] I discuss the significant political considerations that this view of history evokes in Chapter 6.

### 3.3.1 Second Maccabees

Second Maccabees strongly emphasises divine action. This is affirmed frequently throughout the book, in the claims of characters as they explain events in speeches or offer prayers of invocation before battles,[178] and in explicit statements in the narration.[179] Even more striking, however, are the events which unfold in battles, during which, for instance, heavenly, golden horses or people become suddenly involved in the battle, ensuring victory (3.24–40; 5.2–4; 10.29–30; 11.8–9; 12.22; cf. 2.21). The divine is presented as an actor in the events of the narrative, intervening to ensure a desired outcome.[180] Thus, while divine action occupies an extremely prominent place in the narrative, it is almost always described as part of events as they unfold, as God acts to punish or to rescue as the need arises, rather than as part of an overarching divine plan or series of events that might have been foreseen in advance. There are, however, three examples that might be understood as a type of prophetic sign.

In the second letter given at the beginning of 2 Maccabees, the writer describes a tradition about Jeremiah, who is said to have "received an oracle (χρηματισμοῦ)" (2.4). Following this he found a cave in which he placed "the tent and the ark and the altar of incense" (v. 5) and then sealed the entrance to the cave. This preplanning suggests a belief that the disasters to befall the temple were foreseen and that divinely-granted insight enabled Jeremiah to act to protect the sacred objects, until "God gathers his people together again and shows his mercy" (v. 7).[181]

The other two examples share more in common with the kind of interpretations of omens and dreams in texts like those by Valerius, Diodorus, or Polybius. 2 Macc 5.2–4 describes a strange apparition before a military battle,[182] which the people pray is a good omen (lit. "for the good") for the ensuing battle. Here such a portent seems similar to those described by Valerius or Diodorus, including

---

[178] 2 Macc 8.18–20; 8.36; 10.38; 11.13; 12.15–16, 28; cf. 1.11–17, 21; 2.17–18.
[179] 2 Macc 4.16–17, 38; 5.18; 8.5, 11, 24; 9.4–12, 18; 12.11; 13.4, 17; 15.25–27, cf. 15.21–24, 29, 34–35.
[180] See Chapter 5 for discussion of the ways in which divine action interacts with human agency in 2 Maccabees, including as it supports an extended Deuteronomistic view of the events described.
[181] This kind of tradition, associated with Jeremiah, is also found in 2 Bar 6.7–9; cf. 80.2, where angels move the temple objects for their protection. See p. 223 n. 65.
[182] The apparition goes on for some time—almost forty days!—and involves appearances "over all the city," with "golden-clad cavalry charging through the air, in companies fully armed with lances and drawn swords—troops of cavalry drawn up, attacks and counterattacks made on this side and on that, brandishing of shields, massing of spears, hurling of missiles, the flash of golden trappings, and armor of all kinds" (2 Macc 5.2–4).

some element of ambiguity in its interpretation. Having set the narrative up with this sign, however, the narrator initially leaves the question of whether it bodes well or ill uncertain, exploiting a pattern of "relief and reversal" with sudden graphic, violent disasters after moments of reprieve, heightening the emotion for the reader.[183]

And, finally, 2 Macc 15.7–16 describes a situation very like those involving prophetic insights which were exploited by Polybius's characters for a positive military effect—except that in 2 Maccabees, there is no question of the authenticity of the prophetic insight. The narration claims Judas Maccabeus "armed each of them not so much with confidence in shields and spears as with the inspiration of brave words, and he cheered them all by relating a dream, a sort of vision, which was worthy of belief" (15.11). In the dream Judas relates, he received a golden sword from Jeremiah, in the presence of the faithful, recently-deceased, High Priest Onias, and is told that the sword will enable him to defeat his enemies. Like Scipio and Lycurgas in Polybius (10.2.12; 10.11.19), Judas is rallying a group of soldiers when he describes the dream as evidence of divine assurance of success in the upcoming military campaign (2 Macc 15.12–16).[184] This is indeed what then unfolds.

Thus, despite the strong emphasis on divine involvement in the narrative's events, there is only the smallest sense in 2 Maccabees of any events being set in advance. Moreover, these few prophetic insights do not undergird eschatological claims, which in 2 Maccabees are simply stated in either characters' confessions of faith (2 Macc 7.9, 23, 29, 36) or the words of the narrator (12.43–45). Only the story of Jeremiah's oracle and the sealed cave to protect the sacred objects indicates a longer-range prophetic insight, foreseeing the dangers ahead and promising a time of regathering, though there is no indication that this restoration will be in eschatological time. The story of the ambiguous sign in 2 Macc 5.2–4 and the dream recounted in 15.12–16 are instead more akin to prophetic insights described by Valerius or Diodorus Siculus than to the other Jewish texts of this study, except for Josephus, who includes similar types of portentous signs, alongside his additional interests in prophecy.

---

**183** Doran, *2 Maccabees*, 139.
**184** In 2 Maccabees, God is involved in particular events, but the writer does not provide a strong sense of divine guidance of history more broadly. On the role of God in 1 and 2 Maccabees and Acts, see Schwartz, "Circular or Teleological," 128–29 (though I disagree with his portrait of Luke's politics; see my Chapter 6).

## 3.3.2 Josephus's *Jewish War*

Josephus incorporates various approaches to prophecies, which portray the course of history as determined. Similarly to Valerius Maximus and Diodorus Siculus, Josephus describes accurate signs and portents. Herod correctly infers that a building collapsing immediately after he had left it was a good omen for commencing a successful military campaign (*J.W.* 1.331). Various characters experience portentous dreams (1.328; 2.114; 3.354), some Essenes' gift for foretelling the future receives admiration ("seldom, if ever, do they err in their predictions" (2.159)), and Jesus son of Ananias's mournful cry "woe to Jerusalem!" emerges not, as some suspected, as the symptom of mental illness (6.305), but as an inspired seven-year-long witness to Jerusalem's destruction (6.308).[185]

As both character and narrator in the *Jewish War*, Josephus makes authoritative claims about the correct *interpretation* of signs. For instance, after describing storms and earthquakes taking place while the Idumaeans camped outside the city walls, Josephus narrates, "such a convulsion of the very fabric of the universe clearly foretokened (πρόδηλον) destruction for ἄνθρωποι, and the conjecture was natural that these were portents (τὰ τέρατα) of no trifling calamity" (4.287). But whereas the Idumaeans interpret the portent as their destruction and Ananus's people consider it a sign of divine favour, Josephus observes that both "proved mistaken (κακοί) in their divination (στοχασταί) of the future (τῶν μελλόντων)" (4.289), as those who were to die were Ananus and his guards (4.297).[186] Here the misinterpretation is not what leads to the disaster, however, as Josephus asserts that the events took place not by human error but "by the overruling decree of fate (τῆς εἱμαρμένης)" (4.297).[187]

---

[185] Josephus also discusses *false* prophets (*J.W.* 6.285–88). Josephus does not support divination in terms of actively seeking augurs or signs, in keeping with emphases in Deuteronomy (Unnik, "An Attack on the Epicureans," 348–50). Indeed, in *Against Apion* he recounts an anecdote he attributes to Hecataeus, in which a character named Mosollamus, identified multiple times in the text as Jewish and an accurate shot with bow and arrow, shoots dead a bird in the process of being used for augury, with the explanation: "how could any sound information (προϊδών) about our march be given by this creature, which could not provide for its own safety? Had it been gifted with divination (εἰ γὰρ ἠδύνατο προγιγνώσκειν τὸ μέλλον), it would not have come to this spot, for fear of being killed by an arrow of Mosollamus the Jew" (*Ag. Ap.* 1.204). The story serves key elements of Josephus's apology. It presents a critique of augury familiar from Graeco-Roman intellectual traditions, to stave off criticism that Jewish people are gullible to superstition, and it also portrays the Jewish Mosollamus as a fine model by Greek standards; see Barclay, *Against Apion*, 91–95, 115–16.

[186] Attridge notes that the *Jewish War* exhibits greater fatalism than Josephus's approach in the *Antiquities* (Attridge, *The Interpretation of Biblical History*, 183).

[187] Thackeray's LCL translation, modified to reflect the use of εἱμαρμένη.

Josephus's emphasis on accurately interpreting prophetic signs is central to his apologetic purpose in the *Jewish War*. Among the errors he attributes to the revolutionaries lies misinterpretation of prophetic signs on the basis of optimism —"those who had kindled the war readily invented favourable interpretations for them" (*J.W.* 4.297; cf. 1.377; 2.650; Diod. *Library* 16.91 above). They misinterpret "the ambiguous oracle" (χρησμὸς ἀμφίβολος), through which Josephus claims "many of their wise men went astray in their interpretation (περὶ τὴν κρίσιν)" (6.312). They took the prophecy to foretoken a Jewish emperor, though Josephus himself knows that "in reality [it] signified the sovereignty of Vespasian, who was proclaimed Emperor on Jewish soil" (6.313; cf. Tacitus *Hist.* 2.78; 5.13 as above).

Josephus often addresses the reader directly with a formulaic statement that they should make up their own mind about the interpretation of a miracle or other event supposedly brought about through divine action. This is particularly a feature of his narration of biblical material in the *Antiquities* (cf. *Ant.* 1.108; 3.81, 322; 4.158; 10.281; 17.354; cf. 3.268; 8.262; 19.108),[188] but is seen also in the *Jewish War*. For instance, following his claim that the destruction of Jerusalem was brought about through the revolutionaries destroying the city and then the Romans destroying the revolt, thus exonerating the Romans for the destruction while blaming the revolutionaries, he goes on to say, "But let everyone follow their own opinion whither the facts may lead them" (*J.W.* 5.257).[189] Louis Feldman suggests that these statements are part of a larger apologetic trend in Josephus's writing. He notes that Josephus attempts to counter stereotypes of Jewish people as credulous by either downplaying miraculous elements in the biblical narratives or couching them in terminology or stylised stories familiar to non-Jewish audiences.[190] Likewise he suggests that the statements about the readers making up their own minds follow a tradition from both earlier and contemporaneous writers[191] and are "more an expression of courtesy to his pagan

---

**188** Feldman, *Josephus's Interpretation*, 209.
**189** Thackeray's LCL translation, modified for inclusive language.
**190** Feldman cites Horace, *Satires* 1.5.97–103 as evidence of criticism of Jewish people for being credulous. He makes a systematic comparison of Josephus's treatment of passages involving miracles against the biblical text (cf. Feldman, *Josephus's Interpretation*, 209–14), highlighting places where Josephus has played down the miraculous or supernatural elements, and also stories in which the miracle is then recounted in forms familiar from other Graeco-Roman texts. An example of the latter is Josephus's treatment of Elijah's departure via a heavenly chariot, which is narrated in a form parallel to Sophocles's portrait of Oedipus at Colonus (*Ant.* 9.28; p. 212); similarly for Moses' departure (cf. p. 665).
**191** Such statements, found also in Dionysius of Halicarnassus, Lucian, and Pliny, also appear in earlier writers such as Herodotus and Thucydides (see discussion in Feldman, *Josephus's In-*

readers than a confession of his doubt about the veracity of these accounts."[192] Indeed, despite these open statements, the view supported by Josephus in these cases is very clear. He claims to compile sources conscientiously in putting together his account (*Ant.* 3.81; cf. *Ag. Ap.* 1.37), vehemently affirms the prophetic insights of characters such as Daniel (cf. *Ant.* 10.266), and in the case of the interpretation of the causes of the destruction in the war, is extremely clear that the fault lies with the revolutionaries, who have pitted the people against "so great an Ally," the God to whom they now must repent (*J.W.* 5.377, 415).[193]

From his introduction as a character in 2.568, Josephus is a respected military figure (3.142), full of ingenious strategies (3.171–75, 186–88, 271–75). But his insight goes beyond superior military acumen; he is presented in the style of a prophet like Jeremiah and Daniel.[194] Josephus's revelation at Jotapata establishes his prophetic identity (3.352–54; 4.623),[195] though the passage does not disclose the contents of Josephus's dreams, which he indicates took place earlier. Rather, in keeping with his focus on accurate *interpretation* of dreams and prophetic signs, Josephus indicates that the turning point represented by this important event lies in his sudden ability to understand what the dreams meant, namely, in the words of Rebecca Gray's summary: "That God, who had created the Jewish people, had decided to 'punish' them; that 'fortune' (τύχη) has passed to the Romans; and that God had chosen him, Josephus, 'to announce the things that are to come' (τὰ μέλλοντα εἰπεῖν)" (cf. 3.352).[196]

As in the prophetic warnings discussed above, Josephus presents portents and omens both as signs that Jerusalem's destruction had been foreordained to a particular date since long ago (6.250, 313–14)[197] and as warnings which

---

*terpretation*, 209–10). Thackeray suggests Josephus's use of the formula may be taken from Dionysius of Halicarnassus (Thackeray, *Josephus*, 4:82 n. a).
**192** Feldman, *Josephus's Interpretation*, 210.
**193** On Josephus's view of repenting to God and to Rome, and the rule of the stronger, see Chapter 5.
**194** Gray, *Prophetic Figures*, 35; Cohen, "Polybius, Jeremiah, and Josephus," 366–81; Bilde, "Josephus and Jewish Apocalypticism," 55.
**195** Gray, *Prophetic Figures*, 37.
**196** Gray, *Prophetic Figures*, 37. Miller's work on dream-visions in Acts and other ancient literature focuses on texts that he suggests indicate dream-visions were considered unreliable, although he recognises this as a minority view in ancient texts. However, aside from a compelling example in Sir. 34.1–5 (Miller, *Convinced That God Had Called Us*, 56), most of the examples Miller cites relate instead to questions of accurate *interpretation*.
**197** Villalba i Varneda suggests that there are two causes involved in this destruction: God, who has determined that the destruction take place; and another force which has set the date and implemented it (Pere Villalba i Varneda, *The Historical Method of Flavius Josephus*, ALGHJ 19

ought to have been heeded to avert the destruction.¹⁹⁸ Josephus presents his own character drawing on his privileged insight and exhorting his hearers to repent to Rome (5.372) and to God (5.416). As Gray notes, Josephus is unconcerned about the apparent conflict between assessing a prophet's credentials on the basis of the accuracy of their prophecy, and recognising the prophet's vocation as exhorting hearers to alter their behaviour (and thus to avert the foretold, inevitable disaster).¹⁹⁹ When, in the citation above about the "ambiguous oracle" in Book 6, he reminds the reader of his own accurate interpretation which is key to his personal apology in the *Jewish War*, he goes on to conclude: "For all that, it is impossible for ἄνθρωποι to escape their fate (χρεών), even though they foresee it. Some of these portents, then, the Jews interpreted to please themselves, others they treated with contempt, until the ruin of their country and their own destruction convicted them of their folly" (6.314–15).

Finally, unlike Diodorus Siculus or Valerius Maximus, Josephus also demonstrates belief in determinism and divine oversight over the whole course of history and its end, as he also draws on biblical prophecies and applies them to his own context (*Ant.* 10.210; cf. 4.114–17).²⁰⁰ Josephus's interpretation of Daniel, discussed briefly above in relation to the role Josephus attributes to divine πρόνοια, affirms an overarching belief in divine guidance of history that not only explains the past but guarantees the events of the end of history. Josephus portrays Daniel positively both in terms of his wisdom and in his prophetic skill (*Ant.* 10.194, 200, cf. 10.142; 10.237, 239–41). Feldman rightly notes the central place the theme of divine oversight of the course of history and Daniel's prophecies generally occupies for Josephus, who devotes five paragraphs to this discus-

---

(Leiden: Brill, 1986), 49–50). Given how Josephus uses this terminology, however, it is preferable to see these as related and not separate divine forces.

**198** On Klawans's overview of fate and free will in the "compatibilism" of Josephus, see p. 151 n. 78 above. On these questions, see also my Chapter 5 below.

**199** Josephus does come close to presenting this as a conflict in Book 6, by suggesting that he deserves harsher treatments than the abuse he has received from his listeners, for attempting to prevent the destruction that has already been determined (*J.W.* 6.108). The two ideas are explicitly stated together as he claims, through the model of Ahab, readers "should realize that nothing is more beneficial than prophecy (προφητείας) and the foreknowledge (προγνώσεως) which it gives, for in this way God enables us to know what to guard against. And further, with the king's history before our eyes, it behoves us to reflect on the power of Fate (τοῦ χρεὼν ἰσχύν), and see that not even with foreknowledge (προγινωσκόμενον) is it possible to escape it" (*Ant.* 8.418–19), though here the example is also about the king's desire to believe the positive side of a prophecy, thus making (as Josephus implies would always be the case) the inevitable unfold.

**200** Bilde, "Josephus and Jewish Apocalypticism," 53.

sion, concluding not only Book 10 but the biblical material that comprises the first half of the *Antiquities* with it.²⁰¹ Josephus uses Daniel's interpretation to Nebuchadnezzar to claim prophecies show:

> how mistaken are the Epicureans, who exclude Providence (πρόνοιαν) from human life and refuse to believe that God (θεόν) governs (ἐπιτροπεύειν) its affairs or that the universe is directed by a blessed and immortal Being to the end that the whole of it may endure, but say that the world runs by its own movement (αὐτομάτως) without knowing a guide or another's care. If it were leaderless in this fashion, it would be shattered through taking a blind course and so end in destruction, just as we see ships go down when they lose their helmsmen or chariots overturn when they have no drivers. It therefore seems to me, in view of the things foretold (προειρημένοις) by Daniel, that they are very far from holding a true opinion who declare that God takes no thought (πρόνοιαν) for human affairs. For if it were the case that the world goes on by some automatism (αὐτοματισμῷ), we should not have seen all these things happen according to his prophecy. (*Ant*. 10.277–80)

Josephus incorporates various Hellenistic terms, and even polemical treatment of a particular philosophy. But he asserts that history is overseen by θεός (cf. *J.W.* 2.159–166; 5.367; 6.310). Thus, Josephus allows space for human responsibility, particularly for failing to avert the tragic events of the recent past, but he affirms divine guidance over not only particular events within history, but the whole course of history and its end.²⁰²

### 3.3.3 Fourth Ezra and 2 Baruch

As in the *Aeneid*, in 4 Ezra and 2 Baruch the *vaticinia ex eventu* underscore that all of the events included in the prophecies have been set in advance. In this way, the writers interpret the past and present, and give reasons for trusting the claims made about the future.²⁰³ Given the teleological shape of their sche-

---

**201** Feldman, *Josephus's Interpretation*, 639–40. This is also a significant indication that it is appropriate to take these passages on Daniel as an important lens through which to understand Josephus's view of history and divine action more broadly across his work, as argued by Bilde, *Flavius Josephus*, 187–88.
**202** See further discussion of the temporal elements of Josephus's reasoning here in Chapter 5 below.
**203** Rowland, *The Open Heaven*, 12; VanderKam, *Enoch and the Growth*, 142; cf. Loren T. Stuckenbruck, "'Reading the Present' in the Animal Apocalypse (1 Enoch 85–90)," in *Reading the Present in the Qumran Library: The Perception of the Contemporary by Means of Scriptural Interpretations*, ed. Kristin De Troyer and Armin Lange, SymS 30 (Atlanta: Society of Biblical Literature, 2005), 91–92. The discussion in Bockmuehl helpfully emphasises the connection between apocalyptic literature's interest in the revelation of heavenly realities and hope in the present (Markus N. A. Bockmuehl, *Revelation and Mystery in Ancient Judaism and Pauline Christianity*, WUNT

mas of history, the writers' portrayals of determinism and divine guidance over the whole course of history interact importantly with their eschatology.[204]

The term "apocalypse" (ἀποκάλυψις) reflects the centrality of special revelation for texts identified with this form.[205] As noted in Chapter 3, the periodised nature of history itself is part of the content of the divine disclosure in historical apocalypses, as the seer receives a vision of the periods of history unfolding in turn. Rather than merely rhetorical flourishes, these generic features serve claims to privileged access to information about the nature of the world and its end—a special insight which the writer also shares with the implied reader (cf. 4 Ezra 4.22–23; 8.63).[206] Traditions of sealed secrets disclosed to the pseudonymous protagonist from the past (4 Ezra 14.45–8; cf. Dan 12.4) suggest the implied audience sees itself as a select group who have been granted the ability to understand the processes that undergird the world as it really is and history as it will certainly unfold.[207] Fourth Ezra distinguishes general revelation from that

---

2/36 (Tübingen: Mohr Siebeck, 1990), 26–27). Henze on 2 Baruch argues that the interest in determinism across history should not be taken too heavily, as it serves primarily to emphasise divine sovereignty and the certainty of the prophesied end (Matthias Henze, *Jewish Apocalypticism in Late First Century Israel: Reading Second Baruch in Context*, Texts and Studies in Ancient Judaism 142 (Tübingen: Mohr Siebeck, 2011), 280). This is an important theme in Chapter 6 below.

**204** See Chapter 6 below.

**205** This is of course a contemporary term to describe texts grouped according to certain shared attributes. Though Collins, "Apocalypse," is widely taken as the starting point for definitions, debate about various features continues; there is, however, consensus about the central role of revelation. See also Rowland, *The Open Heaven*, 70–72. As they adjust Collins's definition in order to apply it to elements of "apocalypticism" in other texts, see, for instance: Reynolds, "John and the Jewish Apocalypses," 40–41 (on John); Florentino García Martínez, "Apocalypticism in the Dead Sea Scrolls," in Collins, *The Origins of Apocalypticism in Judaism and Christianity*, 264–65 (on the Dead Sea Scrolls); and Hanneken, *The Subversion of the Apocalypses*, 2–3 (the inversion of the form and content in Jubilees). See also G. I. Davies's helpful discussion about "apocalyptic and historiography," including as the ideas relate to Josephus (Davies, "Apocalyptic and Historiography").

**206** Newsom, "The Rhetoric of Jewish Apocalyptic Literature," 202–3.

**207** The tradition of sealed secrets in 4 Ezra 14.45–48 (building on Dan 12.4) confirms that the mystical knowledge included in the written text was authoritatively disclosed in the past. After the seventh episode, 4 Ezra concludes with a scene in which Ezra dictates 94 books over the course of 40 days and nights, and then receives an instruction directly from the Most High: "'Make public the twenty-four books that you wrote first, and let the worthy and the unworthy read them; but keep the seventy that were written last, in order to give them to the wise among your people. For in them is the spring of understanding, the fountain of wisdom, and the river of knowledge.' And I did so" (14.45–48). The emphasis on such true understanding is evident not only in the disclosure of secrets in apocalypses themselves but, for instance, in the theme of

privileged only for the wise (4 Ezra 14.46); 2 Baruch also emphasises purity as an eligibility criterion for receiving revelation. Baruch addresses the Mighty One in his prayer for illumination prior to the vision of dark and bright waters, "You pull down the enclosure for those who are spotless" (54.5; cf. 55.3), claiming that revelation granted to the righteous casts aside the impediments to seeing the world accurately.[208] While the emphasis on privileged knowledge does not necessarily imply a group which wishes its esoteric insights to *remain* secret, it bolsters the claims of the prophecies' accuracy and authority.

Thus, in 2 Baruch, Ramael[209] has been sent by the Mighty One to reveal to Baruch both the times "which have passed and those which in his world will come to pass, from the beginning of his creation until the end" (2 Bar 56.2). Significantly, whereas Ramael goes on to assert that these times "are known by deceit and by truth" (55.2) the narration has already identified Ramael himself as "the angel who is set over true visions" (55.3). The disclosures thus provided by his interpretation are to be trusted by the reader. Similarly in 4 Ezra, despite the rigorous dialogue between Ezra and Uriel in relation to the justice of the events to unfold, the two characters nonetheless agree that the events have been determined. At various points Uriel claims that all of this has been planned from before everything (4 Ezra 6.6; 7.74). For his part, Ezra laments the inevitable events and suffering to be endured while awaiting divine judgement (5.43).[210] Moreover, the messianic lion in 4 Ezra's fifth vision claims to have created four empires (the last being the eagle) to rule, asserting that this was designed to bring about "the end of my times" (11.39). Here divine planning adds a further layer to the determinism, whether or not the writer also attributes responsibility to God for the fourth empire's further atrocities, which the lion goes on to list (11.40–46).

---

sight and blindness exemplified in the *Animal Apocalypse*'s portrayal of decline in key periods of its historical scheme. See p. 292 n. 105 below.

**208** In these apocalypses, most space is devoted to disclosures about the vision's correct *interpretation*, and indeed—in both the vision of the vine and forest (2 Bar 23–30) and the dark and light waters (53–76)—the exposition "goes well beyond what the seer actually saw," setting the stage for the interpretation rather than the vision itself remaining the focus of the text (Henze, *Jewish Apocalypticism*, 272).

**209** This is the only instance of an angelic interpreter in 2 Baruch; the writer normally portrays direct communication with the divine (Henze, *Jewish Apocalypticism*, 272). See further discussion in Henze for connections to other uses of the same name, including in 4 Ezra (p. 272).

**210** Compare Enoch's lament following the *Animal Apocalypse* that all the events he has seen must be fulfilled in order (1 En 90.39–42).

The view of history that emerges from apocalypses is often described as "apocalyptic determinism."[211] Chapter 5 considers any scope these writers envisage for human decisions for faithful practice and divine and human responsibility within this framework (where important differences between 4 Ezra and 2 Baruch emerge), but certainly as they describe the unfolding periods of history, these texts depict history proceeding according to a foretold pattern. Indeed, the prevalence of, for instance, reinterpretations of Daniel's prophecies, even in texts of different genres (4 Ezra 12.11–12; cf. *Ant.* 10.210 above), confirms this is a view late Second Temple Jewish writers frequently share about divine guidance over the periods of history and its end.

### 3.3.4 The War Scroll

In the War Scroll, the writer's claims about the future are couched in terms that assert both their accuracy and the privileged status of the readers (17.8). The War Scroll does not contain prophecies in the form of *vaticinia ex eventu*, but the writer does set out prophetic claims about events to take place in the future, beyond the implied reader's time.[212] The text provides no hint of any question of the accuracy of the scenario outlined in it.

The writer portrays the eschatological war's events as divinely determined, with no scope for change or impact by human actors, despite the active (but also predetermined) roles that humans are to perform as the plan itself unfolds.[213] The day on which the Kittim will fall has been "determined by [the God of Israel] since ancient times" (1QM 1.10; 13.14; 17.5).[214] The hymn to be sung following victory asserts: "for you know our appointed time and today it shines for us" (18.10). The sons of light also enjoy support from significant figures who have been appointed from ancient times[215] and supernatural beings actively engage in the conflict, with "the assembly of the gods and the congregation of men (אנשים)" battling each other amid "the roar of a huge multitude and the

---

211 Popović, "Apocalyptic Determinism," 256.
212 The War Scroll also applies the prediction of a star departing from Jacob and victory over Moab and the sons of Seth in Num 24.17–19 as a prophecy of the Kittim's destruction (1QM 11.6–8).
213 See further Chapter 5 on humans as divine instruments.
214 The writer also finds support for these claims in Isa 31.8 at 1QM 11.11–12.
215 See Chapter 6 regarding the various titles attributed to characters in the War Scroll. However understood in relation to other expectations in Second Temple Judaism, characters like the Prince of Light and the angel Michael confirm divine involvement in the events, certainty of victory, and the eschatological significance of the battle.

shout of gods and of men (אנשים)" (1.10 – 11).²¹⁶ God acts to strengthen the people in battle and, regarding enemies, "will wage war against them from the heavens" (11.17).

Geza Vermes summarises the divinely determined structure of the war:

> The phases of its battle are fixed in advance, its plan established and its duration predetermined. The opposing forces are equally matched and only by the intervention of "the mighty hand of God" is the balance between them to be disturbed when he deals an "everlasting blow" to "Belial and all the host of his kingdom."²¹⁷

The events foretold in the War Scroll describe a divine plan (13.2), in opposition to the plan of Belial (13.4; cf. 17.4 – 6).²¹⁸ According to 13.11, God has created Belial;²¹⁹ though created "for the pit," his purpose is "to bring about wickedness and guilt." The writer seems unconcerned by any resultant questions about divine responsibility for this destructive empire. The Scroll's detailed picture of determinism focuses only on divine sovereignty and the certainty of eschatological victory for the sons of light.

## 3.4 Summary: prophetic signs and determinism

Despite their different ways of portraying these concepts and their different literary forms, writers from Diodorus Siculus to Virgil and the author of 2 Baruch indicate that some form of accurate prophetic insight into the future is possible, which suggests that history is to some extent set in advance. Some texts, like 4 Ezra and 2 Baruch, even state that the foretold events are a result of divine planning. As writers like Valerius, Diodorus, and Tacitus, as well as Josephus, incorporate accounts of portents or dreams, they communicate a sense of inevitability about the ensuing events after the fact. In *vaticinia ex eventu* in the Ae-

---

216 See Chapter 5 for discussion of this plural picture of "gods" engaged in the battle.
217 Vermes, *The Complete Dead Sea Scrolls*, 163.
218 Vermes attempts a fuller reconstruction of the fragmentary text at 1QM 17.4 – 6, reading: "the day appointed by Him for the defeat and overthrow of the Prince of the kingdom of wickedness" (Vermes, *The Complete Dead Sea Scrolls*; cf. García Martínez and Tigchelaar, *The Dead Sea Scrolls*, 141).
219 Dimant argues that 1QM is unique among the DSS for making this claim, though "Belial" terminology is an important marker of sectarian texts (Devorah Dimant, "Between Qumran Sectarian and Non-Sectarian Texts: The Case of Belial and Mastema," in *The Dead Sea Scrolls and Contemporary Culture*, ed. Adolfo D. Roitman, Lawrence H. Schiffman, and Shani Tzoref, STDJ 93 (Leiden: Brill, 2011), 245).

*neid*, Virgil supplies not only a similar sense of inevitability, given all of the events leading up to the end of the historical review were set in advance, but an interpretation of the significance of these events. The view of history evoked by prophecies such as those in 4 Ezra and 2 Baruch, but also present in the War Scroll and Josephus's narratives, affirms divine guidance of the whole course of history including the events of the end.

Thus determinism in history can confirm hope (the promised end to present suffering is assured, as also the events of the past took place as predicted),[220] endorse existing authorities,[221] or underscore the futility of human resistance.[222] In some of the texts of this study, divine forces can drive the course of history as part of a larger plan; in others they simply react in the moment—whether acting through caprice or interacting dynamically with human failures of virtue or their positive contributions to divine priorities. Luke's approach to prophecy in the context of claims about divine guidance of history owes much to the view found in the texts with an overarching account of divine guidance of history discussed here, such as the War Scroll, *Jewish War*, 4 Ezra, and 2 Baruch, though his βουλὴ τοῦ θεοῦ also displays important flexibility and adaptability.

## 4 Prophetic insight and the divine plan in Luke/Acts

Prophecy and its fulfilment plays an important role in Luke's narrative and has attracted considerable scholarly attention.[223] The following treats this motif more narrowly, first highlighting some of the ways in which Luke's approach to prophecy illuminates themes of determinism and divine guidance in history,

---

[220] Cf. 4 Ezra 11–12 and 2 Bar 53–76; predictions of the past also undergird the function of prophecy in the War Scroll, *Jewish War,* and in many ways also Luke/Acts.
[221] This is the effect of determinism in the *Aeneid*.
[222] Valerius frequently presents this view, as in the tragic inevitability of Croesus's son's death (1.7.ext4).
[223] On Luke's "proof from prophecy" see Cadbury, *The Making of Luke-Acts*; Fitzmyer, *The Gospel according to Luke*, 1:179–81; Keener, *Acts*, 1:483–91; Peter Mallen, *The Reading and Transformation of Isaiah in Luke-Acts*, LNTS 367 (London: T&T Clark, 2008), 4–9; Rothschild, *Luke-Acts and the Rhetoric*, 158–84; Holladay, *Acts*, 49–50, 54–55. On Luke's substantiation of the plan of God through a retrospective means of fulfilment, see Sterling, *Historiography and Self-Definition*, 359. Also Moessner, "Luke's 'Plan of God,'" Moessner, "The 'Script,'" and Sterling, "'Opening the Scriptures.'" On prediction as a rhetorical technique, see Rothschild, *Luke-Acts and the Rhetoric*, 158. On ancient uses of scripture, see Fishbane, *Biblical Interpretation*; Sanders, "God Gave the Law."

and then examining Luke's explicit attributions to divine guidance in his portrayal of the divine plan.

Crucially, as in the similar dynamic discussed above in relation to Luke's use of δεῖ, in Luke/Acts, not all events that have been accurately *foretold* have been divinely *planned*. Rather, more frequently, God's capacity to foresee accurately the tragic opposition to the divine βουλή makes possible divine planning to mitigate its effects. In this way, Luke allows for a more dynamic interaction between divine and human agency (a topic to which I return in Chapter 5), and even some diversity in his portrait of divine responsibility for particular events, which shows that Luke is not always strictly consistent or rigid in his presentation of divine guidance. But, Luke indicates, the promises about divine action in the future remain absolutely certain. This confirms again the assurance Luke promises to provide his reader: the dynamic βουλή can be opposed, but it cannot be stopped.

## 4.1 Prophecy in Luke/Acts: interpreting the past and assuring for the future

Luke treats prophecy positively and has his characters demonstrate that the future can be accurately foretold.[224] In many ways, Luke thereby demonstrates some continuity with a great variety of writers discussed above, from Valerius Maximus to the author of 2 Baruch. Agabus's prophecy about a famine is endorsed (Acts 11:28),[225] the prophetic gift of Philip's daughters is portrayed positively (21.9),[226] and Ananias finds things just as he has been told when he goes to help Paul (9.17). Even the girl who prophesies through a Pythian spirit

---

**224** Squires discusses miracles and σημεῖα in Luke/Acts in the category of portents, arguing they are about God's ongoing care and involvement. Although Josephus does connect signs and providence in *J.W.* 6.310, this relates to the signs functioning as warnings. In Luke/Acts, however, as also in Mark, miracles constitute revealed evidence of the world as it really is and of Jesus' true identity. This is also seen in prophecy about signs that will in turn provide the witnesses with information about the significance, and imminence, of the eschatological events they portend (cf. Luke 11.20; 21.5–33). If there is an element of warning, it is about the urgency of repentance and vigilance (Luke 21.34–36; Acts 17.31).
**225** This ensures that Agabus's credibility is already established when he returns in Acts 21.10 to prophesy about Paul's treatment in Jerusalem. Contra those who suggest Agabus is introduced as though a new character in Acts 21.10, the connection to 11.28 provides important background for the reader, supporting Agabus's prophetic abilities and creating an expectation that the prophecy to follow in 21.11 will also be accurate.
**226** Philip's daughters' prophetic abilities both affirm the possibility of accurate prophecy and establish an expectation that it will take place in these scenes (Conzelmann, *Acts of the Apostles*, 178).

is portrayed as accurate (16.16–18),²²⁷ akin to the special insight attributed to unclean spirits across the synoptic tradition (Luke 4.41; 8.28/pars).²²⁸ But Luke's prophecies provide a certainty beyond, for instance, that in Valerius Maximus's anecdotes, where the focus lies on the comic brunt of a victim's ill-fated attempts to escape the inescapable; prophecies in Luke point to the significance of the events unfolding in his narrative about Jesus and his apostolic witnesses, and confirm those further events promised for the future.

### 4.1.1 Prophecy made and fulfilled within Luke's narrative

Several characters offer prophecies which are then fulfilled within the narrative. In addition to confirming the characteristic accuracy and positive portrayal of prophecy in Luke/Acts,²²⁹ these prophecies also interpret the significance of the later events which then unfold in the narrative, simultaneously performing an important literary function.²³⁰ The infancy narratives supply several examples. For instance, following his inspired arrival at the temple (καὶ ἦλθεν ἐν τῷ πνεύματι εἰς τὸ ἱερόν, Luke 2.27),²³¹ Simeon's words over the infant Jesus inform the reader's encounter with later events. Luke has Simeon interpret a key element of Jesus' mission, as he pronounces Jesus "a light for revelation (ἀποκάλυψιν) to the Gentiles (ἐθνῶν), and for glory to your people Israel (λαοῦ

---

**227** For background on Pythian sibyls, see Cancik, "The End of the World," 87, 91, 94–96. Whereas Luke denounces elements of the girl's situation, he does not question her predictions' accuracy. Spencer criticises Luke's perpetuation of cultural norms about women of lower economic status in his stigmatised portrayal of her prophecy, despite its accuracy and the promise of Acts 2.18 (F. Scott Spencer, "Out of Mind, Out of Voice: Slave-Girls and Prophetic Daughters in Luke-Acts," *BibInt* 7 (1999): 146–51). Johnson makes the point about Luke's characteristic attention to wealth and possessions, evident in the slave masters' concerns about their own financial gain, and highlights a contrasting parallel with the generosity of Lydia and her friends in the preceding story (Johnson, *The Acts of the Apostles*, 298).
**228** Conzelmann, *Acts of the Apostles*, 131. See also the lexical connections to Luke 8.8 highlighted by Tannehill, *Narrative Unity*, 2:197.
**229** Rius-Camps and Read-Heimerdinger list examples of positive prophets in Luke and Acts (Rius-Camps and Read-Heimerdinger, *The Message of Acts*, 4:162 n. 108).
**230** Johnson identifies "programmatic prophecy," which interprets the narrative (Johnson, *The Gospel of Luke*, 16).
**231** Green notes there is a poignant irony in the setting for this scene, in which the temple is a location for inspired revelation about the universality of the gospel (see Green, *The Gospel of Luke*, 146; he also notes the similar irony in Acts 22.17–21).

σου Ἰσραήλ)."²³² And, relatedly, he sets a foreboding tone of tragedy, as he prophesies to Mary:

> This child is destined (κεῖται) for the falling (πτῶσιν) and the rising (ἀνάστασιν)²³³ of many in Israel, and to be a sign that will be opposed (σημεῖον ἀντιλεγόμενον) so that the inner thoughts (καρδιῶν διαλογισμοί) of many will be revealed (ἀποκαλυφθῶσιν)—and a sword will pierce your own soul (ψυχήν) too. (Luke 2.34–35)²³⁴

The reader is encouraged to trust Simeon's words: his affinity with the Holy Spirit, repeated three times in the preceding three verses, and the accuracy of his past prophetic insight, portrayed as fulfilled in this encounter with Jesus (that "he would not see death before he had seen the Lord's Messiah," v. 26), underscore his reliability.²³⁵ Thus, Simeon's interpretation of the events to unfold later in the narrative becomes authoritative.²³⁶ The parallel description of Anna's

---

**232** On the tragedy of Israel in Luke/Acts, particularly as established in the infancy narratives, see Robert C. Tannehill, "Israel in Luke-Acts: A Tragic Story," *JBL* 104 (1985): 74.
**233** Ἀνάστασις is used six times in Luke. Each relates to expectations of a resurrection of the righteous, or debate with Sadducees about the resurrection. The 11 uses in Acts refer to the resurrection of the dead as an eschatological event and the proclamation of Jesus' resurrection (see Chapter 6 for further discussion of resurrection as a key theme of the apostles' proclamation). There are no "domestic" meanings of ἀνάστασις. In this context, Simeon's prophecy comes loaded with the idea of Jesus being situated for the *resurrection* of many, with parallel eschatological consequences for the falling of many, brought about by their opposition to Jesus.
**234** See Johnson on the motif of the rejected prophet (Johnson, *The Gospel of Luke*, 16–17). Alexander suggests that this prophecy (as also other elements of Luke 1–4) links in important ways to the ending of Acts (Loveday Alexander, "Reading Luke-Acts from Back to Front," in *Acts in Its Ancient Literary Context: A Classicist Looks at the Acts of the Apostles*, JSNTSup 298 (London: T&T Clark, 2007), 224–26). The tragedy foreshadowed by Simeon perhaps functions like the prophecies with twists discussed above—as their fulfilment is finally narrated, the reader realises the true meaning of the prophecy.
**235** Rothschild attempts to distinguish between "human" and "divine" prophecies in Luke/Acts, arguing that, rhetorically, "human prophecies" make the historiographical narrative more believable to a Hellenistic audience (Rothschild, *Luke-Acts and the Rhetoric*, 182). However, separating the divine from human in these passages is impossible; as even Rothschild notes, "these categories overlap" (p. 176). All accurate prophecy in Luke/Acts requires *spiritual* insight into the world as it really is (see discussion of insight in apocalypses above). Simeon exemplifies the relationship: he is righteous (Luke 2.25) and anticipates God's redemptive action (in light of an earlier revelation, v. 26), but the Holy Spirit facilitates his prophetic insight and guides him to its fulfilment (vv. 25, 27).
**236** Green highlights the emphatic nature of Luke's word order, as Simeon begins speaking with "now": "*now*, you are *releasing* your servant, *Master*" (2.11), which he suggests supports Luke's emphasis on the present nature of salvation already unfolding in these events (Green, *The Gospel of Luke*, 147).

faithfulness and her actions in directing those looking for the redemption of Jerusalem to the infant further confirms the significance of the unfolding events (2.36–38).[237]

Indeed, as prophecies throughout the infancy narratives are fulfilled, they interpret the unfolding events and provide assurance about further claims made about the future. For instance, having told Zechariah that John will prepare the way for the *Lord*, Gabriel simultaneously confirms Jesus' identity (Luke 1.17; cf. also 2.26). The fact that Gabriel is familiar from the vision in Dan 9.24–27, where he describes 70 weeks to take place before the arrival of "an anointed" ruler (9.25) followed by destruction and final vindication, may further underscore the significance of what is happening here in Luke.[238] Gabriel's declaration to Mary, likewise confirmed by the epiphany's accuracy in other respects, must also be trusted: Jesus' kingdom will have no end (Luke 1.33). Epiphanies and dreams in Acts likewise reveal and interpret events that then unfold in the course of the narrative, as discovered, for instance, by Ananias, Peter, Cornelius, and Paul (Acts 9.11–12, 15–16; 10.3–6, 11–20; 27.24).[239]

---

[237] There is some question about whether some infancy predictions are fulfilled or subverted by the narrative. Does Luke suggest Anna's actions confirm the association between Jesus and the redemption of Jerusalem, or is she correcting misunderstanding by pointing people in the correct direction for hope? (Luke 2.38; cf. Luke 1.68–79; Acts 1.7). I suggest the latter is the better reading (contra Gaventa, *Acts*, 65). Similarly, does Zechariah's song of messianic, Davidic hope (Luke 1.68–79) reflect the hopes that will be fulfilled in the narrative, or perhaps expectations that will be reshaped? Likewise cf. Acts 1.6–8 and discussion below at Chapter 6 §5.3.1.

[238] There are some slight differences between the LXX and MT text here; both refer to an anointing, but the MT is more explicit about an anointed prince or ruler in v. 25. It is, however, interesting that the only references to Gabriel in canonical texts come in Dan 8–9 and Luke 1 (with appearances to each of Zechariah and Mary). Wolter suggests in relation to the first reference to Gabriel in Luke 1.19, that a "conscious reference" to Dan 9.21 and its setting at the time of the evening offering (as the appearance to Zechariah likewise happens during an offering in Luke 1.8–22), is "probably not intended" (Michael Wolter, *The Gospel according to Luke*, trans. Wayne Coppins and Christoph Heilig, BMSEC (Waco, TX: Baylor; Tübingen: Mohr Siebeck, 2016–2017), 68), though he does argue that the passage nonetheless refers to eschatological fulfilment (p. 66). Fitzmyer lists additional allusions to Daniel in the scene with Gabriel and Zechariah, and in relation to the motif of the Day of the Lord (Fitzmyer, *The Gospel of Luke*, 1:315–16).

[239] Ananias learns about Saul, his recent experience, and the inevitable response to his future mission (Acts 9.11–12, 15–16); Cornelius and Peter are made aware of each other and events that unfold as indicated—and with considerable repetition in the retelling, to underscore the point (10.3–6, 11–20; see further discussion of this episode in Chapter 5 §6.3.1 below); and Paul is told that he will stand before Caesar in Rome (27.24), simultaneously confirming for the reader that—regardless of shipwrecks or opposition plots—Paul will make it to Rome. See Farahian on the connection between the prophetic dreams in Acts and Peter's quotation from Joel at Pente-

### 4.1.2 Events identified as the fulfilment of biblical prophecy

Luke also identifies the events of his narrative as the fulfilment of biblical prophecy.[240] Much can be (and has been) said about these features of Luke's narrative.[241] Luke's use of prophecy from Jewish scriptures performs several functions,[242] among which is included assurance that the community's present circumstances, as also the death of Jesus, were accurately foretold through the prophets. Luke uses biblical prophecy to confirm that God had foreseen even apparently disastrous events such as the rejection of the Messiah.[243] However, as I argued in the discussion of Luke's use of δεῖ above, Luke does not generally equate these events directly with the divine plan.[244] Rather, prophecy confirms that God has already adapted to the predictable outcome of Jesus' rejection to ensure the promised end (Acts 3.13–26; cf. 17.31).

In two programmatic passages, Luke portrays the events of the narrative as the fulfilment of biblical prophecy. Jesus' speech at Nazareth (Luke 4.16–18) declares the fulfilment "today" (v. 21) of a spliced citation from Isa 58.6 and 61.1–2 (Luke 4.18–19) and establishes key themes of Jesus' ministry, including the negative reception he will receive from "insider" characters, even directly as a result of the priorities of the ministry he was anointed to fulfil.[245] Similarly, Peter's

---

cost (Edmond Farahian, "Paul's Vision at Troas (Acts 16:9–10)," in *Luke and Acts*, ed. Gerald O'Collins and Gilberto Marconi (New York: Paulist, 1991), 204; cf. Spencer, "Out of Mind," 151).
**240** On Mroczek's helpful reminder about the risks of terminology such as "biblical" when considering writers such as Luke in the first century (Mroczek, *The Literary Imagination*, 4–9, 40–41), see discussion above (p. 129–30, nn. 331 and 333). Here I use the language to indicate Luke's use of texts to which he attributes authority, without venturing any claims about the limits of the set of texts he saw in this light.
**241** See n. 223 above.
**242** Moessner, "Luke's 'Plan of God'"; Sterling, "'Opening the Scriptures,'" 217.
**243** Contra Rothschild, who argues that "prediction" is a rhetorical technique: "from its very earliest appearances in Homeric epic, prediction in ancient historical narrative serves to prepare audiences for implausible events of the upcoming narrative. Prediction is redundant in the narration of plausible or widely accepted accounts" (Rothschild, *Luke-Acts and the Rhetoric*, 158). Luke does not simply attempt to validate his narrative through creating prediction and fulfilment relationships, but as Fishbane has also identified in other early Christian and Second Temple Jewish texts (Fishbane, *Biblical Interpretation*), Luke searches scripture for texts that support his claims about the significance of the events he narrates.
**244** The presentation of the divine βουλή in Acts 4.28 may be the exception to this. See §4.2.3 below.
**245** The tendency to describe conflict in Luke/Acts in terms of Jewish and gentile groups is so strong that Johnson even overlays a Jewish/gentile divide over the conflict between Nazareth and Capernaum in Luke 4 (Johnson, *The Gospel of Luke*, 82). However, the tension that arises in this scene, when Jesus speaks about his powerful action outside his hometown, and draws in the biblical examples of Elijah and Elisha as a model for his own ministry, is between "insid-

speech at Pentecost (Acts 2.14–36) makes use of Joel 2.28–32, Ps 16.8–11, and Ps 110.1, and interprets the events of Jesus' death, resurrection, and ascension, as well as the present time in the fledgling discipleship community, as fulfilment of scripture (Acts 2.16, 25, 31–32, 36; cf. 13.34–39).[246]

In particular, Luke's explanations of Jesus' suffering and death make claims about biblical prophecy. Jesus' resurrection appearances, as also Paul's speech before Agrippa, assert that "Moses and the prophets" point to Jesus' suffering (Luke 24.26–27, 44–47; Acts 26.22–23; cf. Luke 16.29, 31; Acts 28.23). As exemplified in the programmatic events at Nazareth, and evident throughout Luke's narrative, that characters will reject the good news and its anointed prophet is predictable. Stephen's speech confirms that obduracy is endemic in the history of God's people (Acts 7).[247] In his similarly broad account of Israel's history in Pisidian Antioch, Paul explicitly names the tragic consequences which arose from the Jerusalem residents' failure to understand the prophets, through which they *ironically* fulfilled those same prophecies in causing Jesus' death (Acts 13.27).[248]

Thus, Luke does not suggest God's faithful guidance of history attempts to create or plans this response, even though the future remains assured. Rather, as divine inspiration allows accurate prophecy that significant groups will reject God's guidance, the divine βουλή may also adapt to ensure that God's ends are ultimately achieved. Carl Holladay observes the major themes in Stephen's speech set "the framework for the overall story of Acts," namely: "When God seeks to achieve the divine purpose among the people of Israel, they typically resist but fail to thwart God's purpose."[249] There is an important note of tragedy inherent in this predictable rejection, foreshadowed first by Simeon's prophecy and evident still in Paul's closing comments in Rome in Acts 28.[250]

---

ers" and "outsiders." Outsiders may be gentiles, as in the case of Naaman the Syrian (cf. Luke 4.27), but they may also be widows, sinners, or tax collectors. And it is Jesus' ministry to outsiders that consistently prompts outrage from insiders. See Kylie Crabbe, "A Sinner and a Pharisee: Challenge at Simon's Table in Luke 7:36–50," *Pacifica* 24 (2011): 251–54, 260–62.
**246** Holladay helpfully points out that the Pentecost event also fulfils promises made earlier in Luke's narrative, such as John the Baptist's pronouncement of a baptism "with the Holy Spirit and fire" (Luke 3.16; cf. 24.49; Acts 1.4–8; Holladay, *Acts*, 89). On this passage see also Chapter 6 §5.2.2.
**247** For further discussion of Acts 7 see Chapter 5.
**248** This passage in Acts 13 is discussed further below in relation to the divine βουλή.
**249** Holladay, *Acts*, 51.
**250** See Chapter 5 below.

### 4.1.3 Events prophesied for the future

Finally, Luke/Acts includes prophecies about events that remain in the future at the end of Acts. In light of the picture of accurate prophecy elsewhere, the reader is invited to trust the promises related to the events of the end in the proclamation of Jesus (Luke 13.22–30; 17.22–37; 21.25–28) and of his apostles (Acts 3.20–21; 17.31; cf. Acts 1.11). In the manner of the *vaticinia ex eventu* discussed above, some prophecies purport to "foretell" events that have already taken place in between the time of the events in Luke's narrative and the time of Luke's writing, such as Jerusalem's destruction (Luke 19.43–44; 21.20–24). Luke 21.5–36 offers an extended account of historical events and events anticipated as part of the end, to which I return in Chapter 6 in discussing Luke's view on the position of the present time in relation to the events of the end.[251] Here again, as in 4 Ezra or 2 Baruch, the readers' capacity to identify the prophesied events in their own experience serves to reassure, by confirming the events were predictable and known to God (and thus the divine plan has already incorporated them). Simultaneously, these prophecies build confidence that the remaining events of the end of history, also prophesied but not yet brought to completion, will likewise inevitably be fulfilled (Luke 17.24, 26–37; 20.42–44; 21.25–28; Acts 3.21; 17.31).

Like Josephus, Luke harbours concerns about false prophets (cf. Luke 17.23; 21.8–9).[252] But his narrative also offers evidence for readers who can read the signs in the appropriate way (cf. Luke 21.20, 28; Acts 2.17). Signs are demonstrated by the healing ministries of the apostles (Acts 3.1–10; 4.16, 22, 30; 5.12), as also the dreams and visions prophesied for the last days in the passage from Joel are fulfilled in the events of Acts (7.55–56; 9.3–7, 11–12, 15–16; 10.3–6, 11–20; 27.24; cf. Acts 2.17–21; Joel 2.28–32). As these prophecies are fulfilled, they fortify claims about the future signs. Here, portents are not indications of

---

251 This pericope has been central to debates about Luke's separation of history and eschatology (cf. Vittorio Fusco, "Problems of Structure in Luke's Eschatological Discourse (Luke 21:7–36)," in O'Collins and Marconi, *Luke and Acts*, 72–92; Conzelmann, *Theology of St Luke*; Mattill, *Luke and the Last Things*; Andrew J. Mattill, "Naherwartung, Fernerwartung, and the Purpose of Luke-Acts: Weymouth Reconsidered," *CBQ* 34 (1972): 276–93; Maddox, *The Purpose*, 115–23; Ellis, "Present and Future Eschatology in Luke," 129–46; Knight, *Luke's Gospel*, 188–89 (responding to Conzelmann)). Though related to many topics within this study, it is particularly relevant to Chapter 6, and thus discussed there.
252 Cf. *J.W.* 6.285–88. In Luke/Acts, false prophets endorse calculations of particular times, rather than maintaining the more important focus on remaining vigilant at *all* times (E. Earle Ellis, "Eschatology in Luke Revisited," in *Eschatology in Luke*, 122; cf. Luke 12.35–40). Despite this polemic, Luke maintains that true prophetic signs enable those who correctly recognise them to understand that the end is imminent (see Chapter 6).

ideal moments to go to war or prophetic insights derived from practices of divination, as in Diodorus Siculus, Valerius Maximus, or Tacitus, but unnatural phenomena associated with eschatological events in Jewish apocalyptic literature.

## 4.2 Assurance of the divine βουλή in Luke/Acts

Beyond prophecies that demonstrate the future can be foreseen, Luke explicitly affirms that God oversees the whole course of history.[253] Although only mentioned six times, the divine βουλή—as a divine purpose, plan, or intention—relates importantly to the way Luke explains the past and provides hope for the future.[254] Other characters also scheme according to a βουλή, but in doing so they draw out a reminder of the βουλή of God through their opposing plan (Luke 23.51).[255] The following considers each use of βουλή that refers to God's purpose in Luke/Acts.[256]

### 4.2.1 Luke 7.29–30

In the first appearance of the term βουλή in his account, Luke refers to the βουλὴ τοῦ θεοῦ in his description of some characters' rejection of the divine purpose, in the narrative aside at Luke 7.29–30. This aside is set within a series of sayings that function around contrasts between those who respond readily to the gospel proclamation and characters who are impossible to please, as Jesus first replies

---

[253] Several recent studies have confirmed the importance of divine oversight for the events of Luke's narrative, in light of emphases in Graeco-Roman or Jewish Hellenistic texts (Shauf, *The Divine*, 181–265; Squires, *The Plan of God*, 1–3 and passim; Uytanlet, *Luke-Acts and Jewish Historiography*, 27–67).

[254] The term βουλή itself appears in Luke and Acts twice and eight times respectively, while once in each of 1 Corinthians, Ephesians, and Hebrews.

[255] Squires, *The Plan of God*, 56. Squires makes a side comment that the existence of rival plans could imply that Jesus' death was not according to God's, but another plan, though he does not develop this idea (p. 65). Regardless, it is clear that characters can reject God's purposes (βουλή), as in a narrative aside at Luke 7.30 (Crabbe, "A Sinner and a Pharisee," 255–56).

[256] In addition to the reference to the βουλή of the council of Chief priests and scribes which schemed Jesus' death and with which Joseph of Arimathea did not agree (Luke 23.51), the term βουλή also appears in relation to a non-divine βουλή twice in Acts 27, as part of the centurion's planning (against Paul's advice) which then leads to the shipwreck (v. 12), and then the soldiers' intention to kill the prisoners so they could not escape (v. 42).

to pointed questions from followers of John the Baptist (7.18–23)[257] and then addresses the gathered crowd (7.24–28, 31–35). Rather than direct speech from Jesus, as in the surrounding verses, here Luke makes his own summary of the events as narrator, intruding into Jesus' speech either side with the claim:

> And all the people who heard this, including the tax collectors, acknowledged the justice of God, because they had been baptised with John's baptism. But by refusing to be baptised by him, the Pharisees and the lawyers rejected God's purpose (τὴν βουλὴν τοῦ θεοῦ) for themselves. (Luke 7.29–30)

The statement confirms not only the *existence* of a divine βουλή, but the possibility that characters can reject it.[258] As Jesus' speech continues, he uses a children's rhyme to illustrate the refusal of "the people of this generation" to embrace what God is doing, first in John and then in Jesus (vv. 31–34).[259] The consequences of the wilful rejection of the divine βουλή are brought home in the final statement, which asserts that the divine purpose will be upheld regardless: "Nevertheless, wisdom is vindicated by all her children" (v. 35).[260]

### 4.2.2 Acts 2.22–24

Set within his long Pentecost speech (2.14–36), Peter's proclamation in Acts 2.22–24 offers a dense description of the divine purpose borne out in Jesus' resurrection, in verses which raise some complications about how Jesus' death itself (and responsibility for this) might relate to the divine βουλή. Verse 23 makes use

---

**257** Byrne highlights that the conclusion of Jesus' words to John's disciples here, with the macarism "blessed is anyone who takes no offense at me" (7.23), indicates that some offence has been taken about the shape of Jesus' ministry, which might seem not to match that which John expected (Byrne, *The Hospitality of God*, 71).
**258** Although the topic here is baptism by John, the passage makes clear that this also fits within the βουλὴ τοῦ θεοῦ, given explicit mention is made of the phrase—notably, the only time in Luke's Gospel.
**259** Green rightly notes (also drawing on Gowler) that this challenge extends to the audience: "Luke's overt commentary in these two verses, then, serves to encourage Luke's audience to join those who 'justify God' and to distance themselves from those who reject God's purpose" (Green, *The Gospel of Luke*, 301).
**260** Cf. Matt 11.19, where Wisdom is vindicated by her deeds; in both texts Wisdom draws on associations with Prov 8 as a reference to the divine, and here in Luke, the certainty of divine justice (see Carroll, *Luke*, 174). For further discussion of the contrasts between those who participate generously, and those who refuse to, particularly as presented by these sayings about tax collectors and sinners and Pharisees and the episode (about a *particular* sinner and a Pharisee) which follows in Luke 7.36–50, see Crabbe, "A Sinner and a Pharisee," 255–56.

of three loaded terms in quick succession: ὁρίζω, βουλή, and πρόγνωσις. Commentators agree that the passage is designed to lay blame at the (Jewish, "insider") characters in the Jerusalem audience,[261] perhaps with some irony at the lesser responsibility attributed to those "outside the law" (ἄνομοι), through whom the audience is said to have killed Jesus. But as they interpret the statement as an apologetic affirmation of divine sovereignty, commentators also frequently import assumptions about "divine necessity" for Jesus' death.[262] A brief discussion of a difficulty in the Greek will help to clarify some of this confusion, before turning to consider what exactly is attributed to the divine βουλή in this passage.

C. K. Barrett observes a significant ambiguity in the passage in the adjective ἔκδοτος, which he notes should appear with a verb, such as παραδίδωμι, λαμβάνω, or a similar verb, but does not.[263] Richard Pervo suggests, perhaps too quickly, that ἔκδοτος is synonymous with παραδοθείς, using this as an opportunity to laud Luke's lexical range.[264] This is a *hapax legomenon* for the NT, and a term absent from the LXX. F. F. Bruce notes that ἔκδοτος could indicate Jesus was handed over by God or by the people.[265] He and F. J. Foakes Jackson direct readers to *Ant.* 6.316, 14.355, and 18.369,[266] but Barrett suggests that, of these, only the last is clear.[267] It is indeed difficult to discern the intended force of the "given

---

[261] Haenchen, *The Acts of the Apostles*, 180. Haenchen also responds to Overbeck's claim that Luke is characteristically anti-Jewish here, countering that "it would be more correct to discover an exoneration of the Romans" (p. 180 n. 10). Despite the lines of ethnicity down which comparisons between different groups in Luke/Acts frequently are divided (cf. Jacob Jervell, "The Divided People of God: The Restoration of Israel and the Salvation of the Gentiles," in *Luke and the People of God: A New Look at Luke-Acts* (Eugene, OR: Wipf & Stock, 2002), 42, and Johnson, *The Gospel of Luke*, 82), the idea of those "outside" the law contrasts with those who comprise Peter's audience and who began the pericope with disdain for the events unfolding. Thus the insider/outsider dynamic remains of primary interest.

[262] Marshall notes the apparent conflict between divine sovereignty and human responsibility but does not develop the point (Marshall, *The Acts of the Apostles*, 75).

[263] Barrett, *A Critical and Exegetical Commentary*, 1:142. Several manuscripts insert λαβόντες, but this is clearly secondary to get around the problem arising from the missing verb.

[264] Pervo, *Acts*, 80.

[265] Bruce, *The Book of Acts*, 123. Zerwick specifies "given up (to you) by God" (Max Zerwick, *A Grammatical Analysis of the Greek New Testament*, 3rd rev. ed. (Rome: Pontifical Biblical Institute, 1988), 354).

[266] F. J. Foakes Jackson et al., *The Beginnings of Christianity: Part 1, The Acts of the Apostles* (London: Macmillan, 1920–1933), 4:23; Bruce, *The Book of Acts*; Conzelmann cites Polybius on ἔκδοτος (Conzelmann, *Acts of the Apostles*, 20).

[267] Barrett, *A Critical and Exegetical Commentary*, 1:142. *Antiquities* 6.316 uses a different construction with a preposition, to describe being given over by sleep (λαβὼν αὐτὸν ἔκδοτον ὑπὸ τοῦ ὕπνου). *Antiquities* 18.369 uses the adjective alongside a verb (παρασχεῖν) as we might expect to see in Acts 2.23, resulting in a more straightforward expression: "for if they had been

over one" on the basis of the adjective. The verb ἐκδίδωμι, which is etymologically related, takes on the mundane meaning of letting property (cf. Luke 20.9/pars), as well as betrayal, killing, giving over, publishing (of texts), but also giving in marriage. LSJ cites meanings for ἔκδοτος which relate to not only a woman being given in marriage, but giving herself fully to her partner.

This reflexive sense is indeed how the adjective is used in *Ant.* 14.355. Here παρέχειν supplies the expected verb in a context in which Herod exhorts each of the distressed Herodians "not to give himself wholly over (παρέχειν αὑτὸν ἔκδοτον) to grief (τῇ λύπῃ)."[268] Could Luke similarly mean to present Jesus giving *himself* over? Such a reading would also rely on a decision about what kind of datives follow in the phrase τοῦτον τῇ ὡρισμένῃ βουλῇ καὶ προγνώσει τοῦ θεοῦ ἔκδοτον. If offering a construction akin to that in *Ant.* 14.355, Luke here could be indicating that Jesus gave "*himself* over *to* the definite plan, and by the foreknowledge of God you [the audience], having crucified him, killed him."[269]

On balance, however, this reading seems unlikely. Apart from the missing verb, Luke also does not include a reflexive pronoun. And the pairing of ὡρισμένῃ βουλῇ and προγνώσει τοῦ θεοῦ between τοῦτον and ἔκδοτον suggests a hendiadys, indicating the two datives should be taken together. The sense of the best reading, therefore, seems to be that Jesus was given over (to the audience) in keeping with the definite plan and foreknowledge of God.[270]

It is important here, however, to avoid either presuming the meaning of παραδίδωμι alongside ἔκδοτος, or conflating the remainder of the sentence with the divine purpose. The verses do not describe a divine plan to *betray* Jesus, but to give him over to God's people. Likewise, the people's response to him—that "having crucified him, you killed him"—reflects the tragic reception of Jesus by his own, not a divine plan or desire for his death.[271] Here, at least,

---

willing to deliver him up, it was not in their power to do so..." (οὐδὲ γὰρ βουλομένοις ἔκδοτον παρασχεῖν δυνηθῆναι).

268 Given Josephus supplies the verb here with αὐτόν, his meaning is clear. Luke's syntax is not clear.

269 Thus, ἔκδοτος becomes the one who dedicates or gives himself.

270 Note that the dative can function differently from the explicit κατὰ τὸ ὡρισμένον (Luke 22.22) frequently cited as a parallel.

271 As I have argued throughout this chapter, elsewhere in Luke/Acts, prediction and planning can normally be distinguished. Wallace likewise suggests on the basis of syntax that the set plan and foreknowledge in 2.23 should be separated (Daniel B. Wallace, *Greek Grammar Beyond the Basics: An Exegetical Syntax of the New Testament* (Grand Rapids: Zondervan, 1997), 288). However, he also readily admits that he makes further decisions about the relationship between the terms and the meaning of ἔκδοτος based not on syntax but on his interpretation of general

Luke remains consistent in his use of the divine βουλή alongside his portrait of the prophet who is sent (even to announce "the year of the Lord's *acceptance*," cf. Luke 4.19), but is then tragically *rejected*. In an ironic twist—evidenced in Acts 2.22–24 as elsewhere—and through divine foresight, such opposition nonetheless becomes the means of furthering the divine purpose (Acts 2.24–36; cf. Acts 8:1, 4).[272] Peter's speech concludes not simply by proclaiming the resurrection of Jesus, but in calling his audience to repent and to be baptised in light of his vindicated, messianic rule (vv. 33–36, 38–39).

### 4.2.3 Acts 4.27–28

A somewhat different accent emerges from the reference to the divine βουλή in Acts 4.24–30, which Robert Tannehill describes as the "chief" instance of a more rigid determinism in Luke's portrait of Jesus' death.[273] Following Peter and John's release with only a warning, they gather with their friends to recount their recent incident with chief priests and elders (cf. Acts 4.1–21), and share a prayer[274] that asserts divine sovereignty as Creator ("Sovereign Lord, who made the heaven and the earth, the sea, and everything in them," v. 24; cf. Acts 17.24) and ultimate political authority (against whom earthly rulers only through vanity take a stand, vv. 26–27). Applying the citation from Ps 2.1–2 to recent events,[275] they go on:

---

themes about the divine plan, which he cites from Bock (p. 288). The sense of "giving over" here might helpfully be read in light also of Paul's reference to the prophets and Moses saying that the Messiah would be capable of or subject to suffering in Acts 26.22–23 (see p. 160 n. 122 above in this chapter's discussion of δεῖ at §2.5 (a term notably absent from these verses) and the fuller discussion of the Acts 26 passage in Chapter 6 at §5.2.1).

272 Tannehill focuses on the ironic fulfilment of the divine plan despite opposition in a similar way (Tannehill, *Narrative Unity*, 1:37; Tannehill, "Israel in Luke-Acts," 74, 77). This follows the similar pattern identified in Bovon's interpretation of Luke 9.22 (Bovon, *Luke: Commentary*, 1:363). Although Holladay seems to give a more deterministic interpretation of Jesus' suffering in Acts (Holladay, *Acts*, 59–60), he nonetheless unpacks the references to God raising Jesus in Acts 2.24 (as also 2.32; 3.15; 4.10; 5.30; 10.40–41; 13.30, 33–34, 37; and 17.31) thus: "God raises Jesus from the dead, thereby righting the wrong done by those who killed him" (p. 63).

273 Tannehill observes that even this kind of approach to divine sovereignty, which leads to identifying opponents as divine instruments, also serves Luke's characteristic explanation of how Jesus' death "ironically fulfilled God's purpose" (Tannehill, *Narrative Unity*, 2:72).

274 Holladay suggests that because of the prayer's length, use (and interpretation) of a biblical citation, and "elevated tone" it should be treated as a speech (Holladay, *Acts*, 130).

275 Holladay collates numerous further parallels between Jesus' trial in Luke and the terms in Ps 2.1–2, which he suggests underscore the connection and thus lead the reader to conclude that in Jesus God has fulfilled the prophecy of Ps 2 (Holladay, *Acts*, 132).

For in this city, in fact, both Herod and Pontius Pilate, with the Gentiles and the peoples of Israel, gathered together against your holy servant Jesus, whom you anointed, to do whatever your hand (ποιῆσαι ὅσα ἡ χείρ σου) and your plan (βουλή) had predestined to take place (προώρισεν γενέσθαι). (Acts 4.27–28)

Having implicated *everyone*—key individuals,[276] as well as Jewish groups and gentiles alike—the believers proclaim absolute divine sovereignty. The speech reflects a strong polemical interest in disempowering the opponents who acted against Jesus and explaining their apparent agency in the matter by asserting that, despite appearances, God was really controlling their actions.[277] Luke's more characteristic explanation of the negative events of the past as the result of tragic opposition is here set aside by this emphatic claim that even opponents are only divine instruments (cf. Luke 23.12) and act by God's hand to do what had already been determined.[278]

### 4.2.4 Acts 5.38–39

Mirroring the similar incident of imprisonment and trial in Acts 4.1–21, the episode narrated in Acts 5.10–42[279] includes controversy that leads to Jewish authorities seizing Peter and the apostles and imprisoning them overnight. Unbeknownst to the Jewish leaders who flamboyantly summon "the Council and the whole body of the elders of Israel" (v. 21) the following day, the apostles have been released overnight by an angel. A humorous, slightly farcical, incident ensues, during which the apostles are sent for, not found at the prison, and eventually retrieved from the synagogue. The chief priest's accusations are then met

---

**276** Note the alliance between Herod and Pilate, which is unique to Luke (cf. Luke 23.12). Haenchen aligns each group with a group in Ps 2.1–2 (Luke's citation is the same as the LXX): Herod, Pilate, Roman soldiers, and Israel correlating with "the kings of the earth," rulers, ἔθνη, and λαοί respectively (Haenchen, *The Acts of the Apostles*, 226–27).
**277** This common technique in explaining the past is evident in earlier texts drawing on Deuteronomistic theology, and the topic of further discussion in Chapter 5. By contrast, Conzelmann finds in these verses evidence that Luke has emphasised the *guilt* of Pilate, "in line with Luke's fundamental view of salvation history" (Conzelmann, *Acts of the Apostles*, 35).
**278** Προορίζω is not a common word. In the NT it also appears twice together in Romans, and once in each of 1 Corinthians and Ephesians, but it is not used in the LXX or the Greek texts of this study. If *praedestineo* is taken to be the Latin equivalent, it also does not feature in this study's Latin texts, including 4 Ezra's Latin text. Note, however, that the Vulgate also does not give *praedestineo* in Acts 4.28, though it does for the other uses in Rom 8. Here it supplies instead *discerno*.
**279** This pericope is normally treated from v. 17, but the Portico scene directly prior sets the context for the arrest.

by a speech from Peter and the apostles, in which they passionately appeal to the need to obey (πειθαρχεῖν δεῖ) God and not humans (5.29; cf. 4.19–20). This offers an important key to understanding the incident: which characters obey God or humans?[280] "The people" themselves are impressed by the apostles as they perform signs and witness to God (v. 13); the apostles attend to God's instruction throughout. By contrast, the Sanhedrin acts in response to their *fear of* the people (v. 26), who are their primary reference point, and eventually choose to listen to a particular person, who is himself identified, perhaps negatively, as popular: Gamaliel.[281]

Gamaliel intervenes when the Sanhedrin is in a rage and, having offered a reflection on other revolutionary movements that had blown over, advises:

> keep away from these men and let them alone; because if this plan (βουλή) or this undertaking is of human origin, it will fail; but if it is of God, you will not be able to overthrow them—in that case you may even be found fighting against God (θεομάχοι εὑρεθῆτε)![282] (vv. 38–39)[283]

---

280 Crabbe, "Being Found Fighting against God," 30.
281 The consequences of Gamaliel's popularity indicates a key difference from the kind of reception enjoyed by the apostles in v. 13. That the people praise the apostles (ἐμεγάλυνεν αὐτούς) is not presented negatively as it does not lead them to listen to people over God. However, that Gamaliel is held in honour by all the people (τίμιος παντὶ τῷ λαῷ) indicates a different status; this makes him a desirable consultant for the Sanhedrin (Darr, "Irenic or Ironic?", 135), given the people are their reference point (who choose to listen to a person, who in turn understands the views of other people, rather than to God). Interestingly, both Luke and Josephus (Steve Mason, "Josephus's Pharisees: The Narratives," in Neusner and Chilton, *In Quest of the Historical Pharisees*, 37–38) criticise Pharisees as popular. Luke seems to portray Gamaliel negatively through stereotype on the basis of popularity, in addition to his inadequate response to the good news (cf. Luke 11.43).
282 The possibility of becoming a θεομάχος comes with a further set of ideas in Graeco-Roman literature, including hubris and the punishment it elicits. See Chapter 5.
283 These conditions employ different constructions. The first, about a human origin for the apostles' movement is expressed in the subjunctive (with ἐάν), while the second is a conditional in the indicative (εἰ δὲ ἐκ θεοῦ ἐστιν). Some translate with emphasis on the second half of the statement to indicate "since this is the case...". In this way, they paint Gamaliel as a positive figure (David B. Gowler, *Host, Guest, Enemy and Friend: Portraits of the Pharisees in Luke and Acts*, Emory Studies in Early Christianity 2 (New York: Lang, 1991), 278; Squires, *The Plan of God*, 58; Raimo Hakola, "'Friendly' Pharisees and Social Identity in Acts," in *Contemporary Studies in Acts*, ed. Thomas E. Phillips (Macon, GA: Mercer University Press, 2009), 199). I follow Darr, who cites Luke 11.19 to demonstrate that the conditional cannot always take this sense. Rather, Darr suggests that while maintaining conditional force, this construction emphases the "more pressing position" (Darr, "Irenic or Ironic?", 136–39). Thus, according to Gamaliel's statement, whether this condition is true is still in question, but the (severe) consequences which follow if it is, are not.

He persuades the council. But he inadvertently assures the reader. Irony lies in the tension between information to which some characters (the apostles) and the reader have access, which is hidden from Gamaliel, creating the "fall guy" who doesn't "get 'it,'" as in Lyons's definition of irony above.[284] For those who know that an angel has just released the apostles from prison, it is completely clear that "this βουλή is of God," and therefore the apodosis holds: the early discipleship community and its proclamation of the resurrection of Jesus cannot be overthrown.[285]

The possibility of being found to be θεομάχοι is real; opponents of God shape the unfolding narrative not only in the events earlier in the account, such as Jesus' death, but for instance in the persecution that breaks out following Stephen's death.[286] But even this is incorporated into the assured progression of the divine plan (cf. 8.1, 4). The challenge for Gamaliel, as also for anyone who similarly remains ambivalent—or even opposes the apostles' proclamation[287]—is

---

[284] Lyons, "The Words of Gamaliel," 29. Interpreters have offered diverse portraits of Gamaliel: secret believer (Lyons, "The Words of Gamaliel," 42; also many early readers, including Bede (*Comm. Acts* 5.34), Chrysostom (*Hom. Acts.* 14), and Pseudo-Clem. (*Clem Rec.* 1.65.4); see Heidi J. Hornik and Mikeal C. Parsons, *The Acts of the Apostles through the Centuries*, Wiley Blackwell Bible Commentaries (Chichester: Wiley-Blackwell, 2017), 88); well-disposed Pharisee (Hakola, "'Friendly' Pharisees," 199; P. J. Tomson, "Gamaliel's Counsel and the Apologetic Strategy of Luke-Acts," in *The Unity of Luke-Acts*, ed. Joseph Verheyden, BETL 142 (Leuven: Leuven University Press, 1999), 603); supporter of the disciples (either intentionally or ironically, Darr, "Irenic or Ironic?", 129); or Paul's teacher in persecution (Johnson, *The Gospel of Luke*, 99), associated with the criticism of Pharisees in the Gospel (Darr, "Irenic or Ironic?", 125). Gamaliel is certainly the victim of irony, but in a manner that has broader implications—despite his wisdom on the unstoppable outworking of the divine plan, Gamaliel fails to recognise what God is doing and to participate. Thus, by failing to appreciate the content of Peter's and the apostles' proclamation, whether distracted by popularity or other pragmatic concerns, Gamaliel demonstrates that he is unable to listen to God. His fence-sitting exposes his inadequate response (Crabbe, "Being Found Fighting against God," 35).

[285] Tannehill suggests an ironic contrast lies between Gamaliel's statement and "the Sanhedrin's impotence" in vv. 17–26 (Tannehill, *Narrative Unity*, 2:74). Pervo compares Luke and Josephus in relation to Gamaliel's statement, suggesting for both "God supports those who have the right understanding (5.35–39). In the most vulgar sense, God is on the side of the winners" (Pervo, *Acts*, 24). While there is a sense of this in Josephus (e.g. *J.W.* 2.345–401; 5.362–419; see Chapter 5), Pervo's analysis overlooks key elements of Luke's treatment of assurance in the face of opposition, based in part upon his reading of the Gamaliel incident.

[286] See Chapter 5.

[287] I take the view that Luke's implied audience are already disciples, although the narrative contains an apologetic edge to support these believers' own proclamation to those outside the community (cf. Sterling, *Historiography and Self-Definition*, 385–86; Squires, *The Plan of God*, 192).

to recognise and accept the invitation offered in this inexorable divine activity. With irony, through Gamaliel's essentially fence-sitting speech, readers are assured (cf. Luke 1.4) that the plan unfolding in the events of Luke's narrative, in the lives of its readers, and promised for the future, is unstoppable.

### 4.2.5 Acts 13.36–37

When Paul accepts the invitation to speak to the people in the synagogue one sabbath at Pisidian Antioch, he offers a long narrative of salvation history (13.16–41).[288] He traces events from the election of Israel and the exodus (vv. 17–19), through demarcated times of the judges, King Saul, and until the reign of David (vv. 20–22)—from which he jumps, based on the messianic connections to this Davidic heritage,[289] to the activity of God in Jesus (v. 23), with a brief nod to the ministry of John the Baptist (vv. 24–25). As he turns to describe Jesus' death, Paul emphasises the same ironic interaction between prophesied events and the after-effects of the rejection of Jesus.[290] He addresses his hearers:

> to us the message of this salvation has been sent. But because the residents of Jerusalem and their leaders did not recognise (ἀγνοήσαντες) him or understand the words of the prophets that are read every sabbath, they fulfilled those words by condemning him. (13.26–27)[291]

He goes on to stress Jesus' innocence (v. 28). And he makes these Jerusalem residents the active agents, who brought about Jesus' death without valid charge and even "took him down from the tree and laid him in the tomb" (v. 29),[292] as an emphatic contrast with God's action: "But God raised him from the dead" (v. 30).

The passage as a whole emphasises continuity of divine oversight over the events from Israel's election until Jesus' resurrection. The promises of the prophets are a source of hope, and yet they have been ironically fulfilled through

---

[288] For tables detailing the progression of the argument in this speech, alongside relevant scriptural references, see Holladay, *Acts*, 275–79.
[289] See Sterling, "Do You Understand?", 107, 114–15, and discussion in p. 117 n. 280.
[290] On the ironic fulfilment of the prophecy, including a further reference to this passage, see above under 4.1.2.
[291] There are numerous textual variants for these verses; see discussion in Pervo, *Acts*, 338.
[292] Haenchen explains this detail (at variance with Luke's passion account) by suggesting Luke simply wanted to condense the story as much as possible (Haenchen, *The Acts of the Apostles*, 410); however, notwithstanding the need for brevity, Luke's contrast between actors ("they" vs. God) is emphatic and central to the point here.

human ignorance, which led ultimately to vindication through further divine action. This is in keeping with many other uses of the divine βουλή across Luke/Acts, as seen from the dynamic in other passages discussed here, and it is also in keeping with the sense of prophecy which both *must* be fulfilled *and* reflects human actions, even failures, that are then turned to divine purposes.

Here, though, the reference to the divine βουλή comes actually in further comments about *David's* role. David is said to have fulfilled the βουλή of God for his generation and then died (v. 36),[293] which is contrasted with the new thing achieved by God in raising Jesus without corruption (v. 37; cf. Acts 2.29–32). David's action as a fulfilment of the divine purpose for his time thus dovetails with the sense that the divine purpose arches over each of the periods recounted in Paul's salvation narrative.

### 4.2.6 Acts 20.27

Finally, Paul refers to the divine βουλή in the context of his emotional farewell speech to the elders in Ephesus (Acts 20.18–35). He asserts his positive contributions to the community during his ministry there, including his proclamation of repentance and faith in Jesus (vv. 18–21),[294] and emphasises his participation in

---

[293] Holladay helpfully suggests that this derives from Luke's attempt to problem-solve how the reference in Ps 16.10 to "your Holy One" is not a reference to David but to Jesus. Thus he aligns David's role with a specific period, before his death and burial, but still affirms that in doing so David fulfilled the divine βουλή (which Holladay consistently translates as "divine will") for his generation (Holladay, *Acts*, 273). Haenchen notes multiple ways of interpreting this sentence, related to whom or what David serves (his generation, or the divine will) and whether he fell asleep by the will of God, or at the time of his generation (dative of time). Haenchen himself settles on "For David, after he had served his own generation, fell asleep by the will of God…," though he recognises that the various translations are equally possible syntactically (Haenchen, *The Acts of the Apostles*, 412).

[294] Interestingly, Pervo highlights similarities between this speech and its call for vigilance, and Jesus' speech in Luke 21, though he asserts: "a difference is that eschatology, the heart of Luke 21, is explicitly absent from this speech" (Pervo, *Acts*, 517). And yet, as the Lukan Paul incorporates themes such as repentance, allegiance to Jesus, proclamation of the kingdom, the serious need for vigilance, ongoing suffering, his own departure (and possible death, as he will not see them again), and, indeed, "the whole purpose of God," readers would perhaps nonetheless still identify the eschatological overtones of the proclamation, as they imbue the call to discipleship throughout Luke/Acts. The connections to Luke 21 make this all the more salient.

It is one of the strange quirks of Lukan studies that the concept of the Kingdom of God in Jesus' and the apostles' preaching, consistently attributed an eschatological and even apocalyptic flavour in Markan studies, can simply be equated by interpreters with preaching the "gospel" in Luke, drawing out further consequences of the habit of viewing Luke as uneschatological (for

practical tasks (vv. 33–35) as well as the ways he has endured suffering (v. 19). He also outlines his further plans to travel to Jerusalem (vv. 22–24). The entire speech is overshadowed by his declaration that none of them will see him again (v. 25).

Before warning the community of further persecutions they will encounter (vv. 28–31), he describes his clear conscience:

> Therefore I declare to you this day that I am not responsible for the blood of any of you, for I did not shrink from declaring to you the whole purpose of God (οὐ γὰρ ὑπεστειλάμην[295] τοῦ μὴ ἀναγγεῖλαι πᾶσαν τὴν βουλὴν τοῦ θεοῦ ὑμῖν). (20.26–27)

It is clear from the context of the speech that this means the Ephesians were made aware that discipleship would entail suffering. Perhaps this phrase could be intended to imply that the suffering itself is part of the divine βουλή. The persecutions, betrayals, and internal conflicts Paul goes on to predict in the community are not attributed a divine purpose, but the idea of the "whole" divine βουλή (only here does Luke use this qualification) could arguably be taken this way.[296] However, the emphasis on Paul's and the community's mission in furthering the gospel proclamation, supporting the weak, and so on, suggests the more likely reading is that suffering comes as a predictable consequence of living according to the priorities of the divine purpose—akin to the interpretation of δεῖ discussed above, in passages such as Acts 14.22.[297] Nonethe-

---

example, Barrett, *A Critical and Exegetical Commentary*, 2:973; Holladay, *Acts*, 369; Pervo, *Acts*, 517). If there are similarities, for instance programmatically in the parallel between Jesus' proclamation at Nazareth in Luke 4.16–30 and his later claim that he "must proclaim the Good News of the Kingdom of God in other cities also; for I was sent for this purpose" (Luke 4.43), it is not that the proclamation of the kingdom is uneschatological, but that Jesus' proclamation elsewhere (including the declaration of release and acceptance at Nazareth) *also* has an eschatological character. This similarity also extends consistently into the references in Acts (1.3; 8.12; 14.22; 19.8; 20.25; 28.23, 31).

295 Cf. use of the same verb at v. 20, there in Paul's claim that he "did not shrink from doing anything helpful."

296 Conzlemann argues the "whole counsel of God" is a proclamation made known publicly, rather than the Gnostics' "esoteric teaching." After some discussion of this tension, he goes on characteristically: "What is actually being affirmed here is the sufficiency of the historical revelation and the transmission of that revelation through the preached word" (Conzelmann, *Acts of the Apostles*, 174).

297 Contrary to the various views I have presented here, Pervo argues here that βουλή does not relate to a "philosophy of history" but simply to "repentance and faith," which Paul has declared to the disciples in Ephesus, and it is up to them to respond as they wish; he claims the reference in Luke 7.30 reflects the same use of βουλή (Pervo, *Acts*, 522).

less, this final reference to the divine βουλή in Acts 20.27 remains uncertain; the Lukan Paul does not draw out any further what he means, perhaps because the finer details are not important to the farewell speech, or because Luke's reader is presumed by this stage in the narrative to understand already the dynamics of the divine βουλή and the opposition it evokes.

Thus, the six references to the divine βουλή in Luke/Acts appear in different literary settings, frequently those in which an apostolic character is proclaiming the good news and explaining both the causes of Jesus' death and divine action in his resurrection. Luke's use of the term does reflect diverse views about determinism and divine guidance found in Luke's setting at some points, such as claims about divine sovereignty to disempower enemies, exemplified in Deuteronomistic theology (as seen in Acts 4.28).[298] But most commonly, it appears in the context of claiming both the inexorable nature of the divine βουλή, and the possibility that human characters can reject (Luke 7.30) or act against those purposes (Acts 5.38–39; 13.36), which in turn is transformed by God into the ironic fulfilment of the prophetic promises (Acts 2.22–24; 13.36–37). This reflects an explanation for divine action which is far more dynamic than the determinism associated in other texts with words like εἱμαρμένη or *fatum*. As it emerges throughout Luke's text, God's βουλή may be (and habitually is) opposed, but it cannot be stopped.

## 5 Conclusion

In Luke/Acts, history unfolds in a way that God (and God's prophets) are able to foresee, and under divine guidance that ensures the remaining events promised as part of the end of history will certainly be fulfilled. The above exploration of determinism and divine guidance in the study's key texts fills out the range of perspectives which illuminate Luke/Acts, and counters some of the findings each of Hans Conzelmann and John Squires offered through their different approaches.

Importantly, the analysis confirms that, by focusing on divine guidance of history, a writer does not necessarily turn attention away from the events of the end of history. Writers of texts such as the War Scroll, 4 Ezra, 2 Baruch, and even Josephus portray divine guidance over the whole teleological course of history. In contrast to Conzelmann's assumptions, Luke likewise asserts the

---

[298] See Chapter 5 for further discussion of the role of Deuteronomistic theology.

divine βουλή extends to the events of the end; it undergirds God's action to raise Jesus (Acts 2.24; 13.36), which simultaneously confirms the final judgement (17.31).

This chapter also demonstrates that Luke's understanding of divine guidance of the course of history is not best understood as an adaptation of the kinds of ideas found in Graeco-Roman historiographies. Even among and within Graeco-Roman texts, I have noted, divine forces such as τύχη/*fortuna* or εἱμαρμένη/*fatum* can be portrayed quite differently. However, not only is Luke's divine plan more than a rhetorical device, in contrast to the assumptions underlying many comparative treatments of ancient historiographies in Lukan studies, Luke generally does not use any of the characteristic language or related concepts for divine personal and impersonal forces. Moreover, even Josephus, whose use of this terminology is striking, adapts the terms to his own account of divine involvement in, and guidance of, the (teleological) course of history.

As Luke likewise emphasises divine guidance over the whole course of history and its end, he demonstrates continuity with most of the Jewish writers of this study, rather than the writers of Graeco-Roman texts with whom he is normally compared. However, this does not lead to a rigid sense of determinism, which might be associated with either some portraits of determinism in apocalypses like 2 Baruch or explanations involving εἱμαρμένη/*fatum*. This flexibility could offer instead one area of connection to the non-Jewish Graeco-Roman texts. Diodorus Siculus's discomfort with inflexible forces, in the way he omits εἱμαρμένη and "diminishes the power" of ἀνάγκη by associating it with τύχη and πρόνοια,[299] also suggests aspects of flexibility in his understanding of determinism and divine guidance of history.[300] Luke's βουλή τοῦ θεοῦ requires human participation, as Diodorus's divine πρόνοια makes use of human servants (*Library* 1.1.3); this will be taken up further in the next chapter.

Finally, the teleological setting of Luke's claims about the inexorable movement of the divine βουλή shapes both the assurance and the challenge provided by the invitation to participate in divine purposes. Luke's presentation of the events of his narrative as the fulfilment of prophecy confirms that even the apparently disastrous events of the recent past were foreseen by God, and the divine plan has adapted accordingly. Indeed, according to Luke, the same divine actor who foresaw these events has nonetheless still made a sure promise of the end.

---

[299] Squires, *The Plan of God*, 160.
[300] Despite the different vocabulary, Sterling notes similarity between Luke's use of the βουλή of God and Josephus's understanding of πρόνοια (Sterling, *Historiography and Self-Definition*, 357–63).

# Chapter 5:
# Human responsibility and freedom

*For myself, I shudder at recounting the works of God to unworthy ears; yet listen, that you may learn that you are warring not against the Romans only, but also against God.*
—Josephus, *J.W.* 5.378

*Reflecting on these things one will find that God has a care for* ἄνθρωποι, *and by all kinds of premonitory signs shows his people the way of salvation, while they owe their destruction to folly and calamities of their own choosing.*
—*J.W.* 6.310

## 1 Introduction

In the fifth book of the *Jewish War*, as tensions are raised and the conflict with Rome is accelerating towards Jerusalem's destruction, Josephus—as a key character in his own account—paces along the city walls and passionately exhorts his compatriots to change their course.[1] He does this even though he says that the destruction of the temple had already been set for a particular day in advance and that God is, regardless, on the side of Rome, while also claiming that Israel's history shows that things always go badly when humans try to get involved rather than leaving things to divine action. Indeed, in his introduction to the *Antiquities* he will later argue that "the main lesson to be learnt from this history" is that prosperity emerges for those who follow the divine will, and "things (else) practicable become impracticable" leading to "irretrievable disasters" for those who do not (*Ant.* 1.14–15). Here in Josephus's speech in Book 5 of the *Jewish War*, the very idea of "warring not against the Romans only, but also against God" (*J.W.* 5.378) reveals a tragic faultline in the causes of events as Josephus sees them: humans may choose their actions, but as God has already determined how things will unfold, any opposition will inevitably fail. Despite the many ways in which Josephus affirms divine guidance of history, even determinism, as discussed in Chapter 4, in explaining the events which led to the destruction of the Jerusalem temple he claims that God seeks to secure a positive out-

---

[1] This is an important speech that has come up before in this study, with its emphasis on divine backing creating Rome's dominance for *now* (see Chapter 3), drawing on the rule of the stronger, and its striking parallel in Agrippa's speech in Book 2.

come, but humans are responsible for bringing about their own downfall.² Josephus is not alone among ancient writers in presenting divergent explanations of divine and human agency and responsibility.

In this chapter I consider how the writers of my key texts depict interactions between divine and human agency, in order to illuminate how Luke apportions *human* responsibility for the events of the past and for action in the present and future. It is not uncommon for writers to explain events through divine and human action in ways that are apparently incompatible, and certainly at times indicate that coherence is not the primary objective. Various theological purposes push writers in different directions in different settings, balancing the (potentially competing) concerns of the sovereignty or freedom of divine and human agents in relation to questions of these agents' culpability.³ For instance, those who affirm divine sovereignty over history face implications of divine *blameworthiness* for negative events, which they resolve in various ways. For many, human responsibility emerges as an important way of explaining historical events without blaming God. As a result, for instance, events can be portrayed as both divinely determined *and* caused by human failings.⁴ Having already discussed the importance of the divine βουλή for assuring the future in Luke/Acts, I suggest that attending to the ways in which different writers approach questions of divine and human agency in the context of different kinds of problems helps to clarify the particular emphases Luke brings to these tensions.

Understandings of the interaction between divine and human agency play a central role in longstanding controversies in Lukan scholarship, such as in questions about Luke's approach to suffering or politics. As set out in Chapter 1, these concerns have been (rightly) associated with eschatological questions. For Ernst Käsemann, perceived consequences of the parousia's delay included an emerging *theologia gloriae*, with implications for interpreting Luke's approach to suffering, the cross, and politics in the indefinitely extended period before Christ's return. For Käsemann, Luke exhibits a triumphalism which affirms divine action

---

2 On the similar dynamic between the conditions τύχη creates and the downfalls caused by a failure of human foresight in Thucydides, see Cornford, *Thucydides Mythistoricus*, 108.
3 In this chapter I often use "sovereignty" to describe aspects of divine agency, but "freedom" for similar elements of human agency. The writers generally do not portray human agency in an equivalent way to the sovereignty divine agents can attain in some accounts.
4 The discussion of determinism and divine guidance in Chapter 4 has already highlighted some interaction between divine and human responsibility in the key texts of this study, including historians contributing to the work of τύχη (Polybius) or divine πρόνοια (Diodorus Siculus), or the way in which human failings prompt τύχη to bring about regime change (also Diodorus).

alongside political conformism.⁵ From a different perspective, Oscar Cullmann considered questions of agency and suffering, but instead argued (beginning with claims about a general NT theology which he then applied to Luke's text) that God's decisive action in Christ meant that evil was constrained as though on a rope in the period between history's "mid-point" (the Christ event) and the end; thus the power of opposing forces "is only an apparent power."⁶ Here Cullmann's otherwise insightful approach regarding biblical salvation history overlooked the ways opposing human agents and other forces genuinely impact upon human experience in the past and present in Luke/Acts. In their different ways, each of these interpreters, and those who followed their lead—notably, a version of Käsemann's conclusions remains common in Lukan studies⁷—neglected the significant connections between Luke's understanding of human agency and his understanding of history and its end.

For Luke, the events of the past show that suffering can be caused both by the unscrupulous actions of other humans or by accident (Luke 13.1–5). Θεομάχοι can and do oppose the divine plan (Luke 22.6; 23.12; Acts 1.16–20; 5.38–9; 8.1–3; 12.1–4, 20–23), and human rejection of divine initiative leads to tragic consequences (Luke 19.41–4; Acts 3.13–15; 28.24–28). But even opposition is turned to divine purposes (Acts 2.36; 3.14–15; 8.4; 11.19–21). Looking to the future, as argued in Chapter 4, the divine βουλή governs the course of history and cannot be stopped. Nonetheless, the following discussion demonstrates that, set among the comparison texts, Luke's narrative displays a notable focus on *human* action. Human freedom and responsibility are important for Luke's explanation of the past, and his challenge to positive human response in the present and imminent future.

---

5 Käsemann, "Das Problem," 143; Käsemann, "Neutestamentliche Fragen," 21. Conzelmann likewise had already introduced questions of suffering and politics (Conzelmann, *Theology of St Luke*, 98–99, 137–49).
6 Cullmann, *Christ and Time*, 198. Cullmann also suggests that an early Christian view of the agency of angels complicated understandings about the power of the state, whereby the state was considered a mediator of divine action. Here Cullmann attributes to early Christians a version of the "yield to the stronger" phenomenon discussed in Chapter 3 in relation to Josephus.
7 These assumptions about Luke remain prevalent in introductory texts and commentaries. Holladay claims Luke presents a portrait of the church as "politically harmless" and "socially appealing" (Holladay, *Acts*, 55–58). Bock concludes his section on the cross in Luke/Acts supporting what he presents as a wider view: "After death came vindication in his resurrection. Some have said that Paul saw 'the Christ of the cross,' whereas Luke saw 'the Christ of glory'" (Bock, *A Theology of Luke and Acts*, 204).

## 2 Interactions of, or conflicts between, divine and human agency

Several recent studies have explored divine and human agency in Second Temple Judaism as a way of illuminating Pauline literature, responding particularly to the emphases of the "New Perspective on Paul."[8] The studies reconceptualise Pauline themes traditionally interpreted as a distinction between "grace" and "works" as a dynamic between divine and human agency. Set against E. P. Sanders's covenantal nomism (summarised as distinguishing the stages of "'getting in' and 'staying in,'" the former involving grace, the latter obedience or works),[9] some argue that the diverse Jewish literature contemporary with Paul shows a greater appreciation for human agency than the New Perspective acknowledges. John Barclay helpfully delineates three contemporary theoretical models[10] for understanding the relationship between divine and human agency that might be illuminating in relation to ancient texts, which are also taken up by Jason Maston and Kyle Wells.[11]

---

[8] Coined by James Dunn in 1982, this title refers to a strand of Pauline interpretation generally traced back to E. P. Sanders's *Paul and Palestinian Judaism*. Several studies have emerged from Durham in recent years, building on Barclay's contribution to a collection of essays (Barclay, "Introduction"), such as that by Maston, doctoral student of Watson (Maston, *Divine and Human Agency*), and Wells, doctoral student of Barclay (Wells, *Grace and Agency*). Divine and human agency remains a central theme in Barclay's more recent work (Barclay, *Paul and the Gift*, 72, 166–75).

[9] Maston, *Divine and Human Agency*, 3; Barclay, *Paul and the Gift*, 157. Barclay addresses Sanders throughout his 2015 publication, but see esp. pp. 151–58.

[10] It is, of course, important to emphasise that this is a *contemporary* scholarly framework. Contemporary theoretical work that seeks to categorise different patterns of thought evident in ancient texts is an aid to analysis. In her 2011 SBL presidential address, Carol Newsom discussed questions of agency, noting that these questions were more often raised in NT studies but that there was a need for work in the HB and Second Temple Jewish texts. She approaches the matter in terms of moral agency, which likewise focuses on the ability of the human agent to act faithfully, and discusses positive claims about moral agency, "impaired" moral agency (which can be restored), and certain texts which deny moral agency (see Carol A. Newsom, "Models of the Moral Self: Hebrew Bible and Second Temple Judaism," *JBL* 131 (2012): 5–25). Taking a different approach, Bobzien focuses on dealing with ancient Stoic thought with its own terms rather than making connections to modern philosophical categories (Bobzien, *Determinism and Freedom*, 1, 14).

[11] Maston compares Sirach, the Hodayot, and Romans 7–8 (Maston, *Divine and Human Agency*); Wells examines biblical and non-biblical Jewish treatments of divine and human agency in order to illuminate Paul (Wells, *Grace and Agency*).

First, Barclay sets out a "competitive" model: if humans have agency then the divine must not, and vice versa.[12] Barclay argues contemporary scholars commonly presume this model, leading to anachronistic interpretations of ancient texts, and that there should be more consideration given to the alternatives he describes.[13] The second, he dubs a "kinship" model: like branches on a tree, humans are "'fragments' of God," and both act in concert. Here, as humans exercise freedom, they nonetheless express a common will and purpose with the divine.[14] The third model, which is described as "non-contrastive transcendence," draws on the systematic theology of Kathryn Tanner.[15] Here, the divine creates the space to allow for human freedom. Thus, divine and human agencies are necessarily unequal: human freedom relies upon divine action to facilitate that freedom. Barclay also argues that the "vertical" dependence upon divine sovereignty creates a freedom "which may be 'horizontally' independent of other created agencies ... Other agents may *affect* human agency, but it is God who *effects* it."[16]

Barclay's framework offers valuable new angles for tackling entrenched difficulties in Pauline scholarship. However, an approach to divine and human agency in which the frame of reference is not only Paul but, implicitly, Pauline *soteriology*, is limited in the types of questions to which it can be applied. The framework omits issues raised by ancient writers who do not seek principally to account for divine and human *participation in the mechanisms of salvation or practices of piety*, but rather *responsibility for the events of history*. Barclay deliberately brackets out the role of further spiritual forces, such as the demonic or

---

**12** Barclay, "Introduction," 6; cf. Maston, *Divine and Human Agency*, 17; Wells, *Grace and Agency*, 17–19. Engberg-Pedersen similarly argues against such an approach in ancient texts, advocating instead for an "overlap" of divine and human agency in Epictetus and Paul (Troels Engberg-Pedersen, *Cosmology and Self in the Apostle Paul: The Material Spirit* (Oxford: Oxford University Press, 2010), 106–9). This also contributes to Engberg-Pedersen's larger project of arguing against a conflict between "apocalypticism" and "philosophy" (suggesting Pauline scholars who stress the former overemphasise divine agency at the expense of human freedom (p. 107)).
**13** Barclay, "Introduction," 7. Maston suggests that Josephus follows the competitive model in his description of the Pharisees' beliefs in *Ant.* 13.172, but in *J.W.* 2.162 he presents the agencies interacting, akin to Barclay's third model below (Maston, *Divine and Human Agency*, 14–15).
**14** Barclay, "Introduction," 6–7.
**15** Barclay, "Introduction," 7. For full discussion of Tanner's understanding of tyranny and divine control of history, see Kathryn Tanner, *God and Creation in Christian Theology: Tyranny or Empowerment* (Oxford: Blackwell, 1988), 42–46.
**16** Barclay, "Introduction," 7.

the power of sin, while acknowledging that these may be factors in Paul.[17] More broadly, Barclay, like Maston and Wells, does not consider questions of *culpability*—either for "protagonist" characters (e.g. Israel), or "opponent" groups (e.g., paradigmatically, Babylon)—or the implications of claims about the freedom or otherwise "opponents" exercise when they act in history. Barclay's caution against presuming a competitive relationship between divine and human agency in ancient texts is helpful. In some circumstances, the texts in this study present divine and human agency in a way which is consistent with either models two or three, and being able to conceptualise in these terms likewise provides helpful clarity. However, in examining the variety of different problems that ancient writers seek to address, this chapter also suggests writers find solutions by placing stress on different agents in different circumstances, without necessarily conceptualising the relationships between agents in a way which is as coherent as the three contemporary models suggest.

I suggest two elements in particular frequently alter how writers present divine and human agency. The first is temporality, focusing on the differences that emerge because of the inherently retrospective nature of explanations of the past and the prospective orientation of claims about the future.[18] The discussion below shows that writers frequently deal differently with the past and future when attributing freedom and responsibility to divine and human agents, characterising agency in ways that are not necessarily coherent because of the different theological or political issues raised by claims about the past or future. These temporal differences also show ways in which approaches to divine and human agency interact with eschatological claims (or the absence of such claims). Importantly, a mismatch emerges in studies which treat these different considerations uniformly. For instance, Maston begins his discussion with the references to fate, God, and human responsibility in Josephus's descriptions of the Jewish sects (*J.W.* 2.119–66; *Ant.* 13.171–73; 18.12–22), as a way of setting out the diver-

---

[17] Barclay, "Introduction," 5. Similarly, Maston, *Divine and Human Agency*, 18 (though he recognises that the presence of these forces will alter the portrayals of divine and human agency). For a treatment of such forces in Pauline theology, with an apocalyptic lens, see Martyn, *Theological Issues*, 62–65.

[18] Barclay's model is helpful for prospective interests, but does not attempt to account for differences in texts' retrospective explanations of events. Writers' claims about divine sovereignty link in important ways to prospective interests—regardless of the causes of suffering in the past, hope for the future very frequently relies on an affirmation that divine action cannot be impeded. Looking forward, writers may also affirm divine benevolence in facilitating the human freedom to respond positively to divine initiative, as in Barclay's third model.

sity of views on divine and human agency in Second Temple Judaism.[19] However, the kinds of questions Maston then seeks to raise about divine and human agency relate to prospective interests, such as agents' contributions to a salvific process and the capacity for human faithfulness.[20] But Josephus's interests in the philosophical school passages relate to questions of divine providential care and human responsibility for the events of history. These issues incorporate a retrospective, explanatory character.[21]

Josephus's passages on the Jewish sects do not address human or divine participation in effecting salvation and piety, and, I suggest, do not straightforwardly map onto Pauline soteriology in the way Maston presumes. Josephus's stance is important, and the similarities between his portrayal of the Pharisees and his analysis of the causes of the destruction of Jerusalem later in the *Jewish War* (*J.W.* 6.305–13; cf. 2.162–63) suggest these passages illuminate his own views. He exemplifies the way writers can explain the events of history through apparently contradictory causes arising from the mix of retrospect and prospect in the explanation. For Josephus, absolute divine sovereignty secures the future, which he demonstrates through claims about divine determinism throughout history,[22] but humans are to be held responsible for the calamities of the recent past.[23] As argued below, similar temporal distinctions illuminate key elements of the attributions of divine and human agency in texts across this study.

Secondly, rather than a homogenised treatment of divine and human agency, writers frequently handle different types of characters differently in terms of the agency attributed to them, especially in the case of opponent and protagonist

---

**19** Maston carefully asserts that he uses these descriptions as examples of the kind of diversity present in Second Temple Judaism, and not as historically accurate accounts of these Jewish groups—though Josephus's distinctions form the basis of Maston's focus on Sirach and the Hodayot, as representatives of the views Josephus attributes to the Sadducees and Essenes respectively (Maston, *Divine and Human Agency*, 10–19).
**20** Maston describes Josephus setting out the relationships between "fate" and "human volition" (Maston, *Divine and Human Agency*, 15), but I suggest the overriding question in these passages is one of *responsibility*.
**21** Such explanations can still underscore exhortation for readers to learn from the past as they act in the present and future. But as this chapter demonstrates, writers also frequently give quite different responses about the human capacity to act differently in the future, as a result of divine assistance (without implicating the divine in the failure to avert disasters that have already taken place).
**22** See Chapter 4.
**23** The differences between retrospective and prospective orientations also allow for a divine capacity to *adapt* to incorporate human opposition or a conflict between human and divine intention within the divine plan. For instance, of the events that led him to Egypt, Joseph tells his brothers: "even though you intended to do harm to me, God intended it for good" (Gen 50.20).

groups. Again, this creates an approach to divine and human agency in which people are considered independently from one another, rather than as part of the same conceptual framework. The resultant tensions reflect the theological and political concerns of the writers as they seek to explain certain events, rather than attempts to conceptualise their claims about different groups in a connected way. Opponents can be passive divine instruments or absolutely culpable (or both!), whereas protagonists might be promised divine assistance to enable piety in the future.

The following discussion demonstrates that, in keeping with Barclay's caution, the study's texts do not present only a competitive relationship between divine and human agencies. There are several texts which portray humans freely acting as an extension of divine action, as in Barclay's second model (for instance, in many descriptions of Judas Maccabeus in 2 Maccabees), or the divine enabling space for humans also to exercise their own agency, as in Barclay's third model (for instance, 4 Ezra's account of God's initiative to enable Ezra and his group to discipline their hearts, or Luke's description of a universal divine invitation which creates the space in which some humans choose to decline the invitation). But there are also other examples which produce different tensions, from differing explanations of divine control and human responsibility, to explaining events through the actions of opposing spiritual forces or gods who act as opponents for human projects. The remainder of this chapter addresses these themes in both the Jewish and non-Jewish texts, the former initially in relation to their extensions of Deuteronomistic themes, before considering the points of connection and difference in Luke's presentation.

## 3 Engaging with Deuteronomistic approaches to divine and human agency

Jewish texts of this period reflect various responses to Deuteronomistic approaches to divine and human agency, which it is helpful to outline first before turning to the key texts that extend these themes. I then discuss two further types of opponents in the Jewish texts of this study: other spiritual forces and humans who are depicted through the literary type θεομάχοι.

## 3.1 Deuteronomistic approaches

This significant strand of theology in Jewish scriptures provides theological reflection on the exile,[24] and a basis from which later Jewish texts build their theological interpretations of experience. Though Deuteronomistic themes are familiar to many readers of the HB, it is helpful to articulate the contours of Deuteronomistic theology from the perspective of divine and human agency, in order to illuminate the pressures which create apparent inconsistency in some key ways. Deuteronomistic explanations for the events of history affirm divine sovereignty. YHWH declares: "There is no god beside me. I kill and I make alive; I wound and I heal; and no one can deliver from my hand" (Deut 32.39). The writers of these texts reject the power of any other people or forces (whether the Babylonians or their divinities) by interpreting suffering as YHWH's punishment (cf. 32.41). Like Pauline theology in E. P. Sanders's interpretation,[25] the reasoning works backwards from solution to plight: given Israel suffers, punishment must have been necessary. Psalm 1 exemplifies the connections between prosperity and righteousness, and suffering and sinfulness, upon which such interpretations of experience rely. The psalmist claims of the righteous, "in all that

---

[24] The adjective "Deuteronomic" refers to elements identified directly in Deuteronomy. This discussion will use "Deuteronomistic" to refer to theology modelled on the pattern found in Deuteronomy but also evident through other parts of the HB, including the texts Noth labelled the "Deuteronomistic History" (Josh–2 Kgs; Martin Noth, *The Deuteronomistic History* (Sheffield: University of Sheffield, 1981)). I focus on the characteristic theological explanations in these texts, without entering the detailed debates about the relationships between biblical texts that display this theology, or the historicity of Israel's past in texts from Deuteronomy and the canonical historiographies. On the former, see Gerhard von Rad, *Old Testament Theology*, trans. D. M. G. Stalker (Edinburgh: Oliver & Boyd, 1962–1965); von Rad, "The Beginnings of Historical Writing in Ancient Israel," in *From Genesis to Chronicles: Explorations in Old Testament Theology*, ed. K. C. Hanson, Fortress Classics in Biblical Studies (Minneapolis: Fortress, 2005), 125–53; Noth, *The Deuteronomistic History*; Lothar Perlitt, *Deuteronomium-Studien*, FAT 8 (Tübingen: Mohr Siebeck, 1994). On the latter, sceptical views about the historical basis for the biblical historiographies are provided by Niels Peter Lemche, *The Israelites in History and Tradition*, ed. Douglas A. Knight, LAI (London: SPCK; Louisville: Westminster John Knox, 1998); Lester Grabbe, *Ancient Israel: What Do We Know and How Do We Know It?* (London: T&T Clark, 2007); Philip R. Davies, *In Search of "Ancient Israel,"* JSOTSup 148 (Sheffield: Sheffield Academic, 1992). Compelling critique of this position can be found in James Barr, *History and Ideology in the Old Testament: Biblical Studies at the End of a Millennium* (Oxford: Oxford University Press, 2000), esp. pp. 59–72.

[25] Sanders's focus is Paul's interpretation of the salvific work of Christ, a "solution" which Paul takes to indicate that the law was inadequate for achieving this purpose (Sanders, *Paul and Palestinian Judaism*, 442–44, 481–85, 497–501; cf. Sanders, "God Gave the Law," 85).

they do, they prosper" (v. 3), and concludes "for the Lord watches over the way of the righteous, but the way of the wicked will perish" (vv. 4, 6).[26]

In Deuteronomy, the description of the wickedness of the previous occupants of the promised land and ensuing dispossession as divine punishment analogously interprets Israel's later exile.[27] Set in an account of Israel's past, the explanation functions like the retrospective "predictions" offered by *vaticinia ex eventu*, providing an authoritative theological commentary on the events of the implied reader's own time.[28] Thus, Deuteronomy's Moses emphasises divine sovereignty and human culpability, within a framework of reward and punishment through the events of history:

> If you do forget the Lord your God and follow other gods to serve and worship them, I solemnly warn you today that you shall surely perish. Like the nations that the Lord is destroying before you, so shall you perish, because you would not obey the voice of the Lord your God. (Deut 8.18–19)

The gift of the land emphasises divine sovereignty, both in punishing the other nations and in honouring the promises made in electing Israel (cf. Deut 7.7–8).[29] Israel has to some extent acted freely in the past, however; having displayed stubbornness in the wilderness, Israel is portrayed as the *undeserving* beneficiary of the divine punishment of the other nations and should not congratulate itself (9.4–8, 12–14, 22–24).[30] But the writer also interprets the events of the historical (as opposed to literary) present to confirm Israel's privileged status. The exile is explained as benevolent divine discipline (8.5).[31] Current experiences

---

[26] Brueggemann suggests Psalm 1 represents a central strain of thought in the HB, against which other texts provide counter-testimony as lived experience calls the Psalm's affirmations into question (Walter Brueggemann, *Theology of the Old Testament: Testimony, Dispute, Advocacy* (Minneapolis: Fortress, 1997), 385).

[27] This does not discount the harrowing uses to which this understanding of dispossession and divine blessing for prosperity has been put in violence and colonial practices of the past and present. For discussion of issues in reading these texts, see Mark G. Brett, *Decolonizing God: The Bible in the Tides of Empire*, Bible in the Modern World (Sheffield: Sheffield Phoenix, 2008), 79–93.

[28] Chapters 4 and 6 deal with this phenomenon in more detail.

[29] See Barclay's discussion of "incongruity" to illuminate the importance of undeserved divine benevolence as one of the "perfections" of grace (Barclay, *Paul and the Gift*, 166–75). I discuss the contrast between writers' interests in protagonist and opponent groups below.

[30] Philip E. Satterthwaite and Gordon McConville, *The Histories*, Exploring the Old Testament 2 (London: SPCK, 2007), 122.

[31] See Weinfeld on temporary suffering in the interests of "a good end" (Moshe Weinfeld, *Deuteronomy and the Deuteronomic School* (Oxford: Clarendon, 1972), 317).

§3 Engaging with Deuteronomistic approaches to divine and human agency — 215

of suffering are not a *direct* result of poor human choices,[32] but a consequence mediated by sovereign action to inflict divine punishment and prompt correction—also action within Israel's control—ultimately in Israel's interest.

When considering the future, the writer describes Israel continuing to enjoy a privileged status. YHWH will not only act to bring the suffering which constitutes punishment to an end, but will also grant Israel's capacity to maintain its side of the covenant. As Moshe Weinfeld notes, it is essential to Deuteronomistic theology that suffering is temporary and leads to restoration.[33] Speaking to the core concerns of Deuteronomy's historical setting, Moses goes on in his speech to promise:

> Even if you are exiled to the ends of the world, from there the Lord your God will gather you, and from there he will bring you back ... Moreover, the Lord your God will circumcise your heart and the heart of your descendants, so that you will love the Lord your God with all your heart and with all your soul, in order that you may live." (Deut 30.1–6;[34] cf. 2 Kgs 24.20; 25.11; 1 Chr 9.1)[35]

Thus, for the protagonists, divine discipline and human culpability explain the past.[36] Israel, though undeserving of its original prosperity and election, has ex-

---

[32] As argued in Chapter 4, in some texts negative events flow directly from the consequences of poor choices.
[33] Weinfeld, *Deuteronomy and the Deuteronomic School*, 316–19. Moreover, in this theological approach, where multiple generations are punished, it is not because a debt has been inherited but because each generation is equally marked by sinful behaviour (p. 319).
[34] These passages promise even greater prosperity, and Deut 30.12–14 sets out that this is explicitly available on earth, accessible for the reader.
[35] This is a fraught area of interpretation, with varied views on whether Deut 30.1–10 accents the priority of human action in turning to YHWH and YHWH then circumcising the heart facilitating further faithfulness, or YHWH's initiative in circumcising the heart that then enables human response. Wells provides a compelling account of syntactical, structural, and literary/thematic justifications for a divine priority reading (Wells, *Grace and Agency*, 31–39). He convincingly makes his case, not that this is the only possible reading of Deuteronomy 30, but that it is a highly plausible reading that interpreters, including Paul, could have taken up (p. 39). Nonetheless, without resolving a competitive, sequential account of divine and human agency, it remains consistent with other texts that writers might simultaneously affirm that it is a divine gift to be able to respond to God, and that humans must faithfully turn to God: both are true at once.
[36] This is not to deny the importance of this theology to these texts. As Sanders points out, although NT scholars are tempted to say these writers simply attribute punishment after the fact, this "would underestimate the degree to which *people believed* in God's providence, or fate, or destiny" (Sanders, "God Gave the Law," 91). Similarly for Graeco-Roman texts: Gottlieb claims "It would be a mistake if we understood these elements of Roman religion as superficial ... the gods

ercised unfettered freedom by straying from its covenant responsibilities. Conversely, for the future, although the people must be reformed and love the Lord, divine activity will also make such faithfulness possible. Thus the elements of Deuteronomistic theology that are orientated towards the protagonist group's future reflect Barclay's third model. YHWH will give Israel the ability to be faithful and Israel will choose to be obedient and be restored to prosperity.

For opponents, by contrast, the prospective orientation in Deuteronomistic theology suggests a less favourable outcome. Opponents like Babylon enjoy no agency of their own, as they have acted merely as instruments of divine punishment (2 Kgs 2.17; 24.20; 1 Chr 9.11; cf. Jer 21.7–10). But within strands of the HB, Babylon also remains culpable and will be punished in the future as part of Israel's restoration (Isa 13.19; 14.22; 21.9; 48.14–20; Jer 25.11–12).[37]

Already within the HB, this theology develops in various directions.[38] Jeremiah describes divine action to enable positive human action, meditating upon the divine initiative of writing the law on hearts so that the people may be faithful (Jer 31.33)—a theme which Paul will also take up in his letter to the Romans (Rom 2.15, 29; cf. Heb 8.8–12; 10.16–17; though, by contrast, Acts 7.51). Inverting Psalm 1, Psalm 73 troubles over the lived experience not only of the righteous suffering, but the wicked prospering. It almost causes the Psalmist to stumble (73.1–3).[39] In other texts, like Job and Proverbs, the writers likewise contemplate justice when the wicked prosper.[40] These preoccupations continue in later texts, which extend or challenge Deuteronomistic themes to resolve the balance between divine and human sovereignty or freedom and responsibility in different ways.

---

are guarantors of victory and are jointly responsible for every public success" (Gottlieb, "Religion in the Politics," 22–23).

[37] It could be, of course, that this serves both purposes (as in Deut 8.18–9.3)—that is, that Babylon is independently deserving of punishment, though this does not justify their prosperity during exile. Second Baruch takes an approach along these lines. By contrast, Josephus's *Jewish War* emphasises Rome's piety. See §3.2.2 and §3.2.3 below.

[38] As set out by Brueggemann; see also, for instance, Jer 12.1–4, and complaint psalms (Brueggemann, *Theology of the Old Testament*, 385–86). On Job, see pp. 386–93; Ecclesiastes, pp. 393–98; and Ps 88, pp. 398–99.

[39] The psalm concludes by affirming a later judgement will befall the wicked (vv. 27–28). In many ways this Psalm undoes the easy confidence of Psalm 1 and its connections between prosperity and righteousness and suffering and sin.

[40] Brueggemann defines theodicy in the HB in terms of "counter-testimony" as protest, and asserts that "Israel has no interest in justifying an unjust world in making excuses for Yahweh" (Brueggemann, *Theology of the Old Testament*, 739). However, as many of this study's key texts and various strands of the HB noted above demonstrate, numerous writers do manage to hold together protest and self-accusation to explain the events of history.

## 3.2 Extensions of Deuteronomistic themes in late Second Temple texts

In the texts of this study, Deuteronomistic themes are extended in 2 Maccabees, Josephus's *Jewish War*, and 2 Baruch. They are also presumed, but in many ways challenged, in 4 Ezra.

### 3.2.1 Second Maccabees

Second Maccabees presents an approach very similar to Deuteronomistic texts,[41] but some attention to post-mortem reward extends the pattern. Events in 2 Maccabees are identified as punishment within history (7.18, 38; cf. 4.38; 8.11) or, correspondingly in relation to success, divine restoration within history (12.15–16). Importantly, the latter becomes possible once divine anger, which was only "for a little while," has abated (5.17, 20; 7.33; cf. 8.5). In a narrative aside that frames the martyrdom stories which follow, 6.12–17 explains that readers should not lose heart because "these punishments were designed not to destroy but to discipline our people" (v. 12; cf. Deut 8.5). The potential benefits of suffering as discipline are not understood as an ascetic or Stoic virtue in assenting to suffering itself. Rather, the benefit lies in satisfying the need for punishment, and reforming behaviour, before it is too late.[42] Being punished "immediately" constitutes "a sign of great kindness" for favoured people (v. 13), rather than "the case of the other nations," in which, as noted in Chapter 3 above, "the Lord waits patiently to punish them until they have reached the full measure of their sins (ἐκπλήρωσιν

---

[41] In his study of Second Temple receptions of Deuteronomy, Lincicum notes that 2 Maccabees cites Deuteronomy's text less than Lincicum's other focus texts, but he claims the pattern of Deut 32 especially remains in the background for this text (David Lincicum, *Paul and the Early Jewish Encounter with Deuteronomy*, WUNT 2/284 (Tübingen: Mohr Siebeck, 2010), 88–89).

[42] Guffey argues for a pattern of change between the biblical book of Job and the Testament of Job that is along these same lines, that is, a movement towards post-mortem reward and punishment (here it is Satan whom God allows to punish the righteous as purification). See Andrew R. Guffey, "Job and the 'Mystic's Solution' to Theodicy: Philosophical Paideia and Internalized Apocalypticism in the Testament of Job," in *Pedagogy in Ancient Judaism and Early Christianity*, ed. Karina Martin Hogan, Matthew J. Goff, and Emma Wasserman (Atlanta: SBL Press, 2017), 235. Although a helpful study, Guffey's idea about an "internalised apocalypticism" is less convincing (pp. 225, 233). The end of the Testament of Job introduces a mystical element which indicates a way of *transcending* suffering even in the present; in many ways, Job's daughters' experiences with the sashes that lead to mystical experiences describe a hope that is less about anticipating the future and more about escaping from the present (TJob 48–50). Nonetheless, Guffey draws out a helpful contrast: "Hellenistic philosophy only prepares one to tolerate the dung-heap and to command the worms, but angelmorphic transformation and ascension to a divine throne actually takes away the pain" (p. 232).

ἁμαρτιῶν)" (v. 14).⁴³ This similarly implies potential incoherence arising from retrospective and prospective interests: Antiochus IV acts as a divine instrument in meting out this deserved punishment (2 Macc 6–7),⁴⁴ yet the writer asserts that he will receive his own punishment for this divinely-orchestrated behaviour (7.17, 19, 31), in turn identified with his later demise (9.4–28).⁴⁵

In addition to these elements shared with Deuteronomistic texts, the writer of 2 Maccabees affirms *post-mortem* restoration. The mother of the seven martyred sons in 2 Macc 7 links her trust in post-mortem restoration with the mysterious divine activity of creation in the womb, concluding: "therefore the Creator of the world, who shaped the beginning of humankind and devised the origin of all things, will in his mercy give life and breath back to you" (7.23, 28–29; cf. 7.9, 14). Although guaranteed for pious martyrs, post-mortem restoration remains uncertain for the soldiers whose deaths are identified with divine punishment for wearing amulets: "it became clear to all that this was the reason these men had fallen" (12.40), though as noted in Chapter 3, Judas arranges a sin offering to seek post-mortem mercy on the group's behalf (vv. 43–45).⁴⁶

Descriptions of battles and reflections on victory consistently attribute success to divine action; Judas and his soldiers for their part approach the battles piously, with prayer calling on God's assistance (cf. 10.38; 11.3; 12.11, 15–16, 28; 13.13–17). More than once divine assistance comes directly in the form of shining horsemen. In 10.29–31, "there appeared to the enemy five resplendent men on horses with golden bridles" (v. 29), two of whom take up position on either side of Judas to protect him and strike down the enemy with "arrows and thunderbolts" (v. 30; similarly, see 11.8 and reference to similar incidents in the past in 8.20).

Judas also appears to maintain his own agency, even when the narration equates Judas and the soldiers' actions with the action of God:

---

**43** See Chapters 3 and 6 in this study for further discussion of this passage and its relationship to 2 Maccabees' portrayal of the end of history. See also other texts with a motif of delayed punishment, such as Valerius Maximus on the Carthaginians below (§4.1).
**44** There is a complex interaction between these themes in the case of Antiochus, about which the writer is not particularly concerned. He is a divine instrument, but also an archetypal θεομάχος (2 Macc 4.17; 5.17–20). See §3.4 for discussion of Antiochus's hubris.
**45** Van Henten observes the verbal connections between the description of Antiochus's death and the earlier description of the torture of the martyrs (van Henten, *The Maccabean Martyrs*, 170–72).
**46** Cf. 4 Ezra 7.102–15, which deals not with intercessions for those who have died, but the prospect of intercession at the time of eschatological judgement (a possibility Uriel entirely rules out).

Nicanor and his troops advanced with trumpets and battle songs, but Judas and his troops met the enemy in battle with invocations to God and prayers. So, fighting with their hands and praying to God in their hearts, they laid low at least thirty-five thousand, and were greatly gladdened by God's manifestation.[47] (2 Macc 15.25–27; cf. 12.22–23)[48]

Judas acts genuinely as an extension of the divine purpose, with his own will directly aligned with the will of God, as in Barclay's second model.[49]

Thus, in 2 Maccabees, those aligned with non-Hellenising forces suffer through benevolent discipline (6.12–17) and may be restored from sinfulness even after death (12.43–45).[50] Conversely, opponents, even when their actions constitute divine imperatives, enjoy no hope of restoration beyond the punishment within history which inevitably still emerges for them (7.14).[51]

### 3.2.2 Josephus's *Jewish War*

Josephus also maintains a strong emphasis on Deuteronomistic interpretations of events. He explains the past in terms of human culpability and divine punishment—Jerusalem's destruction constitutes just punishment for the Jewish people (*J.W.* 3.52–54; 5.378, 395–96, 412), who have compromised the sanctuary

---

[47] This is the battle in which Nicanor dies and, when his body is found, a gruesome incident ensues in which his head and arm are cut off and paraded in victory. His tongue is also removed and ultimately Judas displays his head from the citadel: "a clear and conspicuous sign to everyone of the help of the Lord" (15.35).

[48] In 12.22–23 the appearance of soldiers also aligns with the experience of the presence of God: "But when Judas's first division appeared, terror and fear came over the enemy at the manifestation to them of him who sees all things. In their flight they rushed headlong in every direction, so that often they were injured by their own men and pierced by the points of their owns swords. Judas pressed the pursuit with the utmost vigour, putting the sinners to the sword, and destroyed as many as thirty thousand." Thus, God is identified with Judas and his division of soldiers, the enemy are responsible in part for their own demise, and Judas himself acts with "utmost vigour" but in complete concert with the divine purpose.

[49] This combination of efforts between divine and human agency can also be communal, as in, for instance, reflections after a successful battle: "When they had accomplished these things, with hymns and thanksgivings they blessed the Lord who shows great kindness to Israel and gives them the victory" (10.38). Judas's soldiers accomplish these things, but it is the Lord who gives victory.

[50] Ego distinguishes between the "measure for measure principle," which governs how opponents are dealt with in 2 Maccabees, and benevolent discipline shown towards the protagonists (Beate Ego, "God's Justice: The 'Measure for Measure' Principle in 2 Maccabees," in Xeravits and Zsengellér, *The Books of the Maccabees*, 153–54).

[51] By contrast, cf. 4. Macc 12.18; 18.5; and discussion in p. 92 n. 176.

(4.204–5; 5.18, 364, 401–2),⁵² been beguiled by the revolutionaries (5.407; 6.285), and engaged in revolution instead of allowing God to come to their defence (5.377–78).⁵³ Indeed, in his own speech in Book 5 noted above, Josephus shapes his account of Israel's history to show that God has always provided assistance when Israel was in need of defence, but not when they have taken matters into their own hands (5.377–400).⁵⁴ In Josephus's reckoning, and in keeping with this censure of revolutionary activity, such *human action itself* represents a failure of virtue and leads to becoming opponents of God:

> in short, there is no instance of our forefathers having triumphed by arms or failed of success without them when they committed their cause to God: if they sat still they conquered, as it pleased their Judge, if they fought they were invariably defeated. (*J.W.* 5.390)⁵⁵

Josephus also makes his own adjustments to Deuteronomistic theology. Unlike the portraits of divine instruments in the texts discussed above, Josephus presents the Romans positively. He takes pains to show the superior piety of the Romans (5.363, 372–73). They are instruments of divine punishment of the Jewish people (6.110), but unlike the Babylonians or Antiochus IV in the texts above, they are not culpable. They are more respectful of the sanctuary than the Jewish people themselves (5.363), benevolent in mercy (5.372–74), and studiously devoid of responsibility at the moment of the fire at the temple (6.252), especially Titus (6.254–56, 266).⁵⁶ Indeed, when he exhorts repentance—a response entirely

---

52 Regev, "Josephus, the Temple," 280–83.
53 Josephus's use of Deuteronomistic themes does not imply that he has not also been influenced by Hellenistic traditions; on these questions the Deuteronomistic influences are clear, however. On Josephus's presentation of himself as an inspired prophet, drawing on HB prophetic traditions, see Gray, *Prophetic Figures*. On the impact of Deuteronomistic theology upon Josephus's retrospective interpretation of Jerusalem's destruction, see Crabbe, "Being Found Fighting against God," 23–26.
54 This relates also to Josephus's introduction to the *Antiquities*, noted above, that following the divine will leads to positive outcomes, but by opposing the divine will one will find that "things (else) practicable become impracticable" leading to "irretrievable disasters" (*Ant.* 1.14–15). Connections to Psalm 1 are obvious. Note the discussion in Attridge, *The Interpretation of Biblical History*, 93. So also Josephus's claims about divine providence, through which humans are responsible for the "folly and calamities of their own choosing," in the citation with which this chapter began, *J.W.* 6.310.
55 Sanders compares Josephus's views to ancient Stoicism, arguing that in a Stoic framework: "a person was free to accept willingly his or her place in the causal nexus, or not. Rejection of destiny would not alter events, but only damage one's inner virtue" (Sanders, "God Gave the Law," 89).
56 Here the destruction is also portrayed as an act of purification (*J.W.* 4.323, 388; 5.19, 416–18; Regev, "Josephus, the Temple," 283–84).

§3 Engaging with Deuteronomistic approaches to divine and human agency — 221

consistent with Deuteronomistic theology—Josephus incorporates repentance to not only God (5.415), but also to Rome (5.372–73).

Secondly, Josephus differs from Deuteronomistic texts in how he presents divine and human agency in the future. The events of the end of history are not about a restoration resulting from repentance, so much as divine sovereign action in which humans play no role. Although Rome will inevitably fall as part of the sequence of kingdoms (J.W. 5.367; Ant. 10.210, 276; see Chapter 3), Josephus does not identify Rome's decline as punishment for its treatment of the Jewish people. Moreover, as noted in Chapter 4 above, Josephus portrays the destruction of Jerusalem as predetermined (6.305–13). From his retrospective vantage point, he sees no incoherence between this determinism and human responsibility for the events that led to divine punishment.[57] His theological interests, emphasising divine control and also human failings, enable the two sides of this interpretation to stand.[58]

Finally, Josephus's treatment of the Roman opponents still seems to limit their agency. In the *Jewish War*, as in several of the texts of this study, *who* has freedom is an important question for understanding what Josephus is doing in explaining the past and offering hope for the future. Even his positively portrayed Roman opponents do not appear to enjoy very much agency; the temple fire begins chaotically, the soldier who lit it being driven on by some divine impulse (δαιμονίῳ ὁρμῇ τινι, 6.252).[59] By contrast, the protagonist Jewish groups freely went astray and prompted the need for divine punishment, and they may also repent now.

Nonetheless, having relied on Deuteronomistic interpretations of past events and the present call for repentance, when Josephus turns to consider the events

---

[57] Although Sanders observes some possible awareness of Stoic thought in Josephus (*Life* 12; *Ag.Ap.* 2.168; and perhaps *Ant.* 10.277), he argues rightly that Josephus does not deal directly with these kinds of compatibility problems: "He simply asserts both that God chose to back the Romans and to destroy Jerusalem, and that this came as the consequence of the Jews' transgressions, which they could have avoided" (Sanders, "God Gave the Law," 90). Beginning with Josephus's philosophical school passages, Klawans argues Josephus demonstrates two kinds of compatibilism as he portrays fate and free will with respect to the Pharisees' position. But Klawans emphasises that these views relate to Jewish philosophies seen also in later rabbinic texts, not Stoic compatibilism (Klawans, "Josephus on Fate," 76–81).
[58] Likewise see discussion of *J.W.* 6.108 on related themes in p. 178 n. 199.
[59] As noted above, Josephus considers the Romans to be pious, which is a characteristic that may indicate a measure of agency, though certainly when it comes to events like the destruction of the temple, they are disempowered.

of the end of history, he emphasises only divine sovereignty. This provides hope. And it also avoids uncomfortable political implications in the present.[60]

### 3.2.3 Second Baruch

Second Baruch offers a view deeply shaped by these biblical patterns[61] and yet marked by apocalyptic extensions. In the words of Matthias Henze, "this is Deuteronomic theology propelled to its eschatological extreme."[62] Consistent with its pseudonymous attribution to Jeremiah's scribe, Baruch, the text particularly draws on Jeremiah's themes (2 Bar 2.1; 5.5; 9.1; 10.2–4; 33.1–2; 35.1–4). It describes the destruction of Jerusalem as divine punishment for impiety. After the description of Jerusalem's destruction in the first 8 chapters, Baruch fasts first before a series of laments (9.1–12.4), and then before a dialogue (12.5–20.4). In the words spoken to Baruch at the beginning of this first dialogue, as he stands on Zion, he is given an authoritative interpretation of the events of the destruction as testimony to be given to those asking, "Why has the mighty God brought upon us this retribution?" (13.4). Punishment is indeed the cause of this destruction throughout the text (cf. 33.2; 77.3–4; 79.2–4; cf. 84.2). Later, as he addresses the divine seeking an explanation for his vision of the dark and bright waters, Baruch asserts, "those who do not love your Law are justly perishing. And the torment of judgment will fall upon those who have not subjected themselves to your power" (54.14).

Although interpreted through the lens of the punishment of the people, in 2 Baruch culpability nonetheless lies with individuals. Baruch goes on to reflect in this same prayer, between the vision of the bright and dark waters and its interpretation: "Adam is, therefore, not the cause, except only for himself, but each of us has become our own Adam" (54.19; cf. 54.15).[63] As elsewhere, access to the law gives understanding, through which the people should have avoided sin, but did not (15.5–7).

Opponents are, therefore, divine instruments. In the unfolding description of the destruction, the seer's Lord declares, "the enemy ... shall serve the Judge for a

---

60 Rajak, *Josephus*, 89. See also Chapter 6 below.
61 See direct citations of Deuteronomy, such as in 2 Bar 19.1 (Deut 30.19).
62 Henze, "Torah and Eschatology," 206.
63 The exception, according to Baruch, is the sinless Zion who suffers as a result of the sins of others (2 Bar 76.8–9; 77.10). Like 2 Baruch, 4 Ezra reflects upon Adam's sin brought by Adam, but laments Adam's birth or wishes he had been "restrained" from sinning (7.116–19). Rather than 2 Baruch's claim that all became their own Adam, in 4 Ezra all share the consequence of Adam's sin, though this also manifests as individual sinning.

## §3 Engaging with Deuteronomistic approaches to divine and human agency — 223

time" (5.3). And in Baruch's report to the assembled people after receiving the vision of the twelve periods of calamities, he names Babylonian captivity a "sentence" (33.2).[64] Again, however, this punishment reflects benevolent discipline for the covenant people; the letter at the end of the text asserts that present suffering is "for your good so that you may not be condemned at the end and be tormented" (78.6). And earlier the punishment is explained as though to an outsider audience:

> You who have drunk the clarified wine, you now drink its dregs, for the judgment of the Most High is impartial. Therefore, he did not spare his own sons first, but he afflicted them as his enemies because they sinned. Therefore, they were once punished, that they might be forgiven. But now, you nations and tribes, you are guilty, because you have trodden the earth all this time, and because you have used creation unrighteously. (2 Bar 13.8–11).

As in 2 Macc 6.12–17, the other nations will also be punished, but by then their situation will be more dire.

While affirming human responsibility, however, the writer simultaneously depicts history as utterly planned; things are unfolding exactly as intended (9.1–2; 10.6–19;[65] 14.1; 23.4–7; 27.1; 40.2; 54.1; 56.2; 69.2).[66] The Lord addresses Baruch:

> For as you have not forgotten those who exist and who have passed away, I remember those who will come. For when Adam sinned and death was decreed against those who were to be born, the multitude of those who would be born was numbered. And for that number a place was prepared where the living ones might live and where the dead might be preserved. No creature will live again unless the number that has been appointed is completed. (23.3–5a)[67]

As a result of this mix of determinism and punishment, 2 Baruch's reader is caught between being held responsible and powerlessness. There is no scope within this account for questioning divine faithfulness for creating a situation

---

64 See Chapter 6 on the effects of 2 Baruch's literary setting.
65 As evidence of divine coordination of even these anguished events (9.1–2; 10.6–19), Baruch receives a vision of angels taking the essential temple items prior to the destruction for protection until the end (6.7–9; cf. 80.2; 2 Macc 2.4–7). Although this vision, unlike the exposition in dialogues, could indicate divine adaptation to mitigate a foreseen disaster, the tone of 2 Baruch, including claims such as that cited above, that the opponent will "serve the Judge for a time" (5.3), leads to a rather different interpretation in this text.
66 See Chapter 4.
67 Klijn's translation, modified for inclusive language.

in which divine planning leads inevitably to punishment (unlike key themes in 4 Ezra discussed below).

Prospectively, 2 Baruch's writer asserts that restoration is also determined but, rather than an event within history as in Deuteronomy or Jeremiah, this restoration is now emphatically placed at the end (6.8–9; 15.7–8); in the vision of the forest and the vine, the symbol of the penultimate ruler, the cedar, will certainly be destroyed (36.5–7; 37.1; 39.8–40.4). Maintaining piety is an appropriate human response in the present (32.2; 44.2–3; 45.1–2; 46.5–7; 51.3; 76.5; 84.5–11; 85.4, 9), which also elicits eschatological consequences. On the one hand, the reader is exhorted to "direct and dispose our hearts" (85.4) and to "prepare" (32.1; 46.5; 52.7; 84.9; 85.11), and at one point in the final letter, even the threat of eschatological exclusion seems to remain in some play:

> You should, therefore, prepare your hearts for that which you have believed before, lest you should be excluded from both worlds, namely, that you were carried away into captivity here and tormented there. (83.8)

A long list of reversals follows as part of underscoring the eschatological changes the reader should expect, with a focus on the ultimate punishment the unrighteous will receive (83.10–23). Rhetorically this drives home the exhortation to faithfulness for the implied audience of the final letter.

But on the other hand, even those who will ultimately receive an eschatological reward have been determined, as in the conclusion of the vision of the twelve periods of calamities:

> And it will happen at that time that those treasuries will be opened in which the number of the souls of the righteous were kept, and they will go out and the multitudes of the souls will appear together, in one assemblage, of one mind. (30.2; cf. 52.1–7; 84.6)

Again, incoherence exists for enemies, who are divine instruments but also "will be thoroughly punished" (13.5; cf. 12.4; 14.2), now as part of an eschatological judgement (42.1–2; 44.11–15; 48.29, 40–1, 43, 47; cf. Baruch's words at 54.14–22). The writer affirms absolute divine sovereignty, without concern about its potential incoherence with attributions of human responsibility. It is as though the determinism simply reflects a deeper knowledge of how all people would respond anyway.[68]

---

**68** Perhaps this is akin to the wicked shepherds in the *Animal Apocalypse* (now generally understood to be human and not angelic figures, cf. Patrick A. Tiller, *A Commentary on the Animal Apocalypse of I Enoch*, EJL 4 (Atlanta: Scholars Press, 1993), 51–52; Olson, *A New Reading*, 190 n. 1); God appoints the shepherds for a particular purpose in a highly deterministic setting,

And yet, given the disclosures shared with the reader, the assumption appears to be that readers should consider themselves a part of the privileged group. Buoyed by believing compliance is already determined, readers should embrace the responsibility to keep the law. Rather than concerns about the plight of other groups, questions of justice in 2 Baruch revolve around the promise that opponents (even if divine instruments) will ultimately be punished and the people vindicated, by God's sovereign action.

### 3.2.4 Fourth Ezra

Finally, the writer of 4 Ezra shares many Deuteronomistic assumptions about history's events—for instance, by viewing Jerusalem's destruction as a punishment for sin (3.25–36; 6.55–59; 7.19–25, 72)—but *challenges the justice* of such a reality. As in 2 Baruch, the current situation certainly reflects judgement, but eschatological extensions of this pattern of sin and punishment intensify concerns about present events.[69] In the dialogues, Ezra challenges Uriel regarding God's responsibility for creating a situation in which judgement and punishment were inevitable, given humans are not capable of living faithfully.[70] Ezra laments in the third dialogue:

> Who among the living is there that has not sinned, or who is there among mortals that has not transgressed your covenant? And now I see that the world to come will bring delight to few, but torments to many. For an evil heart has grown up in us, which has alienated us from God, and has brought us into corruption and the ways of death. (7.46–48)

Uriel's response, that rare stones are more precious than the plentiful and thus the rare faithful person will prompt rejoicing (7.52–61; cf. 8.2–3; 9.21), does not console Ezra (7.67–68). He returns several times to the theme (cf. 8.34–35; 9.14). The problem, it seems to Ezra, lies in the way people have been created and the

---

but they also, inevitably, overstep their authority. This may also be the best explanation for the portrayal of Antiochus IV in 2 Maccabees—he enacts divine punishment, but is predictably hubristic and culpable in his own way.

**69** These themes draw on multiple layers in 4 Ezra's text. Judgement is highlighted in: the literary present (post-586 BCE), the historical present (post-70 CE), and the end of history. Divine and human responsibility and the consequences of such judgement are important in each layer.

**70** So Harnisch on 4 Ezra's understanding of the evil heart as excluding human freedom (Harnisch, *Verhängnis und Verheißung*), though this overlooks other elements of the text, particularly future response from the protagonist groups. See below.

conditions in which they exist.[71] Uriel further illustrates the rareness of human faithfulness with the image of a farmer's seeds—not all seeds which are planted will grow (8.41). But Ezra retorts: "if the farmer's seed does not come up, because it has not received your rain in due season, or if it has been ruined by too much rain, it perishes" (v. 43). The implication is incisive: providing the conditions for flourishing remains a divine responsibility. Here, questions of divine responsibility arise precisely *because* humans are culpable. God, the sovereign Creator (v. 44–45; cf. v. 15) and provider of the law (3.19; 7.12) and of understanding (8.62), should have arranged things differently.[72]

As in all interpretation of 4 Ezra, the relationship between the voices of Ezra and Uriel, and between the seven episodes, remains central.[73] Although the text across the episodes comes to affirm Uriel's position—or, more precisely, Uriel's prospective orientation—Ezra's complaint ensures essential concerns about the present are canvassed.

Importantly, the third dialogue offers a conflicted image of freedom for different human subjects. As the dialogue continues, Uriel attempts to move Ezra from his interest in the many created (who will perish) to the few who will be saved (8.55; cf. 9.13, 21–22).[74] He asserts that those who are perishing have exercised freedom in straying from the law (8.56–58; cf. 9.11), though he assures Ezra that, "the root of evil is sealed up from you" (8.53; cf. 2 Bar 31.5–32.2; 54.15–16). Thus, whereas Ezra points out that all mortals who have been born have sinned (8.34) and flourishing requires divinely granted conditions (8.43), Uriel argues that "the many" have made their own choices freely (8.56–58), and this explains their certain perishing later, while those like Ezra have been protected from going astray (8.53; cf. 9.21–22).

---

[71] Ezra's reference to "an evil heart" does not blame God for its emergence (7.48); see Barclay, *Paul and the Gift*, 287, 302. Nor does 4 Ezra blame other spiritual forces. On the intrinsic evil tendency of the human heart in 4 Ezra, see Bilhah Nitzan, "Apocalyptic Ideas in 4 Ezra in Comparison with the Dead Sea Scrolls," in Boccaccini and Zurawski, *Interpreting 4 Ezra and 2 Baruch*, 24–25.

[72] Here Ezra does not distinguish between divine action in creating opposition or permitting opponents to exercise freedom, or even creating opponents to act in their own characteristic manner. In the dialogues, God is seen as responsible because of being sovereign over a situation which, through any of these causes, leads to human suffering. Although the later episodes do not overturn this sentiment, they do highlight future hope in divine sovereignty which ultimately trumps these questions of responsibility, as discussed below.

[73] See Chapter 3 §3.1.

[74] On debates about universalism and particularism, and Ezra and Uriel's voices, see Bruce W. Longenecker, *Eschatology and the Covenant: A Comparison of 4 Ezra and Romans 1–11*, JSNTSup 57 (Sheffield: JSOT Press, 1991); Hogan, *Theologies in Conflict*, 32–33.

Here the writer of 4 Ezra, like the writers discussed above, treats "opponents" and the groups whose interests lie at the heart of the text differently (cf. 8.47). The passion behind the distinction is perhaps exemplified in Uriel's indictment of those who "have even trampled upon his righteous ones, and said in their hearts that there is no God" (8.57–58), which may give an insight into the pain of the historical situation that has prompted the writer's theological reflection. As it explains the past, 4 Ezra attributes freedom and responsibility to opponents, even when they have implemented divine punishment (3.27–8; 8.56–61). However, Ezra and those like him enjoy different potential.[75]

Also in keeping with the texts discussed above, 4 Ezra reflects significant differences between retrospective and prospective orientations in the text. The third dialogue makes this explicit, as Uriel challenges Ezra's focus on mortality, "why have you not considered in your mind what is to come, rather than what is now present?" (7.16; cf. 6.34).[76] The shift evident in the visions of episodes four to seven turns on these types of questions. Indeed, while Deuteronomistic theology is found in the earlier dialogues, the conversation between Ezra and Uriel serves to challenge the *limits* of these kinds of interpretations of suffering. Without refuting the interpretations' accuracy, 4 Ezra ultimately expands the perspective of history in which the present is set,[77] in order to emphasise instead future promise and divine sovereignty throughout history.[78]

While retrospective and prospective orientations shape many of the representations of divine and human agency discussed in this study, leading to a certain sense of incoherence or inconsistency at various points, 4 Ezra's author

---

**75** 4 Ezra 8.59–60 claims God did not intend to destroy, rather people created that situation through sin. Though, given determinism (cf. 7.42), sin and Jerusalem's destruction are inevitable.
**76** Barclay suggests this is a movement towards being able to see from the perspective of the future (Barclay, *Paul and the Gift*, 287, 302).
**77** See Chapters 3 and 6. As rightly asserted by Bachmann: "Ezra's understanding of history (cf. 3.4–27) … is rather enlarged than revised in 4 Ezra" (Veronika Bachmann, "More Than the Present: Perspectives on World History in *4 Ezra* and *The Book of the Watchers*," in Boccaccini and Zurawski, *Interpreting 4 Ezra and 2 Baruch*, 7). It is the "technique" of facing crisis by setting the present in a broader framework of world history (so Collins, "Temporality and Politics") which provides the new perspective, but it does not refute other assumptions about the present.
**78** In her very helpful treatment, Hogan argues that neither Uriel nor Ezra present the author's view, but the text builds towards affirming the perspective of the visions, which in some respects conflict with both voices (Hogan, *Theologies in Conflict*, 2). She suggests that the visions emphasise apocalyptic divine action which overturns the wisdom perspectives of the earlier dialogues (p. 39). I suggest, however, that the retrospective and prospective orientations remain important distinctions for explaining these different emphases in 4 Ezra; the visions expand the perspective, but do not overturn the earlier views.

stands out as one who demonstrates *awareness of the tensions this creates*. Other writers similarly stress divine sovereignty. But 4 Ezra's dialogues provide a penetrating recognition of some of the costs of this emphasis. If the future is ultimately assured by divine sovereignty which governs all of history, then God remains responsible. Moreover, unlike for instance the vision of the forest and the vine in 2 Bar 23–30, where the vine declares that the evil cedar will be destroyed at the end without stating its origins, in 4 Ezra's fifth episode, the (messianic) lion addresses the eagle (representing Rome) to claim responsibility for having created the empires (11.39).[79] The writer of 4 Ezra bites an important bullet: if God is absolutely sovereign, then even the oppressive empires must have been created by God. However, as in other texts which emphasise divine sovereignty when looking ahead, the vision's orientation towards the future ensures that the claim that God created the oppressive empire does not emphasise divine responsibility for the suffering caused by Rome, as in the earlier dialogues, but divine *power over Rome*, and thus the pre-planned endpoint to its rule.

Finally, in 4 Ezra divine sovereignty ultimately guarantees not only the promised end, but the divine capacity to produce human faithfulness. Uriel indicates that, though the existence of an elect is determined, its *membership* at the end remains in question.[80] By the time of Ezra's address to the people after the final episode, the evil heart about which he was worried (7.48) has become a possibility of transformation. He exhorts the people to discipline their hearts and to seek righteousness through Torah observance so they might be included among the few at the end. Following the model of divine rescue from Egypt, Ezra speaks into the (literary) setting of the exile,[81] to communicate a promise for the eschatological future:

---

[79] See also Chapter 4 above.

[80] Rowland describes determinism in apocalypses through the image of a play comprising multiple scenes that have all been written in advance, but have not yet all been acted out on stage (Rowland, *The Open Heaven*, 144; Wright's image of salvation history unfolding over five acts is quite different, see Wright, "How Can the Bible Be Authoritative?", 19). To continue Rowland's image, in texts like 4 Ezra, although the events are all set, it remains unclear which actors will play which roles (cf. 14.34–35).

[81] As noted above, of course, this literary setting addresses a historical setting which is after the destruction of the Second Temple. As a result, this pattern of divine rescue in fact becomes a pattern with an additional layer: deliverance from Egypt where they had been aliens (and without any fault on Israel's part specified, 14.29); from exile following the destruction of the first temple; which morphs for the reader into the promise of rescue following the second temple's destruction. Both destructions are thus aligned with divine punishment to discipline and to take back what had been given.

## §3 Engaging with Deuteronomistic approaches to divine and human agency — 229

> If you, then, will rule over your minds and discipline your hearts, you shall be kept alive, and after death you shall obtain mercy. For after death the judgement will come, when we shall live again; and then the names of the righteous will be made manifest, and the deeds of the ungodly will be disclosed. (14.34–35; cf. 8.3; 14.13–15, 22)[82]

Despite Ezra's concerns about the inevitable failures of virtue that led to divine punishment, protagonist characters (but not opponents)[83] still enjoy the freedom to act virtuously—exercised through divine facilitation (as in Barclay's third model). Looking to the future, readers may be assured that divine sovereignty has not only secured the end, but made human piety possible, thereby exempting a select group from the inevitable culpability and punishment that arises when humans are left to their own devices.[84]

### 3.3 Other spiritual forces in late Second Temple texts

Attributing responsibility to other spiritual forces can eliminate the need to attribute responsibility to *either* humans or the divine. The writers of Jewish texts such as the War Scroll or 2 Baruch describe spiritual forces as opponents. In the battles set out in the **War Scroll**, the human sons of darkness are supported by the host of Belial.[85] The language in 1QM 1 describes a final showdown involving "the assembly of the gods and the congregation of men (אנשים)" (1.10–11); the action involves flurried battles amid "the shout of gods and of men (ואנשים)" (1.11). While the text differentiates the singular God of Israel (thus "God's might" in 1.11, לגבורת אל), it nonetheless presumes numerous gods engaging in the battle alongside their human counterparts.[86] The writer does not downplay the strength of the enemy or the severity of the battles

---

[82] Najman argues 4 Ezra is about a renewal of faithful Torah practice, made possible in the aftermath of the loss of the temple (Najman, *Losing the Temple*, 152–58).
[83] Barclay, *Paul and the Gift*, 307–8.
[84] Willett compares 2 Baruch and 4 Ezra, arguing there are no new answers in 2 Baruch, and no new answers on theodicy in 4 Ezra, except that 4 Ezra discards the idea of a rational answer, like Job, and instead brings together the ends of the spectrum, including religious experience (Tom W. Willett, *Eschatology in the Theodicies of 2 Baruch and 4 Ezra*, JSPSup 4 (Sheffield: JSOT Press, 1989), 125).
[85] See Rowland, *The Open Heaven*, 40.
[86] Rowland emphasises that the War Scroll implies that this battle takes place within history, in which the sons of light are to participate in the divine action of defeating evil. Rather than the quietism of Daniel, this portrays expectations closer to those of the zealots (Rowland, *The Open Heaven*, 41).

and, as noted in Chapter 4, portrays the sides as evenly matched until Israel's God tips the balance.[87] Nonetheless, the overall outcome is assured. Philip Alexander suggests that the War Scroll reflects the interests of a community preparing for war in a manner like that of the zealots.[88] In such a view, the account of divine and human agency reflects Barclay's second model outlined above—humans act in concert with God, exercising freedom but as direct agents of the divine purpose. The community's experiences may suggest to them that an empire of Belial (and his human agents) is at work in history, and the anticipated eschatological war may involve such forces, but the War Scroll's emphasis on the God of Israel's sovereignty—even at the expense of claiming God has created this destructive empire (13.11; see Chapter 4)—ensures that when looking to the future, these other spiritual forces will certainly be overcome.

**Second Baruch**'s vision of the dark and bright waters (2 Bar 53–76) explicitly attributes past negative events to other spiritual forces. Although blackness is said to enter with Adam, the vision employs the tradition of the Watchers to explain further corruption. Ramael's explanation of the vision clarifies that these fallen spiritual beings "possessed freedom in that time" (56.11). Moreover, innumerable other angels "restrained themselves," permitting the Watchers to wreak their havoc without opposition, resulting in the need for the flood (56.14–15).[89] The historical review thus draws on themes found elsewhere.[90] But the claim that the freedom was *granted* to the Watchers, including permission to act unchecked, highlights not only the (partial) agency granted to them, but its time-limited nature. Divine sovereignty prohibits such forces from affecting the divine plan for the future.

Second Baruch does not raise the question of divine responsibility for having granted these forces agency in the first place. Opposing spiritual forces' origins are not addressed. Consequently, the writer avoids implications of either divine responsibility for their existence or—the potential flipside—a challenge to divine sovereignty if these forces exist independently of divine will.[91]

---

87 Vermes, *The Complete Dead Sea Scrolls*, 163.
88 Alexander, "The Evil Empire," 31; cf. Rowland, *The Open Heaven*, 41–42. Alexander argues that, though the war cycle texts come from earlier traditions, it is likely that they were "revived" in the build up to the revolt against Rome (p. 31).
89 The War Scroll presents a challenging battle between opposing forces; similarly 2 Baruch does not negate the power of the Watchers, though they were restrained from exercising that power.
90 See James C. VanderKam, "The Book of Enoch and the Qumran Scrolls," in Lim and Collins, *The Oxford Handbook of the Dead Sea Scrolls*, 264, 268; Rowland, *The Open Heaven*, 93–94.
91 This tension is part of what is at stake in some claims about *creatio ex nihilo*, ensuring the sovereignty of the Creator. See, for instance, Bockmuehl, who notes the War Scroll's assertion

§3 Engaging with Deuteronomistic approaches to divine and human agency —— 231

As noted above, Barclay consciously excludes these forces from his framework for divine and human agency.[92] Certainly texts of Second Temple Judaism do not portray such forces with the agency to influence events of *soteriological* significance, and thus they may reasonably fall outside Barclay's area of interest. However, these forces do exist in some texts. Their activities may instead explain negative events. Again, temporal orientation shapes the way these forces are described: looking back, writers may exclude both divine and human responsibility by assigning agency to other forces (even if the effects of that agency, as in 2 Baruch, are facilitated by righteous forces restraining themselves). But looking forward, divine sovereignty will render these forces impotent.

## 3.4 Θεομάχοι

Finally, for some writers, suffering comes as a result of the behaviours of other humans, who are not in the first instance fulfilling a divine purpose but opposing God. Such attempts to fight God are frequently portrayed with a paradigmatic combination of hubris and dramatic downfalls. In the shorter term, their actions may explain events without attributing divine responsibility, but ultimately God will always win out.

---

that God created Belial (Markus N. A. Bockmuehl, "Creatio ex Nihilo in Palestinian Judaism and Early Christianity," *SJT* 65 (2012): 262; by contrast see Frances Young, "'Creatio ex Nihilo': A Context for the Emergence of the Christian Doctrine of Creation," *SJT* 44 (1991): 139–51). In a discussion of Philo, Sterling notes both the difficulty of discerning a clear view of Philo's understanding of creation, and the core claim about God's superiority over matter, which is common to all of Philo's texts on this question. Philo is aware of the concern, for instance, that to assert that matter was formless prior to the work of the Creator is to equate uncreated matter with the uncreated divine. Sterling argues that Philo can be seen as "a bridge" between Hellenistic philosophy and the early Christians, who would go on to extend this kind of emphasis on divine sovereignty into claims of *creatio ex nihilo* (Gregory E. Sterling, "'The Most Perfect Work': The Role of Matter in Philo of Alexandria," in *Light on Creation: Ancient Commentators in Dialogue and Debate on the Origin of the World*, ed. Geert Roskam and Joseph Verheyden, STAJ 104 (Tübingen: Mohr Siebeck, 2017), 243–57). Some early Christian writers approached the challenge of suffering or evil in creation by attributing creation to the demiurge. On Paul's understanding of the power of other forces such as sin, and "apocalyptic" accounts which disempower human response, see Martyn, *Theological Issues*, 111–13, 120–22, 143–47, and related analysis in Campbell, *The Deliverance of God*, 191–92.
92 Barclay, "Introduction," 6–7.

Archetypal examples of θεομάχοι in Hellenistic Jewish texts include Pharaoh, Goliath, Nebuchadnezzar, and Antiochus IV,[93] who are portrayed through a literary type found in Graeco-Roman tragedy. The term θεομαχέω first appears in Euripides, but it reflects earlier traditions.[94] Non-Jewish Graeco-Roman writers in this tradition detail the tragic consequences of human attempts to fight against the divine. They can variously highlight the justice of Zeus or the doomed valour of the hero.[95] However, as they adapt these traditions, Jewish writers typically emphasise the arrogance and certain failure inherent in any attempt to fight God. Hellenistic Jewish writers draw on this literary type through a constellation of ideas such as hubris and blasphemy, even when the terms θεομάχος/ θεομαχέω are not employed.[96]

Without employing θεομαχία terminology in either the *Antiquities* or *Jewish War*,[97] **Josephus** draws on the concepts associated with this literary tradition, particularly in portraits of characters especially associated with these themes in Second Temple Judaism. His account of biblical history in the *Antiquities* provides numerous examples as he brands characters opponents of God by emphasising their hubris and dramatic downfall. Moses rescues the Hebrews from "Egyptian hubris (ὕβρεως)" (*Ant.* 2.268, cf. 2.261; 4.3, 243; 6.89),[98] and warns Pharaoh that by "hindering them, he should unwittingly have but himself to blame for suffering such a fate as was like to befall him who opposed (τὸν ἀντιπράττοντα) the commands of God," including "dread calamities" (2.291–92).[99] Indeed, Josephus suggests that Pharaoh, being "less fool than knave,[100] though

---

[93] Michael Wolter, "Paulus, der bekehrte Gottesfeind: Zum Verständnis von 1.Tim 1,13," in *Theologie und Ethos im frühen Christentum: Studien zu Jesus, Paulus und Lukas*, WUNT 236 (Tübingen: Mohr Siebeck, 2009), 247.

[94] See J. C. Kamerbeek, "On the Conception of ΘΕΟΜΑΧΟΣ in Relation with Greek Tragedy," *Mnemosyne* 1 (1948): 274.

[95] Kamerbeek, "On the Conception of ΘΕΟΜΑΧΟΣ," 276, 283. See also Wolfgang Speyer, "Gottesfeind," *RAC* 11:996–1043.

[96] Wolter, "Paulus, der bekehrte Gottesfeind," 247.

[97] However, in *J.W.* and *Ant.* Josephus frequently employs a full phrase to describe opposing God (e.g. *Ant.* 2.307). See, though, *Ag. Ap.* 1.246 and 1.263, which use θεομαχέω in the context of the military decisions of a character who did *not* want to fight God.

[98] Rothschild, *Luke-Acts and the Rhetoric*, 158.

[99] Many dramatic incidents in the *Antiquities* are expressed in terms of hubris (cf. 1.60). For a collective representation of opponents of God, see the account of the Babel incident (*Ant.* 1.113–21).

[100] Feldman translates as "induced not so much by stupidity as by wickedness," which he notes is Josephus's addition to the story as outlined in the biblical text (Louis H. Feldman, ed. and trans., *Flavius Josephus: Judean Antiquities 1–4*, Flavius Josephus: Translation and Commentary 3 (Boston: Brill, 2000), 220).

alive to the cause of it all [the plagues], was matching himself against God (ἀντεφιλονείκει τῷ θεῷ)" (*Ant.* 2.307).[101] Similarly, Josephus has David declare that Goliath has "insulted our army and blasphemed our God, who will deliver him into my hands" (*Ant.* 6.183, cf. 186–192, 210); the ensuing downfall contrasts Goliath's arrogance with the humility of David, whose power comes from God (6.181, 186–91; cf. also *Ant.* 10.242). Josephus's Daniel reflects on Nebuchadnezzar's punishment as a result of his "insolence" (ὕβρεις, *Ant.* 10.241) and "impieties" (ἠσέβησε, 10.242)[102] when interpreting signs of disaster for Baltasares, who had failed to learn from this example to avoid arrogant striving beyond human things (10.241–243). And Caligua's death links to his aspirations to be worshipped (19.4).[103] Gruesome deaths, normally attributed to divine πρόνοια (*Ant.* 2.286, 330, 344), likewise fulfil the literary type and assert ultimate divine sovereignty.

Likewise, **2 Maccabees** confirms Antiochus IV and Nicanor as opponents of the divine in both their arrogance and their gruesome ends (4.17, 38; 5.12–17, 21; 9.4). The sixth martyred son's words to Antiochus incorporate the only use of θεομάχος/θεομαχέω terminology in the LXX: "but do not think that you will go unpunished for having tried to fight against God (θεομαχεῖν)!" (7.19). This statement ensures these earlier events in 2 Macc 6–7 are read in light of the end to which they lead: Antiochus's death as a θεομάχος (9.4–28, esp. vv. 11–12).[104] In addition to highlighting this literary tradition for Antiochus, the writer of 2 Maccabees simultaneously portrays Antiochus as a disempowered

---

**101** Rajak also explores the significance of anger in the portrayal of tyrants, as a failure to control the emotions, such as in the contrast between Pharaoh's rage and Moses's superior self-control in *Ant.* 2.284–302 (Tessa Rajak, "The Angry Tyrant," in *Jewish Perspectives on Hellenistic Rulers*, ed. Tessa Rajak, Hellenistic Culture and Society 50 (Berkeley: University of California Press, 2007), 115–16). She notes that such adaptations allow for subversion, not only by critiquing characters through traditional moral conventions, but also by emphasising superior divine anger (p. 125).
**102** Second Baruch's historical review also says Nebuchadnezzar in the eleventh black water period will be arrogant and then fall (67.7–8; cf. 82.9). Numerous further texts censure hubris, noting practical ways in which this leads to downfall (as in Diodorus's *Library*) and even eschatological punishment for pride (4 Ezra 8.50).
**103** See *Ant.* 19.155–56 for further practical causes of Caligua's downfall. Schwartz observes the *Jewish War* does not generally involve the graphic punishments characteristic of the *Antiquities*, though Catullus's death does (*J.W.* 7.453). Schwartz uses his comparison of these themes in the two works to suggest a later dating for *J.W.* 7 (Schwartz, "Josephus, Catullus, and the Date," 399).
**104** Rajak observes that 4 Maccabees' adaptation of the stories of 2 Macc 6–7 particularly accentuates Antiochus's failure to control his excess of emotions, thus drawing on Greek censure of immoderation (Rajak, "The Angry Tyrant," 120).

divine instrument (7.8), as discussed above. Perhaps ironically, part of the arrogance for which Antiochus is punished is believing that he inflicts suffering through his own agency:

> Antiochus was elated in spirit, and did not perceive that the Lord was angered for a little while because of the sins of those who lived in the city, and that this was the reason he was disregarding the holy place. But if it had not happened that they were involved in many sins, this man would have been flogged and turned back from his rash act as soon as he came forward. (5.17–18; cf. 5.21; 7.18–19; 2 Bar 7.1)[105]

Although θεομάχος/θεομαχέω is not used of Nicanor, he also implies the tradition: his arrogance leads him to suppose he can sway the Jewish people from faithful practice (cf. 2 Macc 14.33; 15.1–6, 32), and his death during battle against (the divinely empowered) Judas and his soldiers is celebrated with a grizzly parade through town with his severed head (15.3–7).

One further example of fighting God warrants mention. In **Josephus**'s *Jewish War*, as in the citation with which this chapter began, Josephus's character claims the people as a whole are "warring not against the Romans only, but also against God" (*J.W.* 5.378).[106] Although this differs from the characterisation of individuals as θεομάχοι, in many ways Josephus connects it to similar themes.[107] The people have displayed foolish arrogance to consider themselves capable of victory against Rome (5.365–67; cf. the many parallels in Agrippa's speech in 2.345–401). Moreover, given the might of Rome, they ought to have recognised Rome's divine support (5.368) and "how mighty an Ally you have outraged" (5.377). For Josephus, the events of history so strongly indicate divine purposes that, on the basis of the rule "yield to the stronger" (5.368), the Jewish people ought immediately to have interpreted Rome's dominance over them as divine will. The ensuing downfall constitutes divine punishment for such arrogant opposition.

---

**105** Here Antiochus's behaviour is possible because God has abandoned the people and allowed it; similarly, see *J.W.* 5.412.
**106** For further discussion, see Crabbe, "Being Found Fighting against God," 27 n. 18.
**107** These issues of individual and corporate sin and punishment are significant throughout the HB (see especially Ezekiel), and texts like the Psalms of Solomon. On Ezekiel see Paul Joyce, *Ezekiel: A Commentary*, LHBOTS 482 (New York: T&T Clark, 2007), 79–87; for a more general discussion of individual and corporate aspects of agency, punishment and salvation, see Boccaccini, "Inner-Jewish Debate," 17–18.

## 4 Divine and human responsibility in other texts

The non-Jewish writers of this study also offer accounts of divine action which constitutes punishment, as well as accounts in which the gods themselves are portrayed as the opponents of human projects.

### 4.1 Human responsibility and divine action

Writers like Diodorus Siculus, Valerius Maximus, and Tacitus also associate the events of history with divine punishment or reward. Sometimes this can lead to the sense that humans are not ultimately in control but are nonetheless responsible, or events whose causes include a mix of both "divine wrath and human madness."[108] As discussed in Chapter 4, these writers may recognise a role for personal and impersonal divine forces in history's events, but other priorities, such as moral instruction, lead frequently to attributions of human responsibility.

**Diodorus Siculus**, for instance, identifies the events of the Third Sacred War (16.61–64) as "just retribution from the deity" (16.64.1).[109] This includes a lightning strike that prompts a "divine fire," destroying siege machinery and mercenaries (16.63.3), as well as divine control of events in which humans play a greater role—from being defeated in war by Antipater (16.64.1) to the personal, moral decline of the commanders' wives (16.64.2) and Philip's success (16.64.3).[110] Admittedly, assumptions about divine retribution may be more salient in this setting, where the issue at hand relates to sacrilege.[111] Diodorus portrays the deity as just and the punishment as deserved;[112] likewise, characters such as the commanders' wives have freely brought about their own moral failures.

---

**108** As Griffin observes of Tacitus (Griffin, "Tacitus as a Historian," 170).
**109** On Diodorus's sources for, and possible contradictions within, Book 16, see Hau, "The Burden of Good Fortune," 175.
**110** On themes of hubris and downfall in Diodorus's portrayal of Philip in 16.95.1, see Hau, "The Burden of Good Fortune," 182–83.
**111** Sacks suggests that the focus on divine retribution in Book 16 is consistent with the narrative focus on recounting the Sack of Delphi from the Third Sacred War here (Sacks, *Diodorus Siculus*, 36–37 n. 56).
**112** For discussion of other examples in Diodorus on this theme, see Sacks, *Diodorus Siculus*, 36–37. This dynamic is also present in various other texts of different genres, for instance, Plutarch's *Lives* (cf. Plu. *Thes.* 15.1–2).

**Valerius Maximus** similarly identifies calamitous events as punishments for religion neglected,[113] as well as positive events flowing from correction of religious practice (1.1.16–21, ext.1–4). He also describes gods refraining from intervention. In a sentence not shared with other accounts of these events that might be Valerius's sources,[114] he reflects, "doubtless the immortal gods could have mitigated [Carthaginian] inhuman savagery, but to shed more lustre on Atilius' glory they let the Carthaginians act after their fashion: only to exact just vengeance … in the Third Punic War" (1.1.14). Thus the Carthaginians are culpable, but the gods are complicit in having refrained from intervening earlier.[115]

As he reflects on the piety of "the senate of our community," Valerius offers a mixed portrayal of the gods' disposition. When the senate shortened the official period of mourning, to ensure continuity of religious service, Valerius notes:

> by such resolution in the maintenance of religion the heavenly beings were made much ashamed to wreak further cruelty upon a nation which could not be scared away from their worship even by harshness of injuries. (1.1.15)

Here, then, as portrayed in Valerius's popular text, human agents appear to make some attempt to *manage* the behaviour of the gods, who may themselves be characterised negatively.[116]

Valerius presents human action in diverse other ways alongside the power of the divine forces within which humans act. As discussed in Chapter 4, he relates numerous anecdotes in which humans attempt to alter a portended outcome, where the dramatic tension for the reader lies in knowing that these efforts are sure to fail.[117] Foretold events are so certain that humans are able only to act within these parameters, although in several examples discussed, Valerius expresses frustration that the recipient of an insight into the future did not interpret it as a warning and act to stave off disaster (1.4.2; 1.6.6; 1.6.11; 1.6.ext1b). The implication—although Valerius does not attempt to be consistent across his corpus of miscellaneous anecdotes—is that the forces which control the future are

---

113 These assessments often include the hesitation "it was believed" (e.g. *Doings* 1.1.16).
114 On Valerius's sources here, see Wardle, *Valerius Maximus*, 111–12.
115 Cf. the sentiment in 2 Macc 6.14 discussed above, of allowing the sins of the other nations to accumulate before punishment. This was not an uncommon idea (cf. Wardle, *Valerius Maximus*, 112).
116 Even if Wardle's point (over against Wensky) is taken in relation to translation here (that *iniurias* takes a broader meaning, whereas Wensky emended to *miserias* (Wardle, "Valerius Maximus on the Domus Augusta," 114)), the depiction of the gods as unable to continue punishing the people is rather negative, and reflects a human management strategy.
117 See Chapter 4, §3.1.

impossible to alter but humans are at times also to be held responsible for *not* changing their own behaviour in the attempt to do so. (Of course, characters who have attempted this, and inevitably failed, are also the objects of tragic irony, as in the case of King Croesus, 1.7.ext4). By contrast, Valerius elsewhere affirms human action in assenting to a foretold negative event. As outlined in Chapter 4, he describes Ti. Gracchus correctly interpreting a strange event as a sign that his friend would betray him. But he then affirms Gracchus's virtue in allowing the prophesied events to take place anyway (1.6.8).[118]

**Tacitus** describes events which are identified as divine punishments and accounts of humans acting as divine instruments. In introducing his *Histories*, he notes signs and portents particularly related to the year 69 CE, asserting: "for never was it more fully proved by awful disasters of the Roman people or by indubitable signs that the gods care not for our safety, but for our punishment" (1.3). This observation frames the tumultuous story which follows. And yet, when the *Histories* later reaches the burning of the Capitol, the gods are said to be favourably predisposed towards the human community and the disaster results from human folly. Amid political strife, Tacitus claims it is not even clear which group—the besiegers or besieged—started the fire (3.71),[119] indicating shared responsibility: "so the Capitol burned with its doors closed; none defended it, none pillaged it" (3.71). The "opponents" here are internal: "Rome had no foreign foe; the gods were ready to be propitious if our characters had allowed; and yet the home of Jupiter Optimus Maximus ... was the shrine that the mad fury of emperors destroyed!" (3.72).[120]

Complementing his generally pessimistic tone, as discussed in Chapter 3, Tacitus not only attributes specific events to human failings, but describes characteristic and consistent human weaknesses. He has Galba conclude a portion of direct speech addressing Piso in Book 1 of the *Histories* with a reflection that goes to the heart of Tacitus's disappointment with the people for the failure of the Republic:

---

**118** Plutarch recounts a story with a similar dynamic, but criticises the act of sacrificing oneself by assenting to what is believed to be an oracle (Plu. *Thes.* 32.4).
**119** Though Tacitus later notes that Atticus took responsibility, for which Vitellius, whom Tacitus implies is actually culpable, is grateful (*Hist.* 3.75). In addition to being characteristically pessimistic, Tacitus's treatment here is also characteristically limited to dilemmas within, and not beyond, Rome.
**120** Tacitus's description of Nero in *Ann.* 14.22.4 offers a further example of human behaviour which is portrayed as eliciting divine anger and punishment (Griffin, "Tacitus as a Historian," 169–70).

With us there is not, as among peoples where there are kings, a fixed house of rulers while all the rest are slaves, but you are going to rule over people who can endure neither complete slavery nor complete liberty (*qui nec totam servitutem pati possunt nec totam libertatem*). (1.16.4)[121]

It seems the people could not survive the freedom of the Republic. Under autocratic rule even peace is savage (1.1; cf. 4.4.3)[122] and, although Tacitus is taking advantage of the new freedom under Trajan to write, his unfulfilled plans to address his own present historical period "later," perhaps to avoid current political pressures, underscore that such freedom is all relative.[123]

In the *Annals*, Tacitus disempowers human opponents as divine instruments, perhaps not unlike the portrayal of Babylon or Antiochus IV in texts discussed above. For instance, in Book 4 Sejanus comes to control Tiberius—"less by subtlety (in fact, he was beaten in the end by the selfsame arts) than by the anger of Heaven (*deum ira*) against the Roman realm for whose equal damnation he flourished and fell" (*Ann.* 4.1; cf. 1.24). Here Tacitus's negative assessment shines through his narrative also in the ensuing description of Sejanus (esp. 4.1–3).[124]

By contrast, for **Polybius**, the focus in the interaction between divine and human agency rests on the importance of human action and skill, evident particularly in his portrayal of positive characters.[125] He criticises other historians who deal with great figures by attributing their successes to θεοί or τύχη rather than the man (ἀνήρ) and his foresight (τὴν τούτου πρόνοιαν) and skills (10.9.2–3; cf. 10.2.6; 10.5.8–10). In comparing human foresight and good fortune, Polybius is clear: "one of the two things deserves praise and the other only congratulation" (10.2.7).[126] Humans may act within the parameters of divine forces,

---

**121** Moore and Jackson's LCL translation, modified for inclusive language.
**122** Syme, *Tacitus*, 1:209.
**123** See discussion in Sailor, *Writing and Empire*, 153. There is a general consensus that Tacitus never fulfilled his promise to provide a work about the eras of Trajan and Hadrian, though of course this or some other work may have been written and lost. It seems possible, though, that Tacitus proposed the work as an excuse to avoid addressing this period in the *Histories*, rather than a concrete plan for future work.
**124** Tacitus implies that, while Sejanus was opportunistically employed for the purpose of exacting divine reprisal, Sejanus himself was already a compromised character who was culpable in his own way. Any downfall that might arise for Sejanus thus could be attributed easily to his own personal failings (4.1–3).
**125** Although not a major focus, on change effected by τύχη as a direct punishment, see 15.20.5 (Walbank, "Fortune (*Tychē*) in Polybius").
**126** Eckstein emphasises this is a key theme in Polybius's treatment of Scipio (3.47.6–3.48.12; 10.5.9; Eckstein, *Moral Vision*, 276).

as in τύχη's ability to act as an umpire in determining the scope of the "match" (1.58.1),[127] but human skill and virtue are the focus, as elements over which his readers have control.[128]

Unlike the texts which draw on Deuteronomistic traditions discussed above, these Graeco-Roman texts remain for the most part in retrospective mode when explaining divine and human agency in historical events. There is no equivalent transition from retrospectively identifying, for instance, Babylon as a powerless divine instrument, to prospectively asserting Babylon's culpability and future punishment. As discussed in Chapter 4, without a teleological view of history, these writers' portrayals of the future remain different from the other texts, including Luke/Acts. For instance, any implications for the future that Diodorus Siculus offers simply reflect a generalised moralism derived from warnings about preparing for possible changes of fortune and the obligations of moral agents.[129]

Furthermore, in many cases the negative events these writers describe flow directly from the poor choices of the human agents, without any need for direct divine action. Teresa Morgan observes the centrality of this kind of thinking in popular ethical material, such as the gnomic saying: "evil is its own reward."[130] Here failures of virtue prompt problematic situations which inevitably lead to disasters, without necessarily requiring divine intervention to orchestrate a downfall.

## 4.2 The divine *as* the opponent

Some writers portray divine responsibility for opponents or adverse conditions in a range of ways, not simply within the framework of justified punishment (where, though enacted through divine will, the cause lies in human sin or hubris). Some texts display gods deliberately invoking hardship, though for a greater benefit. Others portray divine forces themselves as opponents, pitted against human protagonists.

As discussed in Chapter 3, **Virgil**'s depiction of a golden age shifts between his earlier and later work. Rather than the extravagant decadence of the age of Saturn (*Aen.* 8.324–35; cf. *Ecl.* 4.4–10; *Georg.* 4), the *Aeneid* focuses on a new age of Jupiter, attained through striving (*Aen.* 6.793). Jupiter, though acting with the

---

**127** See Chapter 4 above.
**128** Walbank, "Fortune (*Tychē*) in Polybius," 350–51, 355; Eckstein, *Moral Vision*, 281–82.
**129** See Chapter 6.
**130** Morgan, *Popular Morality*, 241.

Trojans' interests at heart, imposes obstacles that give new meaning to this era as an achievement. Although in some ways similar to the sentiments discussed in 2 Macc 6.12–17, here the hardship is not about exacting punishment and repentance before it is too late, but a view of labour as itself embodying virtue.

However, not all depictions of divine opposition maintain a sense of divine nobility. Conflict between the gods, often paralleling conflict between the humans to whom the gods are patrons, can also explain events.[131] In the *Aeneid*, characters like Juno may not ultimately be sovereign, but they do need to be managed.[132] Jupiter keeps her ignorant of his plans, although throughout the epic it is clear that Jupiter's superior power[133] will ensure that he (and thus also the Trojans) will not be foiled.[134]

**Valerius Maximus**'s anecdote above, in which humans manage the gods' somewhat petty instincts (1.1.15), also intimates divine opposition without noble purpose. From Homer's characterisation of the gods in *Iliad* 20–21, ancient readers and writers knew a model of epic in which divine characters could be unscrupulous. Though even here, the focus lies in the "contrast with the serious, heroic and tragic human characters."[135] Attic writers such as Xenophanes censured Homer's depiction as exploiting the worst human attributes in an inaccurate portrayal of the gods.[136] But various writers continued to depict the gods negatively in this tradition, whether to focus on human valour in the face of impossible odds, or to draw out more ironic assessments, such as Ovid's portray-

---

[131] See the battle of the gods set out in *Iliad* 20–21, described in terms like a Titanomachy, but involving the divinities from Olympus (Mark W. Edwards, *Books 17–20*, vol. 5 of *The Iliad: A Commentary* (Cambridge: Cambridge University Press, 1991), 287).

[132] Such management, however, takes place between the gods. See *Aen.* 1.20; 12.791–842; and West's discussion of the way Jupiter manages Juno (D. A. West, "The End and the Meaning: *Aeneid* 12.791–842," in *Vergil's Aeneid: Augustan Epic and Political Context*, ed. Hans-Peter Stahl (London: Duckworth, 1998), 303–4). Braund contends, "despite arguments to the contrary, humans seem to be entirely subject to divine will" and cites, for instance, 4.196–278, where there is a focus on Mercury delivering Jupiter's command, to which Aeneas's obedience is then required (Braund, "Virgil and the Cosmos," 211–12).

[133] The inevitability of *fatum* (cf. 1.262–304) also ensures this (see Chapter 4).

[134] See West, "The End and the Meaning," 303–4.

[135] Emily Kearns, "The Gods in Homeric Epics," in *The Cambridge Companion to Homer*, ed. Robert Fowler (Cambridge: Cambridge University Press, 2004), 68.

[136] Xenoph. *frag.* D8 (B11) and D9 (B12), attested by Sext. Emp. *Against the Professors* 9.193 and 1.289 respectively. See also discussion of Heraclitus's criticism of Homer in Kamerbeek, "On the Conception of ΘΕΟΜΑΧΟΣ," 284. Similarly, the reception of Homer is discussed in Robert Lamberton, *Homer the Theologian: Neoplatonist Allegorical Reading and the Growth of the Epic Tradition*, Transformation of the Classical Heritage 9 (Berkeley: University of California Press, 1986), 10.

al of unlikeable, petty, and despotic gods (*Metam.* 1.166, 588–600; cf. *Aen.* 1.148–53).[137]

Impersonal divine forces may also be capricious and unfair. As noted in Chapter 4, Valerius cites examples of *fortuna*'s fickleness, and for Diodorus the unpredictably of τύχη can create difficulties for human projects (though it may also inspire appropriate humility). Tacitus observes that *fortuna* had "disturbed the peace" (*Ann.* 1.1.1). However, *fortuna* fulfils the role of opponent most clearly when aligned with imperial forces.[138] It is in this sense, as noted in Chapter 4, that Stoic writers like Seneca can come to describe human life as a process of striving against *fortuna*.[139]

## 5 Summary: divine and human agency in the key texts

The above discussion supports Barclay's observation that ancient texts do not merely present divine and human agency in a simple competitive relationship. Some texts demonstrate the kinds of dynamic seen in Barclay's models two (like the alignment of Judas Maccabeus's will and action with divine purpose) and three (such as 4 Ezra's account of disciplining the heart). But there are also numerous examples in which the portrait of divine and human agency is perhaps less coherent than the options suggested within this contemporary framework. In particular, many writers respond to the theological pressure to explain the negative events of the past and present in terms which do not implicate the divine, while still finding a way to claim divine power for justice in the future. Here the claims about divine and human agency are not part of a systematic account of the relationship between divine and human agencies, but reflect the different concerns about sovereignty or responsibility that arise for writers as they seek to explain specific kinds of events or future promises.

Two particular kinds of problems seem to draw these differences out: how to deal with the power of opponents, and how to safeguard promises for the future. In a range of ways, these writers explain the negative events of the past through the behaviour of opponents. Such opponents may serve divine purposes (and therefore may or may not be exercising their own freedom), as in the texts which draw on various applications of Deuteronomistic theology or Tacitus's account of Sejanus. Or the opponents may follow their own interests in fighting

---

137 Hejduk, "Ovid and Religion," 50–53.
138 Regarding Lucan's *Civil War* on this, see Braund, ed. and trans., *Lucan*, xxiii.
139 Matthews, "Roman Constructions of Fortuna," 6.

against the divine, as θεομάχοι or other humans or spiritual forces (including Belial of the War Scroll, or the untrustworthy or fickle gods in the *Aeneid* or Valerius's anecdotes), which have a tangible impact on the lives of the characters with whom the reader is invited to identify.

The discussion shows that many writers treat attributions about divine and human agency for the events of the future, including those of soteriological significance, differently from those of the past. In retrospective mode, writers allow not only for direct opposition between divine and human agents (both have agency as they fight each other, even if victory is only likely for one), but may also demonstrate a greater appreciation for ways in which horizontal relationships and malevolent other forces can impact upon the experiences of the people at the heart of the text. In prospective mode, however, writers often remove the power of opponents, as part of assuring readers that divine justice will ultimately reign.

Finally, several of these writers emphasise divine initiative in facilitating positive human response in the present and future (at least for protagonist groups). Here the examples, such as Deuteronomy's account of divine action to circumcise the heart, or the divine gifts which enable piety before the imminent end in 4 Ezra and 2 Baruch, follow most closely the dynamic Barclay set out in his third model.[140] In contrast to the shift between retrospective and prospective approaches in these texts, the non-Jewish Graeco-Roman writers give no sense that the future will be any different in terms of the human *capacity* to live a virtuous life. Indeed, for a writer like Polybius, even though humans work within divine parameters, the accent for individuals remains on human skill and virtue, without very much divine assistance. I suggest Luke shares an interest in human agency. But, as divine initiative in Luke/Acts invites a positive response in the present and future, Luke shows little distinction between "protagonist" or "opponent" characters in the challenge to respond.

## 6 Interactions between divine and human agency in Luke/Acts

As in the texts examined above, in Luke/Acts divine and human agency also interact. Chapter 4 has already outlined Luke's emphasis on divine guidance of

---

[140] This is quite understandable given that these examples also most closely reflect the kinds of interests in Paul that undergird the discussion of divine and human agency by Barclay, "Introduction"; Maston, *Divine and Human Agency*; and Wells, *Grace and Agency*.

history, in which characters can oppose the divine plan, but it cannot be stopped. The following analysis of Luke/Acts demonstrates three things. (1) Unlike the Deuteronomistic interpretations of the past discussed above, Luke's emphasis on divine sovereignty does not generally lead to claims that the negative events of the past constituted divine punishment. Luke has other ways of explaining such events, as either the direct result of other humans' culpable behaviour as they exercise their own freedom, or random accident. (2) Like Josephus and the writer of 2 Maccabees, Luke incorporates the constellation of literary ideas surrounding θεομάχοι, hubris, and downfall, to demonstrate the impossibility of fighting God. He uses the trope to assure his reader that the fledgling discipleship movement is demonstrably supported by God and cannot be stopped. Humans do have agency which means their actions can genuinely affect others (such as in the persecution meted out by Herod in Acts 12). Although some events can be explained by opponents' actions, neither human opposition nor other spiritual actors like Satan will ultimately succeed. (3) Finally, Luke emphasises divine invitation to positive human response, and here reflects more closely Barclay's third model, and—as noted above—without distinction between "opponent" and "protagonist" characters. This leads to important outcomes in three directions: tragic opposition results in very human reversals; humans contribute significantly to the implementation of divine purposes; and God continues to make positive human response possible.

## 6.1 Attributions of responsibility in explanations of the past

Unlike Psalm 1, Luke/Acts does not generally suggest a relationship between suffering and sin. Suffering is not divine punishment, benevolent discipline, or caused by direct divine opposition. Nonetheless, some sections of Luke's text do draw on apparently Deuteronomistic views. In a key passage of historical review, Stephen's speech (Acts 7.2–53) traces the history of Israel through the lens of characteristically unfaithful behaviour: the people of Israel have been consistently stiff-necked, culminating in an almost hubristic attempt to build a temple. The building project is portrayed as a form of idolatry, stemming from a failure to recognise that God had no use for such a dwelling place made "by human hands" (Acts 7.48; cf. 17.24, 29–31; 19.26).[141] Though the speech includes a cita-

---

**141** Christopher Rowland, "The Temple in the New Testament," in *Temple and Worship in Biblical Israel: Proceedings of the Oxford Old Testament Seminar*, ed. John Day, LHBOTS 422 (London: T&T Clark, 2007), 473–75. See discussion by Ooi, who weighs various interpretations of

tion from Amos 5.25–27, which recalls the divine decision to remove the people "beyond Babylon" (Acts 7.43), its emphasis remains on Israel's consistent responsibility for the events that unfold, not the divine punishment or even restoration—unlike the passages from Deuteronomy or Jeremiah discussed above.[142] Similarly, the times of ignorance, though now drawn to a close (Acts 3.17; 14.16; 17.30),[143] do not lead to explanations of the negative events of history as punishment for this ignorance.

The passage with the strongest focus on disempowering enemies by emphasising divine sovereignty has already been discussed in Chapter 4: Acts 4.27–28. Here Luke emphasises that almost everyone concerned—Herod, Pilate, the gentiles, and the people of Israel—were simply directed to implement the divine purpose. Here again, though, the point is not to present what took place in Jesus' death as a divine punishment, but to ensure that matters do not look beyond divine control.[144]

Indeed, most passages in Luke/Acts do not rely on Deuteronomistic interpretations of suffering.[145] Luke's most striking engagement with questions of responsibility for suffering comes in Luke 13.1–9, which directly raises these questions of theodicy and provides a paradigmatic response that connects with Luke's wider themes.[146] This passage, which is unique to Luke, comes after a series of challenging sayings throughout chapter 12 (which forms one scene up until

---

the portrait of the temple in Stephen's speech. He argues that vv. 46–47 could be interpreted in multiple ways, but supports the view that the temple is presented as a source of false security, and that the building project itself is a form of rebellion (Vincent K. H. Ooi, *Scripture and Its Readers: Readings of Israel's Story in Nehemiah 9, Ezekiel 20, and Acts 7*, Journal of Theological Interpretation Supplement Series (Winona Lake, IN: Eisenbrauns, 2015), 168–75). He particularly argues that the negative presentation of the temple here puts this passage at odds with Luke's generally positive portrayal of the temple elsewhere (p. 173).

**142** Deuteronomistic overtones are potentially present in Peter's speech in Acts 3.19, where repentance is exhorted so that the times of refreshing might come. Holladay associates this promise of the times of refreshing with traditions in apocalypses (Holladay, *Acts*, 120), though normally these traditions would not envision the end as prompted by repentance, but by sovereign divine action.

**143** See discussion of the times of ignorance in Chapter 3 §4.1.4.

**144** See Chapter 4 §4.2.3.

**145** By contrast, Sterling sees the Deuteronomistic history as a major influence in light of Luke's understanding of divine providence (Sterling, *Historiography and Self-Definition*, 358–59).

**146** Luke 13.1–9 represents arguably one of only two Gospel passages that deal so explicitly with these questions—the other being John 9.

13.9),¹⁴⁷ to do with preparing for the suddenness of the return of the Son of Man (12.35–46, 54–59), relativisation of worldly concerns like possessions in light of this (vv. 13–21, 33–34), assurance of divine care (vv. 7–8, 11–12, 22–32), and related explanations of divisions between people and judgement (vv. 4–6, 8–10, 47–53).

As chapter 13 opens, some characters ask Jesus his view on "Galileans whose blood Pilate had mingled with their sacrifices" (v. 1). Jesus roundly rejects the unspoken implication that the suffering of these Galileans, or of those killed by the falling tower of Siloam, was associated with sin.¹⁴⁸ However, after overturning the notion that suffering (by either atrocity or accident) represents divine punishment (vv. 2, 4), Jesus unexpectedly introduces repentance and final judgement: "No, I tell you; but unless you repent, you will all perish just as they did" (v. 5; cf. v. 3).¹⁴⁹ The rebuff seems to confirm the characters were raising idle questions or gossiping, as Jesus turns attention from the objects of this speculation to the questioners themselves.

Most importantly, however, Jesus severs the inquirers' presumed relationship between suffering and sin. Through his rhetorical questions—"do you think that they were worse offenders than all the others...?" (v. 4, cf. v. 2)—Jesus not only vindicates these groups of sufferers, but challenges his listeners. The logic is that sin is widespread, others are even greater sinners, but not all currently suffer in this way; thus such suffering cannot simply be the consequence of sin. The most pressing issue, therefore, is not whether these people were sinners, but that —if suffering and sin are thus unrelated—the *absence* of calamity does not indicate blamelessness or that repentance is unnecessary (cf. Acts 14.15–17; 17.30).¹⁵⁰ Those who have not experienced such calamity must still repent. In the parable of the fig tree which follows (vv. 6–9), the emphasis may fall on a further opportunity for fruitfulness and the vinedresser's attempt to create the ideal circum-

---

**147** Green, *The Gospel of Luke*, 476. Green also points out a "leitmotif" in 12.1–13.9 of "vigilance in the face of crisis" (p. 476), and that the scene at 13.1–9 is not only connected, but the climax of the long unit (p. 513).
**148** For the view that Jesus tacitly assumes the traditional association of suffering and sin here, see Fitzmyer, *The Gospel according to Luke*, 2:1008; John Nolland, *Luke*, WBC 35 (Dallas: Word, 1989–1993), 2:718; and Johnson, *The Gospel of Luke*, 211. While I disagree with this view of this passage, and suggest Talbert (*Reading Luke*, 145) offers a better account of the logic of the passage as discussed below, some passages Luke takes from the synoptic tradition do seem to imply a traditional view of the relationship between sin and suffering, in the context of healing and forgiveness (e.g. 5.17–26).
**149** Here the plight becomes an insight into eschatological judgement. See Martin Emmrich, *At the Heart of Luke: Wisdom and Reversal of Fortune* (Eugene, OR: Pickwick, 2013), 118.
**150** Talbert, *Reading Luke*, 145.

stances for growth, but the sense of urgency remains just below the surface: this tree is already into borrowed time for bearing fruit and the moment is short for turning things around.[151] The urgent warnings of Luke 12, fresh in the reader's memory, likewise underscore the seriousness of the situation.

## 6.2 Θεομάχοι in Luke/Acts

Given Luke's emphatic separation of suffering from sin in Luke 13.1–9, it may seem uncharacteristic that his narrative includes graphic accounts of calamities that befall characters as punishments. Unlike Judas's remorseful return of the thirty pieces of silver and later suicide in Matthew 27,[152] in Acts (the only other NT account of Judas's death)[153] Judas falls forward[154] as he is spontaneously disembowelled (1.18). Similarly, Ananias and Sapphira fall to the ground struck dead (5.1–11), and Herod Agrippa I suddenly dies and is eaten by worms (12.20–23; cf. 2 Macc 9.9).[155] Agrippa I brings together key themes about fighting God: rage, hubris, and dramatic death. His extraordinary rage leads him to murder James and threaten Peter. He exhibits extreme hubris as he basks in the crowd's mistaken praise of him as a god. And then he immediately dies (cf. Josephus's complementary portrayal of Agrippa I's hubris as he was lauded as "more than mortal" and then dies at the hands of divine πρόνοια, *Ant.* 19.345–51).[156]

---

151 Green highlights further examples in which Luke has already emphasised the importance of bearing fruit (cf. 3.7–9; 6.43–45; 8.4–15; Green, *The Gospel of Luke*, 515). See Chapter 6 for further discussion of urgency and the events of the end of history in Luke/Acts.
152 It is unhelpful to attempt harmonisation of these stories (Fitzmyer, *The Acts of the Apostles*, 224); Luke's use of the literary trope seeks to make a different point, as also may Matthew's portrayal of Judas's suicide.
153 Papias provides another account (preserved by Apollinarius of Laodicea, frag. 4 of Papias in Ehrman's LCL edition of the *Apostolic Fathers*). Later stories are clearly influenced by Luke/Acts (Pervo, *Acts*, 52).
154 Cf. Wisdom 4.19 (Fitzmyer, *The Acts of the Apostles*, 224).
155 The sense of opposition to divine purposes is also evident in Luke's portrayal of other Herodian characters. Dicken argues that the various different historical figures named as "Herod" in Luke/Acts are portrayed in the narrative as a "composite" character, who is established as a key opponent (Frank Dicken, *Herod as a Composite Character in Luke-Acts*, WUNT 2/375 (Tübingen: Mohr Siebeck, 2014), 71–131). For Dicken this includes "Herod" at Luke 1.5; Luke 3.1–Acts 4.27, and Acts 12, but not Agrippa II in Acts 26.
156 The account of Agrippa I's death in *J.W.* 2.219 is not dramatic. The firm friendship established between Pilate and Herod at Jesus' death, unique to Luke, also builds the sense of tyrants who contribute to the opposition to Jesus' kingship. Although by their friendship, to an extent

As in the accounts of characters like Nebuchadnezzar or Antiochus IV provided by Josephus and the writer of 2 Maccabees, these passages in Luke/Acts portray the fitting end of θεομάχοι. Commentators often note a "punitive miracle" form in these passages,[157] but the Lukan passages go further in drawing on the literary type, already—as discussed above—established in Hellenistic Jewish texts, of θεομάχοι.[158] Opposition to the divine takes the form of hubris and blasphemy, and results in inevitable (and dramatic) downfall for the characters who attempt the impossible: fighting God.

Gamaliel's words in Acts 5.38–39 also function as a clue for interpreting the other passages and a commentary on how opposing God will play out across the text. Gamaliel's use of the term θεομάχοι (a NT *hapax legomenon*) removes any doubt about the literary tradition in play here. As set out in Chapter 4, Gamaliel's advice to the Sanhedrin, advocating judicious fence-sitting in case "this βουλή is of God" (v. 39), ironically confirms for the reader that the discipleship community and its proclamation cannot be stopped. By structuring Gamaliel's advice around the risks of being found θεομάχοι, Luke also highlights that the dramatic incidents involving Judas, Ananias and Sapphira, Agrippa I, and—to an extent—even Paul and the magician Bar-Jesus/Elymas[159] should also be understood through the lens of opposition to divine purposes that cannot be successful.[160]

When Ananias and Sapphira sell property and give only part to the discipleship community (in contrast to Barnabas's positive example of resource sharing immediately preceding), they attempt to deceive the other members of the com-

---

Luke presents both as opponents (Luke 23.12; cf. Acts 4.27), but interestingly he does not also portray Pilate (and his death) in the same literary tradition. Richardson explores historical questions about the friendship (Peter Richardson, *Herod: King of the Jews and Friend of the Romans* (Edinburgh: T&T Clark, 1999), 311–12), though the key issue here is literary.

**157** Highlighted by Gerd Theissen as miracles which enforce religious boundaries (Gerd Theissen, *The Miracle Stories of the Early Christian Tradition*, trans. Francis McDonagh, SNTW (Edinburgh: T&T Clark, 1983). In contrast to words or actions that immediately heal someone, here the miraculous moment confers a punishment.

**158** MacDonald finds numerous parallels between Euripides's *Bacchae* and Luke/Acts; see particularly his discussion of θεομάχοι (MacDonald, *Luke and Vergil*, 34–56). I suggest Luke follows in the tradition of the Jewish Hellenistic writers above who already have an established way of making use of, and adapting, the θεομάχοι theme, rather than requiring direct dependence upon Euripides. See also Wolter, "Paulus, der bekehrte Gottesfeind," 274. As it connects to the θεομάχοι theme, this is sometimes also described as a "death of a tyrant" literary type (e.g. Holladay, *Acts*, 61–62).

**159** Fitzmyer also calls the incident with Elymas/Bar-Jesus (13.6–12) another punitive miracle (Fitzmyer, *The Acts of the Apostles*, 499, 503).

**160** As also in Josephus's descriptions discussed above, which do not use θεομάχος/θεομαχέω language, but nonetheless draw clearly on the literary type.

munity. Moreover, Richard Pervo rightly notes that Peter's observation that they lied to the Holy Spirit and "put the Spirit of the Lord to the test" (5.3, 9; cf. 7.51), suggests their behaviour is tantamount to θεομαχία.[161] The close proximity of the following pericope involving Gamaliel also makes this salient. Commentators who are swift to suggest the text condemns only the deception itself[162] overlook not only the centrality of Luke's concern about attachment to possessions,[163] but also the significance of his portrayal of opposing divine purposes. Likewise commentators who worry about what kind of image of God this incident provides—a divine figure who would strike wrongdoers down so swiftly—have missed the point made by Luke's use of this literary technique (though, of course, Luke/Acts is not without its emphasis on judgement).[164] As always in this literary trope, the punishment confirms the crime. This approach to punishment through events within history is atypical of Luke/Acts.[165] Several examples make this a significant strand within Luke's text, but without the constellation of ideas of hubris, downfall, and so on, other episodes take a different approach. The episodes involving θεομάχοι include several examples in which particular characters are given no further opportunity to repent, which is also unusual in Luke. But by employing a literary type from elsewhere, Luke does not purport to give a full picture of the divine character in these passages, but draws on the reader's knowl-

---

[161] Pervo, *Acts*, 133. Similarly noted by Holladay, *Acts*, 61.
[162] Fitzmyer, *The Acts of the Apostles*, 316.
[163] See Christopher M. Hays, *Luke's Wealth Ethics: A Study in Their Coherence and Character*, WUNT 2/275 (Tübingen: Mohr Siebeck, 2010), 264–69; Robert J. Karris, "Poor and Rich: The Lukan Sitz im Leben," in *Perspectives on Luke-Acts*, ed. Charles H. Talbert (Edinburgh: T&T Clark, 1978), 112–25; J. R. Donahue, "Two Decades of Research on the Rich and the Poor in Luke-Acts," in *Justice and the Holy*, ed. Douglas A. Knight (Atlanta: Harrelson, 1989), 129–44.
[164] Fitzmyer's interest in questions of historicity, although he himself is not arguing for historical detail, is not quite the right slant (Fitzmyer, *The Acts of the Apostles*, 317–20). Here the literary trope does not *counter* Luke's theology, as in my criticism above of rhetoric which contradicts content, but it nonetheless signals a specific theological belief, namely that the divine purpose cannot be opposed.
[165] Importantly, not all negative events reflect punitive divine action, and not all examples of opposition receive these types of punitive responses. See for example the way Jesus dismisses offers to call down fire upon the Samaritan villagers who do not accept him (Luke 9.52–6). Pervo misunderstands when he claims: "The most important punitive action in the book is implicit: the destruction of Judea for its rejection of Jesus" (Pervo, *Acts*, 52). Rather, Luke portrays both the rejection of the gospel by a subset of the Jewish characters as tragic, not divine punishment, and as the natural outworking of the characteristic obduracy by which the people fail to recognise God's activity in their midst (I return to this theme below). I am also not as convinced as Pervo that the incident with the seven sons of Sheva represents the same kind of downfall (cf. Acts 19.13–17; Pervo, *Acts*).

edge of the literary tradition to make one key point: opposing God's purpose is impossible. The overriding message is that Ananias and Sapphira have opposed God and, as a sign of reassurance for readers who seek to follow the divine purpose, such behaviour never ultimately succeeds.

In some cases, characters who oppose the divine purpose are subject to a "punitive miracle" which is temporary rather than final, and enjoys rehabilitative possibilities.[166] Paul is turned around through a period of blindness (Acts 9.8–9), which is perhaps also the model for the blindness of Bar-Jesus later (13.11; cf. Luke 1.18–20). In many ways, Paul's zeal prior to his encounter on the Damascus road demonstrates traits of one going into battle against God— he breathes "threats and murder against the disciples of the Lord" (9.1, not unlike Herod's θυμομαχῶν in 12.20), approves of the murder of Stephen (whom, not long before, the narrator described as looking like an angel, Acts 6.15), and attempts to stamp out the apostles' missionary efforts. Although the blindness is temporary, the divine intervention confirms the nature of Paul's earlier opposition. In the third of his three accounts of Paul's Damascus road experience, Luke employs a stock phrase from Euripides related to θεομαχία. Following "Saul, Saul, why are you persecuting me?", the Lord says, "It hurts you (σκληρόν σοι) to kick against the goads" (Acts 26.14; cf. Euripides *Bacchae* 794.5).[167] The phrase, illustrating the impossibility of going against the grain of divine will (cf. *Ant.* 1.14), underscores that Paul's persecution was a form of fighting God.[168]

Θεομάχοι in Luke/Acts also connect in important ways to Luke's portrayal of the devil/Satan as an opponent of God and actor in the events of the narrative. After challenging Jesus in Luke 4, asserting in particular his reign over all the kingdoms of the world, ὁ διάβολος then departs "until an opportune time" (Luke 4.13).[169] But when ὁ διάβολος/σατανᾶς does appear again, it is to enter Judas (Luke 22.3) and to fill Ananias's heart (thus prompting his opposition to the Holy Spirit, Acts 5.3), or to mislead through the magic of Bar-Jesus (13.10).[170] In the few passages which deal with Satan in the Gospel of Luke, he

---

166 Such flexibility is unusual among examples of the literary trope in other texts, though arguably more in keeping with Luke's emphasis on the continuing possibility of repentance.
167 Kamerbeek, "On the Conception of ΘΕΟΜΑΧΟΣ," 279.
168 Wolter, "Paulus, der bekehrte Gottesfeind," 246–49.
169 See the emphasis Conzelmann places on this, as part of his periodisation of Jesus' ministry (Conzelmann, *Theology of St Luke*, 28).
170 The opposition to the divine βουλή set out in Luke/Acts does relate in some way to spiritual forces. Contra Dicken, however, the claim of ὁ διάβολος in Luke 4.5–6 (the archetypal "liar"), does not indicate the devil has divinely granted authority over all the nations of the world (Dicken, *Herod as a Composite Character*, 143).

is a force holding back the release and acceptance Jesus is bringing—for the woman who has been bleeding for 18 years (Luke 13.16), as also it is the devil who snatches away the seed which falls on the path, in the explanation of the parable of the sower (Luke 8.12).[171] And as part of his description of his call to stop attempting to "kick against the goads" by persecuting the Lord, Paul identifies his vocation as proclamation so that people may no longer be kept in darkness by Satan but rather be released into the light which leads to forgiveness (Acts 26.18; cf. 10.38). These references to Satan and the devil indicate forces which act in opposition to the divine βουλή, and are integrated particularly into the dramatic passages which portray human opposition in the constellation of ideas associated with θεομάχοι.

But, most importantly, for both the human θεομάχοι and the associated spiritual forces, Luke reassures his readers that this opposition will not be successful.[172] In this sense, Luke is consistent with the prospective interests of other texts above which deal with malevolent forces. Satan is, in a crucial sense, already a defeated force, whom Jesus reports having seen fall from heaven (Luke 10.18), even though at the same time (contra Cullmann's claims discussed above)[173] Satan continues to act in some form, with tangible effects for the characters in the story.[174]

Summary passages which confirm the unabated growth of the witness to the word of God frequently follow straight after these events related to θεομάχοι: Ananias and Sapphira's deaths lead into a continued account of people coming to faith (Acts 5.12–16); the persecution surrounding Stephen's martyrdom ironi-

---

[171] Although they reflect the same idea, each synoptic Gospel uses a different term for the one who snatches the seed that falls by the path here: Mark uses σατανᾶς; Matthew ὁ πονηρός; Luke διάβολος.
[172] Holladay is right to note the connection between the θεομαχία literary type and a characteristic pattern he sees throughout Acts: "The threefold template of divine initiative, resistance, and divine vindication" (Holladay, *Acts*, 62). An important difference lies in the usual outcomes for characters who oppose the proclamation of the resurrection: unlike the dramatic downfalls recounted in these passages, scenes involving characters resisting the gospel normally end with the challenge still in the air, leaving the characters' response(s) uncertain, and simultaneously also challenging the reader (cf. Luke 7.36–50; Acts 28.26–30; see below).
[173] Cf. Cullmann, *Christ and Time*, 198.
[174] Talbert, *Reading Luke*, 117 links this verse with the claim that Satan's power is already broken. Flender likewise claims that "the victory [over Satan] has already been won" (Flender, *St Luke*, 103; see also p. 308 n. 160 and p. 310 n. 167 below). Dicken (rightly) observes that Satan's fall "is not a final blow" given his ongoing activity in Luke and Acts (Dicken, *Herod as a Composite Character*, 143). Dicken also puts aside questions about the timing of this fall (p. 143 n. 64); however, I suggest questions of timing do remain important as evidence that Satan's power has already been fundamentally fractured.

cally furthers the spread of the gospel (8.1–4); and Acts 12, which describes the extreme persecution meted out by Agrippa I, culminates in a sudden summary about continued growth (12.24). The attempts at opposition certainly lead to suffering and even martyrdom, but they are unable ultimately to impede the dynamic βουλή of God.

## 6.3 Human response and reversal in Luke/Acts

Most characters in Luke/Acts, however, are not archetypal θεομάχοι. Rather, people are faced with choices about how they will respond to divine initiative, which have real consequences not only in how Luke suggests these choices have shaped the events of the past, but in how things will unfold for various characters into the future. Here Luke does reflect Barclay's third model in how he presents divine and human agency. The divine invitation reflects divine agency which gives space for human freedom. The different ways in which characters then choose to respond shows the freedom they exercise within that space. Some characters' negative responses draw out the tragedy of humans rejecting the divine purpose or simply failing to appreciate the gravity and urgency of a positive response.[175] Other responses disclose the important roles that people play in contributing positively to the unfolding of the divine plan.

### 6.3.1 Tragic opposition to the divine plan and reversal

As rightly highlighted by Robert Tannehill, the reception of Jesus' proclamation in Luke/Acts is imbued with tragedy, foreshadowed even from the infancy narratives.[176] Jesus is a sign who will be opposed (Luke 2.34).[177] Simeon's prophecy, as discussed in Chapter 4, declares that this infant, who is "a light for revelation (ἀποκάλυψιν) to the gentiles" (v. 32), is set to prompt the "falling and rising of many in Israel" and will reveal the thoughts of many. The prophecy establishes the overtone of tragedy that will result in not only a sword piercing Mary's soul (v. 35), but Jesus' own lament over the obduracy of his people (13.34;[178] 19.41–44). The narrative is a tragic account of the ways in which characters who ought to have been keenly attuned to divine activity failed to "recognise

---

[175] For instance, the so-called "positive" or disinterested Roman characters. See below.
[176] Tannehill, *Narrative Unity*, 9, 261; Tannehill, "Israel in Luke-Acts," 171–74.
[177] Those who follow him have the same effect. For instance, Paul is opposed (ἀντιτασσομένων) and shakes the dust off his feet in Macedonia (Acts 18.6).
[178] Also paralleled in Matt 23.37.

the time of their visitation" and "the things that make for peace" (19.42, 44), with the result that they even "killed the author of life" (Acts 3.15; cf. 13.27).

Luke underscores the importance of positive human response to divine initiative with one of his narrative's central motifs: reversal.[179] Frequently associated with Lukan parables, reversal is a key theme across a range of passages in Luke.[180] In a detailed study, John O. York distinguishes between explicit and implicit examples in Luke's Gospel of what he describes as "bi-polar" reversal—that is, instances where both poles are inverted, such as the first and the last swapping places.[181] He identifies seven examples of explicit reversals (or nine if two sets of repeated doublets are counted separately): the Magnificat (1.53–55); blessings and woes (6.20–26); the parables of the rich man and Lazarus (16.19–31), and of the Pharisee and the sinner (18.9–14), plus three sayings of reversal (14.11 and 18.14; 9.24 and 17.33; 13.30).[182] But he argues convincingly that a range of other passages, when read in their literary settings, where narrative and conceptual links to the explicit reversal sayings are present, likewise contribute to the reversal theme. In this category he includes the sayings of Simeon (2.34) and John the Baptist (3.4–6),[183] the episodes involving the sinful woman and Simon the Pharisee (7.36–50) and the rich ruler (18.18–30),[184]

---

[179] See discussion of this central theme in Nave, *The Role and Function of Repentance*; Emmrich, *At the Heart of Luke*; Gregory E. Sterling, "'Turning to God': Conversion in Greek-Speaking Judaism and Early Christianity," in Gray and O'Day, *Scripture and Traditions*, 69–95.

[180] Emmrich argues Wisdom themes run through Luke's approach to reversal, such as in the discussion of the consequences of humbling or exalting oneself (Luke 14.11; 18.14; Emmrich, *At the Heart of Luke*, 102).

[181] John O. York, *The Last Shall Be First: The Rhetoric of Reversal in Luke*, JSNTMS 46 (Sheffield: JSOT Press, 1991). One-way reversals would include rags-to-riches stories, or accounts of high-status individuals falling from grace; the focus here is on references or allusions to two-way reversals. York attributes the language of "bi-polar reversal" to a dissertation by Larry K. Drake (p. 36).

[182] York's discussion of the sayings is helpful, and appropriately situated in their narrative settings; it seems somewhat counter-intuitive that he chooses to refer to them as separate aphorisms, rather than identifying the passages in which they appear as further illustration of Luke's reversal theme (though he does deal with the wider scene in 14.7–24, but separately from his initial treatment of v. 11 (York, *The Last Shall Be First*, 78–79, 133–144)). Importantly, he does note that Luke moves the synoptic saying of 13.30 into an eschatological discourse (pp. 88–89).

[183] This inclusion is perhaps the least convincing in York's list of passages about reversal. See discussion in York, *The Last Shall Be First*, 116–18.

[184] York argues this becomes a "bi-polar" reversal, rather than just one-way, when considered in connection to the following episode with Zaccheus, in Luke 19.1–10 (York, *The Last Shall Be First*, 160).

and the parables of the good Samaritan (10.25–37), great banquet (14.17–24), and lost sons (15.11–32),[185] to which I would also add the inauguration of Jesus' ministry at Nazareth (4.16–30).[186] Though no explicit double-edged reversal sayings are included in Acts, a number of stories may similarly recall the theme to readers of the Gospel, perhaps most explicitly the closing interaction of Acts 28.23–28, discussed in more detail below, where Paul's statement that "this salvation of God" was sent to the gentiles (who will listen) parallels elements of Simeon's prophecy in Luke 2.[187]

Reversal of fortune is a common theme in many of this study's texts.[188] For writers like Diodorus Siculus or Valerius Maximus, the constant possibility of a reversal of fortune stems from the understanding that human freedom exists within divine limits, and a human agent's status is always provisional because of unpredictable (and sometimes vindictive) forces like τύχη/*fortuna*. In 2 Baruch, reversal describes an eschatological expectation which drives home the importance of faithfulness to the reader (who is encouraged to see themselves among those who will benefit from this great reversal, 2 Bar 83.10–23). In Luke's narrative, reversal emerges as a direct result of the varied ways in

---

[185] Other passages may be seen to contribute to a sense of reversal in various ways. Status reversals may be understood more broadly, as they relate to narratives such as Jesus welcoming children, and other kingdom priorities; for helpful discussion see the references to status reversal in Carroll, *Luke*, 551. Brendan Byrne's insight about Lukan triangles, where episodes tend to involve interactions between Jesus and two characters—often an outsider, who has been the focus of traditional interpretation, and an insider, to whom the episode offers the greater challenge (Byrne, *The Hospitality of Luke*, 4–5; see p. 117 n. 278 above), provides insight into episodes that often also portray reversals, such as Luke 7.36–50, 15.11–32, and so on.

[186] As discussed above in Chapter 4, the Nazarene "insiders" cannot accept Jesus' ministry to the "outsider" and, prefiguring later events, threaten Jesus as they react negatively to his proclamation (Luke 4.28–30). In her analysis of status reversal as part of coded messages of resistance, Miller adds the episode at Nazareth in Luke 4.16–30 (Amanda C. Miller, *Rumors of Resistance: Status Reversals and Hidden Transcripts in the Gospel of Luke*, Emerging Scholars (Minneapolis: Fortress, 2014)). Without an explicit saying about reversal, the passage develops the double-sided dynamic of insiders and outsiders who will change places in the course of the Lukan narrative. (Miller's study of status reversals focuses on 1.46–55, 4.16–30, and 16.19–31.)

[187] Luke's theme of reversal differs from the complaint in Thessalonica that these people have been "turning the world upside down" (Acts 17.6). The upset there reflects the political priority of Jesus' lordship over the worldly authorities (see Rowe, *World Upside Down*, 95–99); this does not conflict with other types of reversal and may even remind the reader of some earlier examples about radically reshaping worldly priorities which also incorporate reversal, such as Luke 1.46–55.

[188] See also Chapter 4.

which humans respond to divine initiative—likewise frequently drawing out eschatological consequences.[189]

In Luke/Acts, divine initiative itself is expressed in terms of divine favour, which is neither fickle nor changeable as the favour of τύχη/*fortuna* can be. The angels' tidings to the shepherds affirm peace on earth and good will among all whom God favours (ἐν ἀνθρώποις εὐδοκίας, Luke 2.14) and, as noted above, at Nazareth Jesus confirms divine favour or acceptance, drawing on Isaiah 61.1–2 to declare "the year of the Lord's favour (δεκτόν)," (Luke 4.19).[190] Peter's later realisation in light of his experience with Cornelius's household encapsulates the breadth of the divine invitation: "I truly understand that God shows no partiality (προσωπολήμπτης), but in every nation anyone who fears him and does what is right is acceptable (δεκτός) to him" (Acts 10.34–35). Emphasising that this indiscriminate acceptance stems first from divine initiative, when Peter reports the incident to the disciples in Judea, they respond joyfully: "God has given (ἔδωκεν) even to the gentiles the repentance that leads to life" (11.18). I touch more on repentance as a divine gift below.

In his discussion of "bi-polar" reversals, York attributes some reversals to divine action (Luke 1.53–55; 6.20–26; 16.19–31). Mary's Magnificat certainly attributes much to the divine actor; how the mighty are brought down and the humble raised is not explained more at this point—though it will become clear as the narrative unfolds (cf. 14.11; 18.14). All subsequent explicit reversals are presented as sayings of Jesus, and, as York writes later: "the two sides characterised in these reversals are also sharply divided in their acceptance or rejection of Jesus."[191] Even, for example, the parable of the rich man and Lazarus, which York identifies as one of the three explicit reversals in which action is attributed to the divine, suggests that the mechanism of reversal comes from divine action in light of human action.[192] Despite ample opportunity, the rich man failed to act in response to Lazarus's need and finds himself eschatologically excluded from the company of Abraham,[193] in whose bosom the one the rich man

---

**189** See discussion in Carroll, *Response to the End*, 75 n. 143, 84–86.

**190** See Chapter 3 §4.1.4 and Chapter 4 §4.1.2. Luke notably omits the following verse about the day of God's vengeance (Byrne, *The Hospitality of God*, 50), though cf. Luke 21.22 and discussion of the days of vengeance in my Chapter 3 above.

**191** York, *The Last Shall Be First*, 111; cf. pp. 93, 160–61.

**192** York suggests that because no change is effected in the parable, this places the onus on divine action (York, *The Last Shall Be First*, 71); however the thrust of the parable, in connection also with the preceding parable, is to emphasise the importance of human action for the reader, before it is too late (as it now is for the rich man).

**193** Jeffrey is concerned to emphasise, following Wright, continuities between the welcome of the prodigal and of Lazarus, to temper the judgement in this parable (Jeffrey, *Luke*, 202–5).

had rejected now rests (16.19–31). While the rich man's position in this post-mortem setting has been divinely allocated, it is in light of the man's actions.[194]

In some other texts, the exclusion described is rather the result of human choices. Those who reject the good news bring about, in direct and concrete ways, the "falling and rising of many" and opposition foretold by Simeon (Luke 2.34). By failing to respond positively[195] some characters exclude themselves[196]—that is, through their own choices they place themselves away from the sites of divine action while seemingly distant characters are brought close by choosing to associate with Jesus, the apostles, and what they proclaim. In the parable of the great banquet, the diners in a good social position reject the invitation and through their own choice exclude *themselves* (14.16–24; cf. 7.36–50; 15.25–32).[197] Indeed, even Luke's blessings and woes (Luke 6.20–26) describe the practical outworking of the self-reliance of those who are rich, full, laughing, or spoken well of now (Luke 6.24–26; cf. 14.11; 18.14).

---

While correct to note the ongoing possibility of the brothers' repentance, the rich man's judgement is set (cf. Acts 10.43; 17.31), even if features of the "afterlife" presented are symbolic and not intended to be accurate (cf. Maddox, *The Purpose*, 103).

**194** Similarly, Luke includes the synoptic tradition about the Son of Man being ashamed of those who are ashamed of Jesus (Luke 9.26), likewise implying a stronger sense of divine action to prompt the reversal as a punishment.

**195** Jervell notes that negative human action in Luke/Acts is only possible through divine permission (Jervell, "The Future of the Past," 106–7).

**196** In his study of Wisdom themes in Luke's portrait of reversal, Emmrich notes, for instance, that failures of humility lead to characters being brought down (Emmrich, *At the Heart of Luke*, 102). He is unclear here whether divine action causes the reversal, though later states in relation to responding positively to divine invitation, "Failure to do so will bring its own consequences" (p. 122). He also emphasises that this reversal is intrinsic to Jesus' passion and resurrection (p. 123).

**197** James A. Sanders, "The Ethic of Election in Luke's Great Banquet Parable," in *Essays in Old Testament Ethics (J. Phillip Hyatt, in Memoriam)*, ed. James L. Crenshaw and John T. Willis (New York: Ktav, 1974), 258–59. (Sanders sees Luke 14.15–35 as a "subversion" of Deuteronomistic theology and interpretations of election; cf. Paul H. Ballard, "Reasons for Refusing the Great Supper," *JTS* 23 (1972): 350.) Some sayings in Luke/Acts warn of a kind of reversal in some ways familiar from other texts discussed above, embodying wise advice for those seeking to lead a life of virtue. In the early part of the Luke 14 meal scene, having observed the jostling as guests sought out the best seats, Jesus offers practical advice that would be at home in Graeco-Roman reflections on savvy dining etiquette (vv. 8–11; see, for instance, Plutarch's *Table Talk* 615B–619A), though as he goes on his suggestions become more radical (vv. 12–14; see Willi Braun, *Feasting and Social Rhetoric in Luke 14*, SNTSMS 85 (Cambridge: Cambridge University Press, 1995), 88–97).

Characters in Luke/Acts who do not know their need, like Simon the Pharisee, fail to respond positively to divine initiative (7.36–50).[198] And seemingly innocuous characters like Gamaliel fail to recognise the eschatological urgency of their response.[199] In many cases, though, the passages retain a challenge because the episode draws to a close before the choice is made. Will, for instance, Simon the Pharisee (7.36–50), or the elder son in the parable (15.11–32), respond to the challenge and change their course before it is too late? Will the reader? All who fail to recognise the significance of the divine invitation are warned that, having counted themselves among the first, they may suddenly find themselves last.

This might dovetail with the idea of hubris and downfall found in Graeco-Roman texts, but this principal mode of reversal in Luke[200] does not rely on divine retribution during a person's life, nor suggest the workings of a cosmic pendulum. Rather, though it is certainly good news for the poor and humble who will be exalted (Luke 1.52–53), for those who will fall, Luke's reversal is a direct result of human responses. In keeping with other major themes in his narrative, Luke portrays this as arising from a failure to see past all the things which get in the way of accepting the divine invitation.[201] Here divine action brings about genuine human freedom to choose whether to accept; reversal arises for those who do not. Such reversals reflect a tragedy of human culpability *despite* divine initiative.

Finally, passages about reversal relate not only to Lukan themes about impediments to discipleship but also, as shown by the particular passages discussed above, to Luke's portrait of eschatological consequences and urgency. Tracing the history of scholarship about Lukan reversals, York observes that eschatological elements of reversal in parables have often been distanced from Luke's narrative as an earlier tradition, at times capitalised on as an insight into the historical Jesus, but then presented as somehow separate from Luke's own view. York's assessment is that the tendency to dismiss eschatological elements of reversal in Luke is thus based on "modern theological tastes and a pre-

---

**198** Crabbe, "A Sinner and a Pharisee."
**199** Crabbe, "Being Found Fighting against God," 36–39.
**200** As distinct from the examples of θεομάχοι above.
**201** In various passages this includes a false self-sufficiency that might also be manifest in attachment to possessions or popularity. On the latter, see also Chapter 4 on Gamaliel's popularity, and also Crabbe, "Being Found Fighting against God," 32–33; cf. Mason, "Josephus's Pharisees: The Narratives," 37–38.

conceived understanding of Lukan eschatology."²⁰² Rather, the number of passages unique to Luke which involve reversal, including those with eschatological elements, indicates that these are important themes for Luke.²⁰³

### 6.3.2 Human contributions to the divine plan

Conversely, many characters in Luke/Acts respond positively to divine initiative, and they make crucial contributions to the unfolding divine plan (unlike, for instance, the Romans' function in Josephus's *Jewish War*, who remain passive (if virtuous) instruments of the divine purpose). This underscores again the importance of human freedom as it interacts with divine action: in Luke/Acts the divine plan cannot be stopped, humans choose whether to participate positively, and yet the plan itself relies on human action.

In an exemplary passage, Mary receives Gabriel's extraordinary report about Jesus' impending birth, which ends with the assertion "for nothing will be impossible with God" (Luke 1.37). Gabriel has spoken with assurance; the pregnancy will unfold as he has indicated.²⁰⁴ But Mary's response confirms her willing participation in the plan: "let it be for me according to your word" (v. 38). By contrast, Zechariah fails to embrace the announcement to him and, though this does not stop the events which proceed, it leads to a period of silence (perhaps not unlike Paul or Bar-Jesus' blindness) until he comes to affirm God's activity at John's birth (1.63–64). In Zechariah's case it is clear that the divine purpose, though requiring human participation, could continue with *other* human agents, should he persist in his doubt, but his own canticle confirms that he has been persuaded by what he has experienced and witnessed.

Other characters in Luke/Acts assent to making a positive contribution to divine purposes. Paul's discernment of his ministry direction and assent to suffering in Jerusalem is a key example, though one involving elements of divine intervention and prophecy that interpreters have found perplexing. Paul receives several prophetic insights related to his journey, even including exhortations

---

202 York, *The Last Shall Be First*, 17. York particularly criticises Schottroff and Stegemann for this, though notes the role of eschatological assessments also in work by Nickelsburg (who assesses similarities between Luke and 1 Enoch in these themes) and John Dominic Crossan (see discussion on pp. 10–17).
203 York, *The Last Shall Be First*, 17. York brings the question of eschatology and acceptance/rejection together by noting, "with regard to eschatology, these stories demonstrate present conditions that are reversed, but the reversal is linked to acceptance or rejection of Jesus as the bearer of the Kingdom in the present" (p. 162).
204 See Chapter 4 on reliable prophecies within the text of Luke/Acts.

to *avoid* the direction he then goes on to take. In Acts 16.6–10, the reader is told baldly that the Holy Spirit and then the Spirit of Jesus[205] simply prohibit two courses of action before Paul dreams of a third, which "we" interpret as a divine call to Macedonia (vv. 8–9).[206] Elsewhere, Paul receives prophetic dreams that he must stand before Caesar in Rome (27.24), and the Spirit testifies to him that suffering awaits him in Jerusalem (20.23). The contrast between the prophecies about Rome and Jerusalem is such that Josep Rius-Camps and Jenny Read-Heimerdinger claim, certainly in the Bezan text but also with evidence in the Alexandrian text, that Luke portrays a conflict between Paul's planning (βούλομαι) and the divine θέλημα. They suggest that the theological discomfort arising from the implication that Paul's journey to Jerusalem conflicts with the divine will inhibits most interpreters from correct exegesis of these passages.[207]

Acts 21.4b offers a particularly difficult phrase, declaring the disciples in Tyre speak "through the Spirit" when they tell Paul not to go to Jerusalem. Commentators seek various ways around the phrase, normally either by postulating divergent sources behind the passage or distinguishing an accurate prophetic insight (Paul will suffer in Jerusalem) from the disciples' exhortation not to go (a result of their own distress at the prophecy, and not the Spirit's directive).[208] However, there is no sense of this distinction in the text, which is rather couched as a genuine prophetic utterance, confirmed by the identical formula (διὰ τοῦ πνεύματος)[209] for Agabus's earlier (accurate) prophecy (11.28), and the positive treatment of prophecy throughout Luke's narrative.[210] Indeed, contrasts between the Spirit's intervention to stop travel to Asia and Bithynia in Acts 16.6–7, and

---

205 On these titles, see G. Stählin, "Τὸ πνεῦμα Ἰησοῦ (Apostelgeschichte 16:7)," in *Christ and the Spirit in the New Testament: Studies in Honour of Charles Francis Digby Moule*, ed. Barnabas Lindars and Stephen S. Smalley (Cambridge: Cambridge University Press, 1973), 232–34. While the different titles here are interesting and the Spirit of Jesus is unique to this verse, it seems the titles are intended to indicate the same sense of spiritual guidance.
206 Miller argues that this scene portrays the disciples grappling to interpret the divine call, and the opposite end of the spectrum to the transparent divine direction in the scene with Philip (Acts 8.26–40; Miller, *Convinced That God Had Called Us*, 233–34). Although Miller's reflections are helpful, the key human element in this story remains the choice to accept, not the capacity to interpret, the divine invitation.
207 Rius-Camps and Read-Heimerdinger, *The Message of Acts*, 4:152.
208 Alternative proposals include the assumption that the verse must be secondary (cf. discussion in Haenchen, *The Acts of the Apostles*, 603–4), expressed wrongly (Fitzmyer, *The Acts of the Apostles*, 685; Pervo, *Acts*, 535), or reflect the (incorrect) interpretation of the disciples in Tyre (Conzelmann, *Acts of the Apostles*, 178). See discussion in Crabbe, "Accepting Prophecy."
209 This is the only other use of the full phrase. Acts 1.2 and 4.25 also give διὰ πνεύματος ἁγίου, both describing prophetic inspiration.
210 Rius-Camps and Read-Heimerdinger, *The Message of Acts*, 4:162 n. 108.

the openness of both the call to Macedonia (16.9) and the way to Jerusalem (despite the Spirit's exhortation, 21.4b, 13–15), emphasise the importance of Paul's *choices*. Although it is possible for the Spirit to intervene directly in Paul's travels elsewhere (cf. Acts 16.6–7), Acts 21.1–14 combines the Spirit's wish that Paul not suffer with an openness that enables Paul nonetheless to assent freely to the foretold suffering in the service of his mission.[211]

Conzelmann observes in relation to 21.12–13:

> Luke sees no contradiction that Paul is warned by the Spirit and nevertheless goes to Jerusalem. This is in accord with the common notion of prophecies and prodigies: they are fulfilled, but not to the exclusion of human decision. Paul "must" go, but he freely affirms his destiny.[212]

By contrast, the examples of prodigies and other prophetic insights I discussed in Chapter 4 indicate for the most part that in the non-Jewish Graeco-Roman texts of this study fated events will unfold quite independently of human assent (often ironically so). Nonetheless, Conzelmann identifies something important about the interaction between divine disclosure and human agency here in Acts. Not unlike Valerius Maximus's affirmation of Ti. Gracchus for correctly interpreting a prophetic warning but allowing the prophesied betrayal to take place anyway (1.6.8), discussed above, in Acts Paul gives his own assent to the direction which he has been forewarned will lead to suffering.[213] Further features, such as positive parallels between Paul's journey to Jerusalem and Jesus' journey to Jerusalem, endorse the choice.[214]

---

[211] Given Luke does not portray the divine plan in an inflexible model akin to fate, as discussed above, assenting to the divine plan remains different from Stoic understandings of assenting to fate.

[212] Conzelmann, *Acts of the Apostles*, 178. Conzelmann does, however, suggest earlier that the statement in 21.4b reflects the companions' concern not the Spirit's direction.

[213] This interesting example is in contrast to numerous other anecdotes in which Valerius passionately bemoans the foolishness of characters who fail to avert disaster by responding to a prophetic warning (1.4.2; 1.6.6; 1.6.11; 1.6.ext1b). See also, by way of exception, the rather sceptical comment from Plutarch, who notes he is relating someone else's report, that "in accordance with some oracle he voluntarily gave himself to be sacrificed in front of the line of battle" (Plu. *Thes.* 32.4).

[214] Luke 9.51 supplies both the sense of internal necessity and predictability to do with Jesus' death, and his assent to this course: "When the days drew near for him to be taken up, he set his face to go to Jerusalem" (cf. Luke 22.39–46). On parallels between Jesus and Paul in these journeys, see Joel B. Green, "Internal Repetition in Luke-Acts: Contemporary Narratology and Lucan Historiography," in Witherington, *History, Literature, and Society in the Book of Acts*, 299; Pervo, *Acts*, 533–34.

This is consistent with the open way other characters accept divine invitation rather than being forced to go, such as Philip's dream (Acts 8.26). Both Paul's dream in 16.9 and the inspired exhortation in 21.4b serve to underscore the importance of *human* action, which is confirmed in Paul's climactic acceptance of Agabus's prophecy just prior to his entry into Jerusalem.[215] The result is an emphasis on Paul's virtue in nonetheless choosing to go to Jerusalem.

Thus, across Luke/Acts, various characters respond to an invitation or insight in the form of a dream or other prophecy and become significant participants in the unfolding plan (Acts 8.26–39; 9.10–19; 10.19–24; 16.9–10; 21.3–14; cf. Luke 9.51).[216] Some other characters, such as Gamaliel (5.38–9), Gallio (18.14), the town clerk in Ephesus (19.35), or even Festus and Agrippa (25.13–27; 26.30–2), also serve the divine purpose, but in these cases it is entirely ironic—they do not assent, but without realising it become party to the divine βουλή that cannot be stopped (cf. 13.27).[217] Acting unknowingly, although they support the divine purpose, they remain responsible in the narrative because of their own failure to recognise the significance of what is unfolding in their midst and to choose to get on board.

Although the divine plan will definitely unfold, humans are able to respond and align themselves with "deeds consistent with repentance" (Acts 26.20).[218] The exhortation to do so in Luke/Acts in some ways reflects Ezra's exhortation to the people, "discipline your hearts," in the face of urgent eschatological circumstances (4 Ezra 14.34). However, 4 Ezra's exclusive focus on the one over the many differs importantly from Luke/Acts. Luke's universal invitation also

---

[215] This dynamic is also present in later rabbinic sayings, such as *Pirke Aboth* 3.19, "All is foreknown but freedom of choice is given."

[216] See also n. 220 below, on some tensions in the history of scholarship about whether Peter was "unable" to hinder the baptism of Cornelius's household.

[217] Even here, the characters choose their own course of action—but ironically what they choose also furthers the divine plan. See Chapter 4 §4.2.4 on irony in Acts 5.

[218] Nave describes this as an emphasis on "universal salvation" (what I would describe as universal invitation, which seeks a positive response). Nave rightly identifies the desired response as repentance, which he says requires a fundamental change in both "thinking and living" (Guy D. Nave, *The Role and Function of Repentance in Luke-Acts*, Academia Biblica 4 (Atlanta: Society of Biblical Literature, 2002), 146). Having considered the use of μετανοέω and μετάνοια in Graeco-Roman and Jewish Hellenistic literature, Nave argues that Luke does not attribute an unusual meaning to the terms, "That which may be considered unique is not the meaning of repentance in Luke-Acts, but rather the role and function of repentance within the author's narrative" (p. 145). In this way, Nave also suggests, repentance functions as a means by which humans make contributions to the divine plan; repentance is "a necessary change in thinking and behaviour required of individuals in order to help fulfil God's plan of universal salvation" (p. 145).

emerges as a central challenge within his narrative, as he looks towards the future.

### 6.3.3 Looking ahead: divine initiative and challenge

While humans (or, sometimes, random events)[219] rather than God are generally responsible for negative events of the past in Luke/Acts, humans also remain active agents in the present and future. Nonetheless, divine action is not simply divine initiative (as in the declaration of favour), but God continues to act to make positive human response possible. As people are exhorted to repent, they are also, through the gracious exercise of divine action, *made able to do so* (Acts 2.37–9; 3.17–21, 26). Similarly, Luke affirms humans are made able to cast aside ignorance (Acts 3.17; 17.30) and to stand up straight in the face of God's redemptive activity (Luke 13.12–13, 16; 21.28). Likewise, as Paul assures the Ephesian elders, the word is able to build them up (Acts 20.32).

Indeed, according to Luke, repentance itself—the ability to turn away from sin and align one's life with the divine purpose and the priorities of the kingdom—is a gift. As he addresses the Sanhedrin, including Gamaliel, Peter proclaims that God raised Jesus "that he might give repentance (δοῦναι μετάνοιαν) to Israel and forgiveness of sins" (5.31; cf. v. 32). And, as noted above, the Judean disciples recognise that the gentiles also have been *given* the repentance that leads to life (Acts 11.18).[220] As in Barclay's third model, divine action provides

---

[219] Cf. Luke 13.1–9.
[220] Immediately before making this claim, Peter says of the choice to baptise the household: "who was I that I could hinder God? (ἐγὼ τίς ἤμην δυνατὸς κωλῦσαι τὸν θεόν;)" (Acts 11.17). This has raised some further questions about divine and human agency. Gaventa identifies the rhetoric as authenticating the gentile mission, with a focus on God as a primary actor and the human actors "only secondarily" (Gaventa, *Acts*, 173–75), and Johnson highlights the phrase as the *peroratio* of Peter's defence speech, which shows "unequivocally that his decision was not the result of human calculation, but rather *a response to the divine initiative*, from beginning to end" (Johnson, *The Acts of the Apostles*, 200, emphasis original). Haenchen, by contrast, takes the verse as further evidence of grave problems with Luke's narrative, claiming "here faith loses its true character of decision, and the obedience from faith which Luke would have liked to portray turns into something utterly different: very nearly the twitching of human puppets" (Haenchen, *The Acts of the Apostles*, 362). He presents such a view as a temptation to distance oneself from the responsibility of human decision, a result here of Luke's "allegiance to the outlook of his time," but "dangerous" because it is a temptation also for the Christians of Haenchen's day (p. 363). This illustrates again the powerful concerns behind mid-twentieth-century treatments of Luke, but it also shows an understanding of divine and human agency in competition with one another (with a strong measure of Haenchen's own theological tradition). While the inexorable movement of the divine purpose in Luke/Acts would suggest that the open-

the scope for positive human response, but the people must still freely choose to participate. In Luke/Acts, repentance is a key way of understanding positive human action—it is the appropriate response to Jesus' resurrection (cf. Acts 2.38; 3.19; 5.31; 17.30; 26.20; discussed further in Chapter 6 below), and is bound up in decisions for participation through the *deeds* of repentance (Acts 3.8; 26.20; cf. Luke 3.8/Matt 3.8).[221]

But the most challenging passage regarding divine and human agency in Luke/Acts comes at its end: Acts 28.17–28.[222] The enigmatic finale has prompted much debate, including in relation to whether this constitutes the original ending of Acts (or Luke/Acts).[223] Questions of divine and human agency and responsibility arise particularly from the citation from Isa 6.9–10 LXX.[224] Luke describes Paul's reception by the Jewish characters in Rome, saying they:

---

ing out of the spirit-filled community to include the gentiles could not be stopped, this statement from Peter does not imply that he was compelled independent of his will to be the one to perform the baptism. A stronger sense of the interplay between divine invitation and human response also makes better sense of the experience of Cornelius and his household.

[221] Such fruit may also be demonstrated in gratitude, which takes its place within a cycle of divine and human action. For instance, in a unique Lukan passage, ten people suffering from leprosy encounter Jesus and receive healing, but only one returns to express his gratitude. The incident reflects the dynamic between the universal divine initiative and rarer positive human response. But the one who returns then benefits in other ways, receiving the further blessing: "having been raised (ἀναστάς) go your way; your faith has saved you (σέσωκέν σε)" (11.19). The incident is also reminiscent of the discussion about human response to divine initiative at Simon the Pharisee's table, though there the differing responses stem from the superior gratitude of the one whose greater debt has been forgiven in the parabolic saying (7.41–43), linking to the kinds of causes of reversal discussed above.

[222] See Metzger on v. 29, which is a later addition (Bruce M. Metzger, *A Textual Commentary on the Greek New Testament*, 2nd ed. (Stuttgart: Deutsche Bibelgesellschaft, 1994), 444).

[223] Cf. Johnson, *The Acts of the Apostles*, 474–75. It may seem surprising that the build-up to Rome leads to a dispute with Jewish characters, but the encounter mirrors themes from the beginning of Luke in important ways (cf. Alexander, "Reading Luke-Acts from Back to Front," 226–29). Johnson argues that the reliability of prophecy throughout Luke/Acts suggests readers should simply presume Paul's moment before Caesar has taken place (Johnson, *The Acts of the Apostles*, 475). Furthermore, I suggest the contrasts between Luke/Acts and, for instance, Virgil's portrayal of Rome as the end of history reveal the *importance* of Luke's decision to conclude his narrative here rather than before Caesar. Rome is not the goal of the mission, the "end of the earth" (Acts 1.8; Ellis, "The End of the Earth," 58; cf. Barreto, *Ethnic Negotiations*, 120; contra Moessner, *Luke the Historian*, 290–91), or the end of history. See discussion of the political implications of Virgil's and Luke's portrayals of the end of history in Chapter 6.

[224] For Evans, Isa 6.9–10 and its early Jewish and Christian reception reflects fundamental tensions that emerge as writers seek to explain all experience in light of monotheistic divine sovereignty (Craig A. Evans, *To See and Not Perceive: Isaiah 6.9–10 in Early Jewish and Christian Interpretation*, JSOTSup 64 (Sheffield: JSOT Press, 1989), 16).

disagreed with each other; and as they were leaving, Paul made one further statement: "The Holy Spirit was right in saying to your ancestors through the prophet Isaiah,[225]
'Go to this people and say,
You will indeed listen, but never understand,
and you will indeed look, but never perceive.
For this people's heart has grown dull (ἐπαχύνθη),
and their ears are hard of hearing,
and they have shut (ἐκάμμυσαν) their eyes;
so that they might not look with their eyes,
and listen with their ears,
and understand with their heart and turn—
and I would heal them.'" (Acts 28.25–27)

Luke has reserved the full citation until this climactic moment.[226] Building on Jacques Dupont's distinction between the scene in Rome (28.17–28) and the final summary (vv. 30–31), Loveday Alexander highlights that the last two verses have a prospective orientation, whereas the scene in verses 17–28 looks backwards.[227] This retrospective focus is particularly important for the citation from Isaiah; Luke uses the scriptural passage to interpret events that have unfolded throughout the narrative.[228]

While in the MT, the verbs in Isa 6.10 suggest a divine intention to make hearts fat and to close eyes so that the people will not respond, the LXX translator makes the verbs indicatives, which simply describe the situation: they closed their eyes (ἐκάμμυσαν, Isa 6.10 LXX; Acts 28.27).[229] Luke cites the LXX di-

---

**225** Luke supplies emphatic authority to the citation by attributing the words to the Holy Spirit through Isaiah (cf. also Acts 1.16; 4.25; Holladay, *Acts*, 512).
**226** Luke keeps Isa 6 in the explanation of the parable of the sower (Luke 8.10), but makes the reference shorter (cf. Mark 4.12; Matt 13.14–15; cf. also Mark 8.17–18; John 12.39–40). The possibility that Luke deliberately retained the full citation until the conclusion of his *Doppelwerk* plays a key role in discussions about whether Luke planned Acts when writing the first volume (see Alexander, "Reading Luke-Acts from Back to Front," 216).
**227** Alexander, "Reading Luke-Acts from Back to Front," 214.
**228** Alexander notes that the interrelationships of themes in the prologue to Luke (chapters 1–4) and Acts 28, made salient by reading Luke/Acts from the perspective of the end, support claims to a literary unity of the two volumes from the author's perspective (though not, she argues, a prospective unity from the perspective of the reader; Alexander, "Reading Luke-Acts from Back to Front," 24). Links between the infancy narratives and Acts 28 are also set out in Tannehill, "Israel in Luke-Acts," 71–74.
**229** Evans observes that interpretation of Isa 6.9–10 shifted in Second Temple Judaism, away from focusing on prophetic accusation, as in the Hebrew text, to accenting the promise of restoration when the people turn and are healed. This shift is already in evidence in the LXX (Evans, *To See and Not Perceive*, 163–64).

rectly without significant differences.²³⁰ Luke Timothy Johnson suggests verse 27 (Isa 6.10) introduces a sense of wilfulness.²³¹ This is not an account of divine *intention* to stop up the ears and hearts to ensure the people do not respond and receive forgiveness—after all, Jesus declared a time of favour (Luke 4.16–18) and Peter observed that God shows no partiality (Acts 10.34–35)—but a reflection on what has already happened throughout. Looking back, Luke summarises that some characters have not been able to turn and be forgiven, because they have been unable to hear, see, or allow their hearts to be moved.²³²

However, the reader knows that not all Jewish characters have rejected the proclamation (indeed, Luke reports many thousands have become followers of Jesus in Acts 21.20).²³³ Many have responded positively and become crucial participants in the unfolding divine purpose, or benefited from the reversal caused by differing responses to divine initiative. Whatever opportunities are now closed off, Luke/Acts does not portray a blanket rejection by Jewish people. Even in this final scene, "some were convinced by what [Paul] said,²³⁴ but others disbelieved" (28.24). And, in fact, their departure following Paul's citation from Isaiah 6 and

---

**230** Mallen, *The Reading and Transformation*, 95.
**231** Johnson, *The Acts of the Apostles*, 472. Evans argues that the shift from the Hebrew hiphil to the Greek passive alters the LXX so that the prophet's preaching no longer "causes the heart to be fat, but the prophet preaches *because* (γάρ) the heart is already fat" (Evans, *To See and Not Perceive*, 63). In both Isa 6.10 LXX and Acts 28.27, the verbs escalate in their sense of human culpability: the people's heart has become dull (in the passive, ἐπαχύνθη), their ears hear with difficulty (βαρέως), whereas their eyes they have closed (in the aorist, ἐκάμμυσαν).
**232** As also Johnson, *The Acts of the Apostles*, 476. Johnson asserts that this concludes the defence in which Luke is actually interested—not that before Caesar, but defending God against any accusation of divine responsibility that might arise from the plight of those Jewish people who have rejected the divine visitation, and brought about their own reversal. Barrett argues Luke sees the rejection as part of "God's intention" (Barrett, *A Critical and Exegetical Commentary*, 2:1245), though elsewhere suggests the people reject wilfully—and that Luke does not offer sophisticated theological reflection on the topic (p. 2:1246).
**233** Holladay translates πόσαι μυριάδες even as "tens of thousands" (Holladay, *Acts*, 51; cf. Jervell, "The Divided People," 42, 46). Tannehill divides the final scene into two parts (vv. 17–22, 23–28), and argues that the first makes Luke's core point: Paul and his mission have not been opposed to the Jewish people (cf. esp. v. 20; Tannehill, *Narrative Unity*, 2:344–45). Mallen argues the two parts of this scene mirror those elsewhere, where proclamation is first received in a "polite interchange," and then opposed in the second part of the scene (Mallen, *The Reading and Transformation*, 94; cf. Luke 4.16–30).
**234** Tannehill emphasises the imperfect here, to suggest they were simply in the "process of being persuaded" (Tannehill, *Narrative Unity*, 2:347), arguing Luke intends that such persuasion remains an ongoing possibility (p. 2:347).

announcement that the proclamation will go to the gentiles[235] comes as they disagree among themselves!

Luke does not treat the potential of different groups or individuals differently.[236] Unlike Josephus and the writers of 4 Ezra, 2 Baruch, and many further texts, Luke does not normally divide between "opponent" and "protagonist" groups in the sense of their opportunity for positive response.[237] The comparison between Luke 2 and Acts 28 exposes a contrast between gentiles (whom Simeon says will receive revelation, Luke 2.32,[238] and Paul says will listen, Acts 28.28), and characters in Israel (many of whom will fall and rise, Luke 2.34, and some of whom will ultimately fail to listen, Acts 28.26–27).[239] Nonetheless, in Luke/Acts, all have received the same invitation (cf. Acts 11.18). But characters make different choices—for which they are ultimately responsible.

The prospective elements of Acts 28 leave the challenge in the air, alongside the sense of urgency. Verses 17–28 explain past rejection. But with its open, seemingly unfinished ending, account of mixed reception, and challenging proclamation—and the final summary's claim that Paul still "welcomed all who came to him" (v. 30)[240]—a *prospective* challenge remains. While the options may be closed for these characters whose story has come to a conclusion, the challenge for positive response transfers to the reader, whether insider or outsider, Jew or gentile. Nonetheless, Paul's words remain an ominous warning: time is running short. By the very openness of its ending, Acts underscores the unknown nature of the culmination of history, though the events begun in the res-

---

[235] Cf. Acts 13.45–47; 18.6; Tannehill, *Narrative Unity*, 2:346.
[236] Contra Nave, who suggests that, despite Luke's emphasis on "universal salvation," the response expected of Jewish and gentile characters is different (Nave, *The Role and Function of Repentance*, 224). In analysing the role of repentance in Luke/Acts, Nave also emphasises the importance of the decision to change one's life (and attitude to Jesus, for Jewish characters), but he does not address the dynamic of repentance as divine gift.
[237] The individuals portrayed as θεομάχοι as discussed above are the exceptions. Some of the other texts I have suggested do distinguish between opponent and protagonist groups likewise make use of this literary tradition; key examples of opponents in texts like 2 Maccabees are θεομάχοι, like Antiochus IV and Nicanor. However, in 2 Maccabees as in other texts, these individuals remain a part of larger groups, which are not necessarily described as θεομάχοι but do experience different levels of agency and opportunity for restoration than the protagonist groups enjoy. This is a key difference from Luke/Acts.
[238] Alexander notes Simeon also foresees Jesus bringing "glory" for Israel, and that the hymn here supplies a positive portrait, though Simeon's further words immediately foreshadow struggle (Alexander, "Reading Luke-Acts from Back to Front," 220).
[239] See Tannehill's more detailed comparison of the infancy narratives and Acts 28 (Tannehill, *Narrative Unity*, 2:349–50). Also Alexander, "Reading Luke-Acts from Back to Front," 221–22.
[240] Tannehill notes this is striking given the preceding verses (Tannehill, *Narrative Unity*, 2:351).

urrection of Jesus guarantee that the date for judgement has been set (Acts 17.31).²⁴¹ The decision to exercise human freedom through positive response to divine initiative is urgent.

## 7 Conclusion: human response in Luke/Acts

Luke/Acts also suggests interplay between divine and human agency in various ways, in keeping with Barclay's claim that ancient texts reflect more complex understandings of agency than a simple "competitive" model. Like the Jewish texts that draw on Deuteronomistic themes, Luke addresses issues which raise various kinds of problems for divine and human agency, as he explains the past and present and provides hope for the future. Like Josephus and 2 Baruch, he claims that divine sovereignty secures the future, but he also describes negative events which genuinely affect characters, and which he attributes to the actions of humans. In contrast to Käsemann's criticism that Luke was a proponent of *theologia gloriae*, or Cullmann's suggestion that NT writers including Luke portrayed the divine action in the Christ event as so decisive that evil no longer has an effect, Luke's account includes many examples of humans acting wilfully to cause negative events, evident, for example, in the persecutions throughout Acts.

But, despite his assurance of divine sovereignty, Luke does not generally suggest God is responsible for these negative events.²⁴² They are normally the direct result of poor human choices, sometimes with a role attributed to Satan as he interacts with human opponents of the divine purpose.²⁴³ Nonetheless, Luke shows the divine βουλή adapting, ironically furthering its course even through opposition. Indeed, where God does act to cause negative events, it is to stop a particular type of character: θεομάχοι. While Antiochus in 2 Maccabees is a θεομάχος explicitly connected to Deuteronomistic themes, as the agent of benevolent punishment of the people who is then himself punished (cf. 2 Macc 6.12–17), θεομάχοι in Luke's text are not agents of divine punishment but simply

---

241 See Chapter 6.
242 Unlike the key feature of explanations of the past in texts with a Deuteronomistic focus, Luke does not generally explain the past through divine punishment. Deuteronomistic theology makes a minor appearance in Stephen's speech in Acts 7, but even here Stephen's historical overview focuses on the culpability of those who have always opposed the divine purpose (as his audience will do immediately after the speech, by stoning him), rather than divine punishment. The punishing events, though significant and no doubt salient for any reader familiar with the biblical themes of exile and return, are mentioned here only at 7.43.
243 As in Luke 13.4, Luke suggests negative events can also unfold through random accident.

opponents, whose demise through divine action confirms divine sovereignty. These episodes serve an essentially future-orientated purpose: the divine βουλή cannot be stopped, and those who try will be brought to an end.

Again, similarly to most of the texts, but in contrast to the anguished exploration in 4 Ezra and even Valerius Maximus's implication that humans seem to manage some divine behaviour, Luke's explanations about past negative events do not lead him to anxieties about divine responsibility for creating the conditions which allowed such human actions in the first place. In Luke/Acts, opposition leads into a strong sense of tragedy.

Indeed, Luke emphasises human action, not only in the past but also the future. Human action is a feature of many of the texts discussed above, whether Polybius's affirmation of the importance of human skill and virtue within divine parameters, or the stronger sense of divine facilitation to improve the human capacity for faithful action in the future in 4 Ezra, 2 Baruch, and to an extent 2 Maccabees. But here there is a key difference in Luke/Acts. Unlike writers who portray divine benevolence for protagonist characters differently from the divine attitude towards opponents, Luke emphasises both divine initiative, and the human responsibility to take up the opportunity for positive response, for all characters (and, implicity, readers). In a kind of inversion of the priority for protagonists in other texts, the universal invitation in Luke/Acts ironically offers a particularly biting warning for insider characters, whose choices put them at risk of creating a reversal. Reversals feature in many of the study's texts, often a possibility attributed to a change of heart by fortune, or a reassessment of the pecking order in 2 Bar 83.10–23 (Cf. 1QM 14.5–12; contrast 1QSa 2.7–8), but in Luke/Acts reversal comes about through the outworking of human choices. Somewhat like the pragmatic understandings of Diodorus Siculus, who suggests reversal happens because of the complacency of those in the best positions (though here τύχη plays some role in response), reversals in Luke/Acts frequently unfold because of divergent responses to divine initiative. On the other hand, Luke describes a kind of human action which plays a part (through divine facilitation) in contributing positively to the divine purpose.

Finally, despite some similarities to the Graeco-Roman texts, differences in temporal understanding create further contrasts between these texts and Luke/Acts. While writers like Diodorus Siculus and Valerius Maximus suggest that future conditions will not alter the human capacity for virtue, this is importantly different from the future scenario portrayed by texts such as 4 Ezra, 2 Baruch, and Luke/Acts. Luke's approach remains fundamentally shaped by the eschatological focus that writers such as Polybius, Diodorus, Valerius, or Tacitus do not share. As Luke explains the past and provides assurance for the future, his focus on human freedom ensures a sense of urgency governs his exhortation for appropriate human response in the present. As it draws to a close, Luke/Acts continues to challenge readers to accept divine invitation urgently. Luke's understanding of the present time in relation to the end, as explored in Chapter 6, underscores that response remains possible for a limited time.

# Chapter 6:
# The present and the end of history

*Measure carefully in your mind, and when you see that a certain part of the predicted signs are past, then you will know that it is the very time when the Most High is about to visit the world which he has made. So when there shall appear in the world earthquakes, tumult of peoples, intrigues of nations, wavering of leaders, confusion of princes, then you will know that it was of these that the Most High spoke from the days that were of old, from the beginning...*

—Uriel, 4 Ezra 9.1–2

## 1 Introduction

In 1992, Francis Fukuyama wrote about the end of history.[1] Not unlike many ancient writers, he was affected by the mood of his time. And as the wall came down in Germany and related changes swept through Europe, he declared that the practical and philosophical achievements of liberal democracy signalled that the end of history had already been realised. He was not the first political philosopher to have delved into questions of the end of history. In nineteenth-century Germany, Karl Marx had articulated an ideal towards which history strived. Inspired by Hegel's dialectical account of history,[2] Marx's dialectical materialism *anticipates* the dictatorship of the proletariat that will result in communism at history's end.[3] Although Marx and Fukuyama speak of different things

---

[1] After an initial essay published on the brink of the changes in Europe in 1989, Fukuyama's 1992 publication likewise reflected his enthusiasm about an increasing dominance of liberal democracy (Francis Fukuyama, *The End of History and the Last Man* (New York: Free Press, 1992), xiii–xxiii, 276–86, 341–54). Critiques have challenged both Fukuyama's teleological conception of history and the role he ascribed to liberal democracy within it (see discussion in Gregory Elliott, *Ends in Sight: Marx/Fukuyama/Hobsbawm/Anderson* (London: Pluto, 2008), 34–63, including in response to Fukuyama's subsequent revisions). My interest here is not in Fukuyama's specific theoretical claims, but the contrast between views, based on beliefs about the extent to which the end of history has already been achieved.
[2] G. W. F. Hegel, *Manuscripts of the Introduction and the Lectures of 1822–1823*, vol. 1 of *Lectures on the Philosophy of World History*, trans. Robert F. Brown and Peter C. Hodgson (Oxford: Hoffmann, 2011), 118–19, 133–68 (esp. pp. 166–68).
[3] Karl Marx, *Writings of the Young Marx on Philosophy and Society* (Garden City: Anchor, 1967), 249–59, 285–87; Marx, *Economic and Philosophic Manuscripts of 1844*, trans. Martin Milligan, 4th rev. ed. (Moscow: Progress, 1974); cf. Howard Williams, "The End of History in Hegel and Marx," *The European Legacy: Toward New Paradigms* 2 (1997): 557.

when they consider the end of history, their treatments are each affected in fundamental ways by their understandings of the relationship between the present time and the end of history. These ideologies evoke important distinctions that are also evident in ancient texts: not only do writers' teleological conceptions of history shape their texts, but significant implications also arise from the extent to which the writers consider the end to have been achieved in the present.

In this chapter I examine the ways in which the present time and the end of history are characterised in the study's key texts, in order to illuminate Lukan eschatology. In addition to their particular expectations about the end and views about the significance of the present, writers' understandings of the relationship between these two moments shape how eschatology functions in their texts. Thus, in this chapter I build on the conclusions of Chapter 3, about the essential connection between history and its end in Luke's periodised, teleological schema of history, to address the fraught topic of Luke's expectations about the *imminence* of the end. Chapters 4 and 5 highlighted the ways in which retrospective and prospective interests shaped writers' portrayals of divine and human agency, including presentations of determinism and responsibility for negative events in the past and present. This chapter demonstrates that a writer's understanding of the relationship between the present and the end of history similarly draws out important consequences for his or her portrait of hope and of appropriate political orientation in the present. As noted in Chapter 1, these elements of Luke/Acts have been vigorously debated, in part as an effect of the claims made about Luke's eschatology.

This chapter draws on research into understandings of history and time in late Second Temple Jewish texts, exemplified by recent studies by Loren Stuckenbruck.[4] Stuckenbruck analyses the understandings of time in Pauline literature, contemporaneous Jewish texts, and some of the beliefs attributed to Jesus by historical Jesus researchers.[5] He sets up the problem as one in which understandings of time are integrally connected to making sense of evil, stating:

---

[4] Stuckenbruck, "Overlapping Ages," 320–26; Stuckenbruck, "Posturing 'Apocalyptic,'" 240–56. As noted in earlier chapters, there have been several recent studies of understandings of time and history in Second Temple Judaism, many of which in various ways inform the current study. On ways of securing continuity, rather than rupture, in history in light of the exile, see Mermelstein, *Creation, Covenant*, 11–15. Similarly, in relation to the destruction of the temple in 70 CE, including ways of reinterpreting the past as a resource for making sense of the present, see Najman, *Losing the Temple*, 27–33, 62–67, 153–58.

[5] Stuckenbruck, "How Much Evil?", 145–52.

the way time is understood within both the NT and its Jewish environment has important implications for how a faith perspective, which interprets the past and anticipates the future, can be understood as an effective means to negotiate evil in the present.[6]

Stuckenbruck argues that there are core similarities in the structuring of time in early Jewish and NT texts, including the way in which decisive events of the past provide assurance for future victory, and thereby also shape identity and experience in the present.[7]

Stuckenbruck's account offers welcome nuance to the way in which late Second Temple Jewish texts are frequently employed in comparisons with NT texts.[8] This type of analysis also offers a helpful response to the difficulty I have identified in Oscar Cullmann's otherwise illuminating concept of the "redemptive line of history," in which Cullmann fails to take sufficient account of ongoing experiences of suffering in the period beyond God's decisive action in Christ at history's "mid-point" in NT texts.[9] In Chapter 5 I noted that Cullmann had overlooked Luke's recognition of evil and the tragic consequences brought about by continued opposition to the (nonetheless unstoppable) divine βουλή. But the same difficulty likewise relates to the ways Cullmann failed to account adequately for the tension between the present time (already—I agree with Cullmann—positioned within the ultimate period of history), and its culmination on the date set for judgement (cf. Acts 17.31).

The discussion below demonstrates that writers' characterisations of the present time, end of history, and relationship between the two are all important. It indicates a range of similarities—and some key differences—between the study's Jewish texts (themselves diverse) and Luke/Acts in terms of the placement of the present in relation to the pattern of events expected as part of the end of history. But it also highlights that, for all of the writers discussed, a key aspect of the present time remains crucial: the extent to which further change remains possible in the present time. Even the writers who give no sense of an endpoint to history nonetheless account for the possibility of further change. As a result, the future affects experience in the present in tangible ways, whether as comfort or challenge.

In examining characterisations of the present (including any sense of the broader significance of this moment in history), and its relationship to understandings of the future or end of history, I consider the study's key texts in

---

6 Stuckenbruck, "How Much Evil?", 143.
7 Stuckenbruck, "How Much Evil?", 161, 165.
8 Cf. Stuckenbruck, "Posturing 'Apocalyptic,'" 243–49.
9 Cf. Cullmann, *Christ and Time*, 198, and my Chapter 5 above.

three groups: those which, as demonstrated in Chapter 3, depict history continuing through unending ages, where the *future* rather than *end* plays a key role; Virgil's teleological schema of history in the *Aeneid*, which portrays the goal of history as having been achieved (and is represented as continuing statically *sine fine*); and the Jewish texts, which all to some extent anticipate the end of history, though they identify the historical present in relation to the events of the end in diverse ways. The conclusions illuminate the treatment of Luke/Acts which follows. By exploring the extent to which the end of history is already realised in the present, and the static or dynamic character of the present, this chapter demonstrates that *both* of these elements are essential for understanding how eschatology functions in Luke/Acts.

## 2 The present and the future in non-teleological texts

Polybius, Diodorus Siculus, Valerius Maximus, and Tacitus do not incorporate the sense of an endpoint within the scope of their schemas of history.[10] As argued in Chapter 3, these writers all suppose that empires rise and fall,[11] each in turn indefinitely replaced by the next, and this feature ultimately establishes the non-teleological shape of their histories. Nonetheless, expectations about the *future* still affect the present in these texts, as also the writers' varied attributions of significance to the present time shape their texts in important ways. The present can constitute the climax within the section of history considered or simply the current in a series of equally commonplace historical moments.

As argued throughout, for **Polybius** the present moment is imbued with universal significance. Polybius praises the period "since these times[12] (ἀπὸ δὲ τούτων τῶν καιρῶν)"—that is, the "now" represented by the rise of Rome. As set out in Chapter 3, Polybius describes the former times of disparate events (which were "held together by no unity of initiative, results, or locality") as having been replaced, when τύχη brought together the entire world into one "organic whole" (1.3.3–4; cf. 1.4.1–3; 8.2.2–3).[13] But, as will be clear from earlier chapters of this study, this in itself is an intriguing element of Polybius's historiography. Elsewhere his attention to progress in history emphasises the value of future

---

[10] See Chapter 3 for discussion about the impact of a writer's "scope" or "scale" of history on their depiction of the shape and direction of history underlying a text.
[11] For Tacitus, regime change involves transitions between different Roman regimes. See Chapter 3.
[12] In the LCL, Paton, Walbank, and Habicht translate, "but ever since this date" (1.3.3).
[13] See Walbank, *A Historical Commentary*, 1:44.

generations learning from the mistakes of the past (1.35.6–10; see Chapter 3);[14] his portrayal of τύχη is famously mixed, though frequently τύχη is sidelined in the interests of providing replicable causal explanations where possible (see Chapter 4); and he explicitly praises human skill as the more desirable attribute over good fortune (see Chapter 5). Although for a writer like Valerius Maximus current circumstances are subject to an element of provisionality given the unpredictability of fortune, for Polybius the future predominantly provides an opportunity for improving one's own skills, strategies, and circumstances.

Polybius's allusion to future rotation through empires seems particularly striking, given this emphasis on both Rome's extraordinary ascendancy and human competence. Nonetheless, Scipio's comment at the fall of Carthage (38.21–22), discussed in Chapter 3, intimates that the cause of such collapse—whether of Carthage or as predicted of Rome—lies only in the inevitable progression of one empire to another. Scipio's insight is portrayed as a virtue (38.21.2–3).[15] Despite Polybius's affirmation of Rome, in the aftermath of his own homeland's fall he may proffer a subtle sense of dissent,[16] implying some silver lining lies in the inevitable provisionality of the present time.

Conversely, with the broad scope of his historiography from primordial times and in diverse geographical locations, **Diodorus Siculus** relativises the significance of the particular "moment" in which he writes.[17] As argued in Chapter 3, Diodorus affirms progress in history, including the sense that progress is intrinsically related to the purpose of writing and reading historiography, but this progress does not lead to any particular affirmation of achievement in the present time. Moreover, when individuals look towards the future, Diodorus's advice is simply that everything can change (see Chapter 4). For Diodorus, changes in fortune provide the opportunity not only for those experiencing adverse fortune to look forward to possible improvement, but for those currently enjoying the spoils of good fortune to attain virtue. In the latter case, they may avoid arrogance,[18] by acknowledging that such things do not last, and when things do change, they

---

**14** This development includes both military strategies and moral improvement (Eckstein, *Moral Vision*, 281–82).
**15** The virtue of responding to bad fortune positively is a major interest for Diodorus, but this also features in Polybius's reasoning (Eckstein, *Moral Vision*, 277).
**16** Gruen, "Polybius and Josephus," 152–55.
**17** Sacks, *Diodorus Siculus*, 157.
**18** Sacks describes Diodorus's reasoning as: "because τύχη is capricious, an individual ought to avoid arrogance when blessed with good fortune" (Sacks, *Diodorus Siculus*, 39).

may practice the moral virtue of enduring changes of fortune well (cf. 12.1; 17.38.4–6; 18.60.1; 31.15.1; 38.41.6; 38.42.1).[19] When Diodorus moves beyond individuals to the transitions between empires, he maintains that the continued pattern of rise and fall is inevitable—both because of the changeability of fortune, and because discipline over time seems impossible for those enjoying ruling power, judging for instance by the immoderation and arrogance into which the Carthaginians and Romans alike have fallen (cf. 14.46.4; 37.2–8).[20]

Conversely, **Tacitus**'s account of the present moment and any expectations of the future again revolve around his picture of decline (see Chapter 3). Although he may imply that the period under Trajan is more positive, as Russell Scott argues, Tacitus's treatment of this time is ambiguous and impossible to separate from his own political situation in the present.[21] Given Tacitus's persistent criticism of any conditions that compromise true liberty (cf. *Hist.* 1.2.1; 1.16.3; cf. *Ann.* 1.10), it seems likely that not even a good *princeps* could offer a model to avoid his disappointment.[22] Tacitus engages in nostalgic longing for old customs, illustrated through his contrast between Galba's apparently antiquated civility and the methods of other rulers like Nero and Otho (*Hist.* 1.12–13, 1.18). For Tacitus, the present is part of a grim period of decline, although even this does not make the present period unique or especially significant. His attitude towards the future offers no further hope in relation to the political situation and the characteristic failures of autocratic rulers.

Finally, for **Valerius Maximus**, vulnerability to fortune simply reflects the nature of human existence. Given the great continuity of human circumstances in all times and places (see Chapter 3), Valerius suggests the "now" in which he writes is the same as that of all other times.[23] Although, as argued above, this creates the sense that history itself remains always the same, nonetheless for individuals, the present is always governed by the potential for somewhat fickle changes of fortune in their lives in the future (cf. 6.9.praef; 7.1.praef). In the context of his compilation of exempla, this serves more to provide entertain-

---

[19] Sacks, *Diodorus Siculus*, 39–41. Though Hau notes that Diodorus consistently raises questions about characters' capacity (or incapacity) to achieve moderation and virtue during good fortune (Hau, "The Burden of Good Fortune," 172).
[20] Sacks, *Diodorus Siculus*, 52.
[21] Scott argues that Tacitus's decision not to focus on a period that was considered a great time of expansion and development under Trajan is itself telling (Scott, *Religion and Philosophy*, 50).
[22] Syme, *Tacitus*, 1:208; Sailor, *Writing and Empire*, 191.
[23] Mueller, *Roman Religion in Valerius*, 176; Bloomer, *Valerius Maximus and the Rhetoric*, 205.

ment at the expense of the victims of *fortuna* or *fatum* (cf. 1.6.7; 1.7.ext4),[24] though these constitute irresistible forces to which all must inevitably resign themselves (see Chapter 4). Such expectations about the future on the one hand, as for Diodorus, offer hope of change to those in difficulty, but on the other, given *fortuna*'s unpredictability, reduce the only viable human response in the present to a readiness to face the future as it comes.

Teresa Morgan's treatment of popular morality, in which she also engages with Valerius Maximus, highlights the importance of the dynamic relationship between the present and future in such texts. She observes, "time is the great ethical motivator for those who have few or no other resources. When no other aspect of life seems likely to improve one's situation, one can always hope that things will get better over time."[25] Where this popular material incorporates elements of divine justice, Morgan highlights the explicit provision for delay in that justice being realised. Recognising the tension between the present and the hope represented by possible changes in the future, she observes of the sentiment in the popular texts she studies, "all human life is lived in the meantime."[26]

Thus, the scope for movement and change beyond the present time maintains an important dynamic tension between the present and the future in these texts. The circumstances of the present time are provisional. For Valerius the possible workings of *fortuna* in all times make it a fascinating, if sometimes frightening, force hanging over the future. Polybius portrays an insight into inevitable changes in the future which ascribes provisionality to the present, despite the significance of Rome's moment, as well as opportunities to improve on present circumstances through learning from the past. For Diodorus, the future ought to motivate virtue and moderation in the present, even if on a communal level eventual failure and regime change is inevitable, whereas for Tacitus the gloomy present seems only likely to lead to further decline in the future.[27] Each of these writers offers no guarantees, except that the pattern of regime change will continue inevitably in due course.[28] In all cases, whether dealing with the lives of individuals or an entire empire, the present time remains vulnerable to the future. This serves for some writers to explain the past, provide hope

---

**24** Bloomer notes Valerius's particular interest in "paradoxical" and complicated outcomes brought about by reversals of fortune (Bloomer, *Valerius Maximus and the Rhetoric*, 17).
**25** Morgan, *Popular Morality*, 246.
**26** Morgan, *Popular Morality*, 241. Morgan observes that the solace of possible change over time can also be grounded in beliefs that things were better in an earlier time (pp. 245–46).
**27** Griffin, "Tacitus as a Historian," 172.
**28** See Chapter 3.

for the future, and identify appropriate human response in the present. But when writers deal not only with the *future* but an *end to history*, the consequences of the relationship between the present and the end become more pressing.

## 3 The historical present *is* the *telos*: Virgil's *Aeneid*

In the *Aeneid*, Virgil not only stresses the significance of the present moment, but portrays it as the end and goal of history. Various features of the trajectory leading to this end contribute to a sense of ambiguity, which is essential to many of Virgil's themes in the epic; he introduces double-meanings, plays with time as the plot moves from later events to earlier ones, and builds tension as the characters endure difficulty on the way to reaching their goal. Nonetheless—as argued in Chapter 3 in relation to the teleological nature of Virgil's schema of history in the *Aeneid*, and set out in more detail below in terms of the significance and position of the present time—this ambiguity adds complexity to Virgil's portrait of the past, but it does not ultimately compromise his assertions about the end. Unlike the other key texts of this study, Virgil's alignment of the present with an eternally consistent future produces a static effect, with the result that his account of the end of history functions differently from that of the other writers.

### 3.1 Virgil's portrait of the end

Virgil's portrait of the nature of the end of history emerges from Book 1. According to Jupiter's prophecy (see Chapter 3), the course of events in which Aeneas is a participant leads to *imperium sine fine* (1.279; cf. 1.278, 287; 6.788–797). Jupiter's speech confirms the Romans as the final empire of history. Aeneas prefigures later concord by his military conquests (1.264; cf. 6.889–890), indicating the peace secured through threat of military response embodied by the *pax Romana* (cf. 6.851–3).[29] For Tacitus, such a "peace" is ultimately oppressive (*Hist.* 1.2.1; 4.4.3; *Ann.* 1.10); in Virgil's *Aeneid*, though there may be elements of ambiguity in the course of achievements which have led to this end, this peace reflects, rather, the hard-won accomplishment of Jupiter's renewed age.[30] This is the pic-

---

**29** Galinsky, *Augustan Culture*, 149. Jupiter's revelation about the end centres on newfound peace: "wars shall cease" (1.291), "savage ages (*aspera saecula*) soften" (291), and "the gates of war, grim with iron and close-fitting bars, shall be closed" (293–94).
**30** On Virgil's contrasting picture of the end in the *Georgics* and *Eclogues*, see Chapters 2 and 3 above.

ture of life at the *telos* in the *Aeneid*, constituted by the inverse of those things which are overcome through the epic: war, homelessness, civic unrest, and uncertainty.[31] These are all real in the epic, and add complexity even as the narrative goes back and forth between events—for instance, from Carthage and Dido's palace in Book 1, back to Aeneas's account of the fall of, and departure from, Troy in Book 2.[32]

Virgil does not elucidate metaphysical questions as part of his portrayal of the end. Although metaphysics related to post-mortem conditions are mentioned in Book 6 as part of the scene-setting for the underworld parade, they are not the focus there,[33] nor do such questions enter into Virgil's account of the end of history (aside from key figures who are promised *apotheosis*; cf. 1.290). The picture of the end is not articulated in terms of an afterlife, but as continuous Roman rule, divine favour, and religious piety.

At the conclusion of the epic, continued favour with Jupiter has led also to resolution with Juno, facilitating ongoing piety and Rome's uninterrupted well-being. As Gunther Gottlieb observes in relation to the concluding scene with Juno (12.791–842):

> Jupiter finally succeeds in calming down the angry and grumbling Juno. There are no more obstacles to prevent the happy rise of the *res Romana* in Italy. The new generation growing up will surpass men and gods in piety and will honour even Juno as nobody else does. Vergil refers to the Capitoline triad with Juno as one of the three supreme gods, who in the time of Vergil's readers are the guarantors of Roman welfare and prosperity.[34]

This confirms the end which the *Aeneid* affirms, embodied in Roman rule and divine favour.

---

**31** Cf. 6.889–890, in which the narration follows on after the conclusion of Anchises's speech with an indirect comment about his further revelations to Aeneas: after "kindling [Aeneas's] soul with longing for the glory that was to be, he then tells of the wars that the hero must wage." Aeneas killing Turnus in the epic's final moment (12.939–53) similarly reflects the complex role of struggle and violence in the *Aeneid*: this paves the way to establishing Rome and fulfilling Jupiter's prophecy of unending rule and a renewed golden age of "peace," but the moment communicates the anguish and compromise this requires (Lyne, "Vergil and the Politics," 338).
**32** No doubt readers who had lived through the civil war could identify the absence of these things as a positive historical development (O'Hara, *Death and the Optimistic Prophecy*, 163).
**33** Horsfall, *Virgil, "Aeneid" 6*, 1:xxv–xxvi; cf. Williams, "The Sixth Book," 201–2. O'Hara suggests the inconsistency in metaphysical claims itself is the point (O'Hara, *Inconsistency in Roman Epic*, 94).
**34** Gunther Gottlieb, "Religion in the Politics of Augustus, (*Aeneid* 1.278–91, 8.714–23, 12.791–842)," in Stahl, *Vergil's Aeneid*, 23.

## 3.2 The significance of the "now" in the *Aeneid*

Virgil's portrait of the end of history thus also confirms the significance of the present. In the *Aeneid*, the historical present is easily identified with Augustus's reign; the *vaticinia ex eventu* interpret the events of the past as well as facilitating the readers' ability to identify their own historical present among the events of the historical review.[35] For instance, the closing of the gates of war (1.293–94) pinpoints the moment when the doors of the temple of Janus, traditionally closed during a time of peace, were closed by Augustus in 29 BCE, after standing open for more than 200 years.[36]

For *vaticinia ex eventu* in apocalypses,[37] the accuracy of the insights received by an earlier pseudepigraphal seer, which "predict" events that lie in the *literary* future but *historical* past, serves to interpret history and to assure readers of the accuracy of the events predicted for time *beyond* the historical present.[38] In the *Aeneid*, by contrast, the only elements beyond the historical present included are the expansive claims of *extension* of the present, in Rome's unending rule (1.279; 6.793).[39] In Virgil's text these prophecies thus serve primarily to underscore the significance of the present.

In this way, the present is not only the moment readers will recognise in the unfolding prophecy, but the culmination of the entire historical process. The historical reviews in Books 6 and 8 merge this emphasis on the present moment with praise for Augustus. In his commentary on the underworld parade, Anchises (Aeneas's father) calls out at the moment Augustus appears:

> Turn hither now your two-eyed gaze, and behold this nation, the Romans that are yours. Here is Caesar and all the seed of Iulus destined to pass under heaven's spacious sphere. And this in truth is he whom you so often hear promised you, Augustus Caesar, son of a god (*divi genus*), who will again establish a golden age (*aurea condet saecula*)[40] in Latium amid

---

35 See Chapter 4.
36 Ahl, *Virgil, Aeneid*, 332; Fairclough and Goold, *Virgil*, 1:282.
37 See §4 and Chapter 4.
38 VanderKam, *Enoch and the Growth*, 142.
39 Contra Feeney, who identifies a "genuinely forward-looking" element, with the grief over Marcellus as a thwarted future (Feeney, "History and Revelation," 15). However sincere this grief is (6.860–92), and notwithstanding its connection to the funeral parade imagery (Horsfall, *Virgil, "Aeneid" 6*, 1:xviii), as with the other accounts of struggle, the disaster with Marcellus belongs to the past; Augustus constitutes the present and the end that overcomes the difficulties of the past.
40 The LCL translation by Fairclough and Goold converts the plural "golden ages" in Latin into the singular in English. On Virgil's treatment of the Golden Age, see Chapter 3.

fields once ruled by Saturn; he will advance his empire (*proferet imperium*) beyond the Garamants and Indians to a land which lies beyond our stars. (6.788–97)

The moment is emphatic: this is the end to which the parade has been leading.[41] The underworld experience itself is the final event of the first half of the epic, drawing Virgil's reinterpreted *Odyssey* to a close. Augustus's early mention underscores his significance[42] and allows him to appear next to divine figures.[43] While the parade in the underworld asserts Augustus's centrality to the Roman empire, the *ekphrasis* of Book 8, in which he presides at the centre of Aeneas's shield, presents him as the centre of a *cosmic* picture of history.[44] Augustus himself embodies something of Virgil's portrait of the end of history, and his reign in the present underscores to the reader that the promised *telos* has been achieved.

Virgil's *Aeneid* is therefore certainly Augustan panegyric, but not simplistically so.[45] The epic contains numerous ambiguous elements. Setbacks and delay appear to impede the promised events from unfolding, partially explained prophecies lead to surprising twists,[46] and, in the Book 6 review, identifications of some characters are vague, evidently in order to blur the meaning and allude to multiple historical figures.[47] It seems Virgil allows, indeed encourages, multiple meanings to coexist. D. C. Feeney considers each line of the underworld pa-

---

[41] The Latin gives a strong sense of emphasis in its repetition of demonstratives (cf. 6.788–92). Horsfall's translation maintains the emphasis in "This, this is the man" (791; Horsfall, *Virgil*, "*Aeneid*" 6, 1:55). Ahl's translation, which retains the poetic metre, communicates effectively the emphatic sense of this announcement in its punctuation: "Marshal your eyes' twin gaze this way now! Look at this people, / Look at your Romans! For Caesar is here…" (788–89, Ahl, *Virgil, Aeneid*). Williams identifies the parade as the epic's most patriotic moment (Williams, "The Sixth Book," 202).
[42] Horsfall wonders if the identification of Augustus here, rather than Julius Caesar, should be slightly more controversial (Horsfall, *Virgil*, "*Aeneid*" 6, 2:538).
[43] Ahl, *Virgil, Aeneid*, 376. By moving Augustus earlier, Virgil also glosses over some more difficult patches of Roman history in the chronology.
[44] Hardie, *Virgil's Aeneid*, 350–53.
[45] Galinsky notes that ideological concerns drove twentieth-century (especially post-war) interpretation of Virgil (Galinsky, *Augustan Culture*, 3–5). Interpretations of the *Aeneid*'s politics range from imperial propaganda to clever subversion, leading variously to censure or agreement from the interpreter. See Harrison's overview of twentieth-century interpretation, including his designation of "positive" and "pessimistic" accounts of the *Aeneid* (Harrison, "Some Views of the *Aeneid*," 3–6). See my Chapters 2 and 3 on recent treatments of the *Aeneid* as representing anti-imperial thrust.
[46] See Chapter 4.
[47] Feeney identifies a list of ambiguous figures (Feeney, "History and Revelation," 5–6).

rade, assisted by Lucan's re-presentation of the scene in his *Civil War*, and highlights the various ways in which the grand presentation of individuals belies an underwhelming reality in Virgil's own time; he notes the parade includes families fallen from grace and derelict cities.[48] Feeney argues that "riddles" qualify the whole review.[49]

However, again, temporal elements remain key for interpreting the effect of Virgil's ambiguity. Virgil's "riddles" complicate the attributions he makes about past events. But from the implied reader's historical present, any ambiguity about identifying Rome as the *telos* of this trajectory has been resolved. Even Feeney, having posed the question in light of the first town of the list in the underworld review ("*Nomen-tum*", 6.773), "whether Vergil can conceive of a time when even Rome will be only a name," answers: "it hasn't happened yet."[50] The scene may confirm that it is possible for places once praised to become derelict, but this is not Rome's fate.[51] Feeney likewise concludes that in this historical review Rome is "the τέλος of the way in which the world is ordered" and is "celebrated by the device," even if he also queries other ambiguities in the scene.[52] Indeed, one might add that, in fact, Virgil has framed his epic with a claim very far from the possibility of such obscurity, namely that Rome is fated to enjoy *imperium sine fine* across the breadth of the universe (1.279, 287).

James O'Hara also questions the epic's endpoint, suggesting Juno's acquiescence to Jupiter is merely a temporary truce (12.791–842), given that the Punic Wars remain in the future beyond the poem's conclusion.[53] But, again, temporal considerations clarify the ambiguous elements of these interactions between the

---

**48** Feeney, "History and Revelation," 5, 7.
**49** Feeney, "History and Revelation," 6. The ivory gate of sleep, through which the reader is told "delusive dreams issue upward" (6.896), and through which Aeneas exits the underworld, most likely is a device to explain Aeneas's failure to remember the content of the underworld disclosures in the second half of the epic (Fairclough and Goold, *Virgil*, 1:597). See Chapter 4.
**50** Feeney, "History and Revelation," 8.
**51** Likewise reflecting the way in which Virgil plays with time, Feeney also attributes the insignificance of these cities a further role in light of the *vaticinium ex eventu:* "The glorious future of the independent states is taken away from them before it has even happened, as the poet nudges his audience into remembering their contemporary eclipse" (Feeney, "History and Revelation," 7–8).
**52** For instance, Feeney considers whether Platonic interests qualify or make unclear the value of such achievement (Feeney, "History and Revelation," 15–16). Similarly, although he questions other elements of prophecy in the *Aeneid*, O'Hara still asserts that the underworld parade describes "the historical process that will culminate with Augustus' reestablishment of a Golden Age in Latium" (O'Hara, *Death and the Optimistic Prophecy*, 163–64).
**53** O'Hara, *Death and the Optimistic Prophecy*, 142.

gods and their effects.⁵⁴ From the perspective of the reader, the Punic Wars are already in the past;⁵⁵ the resolution between Juno and Jupiter not only stands but confirms the favour Rome enjoys from both. Moreover, Turnus's death in the concluding moments of the epic, however Aeneas's moment of hesitation and then vengeance is to be interpreted, secures Roman supremacy (12.939–53).⁵⁶

Karl Galinsky rightly observes that Virgil's decision to write an "Aeneid" and not an "Augusteid" shapes the kind of story he presents.⁵⁷ In his *Aeneid*, Virgil offers a commentary on the present through the lens of mythic origins. As a drama played out in the past, the *Aeneid* explores themes such as delay, nostalgia, and suffering, but its picture of the end of history is ultimately represented not by Saturn's golden age of the past, or thwarted hopes, but the reinterpreted golden age of Jupiter.⁵⁸ Readers live in the time of Augustus; the fact of his reign shows delay has been overcome and qualifies the struggles which Virgil depicts leading to the establishment of this new golden age.

The emphatic words of Anchises cut through the intervening time, underscoring the significance of this moment. His call of "now" in the parade resonates with the "now" of the reader: "Turn hither now … Here is Caesar!" (6.791–92).

## 3.3 The consequences of aligning the present with the end

As he compares accounts of the end of history in various ancient texts, Hubert Cancik dubs Jupiter's prophecy in Book 1 of the *Aeneid* "triumphant counterpropaganda" against Rome's enemies and its own fears, which is "not uneschatolog-

---

54 West, "The End and the Meaning," 303.
55 Similarly, concerns that the civil wars undermine the positive picture of the Roman rule may be allayed by the text's identification of the highpoint in the progress of history in the Augustan era (the *Aeneid* contains its own jokes about this, for instance in Carthage building stages in Book 1, on which plays will be performed in hundreds of years; Ahl, *Virgil, Aeneid*, 340).
56 Theodorakopoulos suggests the scene indicates a darker side that is nonetheless essential to the trajectory to Rome (Theodorakopoulos, "Closure," 157), and Quint highlights the role of vengeance (Quint, "Repetition and Ideology," 36). Williams argues that all hesitation ends in the underworld journey in Book 6, as Aeneas sees Augustus and what must and will be fulfilled (Williams, "The Sixth Book," 203).
57 Galinsky, *Augustan Culture*, 125.
58 Galinsky, *Augustan Culture*, 95. Also see Gillian Clark, "Paradise for Pagans? Augustine on Virgil, Cicero, and Plato," in *Paradise in Antiquity: Jewish and Christian Views*, ed. Markus N. A. Bockmuehl and Guy G. Stroumsa (Cambridge: Cambridge University Press, 2010), 168.

ical, but posteschatological."⁵⁹ He makes an important point. Texts that do not include an endpoint to history, such as those by Polybius, Valerius Maximus, or Diodorus Siculus discussed above, may perhaps be classed as *uneschatological*. They exclude the end of history from their scope, but as noted above, there may still be some benefit in the historical present derived from an appreciation for the future, such as consolation in light of the possibility of change or the ability to attain moral virtue by bearing changes of fortune well. In the *Aeneid*, however, the scope extends infinitely, but its character is described in unison with the present. This invites no opportunity for change.

Whereas the relationship between present realities and the future provides a source of consolation in a broad range of other texts of this study, from Valerius's exempla and Diodorus's *Library* to 4 Ezra, the way in which Virgil collapses these categories limits this possibility.⁶⁰ Any reader suffering in the historical present might find in the *Aeneid* a message of sacrifice that leads to hard-won conquest, as well as some space for pathos and grief, in its portrayal of *past* events. But a depiction of the present as the attainment of history's goal eliminates the possibility for change required in order for the future to represent a source of hope.⁶¹ Karl Mannheim offers a contrast between "ideology," a view in which the end of history has been realised already in current political structures, and "utopia," which anticipates an end beyond those structures.⁶² I return to this distinction in relation to the comparison to Luke/Acts below. Here the distinction exposes the impact of Virgil's identification of the end with the present: in Mannheim's terms, Virgil's treatment of the end of history represents "ideology." Coinciding with the end of history, the present is simply static. As a result, the conception of a progressing, teleological trajectory to an end of history already realised in the Augustan empire, which underlies the *Aeneid*, overlooks

---

**59** Cancik, "The End of the World," 119. Krauter makes a similar point in critiquing Bonz's parallels between Luke's narrative and Virgil's *Aeneid*, arguing that despite various similarities in teleological focus, this creates a fundamental difference between the texts (Krauter, "Vergils Evangelium und das lukanische Epos?", 233).

**60** O'Hara argues that Virgil presents himself as a prophet-poet (7.41) in order to indicate that he is being less than truthful, and so to provide consolation, "putting on a brave face for the lie" as O'Hara argues Jupiter did in consoling Venus in Book 1 (O'Hara, *Death and the Optimistic Prophecy*, 176, 184).

**61** Cancik observes, "Rome has its demise behind it," (Cancik, "The End of the World," 119) and so the new era becomes something different and invulnerable.

**62** Karl Mannheim, *Ideology and Utopia: An Introduction to the Sociology of Knowledge* (London: Routledge & Kegan Paul, 1960), 36. Mannheim primarily deals with other epistemological and psychological considerations, which may not be of continuing relevance. But his distinction between ideology and utopia contributes to the current study.

any ongoing experiences of suffering, and portrays a setting in which the possibility of dissent from the ruling political authorities is excluded, both now, and in the eternally consistent future.

## 4 The present and the end of history in late Second Temple texts

By contrast, in the study's Jewish texts the writers play upon the dynamic between present experience and the altered circumstances promised for the end of history. Notwithstanding the diversity across these texts, there is considerable continuity in the writers' accounts of the structure of history and their expectations of the end, thus supporting key features of Stuckenbruck's argument noted above.[63] In Chapter 3, I concluded that the writer of each of these texts depicts a teleological schema of history, although they accent different moments or features of the schema and 2 Maccabees, particularly, does not focus on the end. Here I examine the significance and placement of the present time in relation to the events of the end. Some writers provide only hints of an anticipated end or simply place the present generally within the penultimate period of history before an unending divine reign. For others, current events are already set among the woes which signify the beginning of the events of the end.

### 4.1 The relationship between the present and the end

The writer of **2 Maccabees** supplies minimal detail about the end. As set out in Chapter 3, eschatological expectations are suggested in the summary statement about delayed judgement for the other nations (6.12–17) and in affirmations about resurrection in the martyrdom accounts of 2 Macc 6–7 and the future resurrection of the dead soldiers in 2 Macc 12.43–45. However, these hints do not lead into more systematic accounts of eschatological events. The writer does not outline messianic expectations; there is no reason to attribute messianic features to Judas, despite the moment in which he is identified with God's presence in the battle (12.22).[64] Nor does the narrative interpret any of the sufferings described or anticipated as messianic woes.

---

[63] Stuckenbruck, "How Much Evil?", 161–68; Stuckenbruck, "Overlapping Ages," 320–26.
[64] The passage describes the arrival of Judas and his soldiers as the enemy witnessing "He who sees all things," the same title given to God in 15.2 (cf. discussion in Jonathan A. Goldstein, "How

Some elements of the battles recounted in later chapters could tempt readers to supply eschatological overtones. In Judas's vision of Jeremiah and the recently-martyred high priest Onias, Judas receives a golden sword (15.12–16), which then secures victory in the ensuing battle.[65] The sword itself is reminiscent of the *Apocalypse of Weeks* (1 Enoch 91.12) and the *Animal Apocalypse* (1 Enoch 90.19). In each of these 1 Enoch apocalypses, the Lord strikes the ground and bestows a sword with which the people are victorious in a battle which leads into the complete destruction of evil and installation of divine reign at the end of history.[66] Daniel 10–12 also supplies eschatological imagery for a battle. However, the writer of 2 Maccabees does not suggest Judas's battles should be interpreted eschatologically. Divine assistance (10.38; 12.11, 28; 13.4, 13–14, 17; 15.21–24, 27), and even supernatural reinforcements (10.29–30), feature to Judas's advantage, but the texts to which 2 Maccabees allude explicitly are *Joshua*'s battle (2 Macc 12.15–16; cf. Josh 6.1–21) and the divine help supplied to Hezekiah (2 Macc 8.19; 15.22; cf. Isa 37.36; 2 Kgs 19.35). The battles in 2 Maccabees do not parallel the ultimate battle portrayed in the *Apocalypse of Weeks*, *Animal Apocalypse*, Dan 10–12, or the War Scroll.

Rather, in 2 Maccabees the writer portrays a cycle of divine punishment[67] followed by divine rescue.[68] This cycle remains in the position of divine favour at the end of the narrative; the *literary* present constitutes a significant moment of divine vindication in the aftermath of Judas's victories and continued independence for the Hebrew people (15.37). But the prayers of "Maccabeus and

---

the Authors of 1 and 2 Maccabees Treated the 'Messianic' Promises," in Neusner, Green, and Frerichs, *Judaisms and Their Messiahs at the Turn of the Christian Era*, 88). Schwartz contrasts messianic longing for change to the world order in 1 Maccabees with the absence of these kinds of interests in 2 Maccabees (Schwartz, "Circular or Teleological," 127; cf. Collins, "Messianism in the Maccabean Period," 106).

**65** See also Chapter 4 above.

**66** Note also the debates in relation to interpretation of the *Animal Apocalypse* and whether the ram with a horn is to be interpreted as Judas Maccabeus. While it seems likely that it is (Stuckenbruck, "'Reading the Present,'" 94), the writer does not associate the sword with this ram, nor is the ram to be identified with the Messiah (contra George W. E. Nickelsburg, "Salvation without and with a Messiah: Developing Beliefs in Writings Ascribed to Enoch," in Neusner, Green, and Frerichs, *Judaisms and Their Messiahs*, 55).

**67** See Chapter 5.

**68** In this sense, 2 Maccabees reflects some similarity to the Graeco-Roman texts discussed at §2: the future provides both consolation and warning, as protagonist characters are aware that God will act to punish and to rescue as required throughout the course of history. This feature leads Schwartz to identify a circular understanding of history in 2 Maccabees (Schwartz, "Circular or Teleological," 128), though I suggest the hints of an end do nonetheless affect experience in the present.

his followers," petitioning that God might again punish them should this become necessary in the future (10.4; cf. 6.16; 7.33), and the epitomiser's somewhat apologetic reflections on his chosen endpoint for the narrative (15.37–39), suggest it is possible that experience in the *historical* present of the intended reader may not remain as positive.[69] Both the continued cycle of divine punishment and rescue, and the hint of the end, shape experience in the present as it remains subject to future change.

**Josephus** engages more directly with a particular portrait of the end of history through his understanding of the succession of empires leading to divine reign. As noted in earlier chapters, Josephus explicitly affirms the five-kingdom framework of Dan 2 in *Ant.* 10.203–10, (cf. also 10.266–81), which is paradigmatic for his understanding of history elsewhere (cf. *J.W.* 5.367).[70] Daniel particularly attracts Josephus's praise because "he was not only wont to prophesy future things, as did the other prophets, but he also fixed the time at which these would come to pass" (*Ant.* 10.267).[71]

But most importantly for the current chapter, as he applies Daniel's prophecies to his own historical context,[72] Josephus not only provides a broader schema of teleological history, but he also identifies the present time. In the passage in which he discusses Dan 8, Josephus specifies the penultimate empire as Rome,[73] though he does not focus on the regime's end here but rather moves into his af-

---

**69** Schwartz, *2 Maccabees*, 556. It is generally accepted that the epitomiser had access to further historical material. Doran suggests the narrative is structured around defence of the temple and the endpoint relates to drawing together festival themes (Doran, *2 Maccabees*, 10).
**70** Bilde, "Josephus and Jewish Apocalypticism," 47.
**71** Davies even argues that it is this emphasis on Daniel's ability as a prophet, alongside Josephus's positive attitude towards prophecy, which confirms that Josephus did anticipate the end of Rome and the installation of a final, divine kingdom, however subtly he expressed it (Davies, "Daniel in the Lion's Den," 174).
**72** Bilde also highlights that Josephus's interpretation of Numbers 22–24 in *Ant.* 4.100–31 expands on the biblical text to identify the prophesied suffering with the events of his own recent past (Bilde, "Josephus and Jewish Apocalypticism," 52–53).
**73** Begg and Spilsbury note a number of ambiguities in translating the reference to the Roman empire and that "it" would be "laid waste by them" in Josephus's interpretation of Dan 8 in *Ant.* 10.276. Their main argument against reading this passage as foretelling the destruction of Rome is that it is unlikely Josephus would "make such a bold statement;" they find an alternate interpretation by following Chrysostom's reading of Josephus here, though, drawing on earlier work by Begg, they also note the possibility that Josephus intended the reference to be ambiguous and read differently by Jewish and Roman readers (Begg and Spilsbury, *Judean Antiquities 8–10*, 314 n. 1177). Although Josephus may at times veil his convictions about the end of Rome, for obvious political reasons, this study highlights numerous places where he hints that he does hold the view that Begg and Spilsbury take to be surprisingly "bold."

firmation of divine guidance of all of history (10.266–81).⁷⁴ By contrast, his account of Daniel's interpretation of Nebuchadnezzar's dream in Dan 2 stresses the total destruction of the statue comprised of four materials that signifies the four empires (10.207).⁷⁵ His reticence to spell out the consequences of this decisive and sudden transition to the ultimate reign (10.210; cf. 281) itself confirms his interpretation of the prophecy as the end of Rome's reign.⁷⁶ This understanding likewise illumines his claims in the *Jewish War*, as discussed in more detail in Chapter 3, about the divine favour that rests upon Italy "now" (*J.W.* 5.367), with concomitant implications for his view of the significance of the present time.

Thus, Josephus identifies the present in the period of the penultimate regime of Daniel's prophecy, but he is no more specific about how imminent the end of that reign is.⁷⁷ Similarly, in the *Jewish War* the gruesome events of the recent past are significant as a demonstration of divine punishment of the Jewish people and favour for Rome, but Josephus does not identify them with messianic woes.

Indeed, for Josephus political dissent has no place in the present and, although the divine reign will be installed at the end of history, this will take place in God's own time and cannot be rushed.⁷⁸ The metric Josephus associates with the "rule of the stronger"—affirmed by both Agrippa (*J.W.* 2.345–401) and Josephus's speeches (5.362–419; cf. *Life* 17–18)—continues in effect into the present. In this thinking, the stronger party must enjoy divine assistance and thus should not be opposed. Moreover, as discussed in Chapter 3, if the Jewish people follow Josephus's advice and repent to Rome, then they will discover that the remaining time of Rome's reign can even be positive. Thus, although for Josephus history has a definite endpoint and Rome is the last political empire before it, he does not give any indication that the events of the end have already begun.

---

**74** See Chapter 4.

**75** This sudden and total destruction in *Ant.* 10.207 is unlike the biblical account of the feet being destroyed by the stone, which then causes the remainder of the statue to be destroyed (Dan 2.34). In the biblical account the fourth material is itself a mixture (Dan 2.33), but Josephus describes the feet as simply iron (*Ant.* 10.206–7). Also in the *Antiquities*, the stone is simply broken off from a mountain, omitting the biblical phrase about the stone being cut out, "not by human hands" (Dan 2.34, 45; cf. 4 Ezra 13.36).

**76** In Chapter 3, I observed that Josephus's apocalyptic and eschatological interests are frequently overlooked in NT comparisons, though studies of Josephus frequently highlight these topics.

**77** Although Josephus does not detail specific expectations about the end, his criticism of the Sadducees (*J.W.* 2.164–66) suggests he anticipates resurrection.

**78** Further stressing political conformity, Josephus takes pains to describe the positive attitude of the kings to Daniel, despite the bad news he supplies (10.242–44).

The War Scroll, 4 Ezra, and 2 Baruch provide more detailed accounts of end-time events. In addition to the central theme of the eschatological war, the **War Scroll**'s picture of the end encompasses elements such as enlightenment for a select group (17.8), divine judgement (6.5–6; 11.13–7), eternal destruction of the wicked (1.5–7; 9.5–6; 15.2, 12; 18.1), and vindication of Israel (1.8–9; 19.2–8).[79] The writer associates ultimate divine judgement with the events of the war itself. Judgement resounds through descriptions of battle shields, spears, and swords that are to be used "to fell the dead by the judgement of God and to humiliate the enemy line by God's might, to pay the reward of their evil to every people of futility" (6.5; cf. 1.5–7; 11.13–17; 15.2; 18.1–4).

Though John Collins protests that the War Scroll's dependence on Dan 10–12 extends to Daniel's quietist emphasis on waiting upon God's action,[80] the narration of the war itself contains violent language in its exhortation to engage in the destruction of the enemy (12.10–15; cf. 19.2–8) and pillaging of valuables (12.4; cf. 19.6–7).[81] As noted by Sharon Mattila, rather than an idyllic picture of peace and universal conversion to the way of Israel's Lord (as in 4Q426), in 1QM characters belong to either the camp of darkness or that of light, and all of the sons of darkness are utterly annihilated.[82]

---

**79** The detail of the battle also implies that it is expected to extend for some time; instructions are provided for the tasks to be fulfilled by the different groups within the community, over days, weeks, seasons, and the whole course of years (1QM 2.5). According to the War Scroll, life at the culmination of history continues through further "eternal seasons" (14.17). The writer describes the restoration of Israel in keeping with the covenant (12.6; 17.7–8; 19.2–8), though the reference to the violators of the covenant who help the Kittim (1.2; cf. 12.1) suggests vindication extends only to a righteous subset of Israel. This end-time portrait however does not include any explicit references to resurrection. As noted in Chapter 3, the ideal picture of life of the end of history in 1QM is one in which the sons of light continue celebrating pious practices through further, unending periods, unimpeded by any forces of evil (1.8–9; 15.1; 18.11–12). Here, the righteous are depicted filling out their length of days and enjoying *long* life, rather than eternal life (1.9). See discussion at p. 96 n. 194.
**80** See animated discussion on aspects of these arguments as outlined by John J. Collins, "The Mythology of Holy War in Daniel and the Qumran War Scroll: A Point of Transition in Jewish Apocalyptic," *VT* 25 (1975): 596–612, and the response this prompted from Philip Davies, "Dualism and Eschatology in the Qumran War Scroll," *VT* 28 (1978): 28–36; Collins, "Short Notes: Dualism and Eschatology in 1 QM: A Reply to P. R. Davies," *VT* 29 (1979): 212–15; and Davies, "Dualism and Eschatology in 1QM: A Rejoinder," *VT* 30 (1980): 93–97.
**81** The reference to a "peaceful return" on one of the trumpets in 3.11 does not relate to concern about the enemy, which will be utterly destroyed and humiliated—both the human sons of darkness and their supernatural counterparts (14.16; 18.1, 11).
**82** Mattila, "Two Contrasting Eschatologies," 533, 538.

Some characters in the War Scroll are attributed key roles and titles but, as noted in Chapter 3, none is explicitly messianic.[83] One character's role appears clearer: column 17 refers to "the majestic angel, Michael" (17.6–7), sharing understandings of Michael's role as outlined in Dan 10.13, 21; 12.1.[84] Rather than a messianic character, Michael is described as the preeminent angelic commander. His presence confirms the eschatological significance of the war and imminence of the inauguration of divine reign, as in Dan 12.1.[85]

Nonetheless, there is no sense that the writer considers the angelic figure Michael to be present in the community already, nor that final events involving judgement and vindication have begun. The so-called "sectarian" texts from Qumran[86] have frequently sparked questions about writers' conceptions of the

---

[83] See, for instance, the "Prince of the whole Congregation" (5.1), though the details of his role are not specified. Likewise, the "Hero of War" (12.9; though cf. more domestic use of "hero" at 19.2–5), the "Prince of Light" (13.10), and, in a Cave 4 fragment, the "Prince of the Battle" (4Q492; Vermes, *The Complete Dead Sea Scrolls*, 183). It is unclear whether these characters should be equated with one another or any relationship be presumed to messianic figures anticipated in other texts, such as the Priestly and Davidic Messiahs described in 1QSa. Davies argues there is no evidence of the Davidic Messiah in 1QM and, given it describes events in which one may easily be expected, he believes this provides strong evidence against messianic belief (alternatively, he notes the reference to the Messiah in 4Q285; Davies, "War of the Sons of Light," 968). See also Shemaryahu Talmon, "Waiting for the Messiah: The Spiritual Universe of the Qumran Covenanters," in Neusner, Green, and Frerichs, *Judaisms and Their Messiahs*, 111–37. By contrast, although none of these roles is clearly specified and none can easily be attributed a messianic status, Collins argues for a Davidic messianic influence on 1QM, and suggests that the onus lies with those who would disagree to prove their case (Collins, *The Scepter and the Star*, 59).

[84] Stuckenbruck, "The Formation and Re-Formation," 128–29. See also 11QMelch; Rev 12.

[85] Philip R. Davies, "Qumran and Apocalyptic or *Obscurum per Obscurius*," *JNES* 49 (1990): 133. Connections elsewhere to the list of the just (Dan 12.1–2) and references to the Kittim evoke further traditions shared with Daniel (Stuckenbruck, "The Formation and Re-Formation," 129). Vermes also uses the reference to the Kittim as the "masters of the world" to date the text (Vermes, *The Complete Dead Sea Scrolls*, 163; similarly, see Davies's argument that use of Kittim to denote Rome confirms a later date for 1QM (and a different setting, he argues, for Pesher Habakkuk; Davies, "Daniel in the Lion's Den," 168–70)). Later versions of Daniel also come to associate the Kittim with Rome (Collins, *Daniel*, 7; see earlier discussion in Chapter 3). 1QpHab 3.11 also makes connections between the Kittim and an eagle (cf. 4 Ezra 11–12; Stone, *Fourth Ezra*, 350).

[86] See Chapter 2 above for notes on the nature of the collection at Qumran. Texts that have been labelled "sectarian" in past scholarship are not necessarily from the same community and many scrolls appear to have been brought to the site from elsewhere (as confirmed by the Cairo Geniza copy of CD). Collins's suggestion that it is "easy enough to arrive at a core group of sectarian texts" (Collins, *The Scepter and the Star*, 10) is perhaps no longer accepted so straightforwardly. This does not preclude considering beliefs potentially shared between various texts.

present time in relation to the events of the end.[87] The Habakkuk Pesher offers an important example.[88] In interpreting Habakkuk with insights attributed to the Teacher of Righteousness (1QpHab 7.1–4), the writer incorporates historical details of events from his or her own time, identifying these events as fulfilment of Habakkuk's prophecy.[89] Notably, the pesher allows for flexibility in calculating the end and suggests some adaptation of the expectation as the period from the death of the Teacher extended.[90] Thus, although the text is profoundly eschatologically orientated and presents the decisive action at the end of history as certain, the end remains in the future. The writer thereby explains how the end can have been delayed (7.9–10), and yet remain imminently anticipated.

John Collins's study of the phrase "the end of days" similarly underscores the eschatological consciousness of the Qumran texts' writers. In the most explicit case, 4QMMT declares, "this is the end of days" (4QMMT C21=4Q398 f11–13.4).[91] However, even here, Collins argues, the writer stops short of suggesting that the community lives in the final period of history. Although the phrase "end of days" may include the woes leading up to the final period of history, the writer does not suggest the Messiah has already come, and Collins points out that, despite some diversity and ambiguity among the Dead Sea Scrolls, they do not suggest that other positive elements of what is expected at the end have already begun.[92]

In the War Scroll, although the end-time events, including the eschatological war itself, have not begun, some hints of present circumstances suggest they are anticipated imminently. The War Scroll allows only minimal reconstruction of its historical setting, but the allusions to internal division and betrayal by the "vio-

---

**87** See Stuckenbruck, "Temporal Shifts," 124–49; Collins, *The Scepter and the Star*, 105–6; Davies, "Eschatology at Qumran," 39, 48.
**88** Collins notes that the varied purposes of the texts work against mixing their presentations of the end (Collins, *The Scepter and the Star*, 10).
**89** Stuckenbruck considers the use of perfect and imperfect verbs in Pesher Habakkuk, in an attempt to determine the extent to which the writer indicates the end has already arrived (Stuckenbruck, "Temporal Shifts," 124–49). See discussion of this phenomenon in relation to reinterpretations of Daniel's prophecies below §4.2.
**90** Collins, "Expectations of the End," 85. Davies makes a less convincing argument that the Teacher of Righteousness was "a *pre-Qumran* title for an eschatological figure" (Davies, "Eschatology at Qumran," 54).
**91** Collins, *The Scepter and the Star*, 106. 4QMMT indicates a time when the writer and their implied readers believed they were those who had been chosen in the seventh week of the *Apocalypse of Weeks* (VanderKam, "The Book of Enoch and the Qumran Scrolls," 266–67).
**92** On the presence of the messianic woes, Collins says "the language of the Scrolls is often ambiguous" (Collins, "Expectations of the End," 80, 82).

lators of the covenant" who are assisting the Kittim of Ashur (1.2), coupled with the list of surrounding nations (1.1),[93] indicate present circumstances the writer longs to have reversed. Similarly, although the words come in the context of the Priests and Levites' praise at the defeat of enemies later in the text, the affirmation that "for the sake of your [co]venant [you have remo]ved our misery in your goodness towards us" (18.8) also invites the reader to identify in the present with such misery, which will be removed. And the connection between the Kittim and Rome[94] identifies concrete and present enemies who, along with the supernatural counterparts of the empire of Belial, will be participants in the war. The sense of animosity and conflict suggests the war is expected imminently.

Finally, some Qumran texts attribute additional significance to the present moment in relation to the end. Here the present is not merely nearer to or further from the events of the end temporally, but people in the present seek to *emulate* the end. Thus, as patterns of piety will continue unimpeded through the "eternal seasons" (1QM 14.17)[95] after the decisive defeat of evil, practices in the present are also designed to mirror that end-time existence.[96] Correlations between the Rule of the Community and the Rule of the Congregation (1QS 2.22; 5.23–4; 6.2; 1QSa 2.5–7; cf. 1QM 2.10),[97] in which liturgical and community practice continues essentially identically in the period before and at the time of the end of days, with the exception of the presence of the Priestly and Davidic Messiahs, support the hypothesis that at least some of the writers of the Qumran texts and their community/communities[98] understood current practice as an anticipation of the end. Texts such as the Hodayot also provide some sense in which present liturgical practices enable participation in heavenly realities.[99]

Although all of the War Scroll's instructions relate to the time of the eschatological war, the strong focus on recounting faithful divine acts in the past may

---

[93] The list of nations itself comes from Genesis; the historical reality behind these references suggests a more general sense of other nations as opponents (Alexander, "The Evil Empire," 27).
[94] See n. 85 above.
[95] See Chapter 3.
[96] Knibb claims that scholarly characterisations of the Dead Sea Scrolls tend to overemphasise eschatological elements at the expense of the texts' focus on proper observance of Torah (Michael Knibb, "Apocalypticism and Messianism," in Lim and Collins, *The Oxford Handbook of the Dead Sea Scrolls*, 415), although frequently these come together.
[97] On the relationship between 1QSa and 1QM, see Schultz, *Conquering the World*, 327–65.
[98] See n. 86 above.
[99] This spatial dimension does not remove a temporal element, but these liturgical practices bridge the two realities in the interim. Jubilees, a text which appears to have been important at Qumran, also reflects a sense of concurrent, even combined, worship in heavenly and earthly spheres. See discussion in Moore, *Repetition in Hebrews*, 40–46.

indicate a similar emphasis on this practice in the present. The reviews of God's saving acts in the past invite the reader to reflect on God's sovereignty, as demonstrated in creation and powerful acts in the past, and the favourable status of Israel (13.7–10; 14.4–5, 8–10; cf. 17.6–9; 18.7–9). This not only indicates pious practices that will be followed when the enemy has been defeated, but implies a hymnic model to be emulated in the present. Such a practice might also serve to provide assurance of the promised final events, in keeping with the reminders of divine faithfulness in the past.

The historical reviews in **4 Ezra** and **2 Baruch** set out very detailed expectations for the pattern of events at the end of history though, as noted in Chapter 3, various episodes present these expectations in slightly different ways in each text, depending on the focus of particular pericopes.[100] Each text includes references to messianic woes (4 Ezra 5.1–12; 6.21–24; 2 Bar 26–28; 70.7), special insight (4 Ezra 6.20; 12.36–38; 13.53–56; 14.26, 45–47; 2 Bar 27.15; 48.3, 33), the revelation of the Messiah (4 Ezra 7.28; 12.32; 13.26, 52; 2 Bar 30.1),[101] judgement (4 Ezra 7.70; 9.18; 12.34; 13.58; 2 Bar 44.15), a messianic period (4 Ezra 7.29–31; cf. 2 Bar 29–30), resurrection (4 Ezra 7.32; 14.34–35; 2 Bar 30.1–2), and vindication for the righteous (4 Ezra 8.51–61; 2 Bar 15.2; 51.11–13; 54.15–16; 73.1–74.2). While some passages reflect a general interest in setting out the periods of history and answering metaphysical questions about, for instance, the eschatological status of those who die before the end (4 Ezra 7.26–44), others focus on the events which function as signs of the end and imminent divine action to defeat the current (final) worldly regime (4 Ezra 11–12; 13).

Indeed, in the quotation with which this chapter began, Uriel explicitly instructs Ezra how to attend to the events of history in such a way as to recognise the precursors to the end:

> Measure carefully in your mind, and when you see that some of the predicted signs have occurred, then you will know that it is the very time when the Most High is about to visit the world that he has made. (4 Ezra 9.1)

---

**100** This is particularly marked in the comparison between the metaphysical interests and account of the messianic period in 4 Ezra's third episode (6.35–9.25), and the focus in other episodes. See Stone's examination of "the end" in 4 Ezra (Stone, "Coherence and Inconsistency," 295–312), and my further discussion in Chapter 3 above.
**101** Stone considers it significant that 4 Ezra does not associate royal features with the Messiah (Stone, *Fourth Ezra*, 42).

Uriel's words explain how to read any *vaticinium ex eventu* and set the reader up for the later visions.[102] In the eagle vision in 4 Ezra's fifth episode, the eagle is explicitly identified as the penultimate regime in Daniel's vision (12.11; cf. 11.40). The political events described in metaphor through the various wings of the eagle and its heads (which reflect various Roman rulers, the heads being associated with the Flavian emperors),[103] invite readers to recognise their own historical time. The tumult of the last two small wings of the eagle (12.2–3) clarifies the timing of the historical present, which is also the time of greatest affliction, and looks to the imminent destruction of the eagle and installation of a just divine reign.

In 4 Ezra and 2 Baruch, the writers also make assertions about the timing of the present through their claims that only a privileged group will understand the significance of the times as they unfold. Given the revealed knowledge provided through the texts themselves, these apocalypses confirm that the communities to which the texts are addressed *are* this privileged group.[104] Thus, in keeping with the events set out in the *vaticinia ex eventu*, they claim the current time is the "now" in which the people will receive enlightenment and the events of the end will begin.[105] In 2 Baruch, the community's secret knowledge is also explained by claims such as, "those who live on the earth in those days will not understand that it is the end of times" (27.15), and people who continue living a peaceful life can do so because they do not realise that divine judgement

---

[102] On reading *vaticinia ex eventu*, see Chapter 4. The method of interpreting the past, identifying the present, and thereby also offering hope for the future functions similarly in Deuteronomy's "prediction" of the exile (Deut 30.1–5; see Chapter 5). See also discussion of Jesus' prophecy in Luke 21 (§5.3.1 below and Chapter 4).

[103] Bizzarro, "The 'Meaning of History,'" 34; Hogan, *Theologies in Conflict*, 199–200.

[104] The writer of 4 Ezra asserts that God revealed the *temporum finis* to Abraham (4.26) and it is in this company that Ezra is listed as a seer enabled by God to recognise the current times (Stone, *Fourth Ezra*, 100).

[105] The traditional method of identifying the date of such a prophecy lies in noting the increasing detail during the writer's present, and the point at which further predictions become less specific (VanderKam, *Enoch and the Growth*, 142). However, claims to special insight may be viewed as a further confirmation of the position of the historical present in the review. Likewise, in *Apocalypse of Weeks* (1 Enoch 93.10; 91.14), *Animal Apocalypse* (1 Enoch 90.9), Daniel 11.33, 4 Ezra 6.20, and 2 Baruch 28.1, the righteous receive enlightenment at a particular moment in the schema. Fourth Ezra also places Ezra within the tradition of being given secret knowledge to record in sealed books (4 Ezra 14.1–6, 44–48, cf. Dan 12.9).

"has come near" (48.33; cf. 48.3; 54.4–5; 4 Ezra 12.36–38; 13.53–56; 14.13, 20, 26, 45–48).[106]

Significantly, these writers appear to identify present experiences as part of the eschatological woes. In 2 Baruch, the Lord tells Baruch, "and the time will come of which I spoke to you and that time is appearing which brings affliction" (2 Bar 48.31; cf. 25.2–3); the woes are already starting to appear. Likewise in 4 Ezra, the decline portrayed merges into the calamities of the eschatological woes and the nadir of history, which is both the sign and catalyst of imminent divine action. Uriel promises Ezra before the eagle vision that he will see events to take place "in the last days" (4 Ezra 10.58–59; cf. 12.9), with which some elements of the vision are then identified, such as the death of the emperor represented by the third head of the eagle (12.28). Notably, the historical event corresponding to this imagery has already taken place before the time of writing.[107] Similarly, the lion identified as the Messiah speaks *before* the final tumultuous reign of the last two little wings, and already declares: "the Most High has looked at his times (*sua tempora*); now they have ended (*ecce finita sunt*), and his ages have reached completion (*saecula eius conpleta sunt*)" (11.44). The calamities caused by the eagle's reign, which are already recognisable in the historical present, constitute the messianic woes themselves.[108]

That the woes are already unfolding in both 4 Ezra and 2 Baruch underscores the imminence of the remaining events anticipated as part of the end, which each text also states outright. In 4 Ezra's first episode Uriel reveals, "the world is hastening quickly to its end" (4.26), and in the sixth episode, "the days are coming when the Most High will deliver those who are on the earth" (13.29). Uriel confirms that the end cannot be delayed (to allow further time for repentance), just as a birth cannot be delayed when the time of labour arrives (4.40), and the events that can already be identified show that the unstoppable process towards the end is in train. The final episode underscores the imminence of the end by outlining the proportion of time that has already passed in Ezra's (the character's) time, from which further calculations towards the end can be made (14.11–12, 18).

In 2 Baruch, the Lord expresses the acceleration towards the end:

---

**106** Here 2 Baruch extends the claim to the (few) intelligent ones keeping silent: then "there will not be found many wise men and there will also be not many intelligent ones, but, in addition, they who know will be silent more and more" (2 Bar 48.33).
**107** Stone, *Fourth Ezra*, 368 (though Stone also notes some distinction between historical accuracy and popular belief about the events themselves).
**108** Stone, *Fourth Ezra*, 251–52.

therefore, behold, the days will come and the times will hasten, more than the former, and the periods will hasten more than those which are gone, and the years will pass more quickly than the present ones. Therefore I now took away Zion to visit the world in its own time more speedily. (20.1–2; cf. v. 6; 23.7; 36.9)

And the letter to the nine-and-a-half tribes at the end of 2 Baruch[109] reintroduces the imagery from the earlier discussion about the futility of beginnings that do not lead to an end, such as starting out on a sea voyage.[110] Thus also here, the writer asserts:

> For the youth of this world has passed away, and the power of creation is already exhausted, and the coming of the times is very near and has passed by. And the pitcher is near the well, and the ship to the harbour, and the journey to the city, and life to its end. Further, prepare yourselves so that, when you sail and ascend from the ship, you may have rest and not be condemned when you have gone away. For behold, the Most High will cause all these things to come. There will not be an opportunity to repent anymore... (85.10–12; cf. 83.1–2, 4)[111]

Despite nostalgic features such as the return to manna from heaven during the messianic age (2 Bar 29.8), the schema of history in 2 Baruch remains linear, as discussed in Chapter 3. Some elements of the writer's description of idyllic life draw on earlier types, such as in the reference to manna. But the end itself is a transition to a renewed version of these earlier types. It is on the brink of this reality that the writer suggests the reader lives.[112] In the vision of the dark and bright waters, the end is the period of *brightest* water (74.2–4). Baruch relates his insight to the people, having observed the passing nature of present things, proclaiming: "for there is a time that does not pass away. And that period

---

[109] Henze highlights elements of the letter which draw out key features of 2 Baruch as a whole (rather than searching for a single theme in 2 Baruch): the focus on Torah and faithfulness, reflecting on the end as a source of hope in the present, Deuteronomistic theology, and the use of diverse intertextual imagery (Henze, "Torah and Eschatology," 201–4).
[110] See Chapter 3.
[111] Henze argues the Deuteronomistic themes parallel Baruch with Moses, though the eschatological urgency highlights differences in the leadership Baruch will be called to exercise (Henze, "Torah and Eschatology," 203).
[112] Henze helpfully clarifies that the writer of 2 Baruch is interested in the future "in order to spell out how such knowledge about the End Time has an immediate effect on the Mean Time, i.e., the time of the author and his original audience" (Henze, "Torah and Eschatology," 202). For an excellent discussion of the focus on the present in apocalypses, see Collins, "Temporality and Politics," 40–41.

is coming which will remain forever; and there is the new world which does not carry back to corruption those who enter into its beginning" (44.11).[113]

Thus each of 4 Ezra and 2 Baruch identifies the present time as already at the beginning of the events of the end of history. Enlightenment for a privileged elect aligns with the beginning of these last events, and the decline in the present is already a part of the eschatological woes. However, neither suggests that the Messiah has already acted (the lion in 4 Ezra's eagle vision provides commentary on the unfolding events, but does not act to destroy the eagle before the events associated with the historical present). Resurrection, judgement, and vindication of the righteous are still awaited. And, indeed, further exhortation to piety (notwithstanding, for instance, 2 Baruch's emphasis on determinism) remains in place; turning to right practice of the law is still possible in this period, though time is running short.

In sum, the writers of the Jewish key texts of this study each indicate some claims about the end of history. In 4 Ezra and 2 Baruch, the events are set out in considerable detail (even if some features vary between passages). The War Scroll similarly describes the events leading up to and including the end of history, identifying eschatological judgement with the events of the war itself and anticipating an ongoing cycle of periods at the end, during which the sons of light will continue in piety unimpeded. Josephus and the writer of 2 Maccabees provide less detailed accounts of the end, though Josephus affirms Daniel's vision of the destruction of the final worldly political regime and installation of an unending divine reign. In each case, the ways in which these writers interpret the significance of the present time, and their expectations about the end, suggest some shared understandings about how time is structured.[114] However, some important differences also arise regarding the consequences of how these writers portray the present in relation to the pattern of events of the end.

---

**113** Stuckenbruck refers to ways in which late Second Temple texts consider the end as in some sense a return to the beginning, in part while discussing the ways in which creation functions as assurance for the end (Stuckenbruck, "How Much Evil?", 167). While I agree that creation provides this assurance (in relation to both divine will and capacity to create and thus also to restore), I do not think that this creates a circular section ("loops back," p. 167) in the structure of history. For these writers, whatever similarities there are between earlier periods and the end of history, it is crucial that the final end is different—it has moved, in the words of 2 Baruch, from corruptibility into incorruptibility.

**114** Collins notes the sense of inevitably in Jewish texts as it is borne out through lived experience: "The conviction that 'Babylon will fall' has always been proved right, eventually, even if the fulfilment is sometimes deferred for hundreds of years" (Collins, "Temporality and Politics," 42).

## 4.2 Consequences of the dynamic relationship between the present and the end

Each of the Jewish key texts of this study therefore reflects a dynamic relationship between the present and the end of history (or, in the case of 2 Maccabees, a focus more on the dynamic created with the future). Although the writers situate the present time in different positions in relation to the pattern of events of the end, in all cases some further change in conditions is anticipated. Their interpretations of past events are also used to confirm the reliability of claims made about divine action in the future. The dynamic relationship between the present and the end ensures that understandings of the end of history shape present experience in ways that are starkly different from Virgil's portrait in the *Aeneid* discussed above, even though the writers of all of these texts portray history as teleological. Indeed, the ways in which expectations about the *future* shape experience in the present for the other non-Jewish Graeco-Roman writers discussed above may evoke more similar effects than in Virgil's static present, despite his teleological approach.

Given the focus on cycles of divine punishment and rescue within history in **2 Maccabees**, the sense of provisionality in the present time functions similarly to the way it does for Diodorus Siculus or Valerius Maximus. The possibility of future punishment, or rescue, ensures that the future provides a constant warning or source of consolation. This consciousness shines through even in the narrative style, as the narrator makes intrusions into the text such as, in relation to Heliodorus: "It is no light thing to show irreverence to the divine laws—a fact that later events will make clear" (4.17). Or the observation that Nicanor acts without realising "the judgment from the Almighty that was about to overtake him" (8.11; cf. 7.17). To the extent that the *end* of history affects experience in the present for the writer of 2 Maccabees, it acts as an explanation for the behaviour and possible success of opponents, and reassurance that this will be brought to an end (6.12–16). For readers experiencing further hardship, the exhortation to steadfast faith in the face of temptation to compromise, promise of post-mortem reward, and affirmation of divine sovereignty (2 Macc 6–7) may continue to offer consolation and encouragement. However, as the writer describes decisive divine action it is predominantly depicted in the arena of human history, demonstrated for instance when God turns from wrath to mercy and acts in the interests of God's people (8.5).

Josephus and the writers of the War Scroll, 4 Ezra, and 2 Baruch set up the dynamic between the present and the end of history in ways that are more similar to one another. Expectations about the end shape their interpretations of present experience, as they also reinterpret earlier prophecies to make sense in the present. For instance, each draws in significant ways on the visions in Daniel (1QM 1.2, 8; 17.6–7;[115] *Ant.* 10.205–210, 272–276; 4 Ezra 11–12; 2 Bar 35–40).[116] The writers reapply the earlier prophecy to their own settings. They continue to identify the present time with the penultimate empire of Daniel's five-kingdom paradigm, but reinterpret the empire's identity. Thus, what for Daniel initially described the Greek empire,[117] for each of 4 Ezra, 2 Baruch, and Josephus's *Antiquities* has become Rome. In 4 Ezra's eagle vision, the lion even acknowledges the adaptation, explaining: "the eagle that you saw coming up from the sea is the fourth kingdom that appeared in a vision to your brother Daniel. But it was not explained to him as I now explain to you or have explained it" (12.11–12). The revealed knowledge here has been updated, as also the prophecies in Dan 9 had updated Jeremiah (Dan 9.2, 24–27; cf. Jer 25.11–12).[118] In this way, the promises for the end can still be sustaining—even if there appears to be some delay. The structure of history remains the same and the end therefore still remains imminently expected.

While **Josephus** maintains a dynamic relationship between the present and the end, other elements elicit somewhat different effects, such as in the way his understanding of the end might shape his politics or interpretation of suffering in the present. Although Josephus's interpretation of Daniel places Rome's reign as the final empire before God's decisive action to end the succession of empires and install an eternal divine reign, his generally positive portrayal of Rome and emphasis on leaving all defence to God shapes the consequences of this view. For Josephus, flexibility in the present leaves the possibility of repentance open, but there is no sense of imminence to the end of Rome's reign. His understanding of the end ultimately affects the present by encouraging amicable rela-

---

115 Cf. Stuckenbruck, "The Formation and Re-Formation," 128–29.
116 Cf. *Animal Apocalypse*, which also includes a succession of four empires during the period from the exile until the eschatological war (Olson, *A New Reading*, 190). The use in the *Animal Apocalypse* is of particular interest because it is incorporated into the framework of an *Urzeit zu Endzeit* review, which largely follows a Deuteronomistic interpretation of history until the exile, and then the more deterministic framework associated with apocalypses from the time of these four highly-structured periods presented under the leadership of rogue (though predictably unjust) angelic shepherds. For the shepherds as angels, see Tiller, *A Commentary*, 51–52.
117 Collins, *Daniel*, 36, 312. Collins also notes that in the Old Greek version of Daniel the translation into a new context has already been made, with the Kittim persistently referred to as Romans (p. 7). For a fuller discussion of the various texts of Daniel and possible relationships between them, see Collins, *Daniel*, 3–11. On various reinterpretations of the paradigm in later Jewish texts, see Davies, "Daniel in the Lion's Den."
118 Bizzarro, "The 'Meaning of History,'" 35–37.

tionships with Rome in the interim, while passively awaiting the decisive action of the end in God's own time.

For the writers of the War Scroll, 4 Ezra, and 2 Baruch, the relationship between the present and the end remains similarly dynamic, given their expectations about future change. But the end affects the present in more urgent ways given its imminence and the implied portrait of difficult conditions in the present. Importantly, these writers draw on their interpretations of divine action in the past to provide assurance of the divine action promised in the future, as Stuckenbruck has highlighted is common in Jewish texts of this time.[119] Stuckenbruck argues that NT theology which makes eschatological claims about the certainty—indeed partial fulfilment—of God's decisive action at the end of history on the basis of past events reflects continuity with the kind of claims frequently made in late Second Temple texts about the certainty of the future on the basis of completed events in the past.[120] These observations helpfully illuminate similarities in the structure of writers' claims about the past and the future, and interpretations of experience in the present, which is taken up again in relation to Luke/Acts below. However, the uniqueness of certain eschatological events clarifies that these earlier events, though characteristic of divine action, are not the same as the decisive events described as part of the end.[121] This creates important distinctions between texts on the basis of where their writers place the present time in relation to the pattern of end-time events.

For instance, the **War Scroll** includes historical reviews of divine action in creation and covenant (1QM 10.11–16; 11.1–9; 14.4–18; 15.7–18), as well as claims about characteristic divine behaviour. In 1QM 11, the line "for the battle is yours!" is repeated several times in address to God (11.1, 2, 4), recounting archetypal vic-

---

[119] Stuckenbruck, "Overlapping Ages," 320–26; Stuckenbruck, "Posturing 'Apocalyptic,'" 240–56.
[120] Stuckenbruck, "Overlapping Ages," 320–26. Contra Davies, who argues for a stark difference between Jewish and Christian applications of the Danielic paradigm, though by his own admission with very little discussion of the Christian texts (Davies, "Daniel in the Lion's Den," 167, 177). Admittedly, Christian texts after Constantine do draw this tension more starkly and without the kind of provisionality that Stuckenbruck rightly notes is inherent in both Second Temple Jewish and NT texts (Stuckenbruck, "How Much Evil?", 168; see below).
[121] In an earlier article Stuckenbruck suggests that these earlier saving moments function similarly to the assurance provided in Pauline epistles by the death and resurrection of Jesus (Stuckenbruck, "Overlapping Ages," 320–26). Particularly in his most recent publication, Stuckenbruck recognises the unique elements of the claims made in NT texts (Stuckenbruck, "How Much Evil?", 167). I suggest that both the *similarities* in the structuring of history, and the *differences* in the kind of events NT writers claim have already taken place, are important in analysing these texts.

tories, such as that over Goliath and the Philistines, and Pharaoh. The passage affirms, "by the hand of our kings, besides, you saved us many times" (11.3), which is mirrored also in the affirmation "You have opened for us many times the gates of salvation" (18.7). Stuckenbruck rightly observes that these kinds of claims about the events of the past demonstrate writers' beliefs about the way in which time is structured, and this understanding of time undergirds their portrayals of hope for the future. In the War Scroll, these events of the past become the model for God's decisive (but notably still future) action: "You shall treat them like Pharaoh, like the officers of his chariots in the Red Sea" (11.9–10; cf. 11.13). In this context, the refrain "the battle is yours!" becomes not a temporal claim about the battle already having been completed, but an affirmation of God's character and sovereignty in *all* contexts—the battle, though still in the future, is indeed as good as won.

However, the future divine action anticipated in the War Scroll, though consistent with, and assured by, God's action in the past, remains unique. The utter and final destruction of the sons of darkness, comprising not only human opponents but all the lot of Belial, indeed the *empire* of Belial (14.9), ensures that the promised events are not merely further cycles of divine rescue (as in the battles in 2 Maccabees) but a unique transition in history.[122] As frequently noted, despite the parallels between life in the present, in the Rule of the Community, and the messianic age, in the Rule of the Congregation, discussed above, there is no evidence in the text that the writer believes the Messiah is already present in the life of the community. Similarly, I noted above that there is no hint in the War Scroll that key eschatological figures such as Michael have appeared in the community already. The present time falls earlier in the pattern of end-time events, and these decisive events are still awaited.

The writers of **4 Ezra** and **2 Baruch** also draw on their interpretations of the past in ways that affect experience in the present, but their expectations about the final events likewise still look towards a unique transition in history. In both texts, the writers provide consolation by overlaying the literary setting of the time following the destruction of the first temple in 586 BCE onto the historical setting of the second temple's destruction.[123] In 2 Baruch, a reminder about the fall of Nebuchadnezzar confirms that in this time also divine action will prevail (67.7–8). In 4 Ezra's fourth episode, the humiliation of Zion is laid out in terms recognisable to its readers. Grief and hope are aligned in this episode,

---

**122** See Chapter 3.
**123** Najman argues that by aligning the present with the first destruction, the writer performs a "bold reboot," which skips over the second temple and emphasises instead hope in the "renewal of scripture" (Najman, *Losing the Temple*, 67, cf. pp. 153–58).

in which Ezra offers his final lament,[124] and then encounters a mourning woman/Zion who is transformed into a glorious Zion. The episode calls to mind current experience in graphic terms:

> For you see how our sanctuary has been laid waste, our altar thrown down, our temple destroyed ... our holy things have been polluted, and the name by which we are called has been almost profaned ... our Levites have gone into exile ... our young men have been enslaved. (10.21–22)

While the creative tension between the literary and historical settings throughout 4 Ezra might imply some solace—the temple was rebuilt once, this too can happen again—in fact the writer takes a different direction. *Both* temples are juxtaposed with the transcendent Zion (10.25–38), which has not been produced through human effort and therefore cannot be destroyed in such a way either.[125] In Ezra's vision, this glorious city is in the process of being built (10.27, cf. v. 44), but it is also revealed (10.54). The promise here is at once spatial and temporal: the city which is disclosed to Ezra is portrayed as *real* (part of the proof here is said to lie in the vision taking place in a field which could not already contain other foundations built by humans, though the size of the glorious Zion's foundations is explicitly noted, 10.27, 51–54)—and yet it still remains promised. In this vision of the future, which is at the same time an insight into a transcendent reality, grief is transformed. Indeed, it is almost performative: in the promise itself, absolutely certain as it is, the grief is altered. Ezra seems to experience this assurance himself, as he shifts his focus from the orientation of the earlier dialogues to the remaining three visions.[126]

---

**124** Hermann Lichtenberger, "Zion and the Destruction of the Temple in 4 Ezra 9–10," in *Gemeinde ohne Tempel: Zur Substituierung und Transformation des Jerusalemer Tempels und seines Kults im alten Testament, antiken Judentum und frühen Christentum*, ed. Beate Ego et al. (Tübingen: Mohr, 1999), 245.
**125** See discussion in Bruce W. Longenecker, *2 Esdras*, Guides to the Apocrypha and Pseudepigrapha (Sheffield: Sheffield Academic, 1995), 68. Zion and the temple are aligned here: the barrenness of the woman, who is said to represent Zion, is identified as the three thousand years before offerings were made, prior to Solomon building the city and offerings commencing (10.45–46).
**126** This assurance is provided without undermining the extremity of current circumstances, which is attested throughout the seven episodes. This portrait of the future is central to the exhortation to view the present from the perspective of the future, which addresses Ezra's concerns also from the earlier dialogue (Barclay, *Paul and the Gift*, 287, 302).

As discussed above, for Stuckenbruck a key question that emerges from the structuring of time in late Second Temple Judaism lies in the extent to which these views provide the writers with resources to explain and deal with evil in the present.[127] I have suggested that, unlike Virgil's static portrayal of the present and the end, the dynamic possibilities of further change between the present and the end in these late Second Temple texts provide hope. Whereas in 2 Maccabees possible future changes in divine favour shape experience in the present, and for Josephus divine action at the end of history suggests readers should work for political stability in the present, for the writers of the War Scroll, 4 Ezra, and 2 Baruch, the end of history supplies hope in the present as readers are also exhorted to practise piety in the short time remaining. Luke likewise shares numerous similarities in his understanding of the structure of history, expectations of the end, and portrayal of a dynamic relationship between the present time and events of the end still anticipated. Nonetheless, in Luke/Acts the assurance for the future provided by the events of the recent past is amplified, because these events already constitute the decisive divine action of the end.

## 5 The present and the end of history in Luke/Acts

Set among the diverse views present in Luke's broader literary context, the similarities and differences of his perspective become clearer. After outlining references to events anticipated as part of the end of history in Luke/Acts, I extrapolate on evidence that Luke's text presents the final period—itself characterised by the continued unfolding of end-time events—as having already begun, and his related portrait of the present time, before turning to some of the consequences of his treatment of the present and end of history to conclude.

### 5.1 The events of the end in Luke/Acts

In his assumptions about the events of the end of history, Luke shares many of the features spelt out systematically in apocalypses with historical reviews like 4 Ezra and 2 Baruch, although common across many contemporaneous Jewish texts. The Lukan Jesus describes messianic woes, in both unique material (Luke 23.28–31) and that shared with Matthew and Mark (Luke 21.25–26; cf.

---

127 Stuckenbruck, "How Much Evil?", 143.

Matt 24.29; Mark 13.24–25).[128] Expectation of a Messiah is present throughout,[129] not only when the narrative explicitly identifies Jesus as the Messiah (Luke 2.11, 29–30; 4.41; 9.20; 24.26, 46; Acts 2.36; 3.18, 20; 5.42; 8.5; 9.22; 17.3; 18.5, 28; 26.23; cf. Luke 1.69), but also as an expectation which Luke paints various characters holding independently of experience with Jesus and the apostles (Luke 2.26; 3.15; 22.67; Acts 2.31). This also serves his rhetorical purpose of claiming belief in Jesus to be consistent with Jewish heritage (cf. Luke 24.26–27; Acts 2.31; 26.22–23).[130]

Luke refers to the resurrection of the dead, sometimes as an event anticipated for all and leading to judgement (Acts 24.15),[131] at other times as an event only for the righteous (Luke 20.27–38; cf. Luke 10.20; 21.19).[132] As in Mark and Matthew, the Lukan Jesus refers to a future day of judgement, over which he will preside (Luke 22.30; cf. Matt 19.28–29; Luke 21.34–36; cf. Matt 24.43–51; 25.13; Mark 13.33–37;[133] Acts 10.42; 17.31). The timing of this judgement will be unexpected, and is associated with the return of the Son of Man (Luke 12.35–40; Acts 1.7, 11). The judgement may represent a fearful prospect to the unprepared, but to the righteous it is a promise of vindication (Luke 21.28). Hospitality (Luke 10.25–37; 14.14),[134] renouncing weath (Luke 16.19–31; 18.18–27), following Jesus (Luke 18.28–30), and enduring persecution (Luke 21.19; Acts 14.22) lead to post-mortem reward.[135] This reflects also an implicit extension of Luke's emphasis on reversal.[136]

---

**128** Wolter rightly argues that, whatever other differences in eschatology interpreters claim to find in Luke/Acts, Luke expects the same end-time events as other NT writers (Wolter, "Eschatology," 93).
**129** Many texts included in this study refer to a divine agent with a key role within the unfolding of the divine plan for history, though messianic expectations in Jewish texts of this period are notoriously uncertain (Collins, "Messianism in the Maccabean Period," 97–109).
**130** See discussion below in relation to Acts 26.22–23.
**131** Cf. Luke 11.31 (Matt 12.38–42; Mark 8.11–12), which presents the striking eschatological scene in relation to the sign of Jonah, in which resurrection relates to judgement.
**132** Note that in 20.27–38 the Lukan Jesus may still mean that all are resurrected, then judged, and only the righteous enter into the new age.
**133** See Maddox's redaction-critical comparisons (Maddox, *The Purpose*, 111–23).
**134** Byrne, *The Hospitality of God*, 123, cf. pp. 4–5. See other instances of Luke's accounts of banquet scenes with eschatological and judgement overtones: Luke 5.27–32; 7.36–50; 11.37–52; 14.7–24 (Crabbe, "A Sinner and a Pharisee," 250–51; Arthur A. Just Jr., *The Ongoing Feast: Table Fellowship and Eschatology at Emmaus* (Collegeville: Liturgical Press, 1993), 139).
**135** Cunningham, "Through Many Tribulations," 14.
**136** Tannehill, "Israel in Luke-Acts"; Mihamm Kim-Rauchholz, *Umkehr bei Lukas: Zu Wesen und Bedeutung der Metanoia in der Theologie des dritten Evangelisten* (Neukirchen-Vluyn: Neukirchener, 2008), 79–165; John O. York, *The Last Shall Be First: The Rhetoric of Reversal in Luke,*

In these various ways, Luke's narrative indicates expectations of events which cohere with those evident in other contemporaneous texts. There are of course important differences across the texts discussed, particularly in relation to messianic expectation and individual eschatology. But Luke's expectations fit within the pattern of eschatological claims seen across the texts. Indeed, Luke/Acts shares notable common themes: eschatological woes and judgement (with related vindication) are common across the War Scroll, 4 Ezra, and 2 Baruch. Resurrection, whether of all or of only the righteous, features in 2 Maccabees, 4 Ezra, and 2 Baruch, while all of the teleological texts of this study, including the *Aeneid*, describe ongoing life under a final reign.[137]

## 5.2 The placement of the present in Luke's schema of history

Importantly, as for other texts that draw on teleological understandings of history, the placement of the present time within Luke's schema of history shapes his account. As noted, of the texts discussed above, only the *Aeneid* situates the present time at the end, although 4 Ezra and 2 Baruch appear to equate present experience with the eschatological woes on the cusp of the events of the end. Moreover, although many texts point to saving moments in the past as assurance of God's action at the end of history (eg. 1QM, *Jewish War*, 4 Ezra, and 2 Baruch),[138] and some even display such intense orientation towards the future that current practices are modelled on the end, in all cases key events such as the appearance of the Messiah or resurrection remain in the future.[139] However, in Luke/

---

JSNTSup 46 (Sheffield: JSOT Press, 1991); Emmrich, *At the Heart of Luke*. As reversal relates to Jesus' suffering and Luke's understanding of salvation, see Eben Scheffler, *Suffering in Luke's Gospel*, ATANT 81 (Zürich: TVZ, 1993), 152, 158. See also Chapter 5 above.

**137** On the War Scroll's expectations of Israel's ongoing existence, and individuals' "long life," see p. 287 n. 79 and Chapter 3.

**138** This common technique is seen across Second Temple texts and evident in the rewritten Bible tradition. See Mermelstein on post-exilic writers retelling history from creation, rather than the establishment of covenant with YHWH, in the face of crises that might be interpreted as signs of the end of the covenant (Mermelstein, *Creation, Covenant*, 1–3).

**139** So also Rajak, "Jewish Millenarian Expectations," 165. Kim rightly notes the complexity of messianic belief in Second Temple Judaism, with diverse views coexisting, including views about a "second coming" of God in the manner of the description of God walking the earth in Gen 2 (Kim, *Die Parusie bei Lukas*, 139–40). It should be noted, though, that it is not clear whether 2 Maccabees anticipates individual resurrection for the pious martyrs in a heavenly location immediately following their death, though this would also not seem to indicate the type of end-time resurrection anticipated in 2 Macc 12.43–45.

Acts, the kind of events that have already taken place suggest that, for Luke, God's decisive action in inaugurating the final period of history is no longer anticipated, but already in the past, demonstrated through the resurrection, descent of the Spirit, and placement of Jesus.

### 5.2.1 Resurrection as the turning point and confirmation of Jesus as Messiah

In Acts, Jesus' resurrection confirms the transition to the new era. In ten speeches or shorter statements, his resurrection forms the key content of the apostles' witness (Acts 1.22; 2.24, 29–32; 3.15; 5.29–32; 10.39–41; 13.26–37; 17.30–31; 23.6;[140] 24.15–21; 26.6–8, 23).[141] This belief causes the greatest controversy, and is revealed as the radical element of the apostles' proclamation.

Paul's speech to Agrippa in Acts 26 confirms the radical nature of claims regarding Jesus' resurrection. The question is not *whether* God raises the dead, but the significance of claims that in Jesus *God has already done so*. Here Luke's Paul claims to draw upon existing beliefs about resurrection, highlighting that it is strange that people who understand, or even participate in, relevant Jewish traditions should hold these beliefs and yet find it "incredible (ἄπιστον) ... that God raises the dead" (Acts 26.8). As the speech progresses, recounting his own story of conversion and call, Paul asserts: "So I stand here, testifying to both small and great, saying nothing but what the prophets and Moses said would take place: that the Messiah would suffer,[142] and that, by being the first to rise from the dead, he would proclaim light both to our people and to the Gentiles" (vv. 22–23).

These verses contain the key to Paul's speech here and support the significance of testimony regarding the resurrection across Acts. Here Luke approaches the kind of "first fruits" theology found in the Pauline epistles, in which Jesus is the first to be raised from the dead as part of a new era of resurrection (cf. 1 Cor. 15.12–24; 2 Cor. 4.14).[143] The verse presents some difficulties for transla-

---

[140] In this pericope, part of the function of the references to resurrection is likely polemical and strategic; Paul may be presented as raising questions of resurrection in order to arouse sectarian disagreement deliberately.

[141] See also Acts 17.3, 18, 32, and 25.19, in which the centrality of resurrection to the apostles' witness is confirmed by other characters or the narrator.

[142] This is the NRSV, with a change only to the English verb (from the adjective παθητός) from "must suffer" to "would suffer;" see discussion below.

[143] Haenchen cautions against importing material from Pauline literature (Haenchen, *The Acts of the Apostles*, 687); however it may well be illuminating on this point. Also contra Drury, who expounds, with clear if unstated influence from Conzelmann: in Luke "there is a levelling down of Paul's doctrine of the unique interruption, a muffling of the crash of the descent of the Re-

tion.¹⁴⁴ By rendering the phrase as "that the Christ/Messiah must suffer," the ESV and NRSV unhelpfully obscure the Greek behind what looks like a translation of one of Luke's δεῖ clauses.¹⁴⁵ However, the translation comes instead from the combined use of εἰ with παθητός, here translated as "must suffer,"¹⁴⁶ but tied to the sense of "being capable of or subject to suffering."¹⁴⁷ The emphasis in its context lies not on questions of necessity regarding Jesus' suffering,¹⁴⁸ but the claim that all of this was prophetically foretold about the Messiah. Regardless of the accuracy of the Lukan Paul's use of Jewish tradition at this point, the recipient of his rhetoric is placed in the position of having to affirm that Moses and the prophets point to such a resurrection, with the immediate consequence that

---

deemer causing a radical discontinuity in the conditions of life. Instead we have a Jesus who is a link in time's chain, himself the ligature of old and new, the middle of time. History is no longer, as in Paul, the anvil on which God hammers out salvation at white heat, but the medium in which he is known in its rhythm of prophecy and fulfillment. Eschatology is subtly affected. It remains but is very deliberately 'not yet.' Jesus is not the end but its prophet" (Drury, *Tradition and Design*, 9). By contrast, Ellis suggests it is appropriate to consider Lukan and Pauline theology as they illuminate each other, and rightly argues that even Paul includes elements of salvation history (Ellis, *The Gospel of Luke*, 49).

**144** The Greek reads: οὐδὲν ἐκτὸς λέγων ὧν τε οἱ προφῆται ἐλάλησαν μελλόντων γίνεσθαι καὶ Μωϋσῆς, εἰ παθητὸς ὁ χριστός, εἰ πρῶτος ἐξ ἀναστάσεως νεκρῶν φῶς μέλλει καταγγέλλειν τῷ τε λαῷ καὶ τοῖς ἔθνεσιν (Acts 26.22b–23). The two somewhat confusing uses of εἰ are best translated as indirect interrogatives indicating questions about *what* Moses and the prophets have said (so Pervo, *Acts*, 624). They may also be translated, as Johnson does, with the sense of a conditional introducing, as a topic for debate, not whether Jesus has been raised but whether Moses and the prophets point to this: "I say nothing other than the things the prophets as well as Moses said were going to happen, whether (εἰ) the Messiah would suffer, whether (εἰ) as first from the resurrection of the dead he would proclaim light both to the people and to the Gentiles" (26.22b–23; translation by Johnson, *The Acts of the Apostles*, 431, 442; so also Zerwick, *A Grammatical Analysis*, 446).

**145** See extended discussion of Luke's use of δεῖ in Chapter 4, where I provide evidence that Luke does not use the term simply to indicate "divine necessity." Importantly, δεῖ and the divine βουλή are not equivalent in Luke's understanding.

**146** The term, a verbal adjective (not verb as in the ESV and NRSV translations), has the sense of being subject to suffering (BDAG, 748), or "capable of suffering" (BDF 65.3). Johnson emphasises that this is not another use of a δεῖ clause (Johnson, *The Acts of the Apostles*, 438). Indeed, given that Luke frequently uses δεῖ elsewhere, caution should be exercised in importing the same meaning into another construction. Unhelpfully, Witherington introduces δεῖ into the Greek, and then footnotes the correct term (Ben Witherington III, *The Acts of the Apostles: A Socio-Rhetorical Commentary* (Grand Rapids: Eerdmans, 1998), 748).

**147** Bruce notes this is a *hapax legomenon* in the NT, though a term taken up later by Ignatius and Justin (Bruce, *The Book of Acts*, 390).

**148** Conzelmann, *Acts of the Apostles*, 171 n. 2, and Haenchen, *The Acts of the Apostles*, 687, focus on this sense of the necessity of suffering.

Jesus must be viewed as the Messiah and thus the sign of a new era in history (cf. also Luke 16.31; 20.37–38; Acts 3.21b–25).¹⁴⁹

This fits with the kind of scandal caused by the testimony. The immediate interruption of Festus, who questions Paul's sanity, highlights the significance of Paul's statement. Here Festus fulfils the role of a naïve character who acts as an ironic foil, unaware of the true significance of the kind of claims at work.¹⁵⁰ To Festus claiming someone has returned from the dead is insane, but he is oblivious to the expectations about the pattern of end-time events that underlie it. Agrippa understands Paul's proclamation better. He sees immediately that accepting the testimony that Jesus is the first to be raised from the dead would have significant consequences, necessarily leading to following him, and thus "quickly persuading [Agrippa] to become a Christian" (v. 28).¹⁵¹ Luke's Paul draws on these traditions about resurrection but his conclusions are different; the other Jewish texts discussed anticipate resurrection, as noted above, but they do not claim that this has ever taken place.¹⁵²

Speeches in Acts also draw connections between the proclamation of Jesus' resurrection and his identity as Messiah. Again, identifying an individual with the Messiah demonstrates a clear difference from texts like 4 Ezra or 2 Baruch, where the Messiah remains imminently expected and is not identified with any historical individual. Moreover, despite the significance attributed to the Teacher of Righteousness in texts such as the Damascus Document and Pesher Habakkuk, even these texts do not approach claims similar to the NT affirmation of Jesus as Messiah.¹⁵³ In Peter's speech in Acts 2.17–36, Psalm 16 is cited as sup-

---

**149** Those who argue that Acts does not contain imminent eschatological expectation (e.g. Adams, *The Stars Will Fall*, 179 n. 222; Pervo, *Acts*, 25) overlook the interrelation of these ideas about resurrection, "first fruits," and the final judgement (cf. Acts 10.42; 17.31; 26.22–23). In their overview of reception history of Acts, Hornik and Parsons outline the role of this passage in Robinson's argument for the earliest christology revolving around Jesus becoming the Messiah at the parousia (Hornik and Parsons, *The Acts of the Apostles*, 68–69).
**150** See Chapter 4 on a similar irony in the incident involving Gamaliel in Acts 5.
**151** See Barrett on the question of whether this is to be taken as serious or ironic—that is, lightly "playing the Christian" or being made a Christian with little effort (C. K. Barrett, *The Acts of the Apostles: A Shorter Commentary* (London: T&T Clark, 2002), 392–93). Given Paul takes the comment seriously in his response I suggest that is the more likely reading, even if Agrippa's response is also incredulous. Contra Bruce, Agrippa's statement is not likely a sign of his embarrassment for having religious discussions in front of Festus (Bruce, *The Book of Acts*, 471).
**152** Cullmann uses similar observations to claim a "radical difference" between Jewish and Christian understandings of time (Cullmann, *Christ and Time*, 83).
**153** Understanding the status of the Teacher of Righteousness is important, though exact attributions are difficult to uncover. Despite Davies's claims discussed above (Davies, "Eschatology

port for resurrection without corruption being a sign of the Messiah (vv. 25–28, 31, 36) with connections also to Psalm 110 and sitting at God's right until enemies are made a footstool (vv. 34–35).[154] Peter concludes his speech by asserting that in raising Jesus God has proven Jesus is both Lord and Messiah (v. 36; cf. Acts 5.42). Furthermore, Jesus' resurrection is intrinsically connected to the completion of these end-time events. Paul tells the Athenians that the fact of Jesus' resurrection simultaneously provides the confidence (πίστις) that God has set a date for judgement (Acts 17.31).[155]

Thus, Jesus' resurrection plays a central role in signalling the position of the historical present in Luke's schema of history.[156] In his resurrection, Jesus is confirmed as the Messiah and divinely appointed judge, roles associated with the end of history. At the same time, the decisive action of God in raising him confirms the entry into a new and ultimate period of history.

### 5.2.2 The presence of the Spirit

Luke interprets the drama of Pentecost with words from Joel (Acts 2.17–21; cf. Joel 2.28–32). He evokes a picture of inspired prophecy, renewal of the old and vision of the young.[157] In itself, particularly in the context of the dramatic Pentecost account, it could give the sense of a new eschatological period. But, perhaps in order to be completely clear, Luke adds the time reference "in the last days" to the LXX quotation (Acts 2.17; cf. Joel 2.28–32; LXX 3.1–5).[158] Both the LXX

---

at Qumran," 54), Qumran texts do not seem to identify him with the Messiah and thus claims about the Teacher differ in this crucial way from the NT's claims about Jesus.

**154** Cf. also Luke 20.41–44, which makes these connections between Ps 110, messianic status, and sitting at the right of God, ready for application to Jesus in Acts 2.34–35.

**155** See Chapter 3 for my argument for interpreting the καιροί established by God in Acts 17.26 as historical periods and not annual seasons. On Acts 17.31 and Luke's expectation of an imminent end, see below (§5.3.1).

**156** Following Conzelmann, several Lukan scholars debated the placement of transition in Luke's historical schema, but their focus was a transition postulated between the time of Jesus and the church, not the end, particularly in relation to verses such as Luke 16.16. See Chapters 1 and 3.

**157** For further discussion of NT reception of Joel, see John Strazicich, *Joel's Use of Scripture and Scripture's Use of Joel: Appropriation and Resignification in Second Temple Judaism and Early Christianity*, BibInt 82 (Leiden: Brill, 2007), 371–75.

**158** Barrett argues that the descent of the Spirit and the phrase "in the last days" here confirm a separate time of the church, indicated also by the ascension, with obvious connections to Conzelmann's salvation-historical periods (Barrett, *The Acts of the Apostles: A Shorter*, li–lii; cf. Conzelmann, *Theology of St Luke*). By contrast, Witherington argues that these events indicate the beginning of the eschatological age, though elsewhere he argues for an anti-eschatological out-

and MT begin this passage with less precise time references to "after" events just described.¹⁵⁹ Luke's addition underscores the eschatological significance of the event and its position in his schema of history; the activity unfolding before the hearers was prophesied to take place in the ultimate period of history.

### 5.2.3 The position of the exalted Jesus

Jesus' position at the right of God also functions to confirm the new eschatological era. In a convincing study of Luke 22.66–71 and Acts 7.54–60, Martin Bauspieß notes the significance of Jesus' response to interrogation in the trial scene of Luke 22, namely the announcement that "from now on (ἀπὸ τοῦ νῦν) the Son of Man shall be seated at the right hand of the power of God" (Luke 22.69).¹⁶⁰ Importantly, Luke's wording differs from that in Mark 14.62.¹⁶¹ Luke has added the ἀπὸ τοῦ νῦν, thus describing a reality which is in place if not "from now" at the point of the trial, certainly from the time of the ascension. Bauspieß argues that Luke has deliberately drawn connections between this trial scene and Stephen's vision at the point of his martyrdom in order to present Jesus' placement at God's right as a hidden reality already in place throughout Acts¹⁶² (cf. Acts 2.33).

---

look of Acts (Witherington, *The Acts of the Apostles*, 140, cf. 111). Holladay names a longstanding tradition of associating the passage from Joel with the end of history and then suggests that Luke's redaction must be taken to associate the events of this episode with the end of history, even if as a "proleptic fulfilment" of the prophecy; Holladay notes various ways in which the events recounted in Acts 2 mirror those prophesied in Joel 2, in order not simply to tell, but to show the reader that this is so (Holladay, *Acts*, 101–2).

**159** καὶ ἔσται μετὰ ταῦτα (LXX); והיה אחרי־כן (MT).

**160** Martin Bauspieß, "Die Gegenwart des Heils und das Ende der Zeit: Überlegungen zur lukanischen Eschatologie im Anschluss an Lk 22,66–71 und Apg 7,54–60," in *Eschatologie—Eschatology: The Sixth Durham-Tübingen Research Symposium: Eschatology in Old Testament, Ancient Judaism and Early Christianity (Tübingen, September, 2009)*, ed. Hans-Joachim Eckstein, Christof Landmesser, and Hermann Lichtenberger (Tübingen: Mohr Siebeck, 2011), 125–48. See also Maddox's affirmation of the centrality of this passage for Lukan eschatology and christology (Maddox, *The Purpose*, 108). Although Flender generally associates the ascension with the new era (see n. 167 below), he also notes other passages, such as Jesus' claim that he saw Satan fall from heaven in Luke 10.18, and argues "the imperfect ἐθεώρουν leaves no doubt that the victory has already been won" (Flender, *St Luke*, 103).

**161** The text is also different from Matt 26.64, but Matthew communicates a similar sense, through ἀπ' ἄρτι (see the comparison in Bauspieß, "Die Gegenwart des Heils," 130). Luke also does not include the future time reference "you will see (ὄψεσθε)," which is found in both Mark and Matthew.

**162** Bauspieß, "Die Gegenwart des Heils," 139. Nielsen argues that the certainty of the parousia is related to the ascension and the enthronement of Jesus which has already taken place, and helpfully highlights the explicit connection between the ascension and parousia in Acts 1.11 (An-

Importantly, insight into this reality is not available to all characters. Stephen can only describe the vision to others who are present but cannot see it.[163] And upon hearing his report, the characters are also unable truly to hear the significance of his testimony (even covering their ears! v. 57), and then carry on the stoning. But the two spatial realities—the world seen by all the characters and the world of the exalted Christ—have been revealed to Stephen and to any readers with ears to hear.

Although Luke presents Jesus' exaltation as a transcendent reality that is already in place, it is also a reality which provides further assurance of the final events that will yet bring suffering to an end. Matthew Sleeman is right when, countering scholars who only attend to the historical review in Stephen's speech, he highlights the spatial elements confirmed in the vision with which it ends.[164] But this spatial reality is the basis for hope in a further temporal transition also. In some ways like Ezra's vision of the glorious Zion, Stephen sees the truth of this transcendent reality. And yet, while in 4 Ezra the unveiling of Zion is imminently anticipated and hope in this tangibly affects experience in the present, in Acts Jesus' exaltation has already placed him in a position of ultimate authority at God's right. The final events—including the resurrection of Jesus as the first to be raised from the dead (26.22–23), which also constitutes proof that the final judgement has been set (17.31)—have already begun.[165]

## 5.3 The character of life in the present according to Luke

Despite these signs that the ultimate period of history has begun, the promise of the return of the Son of Man, the call to repentance, and recognition of current experiences of suffering ensure that the fraught question of Luke's expectations of a final culmination to history remains in play. With the resurrection in the past, the present time is neither beyond the culmination of all things, nor simply

---

ders E. Nielsen, "The Purpose of the Lucan Writings with Particular Reference to Eschatology," in *Luke-Acts: Scandinavian Perspectives*, ed. Petri Luomanen (Göttingen: Vandenhoeck & Ruprecht, 1991), 83).
**163** Bauspieß, "Die Gegenwart des Heils," 141.
**164** Matthew Sleeman, *Geography and the Ascension Narrative in Acts*, SNTSMS 146 (New York: Cambridge University Press, 2009), 172–73.
**165** Ironically, Stephen's death, and the persecution it begins, prompts the dispersal of believers which leads to further proclamation of the Gospel (8.1). This is a kind of irony at work throughout Luke/Acts. Even those attempts to oppose the divine plan are diverted into its service (Acts 2.22–23). See Chapter 4 above.

another period akin to those of the past.¹⁶⁶ Instead, the present is characterised by the ongoing unfolding of end-time events. That readers should anticipate their continued unfolding up to and including the return of the Son of Man confirms an expectation of imminent eschatological expectation, while the call to repentance points to the further changes still possible in this dynamic present time before the final judgement takes place.

### 5.3.1 The return of the Son of Man

Luke 22.69 and Acts 7.56, as well as the accounts of the ascension (Luke 24.50 – 53; Acts 1.6 – 10), confirm that Jesus is already placed at God's right, but the promise of his return acknowledges that the situation is not ultimately resolved. At the conclusion of the Acts account of the ascension, the men in white robes declare that Jesus will come again in the same manner as his departure (Acts 1.11), while the Lukan Jesus himself points to a future coming of the Son of Man on clouds (Luke 21.27), in apparent contrast to his description of an ongoing reality of the Son of Man seated at God's right "from now" in Luke 22.69.

It could be that Luke understands these two realities as coexisting indefinitely, with some mediation between the two spaces to be performed by the Son of Man and/or the Spirit.¹⁶⁷ However, this seems unlikely given Acts 3.21, in which Jesus' place at the right of God is described as a reality that must endure "until

---

**166** This not only counters Conzelmann's hypothesis that Luke inserted an extended period of the church before the distant end (Conzelmann, *Theology of St Luke*, 135), but also contrasts with the views of others who identify a separate historical period of soteriological value after Jesus, such as Wright's understanding of salvation history, with the church the next "act" in the "play" following the time of Israel (Wright, "How Can the Bible Be Authoritative?", 19), or the approach of those who see the culmination of history in Luke/Acts as actively held off until the universal mission has been completed (Smith, "History and Eschatology in Luke-Acts," 881–901; cf. Tannehill, *Narrative Unity*, 1:258 – 61).

**167** This spatial solution is offered, for instance, by Flender, *St Luke*, 98, 100 – 1, 106. Though, given he still sees the parousia as a future event, he argues that the ascension represents the end of OT history and the fulfilment of the eschatological era in a heavenly realm, which must still be brought to completion on earth (p. 106). Bockmuehl identifies in Luke's narrative a dialectical tension between Jesus' absence from the discipleship community following his ascension in Acts, and his presence in some form through his name and the Spirit (Markus N. A. Bockmuehl, "The Gospels on the Presence of Jesus," in *The Oxford Handbook of Christology*, ed. Francesca Aran Murphy (Oxford: Oxford University Press, 2015), 95 – 97). Although Jesus remains in the authoritative position to the right of God throughout the narrative of Acts, any sense of absence seems to underscore the importance of the promised restoration of his presence (cf. Acts 3.21).

the time" of universal restoration.[168] Thus, the promised time of judgement (Acts 17.30–31, cf. 10.42), and coming of the Son of Man, is best understood as a final point in history which draws the separation of these realities to a close.

At four points in Luke/Acts, characters either explicitly or implicitly raise questions about "when" eschatological events still anticipated will take place: Luke 17.20; 19.11; 21.7; Acts 1.6.[169] Although not all of these questions are centred on the return of the Son of Man, the passages in which these questions appear have each in their own way played a part in the contentious debates about the imminence or otherwise of Luke's understanding of the parousia.[170] The following addresses each in turn, in addition to a further statement by Paul about the final judgement, in Acts 17.31.

## Luke 17.20–18.8

Luke 17.20a begins a new scene,[171] introducing a question from Pharisees about the timing of the coming of the kingdom of God. After Jesus' initial response to

---

[168] Sleeman's study of geography and the ascension, through which he develops the idea of "third-space," valuably emphasises the ways in which Jesus' placement following the ascension both affects life in the present *and* remains a time-limited reality until the time of restoration promised in Acts 3.21 (Sleeman, *Geography and the Ascension*, 108–9).
[169] Conzelmann notes these questions as part of structuring his response on Lukan eschatology (Conzelmann, *Theology of St Luke*, 121). Carroll argues this is a typically Lukan strategy, to introduce material with a question like this, noting the three Lukan examples of questions which prompt discussions of "eschatological teaching" (they are all about timing), and the fourth example shared with Mark (Luke 21.7) (see Carroll, *Response to the End*, 77).
[170] Wolter suggests that questions about Luke's expectations about the timing of the Son of Man's return, though once fraught, are now "settled" (Wolter, "Eschatology," 103), with the understanding that Luke emphasises "the proper conduct of life for the Christians," given an attitude of uncertainty about the parousia (involving implicit delay but some small possibility that it *might* be sooner; p. 105).
[171] The previous episode describes Jesus' interactions with ten people with leprosy (Luke 17.11–19). Wolter discusses vv. 20–21 as part of the previous scene, though as a separate two-verse unit, stressing the change of audience for the two verses (Wolter, *Gospel according to Luke*, 2:300). However, the series of repeated terms, such as "Look!", "here," "there," in vv. 21 (ἰδοὺ ὧδε ἤ ἐκεῖ) and 23 (ἰδοὺ ἐκεῖ, ἰδοὺ ὧδε), confirm that the passages should be considered together, as a pairing where an interaction with an external group (the Pharisees) leads into further instruction to the disciples on a related theme. So also Conzelmann, though he draws from the connections in themes across these verses a quite different conclusion (Conzelmann, *Theology of St Luke*, 123). Moreover, Carroll notes an "inversion-arrangement" structure in the audience across this section, 17.20–21 (to Pharisees), 17.22–37 (to the disciples), 18.1–8 (to the disciples), 18.9–14 (by implication, to the Pharisees; see Carroll, *Response to the End*, 72). This

the Pharisees (vv. 20b–21), he takes the themes further with instructions to the disciples on the days and day of the Son of Man (vv. 22–37)[172] and a parable, also addressed to the disciples, about a widow and an unjust judge (18.1–8).[173]

Jesus' response to the Pharisees' question is to refute their method of looking to the future, indeed they fail already to notice the signs of the kingdom in their midst. He answers them, "The kingdom of God is not coming with things that can be observed (μετὰ παρατηρήσεως); nor will they say, 'Look, here it is!' or 'There it is!' For, in fact, the kingdom of God is among you (ἐντὸς ὑμῶν)" (vv. 20b–21). Two *hapax legomena* have somewhat complicated debates about interpretation. The observable signs (from παρατήρησις) are described with the language of medical observation or, John Carroll suggests, the language of divination, with potential allusions to hostile observation in the related verb παρατηρέω.[174] Whether to be taken as a rational, empirical kind of observation, or astrological, the Pharisees cannot discover the timing of God's final activity

---

likewise holds the section discussed here together with the parable that follows, and shows how, alongside the shared themes, a change of audience can in fact hold a passage together.

**172** On the days and day of the Son of Man, see also Chapter 3, §4.1.3. Although I appreciate Carroll's distinction between plural and singular times, so that, for instance, the last "days" describes a period that leads up to the last "day" (Carroll, *Response to the End*, 143), Luke's language is not consistent enough to support this as a general pattern. Such a reading does not account for the longing for "just one of the days of the Son of Man" described here, which is better understood as longing for just part of the end-time existence (which Carroll also recognises, p. 93 n. 211).

**173** There are numerous thematic connections also in the passages which follow. The parable of the Pharisee and the tax collector is addressed to "some who trusted in themselves that they were righteous and regarded others with contempt" (18.9)—the kind of language Luke frequently uses to describe Pharisees, which is also borne out by the content of the parable; this connects back to the earlier question from the Pharisees at 17.20–21. But related themes continue in the subsequent passages too, including the example of those who will enter the kingdom of God, children (in 18.15–17), and the rich ruler's struggle with the demands of inheriting eternal life (18.18–27), in turn connected to Jesus' response to Peter and the disciples following (18.28–30), which also comes back to a statement about the suffering prophesied for the Son of Man and prediction of his death and resurrection (18:31–34). Given the change in audience at 18.9, however, I have chosen to deal with 17.20–18.8 as one unit, while recognising the numerous connections that continue beyond 18.8.

**174** Carroll, *Response to the End*, 77. Although the noun is a *hapax legomenon* in the NT, Carroll notes that the related verb, παρατηρέω, appears in Luke 6.7, 14.1, 20.20, and Acts 9.24, where the kind of watching involved is hostile. BDAG lists more domestic and technical uses, including for divination of the future, and in medicine for the observation of symptoms. *TDNT* concludes that the type of observation Jesus rejects here is a "rational-empirical observation and fixing of signs and symptoms" (*TDNT* 8:150, cf. pp. 148–51). Nolland also relates the term to medical observation (Nolland, *Luke*, 2:852).

through such means. However, in a strange irony, it seems, as they ask about the *future* coming they overlook the signs of the kingdom already in their midst (the sense of the other *hapax legomenon*, ἐντός, v. 21),[175] which are to be found in the effects of Jesus' ministry (cf. 7.18–35; 11.20).[176]

Rather than viewing 20b–21 as evidence of either realised eschatology or delayed parousia, the connections to the following verses show this is part of the same larger conversation. To the disciples, Jesus gives more information about the future events anticipated: the Son of Man will have his future day, but they shouldn't rush off elsewhere responding to others' claims about its arrival (expressed in similar phrasing to v. 21), because it will be unmistakable—as clear as lightning that lights up the whole night sky (cf. Matt 24.23–27).[177]

The following verse (v. 24) then takes a temporal step backwards from the day of the Son of Man, to predict the suffering and rejection of the Son of Man—still to come in the narrative, but in the past for all of Luke's readers.[178] Jesus then immediately returns to describing the harsh realities of the coming judgement, with two analogous examples of severe judgement from the past: the destruction by the flood (vv. 26–27)[179] and the rains of fire and sulphur that destroyed Sodom (vv. 28–29). The effects of the revelation of the day of the Son of Man will also be severe, people will be separated through a final judgement (vv. 31–35), and those left for dead will be subject to the gathering

---

**175** There is no justification in the context for taking the other *hapax legomenon*, ἐντός, to indicate that the kingdom of God is within individuals; Luke does not present the kingdom in such individualistic, spiritualised terms (as also noted by Conzelmann, *Theology of St Luke*, 122, 124–25). The term should rather be read as "among you (plural)" (see BDAG; so also Carroll, *Response to the End*, 79). By contrast, see Nolland, who identifies four possible interpretations and favours Bultmann's view that the term here refers to "a sudden and unheralded arrival of the kingdom of God" (Nolland, *Luke*, 2:853–54). Conzelmann argues that it is only the preaching of the kingdom, not the kingdom itself, which is a present reality, arguing on the basis of Luke 19.11 that Luke's understanding of the kingdom is necessarily future (Conzelmann, *Theology of St Luke*, 122–23).
**176** Carroll helpfully suggests, "In the light of v. 20b, the implied continuation of the saying is: "(Look! The kingdom of God is among you) *and you do not observe it*" (Carroll, *Response to the End*, 80, emphasis original). Bovon translates, "For, in fact, the kingdom of God is in the space that belongs to you" (Bovon, *Luke: Commentary*, 2:515–17).
**177** See discussion in Carroll, *Response to the End*, 89.
**178** Similar steps backwards in time are given in the prophecy of Luke 21.5–36, as discussed below.
**179** This first analogy is also used in the same context in Matt 24.37–39. It is interesting that the flood appears as an analogy for final judgement, but it is not without precedent; the *Apocalypse of Weeks* (1 Enoch 93.4) and the *Animal Apocalypse* (1 Enoch 89.1–9) likewise present this flood as an earlier precursor to a final, definitive judgement and restoration.

vultures (v. 37). As in Matthew's version, which also suits Luke's characteristic themes, the Lukan Jesus describes the people in the days of Noah carrying on with the distractions of everyday life when they were overtaken by judgement (v. 27; cf. Matt 24.37–39); Luke adds the parallel phrase about the days of Lot (v. 28). The effect is to underscore the importance of remaining alert (cf. 12.35–48). The claim that no one should hesitate on that day, looking back, or going indoors to gather up possessions (vv. 31–32), furthers the sense of warning.

The following parable continues the themes of timing, questioning whether there will be delay and affirming speedy justice.[180] Although the introductory verse is often taken as evidence that Luke's primary concern is continued delay of the parousia ("Then Jesus told them a parable about their need to pray always and not to lose heart," 18.1),[181] the *a fortiori* reasoning of the parable stresses the promise of a much swifter response from God than from the unmotivated, self-interested judge. At the conclusion of the parable, Jesus asks: "And will not God grant justice to his chosen ones who cry to him day and night? Will he delay long in helping them? I tell you, he will quickly grant justice to them. And yet"—the more pressing concern that immediately arises in light of the anticipated rapid justice—"when the Son of Man comes, will he find faith on earth?" (vv. 7–8). In a move familiar from the recalibration of timing to affirm that divine action remains imminent in Daniel's reinterpretation or Jeremiah, or 4 Ezra's reinterpretation of Daniel, whatever delay has already elapsed, Luke's reader should continue to anticipate a swift response. Coming straight after the verses about the harsh realities of the coming judgement (17.30–37), the need for constant prayer is both a source of solace ("and not lose heart") and a caution about remaining among those who will be found faithful when the Son of Man comes (18.8).[182]

---

[180] The textual development of this passage has been much debated, though given the parable only appears in Luke conclusions are not possible (or necessarily helpful, given the need to deal with the text as it appears in its manuscripts). Claims to distinguish between material that is "Lukan" or not can simply reflect initial presuppositions, for instance Bovon, "Apocalyptic Traditions in the Lukan Special Material," 51–58; cf. p. 13 n. 51 above. See the detailed discussion of reconstructions in Bovon, *Luke: Commentary*, 2:529–32; Fitzmyer, *The Gospel according to Luke*, 2:1176–78.

[181] Fitzmyer, *The Gospel according to Luke*, 2:1177; Conzelmann, *Theology of St Luke*, 112, 123.

[182] Exhortations to constant prayer in biblical texts that are not presumed to have moved away from an imminent eschatological expectation, such as in Rom 12.12 or 1 Thess 5.17, are not read as a sign of delayed eschatology. That the parable suggests imminent justice despite any delay that has already elapsed is also argued by Carroll, *Response to the End*, 95–96; Green, *Gospel according to Luke*, 637.

Interpretations of this passage inspired by Conzelmann's theory tend to dismiss eschatology in 17.21, with the future expectation reduced to the far distance through a presumed focus on delay in the parable of Luke 18.1–8.[183] However, the elements of the kingdom that the text suggests may be discerned in the present are not portrayed in opposition to the further events anticipated. Rather they are part of the same eschatological process already breaking in through Jesus' ministry, leading to the suffering and death of the Son of Man, and the final events—death to those who seek to make their lives secure, but life to those who lose their lives (17.33)—which will bring the swift justice for "the chosen ones," for whose sake he will not delay long (18.7–8).

### Luke 19.11–27

Jesus tells the composite parable of the throne claimant and the pounds in 19.12–27[184] as a response to an implicit question about eschatological timing (v. 11).[185] Because verse 11 states that "they supposed that the kingdom of God was to appear immediately (παραχρῆμα μέλλει ἡ βασιλεία τοῦ θεοῦ ἀναφαίνεσθαι)," and that Jesus tells the parable because of this (mistaken) expectation, the verse is frequently cited as evidence of Luke's preoccupation with the theme of the delayed parousia.[186] However, Michael Wolter rightly argues that the dampening down of expectations of an immediate inauguration

---

[183] See, for instance, Fitzmyer, *The Gospel according to Luke*, 2:1177.
[184] The multiple themes within this parable, in addition to its mixed relationship to other synoptic texts (especially Matt 25.14–30, but also Mark 13.33–37), have prompted diverse opinions on its origins and stages of development. For those committed to a two- (or four-) source theory of synoptic relationships, it has prompted further complex hypotheses about which form would be plausible in Q and which of Matthew or Luke would be the more likely to have made significant changes (see, for example, discussion in Fitzmyer, *The Gospel according to Luke*, 2:1228–32 —the argument that each of M and L had a version of the parable (see p. 2:1230) is even more convoluted). It is clear that there is something unusual in the parable's formulation. This is evident particularly in the similarity between the Matthean version and a section of Luke's version, as well as the move from ten servants being entrusted with an investment in the master's absence, to only three then being called to account. But these difficulties need not dominate the interpretation of the issues considered here.
[185] This parable forms one scene since Jesus' arrival in Jericho at 19.1, and his interactions with Zacchaeus. Following the parable, in verse 28 Luke states that Jesus continues his journey towards Jerusalem.
[186] See, for instance, Fitzmyer, *The Gospel according to Luke*, 2:1232; Conzelmann, *Theology of St Luke*, 113, 121.

of the kingdom of God is not related here to the setting of Luke's audience, but the situation for the characters in the unfolding narrative.[187]

Elements of the story both directly before and after this parable make this plain. Indeed, verse 11 already makes explicit links in both directions. The verse begins "As they were listening to this, he went on to tell a parable," tying the parable back into the story of Zacchaeus.[188] At the same time, the travel narrative is reaching its culmination, having built expectation about Jerusalem since 9.51.[189] Indeed, according to verse 11, Jesus tells the parable *"because he was near Jerusalem, and* because they supposed that the kingdom of God was to appear immediately."[190] The importance of the nearness to Jerusalem is confirmed as it is repeated in the verse following the parable (v. 28). Both the declaration to Zacchaeus ("today, salvation has come to this house," 19.9),[191] and the rising expectations about Jesus' arrival at Jerusalem have characters expecting the final inauguration of divine reign once Jesus gets there.[192] As in passion predictions which correct inappropriate expectations about the nature of Jesus' messiahship by foretelling his suffering and death,[193] the parable functions to explain the further steps still to take place before the culmination of the kingdom.[194]

---

[187] Wolter, *Gospel according to Luke*, 2:353.

[188] Green, *Gospel according to Luke*, 674–75.

[189] Jesus telling this parable is the last episode before the triumphal entry and brings the travel narrative to a close.

[190] Emphasis added.

[191] These are the words which verse 11 implies the crowd are listening to, as Jesus decides to tell them a parable, and Green rightly notes they raise these questions of timing for those present (Green, *Gospel according to Luke*, 674–75).

[192] Although Wolter is correct to note that the kingdom of God and the return of the Son of Man are not the same thing, the sense in which the kingdom of God is used here is in relation to a final and full inauguration of divine reign (admittedly different from some other uses in Luke, such as Luke 11.20 or 17.21, discussed above; see Wolter, *Gospel according to Luke*, 2:300). In the words of Joel Green, the kingdom of God in 19.11 "refers to the end-time scenario" (Green, *The Gospel of Luke*, 678). In this sense, the end-time inauguration of the kingdom of God and the return of the Son of Man both describe final eschatological events in Luke's expectation. Wolter likewise also cites examples of Second Temple Jewish texts which describe expectation of some kind of theophany at the time of the inauguration of the kingdom of God, which also indicates an end-time expectation (Wolter, *Gospel according to Luke*, 2:354).

[193] Notably, the passion predictions also seek to correct expectations about what will happen once Jesus arrives in Jerusalem, as recently in 18.31–34.

[194] After a helpful critique of Johnson's interpretation of the parable as related not to eschatological matters but to Jesus' entry into Jerusalem, Carroll concludes: "Luke 19.11–27 both interprets the decisive turn in the story which the arrival of Jerusalem represents, and clarifies the

Multiple hints in the parable, including the introductory verse to direct interpretation, favour an allegorical reading which presents Jesus as the throne claimant, who is rejected and entrusts servants to manage things in his absence, then travels to have his authority confirmed in an enthronement elsewhere, and returns to pass judgement on the efforts of his servants and on those who had originally rejected his authority as king.[195] The parable therefore certainly describes some delay, but the additional steps outlined to counter the characters' assumptions describe the time from Jesus' arrival in Jerusalem until the time of his ascension (the enthronement, in the terms of the parable). From the perspective of the reader, the only step therefore remaining is his return and the associated judgement, and there is no sense in the parable that this should involve further delay now that these other events have been fulfilled.[196] Rather, the parable's focus lies in characteristic concern about the consequences of being found faithful or not at that time,[197] and the vindication through judgement upon those who have rejected Jesus.[198]

---

relation of the Jerusalem narrative to the end-time" (Carroll, *Response to the End*, 103, cf. 100–3; Carroll's critique is also taken up by Green, *Gospel according to Luke*, 675 n. 220).

**195** Understandable discomfort about the characterisation of the throne claimant in the parable, and his severe, uncompromising attitude arises for many interpreters as they consider the limits of allegorical reading (see, for instance, Green, *Gospel according to Luke*, 675–6). Some find connections to real-life examples in Josephus, which correlate with the details of the case (see Wolter, *Gospel according to Luke*, 2:354). It may be that the severity belongs more to the world of the parable than the theological claims drawn from it, though elsewhere Luke also describes dire consequences of failing to align oneself with the priorities of the kingdom before it is too late (e. g. Luke 16.19–31; see Chapter 5; the focus is on exhorting urgent change *before* then.

**196** Green suggests the passage does not imply a long time but stresses the importance of readiness (Green, *Gospel according to Luke*, 675, esp. n. 218).

**197** Hays rightly argues that Luke 17.20–37 and 19.11–27 contain teaching about how to live until the time of the return of the Son of Man (Hays, *Luke's Wealth Ethics*, 164–65). But this does not require a long intervening time; indeed, the severity of the consequences at that time rather stress a sense of urgency.

**198** There is also no reason to associate this judgement explicitly with judgement upon Israel or the inhabitants of Jerusalem, or to see the parable as a description of the destruction of Jerusalem as punishment (so Wolter, *Gospel according to Luke*, 2:361; contra Fitzmyer, *The Gospel according to Luke*, 2:1238; Maddox, *The Purpose*, 47). As elsewhere, the tension is between those who oppose the activity of Jesus and those who accept it, frequently insiders and outsiders (rather than Jewish and gentile characters), as the previous episode involving Zacchaeus and disdainful Pharisees demonstrates.

## Luke 21.5–36

In Luke 21.5–36[199] Jesus likewise prophesies about events that are to take place in the time beyond the literary present of his ministry. As in the *vaticinia ex eventu* discussed above, Luke's original readers know that some of these events have taken place by their own time, while others still await fulfilment. Although this pericope has featured in the studies of those who argue Luke has separated history from eschatology, reading the passage with an awareness of the other models discussed above, I suggest, clarifies the import of this passage.[200] Luke's approach and the structuring of history which he employs here shows striking similarities to that discussed above in texts like 4 Ezra and 2 Baruch, and for a similar purpose.

The passage opens with Jesus prophesying the destruction of the temple (vv. 5–6), eliciting the question which then prompts Jesus' longer speech: "Teacher, when will this be, and what will be the sign (σημεῖον) that this is about (μέλλῃ) to take place?" (v. 7; cf. 4 Ezra 8.63).[201] It is significant that the speech in verses 8–36 is a response to this question about *how to read the times* in light of prophecy. The speech can then be set out as:

vv. 8–9       Jesus warns about false prophets,[202] before turning to his own prophecies:

---

[199] Cf. Mark 13.5–31; Matt 24.1–35.

[200] This is a key text in interpretation since the mid-twentieth century. Debate has been particularly fraught over which events Luke associates with the literary present of Jesus' prophecy, his own historical present, and events still to be fulfilled in the future. Whether to view the destruction of Jerusalem as part of the events of the end has also been contentious. Conzelmann says explicitly at the beginning of his treatment of Luke 21, from verse 7: "Mark's saying has the sense of eschatological fulfilment, but Luke is concerned in what follows with events which do not belong to the Eschaton" (Conzelmann, *Theology of St Luke*, 126). Indeed, he argues that in this speech, presented as prophecy in Jesus' words, Luke provides "a polemical excursus about matters which are mistakenly included among the eschatological events," namely the destruction of Jerusalem and the temple (p. 128). For a similar view see Fitzmyer, *The Gospel according to Luke*, 2:1327; and contrasting views by Mattill, *Luke and the Last Things* and Knight, *Luke's Gospel*, 188–89 (responding to Conzelmann). Bovon seeks to address the problems through source criticism (Bovon, *Luke: Commentary*, 3:106–9). Ongoing concern about these interpretative issues is evident, for instance, in Jeffrey's discomfort with N. T. Wright's interpretation (Jeffrey, *Luke*, 243–51). Maddox argues, "it is not true, for example, as has often been alleged, that in Luke 21.20–24 and 25–27 the evangelist drives a wedge between the fall of Jerusalem and the earthly and cosmic catastrophes leading up to the coming of the Son of Man on a cloud," although Maddox goes on to claim, "but *theologically* speaking the destruction of Jerusalem *is* part of the last judgement" (Maddox, *The Purpose*, 146 n. 34, emphasis original).

[201] On μέλλω, see below.

[202] Cf. Luke 17.23.

| vv. 10–11 | Tumult, violence, and portents (most likely associated with the Jewish war). |
| vv. 12–19 | Predicted persecution, explicitly positioned "before all this" (v. 12; cf. 17.25), thus beginning prior to Jerusalem's destruction. |
| vv. 20–24 | Jerusalem surrounded and its inhabitants to flee—*beginning* with an instruction about recognising this time of destruction (v. 20). |
| vv. 25–28 | Further signs (employing traditional eschatological language), the return of the Son of Man, and the nearness of redemption—*ending* with a further instruction about recognising this time (v. 28). |
| vv. 29–36 | Further exhortation about recognising the time, including the analogy of the fig tree (vv. 29–33). |

After warning about false prophets, Jesus then offers an initial prophecy of tumult, violence, and portents, before going back "before all this" to foretell persecution,[203] followed by Jerusalem's destruction, and then further signs in eschatological language.[204] The beginning of verses 22–24 on Jerusalem's destruction and the ending of verses 25–28 on eschatological signs provide instruction on recognising the times (cf. 12.54–56), which is also the theme of the further exhortation of verses 29–36, including the analogy of attending to the fig tree to recognise the imminent arrival of summer.

The time reference to "before all this" has caused more difficulty than necessary, and led to complicated source-critical theories such as that Luke here drew on freestanding eschatological sayings and put them together into a random collection.[205] However, as Vittorio Fusco observes in his detailed study of the structural issues in the passage, including the shift to an earlier time reference in verse 12, when assumptions that Luke has redacted the passage to distance the parousia are set aside, the continuity of events leading into eschatological events is clearly recognisable.[206] Similarly, that the end will not come immediately (ἀλλ' οὐκ εὐθέως τὸ τέλος, v. 9)[207] is an observation embedded in

---

[203] Fusco discusses the structural issues of the passage, including this shift to an earlier time reference, in detail (Fusco, "Problems of Structure," 84).
[204] The "signs and portents" appear to escalate across these verses (Nolland, *Luke*, 3:1006), though "that day" (v. 34) will still come suddenly (Adams, *The Stars Will Fall*, 177 n. 218).
[205] Bovon, *Luke: Commentary*, 3:106–9.
[206] Fusco, "Problems of Structure," 91–92.
[207] Jervell connects the unknown timing of the end with claims that Luke "obviously thought that he was living in the last days, although the end was not yet" (Jervell, *The Unknown Paul*, 25). Fitzmyer argues that "the end" in view in 21.9 is the end of Jerusalem, as the focus in the first half of the prophecy, quite separate from the focus on the parousia in the second half (Fitzmyer, *The Gospel according to Luke*, 2:1327), but this overlooks the explicit way in which Luke takes the reader back to an earlier time in verse 12.

the *vaticinium ex eventu*, explaining the further incidents which will unfold (and largely have unfolded) before the last events foretold.[208]

Whether or not Luke's text indicates that the persecution in verses 12–19 continues into his readers' present time, it is clear that the persecution at least begins earlier, being identified with occurrences that predate the fall of Jerusalem and connect to the stories in Acts.[209] Here Luke has added the comments at verses 10–11 (cf. Mark 13.8).[210] For Conzelmann, Luke's attention to Jerusalem here confirms his shift to identifying divine action in the events of history, severed from those of the end time.[211] On the contrary: by setting out events of the past in a sequence which leads to the events of the end, Luke instead brings into focus the connections between these events. Real historical incidents actually support eschatological expectation in such prophecies. As in the *vaticinia ex eventu* discussed above, being able to identify the events of their own experience in the historical review enables readers to confirm their own position within the unfolding events and thus the imminence of the end.

This is in keeping with the question which prompted the prophecy and the exhortation to which it leads. Jesus returns to the question about the signs and how to read them at several points (vv. 20, 28), including in the closing parable (vv. 29–33) and the exhortation to vigilance (vv. 34–36). By attending to the signs in this unfolding series of events, Luke's readers recognise that they live among the circumstances of verses 20–24. But there is no indication of a long

---

**208** In contrast to claims that Luke's redaction here reflects a delayed parousia, note that Mark and Matthew include "for the end is not yet" (Mark 13.7; Matt 24.6; see Bauspieß, "Die Gegenwart des Heils," 130). Thus, Luke's amendment does not *remove* eschatological interest, but rather reflects this possibility of an ultimate period which has already begun but not yet come to completion, perhaps also made clearer by an appreciation for Luke's periodisation of history.

**209** Maddox, *The Purpose*, 116. France argues that the prophecy in Luke 21 refers only to the timing of the destruction of Jerusalem until "at least" verse 33, and possibly even beyond (R. T. France, *Luke* (Grand Rapids: Baker, 2013), 332–36). By contrast, Ringe argues, "The destruction of Jerusalem, ten to twenty years before Luke's Gospel was written, serves as a second sign (21.9–10). Many understood the horror of those days to be God's final condemnation of the people, and as already participating in the events of the final judgement. Luke's reading is different. The fall of the city (sketched in vivid images in 21.20–24a) is a sign only that those events of the end-time lie ahead" (Sharon Ringe, *Luke* (Louisville: Westminster John Knox, 1995), 252).

**210** Maddox, *The Purpose*, 115. See also Adams's redaction-critical comparison (Adams, *The Stars Will Fall*, 172–79).

**211** Conzelmann, *Theology of St Luke*, 95–136. Again, this also does not require that the destruction itself is divine punishment, contra Maddox, *The Purpose*, 146 n. 34.

gap before the next events,[212] just as in 4 Ezra and 2 Baruch the emphasis lies on the imminence of what is due to unfold next in the schema. Indeed, Jesus establishes the analogy between recognising summer's arrival by the fig tree's leaves, and "so also, when you see these things taking place, you know that the kingdom of God is near" (v. 31). He then asserts the time's imminence: "Truly I tell you, this generation will not pass away until all things have taken place" (v. 32).[213] Having exhorted vigilance and "prophesied" events of the recent past, Jesus' speech concludes by asserting the nearness of the time of redemption (v. 28).

**Acts 1.3 – 11**

The final passage involving a temporal question that frequently features in discussion of the imminence or otherwise of Luke's eschatological expectation relates to the disciples' query of the resurrected Jesus in Acts 1.6: "Lord, is this the time when you will restore the kingdom to Israel?" Again the question specifies the kingdom rather than the return of the Son of Man (although the topic of Jesus' return also features in the broader passage, at v. 11).[214] The question comes after Jesus' description of the baptism by the Holy Spirit to take place "not many days from now" (v. 5); a claim which appears to prompt the disciples' assump-

---

212 Contra Adams, who suggests Luke has inserted the time of the gentiles between the fall of Jerusalem and the end-time events as an indefinite interim period (Adams, *The Stars Will Fall*, 176).
213 Conzelmann attempts to get around problems raised by this text by saying that "this generation" refers to "humanity in general" (Conzelmann, *Theology of St Luke*, 131). Maddox argues of the prophecy in Luke 21: "However awkward it may be for the theories now widely accepted about Luke's eschatology, Luke 21.32 can only mean that the generation of Jesus' contemporaries will not completely die out before 'all things happen'" (Maddox, *The Purpose*, 115). Similarly, he suggests that the use of the synoptic saying in Luke 9.27, "But truly I tell you, there are some standing here who will not taste death before they see the kingdom of God" together with the saying of the previous verse, "Those who are ashamed of me and of my words, of them the Son of Man will be ashamed when he comes in his glory and the glory of the Father and of the holy angels" is best explained as indicating an assumption that some early disciples would still be alive at the time of the parousia (pp. 109 – 10). He notes also the similar phrasing in relation to the fulfilment of the earlier prophecy to Simeon in Luke 2.26 – 32 (p. 109).
214 The reference to the kingdom in verse 6 does not include τοῦ θεοῦ, though the earlier reference back in verse 3 clarifies that this is the same theme, though it is the focus on Israel in the disciples' expectations that is shifted in Jesus' response, as discussed further below. See n. 222 below.

tion that this may constitute the time of the restoration of the kingdom (to Israel).²¹⁵ Jesus responds, as discussed in detail in Chapter 3:

> It is not for you to know the times or periods (χρόνους ἢ καιρούς) that the Father has set by his own authority. But you will receive power when the Holy Spirit has come upon you; and you will be my witnesses in Jerusalem, in all Judea and Samaria, and to the ends of the earth. (vv. 7–8)

Noting that Jesus does not directly answer the disciples' question, Conzelmann and many who have followed his lead have taken this as evidence that Luke wanted to redirect attention away from the (delayed) parousia and onto the time of the church.²¹⁶ Alongside this, many have interpreted the geographical references in verse 8 as "something like a table of contents" for Acts,²¹⁷ as the mission progresses from Jerusalem to Rome. (However, Robert Tannehill demon-

---

**215** The narration ties Jesus' statement to the disciples' question, with the "therefore" of the following verse: "Οἱ μὲν οὖν συνελθόντες ἠρώτων..." (v. 6). Thus the disciples may be equating the promise Jesus is speaking about (which will unfold at Pentecost) with the "restoration of the kingdom to Israel" (v. 6). Holladay reads this as the disciples misunderstanding "Jesus' vision of God's reign" (Holladay, *Acts*, 73–74). For Gaventa, the disciples' question is "rejected" by Jesus (as their wondering will also be "rejected" by the two messengers in v. 11), but it is rejected because of its temporal concerns, not because of its focus on Israel. She points out that the restoration of Israel also features in Zechariah's canticle in Luke 1.32–33 (Gaventa, *Acts*, 65), so these expectations are not simply overturned in Luke/Acts (p. 62). However, I suggest below that a contrast between the disciples' emphasis on Israel, and Jesus' description of proclamation to the end of the earth, does suggest a shift in focus.

**216** Conzelmann, *Acts of the Apostles*, 6; Haenchen, *The Acts of the Apostles*, 143; Keener, *Acts*, 1:686–87. Although Barrett approaches the text with the assumption that Luke's account reflects an attempt to respond to the parousia's delay, after observing that Acts 1.7 could reflect this overarching dilemma for Luke, he argues it seems more related to the Spirit's and the apostles' witness, which follows in the next verse (Barrett, *Acts*, 1:78).

Fitzmyer interprets this episode in light of his overall affirmation of Conzelmann's salvation-historical schema, but with minor amendments: "The question about 'the time' makes it clear that Luke thinks of a period now beginning, the Period of the Church under Stress, as different from the Period of Jesus, the period of his earthly ministry. This is why the three-phase division of Lucan salvation history advocated by Conzelmann has to be maintained, even if it must be slightly modified" (Fitzmyer, *The Acts of the Apostles*, 201). Fitzmyer goes on to argue that Acts 1.6 supports placing the division between salvation-historical periods and the beginning of the period of the church at the time of the ascension.

**217** Gaventa, *Acts*, 65; cf. Fitzmyer, *Acts*, 201. See also Farrell, "The Eschatological Perspective," 266–79. Gaventa's numerous options for which stories in Acts would describe the "end of the earth," spanning from Acts 8 to 28 or beyond the end of the narrative (pp. 65–66), undermine her suggestion that the series of locations in verse 8 frame a table of contents for "the entire book of Acts" (p. 65).

strates that the geographical signposts do not really map onto the Acts story as it unfolds, and E. Earle Ellis rightly shows that designating Rome as "the end of the earth" is inappropriate).[218] Placing the emphasis elsewhere, others have suggested that the passage focuses on Jesus correcting the political elements of the disciples' expectations about restoration *to Israel*.[219]

Nonetheless, despite the element of political critique in Jesus' response, the mention of "times or periods (χρόνους ἢ καιρούς)" confirms that the primary concern is temporal. But he still does not seem to answer their question. He also does not give a direct answer to the "when" question, for example, in Luke 21.5–36. But there his answer nevertheless focuses on how to discern the time in light of events, and in the process supplies sufficient information for his reader to be assured, given the events that still remain, that they live on the cusp of the Son of Man's return.

Acts 1.7–8 does not provide any framework for discerning the timing of either the inauguration of the kingdom (v. 6)[220] or the return of the Son of Man (v. 11). Indeed, it reasserts the idea of *not* knowing when God has set such dates, as found in the parables of crisis and in statements about the need for vigilance in the Gospel (cf. Luke 12.35–48).[221] Instead, it communicates an assumption that history is comprised of a succession of periods (as discussed in Chapter 3) and the importance of what will take place in Jerusalem in Acts 2 (confirmed also by the emphasis in vv. 4–5), while declaring that the proclama-

---

[218] Even those who would claim that Acts portrays the geographical progress of the mission across all the world, represented by the poles of Rome and Jerusalem, as a necessity which must be fulfilled before the inauguration of the kingdom of God, cannot use this in support of a theory of continued delay of the parousia (see Smith, "History and Eschatology in Luke-Acts," 881–901; cf. Tannehill, *Narrative Unity*, 1:258–61). By the end of Acts, the gospel has been proclaimed in Rome. What might appear delay to the characters in Acts 1 is, for the reader beyond the events of Acts 28, already in the past.

[219] On expectations about the restoration of Israel, see Keener, *Acts*, 1:687–88; Maddox, *The Purpose*, 106–8. Holladay rightly sees the Acts account describing "an alternative vision of the future" (Holladay, *Acts*, 74), though this is not simply a Spirit-filled church, but an eschatological vision of a kingdom for all. See also n. 222 below.

[220] The proximity to the ascension, which takes place in the following verse, confirms that the restoration of the kingdom to Israel and the ascension should not be equated (v. 9, cf. v. 2). Likewise the events of Pentecost cannot represent the kingdom's restoration, given the specific time reference for Pentecost in verse 5 and the statement "it is not for you to know" in verse 7. The Pentecost event is also not to be equated with Jesus' return, contra Holladay, *Acts*, 76.

[221] Rius-Camps and Read-Heimerdinger suggest that Acts 1.7 reflects the same idea as Mark 13.32, about not knowing the hour, and that Luke has deliberately held the saying over for this passage (Rius-Camps and Read-Heimerdinger, *The Message of Acts*, 1:74–75).

tion the apostles will make is of universal significance.²²² Thus, some eschatological interest still flavours the episode. While using language also found in Daniel for the succession of empires, and in 1 Thessalonians about the Day of the Lord,²²³ it directs attention to an event which will, as discussed above, be identified as the fulfillment of events which Luke says were prophesied for "the last days" (Acts 2.17). Without answering their question about the restoration of the kingdom to Israel, Jesus has nonetheless illuminated one further part of the pattern of end-time events unfolding in their midst.

**Acts 17.30–31**

One further passage in Acts, though not prompted by a question about the eschatological schedule, illuminates Luke's understanding of the timing of Jesus' return. Paul concludes his speech in Athens by asserting that God "has fixed a day on which he will have (ἐν ᾗ μέλλει) the world judged (κρίνειν) in righteousness." As noted above, it is the resurrection which confirms both that this will take place and that it is Jesus who has been appointed as judge. In identifying Jesus with this role, F. F. Bruce argues, Luke "has in mind" the "one like a son of man" from Dan 7.13.²²⁴ The text clearly identifies Jesus, but rather than using his name, it says "by a man (ἐν ἀνδρί)," thus potentially supporting the Danielic allusion.

---

**222** Rather than locating a specific city or region as "the end of the earth," the universal scope of the proclamation, in contrast to the disciples' focus on the restoration of the kingdom to Israel, is the more likely focus of this phrase. In several places the picture at the culmination of history is presented in nationalist terms. The disciples ask about the time of restoration of the kingdom to Israel in Acts 1.7. And Anna is presented as pious as she speaks about Jesus "to all who were looking for the redemption of Jerusalem" (Luke 2.38). However, in these examples, there is something of a correction at work in the text: Anna's pointing to Jesus constitutes hope in something more than the restoration of Jerusalem, as also does Jesus' response here in Acts 1.6–8. Although characters may speak in terms focused on Israel, as noted in Chapter 5, the divergent responses to Jesus across Luke/Acts drive the picture of Israel and the gentile mission, which ultimately can perhaps better be understood as a contrast between "insiders" and "outsiders." Luke/Acts suggests an end time picture of a community that stands in continuity with God's people throughout the periods of history, but has been reconfigured to be comprised of those who listen and respond positively to the proclamation of Jesus and his apostles (cf. Acts 28.23–28).
**223** See Chapter 3 §4.1.2.
**224** Bruce, *The Book of Acts*, 341. Bruce goes on to argue, having also cited 1 Thess 1.10, "The terms in which Jesus is introduced here at Athens are as thoroughly eschatological as those in which he was introduced at Thessalonica" (p. 342).

But the term μέλλω introduces also an element of imminence.²²⁵ Although in a "weakened" form it can simply indicate the future²²⁶ or (counter-intuitively) delay or lingering,²²⁷ other meanings reflect inevitability or determinism²²⁸ or a sense of imminence—that something is about to happen.²²⁹ Indeed, A. J. Mattill argues that imminence is the term's basic meaning.²³⁰ Certainly this is the sense in which it is used in Luke 21.7, in the question about how one can know when the prophesied events are "about (μέλλῃ) to happen (γίνεσθαι)."²³¹ In an important critique, Mattill observes that translations of μέλλω in Luke/Acts have been constrained by existing assumptions about Luke's eschatology, rather than detailed engagement with the meaning of the term in its literary setting.²³² In Acts 17.31 the term adds further urgency to a statement that also stresses the need for repentance now that the times of ignorance are over (v. 30). The resurrection shows already that Jesus has been appointed to the key role in the judgement, which is about to take place.

Thus, in Luke/Acts the transition in history brought about by Jesus' resurrection begins a time which is characterised by further end-time events still cascading into the characters' experience. The ascension shows that Jesus is authoritatively in place at the right of God throughout the events of Acts; the "power from on high" (Luke 24.49; cf. Acts 1.5) experienced at Pentecost confirms that these are "the last days" (Acts 2.17). Rather than viewing the first readers' present

---

**225** Contra Barrett, who claims ἐν ᾗ μέλλει makes "little or no difference in meaning" (Barrett, *Acts*, 2:852).
**226** BDAG meaning 1β (pp. 627–28).
**227** BDAG meaning 4, in the sense: "why are you delaying?"
**228** BDAG meaning 2.
**229** BDAG meaning 1. In relation to Acts 17.31, BDAG specifies "intended action" (meaning 1γ) with the present infinitive, though Mattill argues compellingly against this case (Mattill, "Naherwartung, Fernerwartung," 279). The remainder of Acts 17.31 supports the case for a stronger sense of the term, including the reference to having "fixed a day (ἔστησεν)" and the assurance provided by the past event of Jesus' resurrection.
**230** Mattill, "Naherwartung, Fernerwartung," 279.
**231** Mattill provides a list of uses with the meaning of "soon" in Luke/Acts, noting the majority of its uses across the NT, including in Luke/Acts, take this sense (Mattill, "Naherwartung, Fernerwartung," 280–81).
**232** Mattill, "Naherwartung, Fernerwartung," 269, 276. Mattill's criticism is justified. The *EDNT* entry for μέλλω by Radl simply asserts: "in Acts μέλλω contains no suggestion of a near future (against Mattill)" (2:404), without any evidence in support. By contrast, the thrust of the question in Luke 21.7, at least, *requires* a sense of imminence. Similarly, the treatment by Schneider in *TDNT* deals mostly with references in epistles, and simply cites Conzelmann's "Eschatologie im Urchristentum" as one of the key references (1:325–27).

time as a point within eschatological events that are continuing to unfold, the delayed parousia hypothesis led interpreters to presume Luke intended further delay and to read this into the passages that address questions about "when." The above analysis suggests that this is not the best reading.

The passages which include questions about timing do not all make the same point, though none of them gives a straightforward answer about timing. Luke certainly draws on the tradition of the unknown nature of the timing of the end (Luke 12.35–48; Acts 1.7; cf. Mark 13.32), including rejection of false prophets who claim to know specifics (Luke 17.21–24; 21.8), though this common correction is itself unrelated to further delay.[233] But he does include hints in language recognisable to readers familiar with the traditions of Daniel, as also in 4 Ezra, 2 Baruch, and so on, discussed above. The *vaticinium ex eventu* of Luke 21.5–36 uses the same model of enabling the audience to identify their present time (as opposed to the literary present in the narrative context). Even Acts 1.3–11, one of the passages least focused on the timing of final events of those discussed here, points to the last days in the events of Acts 2 while using the language of the periodisation of history. And in the parable of the widow and the unjust judge—the text which explicitly mentions delay—it is mentioned in order to refute that God would delay in bringing justice (Luke 18.7–8). If this seems strange, it is perhaps because we are more used to the delayed parousia hypothesis than we are with the frequent attempts in Second Temple literature to recalibrate eschatological expectation to ensure that the promised divine action remains imminently anticipated.

### 5.3.2 Repentance

While eschatological events continue to unfold, other elements of the present time show that further change remains possible—both in terms of the ability of humans to respond positively in aligning their lives with divine priorities, and in the promise of divine action to bring an end to current suffering. Each of these aspects of Luke's portrait of the present time warrants some brief discussion.

Chapter 5 discussed repentance in Luke/Acts, in terms of human response to divine action. The discussion here does not repeat that, but simply highlights the ways in which the present time in the context of the end affects this theme in

---

[233] By stressing the importance of vigilance, passages which assert the unknown timing of the Son of Man's return (Luke 12.35–48; cf. Mark 13.32) incorporate a sense of urgency.

Luke's narrative. In seven speeches from apostles in Acts the proclamation of good news about Jesus leads into an exhortation to repentance and promise of forgiveness (Acts 2.38; 3.19; 5.31; 11.18; 17.30; 20.21; 26.20). Five of these instances are also those speeches discussed above, in which the resurrection forms a key element in the proclamation (Acts 2.38; 3.19; 5.31; 17.30; 26.20). In each of these cases the speaker identifies repentance as the required discipleship response following claims about Jesus' resurrection.[234]

Although the reader is assured that the time of judgement has already been appointed, the consequences of this for individuals remain contingent upon characters' openness to participation through repentance (Luke 7.18–50; 13.1–9; 14.1–24) and in aligning lives to the deeds of repentance—that is, the priorities of this new reign (Acts 26.20).[235] This creates a dynamic akin to that in 4 Ezra's call to discipline hearts in order to be counted among the "few" faithful at the end (4 Ezra 8.56–58; 14.34–35; cf. 2 Bar 83.8–23; 85.4). In Luke/Acts some characters respond wholeheartedly (Luke 5.27–32; 7.44–50; 19.1–10; Acts 2.41; 10.33, 44–48); others hover uncertainly or with hostility (Luke 7.44–46; 15.2; Acts 5.35–39; 17.32; 26.28–32).[236] But even beyond the end of the narrative, as Paul continues to "welcome all who came to him" (Acts 28.30), the possibility of repentance remains open for readers.[237] Thus, the dynamic nature of the present time, even within the end-time events, continues to offer a challenge.

### 5.3.3 Accounting for suffering in the present

Finally, as discussed in Chapter 5, suffering remains a real part of life in Luke's portrayal of the present time. In texts like 4 Ezra, longing for an end to suffering is one of the signs that the present time is positioned at the point of history's nadir, which heralds that divine action for justice and vindication is imminent.

---

[234] On the importance of repentance as a response to further the divine plan, see Nave, *The Role and Function of Repentance*, 145. See also Emmrich, *At the Heart of Luke;* Sterling, "Turning to God," 69–95; and discussion in Chapter 5 §6.3.3.
[235] Green refers multiple times to repentance as aligning to God's priorities (Green, *The Theology*, 35, 37, 70). See also the political imperative Rowe discerns in Acts (Rowe, *World Upside Down*, 88–89).
[236] See Chapter 5. Even pericopes in which characters respond with hostility tend to come to a close before the character has decided how to respond, for instance Simon the Pharisee's uncertain position at Luke 7.50 serves to challenge the reader (Crabbe, "A Sinner and a Pharisee," 264). Though it is true that by the end of his ministry, Jesus has stopped dining with Pharisees, following his own advice of eating with those who cannot repay the favour (Luke 19.1–10; cf. Luke 14.12–13; Braun, *Feasting and Social Rhetoric*, 175).
[237] See p. 199 n. 287 on Luke's audience.

But in Luke/Acts, though the resurrection marks a decisive transition in history, it has not put an end to suffering.[238] If the present time were identified with the end in a static way, as discussed of the *Aeneid* above, then either suffering would need to be somehow imaginary (perhaps like Cullmann's account of evil only appearing to have an effect), or something to which characters and readers resign themselves. But the suffering of those who follow Jesus, paralleled by his own suffering, mitigates against such a view of the present.[239]

Luke's emphasis on the resurrection has been in part the basis for criticism that Luke focuses on *theologia gloriae* at the expense of *crucis*.[240] But the inherent connection between the cross and God's vindication in raising Jesus (Acts 2.36; 3.13–15)[241] undermines this conclusion. And in a similar way, rather than triumphalism, Acts 14.22 describes tribulations suffered by the apostles in the time after the resurrection that will yet be vindicated. Luke recognises that suffering exists in the life of the Acts community, as well as in the events that have taken place between the time of the narrative's literary present and Luke's audience's historical present, such as the destruction of Jerusalem (Luke 21.6, 20–21). Even the placement of the exalted Christ at the right hand of God and the descent of the Spirit into the life of the discipleship community do not preclude the possibility of suffering.

By recognising the final events of the end of history still to be fulfilled, Luke maintains the kind of dynamic approach to the present which allows for repentance and overcoming the imperfections of present experience, as also in the Jew-

---

**238** A similar structure to history is evident in the Book of Revelation. The vision of the heavenly court in Rev 4 provides assurance of transcendent authority already in place, which in turn enables the recipients of John's report to live in the present with confidence. Revelation 4 and 5 deal with past events, while present events are attributed the status of messianic woes. The interspersed focus on judgement, the messianic age, and a new heaven and new earth (esp. Rev 7; 20–22) provides confidence to readers, with which they may face suffering.

**239** Schleffer sets out a table that compares Jesus' predictions of suffering in Luke 21, his own sufferings, and those of the apostles (Scheffler, *Suffering in Luke's Gospel*, 148–49).

**240** See discussion and examples in Fitzmyer, *The Gospel according to Luke*, 1:22–23. Cunningham attributes such views to an over-emphasis on redaction criticism, for which he criticises Conzelmann (Cunningham, "Through Many Tribulations," 17). Moessner similarly refutes these longstanding assumptions by highlighting Luke's presentation of Jesus in the tradition of biblical prophets who suffer, concluding the cross is essential to Luke's understanding of scriptural attestation of the divine plan (Moessner, "The 'Script,'" 249). See also Bovon's treatment of Schütz, who holds the suffering of Christ to be central to Luke's message to the church (Bovon, *Luke the Theologian*, 33).

**241** Bauspieß, "Die Gegenwart des Heils," 140. See also Fitzmyer's reflections on Jesus' promise "Today you will be with me in paradise" (Luke 23.43) in Fitzmyer, *The Gospel according to Luke*, 1:23.

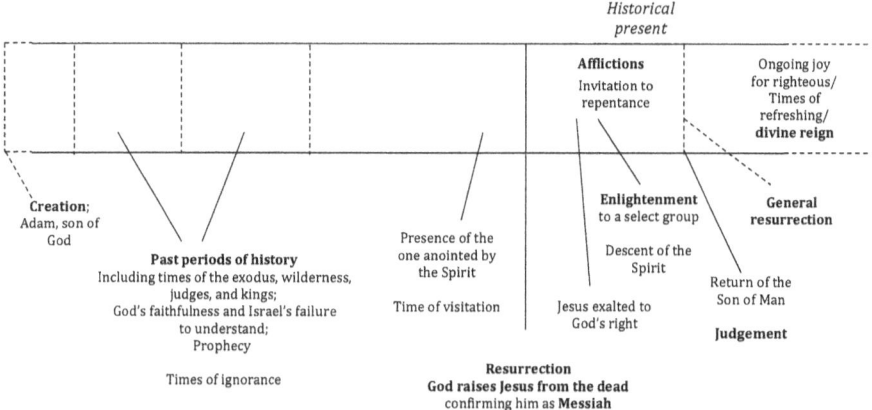

**Fig. 1:** The position of the historical present in Luke's schema of history

ish texts discussed above, without collapsing his vision of the end into a static picture of the present, as I have argued is the effect in the *Aeneid*. Luke's treatment of afflictions, as indeed of repentance, confirms that he is not uninterested in the question of the culmination of history. Without designating dates, Luke remains focused on the sudden and unknown nature of the final date (Luke 12.20–21, 35–40, 43–46; cf. Matt 24.42–51; 25.1–13), but also its imminence (Luke 12.56; 18.7–8; 21.5–36; Acts 17.31).[242]

The diagram (Fig. 1) sets out key elements of the schema of history in Luke/Acts, noting (in the bold print) the type of events shared with the Second Temple comparison texts discussed above. As argued in Chapters 3 and 4, the past periods of history and divine guidance across all of history remain important for Luke/Acts, as they are also for texts such as the War Scroll, Josephus's *Jewish War*, 4 Ezra, and 2 Baruch. As in all of these texts, the events of the past provide assurance for the events still anticipated. Unlike the additional period for the time of the church Conzelmann identified in Luke/Acts,[243] however, for Luke the decisive event of Jesus' resurrection has prompted the transition into a period which itself is comprised of the end-time events, whose continued unfolding is imminently expected. This is where Luke situates the historical present.

---

**242** Ellis, *The Gospel of Luke*, 49; contra Pervo, *Acts*, 25.
**243** Conzelmann, *Theology of St Luke*, 135.

# 6 Conclusion: hope, politics, and invitation at the end of history

The relationship between the present and the end of history in a given text has profound consequences for the text's message to those who suffer and the kind of politics it encourages. As set out in Chapter 1, these have been controversial aspects of Lukan theology, flowing in the most part from a particular view of Luke's eschatology, in which interpreters claimed, following Conzelmann, that Luke had removed all imminent eschatological expectation from his account.[244] It is through this lens that the different incidents with civic authorities in Acts (16.35–40; 17.5–9; 18.12–17; 19.35–41) have been interpreted as advocating complicity with ruling authorities,[245] rather than due attention being given to the implications of the proclamation of Jesus' lordship and the urgent call for characters and readers to align their priorities with his reign.[246] Similarly, by presuming

---

[244] Conzelmann, *Theology of St Luke*, 14, 131–32; Conzelmann, *Acts of the Apostles*, xlv. This view is also taken in Haenchen, *The Acts of the Apostles*, 94; Drury, *Tradition and Design*, 9; Fitzmyer, *The Gospel according to Luke*, 1:182–87; and by many who have continued to build on their interpretations since. See Chapter 1.

[245] Walaskay paints Luke as more politically complicit than other early church figures, seeking to present Rome positively to the church, and identifying divine justification for secular rule, which Walaskay links directly to Conzelmann's delayed parousia hypothesis (Paul W. Walaskay, *"And So We Came to Rome": The Political Perspective of St Luke*, SNTSMS 49 (Cambridge: Cambridge University Press, 1983), 64–67). See a critical summary of earlier accounts of Luke's politics in Rowe, *World Upside Down*, 5–6. See also Walton's summary and evaluation of five types of arguments about Lukan politics he identifies (Steve Walton, "The State They Were In: Luke's View of the Roman Empire," in *Rome in the Bible and the Early Church*, ed. Peter Oakes (Grand Rapids: Baker Academic, 2002), 2–12, 29–33). Walton advocates a middle way (amicable relationships with authorities but witness to Jesus, p. 35) though, despite his focus on the centrality of God's action in Luke's narrative, he does not consider eschatological elements of Luke's politics. See also Bonz's parallels between Lukan politics and epic themes (Bonz, *The Past as Legacy*, 56–57, 182–83), through which she still, nonetheless, argues the parousia's delay drove Luke's restructuring of the kerygma in this form (p. 193).

[246] This remains the dominant approach to Lukan politics, demonstrated by the dedicated focus on politics in Acts at a special session of the Society of Biblical Literature Annual Meeting in November 2014, during which eschatology played no part in the discussion. In contrast to my argument here, Schwartz identifies parallels between 2 Maccabees and Acts in terms of circular history and political stability (Schwartz, "Circular or Teleological," 124). Rowe offers welcome attention to the eschatological features of Luke's politics. He argues that two differing trends in Acts capture on the one hand the claim to divine lordship that relativises all other worldly powers, and on the other the desire to ward off any accusations of insurrection by presenting positive relationships with civic leaders, who in turn declare the innocence of Jesus (Luke

§6 Conclusion: hope, politics, and invitation at the end of history — 331

a schema of extended civic life from which forward-orientated longing for God's final action is deemed absent, interpreters have viewed the proclamation of the resurrection as triumphalist *theologia gloriae*.[247]

However, seen in the context of the discussion above, a writer's depiction of the relationship between the present and the end of history, *and* the character of the present, play significant roles in shaping approaches to politics and suffering. These are important *effects* of a writer's eschatology. It is central for the assurance Luke provides that through Jesus' resurrection the ultimate period of history has been entered, which relativises everything else.[248] And it is also crucial to Luke's account that some movement through human response and final divine action remains possible. The combination of these features facilitates hope.

Where writers equate the completion of history with current political realities an entirely different picture emerges, as in Karl Mannheim's distinction between ideology and utopia.[249] As noted above, according to Mannheim's terminology, "utopia" reflects a hope yet to be fulfilled beyond current structures, while "ideology" considers such fulfilment to have been realised already within those worldly structures.[250] Understandably, ideology tends to be associated with the powerful, utopia with the disempowered.[251] In an article in which he draws

---

23.47) and Paul (Acts 26.31–32) alike, and that these strands have caused the polarised treatments of Luke's politics (Rowe, *World Upside Down*, 88–89).
247 See, for instance, Käsemann, "Neutestamentliche Fragen," 21, and Chapter 1 above.
248 Drawn out well by Rowe, *World Upside Down*, 89.
249 Mannheim, *Ideology and Utopia*, 36.
250 Steven Schweitzer takes a very different view of Acts. Following Roland Boer (and noting the influence of theorist Lyman Sargent), he applies utopian theory to Chronicles. It is through this lens that he approaches Acts, arguing that the Chronicler focuses on maintaining political order, and Luke does likewise in Acts (Steven Schweitzer, *Reading Utopia in Chronicles*, LHBOTS 442 (New York: T&T Clark, 2007), 131). His brief treatment does not benefit from the kind of insights Rowe has brought to the study of politics in Acts (Rowe, *World Upside Down*), nor deal with eschatological considerations. See also Weinfeld, who applies these ideas on ideology and utopia to various strands in the HB related to Zion and kingship (Moshe Weinfeld, "Zion and Jerusalem as Religious and Political Capital: Ideology and Utopia," in Friedman, *The Poet and the Historian*, 75–115).
251 Collins discusses "relative deprivation theory," in which writers' claims of various groups' suffering and disempowerment relates to the groups' own perceptions rather than particular historical claims. He also uses this to reconsider traditional claims that apocalypses arise from situations of crisis (Collins, "Temporality and Politics," 27–28). For similar claims that the conflict depicted in the stories of the first half of the Book of Daniel does not reflect historical persecution, but rather the writer's ideological commitments in portraying allegiance to God and any resultant conflict with the king's sovereignty (which Davies argues is resolved by winning the king over, so that these two forms of "imperium" can coexist), see Davies, "Daniel in the Lion's Den," 163–64. However, Daniel does not so easily affirm worldly leaders, but rather

on Mannheim's approach, John Collins captures the explanatory power of this distinction in relation to the politics of apocalypses:

> Imperial propagandists and apocalyptic dissenters had similar views of the structure of history—a sequence of transitory kingdoms followed by a definitive rule that would last forever. The crucial difference was one of vantage point and location on the time scale. For the triumphalist, the final kingdom has already arrived; for the visionary the kingdom of the present is passing away. Whether the advent of the final kingdom is imminent or deferred to some time in the future does not make an essential difference so long as the conviction is real that an end to the present order is assured.[252]

Collins rightly draws attention to shared views for writers whose schemas of history are periodised and teleological,[253] and the way in which their understandings of the present time in relation to the end shape political perspectives. Virgil's *Aeneid* offers an archetypal version of Mannheim's "ideology," in which (despite some more ambiguous or nuanced approaches to the past) the present and future are collapsed into a static continuity, and the ruling empire emerges triumphant. Virgil is not alone in depicting Rome in such a way,[254] nor are Christian texts distinct from these approaches; such ideology emerges from later Christian writers of the empire like Eusebius or Orosius.[255]

By basing readings of Luke/Acts on the delayed parousia hypothesis, however, interpreters have suggested that for Luke the events of the end are not only distant but irrelevant—thereby, I suggest, overlooking key ways in which Luke's understanding of the end shapes his portrayal of the priorities of, and basis for hope in, the present.[256] From this perspective it is possible to see

---

their comprehensive destruction through the installation of uncompromised divine rule, which Davies does also note through reflection on the ultimately provisional nature of the resolution in each of the stories in Dan 1–6 (p. 164).

**252** Collins, "Temporality and Politics," 42.

**253** See Chapter 3.

**254** Collins notes the inherent difficulties of utopian thinking becoming ideology as revolution leads into political power (Collins, "Temporality and Politics," 42–43).

**255** Nobbs claims Acts and Eusebius's *Ecclesiastical History* share optimistic, triumphalist elements and their "underlying message" (Alanna Nobbs, "Acts and Subsequent Ecclesiastical Histories," in Winter and Clarke, *The Book of Acts in Its Ancient Literary Setting*, 158); my assessment of Luke/Acts here is different. See Davies's brief mention of the transformation of the fourth kingdom in Daniel's paradigm in post-Constantinian Christian texts (Davies, "Daniel in the Lion's Den," 178).

**256** After his extensive overview of Lukan studies on the theme, Bovon argues that according to Luke, "the Parousia, or at least the date of the end, loses its importance. Only the ἀρχή counts. The τέλος, the end, depends on it, not by reason of a historical determinism but rather by theological necessity" (Bovon, *Luke the Theologian*, 85).

that, although the distinction between present and future realisation of the end may be primary, Collins is too ready to endorse simply a binary distinction between writers who depict the end of history in the present and those who keep it in the future, however distantly.[257] As seen in the discussion above, some writers do maintain a focus on the present which reduces the impact of their expectations about the end of history. Second Maccabees focuses on rescue through divine action *within* history with less concern about the culmination of history aside from post-mortem reward for martyrs, and Josephus exhorts readers to repent from revolutionary dissent in order to create harmonious relationships with Rome as they wait for God to intervene at the end of history, according to a divine timetable.[258] The affirmations about divine vindication for writers who expect the end imminently, such as the authors of 4 Ezra and 2 Baruch, offer quite different implications for readers who identify their own experiences with the negative events interpreted as signs of history in decline, or even eschatological woes, and long for the promised end to suffering. Thus, in contrast to Collins's claims, the sense of imminence to the end *does* matter, and most particularly to those who writers imply are suffering in the present.

But it also matters to Luke that the final events of history have already begun and, although the timing of the final culmination remains unknown, as end-time events continue to unfold it should be constantly anticipated. Stuckenbruck is right to highlight important continuities between NT and contemporaneous Jewish texts in their writers' understandings of the structure of time,[259] including a sense of continuity between the kind of assurance offered by NT texts and apocalypses, as well as by other texts such as the War Scroll and Pesher Habakkuk. Luke's promise of assurance, which draws on earlier divine acts, sits in continuity with this late Second Temple tradition.

However, there are also important differences in NT texts.[260] When Luke has Paul proclaim in Acts 17.31 that "God has set a date on which he is about to have[261] the world judged and of this he has given assurance by raising him from the dead," the past event which provides assurance, namely Jesus' resurrection, is a unique, decisive event. It is analogous to the events anticipated in

---

**257** Rajak distinguishes between general expectations of the end and belief in its imminence in Jewish millenarian thought (Rajak, "Jewish Millenarian Expectations," 164).
**258** Bilde, "Josephus and Jewish Apocalypticism," 188.
**259** Stuckenbruck, "Overlapping Ages," 320–26; Stuckenbruck, "How Much Evil?", 145–52. See discussion of continuity versus rupture in the interpretation of understandings of history in the New Testament and contemporaneous Jewish texts in Chapter 3.
**260** See n. 238 above on the Book of Revelation.
**261** On this modification of the NRSV translation, see §5.3.1 above.

the War Scroll, where the final battle of the eschatological war constitutes a unique annihilation of evil. Though of course the certainty of this future action in the War Scroll is in turn also based on God's faithful action in the past, those past events are a different kind of action—characteristic of God but not decisively named among the events of the end in the same manner as the eschatological war in the War Scroll, the Messiah's arrival in 4 Ezra, or the first person raised from the dead (Acts 26.23), whose resurrection itself constitutes evidence that he has been vindicated by God as the Messiah (Acts 2.24; 3.15), in Luke/Acts.

Thus, Jesus' resurrection is *unlike* the military action of Judas Maccabeus, which, though made unstoppable by divine favour, may lead into future times of trial if the people again require disciplining (2 Macc 10.4) until the (distantly anticipated) final resurrection. And, despite some similarities in the dynamic relationship between the present and the future according to non-Jewish Graeco-Roman writers such as Diodorus Siculus and Valerius Maximus, Luke's understanding of the future addresses a type of definitive action which is unfamiliar to these writers. Again, this demonstrates that those texts with which Luke/Acts shares greatest generic similarity, and with which it is most often compared, are not those with which Luke shares key elements of his conception of history.

Yet, although according to Luke the events of the end have already begun, Luke's narrative is also unlike the triumphalism of the *Aeneid*, because of the ongoing possibility for change in the present in Luke/Acts. This understanding of the present time also overcomes the kind of problematic conclusions Oscar Cullmann came to, in which his understanding of what had been achieved by God's decisive action in raising Jesus at the "mid-point" in time essentially introduced into NT texts a static relationship between the "mid-point" and the end of history. This meant that, according to Cullmann's interpretation, evil was constrained in the present time, and the events of the end merely constituted paperwork to confirm what was already the case.[262] Despite the differences between Luke/Acts and the *Aeneid*, Cullmann's assessment of these themes in NT salvation history, including in Luke/Acts, thus edged towards Virgil's interpretation of the end of history.

However, this chapter has demonstrated that a dynamic character to the present is important for a great range of writers, including the ways in which future changes of fortune impact upon present experience and moral imperatives in the other non-Jewish Graeco-Roman texts discussed, as also in the Jewish texts examined. When this dynamic relates to the end of history, a writer's recognition of the need to explain suffering in the present inherently calls final claims into

---

[262] Cullmann, *Christ and Time*, xix, 84; Cullmann, *Salvation in History*, 169.

some question. Having compared the structure of time in a range of texts and noted some unique features NT writers introduced, Stuckenbruck concludes: "in relation to evil, the most important point to make is that in the NT, no less than in contemporary Jewish apocalyptic, the solution to the problem of sin and suffering, though presented as definitive, nevertheless remains provisional."[263] He rightly highlights that all such frameworks, as they seek to explain evil in the present by looking towards future divine action, ultimately retain a level of provisionality, which reflects the need for further change. Despite the post-war criticisms levelled at Luke for being triumphalist, Luke also still communicates that future action remains necessary, because the present remains marred by ongoing experiences of imperfection, including persecution and rejection of the apostles' proclamation.[264]

Nonetheless, in Luke/Acts, present experience is already qualitatively affected by its position within the final period of history. The transcendent reality of Jesus at the right of God *changes* the present, even though the return of the Son of Man remains anticipated. Herein Luke affirms the grounds for hope. This in turn leads to the central invitation of Luke/Acts: readers are exhorted to urgent repentance and thereby to aligning their priorities with those of the divine purpose. In Luke/Acts life is lived conscious of the present time within the final period of history, and with confidence that the remaining end-time events are still unfolding—indeed, the resurrection of Jesus proves that divine action to this *telos* is already underway.

---

[263] Stuckenbruck, "How Much Evil?", 168.
[264] I refer here to the implied portrait of present suffering (also drawing on the understanding of "relative deprivation;" see Collins, "Temporality and Politics," 28 and n. 251 above), rather than relying on historical claims about how widespread any first-century persecution actually was.

# Chapter 7: Conclusion

> *Our experience has made a theology of history suspect for us from the very outset, whatever the reasons may be which are urged in its support. It determined the liberalism whose faith in progress was finally shattered by the First World War. However erroneously and improperly, it was capable of serving as a shield for Nazi eschatology.*
> —Ernst Käsemann, US Lectures, first delivered in 1965–1966[1]

Luke's understanding of the end of history is central to his account. It not only shapes the continuity he sees across the whole course of history, but his portrayal of divine and human agency and of the significance of the present moment in the final period of history. But Lukan eschatology has been obscured by assumptions about the incompatibility of history and eschatology that go back to the mid-twentieth century, compounded by diminished interest in these questions in recent studies. Ernst Käsemann's words above speak to the profound concerns that arose from the post-war setting, where salvation history was deemed to reflect a distortion of Jesus' message and so was excluded from portraits of Paul and denounced in readings of Luke/Acts. These particular tensions have lessened in the intervening period, and the contemporary scholarly landscape no longer gives rise to articles like Werner Georg Kümmel's "Current Theological Accusations against Luke."[2] But the conclusions of the exegesis in that era remain influential. This study has attempted to offer a fresh approach.

## 1 Luke's eschatology and its effects

This study has shown that Luke's understanding of the end, far from being severed from his understanding of history, is integral to each of the other features of history examined across the book. In Chapter 3, I considered the direction and shape of history in the study's key texts and argued that, while the writers of the non-Jewish texts depict different scales of history, at times within an overall trajectory of improvement or decline, most of these writers describe a continuous pattern of rising and falling empires which is not expected to reach an end. By contrast, Virgil's *Aeneid*, all of the Jewish texts (though to a lesser extent in 2

---

[1] Käsemann, "Justification and Salvation History," 64. Käsemann originally gave this paper in a series of lectures in the United States in 1965 and 1966, and revised it for publication in *Paulinische Perspektiven* (1969; ET 1971).
[2] Kümmel, "Current Theological Accusations," 131–45.

Maccabees), and Luke/Acts indicate a teleological understanding of history—that is, a belief that history follows a linear shape that draws to some sort of conclusion at its end.

Moreover, contrary to Conzelmann's hypothesis about the function and uniqueness of Luke's periodised view of salvation history, periodisation is evident in almost all of the texts examined. Indeed, the highly-structured historical reviews of texts such as 4 Ezra and 2 Baruch demonstrate that periodisation itself does not indicate that a writer views history as severed from eschatology or is uninterested in the imminence of the end. Rather, I suggested that periodisation enables writers to provide a sense of continuity across history in a way which also allows for significant change without *rupture* in history. Luke's periodised, teleological view of history is likewise able to hold history and eschatology together, balancing what Luke presents as the cataclysmic change brought about by God's action in raising Jesus from the dead with a sense of continuity across the full sweep of history.

In examining evidence of beliefs about determinism and divine guidance of history in the key texts, in Chapter 4 I also noted ways in which Luke's understanding of the end of history shapes his portrayal of divine guidance. Although a variety of writers, including Josephus and the authors of the non-Jewish texts, describe determinism and divine involvement in history through the actions of divine forces like τύχη/*fortuna* or εἱμαρμένη/*fatum*, they do not all use the terms in the same way. My exploration demonstrated that not only are these characteristic terms absent from Luke/Acts, but Luke's understanding of divine guidance is shaped in significant ways by his claims about the end of history: for Luke, divine action is not merely a form of moral accountability or way of explaining unpredictable changes of fortune in human experience, but the basis for assurance about the end.

Differences in the role of prophecy in the key texts also relate to the writers' portrayals of the end of history (or lack thereof). For writers like Valerius Maximus or Diodorus Siculus, prophetic insights confirm that a predicted event (which also took place prior to writing) was set in advance, whereas for the writers of 4 Ezra, 2 Baruch, and Luke/Acts, accurate prophecies in the past confirm the accuracy of prophecy *yet to be fulfilled*. However, Luke's understanding of the divine βουλή and even his use of the term δεῖ are also different from the elements of determinism in 4 Ezra, 2 Baruch, and the War Scroll. For Luke, the divine βουλή can be opposed, as evidenced by numerous events of the past and present, exemplified in the rejection of Jesus and those who proclaim his resurrection. But, looking to the future, the divine βουλή remains the basis of the assurance that, just as God and God's prophets foresaw this rejection, so will divine action adapt to ensure that the events of the end will certainly unfold as promised.

These conclusions led directly into the discussion of Chapter 5, in which I examined the ways in which the writers of this study's key texts portrayed the relationship between divine and human agency, in order to illuminate Luke's understanding of human responsibility and freedom. In keeping with John Barclay's framework,[3] I noted that the study's texts did not simply present a competitive relationship between divine and human agencies, but often reflect some interplay as suggested by Barclay. But I noted some particular problems tended to draw out inconsistencies. The writers often attribute events to divine sovereignty and responsibility, or human freedom and responsibility, differently depending on whether writers were seeking to *explain the events of the past* or *provide hope for the future*. I also observed that many of the texts made clear distinctions between "opponent" and "protagonist" characters in portrayals of responsibility and freedom. By contrast, Luke generally explains negative events in the past as the result of tragic opposition, maintaining a notable appreciation for human freedom exercised in the choices of almost all characters. And when Luke looks to the future, an (urgent) universal invitation confirms the human freedom for all to respond positively (without distinctions between different types of characters), though repentance itself is also portrayed as a divine gift.

Finally, in Chapter 6 I examined the writers' portrayals of the present and the end of history and the relationship between the two. I noted the ways in which possible change in the future contributes a dynamic element to the present time even for writers who do not anticipate an end to history, facilitating either comfort or challenge in response to a reader's present experience. The structure of history in the Jewish texts confirmed a similar dynamic for life in the present, whereas Virgil's static alignment of the *telos* of history with the present has a quite different effect, prompting a kind of "ideology" over "utopia" which limits the possibilities for hope in the present.[4]

Thus, the structure of history in Luke/Acts is most similar to that in the Jewish texts, where assurance of the past provides confidence in the end, and some final events are still anticipated. However, while the late Second Temple writers locate the present time at different points within the pattern of events anticipated at the end of history (and 4 Ezra and 2 Baruch even identify current events with the eschatological woes), none place the present after such decisive events as the presence of the Messiah or the first one raised from the dead. In Luke/

---

[3] Barclay, "Introduction," 6–7.
[4] Cf. Mannheim, *Ideology and Utopia*, 36.

Acts, Jesus' resurrection, the presence of the Spirit, and the location of the ascended Christ all confirm that the final period of history has begun. Nonetheless, despite the possible similarities between the *Aeneid* and Luke/Acts, both of which locate the present in the final period of history, the character of the present causes their eschatologies to function in starkly different ways. In Luke the present time is characterised by further end-time events, continuing to cascade into experience. By exploring the extent to which the end of history is already realised in the present, and the static or dynamic character of the present, this analysis demonstrated that *both* of these elements are essential for understanding how eschatology functions in Luke/Acts.

Together these features facilitate hope and bring about crucial *effects* of Luke's eschatology. The possibility of future change at the culmination of history reassures those who suffer (unlike Luke's alleged *theologia gloriae*), whereas Jesus' presence already at the right of God relativises other political claims (contrary to concerns about political complicity). Indeed, I suggest the frequent failure to consider Luke's understanding of the present and the end of history in studies of Luke's politics has led to misrepresentations of his politics.

Therefore, I suggest, Luke's understanding of the *end* of history is essential to his conception of history. In each of these areas, Luke's eschatological consciousness shapes his text in crucial ways: divine faithfulness in the past confirms that divine guidance governs all of history, including its end, even as the unstoppable divine βουλή adapts to the tragic consequences of opposition. Contrary to Conzelmann's reading, in which the end has become so distant as to be irrelevant, Luke's attention to the end provides assurance of the culmination of faithful divine action and underscores the urgency of human response. To Luke, from his perspective within the final period of history, the end-time events leading to judgement are already underway.

## 2 Assessment of method

The methodology employed in this study is based on my argument that numerous features of a text—such as those that reflect the writer's understanding of history and its end, and portrayal of divine and human agency in history—*transcend genre*. Just as an ancient writer does not need to write philosophical treatises in order to hold Stoic beliefs about the world and for these to impact on their writing, so they do not need to write histories in order to hold a view about divine involvement in history, nor to write an apocalypse to have expectations about the end of history. It remains important to attend to the generic features of a text, which create a framework of expectations for competent contemporaneous readers, and thus shape their interpretations. But ancient writers may communicate their particular beliefs on topics like the end of history as they write in any one of a variety of genres. Given this study's focus, therefore, I have argued that it is not only possible but necessary to engage in cross-genre comparison, in order to fill out the set of beliefs about these themes evident in Luke's broader context.

In assessing this method in practice, I wish to make three principal observations. (1) By comparing Luke/Acts to ten texts of the Graeco-Roman period (five Jewish and five non-Jewish) from a range of genres—including historiography, epic, and apocalypse—this study has shown that it is possible and effective to compare such diverse texts on their writers' depictions of the shape and direction of history, divine guidance of history, human freedom and responsibility, and the relationship between the end of history and the present time. That is, it is possible and effective to compare diverse texts in relation to features that transcend genre.

(2) This method has demonstrated that on these important topics, Luke/Acts holds more in common with texts of other genres than with the Graeco-Roman historiographies which share its genre. This is particularly important, given the tendency in recent Lukan studies (which is less marked in studies of other parts of the NT) to limit comparison texts to those which interpreters identify as the same genre as Luke/Acts, even when dealing with a theological theme such as the presentation of the divine or the nature of the divine plan in Luke/Acts.

(3) Finally, the broad sample of comparison texts enabled the study to counter the tendency to find (or dismiss) parallels when considering a more limited set of texts. Indeed, the history of interpretation of Luke/Acts since the mid-twentieth century can be expressed in part as a series of consequences arising from the kinds of decisions interpreters have made about comparison texts. Conzelmann's redaction-critical approach led him to overstate Luke's uniqueness in relation to the other synoptic Gospels,[5] as Philipp Vielhauer's treatment of Luke and Paul had also accentuated differences between these two biblical writers.[6] Combined with a set of assumptions about the way in which eschatological consciousness changed over the first generations of disciples, the portrait that emerged from these studies emphasised only Luke's *difference*.

More recent studies, inspired by Luke's style and linguistic skills, have likewise assumed Luke's difference from the other evangelists, and limited compar-

---

[5] Conzelmann, *Theology of St Luke*.
[6] Vielhauer, "Zum 'Paulinismus,'" 12–15.

isons to (generally) other Hellenistic historiographies. As interpreters have made claims about the ways in which these comparisons have illuminated Luke/Acts, they have tended to focus on rhetorical devices or themes they consider the texts to share, excluding other themes from the field of vision and overstating the *similarities* between Luke/Acts and the non-Jewish Graeco-Roman texts.

By contrast, the broad range of texts considered as detailed case studies here has enabled, I hope, greater sensitivity in comparisons. For instance, aside from Virgil's approach in the *Aeneid*, none of the non-Jewish writers were found to portray a teleological view of history—which is crucially important for considering Luke's understanding of history. However, the study's writers did portray history as periodised in some form. The study has also shown that there are important ways in which an understanding of the human capacity to contribute to divine πρόνοια, as suggested by Diodorus Siculus, might illuminate Luke's understanding of human participation in the βουλὴ τοῦ θεοῦ, while the overall structure of history in texts such as 4 Ezra and 2 Baruch, in which the events of the past provide confidence in divine action for events promised in the future, comes closest to Luke's understanding of assurance for future hope.

Therefore, I suggest that the method employed in this study has been effective. By extending the comparison to a wider range of texts, it has built up a fuller picture of ways of thinking about history, or relevant "mental tools," available in Luke's setting. In so doing, the analysis has supported a more nuanced portrait of the similarities and differences between these texts and Luke/Acts in relation to the features of their writers' underlying understandings of history.

As noted in setting out the study, inevitably any selection of comparison texts will be limited. Given constraints on the number of ancient sources with which the study could engage effectively, other NT texts were excluded from detailed consideration, recognising also that they had been the focus of previous studies. However, I believe these findings in relation to history and eschatology in Luke/Acts and the Jewish and non-Jewish literature from Luke's broader context would likewise illuminate assumptions about the relationship between history and eschatology in other NT texts. Future research could incorporate some key NT texts, using a similar method of diverse case studies, to explore how closely Luke/Acts reflects the understanding of history in other NT texts. Indeed, the issues that drove post-war assumptions in Lukan studies reflect tensions that run throughout NT interpretation.

## 3 Salvation history and post-war concerns

As noted in Chapter 1, François Bovon identified "history and eschatology" as the beginning of "everything" in his analysis of Lukan scholarship in the second half of the twentieth century.[7] In so many ways he is, of course, right. But the prior question about *why* these themes became the beginning of such fraught debate in Lukan studies demonstrates the crucial impact of the post-war context upon the complex of issues considered in this investigation, and underscores why this study's reconsideration of Lukan eschatology, in light of the enduring influence of scholarship from that era in particular, has been necessary. It also highlights further areas for exploration that touch on these big picture topics in NT studies.

Käsemann's lecture, cited above, reflects on the reasons why interpreters of Romans had viewed justification and salvation history as antitheses, the latter being associated with "a conception of salvation history which broke in on us in secularised and political form with the Third Reich and its ideology."[8] Conzelmann's influential thesis is grounded in the same powerful worry about salvation history, seen as a distortion of the kerygma.[9] Similar concerns shine through other treatments, like Helmut Flender's emphasis on the transcendence of the kingdom inaugurated by Jesus' ascension, as an emphatic counter to the "false sacralisation of history," or the "fall into historical pantheism."[10] Mid-twentieth-century secular philosophy of history shows the same anxiety about "Meaning in History" in response to the war.[11] And even Oscar Cullmann's choice of military imagery tied to particular historical events—"D-Day" and "V-Day"—to describe God's decisive action, in Christ and at the end of history, itself seems, to a present-day reader, extraordinary.[12] It is perhaps no wonder that Cullmann elicited criticism from Karl Barth,[13] using historical events as an analogy for divine action—and such complex and harrowing events at that. But the salience of war-

---

7 Bovon, *Luke the Theologian*, 11.
8 Käsemann, "Justification and Salvation History," 64.
9 Conzelmann, *Theology of St Luke*. See also Conzelmann, "Zur Lukasanalyse," 16–33; Conzelmann, *Luke's Place*, 298–316; Conzelmann, *Acts of the Apostles*.
10 Flender, *St Luke*, 5, 106. See also Drury, *Tradition and Design*, 12.
11 Löwith's approach in his book of this title (Löwith, *Meaning in History*), as well as his autobiographical reflections in *My Life in Germany before and after 1933* (Karl Löwith, *My Life in Germany before and after 1933: A Report*, trans. Elizabeth King (London: Athlone, 1994)), demonstrate the entanglement of influences in the post-war context and approaches to history.
12 Cullmann, *Christ and Time*, xix, 84.
13 Cullmann, *Christ and Time*, xxv.

time imagery for Cullmann offers a telling reminder of the impact of the setting upon these interpreters.

Intellectual tensions about salvation history run in different directions through NT scholarship. It is not the task of this study to delve further into the mid-twentieth-century setting and its divergent influence upon the interpretation of texts like Romans or Galatians, or assumptions about the "early catholic" tendencies of NT texts attributed to later generations of disciples—though I hope that this discussion has demonstrated the need for further reflection on this. Perhaps particularly in relation to later texts dubbed "early catholic," these questions arising from mid-twentieth-century assumptions have been less often considered. But it is important to emphasise that this pattern of assumptions about Luke/Acts fits into a broader post-war cultural context, and a set of presuppositions about the relationships between NT texts. Although new interpretative methods have been employed in Lukan studies since, recent commentaries, introductory textbooks, and even specialised studies on other Lukan topics have nonetheless frequently maintained the same core assumptions about Luke's setting and de-eschatologising tendencies.

History and eschatology may have been issues at the heart of a new and influential era in Lukan interpretation, as Bovon argues. But *also,* from the beginning, it was a caricatured portrayal of the contrasts between Paul and Luke which emphasised history over eschatology in the latter, and drove further conclusions about the *effects* of Luke's (allegedly absent) eschatological consciousness, such as culpably comfortable politics and *theologia gloriae.*

This study has attempted a new approach to the question of Lukan eschatology. The analysis has shown that in Luke/Acts, as in 4 Ezra and 2 Baruch, and even Josephus's *Jewish War,* history and eschatology go together. The past confirms continuity with the end. Moreover, for Luke, negative events of the past are attributed to the tragic choices of humans who reject the divine plan, even as God enabled the prophets to foresee that they would. But the dynamic divine plan cannot be stopped. As opposition to this plan has already been transformed, so, Luke's narrative asserts, even while end-time events continue to unfold, readers may be assured that the promised events yet to be fulfilled will certainly take place. Yet, even within the final period of history, the present time provides further opportunity for change and grounds for hope that current suffering will yet be brought to an end. Therefore, humans in the present are called to repent and align themselves urgently with the priorities of the kingdom and to recognise the lordship of the one who is already at the right of God. Time is running short, which makes this message one of comfort and of challenge. Indeed, the resurrection of Jesus confirms that divine action towards the final culmination is already underway:

While God has overlooked the times of human ignorance, now he commands all people everywhere to repent, because he has fixed a day on which he will have the world judged in righteousness by a man whom he has appointed, and of this he has given assurance to all by raising him from the dead. (Acts 17.30–31)

# Appendices

## Appendix 1: ὁ αἰών in the Gospels and Acts

| | Matt | Mark | Luke | John | Acts | Totals |
|---|---|---|---|---|---|---|
| **Duration/period:** | | | | | | |
| → This age | 12.32; 13.22 | *4.19*[1] | 16.8; 20.34 | | | 5 |
| → Specific reference to the *end* of the age | 13.39, 40, 49; 24.3;[2] 28.20 | | | | | 5 |
| → Coming age | [12.32][3] | *10.30*[4] | 18.30; 20.35 | | | 3 [4] |
| Forever/always/never | 21.19 | 3.29; 11.14 | 1.33, 55[5] | 4.14; 6.51, 58; 8.35 (x2), 51, 52; 9.32; 10.28; 11.26; 12.34; 13.8; 14.16 | | 18 |
| Of old (ἀπ' αἰῶνος) | | | 1.70 | | 3.21; 15.18 | 3 |
| **Totals** | 8 [9] | 4 | 7 | 13 | 2 | 34 [35] |

\* Italics indicates the same term is used in a synoptic parallel.

---

1 In Luke's parallel account of the parable of the sower he does not use "the cares of this αἰών," but "the cares and riches and pleasures of life (βίου)" (Luke 8.14).
2 Matthew introduces his characteristic phrase "end of the age" into the disciples' question before Jesus' prophecy; the prophecy is paralleled in the other synoptics, but not the use of αἰών.
3 The noun is implied from earlier use in the verse, now to denote the coming (as opposed to present) age with οὔτε ἐν τῷ μέλλοντι, but the noun is not restated. Although not the same phrasing, this passage is paralleled in Mark 3.29, where αἰών is also used, but slightly differently.
4 In Mark 3.29, 10.30, Luke 18.30, John 4.14, and 10.28, in addition to the noun, the adjective αἰώνιος (eternal) also appears.
5 All of these synoptic references, plus all but one of the Johannine references in this category, use the phrase εἰς τὸν αἰῶνα (Luke 1.33 uses the plural; John 9.32 uses a negative with ἐκ τοῦ αἰῶνος to indicate "never").

## Appendix 2: ὁ καιρός in the Gospels and Acts

| | Matt | Mark | Luke | John | Acts | Totals |
|---|---|---|---|---|---|---|
| Positioning in the narrative (ἐν ἐκείνῳ τῷ καιρῷ) | 11.25; 12.1; 14.1 | | 13.1 | | 7.20; 12.1; 19.23 | 7 |
| **A moment:** | | | | | | |
| → A point in time (often eschatologically significant) | 8.29; 26.18 | 13.33 | 4.13; 21.8 | | | 5 |
| → An opportunity, proper time, (including harvest moment) | 13.30;[6] 21.34;[7] 24.45 | 12.2 | 1.20; 12.42; 20.10[8] | | 24.25 | 8 |
| **Duration of time:** | | | | | | |
| → Period of time (general sense of duration) | | | 8.13 (x2); | | 13.11 | 3 |
| → Period of time (including formal historical periodisation) | | 1.15 | 19.44; 21.24 | 7.6 (x2)[9]; 7.8[10] | 1.7; 3.20; 17.26 | 9 |
| → Season (often connected to fruit, though can still have eschatological meaning in context) | 21.41 | 11.13 | | | 14.17 | 3 |
| → *This* time (period of significance; may be contrasted with the coming αἰών) | 16.3 (plural)[11] | 10.30 | 12.56; 18.30 | | | 4 |
| Always | | | 21.36 | | | 1 |
| **Totals** | 10 | 5 | 13 | 3 | 9 | 40 |

---

**6** The time of harvest in this parable of the wheat and weeds is given an edge of eschatological significance through the wider story, which is confirmed by the use of αἰών in the explanation in 13.30.

**7** Note that this reference to the "time for fruit drawing near" does also give the sense of urgency of the harvest time that might indicate an eschatological edge, as in 13.30.

**8** The context implies that the time here is the time for harvesting, though it does not say that.

**9** Here John's Jesus contrasts his time (which has not yet come) with "your time" which is "always here." This suggests a duration of time, but also a sense of an appropriate and fitting moment, which sees these fulfilled. In this sense, perhaps John's use does not quite fit into any single category.

**10** The ESV and NRSV both translate this verse in a rather interpretative (and inaccurate!) way, for ὁ ἐμὸς καιρὸς οὔπω πεπλήρωται they translate "my time has not yet fully come," adding some kind of hint of a partial fulfilment, though the Greek simply says "my time has not yet been fulfilled."

**11** There is a textual difficulty with Matt 16.2–3 and whether the verses including the reference to understanding the "signs of the times" were added by a scribe who was already familiar with the Lukan parallel, or deleted by scribes in geographical areas where the weather patterns described in the explanation were not relevant. In his textual commentary, Metzger describes the committee's decision to retain the verses but in square brackets to reflect this uncertainty.

## Appendix 3: ὁ χρόνος in the Gospels and Acts

| | Matt | Mark | Luke | John | Acts | Totals |
|---|---|---|---|---|---|---|
| **A moment:** | | | | | | |
| → A moment of time, including a specific time of day | 2.7, 16 | | 1.57; 4.5 | | | 4 |
| → A moment in the broader sweep of history | | | | | 1.6; 7.17 | 2 |
| **Duration of time:** | | | | | | |
| → Narrative description about a period of time (a long time; for a while) | 25.19 | 2.19; 9.21 | 8.27; 18.4; 20.9; 23.8 | 5.6; 7.33; 12.35; 14.9 | 1.21; 8.11; 14.3, 28; 15.33; 18.20, 23; 19.22; 20.18; 27.9 | 21 |
| → A historical period | | | | | 1.7; 3.21; 17.30 | 3 |
| → A year | | | | | 7.23; 13.18 | 2 |
| Many occasions | | | 8.29[12] | | | 1 |
| **Totals** | 3 | 2 | 7 | 4 | 17 | 33 |

---

[12] The phrasing in the Greek is unclear. This follows Bovon (see discussion in Bovon, *Luke: Commentary*, 1:328 n. 46; contra Zerwick, *A Grammatical Analysis*, 207).

# Appendix 4: ἡ ὥρα in the Gospels and Acts

|  | Matt | Mark | Luke | John | Acts | Totals |
|---|---|---|---|---|---|---|
| **Time of day:** | | | | | | |
| → Late hour | 14.15 | 6.35 (x2); 11.11 | | | | 4 |
| → Specific time | 20.3, 5, 9; 27.45–46 (x3) | 15.25, 33–34 (x3) | 23.44 (x2) | 1.39; 4.6, 52–53 (x3); 19.14 | 2.15; 10.3, 9, 30; 23.23 | 23 |
| → Time of liturgical practice | | | 1.10 | | 3.1 | 2 |
| **Significant moment:** | | | | | | |
| → Hour of need (may include elements of eschatological woes) | 10.19 | 13.11 | 12.12 | 16.2, 4, 21, 32 | | 7 |
| → Jesus' hour, or hour of arrest | 26.45 | 14.41, 35 | | 2.4; 7.30; 8.20; 12.23, 27 (x2); 13.1; 17.1 | | 11 |
| → Hour of opponents | | | 22.53 | | | 1 |
| → The coming hour (eschatologically significant, also described through parables) | 24.36, 44, 50; 25.13 | 13.32 | 12.39, 40, 46 | 4.21, 23; 5.25, 28; 16.25 | | 13 |
| Length of time | 20.12; 26.40 | 14.37 | 22.59 | 5.35; 11.9 | 5.7; 19.34 | 8 |
| Narrative detail: at that very moment[13] | 8.13; 9.22; 15.28; 17.18; 18.1; 26.55 | | 2.38; 7.21; 10.21; 13.31; 14.17; 20.19; 22.14; 24.33 | 19.27 | 16.18, 33; 22.13 | 18 |
| **Totals** | 21 | 12 | 17 | 26 | 11 | 87 |

---

[13] Often emphatic.

# Appendix 5: ἡ ἡμέρα in the Gospels and Acts

|  | Matt | Mark | Luke | John | Acts | Totals |
|---|---|---|---|---|---|---|
| **Narrative timing:**[14] | | | | | | |
| → The same day/many days/these days of the events narrated | 3.1; 13.1; 22.23 | 1.9; 2.1; 4.35; 8.1 | 1.24, 25, 39; 2.1; 4.2; 5.17; 6.12; 8.22; 9.12, 36–37, 51; 15.13; 19.42; 20.1; 23.7; 24.13, 18 | 1.39; 2.12; 4.40; 20.19 | 1.5, 15; 2.41; 6.1; 7.26; 8.1; 9.19, 23, 37, 43; 10.48; 11.27; 13.31; 15.36; 16.12, 18; 18.18; 20.26; 21.5, 10, 15, 26, 38; 24.24; 25.13, 14; 27.7, 20 | 57 |
| → A specific number of days | 4.2; 15.32; 17.1; 26.2 | 1.13; 8.2; 9.2; 14.1 | 1.59; 2.21, 46; 4.2; 9.28; 24.21 | 2.1; 4.43; 11.6, 17; 12.1; 20.26 | 1.3; 7.8; 9.9; 10.30; 20.6 (x2); 21.4, 7, 27; 24.1, 11; 25.1, 6; 27.33; 28.7, 12, 13, 14, 17 | 39 |

---

14 This category includes uses both of expressions like "after six days" and "that same day." Although I have a separate category for references to Jesus' death and resurrection after "three days" and uses of the "day" as a theologically significant moment, I include all other references to a number of days in the narration in this category, even if there may be some further symbolic significance to the reference, such as Lazarus having died four days earlier (John 11.17) or the three days after which the missing child Jesus was found in the temple (Luke 2.46).

|  | Matt | Mark | Luke | John | Acts | Totals |
|---|---|---|---|---|---|---|
| → Three days related to Jesus' death and resurrection (including metaphorical/parabolic uses) | 12.40 (x2); 16.21; 17.23; 20.19; 26.61; 27.40, 63, 64 | 8.31; 9.31; 10.34; 14.58; 15.29 | 9.22; 18.33; 24.7, 46 | 2.19, 20 | 10.40 | 21 |
| **Duration:** | | | | | | |
| → Generic day period | 6.34; 20.2, 6, 12 | | 2.44; 13.14; 17.4; 24.29 | 11.9 | 2.15; 10.3; 26.13 | 12 |
| → Political or historical period (e.g. the days of Herod) | 2.1; 11.12; 23.30; 24.37, 38 | | 1.5; 4.25; 17.26 (x2), 28 | | 5.36, 37; 7.41, 45; 13.41; 15.7 | 16 |
| → Those days (in the sense of anticipated days, including eschatol woes) | 9.15; 24.19, 22 (x2), 29 | 2.20 (x2); 13.17, 19–20 (x3), 24 | 5.35 (x2); 6.23; 17.22; 19.43; 21.6, 22, 23; 23.29 | | 2.17, 18; 3.24 | 24 |
| **Moment:** | | | | | | |
| → Time of an event or opportunity | 22.46; 24.38; 28.15[15] | 6.21 | 1.20, 80; 2.6; 17.27, 29; 23.12 | 8.56; 11.53; 12.7; 14.20 | 1.2, 22; 2.29; 12.21; 20.18; 23.1; 26.22; 28.23 | 22 |
| → That day (eschatologically significant, including day of the Son of Man, last day, judgement day; including in parables) | 7.22; 10.15; 11.22, 24; 12.36; 24.36, 42, 50; 25.13; 26.29 | 13.32; 14.25 | 10.12; 12.46; 17.22, 24, 30, 31; 21.34 | 6.39, 40, 44, 54; 11.24; 12.48; 16.23, 26 | 2.20; 17.31 | 29 |

---

[15] Textual variant; see discussion in Metzger, *A Textual Commentary*, 60.

|  | Matt | Mark | Luke | John | Acts | Totals |
|---|---|---|---|---|---|---|
| Festival or liturgical time |  | 14.12 | 1.23; 2.22, 43; 4.16; 13.14, 16; 14.5; 22.7; 23.54 | 5.9; 7.37; 9.14; 19.31 | 2.1; 12.3; 13.14; 16.13; 20.6, 16; 21.26 | 21 |
| Day, as opposed to night time |  |  | 4.42; 6.13; 22.66 | 9.4; 11.9 | 12.18; 16.35; 23.12; 27.29, 33, 39 | 11 |
| Constantly, daily | 26.55; 28.20 | 4.27; *5.5*; *14.49* | 1.75; 2.37; 9.23; 11.3; 16.19; 18.7; 19.47; 21.37; *22.53* |  | 2.46, 47; 3.2; 5.42; 9.24; 16.5; 17.11, 17; 19.9; 20.31; 26.7 | 25 |
| Age (advanced in days) |  |  | 1.7, 18; 2.36 |  |  | 3 |
| Totals | 45 | 27 | 83 | 31 | 94 | 280 |

# Bibliography

Adams, Edward. *The Stars Will Fall from Heaven: Cosmic Catastrophe in the New Testament and Its World*. LNTS 347. London: T&T Clark, 2007.
Adams, Sean A. "Luke's Preface and Its Relationship to Greek Historiography: A Response to Loveday Alexander." *JGRChJ* 3 (2006): 177–91.
—— *The Genre of Acts and Collected Biography*. SNTSMS 156. Cambridge: Cambridge University Press, 2013.
Aitken, James. "The Language of the Septuagint and Jewish-Greek Identity." Pages 120–34 in *The Jewish-Greek Tradition in Antiquity and the Byzantine Empire*. Edited by James Aitken and James Carleton Paget. Cambridge: Cambridge University Press, 2014.
Alexander, Loveday. *The Preface to Luke's Gospel: Literary Convention and Social Context in Luke 1:1–4 and Acts 1:1*. SNTSMS 78. Cambridge: Cambridge University Press, 1993.
—— "Reading Luke-Acts from Back to Front." Pages 207–29 in *Acts in Its Ancient Literary Context: A Classicist Looks at the Acts of the Apostles*. JSNTSup 298. London: T&T Clark, 2007.
Alexander, Phillip S. "The Evil Empire: The Qumran Eschatological War Cycle and the Origins of Jewish Opposition to Rome." Pages 17–31 in *Emmanuel: Studies in Hebrew Bible, Septuagint, and Dead Sea Scrolls in Honor of Emanuel Tov*. Edited by Shalom M. Paul, Robert A. Kraft, Lawrence H. Schiffman, and Weston W. Fields. VTSup 94. Leiden: Brill, 2003.
—— "The Rabbis, the Greek Bible and Hellenism." Pages 229–46 in *The Jewish-Greek Tradition in Antiquity and the Byzantine Empire*. Edited by James Aitken and James Carleton Paget. Cambridge: Cambridge University Press, 2014.
Alter, Robert. *The Art of Biblical Narrative*. Rev. ed. New York: Basic Books, 2011.
Ashton, John. "Intimations of Apocalyptic: Looking Back and Looking Forward." Pages 3–35 in *John's Gospel and Intimations of Apocalyptic*. Edited by Christopher Rowland and Catrin H. Williams. London: Bloomsbury, 2013.
Attridge, Harold W. *The Interpretation of Biblical History in the Antiquitates Judaicae of Flavius Josephus*. HDR 7. Missoula, MT: Scholars Press, 1976.
—— "Jewish Historiography." Pages 311–43 in *Early Judaism and Its Modern Interpreters*. Edited by Robert A. Kraft and George W. E. Nickelsburg. BMI 2. Philadelphia: Fortress, 1986.
Aune, David E. "Genre Theory and the Genre-Function of Mark and Matthew." Pages 25–56 in *Jesus, Gospel Tradition and Paul in the Context of Jewish and Greco-Roman Antiquity: Collected Essays II*. Edited by David E. Aune. WUNT 303. Tübingen: Mohr Siebeck, 2013.
Austin, R. G. P. *Vergili Maronis, Aeneidos: Liber Sextus*. Oxford: Clarendon, 1977.
Bachmann, Veronika. "More than the Present: Perspectives on World History in *4 Ezra* and *The Book of the Watchers*." Pages 3–21 in *Interpreting 4 Ezra and 2 Baruch: International Studies*. Edited by Gabriele Boccaccini and Jason M. Zurawski. LSTS 87. London: Bloomsbury, 2014.
Balch, David L. "Two Apologetic Encomia: Dionysius on Rome and Josephus on the Jews." *JSJ* 13 (1982): 102–22.
Ballard, Paul H. "Reasons for Refusing the Great Supper." *JTS* 23 (1972): 341–50.
Balz, Horst, and Gerhard Schneider, eds. *Exegetical Dictionary of the New Testament*. 3 vols. Grand Rapids: Eerdmans, 1990–1993.

Barchiesi, Alessandro. "Virgilian Narrative: Ecphrasis." Pages 271–81 in *The Cambridge Companion to Virgil*. Edited by Charles Martindale. Cambridge: Cambridge University Press, 1997.
Barclay, John M. G., ed. and trans. *Flavius Josephus: Against Apion*. Flavius Josephus: Translation and Commentary 10. Boston: Brill, 2006.
— "Introduction." Pages 1–8 in *Divine and Human Agency in Paul and His Cultural Environment*. Edited by John M. G. Barclay and Simon J. Gathercole. T&T Clark Biblical Studies. London: T&T Clark, 2008.
— *Jews in the Mediterranean Diaspora: From Alexander to Trajan (323 BCE–117 CE)*. Edinburgh: T&T Clark, 1996.
— *Paul and the Gift*. Grand Rapids: Eerdmans, 2015.
Barr, James. *Biblical Words for Time*. 2nd rev. ed. SBT 33. London: SCM, 1969.
— *History and Ideology in the Old Testament: Biblical Studies at the End of a Millennium*. Oxford: Oxford University Press, 2000.
Barreto, Eric D. *Ethnic Negotiations: The Function of Race and Ethnicity in Acts 16*. WUNT 2/294. Tübingen: Mohr Siebeck, 2010.
Barrett, C. K. *The Acts of the Apostles: A Shorter Commentary*. London: T&T Clark, 2002.
— *A Critical and Exegetical Commentary on the Acts of the Apostles*. 2 vols. ICC. Edinburgh: T&T Clark, 1994–1998.
— *Luke the Historian in Recent Study*. A. S. Peake Memorial Lecture 6. London: Epworth, 1961.
— "Theologia Crucis—In Acts?" Pages 73–84 in *Theologia Crucis—Signum Crucis: Festschrift für Erich Dinkler zum 70. Geburtstag*. Edited by Carl Andresen and Günter Klein. Tübingen: Mohr Siebeck, 1979.
Barton, John. *The Biblical World*. 2 vols. London: Routledge, 2002.
Bauer, W., F. W. Danker, W. F. Arndt, and F. W. Gringrich. *A Greek-English Lexicon of the New Testament and Other Early Christian Literature*. 3rd. ed. Chicago: Chicago University Press, 2000.
Bauspieß, Martin. "Die Gegenwart des Heils und das Ende der Zeit: Überlegungen zur lukanischen Eschatologie im Anschluss an Lk 22,66–71 und Apg 7,54–60." Pages 125–48 in *Eschatologie—Eschatology: The Sixth Durham-Tübingen Research Symposium: Eschatology in Old Testament, Ancient Judaism and Early Christianity (Tübingen, September, 2009)*. Edited by Hans-Joachim Eckstein, Christof Landmesser, and Hermann Lichtenberger. Tübingen: Mohr Siebeck, 2011.
— *Geschichte und Erkenntnis im lukanischen Doppelwerk: Eine exegetische Untersuchung zu einer christlichen Perspektive auf Geschichte*. Arbeiten zur Bibel und ihrer Geschichte 42. Leipzig: Evangelische Verlagsanstalt, 2012.
Becker, Eve-Marie. *The Birth of Christian History: Memory and Time from Mark to Luke-Acts*. AYBRL. New Haven: Yale University Press, 2017.
Begg, Christopher T., and Paul Spilsbury, eds. and trans. *Flavius Josephus: Judean Antiquities 8–10*. Flavius Josephus: Translation and Commentary 5. Leiden: Brill, 2005.
Ben Zeev, Miriam Pucci. "Polybius, Josephus, and the Capitol in Rome." *JSJ* 27 (1996): 21–30.
Bergren, Theodore A. "Christian Influence on the Transmission History of 4, 5, and 6 Ezra." Pages 102–27 in *The Jewish Apocalyptic Heritage in Early Christianity*. Edited by James C. VanderKam and William Adler. CRINT 4. Minneapolis: Fortress, 1996.
Berthelot, Katell. "Philo's Perception of the Roman Empire." *JSJ* 42 (2011): 166–87.

Bilde, Per. *Flavius Josephus, between Jerusalem and Rome: His Life, His Works, and Their Importance.* JSPSup 2. Sheffield: JSOT Press, 1988.
—— "Josephus and Jewish Apocalypticism." Pages 35–61 in *Understanding Josephus: Seven Perspectives.* Edited by Steve Mason. JSPSup 32. Sheffield: Sheffield Academic, 1998.
Bizzarro, Laura. "The 'Meaning of History' in the Fifth Vision of *4 Ezra.*" Pages 32–38 in *Interpreting 4 Ezra and 2 Baruch: International Studies.* Edited by Gabriele Boccaccini and Jason M. Zurawski. LSTS 87. London: Bloomsbury, 2014.
Bloomer, W. Martin. *Valerius Maximus and the Rhetoric of the New Nobility.* London: Duckworth, 1992.
Bobzien, Susanne. *Determinism and Freedom in Stoic Philosophy.* Oxford: Clarendon, 1998.
Boccaccini, Gabriele. "Inner-Jewish Debate on the Tension between Divine and Human Agency in Second Temple Judaism." Pages 9–26 in *Divine and Human Agency in Paul and His Cultural Environment.* Edited by John M. G. Barclay and Simon J. Gathercole. T&T Clark Biblical Studies. London: T&T Clark, 2008.
—— *Middle Judaism: Jewish Thought, 300 BCE to 200 CE.* Minneapolis: Fortress, 1991.
Bock, Darrell L. *A Theology of Luke and Acts: God's Promised Program, Realized for All Nations.* Biblical Theology of the New Testament. Grand Rapids: Zondervan, 2011.
Bockmuehl, Markus N. A. "Creatio ex Nihilo in Palestinian Judaism and Early Christianity." *SJT* 65 (2012): 253–70.
—— "The Gospels on the Presence of Jesus." Pages 87–102 in *The Oxford Handbook of Christology.* Edited by Francesca Aran Murphy. Oxford: Oxford University Press, 2015.
—— *Revelation and Mystery in Ancient Judaism and Pauline Christianity.* WUNT 2/36. Tübingen: Mohr Siebeck, 1990.
—— "Why Not Let Acts Be Acts? In Conversation with C. Kavin Rowe." Pages 70–73 in *Rethinking the Unity and Reception of Luke and Acts.* Edited by Andrew Gregory and C. Kavin Rowe. Columbia: University of South Carolina Press, 2010.
Bonz, Marianne Palmer. *The Past as Legacy: Luke-Acts and Ancient Epic.* Minneapolis: Augsburg Fortress, 2000.
Bovon, François. "Apocalyptic Traditions in the Lukan Special Material: Reading Luke 18.1–8." Pages 51–58 in *Studies in Early Christianity.* Grand Rapids: Baker Academic, 2003.
—— *Luke.* Translated by Christine M. Thomas, Donald S. Deer, and James Crouch. 3 vols. Hermeneia. Minneapolis: Fortress, 2002–2013. Translation of *Das Evangelium nach Lukas.* 4 vols. EKKNT. Neukirchen-Vluyn: Neukirchener, 1989–2009.
—— *Luke the Theologian: Fifty-Five Years of Research (1950–2005).* 2nd rev. ed. Waco, TX: Baylor University Press, 2006.
Brandenburger, Egon. *Die Verborgenheit Gottes im Weltgeschehen: Das literarische und theologische Problem des 4. Esrabuches.* ATANT 68. Zürich: Theologischer Verlag, 1981.
Braun, Willi. *Feasting and Social Rhetoric in Luke 14.* SNTSMS 85. Cambridge: Cambridge University Press, 1995.
Braund, S. H., ed. and trans. *Lucan: Civil War.* Oxford: Clarendon, 1992.
Braund, Susanna Morton. "Virgil and the Cosmos: Religious and Philosophical Ideas." Pages 204–21 in *The Cambridge Companion to Virgil.* Edited by Charles Martindale. Cambridge: Cambridge University Press, 1997.
Brett, Mark G. *Decolonizing God: The Bible in the Tides of Empire.* Bible in the Modern World. Sheffield: Sheffield Phoenix, 2008.

Bruce, F. F. *1 & 2 Thessalonians*. WBC 45. Waco, TX: Word, 1982.
—— *The Book of Acts*. Rev. ed. NICNT. Grand Rapids: Eerdmans, 1988.
Brueggemann, Walter. *Theology of the Old Testament: Testimony, Dispute, Advocacy*. Minneapolis: Fortress, 1997.
Bultmann, Rudolf. *History and Eschatology*. The Gifford Lectures 1955. Edinburgh: Edinburgh University Press, 1957.
—— *Theology of the New Testament*. Translated by Kendrick Grobel. 2 vols. London: SCM, 1952–1955. Translation of *Theologie des neuen Testaments*. 3 vols. Tübingen: Mohr, 1948–1953.
Burke, Peter. "Strengths and Weaknesses of the History of Mentalities." Pages 442–56 in vol. 2 of *The Annales School: Critical Assessments*. Edited by Stuart Clark. London: Routledge, 1999.
Burridge, Richard. *What Are the Gospels? A Comparison with Graeco-Roman Biography*. SNTSMS 70. Cambridge: Cambridge University Press, 1992.
Burton, Anne. *Diodorus Siculus, Book I: A Commentary*. Leiden: Brill, 1972.
Busse, Ulrich. "Eschatologie in der Apostelgeschichte." Pages 141–78 in *Eschatology of the New Testament and Some Related Documents*. Edited by Jan G. van der Watt. WUNT 2/315. Tübingen: Mohr Siebeck, 2011.
Byrne, Brendan. *The Hospitality of God: A Reading of Luke's Gospel*. Strathfield: St Pauls, 2000.
Cadbury, Henry J. "Acts and Eschatology." Pages 300–21 in *The Background of the New Testament and Its Eschatology: Studies in Honour of C. H. Dodd*. Edited by W. D. Davies and D. Daube. Cambridge: Cambridge University Press, 1956.
—— *The Making of Luke-Acts*. 2nd ed. London: SPCK, 1958.
Campbell, Douglas A. *The Deliverance of God: An Apocalyptic Rereading of Justification in Paul*. Grand Rapids: Eerdmans, 2009.
Cancik, Hubert, ed. *Brill's New Pauly: Encyclopedia of the Ancient World*. 22 vols. Leiden: Brill, 2002–2011.
—— "The End of the World, of History, and of the Individual in Greek and Roman Antiquity." Pages 84–125 in *The Origins of Apocalypticism in Judaism and Christianity*. Vol. 1 of *The Encyclopedia of Apocalypticism*. Edited by John J. Collins. New York: Continuum, 1998.
—— "The History of Culture, Religion, and Institutions in Ancient Historiography: Philological Observations Concerning Luke's History." *JBL* 116 (1997): 673–95.
Carroll, John T. *Luke: A Commentary*. NTL. Louisville: Westminster John Knox, 2012.
—— *Response to the End of History: Eschatology and Situation in Luke-Acts*. SBLDS 92. Atlanta: Scholars Press, 1988.
Carter, C. J. "Valerius Maximus." Pages 26–56 in *Empire and Aftermath: Silver Latin II*. Edited by T. A. Dorey. Greek and Latin Studies: Classical Literature and Its Influence. London: Routledge & Kegan Paul, 1975.
Chandler, Daniel. "An Introduction to Genre Theory." Rev. ed. 2000. https://www.researchgate.net/publication/242253420_An_Introduction_to_Genre_Theory
Chandler, Daniel, and Rod Munday. "Genre." Page 173 in *A Dictionary of Media and Communication*. Oxford: Oxford University Press, 2011.
Chartier, Roger. *Cultural History: Between Practices and Representations*. Translated by Lydia G. Cochrane. Cambridge: Polity, 1988.
Childs, Brevard S. *Isaiah*. OTL. Louisville: Westminster John Knox, 2001.

Clark, Gillian. "Paradise for Pagans? Augustine on Virgil, Cicero, and Plato." Pages 166–78 in *Paradise in Antiquity: Jewish and Christian Views.* Edited by Markus N. A. Bockmuehl and Guy G. Stroumsa. Cambridge: Cambridge University Press, 2010.
Clarke, Katherine. *Making Time for the Past: Local History and the Polis.* Oxford: Oxford University Press, 2008.
Cohen, Ralph. "Introduction." *New Literary History* 34 (2003): v–xv.
Cohen, Shaye J. D. "Polybius, Jeremiah, and Josephus." *History and Theory* 21 (1982): 366–81.
Collins, Adela Yarbro. "Apocalypses and Apocalypticism: Early Christian." *ABD* 1:288–92.
Collins, John J. "Apocalypse: The Morphology of a Genre." *Semeia* 14 (1979): 1–19.
—— *Daniel: A Commentary on the Book of Daniel.* Hermeneia. Minneapolis: Fortress, 1993.
—— "Expectations of the End in the Dead Sea Scrolls." Pages 74–90 in *Eschatology, Messianism, and the Dead Sea Scrolls.* Edited by Craig A. Evans and Peter W. Flint. Studies in the Dead Sea Scrolls and Related Literature 1. Grand Rapids: Eerdmans, 1997.
—— "Messianism in the Maccabean Period." Pages 97–109 in *Judaisms and Their Messiahs at the Turn of the Christian Era.* Edited by Jacob Neusner, William Scott Green, and Ernest Frerichs. Cambridge: Cambridge University Press, 1987.
—— "The Mythology of Holy War in Daniel and the Qumran War Scroll: A Point of Transition in Jewish Apocalyptic." *VT* 25 (1975): 596–612.
—— *The Scepter and the Star: The Messiahs of the Dead Sea Scrolls and Other Ancient Literature.* ABRL. New York: Doubleday, 1995.
—— "Short Notes: Dualism and Eschatology in 1 QM: A Reply to P. R. Davies." *VT* 29 (1979): 212–15.
—— "Temporality and Politics in Jewish Apocalyptic Literature." Pages 26–43 in *Apocalyptic in History and Tradition.* Edited by Christopher Rowland and John Barton. JSPSup 43. Sheffield: Sheffield Academic, 2002.
Conzelmann, Hans. *Acts of the Apostles.* Translated by James Limburg, A. Thomas Kraabel, and Donald H. Juel. Hermeneia. Philadelphia: Fortress, 1987. Translation of *Die Apostelgeschichte.* HNT 7. Tübingen: Mohr, 1963.
—— "Fragen an Gerhard von Rad." *EvT* 24 (1964): 113–25.
—— "Luke's Place in the Development of Early Christianity." Pages 298–316 in *Studies in Luke-Acts: Essays Presented in Honor of Paul Schubert.* Edited by Leander E. Keck and J. Louis Martyn. Nashville: Abingdon, 1966.
—— *The Theology of St Luke.* Translated by Geoffrey Buswell. London: Faber, 1960. Translation of *Die Mitte der Zeit: Studien zur Theologie des Lukas.* BHT 17. Tübingen: Mohr Siebeck, 1954.
—— "Was von Anfang war." Pages 194–201 in *Neutestamentliche Studien für Rudolf Bultmann, zu seinem siebzigsten Geburtstag am 20. August 1954.* Edited by Walther Eltester. BZNW 21. Berlin: Töpelmann, 1954.
—— "Zur Lukasanalyse." *ZTK* 49 (1952): 16–33.
Cornford, Francis MacDonald. *Thucydides Mythistoricus.* London: Arnold, 1907.
Cosgrove, Charles H. "The Divine ΔΕΙ in Luke-Acts: Investigations into the Lukan Understanding of God's Providence." *NovT* 26 (1984): 168–90.
Crabbe, Kylie. "Accepting Prophecy: Paul's Response to Agabus with Insights from Valerius Maximus and Josephus." *JSNT* 39 (2016): 188–208.

— "Being Found Fighting against God: Luke's Gamaliel and Josephus on Human Responses to Divine Providence." *ZNW* 106 (2015): 21–39.
— "A Sinner and a Pharisee: Challenge at Simon's Table in Luke 7:36–50." *Pacifica* 24 (2011): 247–66.
Culler, Jonathan D. *Structuralist Poetics: Structuralism, Linguistics and the Study of Literature.* London: Routledge & Kegan Paul, 1975.
Cullmann, Oscar. *Christ and Time: The Primitive Christian Conception of Time and History.* Translated by Floyd V. Filson. Rev. ed. London: SCM, 1962. Translation of *Christus und die Zeit: Die urchristliche Zeit- und Geschichtsauffassung.* Zollikon-Zürich: Evangelischer Verlag, 1946.
— *Salvation in History.* Translated by Sidney G. Sowers. London: SCM, 1967. Translation of *Heil als Geschichte.* Tübingen: Mohr, 1965.
Cunningham, Scott. *"Through Many Tribulations": The Theology of Persecution in Luke-Acts.* JSNTSup 142. Sheffield: Sheffield Academic, 1997.
Darr, John A. "Irenic or Ironic? Another Look at Gamaliel before the Sanhedrin (Acts 5:33–42)." Pages 121–40 in *Literary Studies in Luke-Acts: Essays in Honor of Joseph B. Tyson.* Edited by Richard P. Thompson and Thomas E. Phillips. Macon, GA: Mercer University Press, 1998.
— Review of *The Plan of God in Luke-Acts*, by John T. Squires. *CBQ* 57 (1995): 191–92.
Davies, G. I. "Apocalyptic and Historiography." *JSOT* 5 (1978): 15–28.
Davies, J. P., "Paul Among the Apocalypses? An Evaluation of the "Apocalyptic Paul" in the Context of Jewish and Christian Apocalyptic Literature." LNTS 562. London: T&T Clark, 2016.
Davies, Philip R. "Daniel in the Lion's Den." Pages 160–78 in *Images of Empire.* Edited by Loveday Alexander. JSOTSup 122. Sheffield: JSOT Press, 1991.
— "Death, Resurrection, and Life after Death in the Qumran Scrolls." Pages 189–212 in *Death, Life after Death, Resurrection and the World-to-Come in the Judaisms of Late Antiquity.* Edited by Alan J. Avery-Peck and Jacob Neusner. Judaism in Late Antiquity 4. Leiden: Brill, 2000.
— "Dualism and Eschatology in 1QM: A Rejoinder." *VT* 30 (1980): 93–97.
— "Dualism and Eschatology in the Qumran War Scroll." *VT* 28 (1978): 28–36.
— "Eschatology at Qumran." *JBL* 104 (1985): 39–55.
— *In Search of "Ancient Israel."* JSOTSup 148. Sheffield: Sheffield Academic, 1992.
— "Qumran and Apocalyptic or *Obscurum per Obscurius.*" *JNES* 49 (1990): 127–34.
— "War of the Sons of Light against the Sons of Darkness." Pages 965–68 in vol. 2 of *Encyclopedia of the Dead Sea Scrolls.* Edited by Lawrence H. Schiffman and James C. VanderKam. New York: Oxford University Press, 2000.
Dibelius, Martin. *Studies in the Acts of the Apostles.* London: SCM, 1956. Translation of *Aufsätze zur Apostelgeschichte.* FRLANT 60. Göttingen: Vandenhoeck & Ruprecht, 1951.
Dick, Bernard F. "*Fatum* and *Fortuna* in Lucan's *Bellum Civile.*" *Classical Philology* 62 (1967): 235–42.
Dicken, Frank. *Herod as a Composite Character in Luke-Acts.* WUNT 2/375. Tübingen: Mohr Siebeck, 2014.
Dimant, Devorah. "4 Ezra and 2 Baruch in Light of Qumran Literature." Pages 31–61 in *Fourth Ezra and Second Baruch: Reconstruction after the Fall.* Edited by Matthias Henze,

Gabriele Boccaccini, and Jason M. Zurawski. Supplements to the Journal for the Study of Judaism 164. Leiden: Brill, 2013.

—— "Between Qumran Sectarian and Non-Sectarian Texts: The Case of Belial and Mastema." Pages 235–56 in *The Dead Sea Scrolls and Contemporary Culture: Proceedings of the International Conference Held at the Israel Museum, Jerusalem (July 6–8, 2008)*. Edited by Adolfo D. Roitman, Lawrence H. Schiffman, and Shani Tzoref. STDJ 93. Leiden: Brill, 2011.

Diodorus Siculus. *The Library of History*. Translated by C. H. Oldfather. 12 vols. LCL. Cambridge: Harvard University Press, 1933–1967.

Dodds, E. R. *The Ancient Concept of Progress and Other Essays*. Oxford: Clarendon, 1973.

Donahue, J. R. "Two Decades of Research on the Rich and the Poor in Luke-Acts." Pages 129–44 in *Justice and the Holy*. Edited by Douglas A. Knight. Atlanta: Harrelson, 1989.

Doran, Robert. *2 Maccabees: A Critical Commentary*. Hermeneia. Minneapolis: Fortress, 2012.

—— "2 Maccabees and 'Tragic History.'" *HUCA* 50 (1979): 107–14.

—— "Independence or Co-Existence: The Responses of 1 and 2 Maccabees to Seleucid Hegemony." Pages 94–103 in *Society of Biblical Literature, 1999 Seminar Papers*. SBLSPS 38. Atlanta: Society of Biblical Literature, 1999.

Doty, William G. "The Concept of Genre in Literary Analysis." Pages 413–48 in *Seminar Papers: The Society of Biblical Literature, 108th Annual Meeting*. Edited by Lane C. McGaughy. Missoula, MT: SBL Press, 1972.

Dräger, Paul. "Ananke." *BNP* 1:642.

Dreyer, Boris. "Polybius." *BNP* 11:495–503.

Drury, John. *Tradition and Design in Luke's Gospel: A Study in Early Christian Historiography*. London: Darton, Longman & Todd, 1976.

Dubrow, Heather. *Genre*. The Critical Idiom 42. London: Methuen, 1982.

Dunn, James D. G. "The Book of Acts as Salvation History." Pages 385–401 in *Heil und Geschichte: Die Geschichtsbezogenheit des Heils und das Problem der Heilsgeschichte in der biblischen Tradition und in der theologischen Deutung*. Edited by Jörg Frey, Stefan Krauter, and Hermann Lichtenberger. WUNT 248. Tübingen: Mohr Siebeck, 2009.

Eckstein, Arthur M. *Moral Vision in the Histories of Polybius*. Hellenistic Culture and Society 16. London: University of California Press, 1995.

Edelstein, Ludwig. *The Idea of Progress in Classical Antiquity*. Baltimore, MD: Johns Hopkins Press, 1967.

Edwards, Mark. "Gospel and Genre: Some Reservations." Pages 51–62 in *The Limits of Ancient Biography*. Edited by Brian McGing and Judith Mossman. Swansea: Classical Press of Wales, 2006.

Edwards, Mark W. *Books 17–20*. Vol. 5 of *The Iliad: A Commentary*. Cambridge: Cambridge University Press, 1991.

Ego, Beate. "God's Justice: The 'Measure for Measure' Principle in 2 Maccabees." Pages 141–54 in *The Books of the Maccabees: History, Theology, Ideology: Papers of the Second International Conference on the Deuterocanoncial Books, Pápa, Hungary, 9–11 June, 2005*. Edited by Géza G. Xeravits and József Zsengellér. Supplements to the Journal for the Study of Judaism 118. Leiden: Brill, 2007.

Eliade, Mircea. *The Myth of the Eternal Return: Cosmos and History*. Translated by Willard R. Trask. Bollingen Series 46. Princeton: Princeton University Press, 2005. Translation of *Le mythe de l'éternel retour: Archétypes et répétition*. Paris: Gallimard, 1949.

Elliott, Gregory. *Ends in Sight: Marx/Fukuyama/Hobsbawm/Anderson*. London: Pluto, 2008.
Ellis, E. Earle. "The End of the Earth (Acts 1:8)." Pages 53–63 in *History and Interpretation in New Testament Perspective*. BibInt 54. Leiden: Brill, 2001.
— "Eschatology in Luke." Pages 105–19 in *Eschatology in Luke*. FBBS 30. Philadelphia: Fortress, 1972. Translation of "Die Funktion der Eschatologie im Lukasevangelium." *ZTK* 66 (1969): 387–402.
— "Eschatology in Luke Revisited." Pages 120–28 in *Eschatology in Luke*. FBBS 30. Philadelphia: Fortress, 1972.
— *The Gospel of Luke*. Rev. ed. NCB. London: Oliphants, 1974.
— "Present and Future Eschatology in Luke." Pages 129–46 in *Eschatology in Luke*. FBBS 30. Philadelphia: Fortress, 1972.
Elvers, Karl-Ludwig. "Strabo." *BNP* 13:865–69.
Emmrich, Martin. *At the Heart of Luke: Wisdom and Reversal of Fortune*. Eugene, OR: Pickwick, 2013.
Engberg-Pedersen, Troels. *Cosmology and Self in the Apostle Paul: The Material Spirit*. Oxford: Oxford University Press, 2010.
Errington, R. M. "The Chronology of Polybius' Histories, Books I and II." *The Journal of Roman Studies* 57 (1967): 96–108.
Evans, Craig A. *To See and Not Perceive: Isaiah 6.9–10 in Early Jewish and Christian Interpretation*. JSOTSup 64. Sheffield: JSOT Press, 1989.
Fantham, Elaine, ed. *Virgil: Aeneid*. Translated by Frederick Ahl. Oxford World's Classics. Oxford: Oxford University Press, 2007.
Farahian, Edmond. "Paul's Vision at Troas (Acts 16:9–10)." Pages 197–207 in *Luke and Acts*. Edited by Gerald O'Collins and Gilberto Marconi. New York: Paulist, 1991.
Farrell, Hobert Kenneth. "The Eschatological Perspective of Luke-Acts." PhD diss., Boston University Graduate School, 1972.
Farrell, Joseph. "Classical Genre in Theory and Practice." *New Literary History* 34 (2003): 383–408.
Fascher, Erich. "Theologische Beobachtungen zu δεῖ." Pages 228–54 in *Neutestamentliche Studien für Rudolf Bultmann, zu seinem siebzigsten Geburtstag am 20. August 1954*. Edited by Walther Eltester. BZNW 21. Berlin: Töpelmann, 1954.
Febvre, Lucien. *The Problem of Unbelief in the Sixteenth Century: The Religion of Rabelais*. Translated by Beatrice Gottlieb. Cambridge: Harvard University Press, 1982. Translation of *Le problèm de l'incroyance au XVIe siècle: La religion de Rabelais*. Paris: Michel, 1942.
Fee, Gordon D. *The First and Second Letters to the Thessalonians*. NICNT. Grand Rapids: Eerdmans, 2009.
Feeney, D. C. *The Gods in Epic: Poets and Critics of the Classical Tradition*. Oxford: Clarendon, 1991.
— "History and Revelation in Vergil's Underworld." *Proceedings of the Classical Philological Society* 32 (1986): 1–24.
Feldman, Louis H., ed. and trans. *Flavius Josephus: Judean Antiquities 1–4*. Flavius Josephus: Translation and Commentary 3. Boston: Brill, 2000.
— *Josephus's Interpretation of the Bible*. Hellenistic Culture and Society. Berkeley: University of California Press, 1998.

— *Studies in Josephus' Rewritten Bible*. Supplements to the Journal for the Study of Judaism 58. Leiden: Brill, 1998.
Fishbane, Michael A. *Biblical Interpretation in Ancient Israel*. Oxford: Oxford University Press, 1985.
Fitzmyer, Joseph A. *The Acts of the Apostles*. AB 31. New York: Doubleday, 1998.
— *The Gospel according to Luke*. 2 vols. AB 28 & 28 A. New York: Doubleday, 1981–1985.
Flannery Dailey, Frances. "Non-Linear Time in Apocalyptic Texts: The Spiral Model." Pages 231–45 in *Society of Biblical Literature, 1999 Seminar Papers*. SBLSPS 38. Atlanta: Society of Biblical Literature, 1999.
Flender, Helmut. *St Luke: Theologian of Redemptive History*. Translated by Reginald H. Fuller and Ilse Fuller. London: SPCK, 1967. Translation of *Heil und Geschichte in der Theologie des Lukas*. BZET 41. Erlangen: Universität Erlangen-Nürnberg, 1965.
Foakes Jackson, F. J., Kirsopp Lake, James Hardy Ropes, and Henry J. Cadbury. *The Beginnings of Christianity: Part 1, The Acts of the Apostles*. 5 vols. London: Macmillan, 1920–1933.
Fowler, Alastair. "The Formation of Genres in the Renaissance and After." *New Literary History* 34 (2003): 185–200.
— *Kinds of Literature: An Introduction to the Theory of Genres and Modes*. Oxford: Clarendon, 1982.
France, R. T. *Luke*. Teach the Text Commentary Series. Grand Rapids: Baker, 2013.
Francis, Fred O. "Eschatology and History in Luke-Acts." *JAAR* 37 (1969): 49–63.
Franke, Thomas, and Egon Flaig. "Tacitus." *BNP* 14:105–12.
Franklin, Eric. "The Ascension and the Eschatology of Luke-Acts." *SJT* 23 (1970): 191–200.
Freedman, David Noel, ed. *The Anchor Bible Dictionary*. 6 vols. New York: Doubleday, 1992.
Fukuyama, Francis. *The End of History and the Last Man*. New York: Free Press, 1992.
Fusco, Vittorio. "Problems of Structure in Luke's Eschatological Discourse (Luke 21:7–36)." Pages 72–92 in *Luke and Acts*. Edited by Gerald O'Collins and Gilberto Marconi. New York: Paulist, 1991.
Galinsky, Karl. *Augustan Culture: An Interpretive Introduction*. Princeton: Princeton University Press, 1996.
García Martínez, Florentino. "Apocalypticism in the Dead Sea Scrolls." Pages 162–92 in *The Origins of Apocalypticism in Judaism and Christianity*. Vol. 1 of *The Encyclopedia of Apocalypticism*. Edited by John J. Collins. New York: Continuum, 1998.
García Martínez, Florentino, and Eibert J. C. Tigchelaar. *The Dead Sea Scrolls Study Edition*. 2 vols. Leiden: Brill, 1997.
Gaventa, Beverly Roberts. *Acts*. ANTC. Nashville: Abingdon, 2003.
— ed. *Apocalyptic Paul: Cosmos and Anthropos in Romans 5–8*. Waco, TX: Baylor University Press, 2013.
— "The Eschatology of Luke-Acts Revisited." *Encounter* 43 (1982): 27–42.
Goldstein, Jonathan A. "How the Authors of 1 and 2 Maccabees Treated the 'Messianic' Promises." Pages 69–96 in *Judaisms and Their Messiahs at the Turn of the Christian Era*. Edited by Jacob Neusner, William Scott Green, and Ernest Frerichs. Cambridge: Cambridge University Press, 1987.
— *II Maccabees*. AB 41 A. Garden City, NY: Doubleday, 1983.

Gottlieb, Gunther. "Religion in the Politics of Augustus (*Aeneid* 1.278–91, 8.714–23, 12.791–842)." Pages 21–36 in *Vergil's Aeneid: Augustan Epic and Political Context*. Edited by Hans-Peter Stahl. London: Duckworth, 1998.

Goulder, M. D. *Type and History in Acts*. London: SPCK, 1964.

Gowler, David B. *Host, Guest, Enemy and Friend: Portraits of the Pharisees in Luke and Acts*. Emory Studies in Early Christianity 2. New York: P. Lang, 1991.

Grabbe, Lester L. *Ancient Israel: What Do We Know and How Do We Know It?* London: T&T Clark, 2007.

— "Eschatology in Philo and Josephus." Pages 163–85 in *Judaism in Late Antiquity, Part Four: Death, Life-after-Death, Resurrection and the World-to-Come in the Judaisms of Antiquity*. Edited by Alan J. Avery-Peck and Jacob Neusner. HdO. Leiden: Brill, 2000.

Grässer, Erich. "Das Problem der Parusieverzögerung in den synoptischen Evangelien und in der Apostelgeschichte." Pages 99–127 in *Les Actes des Apôtres: Traditions, Rédaction, Théologie*. Edited by Jacob Kremer. BETL. Gembloux: J. Duculot; Leuven: Leuven University Press, 1979.

Gray, Rebecca. *Prophetic Figures in Late Second Temple Jewish Palestine: The Evidence from Josephus*. Oxford: Oxford University Press, 1993.

Green, Anna. *Cultural History*. Theory and History. Basingstoke: Palgrave Macmillan, 2007.

Green, Joel B. *The Gospel of Luke*. NICNT. Grand Rapids: Eerdmans, 1997.

— "Internal Repetition in Luke-Acts: Contemporary Narratology and Lucan Historiography." Pages 283–99 in *History, Literature, and Society in the Book of Acts*. Edited by Ben Witherington III. Cambridge: Cambridge University Press, 1996.

— *The Theology of the Gospel of Luke*. New Testament Theology. Cambridge: Cambridge University Press, 1995.

Green, Joel B., and Michael C. McKeever. *Luke-Acts and New Testament Historiography*. IBR Bibliographies 8. Grand Rapids: Baker, 1994.

Gregory, Andrew. "The Reception of Luke and Acts and the Unity of Luke-Acts." *JSNT* 29 (2007): 459–72.

Gregory, Andrew, and C. Kavin Rowe, eds. *Rethinking the Unity and Reception of Luke and Acts*. Columbia: University of South Carolina Press, 2010.

Grethlein, Jonas. *Experience and Teleology in Ancient Historiography: "Futures Past" from Herodotus to Augustine*. Cambridge: Cambridge University Press, 2013.

Griffin, Miriam T. "Tacitus as a Historian." Pages 168–83 in *The Cambridge Companion to Tacitus*. Edited by A. J. Woodman. Cambridge: Cambridge University Press, 2009.

Gruen, Erich S. "Polybius and Josephus on Rome." Pages 149–62 in *Flavius Josephus: Interpretation and History*. Edited by Jack Pastor, Pnina Stern, and Menahem Mor. Supplements to the Journal for the Study of Judaism 146. Leiden: Brill, 2011.

Guffey, Andrew R. "Job and the 'Mystic's Solution' to Theodicy: Philosophical Paideia and Internalized Apocalypticism in the Testament of Job." Pages 215–39 in *Pedagogy in Ancient Judaism and Early Christianity*. Edited by Karina Martin Hogan, Matthew J. Goff, and Emma Wasserman. Atlanta: SBL Press, 2017.

Gundry, Robert H. *Mark: A Commentary on His Apology for the Cross*. Grand Rapids: Eerdmans, 1993.

Gunkel, Heidrun. *Der Heilige Geist bei Lukas: Theologisches Profil, Grund und Intention der lukanischen Pneumatologie*. WUNT 2/389. Tübingen: Mohr Siebeck, 2015.

Gunkel, Hermann. "Das vierte Buch Esra." Pages 331–402 in vol. 2 of *Die Apokryphen und Pseudepigraphen des alten Testaments*. Edited by E. Kautzsch. Tübingen: Mohr, 1990.
Gurtner, Daniel M. "Eschatological Rewards for the Righteous in 2 Baruch." Pages 107–15 in *Interpreting 4 Ezra and 2 Baruch: International Studies*. Edited by Gabriele Boccaccini and Jason M. Zurawski. LSTS 87. London: Bloomsbury, 2014.
Haaland, Gunnar. "What Difference Does Philosophy Make? The Three Schools as a Rhetorical Device in Josephus." Pages 262–88 in *Making History: Josephus and Historical Method*. Edited by Zuleika Rodgers. Supplements to the Journal for the Study of Judaism 110. Leiden: Brill, 2007.
Haenchen, Ernst. *The Acts of the Apostles: A Commentary*. Translated by Bernard Noble, Gerald Shinn, and R. McL. Wilson. Oxford: Blackwell, 1971. Translation of *Die Apostelgeschichte*. Göttingen: Vandenhoeck & Ruprecht, 1955.
Hakola, Raimo. "'Friendly' Pharisees and Social Identity in Acts." Pages 181–200 in *Contemporary Studies in Acts*. Edited by Thomas E. Phillips. Macon, GA: Mercer University Press, 2009.
Hall, R. G. *Revealed Histories: Techniques for Ancient Jewish and Christian Historiography*. JSPSup 6. Sheffield: JSOT Press, 1991.
Hanks, William F. "Discourse Genres in a Theory of Practice." *American Ethnologist* 14 (1987): 668–92.
Hanneken, Todd R. *The Subversion of the Apocalypses in the Book of Jubilees*. EJL. Atlanta: Society of Biblical Literature, 2012.
Hardie, Philip. *Virgil's Aeneid: Cosmos and Imperium*. Oxford: Oxford University Press, 1986.
Harnisch, Wolfgang. *Verhängnis und Verheißung der Geschichte: Untersuchungen zum Zeit- und Geschichtsverständnis im 4. Buch Esra und in der syr. Baruchapokalypse*. FRLANT 97. Göttingen: Vandenhoeck & Ruprecht, 1969.
Harrington, Daniel J. *The Maccabean Revolt: Anatomy of a Biblical Revolution*. OTS 1. Wilmington, DE: Glazier, 1988.
Harrison, S. J. *Generic Enrichment in Vergil and Horace*. Oxford: Oxford University Press, 2011.
——— "Some Views of the *Aeneid* in the Twentieth Century." Pages 1–20 in *Oxford Readings in Vergil's Aeneid*. Edited by S. J. Harrison. Oxford: Oxford University Press, 1990.
Hau, Lisa Irene. "The Burden of Good Fortune in Diodorus of Sicily: A Case for Originality?" *Historia* 58 (2009): 171–97.
Hays, Christopher M. *Luke's Wealth Ethics: A Study in Their Coherence and Character*. WUNT 2/275. Tübingen: Mohr Siebeck, 2010.
Hegel, G. W. F. *Manuscripts of the Introduction and the Lectures of 1822–1823*. Vol. 1 of *Lectures on the Philosophy of World History*. Translated by Robert F. Brown and Peter C. Hodgson. Oxford: Reinhold Hoffmann, 2011.
Hejduk, Julia Dyson. "Ovid and Religion." Pages 45–58 in *A Companion to Ovid*. Edited by Peter E. Knox. Blackwell Companions to the Ancient World. Chichester: Wiley-Blackwell, 2009.
Hengel, Martin. *Judaism and Hellenism: Studies in Their Encounter in Palestine during the Early Hellenistic Period*. Translated by John Bowden. 2 vols. London: SCM, 1974. Translation of *Judentum und Hellenismus: Studien zu ihrer Begegnung unter besonderer Berücksichtigung Palästinas bis zur Mittes des 2. Jh.s v.Chr.* WUNT 10. Tübingen: Mohr, 1973.

Hengel, Martin, and Christoph Markschies. *The "Hellenization" of Judea in the First Century after Christ*. Translated by John Bowden. London: SCM; Philadelphia: Trinity International, 1989.

Henten, Jan Willem van. *The Maccabean Martyrs as Saviours of the Jewish People: A Study of 2 and 4 Maccabees*. Supplements to the Journal for the Study of Judaism 57. Leiden: Brill, 1997.

Henze, Matthias. *Jewish Apocalypticism in Late First Century Israel: Reading Second Baruch in Context*. Texts and Studies in Ancient Judaism 142. Tübingen: Mohr Siebeck, 2011.

—— "Torah and Eschatology in the Syriac Apocalypse of Baruch." Pages 201–15 in *The Significance of Sinai: Traditions about Sinai and Divine Revelation in Judaism and Christianity*. Edited by George J. Brooke, Hindy Najman, and Loren T. Stuckenbruck. TBN 12. Leiden: Brill, 2008.

Hernadi, Paul. *Beyond Genre: New Directions in Literary Classification*. Ithaca: Cornell University Press, 1972.

Hill, Charles E. *Regnum Caelorum: Patterns of Millennial Thought in Early Christianity*. 2nd ed. Grand Rapids: Eerdmans, 2001.

Hobbins, John F. "Resurrection in the Daniel Tradition and Other Writings at Qumran." Pages 395–420 in vol. 2 of *The Book of Daniel: Composition and Reception*. Edited by John J. Collins and Peter W. Flint. VTSup 83. Leiden: Brill, 2001.

Hoekstra, Kinch, and Mark Fisher. "Thucydides and the Politics of Necessity." Pages 373–88 in *The Oxford Handbook of Thucydides*. Edited by Sara Forsdyke, Edith Foster, and Ryan Balot. New York: Oxford, 2017.

Hogan, Karina Martin. *Theologies in Conflict in 4 Ezra: Wisdom Debate and Apocalyptic Solution*. Supplements to the Journal for the Study of Judaism 130. Boston: Brill, 2008.

Holladay, Carl R. *Acts: A Commentary*. NTL. Louisville: Westminster John Knox, 2016.

Hornik, Heidi J., and Mikeal C. Parsons. *The Acts of the Apostles through the Centuries*. Wiley Blackwell Bible Commentaries. Chichester: Wiley-Blackwell, 2017.

Horsfall, Nicholas. *Virgil, "Aeneid" 6: A Commentary*. 2 vols. Berlin: de Gruyter, 2013.

Horst, Pieter W. van der, ed. and trans. *Philo: Flaccus: The First Pogrom*. PACS 2. Leiden: Brill, 2003.

Jeffrey, David Lyle. *Luke*. Brazos Theological Commentary on the Bible. Grand Rapids: Brazos, 2012.

Jervell, Jacob. "The Divided People of God: The Restoration of Israel and the Salvation of the Gentiles." Pages 41–74 in *Luke and the People of God: A New Look at Luke-Acts*. Eugene, OR: Wipf & Stock, 2002.

—— "The Future of the Past: Luke's Vision of Salvation History and Its Bearing on His Writing of History." Pages 104–26 in *History, Literature, and Society in the Book of Acts*. Edited by Ben Witherington III. Cambridge: Cambridge University Press, 1996.

—— *The Unknown Paul: Essays on Luke-Acts and Early Christian History*. Minneapolis: Augsburg, 1984.

Johnson, Luke Timothy. *The Acts of the Apostles*. SP 5. Collegeville: Liturgical Press, 1992.

—— *The Gospel of Luke*. SP 3. Collegeville: Liturgical Press, 1991.

—— "Literary Criticism of Luke-Acts: Is Reception History Pertinent?" Pages 66–69 in *Rethinking the Unity and Reception of Luke and Acts*. Edited by Andrew Gregory and C. Kavin Rowe. Columbia: University of South Carolina Press, 2010.

*Josephus*. Translated by H. St. J. Thackeray. 10 vols. LCL. Cambridge: Harvard University Press, 1926–1965.
Joyce, Paul. *Ezekiel: A Commentary*. LHBOTS 482. New York: T&T Clark, 2007.
Just, Arthur A., Jr. *The Ongoing Feast: Table Fellowship and Eschatology at Emmaus*. Collegeville: Liturgical Press, 1993.
Kamerbeek, J. C. "On the Conception of ΘΕΟΜΑΧΟΣ in Relation with Greek Tragedy." *Mnemosyne* 1 (1948): 271–83.
Karris, Robert J. "Poor and Rich: The Lukan Sitz im Leben." Pages 112–25 in *Perspectives on Luke-Acts*. Edited by Charles H. Talbert. Edinburgh: T&T Clark, 1978.
Käsemann, Ernst. "Das Problem des historischen Jesus." *ZTK* 51 (1954): 12–53.
—— "Justification and Salvation History in the Epistle to the Romans." Pages 60–78 in *Perspectives on Paul*. Translated by Margaret Kohl. NTL. London: SCM, 1971. Translation of "Rechtfertigung und Heilsgeschichte im Römerbrief." Pages 108–39 in *Paulinische Perspektiven*. Tübingen: Mohr Siebeck, 1969.
—— "Neutestamentliche Fragen von Heute." *ZTK* 54 (1957): 1–21.
Kearns, Emily. "The Gods in Homeric Epics." Pages 59–73 in *The Cambridge Companion to Homer*. Edited by Robert Fowler. Cambridge: Cambridge University Press, 2004.
Keener, Craig S. *Acts: An Exegetical Commentary*. 4 vols. Grand Rapids: Baker Academic, 2012–2015.
Kenney, E. J. "The *Metamorphoses*: A Poet's Poem." Pages 140–53 in *A Companion to Ovid*. Edited by Peter E. Knox. Blackwell Companions to the Ancient World. Chichester: Wiley-Blackwell, 2009.
Ker, James. "Seneca, Man of Many Genres." Pages 19–41 in *Seeing Seneca Whole: Perspectives on Philosophy, Poetry and Politics*. Edited by Katharina Volk and Gareth D. Williams. Columbia Studies in the Classical Tradition 28. Leiden: Brill, 2006.
Kim, Young Ho. *Die Parusie bei Lukas: Eine literarisch-exegetische Untersuchung zu den Parusieaussagen im lukanischen Doppelwerk*. BZNW 217. Berlin: de Gruyter, 2016.
Kim-Rauchholz, Mihamm. *Umkehr bei Lukas: Zu Wesen und Bedeutung der Metanoia in der Theologie des dritten Evangelisten*. Neukirchen-Vluyn: Neukirchener, 2008.
Kittel, Gerhard, and Gerhard Friedrich, eds. *Theological Dictionary of the New Testament*. Translated by Geoffrey W. Bromiley. 10 vols. Grand Rapids: Eerdmans, 1964–1976.
Klauser, Theodor, et al., eds. *Reallexikon für Antike und Christentum*. Stuttgart: Hiersemann, 1950–.
Klawans, Jonathan. *Josephus and the Theologies of Ancient Judaism*. Oxford: Oxford University Press, 2012.
—— "Josephus on Fate, Free Will, and Ancient Jewish Types of Compatibilism." *Numen* 56 (2009): 44–90.
Klein, Günter. "Lukas, 1, 1–4 als theologisches Programm." Pages 183–216 in *Zeit und Geschichte: Dankesgabe an Rudolf Bultmann zum 80. Geburtstag*. Edited by E. Dinkler. Tübingen: Mohr, 1964.
Klijn, A. F. J., ed. and trans. "2 (Syriac Apocalypse of) Baruch." Pages 615–52 in *Apocalyptic Literature and Testaments*. Vol. 1 of *The Old Testament Pseudepigrapha*. Edited by James H. Charlesworth. ABRL. Garden City, NY: Doubleday, 1983.
Knauer, G. N. "Vergil's *Aeneid* and Homer." Pages 390–412 in *Oxford Readings in Vergil's Aeneid*. Edited by S. J. Harrison. Oxford: Oxford University Press, 1990.

Knibb, Michael. "Apocalypticism and Messianism." Pages 403–32 in *The Oxford Handbook of the Dead Sea Scrolls*. Edited by Timothy Lim and John J. Collins. New York: Oxford University Press, 2010.
Knight, Jonathan. *Luke's Gospel*. New Testament Readings. London: Routledge, 1998.
Kovacs, Judith, and Christopher Rowland. *Revelation: The Apocalypse of Jesus Christ*. Wiley Blackwell Bible Commentaries. Oxford: Blackwell, 2004.
Kraus, C. S. "Sallust." Pages 10–50 in *Latin Historians*. Edited by C. S. Kraus and A. J. Woodman. Oxford: Oxford University Press, 1997.
Kraus, Hans-Joachim. *Psalms 1–59*. Translated by Hilton C. Oswald. Minneapolis: Augsburg, 1988. Translation of vol. 1 of *Psalmen*. Neukirchen-Vluyn: Neukirchener, 1961.
Krauter, Stefan. "Vergils Evangelium und das lukanische Epos? Überlegungen zu Gattung und Theologie des lukanischen Doppelwerkes." Pages 214–43 of *Die Apostelgeschichte im Kontext antiker und frühchristlicher Historiographie*. Edited by Jörg Frey, Clare K. Rothschild, and Jens Schröter. BZNW 162. Berlin: de Gruyter, 2009.
Kümmel, Werner Georg. "Current Theological Accusations against Luke." ANQ 16 (1975): 131–45.
— *Introduction to the New Testament*. Translated by A. J. Mattill. Rev. ed. NTL. London: SCM, 1975. Translation of *Einleitung in das neue Testament*. Heidelberg: Quelle & Meyer, 1965.
— *Promise and Fulfilment: The Eschatological Message of Jesus*. Translated by Dorothea M. Barton. 3rd rev. ed. SBT 23. London: SCM, 1957. Translation of *Verheißung und Erfüllung: Untersuchungen zur eschatologischen Verkündigung Jesu*. Basel: H. Majer, 1945.
Lamberton, Robert. *Homer the Theologian: Neoplatonist Allegorical Reading and the Growth of the Epic Tradition*. Transformation of the Classical Heritage 9. Berkeley: University of California Press, 1986.
Law, T. M., and A. Salvesen. *Greek Scripture and the Rabbis*. Contributions to Biblical Exegesis and Theology 66. Leuven: Peeters, 2012.
Lee, DooHee. *Luke-Acts and "Tragic History": Communicating Gospel with the World*. WUNT 2/346. Tübingen: Mohr Siebeck, 2013.
Lemche, Niels Peter. *The Israelites in History and Tradition*. Edited by Douglas A. Knight. LAI. London: SPCK; Louisville: Westminster John Knox, 1998.
Leoni, Tommaso. "The Text of the Josephan Corpus: Principal Greek Manuscripts, Ancient Latin Translations, and the Indirect Tradition." Pages 307–21 in *A Companion to Josephus in His World*. Edited by Honora Howell Chapman and Zuleika Rodgers. Chichester: Wiley & Sons, 2016.
Lichtenberger, Hermann. "Zion and the Destruction of the Temple in 4 Ezra 9–10." Pages 239–49 in *Gemeinde ohne Tempel: Zur Substituierung und Transformation des Jerusalemer Tempels und seines Kults im alten Testament, antiken Judentum und frühen Christentum*. Edited by Beate Ego, Armin Lange, Kathrin Ehlers, and Peter Pilhofer. Tübingen: Mohr, 1999.
Liebeschuetz, J. H. W. G. *Continuity and Change in Roman Religion*. Oxford: Clarendon, 1989.
Lincicum, David. *Paul and the Early Jewish Encounter with Deuteronomy*. WUNT 2/284. Tübingen: Mohr Siebeck, 2010.
Longenecker, Bruce W. *2 Esdras*. Guides to the Apocrypha and Pseudepigrapha. Sheffield: Sheffield Academic, 1995.

—— *Eschatology and the Covenant: A Comparison of 4 Ezra and Romans 1–11*. JSNTSup 57. Sheffield: JSOT Press, 1991.
Löwith, Karl. *Meaning in History*. Phoenix Books. Chicago: University of Chicago Press, 1949.
—— *My Life in Germany before and after 1933: A Report*. Translated by Elizabeth King. London: Athlone Press, 1994.
Luce, T. J. "Livy and Dionysius." *Papers of the Leeds International Latin Seminar* 8 (1995): 225–39.
Luther, Susanne. "'Jesus Was a Man, … but Christ Was a Fiction': Authentizitätskonstruktion in der antiken narrativen Historiographie am Beispiel lukanischer Gleichniserzählungen." Pages 181–208 in *Wie Geschichten Geschichte schreiben: Frühchristliche Literatur zwischen Faktualität und Fiktionalität*. WUNT 2/395. Tübingen: Mohr Siebeck, 2015.
Lyne, R. O. A. M. "Vergil and the Politics of War." Pages 316–38 in *Oxford Readings in Vergil's Aeneid*. Edited by S. J. Harrison. Oxford: Oxford University Press, 1990.
Lyons, William John. "The Words of Gamaliel (Acts 5.38–39) and the Irony of Indeterminacy." *JSNT* 68 (1997): 23–49.
MacDonald, Dennis R. *The Gospels and Homer: Imitations of Greek Epic in Mark and Luke-Acts*. New Testament and Greek Literature 1. Lanham: Rowman & Littlefield, 2015.
—— *Luke and Vergil: Imitations of Classical Greek Literature*. New Testament and Greek Literature 2. Lanham: Rowman & Littlefield, 2015.
Maddox, Robert. *The Purpose of Luke-Acts*. SNTW. Edinburgh: T&T Clark, 1982.
Mallen, Peter. *The Reading and Transformation of Isaiah in Luke-Acts*. LNTS 367. London: T&T Clark International, 2008.
Mannheim, Karl. *Ideology and Utopia: An Introduction to the Sociology of Knowledge*. London: Routledge & Kegan Paul, 1960.
Marguerat, Daniel. *The First Christian Historian: Writing the 'Acts of the Apostles.'* Translated by Ken McKinney, Gregory J. Laughery, and Richard Bauckham. SNTSMS 121. Cambridge: Cambridge University Press, 2002.
Marincola, John. *Authority and Tradition in Ancient Historiography*. Cambridge: Cambridge University Press, 1997.
—— "Speeches in Classical Historiography." Pages 118–32 in vol. 1 of *A Companion to Greek and Roman Historiography*. Edited by John Marincola. Blackwell Companions to the Ancient World. Malden, MA: Blackwell, 2007.
Marshall, I. Howard. *The Acts of the Apostles: An Introduction and Commentary*. Leicester: InterVarsity Press, 1980.
—— Howard. *Luke: Historian and Theologian*. Exeter: Paternoster, 1970.
Martin, Ronald. *Tacitus: Annals V & VI*. Warminster: Aris & Phillips, 2001.
Martyn, J. Louis. *Theological Issues in the Letters of Paul*. London: T&T Clark Continuum, 1997.
Marx, Karl. *Economic and Philosophic Manuscripts of 1844*. Translated by Martin Milligan. 4th rev. ed. Moscow: Progress Publishers, 1974.
—— *Writings of the Young Marx on Philosophy and Society*. Garden City, NY: Anchor Books, 1967.
Mason, Steve. *Josephus and the New Testament*. Peabody, MA: Hendrickson, 1992.
—— "Josephus's Pharisees: The Narratives." Pages 3–40 in *In Quest of the Historical Pharisees*. Edited by Jacob Neusner and Bruce D. Chilton. Waco, TX: Baylor University Press, 2007.

—— "Josephus's Pharisees: The Philosophy." Pages 41–66 in *In Quest of the Historical Pharisees*. Edited by Jacob Neusner and Bruce D. Chilton. Waco, TX: Baylor University Press, 2007.

Maston, Jason. *Divine and Human Agency in Second Temple Judaism and Paul: A Comparative Study*. WUNT 2/297. Tübingen: Mohr Siebeck, 2010.

Matthews, Lydia. "Roman Constructions of Fortuna." DPhil diss., University of Oxford, 2012.

Mattila, Sharon Lea. "Two Contrasting Eschatologies at Qumran (4Q246 vs 1QM)." *Biblica* 75 (1994): 518–38.

Mattill, Andrew J. *Luke and the Last Things: A Perspective for the Understanding of Lukan Thought*. Dillsboro, NC: Western North Carolina Press, 1979.

—— "Naherwartung, Fernerwartung, and the Purpose of Luke-Acts: Weymouth Reconsidered." *CBQ* 34 (1972): 276–93.

McKim, Donald K., ed. *Dictionary of Major Biblical Interpreters*. 2nd ed. Downers Grove, IL: Intervarsity Press, 2007.

Meister, Klaus. "Diodorus Siculus." *BNP* 2:444–46.

Mermelstein, Ari. *Creation, Covenant, and the Beginnings of Judaism: Reconceiving Historical Time in the Second Temple Period*. Supplements to the Journal for the Study of Judaism 168. Leiden: Brill, 2014.

Metzger, Bruce M., ed. and trans. "The Fourth Book of Ezra." Pages 516–59 in *Apocalyptic Literature and Testaments*. Vol. 1 of *The Old Testament Pseudepigrapha*. Edited by James H. Charlesworth. ABRL. Garden City, NY: Doubleday, 1983.

—— *A Textual Commentary on the Greek New Testament*. 2nd ed. Stuttgart: Deutsche Bibelgesellschaft, 1994.

Meyers, Eric M. "Khirbet Qumran and Its Enrivons." Pages 21–43 in *The Oxford Handbook of the Dead Sea Scrolls*. Edited by Timothy Lim and John J. Collins. New York: Oxford University Press, 2010.

Millar, Fergus. "Ovid and the Domus Augusta: Rome Seen from Tomoi." *The Journal of Roman Studies* 83 (1993): 1–17.

Miller, Amanda C. *Rumors of Resistance: Status Reversals and Hidden Transcripts in the Gospel of Luke*. Emerging Scholars. Minneapolis: Fortress, 2014.

Miller, John B. F. *Convinced That God Had Called Us: Dreams, Visions and the Perception of God's Will in Luke-Acts*. BibInt 85. Leiden: Brill, 2007.

Minear, Paul S. "Luke's Use of the Birth Stories." Pages 111–30 in *Studies in Luke-Acts: Essays Presented in Honor of Paul Schubert*. Edited by Leander E. Keck and J. Louis Martyn. Nashville: Abingdon, 1966.

Moessner, David P. "'Completed End(s)ings' of Historiographical Narrative: Diodorus Siculus and the End(ing) of Acts." Pages 193–221 in *Die Apostelgeschichte und die hellenistische Geschichtsschreibung: Festschrift für Eckhard Plümacher zu seinem 65. Geburtstag*. Edited by Cilliers Breytenbach and Jens Schröter. AGJU 57. Leiden: Brill, 2004.

—— *Luke the Historian of Israel's Legacy, Theologian of Israel's "Christ": A New Reading of the "Gospel Acts" of Luke*. BZNW 182. Berlin: de Gruyter, 2016.

—— "Luke's 'Plan of God' from the Greek Psalter: The Rhetorical Thrust of 'The Prophets and the Psalms' in Peter's Speech at Pentecost." Pages 223–38 in *Scripture and Traditions: Essays on Early Judaism and Christianity in Honor of Carl R. Holladay*. Edited by Patrick Gray and Gail R. O'Day. NovTSup 129. Leiden: Brill, 2008.

—— "'Managing the Audience': The Rhetoric of Authorial Intent and Audience Comprehension in the Narrative Epistemology of Polybius of Megalopolis, Diodorus Siculus, and Luke the Evangelist." Pages 179–97 in *The Word Leaps the Gap: Essays on Scripture and Theology in Honor of Richard B. Hays*. Edited by J. Ross Wagner, C. Kavin Rowe, and A. Katherine Grieb. Grand Rapids: Eerdmans, 2008.

—— "The 'Script' of the Scriptures in Acts: Suffering as God's 'Plan' (βουλή) for the World for the 'Release of Sins.'" Pages 218–50 in *History, Literature, and Society in the Book of Acts*. Edited by Ben Witherington III. Cambridge: Cambridge University Press, 1996.

Molthagen, Joachim. "Geschichtsschreibung und Geschichtsverständnis in der Apostelgeschichte im Vergleich mit Herodot, Thukydides und Polybios." Pages 159–81 in *Die Apostelgeschichte im Kontext antiker und frühchristlicher Historiographie*. Edited by Jörg Frey, Clare K. Rothschild, and Jens Schröter. BZNW 162. Berlin: de Gruyter, 2009.

Momigliano, Arnaldo. "The Origins of Universal History." Pages 133–54 in *The Poet and the Historian: Essays in Literary and Historical Biblical Criticism*. Edited by Richard Elliott Friedman. HSS. Chico, CA: Scholars Press, 1983.

—— "Popular Religious Beliefs and the Late Roman Historians." Pages 141–59 in *Essays in Ancient and Modern Historiography*. Blackwell's Classical Studies. Oxford: Blackwell, 1977.

—— "Time in Ancient Historiography." Pages 179–204 in *Essays in Ancient and Modern Historiography*. Blackwell's Classical Studies. Oxford: Blackwell, 1977.

Moore, Nicholas J. *Repetition in Hebrews: Plurality and Singularity in the Letter to the Hebrews, Its Ancient Context, and the Early Church*. WUNT 2/388. Tübingen: Mohr Siebeck, 2015.

Morgan, Teresa. *Popular Morality in the Early Roman Empire*. Cambridge: Cambridge University Press, 2007.

—— *Roman Faith and Christian Faith: Pistis and Fides in the Early Roman Empire and Early Churches*. Oxford: Oxford University Press, 2015.

Mowery, Robert L. "The Divine Hand and the Divine Plan." Pages 558–75 in *Society of Biblical Literature, 1991 Seminar Papers*. Edited by Eugene H. Lovering Jr. SBLSPS 30. Atlanta: Society of Biblical Literature, 1991.

Mroczek, Eva. *The Literary Imagination in Jewish Antiquity*. New York: Oxford University Press, 2016.

Mueller, Hans-Friedrich. *Roman Religion in Valerius Maximus*. Routledge Classical Monographs. London: Routledge, 2002.

Najman, Hindy. "The Idea of Biblical Genre: From Discourse to Constellation." Pages 307–21 in *Prayer and Poetry in the Dead Sea Scrolls and Related Literature: Essays in Honor of Eileen Schuller on the Occasion of Her 65th Birthday*. Edited by Eileen M. Schuller, Jeremy Penner, Ken M. Penner, and Cecilia Wassen. Leiden: Brill, 2012.

—— *Losing the Temple and Recovering the Future: An Analysis of 4 Ezra*. Cambridge: Cambridge University Press, 2014.

Nave, Guy D. *The Role and Function of Repentance in Luke-Acts*. Academia Biblica 4. Atlanta: Society of Biblical Literature, 2002.

Newsom, Carol A. "Models of the Moral Self: Hebrew Bible and Second Temple Judaism." *JBL* 131 (2012): 5–25.

— "The Rhetoric of Jewish Apocalyptic Literature." Pages 201–17 in *The Oxford Handbook of Apocalyptic Literature*. Edited by John J. Collins. New York: Oxford Unviersity Press, 2014.

Nickelsburg, George W. E. "1 and 2 Maccabees: Same Story, Different Meaning." Pages 659–74 in *George W. E. Nickelsburg in Perspective: An Ongoing Dialogue of Learning*. Leiden: Brill, 2003.

— *Jewish Literature between the Bible and the Mishnah: A Historical and Literary Introduction*. Philadelphia: Fortress, 1981.

— *Resurrection, Immortality, and Eternal Life in Intertestamental Judaism and Early Christianity*. Expanded ed. Cambridge: Harvard University Press, 2006.

— "Salvation without and with a Messiah: Developing Beliefs in Writings Ascribed to Enoch." Pages 49–68 in *Judaisms and Their Messiahs at the Turn of the Christian Era*. Edited by Jacob Neusner, William Scott Green, and Ernest Frerichs. Cambridge: Cambridge University Press, 1987.

Nicklas, Tobias. "Irony in 2 Maccabees?" Pages 101–11 in *The Books of the Maccabees: History, Theology, Ideology: Papers of the Second International Conference on the Deuterocanoncial Books, Pápa, Hungary, 9–11 June, 2005*. Edited by Géza G. Xeravits and József Zsengellér. Supplements to the Journal for the Study of Judaism 118. Leiden: Brill, 2007.

Nielsen, Anders E. "The Purpose of the Lucan Writings with Particular Reference to Eschatology." Pages 76–93 in *Luke-Acts: Scandinavian Perspectives*. Edited by Petri Luomanen. Göttingen: Vandenhoeck & Ruprecht, 1991.

Nitzan, Bilhah. "Apocalyptic Ideas in 4 Ezra in Comparison with the Dead Sea Scrolls." Pages 22–31 in *Interpreting 4 Ezra and 2 Baruch: International Studies*. Edited by Gabriele Boccaccini and Jason M. Zurawski. LSTS 87. London: Bloomsbury, 2014.

Nobbs, Alanna. "Acts and Subsequent Ecclesiastical Histories." Pages 153–62 in *The Book of Acts in Its Ancient Literary Setting*. Edited by Bruce W. Winter and Andrew D. Clarke. BAFCS 1. Grand Rapids: Eerdmans, 1993.

Nolland, John. *Luke*. 3 vols. WBC 35. Dallas, TX: Word, 1989–1993.

Noth, Martin. *The Deuteronomistic History*. Sheffield: University of Sheffield, 1981. Translation of *Überlieferungsgeschichtliche Studien*. Halle: Niemeyer, 1943.

O'Hara, James J. *Death and the Optimistic Prophecy in Vergil's Aeneid*. Princeton: Princeton University Press, 1990.

— *Inconsistency in Roman Epic: Studies in Catullus, Lucretius, Vergil, Ovid and Lucan*. Roman Literature and Its Contexts. Cambridge: Cambridge University Press, 2007.

Olson, Daniel C. *A New Reading of the Animal Apocalypse of 1 Enoch: "All Nations Shall Be Blessed."* Boston: Brill, 2013.

Ooi, Vincent K. H. *Scripture and Its Readers: Readings of Israel's Story in Nehemiah 9, Ezekiel 20, and Acts 7*. Journal of Theological Interpretation Supplement Series. Winona Lake, IN: Eisenbrauns, 2015.

Palmer, Darryl W. "Acts and the Ancient Historical Monograph." Pages 1–29 in *The Book of Acts in Its Ancient Literary Setting*. Edited by Bruce W. Winter and Andrew D. Clarke. BAFCS 1. Grand Rapids: Eerdmans, 1993.

Panagopoulos, Johannes. "Zur Theologie der Apostelgeschichte." *NovT* 14 (1972): 137–59.

Parsons, Mikeal C. *Acts*. Paideia. Grand Rapids: Baker Academic, 2008.

Parsons, Mikeal C., and Richard I. Pervo. *Rethinking the Unity of Luke and Acts*. Minneapolis: Fortress, 1993.
Penner, Todd. "Madness in the Method? The Acts of the Apostles in Current Study." *CurBR* 2 (2004): 223–93.
Perlitt, Lothar. *Deuteronomium-Studien*. FAT 8. Tübingen: Mohr Siebeck, 1994.
Pervo, Richard I. *Acts: A Commentary*. Hermeneia. Minneapolis: Fortress, 2009.
— *Dating Acts: Between the Evangelists and the Apologists*. Santa Rosa, CA: Polebridge, 2006.
— *Profit with Delight: The Literary Genre of the Acts of the Apostles*. Philadelphia: Fortress, 1987.
Peterson, David. *The Acts of the Apostles*. The Pillar New Testament Commentary. Grand Rapids: Eerdmans, 2009.
Phillips, Thomas E. "The Genre of Acts: Moving toward a Consensus?" *CurBR* 4 (2006): 365–96.
Polybius. *The Histories*. Translated by W. R. Paton, F. A. Walbank, and Christian Habicht. Rev. ed. 6 vols. LCL. Cambridge: Harvard University Press, 2010–2012.
Popović, Mladen. "Apocalyptic Determinism." Pages 225–70 in *The Oxford Handbook of Apocalyptic Literature*. Edited by John J. Collins. New York: Oxford University Press, 2014.
Puech, Emile. "Messianism, Resurrection, and Eschatology at Qumran and in the New Testament." Pages 235–56 in *The Community of the Renewed Covenant: The Notre Dame Symposium on the Dead Sea Scrolls*. Edited by E. C. Ulrich and James C. VanderKam. Notre Dame: University of Notre Dame Press, 1994.
Quint, David. "Repetition and Ideology in the *Aeneid*." *Materiali e discussioni per l'analisi dei testi classici* 23 (1989): 9–54.
Rad, Gerhard von. "Antwort auf Conzelmanns Fragen." *EvT* 24 (1964): 388–94.
— "The Beginnings of Historical Writing in Ancient Israel." Pages 125–53 in *From Genesis to Chronicles: Explorations in Old Testament Theology*. Edited by K. C. Hanson. Fortress Classics in Biblical Studies. Minneapolis: Fortress, 2005. Translation of "Der Anfang der Geschichtsschreibung im alten Israel." *Archiv für Kulturgeschichte* 32 (1944): 1–42.
— *Genesis: A Commentary*. Translated by John H. Marks. Rev. ed. OTL. London: SCM, 1972. Translation of *Das erste Buch Mose: Genesis*. Göttingen: Vandenhoeck & Ruprecht, 1961.
— *Old Testament Theology*. Translated by D. M. G. Stalker. 2 vols. Edinburgh: Oliver & Boyd, 1962–1965. Translation of *Theologie des alten Testaments*. Munich: Kaiser Verlag, 1957–1960.
Rajak, Tessa. "The Angry Tyrant." Pages 110–29 in *Jewish Perspectives on Hellenistic Rulers*. Edited by Tessa Rajak. Hellenistic Culture and Society 50. Berkeley: University of California Press, 2007.
— "Friends, Romans, Subjects: Agrippa II's Speech in Josephus's *Jewish War*." Pages 122–34 in *Images of Empire*. Edited by Loveday Alexander. JSOTSup 122. Sheffield: JSOT Press, 1991.
— "Jewish Millenarian Expectations." Pages 164–88 in *The First Jewish Revolt: Archaeology, History, and Ideology*. Edited by Andrea M. Berlin and J. Andrew Overman. London: Routledge, 2002.
— *Josephus: The Historian and His Society*. 2nd ed. London: Duckworth, 2002.
— "The Sense of History in Jewish Intertestamental Writing." Pages 124–45 in *Crises and Perspectives: Studies in Ancient Near Eastern Polytheism, Biblical Theology, Palestinian*

*Archaeology, and Intertestamental Literature*. Edited by Johannes C. de Moor. OtSt 24. Leiden: Brill, 1986.

Rapske, Brian. "Opposition to the Plan of God and Persecution." Pages 235–56 in *Witness to the Gospel: The Theology of Acts*. Edited by I. Howard Marshall and David Peterson. Grand Rapids: Eerdmans, 1998.

Rasco, Emilio. "Hans Conzelmann y la 'Historia Salutis': A Propósito de 'Die Mitte der Zeit' y 'Die Apostelgeschichte.'" *Gregorianum* 46 (1965): 286–319.

Regev, Eyal. "Josephus, the Temple, and the Jewish War." Pages 279–93 in *Flavius Josephus: Interpretation and History*. Edited by Jack Pastor, Pnina Stern, and Menahem Mor. Supplements to the Journal for the Study of Judaism 146. Leiden: Brill, 2011.

Reynolds, Benjamin. "John and the Jewish Apocalypses: Rethinking the Genre of John's Gospel." Pages 36–57 in *John's Gospel and Intimations of Apocalyptic*. Edited by Christopher Rowland and Catrin H. Williams. London: Bloomsbury, 2013.

Richardson, Peter. *Herod: King of the Jews and Friend of the Romans*. Edinburgh: T&T Clark, 1999.

Ringe, Sharon. *Luke*. Louisville: Westminster John Knox, 1995.

Rius-Camps, Josep, and Jenny Read-Heimerdinger. *The Message of Acts in Codex Bezae: A Comparison with the Alexandrian Tradition*. 4 vols. London: T&T Clark International, 2004–2009.

Robinson, William Childs. "Theological Context for Interpreting Luke's Travel Narrative." *JBL* 79 (1960): 20–31.

Rosenmeyer, Thomas G. *Senecan Drama and Stoic Cosmology*. Berkeley: University of California Press, 1989.

Rosmarin, Adena. *The Power of Genre*. Minneapolis: University of Minnesota Press, 1985.

Rosner, Brian S. "Acts and Biblical History." Pages 65–82 in *The Book of Acts in Its Ancient Literary Setting*. Edited by Bruce W. Winter and Andrew D. Clarke. BAFCS 1. Grand Rapids: Eerdmans, 1993.

Rothschild, Clare K. *Luke-Acts and the Rhetoric of History: An Investigation of Early Christian Historiography*. WUNT 2/175. Tübingen: Mohr Siebeck, 2004.

Rowe, C. Kavin. "Literary Unity and Reception History: Reading Luke-Acts as Luke and Acts." *JSNT* 29 (2007): 449–57.

——— *World Upside Down: Reading Acts in the Graeco-Roman Age*. Oxford: Oxford University Press, 2009.

Rowland, Christopher. *Christian Origins: An Account of the Setting and Character of the Most Important Messianic Sect of Judaism*. London: SPCK, 1985.

——— *The Open Heaven: A Study of Apocalyptic in Judaism and Early Christianity*. Eugene, OR: Wipf & Stock, 2002.

——— "The Temple in the New Testament." Pages 469–83 in *Temple and Worship in Biblical Israel: Proceedings of the Oxford Old Testament Seminar*. Edited by John Day. LHBOTS 422. London: T&T Clark, 2007.

Sacks, Kenneth S. *Diodorus Siculus and the First Century*. Princeton: Princeton University Press, 1990.

——— *Polybius on the Writing of History*. Berkeley: University of California Press, 1981.

Sailor, Dylan. *Writing and Empire in Tacitus*. Cambridge: Cambridge University Press, 2008.

Sallmann, Klaus. "Pliny (the Elder)." *BNP* 11:383–90.

Sanders, E. P. "God Gave the Law to Condemn: Providence in Paul and Josephus." Pages 78–97 in *The Impartial God: Essays in Biblical Studies in Honor of Jouette M. Bassler*. Edited by Calvin J. Roetzel and Robert L. Foster. New Testament Monographs 22. Sheffield: Sheffield Phoenix, 2007.
— *Paul and Palestinian Judaism: A Comparison of Patterns of Religion*. London: SCM, 1977.
Sanders, James A. "The Ethic of Election in Luke's Great Banquet Parable." Pages 245–71 in *Essays in Old Testament Ethics (J. Phillip Hyatt, in Memoriam)*. Edited by James L. Crenshaw and John T. Willis. New York: Ktav, 1974.
Satterthwaite, Philip E., and Gordon McConville. *The Histories*. Exploring the Old Testament 2. London: SPCK, 2007.
Scheffler, Eben. *Suffering in Luke's Gospel*. ATANT 81. Zürich: Theologischer Verlag, 1993.
Schlapbach, Karin. "Providentia." *BNP* 12:82.
Schlaudraff, Karl-Heinz. *"Heil als Geschichte?" Die Frage nach dem heilsgeschichtlichen Denken, dargestellt anhand der Konzeption Oscar Cullmanns*. Tübingen: Mohr Siebeck, 1988.
Schultz, Brian. *Conquering the World: The War Scroll (1QM) Reconsidered*. STDJ. Leiden: Brill, 2009.
Schulz, Siegfried. *Die Stunde der Botschaft: Einführung in die Theologie der vier Evangelisten*. Hamburg: Furche, 1967.
— "Gottes Vorsehung bei Lukas." *ZNW* 54 (1963): 104–16.
Schwartz, Daniel R. *2 Maccabees*. CEJL. Berlin: de Gruyter, 2008.
— "Circular or Teleological, Universal or Particular, with God or Without? On 1–2 Maccabees and Acts." Pages 119–29 in *Die Apostelgeschichte im Kontext antiker und frühchristlicher Historiographie*. Edited by Jörg Frey, Clare K. Rothschild, and Jens Schröter. BZNW 162. Berlin: de Gruyter, 2009.
— "Josephus, Catullus, and the Date of the Judean War." Pages 331–52 in *Flavius Josephus: Interpretation and History*. Edited by Jack Pastor, Pnina Stern, and Menahem Mor. Supplements to the Journal for the Study of Judaism 146. Leiden: Brill, 2011.
Schweitzer, Albert. *The Mysticism of Paul the Apostle*. Translated by William Montgomery. London: Black, 1931. Translation of *Die Mystik des Apostels Paulus*. Tübingen: Mohr Siebeck, 1930.
— *The Quest of the Historical Jesus: A Critical Study of Its Progress from Reimarus to Wrede*. Translated by William Montgomery. London: Black, 1910. Translation of *Von Reimarus zu Wrede: Eine Geschichte der Leben-Jesu-Forschung*. Tübingen: Mohr Siebeck, 1906.
Schweitzer, Steven. *Reading Utopia in Chronicles*. LHBOTS 442. New York: T&T Clark, 2007.
Schweizer, Eduard. *The Good News according to Luke*. Translated by David E. Green. Atlanta: John Knox, 1984.
Scott, James M. *On Earth as in Heaven: The Restoration of Sacred Time and Sacred Space in the Book of Jubilees*. Supplements to the Journal for the Study of Judaism 91. Leiden: Brill, 2005.
Scott, Russell T. *Religion and Philosophy in the Histories of Tacitus*. Papers and Monographs of the American Academy in Rome 22. Rome: American Academy, 1968.
Seitel, Peter. "Theorizing Genres: Interpreting Works." *New Literary History* 34 (2003): 275–97.
Shauf, Scott. *The Divine in Acts and Ancient Historiography*. Minneapolis: Fortress, 2015.

— *Theology as History, History as Theology: Paul in Ephesus in Acts 19.* BZNW 133. Berlin: de Gruyter, 2005.
Shillington, V. George. *An Introduction to the Study of Luke-Acts.* T&T Clark Approaches to Biblical Studies. London: Bloomsbury, 2015.
Skidmore, Clive. *Practical Ethics for Roman Gentlemen: The Work of Valerius Maximus.* Exeter: University of Exeter Press, 1996.
Sievers, Joseph. "Josephus and the Afterlife." Pages 20–34 in *Understanding Josephus: Seven Perspectives.* Edited by Steve Mason. JSPSup 32. Sheffield: Sheffield Academic, 1998.
Slater, D. A. "Was the Fourth Eclogue Written to Celebrate the Marriage of Octavia to Mark Antony? A Literary Parallel." *Classical Review* 26 (1912): 114–19.
Sleeman, Matthew. *Geography and the Ascension Narrative in Acts.* SNTSMS 146. New York: Cambridge University Press, 2009.
Smith, Daniel L., and Zachary L. Kostopoulos. "Biography, History and the Genre of Luke-Acts." *NTS* 63 (2017): 390–410.
Smith, Robert H. "History and Eschatology in Luke-Acts." *CTM* 29 (1958): 881–901.
Sparks, H. D. F. Review of *Die Mitte der Zeit: Studien zur Theologie des Lukas* (3rd ed.), by Hans Conzelmann. *JTS* 14 (1963): 454–66.
— "The Syriac Apocalypse of Baruch." Pages 835–96 in *The Apocryphal Old Testament.* Edited by H. D. F. Sparks. Oxford: Clarendon, 1984.
Spencer, F. Scott. "Out of Mind, Out of Voice: Slave-Girls and Prophetic Daughters in Luke-Acts." *BibInt* 7 (1999): 133–55.
Speyer, Wolfgang. "Gottesfeind." *RAC.* 11:996–1043.
Squires, John T. *The Plan of God in Luke-Acts.* SNTSMS 76. Cambridge: Cambridge University Press, 1993.
Stählin, G. "Τὸ πνεῦμα Ἰησοῦ (Apostelgeschichte 16:7)." Pages 229–51 in *Christ and the Spirit in the New Testament: Studies in Honour of Charles Francis Digby Moule.* Edited by Barnabas Lindars and Stephen S. Smalley. Cambridge: Cambridge University Press, 1973.
Stemberger, Günter. "Jews and Graeco-Roman Culture: From Alexander to Theodosius II." Pages 15–36 in *The Jewish-Greek Tradition in Antiquity and the Byzantine Empire.* Edited by James Aitken and James Carleton Paget. Cambridge: Cambridge University Press, 2014.
Sterling, Gregory E. "'Do You Understand What You Are Reading?' The Understanding of the LXX in Luke-Acts." Pages 101–18 in *Die Apostelgeschichte im Kontext antiker und frühchristlicher Historiographie.* Edited by Jörg Frey, Clare Rothschild, and Jens Schröter. BZNW 162. Berlin: de Gruyter, 2009.
— "Explaining Defeat: Polybius and Josephus on the Wars with Rome." Pages 135–51 in *Internationales Josephus-Kolloquium Aarhus 1999.* Edited by J. U. Kalms. Münsteraner Judaistische Studien 6. Münster: Institutum Judaicum Delitzschianum, 2000.
— *Historiography and Self-Definition: Josephos, Luke-Acts, and Apologetic Historiography.* NovTSup 64. Leiden: Brill, 1991.
— "'The Most Perfect Work': The Role of Matter in Philo of Alexandria." Pages 243–57 in *Light on Creation: Ancient Commentators in Dialogue and Debate on the Origin of the World.* Edited by Geert Roskam and Joseph Verheyden. STAJ 104. Tübingen: Mohr Siebeck, 2017.

— "'Opening the Scriptures': The Legitimation of the Jewish Diaspora and Early Christian Mission." Pages 199–225 in *Jesus and the Heritage of Israel: Luke's Narrative Claim upon Israel's Legacy*. Edited by David P. Moessner. Luke the Interpreter of Israel 1. Harrisburg, PA: Trinity, 1999.
— "'Turning to God': Conversion in Greek-Speaking Judaism and Early Christianity." Pages 69–95 in *Scripture and Traditions: Essays on Early Judaism and Christianity in Honor of Carl R. Holladay*. Edited by Patrick Gray and Gail O'Day. NovTSup 129. Leiden: Brill, 2008.
Stone, Michael E. *Ancient Judaism: New Visions and Views*. Grand Rapids: Eerdmans, 2011.
— "Coherence and Inconsistency in the Apocalypses: The Case of 'The End' in 4 Ezra." *JBL* 102 (1983): 229–43.
— "The Concept of the Messiah in IV Ezra." Pages 295–312 in *Religions in Antiquity: Essays in Memory of Erwin Ramsdell Goodenough*. Edited by Jacob Neusner. SHR 14. Leiden: Brill, 1968.
— *Fourth Ezra: A Commentary on the Book of Fourth Ezra*. Hermeneia. Minneapolis: Fortress, 1990.
— "The Question of the Messiah in 4 Ezra." Pages 209–24 in *Judaisms and Their Messiahs at the Turn of the Christian Era*. Edited by Jacob Neusner, William Scott Green, and Ernest Frerichs. Cambridge: Cambridge University Press, 1987.
Stone, Michael E., and Matthias Henze, eds. and trans. *4 Ezra and 2 Baruch*. Minneapolis: Fortress, 2013.
Strazicich, John. *Joel's Use of Scripture and Scripture's Use of Joel: Appropriation and Resignification in Second Temple Judaism and Early Christianity*. BibInt 82. Leiden: Brill, 2007.
Stuckenbruck, Loren T. "The Formation and Re-Formation of Daniel in the Dead Sea Scrolls." Pages 101–30 in *Scripture and the Scrolls*. Vol. 1 of *The Bible and the Dead Sea Scrolls*. Edited by James H. Charlesworth. Princeton Symposium on Judaism and Christian Origins 2. Waco, TX: Baylor University Press, 2006.
— "How Much Evil Does the Christ Event Solve? Jesus and Paul in Relation to Jewish 'Apocalyptic' Thought." Pages 142–68 in *Evil in Second Temple Judaism and Early Christianity*. Edited by Chris Keith and Loren T. Stuckenbruck. WUNT 2/417. Tübingen: Mohr Siebeck, 2016.
— "Overlapping Ages at Qumran and 'Apocalyptic' in Pauline Theology." Pages 309–26 in *The Dead Sea Scrolls and Pauline Literature*. Edited by Jean-Sébastien Rey. STDJ 102. Leiden: Brill, 2014.
— "Posturing 'Apocalyptic' in Pauline Theology: How Much Contrast with Jewish Tradition?" Pages 240–56 in *The Myth of Rebellious Angels: Studies in Second Temple Judaism and New Testament Texts*. WUNT 335. Tübingen: Mohr Siebeck, 2014.
— "'Reading the Present' in the Animal Apocalypse (1 Enoch 85–90)." Pages 91–102 in *Reading the Present in the Qumran Library: The Perception of the Contemporary by Means of Scriptural Interpretations*. Edited by Kristin De Troyer and Armin Lange. SymS 30. Atlanta: Society of Biblical Literature, 2005.
— "Temporal Shifts from Text to Interpretation: Concerning the Use of the Perfect and Imperfect in the *Habakkuk Pesher* (1QpHab)." Pages 124–49 in *Qumran Studies: New Approaches, New Questions*. Edited by Michael Thomas Davis and Brent A. Strawn. Grand Rapids: Eerdmans, 2007.

Stylianou, P. J. *A Historical Commentary on Diodorus Siculus Book 15*. Oxford Classical Monographs. Oxford: Clarendon, 1998.
— Review of *Diodorus Siculus and the First Century*, by Kenneth S. Sacks. *Bryn Mawr Classical Review* 2 (1991): 388.
Syme, Ronald. *Tacitus*. 2 vols. Oxford: Clarendon, 1958.
Tacitus. *The Histories and the Annals*. Translated by Clifford H. Moore and John Jackson. 4 vols. LCL. Cambridge: Harvard University Press, 1925–1937.
Talbert, Charles H. "Conzelmann, Hans Georg (1915–1989)." *DMBI* 324–28.
— *Literary Patterns, Theological Themes, and the Genre of Luke-Acts*. SBLMS 20. Missoula, MT: Society of Biblical Literature and Scholars Press, 1974.
— *Luke and the Gnostics: An Examination of the Lucan Purpose*. Nashville: Abingdon, 1966.
— *Reading Luke: A Literary and Theological Commentary on the Third Gospel*. New York: Crossroad, 1982.
— "Shifting Sands: The Recent Study of the Gospel of Luke." *Interpretation* 30 (1976): 381–95.
Talmon, Shemaryahu. "Waiting for the Messiah: The Spiritual Universe of the Qumran Covenanters." Pages 111–37 in *Judaisms and Their Messiahs at the Turn of the Christian Era*. Edited by Jacob Neusner, William Scott Green, and Ernest Frerichs. Cambridge: Cambridge University Press, 1987.
Tannehill, Robert C. "Israel in Luke-Acts: A Tragic Story." *JBL* 104 (1985): 79–81.
— *The Narrative Unity of Luke-Acts: A Literary Interpretation*. 2 vols. FF. Philadelphia: Fortress, 1986–1990.
— Review of *The Plan of God in Luke-Acts*, by John T. Squires. *Biblica* 75 (1994): 425–28.
Tanner, Kathryn. *God and Creation in Christian Theology: Tyranny or Empowerment?* Oxford: Blackwell, 1988.
Taubes, Jacob. *Occidental Eschatology*. Translated by David Ratmoko. Cultural Memory in the Present. Stanford, CA: Stanford University Press, 2009. Translation of *Abendländische Eschatologie*. Bern: Francke, 1947.
Theissen, Gerd. *The Miracle Stories of the Early Christian Tradition*. Translated by Francis McDonagh. SNTW. Edinburgh: T&T Clark, 1983.
Theodorakopoulos, Elena. "Closure: The Book of Virgil." Pages 155–65 in *The Cambridge Companion to Virgil*. Edited by Charles Martindale. Cambridge: Cambridge University Press, 1997.
Thomas, Richard F. "Ovid's Reception of Virgil." Pages 294–307 in *A Companion to Ovid*. Edited by Peter E. Knox. Blackwell Companions to the Ancient World. Chichester: Wiley-Blackwell, 2009.
Thompson, Alan J. *The Acts of the Risen Lord Jesus: Luke's Account of God's Unfolding Plan*. New Studies in Biblical Theology 27. Downers Grove: InterVarsity Press, 2011.
Tiller, Patrick A. *A Commentary on the Animal Apocalypse of I Enoch*. EJL 4. Atlanta: Scholars Press, 1993.
Todorov, Tzvetan. *Genres in Discourse*. Translated by Catherine Porter. Cambridge: Cambridge University Press, 1990.
Tomson, P. J. "Gamaliel's Counsel and the Apologetic Strategy of Luke-Acts." Pages 585–604 in *The Unity of Luke-Acts*. Edited by Joseph Verheyden. BETL 142. Leuven: Leuven University Press, 1999.

Tov, Emanuel. *Scribal Practices and Approaches Reflected in the Texts Found in the Judean Desert*. Studies on the Texts of the Desert of Judah 54. Leiden: Brill, 2004.
Unnik, W. C. van. "An Attack on the Epicureans by Flavius Josephus." Pages 341–55 in *Romanitas et Christianitas: Studia Iano Henrico Waszink A. D. VI Kal. Nov. A. MCMLXXIII XIII lustra complenti oblata*. Edited by W. den Boer, P. G. van der Nat, C. M. J. Sicking, and J. C. M. van Winden. Amsterdam: North-Holland Publishing Company, 1973.
Uytanlet, Samson. *Luke-Acts and Jewish Historiography: A Study on the Theology, Literature, and Ideology of Luke-Acts*. WUNT 2/366. Tübingen: Mohr Siebeck, 2014.
Valerius Maximus. *Memorable Doings and Sayings*. Translated by D. R. Shackleton Bailey. 2 vols. LCL. Cambridge: Harvard University Press, 2000.
Van Seters, John. *Prologue to History: The Yahwist as Historian in Genesis*. Louisville: Westminster John Knox, 1992.
VanderKam, James C. "The Book of Enoch and the Qumran Scrolls." Pages 254–77 in *The Oxford Handbook of the Dead Sea Scrolls*. Edited by Timothy Lim and John J. Collins. New York: Oxford University Press, 2010.
—— *Enoch and the Growth of an Apocalyptic Tradition*. CBQMS 16. Washington: Catholic Biblical Association of America, 1984.
Vermes, Geza. *The Complete Dead Sea Scrolls in English*. London: Penguin, 1997.
—— "Josephus' Treatment of the Book of Daniel." *JJS* 42 (1991): 149–66.
Vielhauer, Philipp. "Zum 'Paulinismus' der Apostelgeschichte." *EvT* 10 (1950–1951): 1–15.
*Virgil*. Translated by H. R. Fairclough and G. P. Goold. Rev. ed. 2 vols. LCL. Cambridge: Harvard University Press, 1999–2000.
Villalba i Varneda, Pere. *The Historical Method of Flavius Josephus*. ALGHJ 19. Leiden: Brill, 1986.
Vogel, Manuel. "Traumdarstellungen bei Josephus und Lukas." Pages 130–56 in *Die Apostelgeschichte im Kontext antiker und frühchristlicher Historiographie*. Edited by Jörg Frey, Clare K. Rothschild, and Jens Schröter. BNZW 162. Berlin: de Gruyter, 2009.
Vovelle, Michel. *Ideologies and Mentalities*. Translated by Eamon O'Flaherty. Cambridge: Polity, 1990. Translation of *Idéologies et Mentalités*. Paris: Maspero, 1982.
Waanders, F. M. J. *The History of ΤΕΛΟΣ and ΤΕΛΕΩ in Ancient Greek*. Amsterdam: Grüner, 1983.
Walaskay, Paul W. *"And So We Came to Rome": The Political Perspective of St Luke*. SNTSMS 49. Cambridge: Cambridge University Press, 1983.
Walbank, Frank W. "Fortune (*Tychē*) in Polybius." Pages 349–55 in vol. 2 of *A Companion to Greek and Roman Historiography*. Edited by John Marincola. Blackwell Companions to the Ancient World. Malden, MA: Blackwell, 2007.
—— *A Historical Commentary on Polybius*. 3 vols. Oxford: Clarendon, 1957.
—— "History and Tragedy." *Historia* 9 (1960): 216–34.
—— "The Idea of Decline in Polybius." Pages 193–211 in *Polybius, Rome and the Hellenistic World: Essays and Reflections*. Cambridge: Cambridge University Press, 2002.
—— "Supernatural Paraphernalia in Polybius' *Histories*." Pages 245–57 in *Polybius, Rome and the Hellenistic World: Essays and Reflections*. Cambridge: Cambridge University Press, 2002.
Wallace, Daniel B. *Greek Grammar Beyond the Basics: An Exegetical Syntax of the New Testament*. Grand Rapids: Zondervan, 1997.

Walters, Patricia. *The Assumed Authorial Unity of Luke and Acts: A Reassessment of the Evidence*. SNTSMS 145. Cambridge: Cambridge University Press, 2009.

Walton, Steve. "The State They Were In: Luke's View of the Roman Empire." Pages 1–41 in *Rome in the Bible and the Early Church*. Edited by Peter Oakes. Grand Rapids: Baker Academic, 2002.

Wardle, D., ed. and trans. *Valerius Maximus: Memorable Deeds and Sayings, Book 1*. Clarendon Ancient History. Oxford: Clarendon, 1998.

―― "Valerius Maximus on the Domus Augusta, Augustus, and Tiberius." *The Classical Quarterly* 50 (2000): 479–93.

Waterfield, Robin, and Brian McGing, eds. and trans. *Polybius: The Histories*. Oxford World's Classics. Oxford: Oxford University Press, 2010.

Weinfeld, Moshe. *Deuteronomy and the Deuteronomic School*. Oxford: Clarendon, 1972.

―― "Zion and Jerusalem as Religious and Political Capital: Ideology and Utopia." Pages 75–115 in *The Poet and the Historian: Essays in Literary and Historical Biblical Criticism*. Edited by Richard Elliott Friedman. HSS. Chico, CA: Scholars Press, 1983.

Wells, Kyle B. *Grace and Agency in Paul and Second Temple Judaism: Interpreting the Transformation of the Heart*. NovTSup 157. Leiden: Brill, 2014.

West, D. A. "Cernere Erat: The Shield of Aeneas." Pages 295–304 in *Oxford Readings in Vergil's Aeneid*. Edited by S. J. Harrison. Oxford: Oxford University Press, 1990.

―― "The End and the Meaning: *Aeneid* 12.791–842." Pages 303–18 in *Vergil's Aeneid: Augustan Epic and Political Context*. Edited by Hans-Peter Stahl. London: Duckworth, 1998.

White, Hayden. "Anomalies of Genre: The Utility of Theory and History for the Study of Literary Genres." *New Literary History* 34 (2003): 597–615.

Wilckens, Ulrich. "Interpreting Luke-Acts in a Period of Existentialist Theology." Pages 60–83 in *Studies in Luke-Acts: Essays Presented in Honor of Paul Schubert*. Edited by Leander E. Keck and J. Louis Martyn. Nashville: Abingdon, 1966.

Willett, Tom W. *Eschatology in the Theodicies of 2 Baruch and 4 Ezra*. JSPSup 4. Sheffield: JSOT Press, 1989.

Williams, Gordon. *Change and Decline: Roman Literature in the Early Empire*. Sather Classical Lectures 45. Berkeley: University of California Press, 1978.

Williams, Howard. "The End of History in Hegel and Marx." *The European Legacy: Toward New Paradigms* 2 (1997): 557–66.

Williams, R. D. "The Sixth Book of the *Aeneid*." Pages 191–207 in *Oxford Readings in Vergil's Aeneid*. Edited by S. J. Harrison. Oxford: Oxford University Press, 1990.

Wilson, S. G. "Lukan Eschatology." *NTS* 16 (1970): 330–47.

Witherington, Ben, III. *The Acts of the Apostles: A Socio-Rhetorical Commentary*. Grand Rapids: Eerdmans, 1998.

―― *The Gospel of Mark: A Socio-Rhetorical Commentary*. Grand Rapids: Eerdmans, 2001.

Wolter, Michael. "Eschatology in the Gospel according to Luke." Pages 91–108 in *Eschatology of the New Testament and Some Related Documents*. Edited by Jan G. van der Watt. WUNT 2/315. Tübingen: Mohr Siebeck, 2011.

―― *The Gospel according to Luke*. Translated by Wayne Coppins and Christoph Heilig. BMSEC. Waco, TX: Baylor; Tübigen: Mohr Siebeck, 2016–2017. Translation of *Das Lukasevangelium*. Tübingen: Mohr Siebeck, 2008.

— "Paulus, der bekehrte Gottesfeind: Zum Verständnis von 1.Tim 1,13." Pages 241–57 in *Theologie und Ethos im frühen Christentum: Studien zu Jesus, Paulus und Lukas*. WUNT 236. Tübingen: Mohr Siebeck, 2009.
Woude, Adam S. van der. "Fifty Years of Qumran Research." Pages 1–45 in vol. 1 of *The Dead Sea Scrolls after Fifty Years: A Comprehensive Assessment*. Edited by Peter W. Flint and James C. VanderKam. Leiden: Brill, 1998.
Wright, N. T. "How Can the Bible Be Authoritative? (The Laing Lecture for 1989.)" *VE* 21 (1991): 7–32.
— *The New Testament and the People of God*. London: SPCK, 1992.
— *Paul and the Faithfulness of God*. 2 vols. London: SPCK, 2013.
— *The Resurrection of the Son of God*. London: SPCK, 2003.
York, John O. *The Last Shall Be First: The Rhetoric of Reversal in Luke*. JSNTSup 46. Sheffield: JSOT Press, 1991.
Young, Frances. "'Creatio ex Nihilo': A Context for the Emergence of the Christian Doctrine of Creation." *SJT* 44 (1991): 139–51.
Zerwick, Max. *A Grammatical Analysis of the Greek New Testament*. 3rd rev. ed. Rome: Pontifical Biblical Institute, 1988.

# Index of ancient sources

## Hebrew Bible / Septuagint

**Genesis**
| | |
|---|---|
| 1–11 | 21 |
| 30.11 | 145n45 |
| 50.20 | 211n23 |
| 50.24–25 | 127n321 |

**Exodus**
| | |
|---|---|
| 3.16 | 127n321 |

**Leviticus**
| | |
|---|---|
| 4.2 | 161n125 |
| 5.17 | 159n115, 161n125 |

**Numbers**
| | |
|---|---|
| 10.9 | 96 |
| 22–24 | 285n72 |
| 24.17–19 | 182n212 |

**Deuteronomy**
| | |
|---|---|
| 7.7–8 | 214 |
| 8.5 | 214, 217 |
| 8.18–19 | 214 |
| 8.18–9.3 | 216n37 |
| 9.4–8 | 214 |
| 9.12–14 | 214 |
| 9.22–24 | 214 |
| 20.2–5 | 96 |
| 30.1–5 | 292n102 |
| 30.1–6 | 215 |
| 30.1–10 | 215n35 |
| 30.12–14 | 215n34 |
| 30.19 | 222n61 |
| 32.39 | 213 |
| 32.41 | 213 |

**Joshua**
| | |
|---|---|
| 3.1–21 | 284 |

**1 Samuel**
| | |
|---|---|
| 2.1–10 | 98n197, 146n51 |

**2 Kings**
| | |
|---|---|
| 2.17 | 216 |
| 7–23 | 31 |
| 17.7a | 31 |
| 19.35 | 284 |
| 24.20 | 215–16 |
| 25.11 | 215 |

**1 Chronicles**
| | |
|---|---|
| 9.1 | 215 |
| 9.11 | 216 |

**Nehemiah**
| | |
|---|---|
| 10.35 | 121n296 |
| 13.31 | 121n296 |

**Esther**
| | |
|---|---|
| 1.15 | 161n125 |

**Job** 216, 216n38

**Psalms**
| | |
|---|---|
| 1 | 30–31, 213–14, 214n26, 216, 216n39, 220n54, 243 |
| 1.3–6 | 214 |
| 2.1–2 | 196, 196n275, 197n276 |
| 16 | 130, 306–7 |
| 16.8–11 | 190 |
| 16.10 | 201n293 |
| 73 | 216 |
| 73.1–3 | 216 |
| 73.27–28 | 216n39 |
| 88 | 216n38 |
| 93.12–13 LXX | 90 |
| 110 | 130 |
| 110.1 | 190 |
| 118 | 130 |

**Proverbs**
| | |
|---|---|
| | 216 |
| 8 | 193n260 |

Index of ancient sources — **381**

| Ecclesiastes | 216n38 | 2.45 | 286n75 |
|---|---|---|---|
| | | 4.37 | 121 |
| **Isaiah** | | 7 | 39, 103, 104n231, 108, |
| 6 | 263n226 | | 112n263 |
| 6.9–10 | 262, 262n224, 263n229 | 7.13 | 324 |
| 6.10 | 263–64, 264n231 | 7.25 | 95n191, 120n289, 121 |
| 13.19 | 216 | 8 | 285, 285n73 |
| 14.22 | 216 | 8–9 | 188n238 |
| 21.9 | 216 | 8.3–14 | 104 |
| 31.8 | 182n212 | 8.4 | 92n175 |
| 37.36 | 284 | 9 | 105n234 |
| 48.14–20 | 216 | 9–12 | 104n231 |
| 54.7–8 | 90 | 9.2 | 297 |
| 58.6 | 189 | 9.21 | 188n238 |
| 61.1–2 | 189, 254 | 9.24–27 | 188, 297 |
| 61.2 | 127 | 9.25 | 188n238 |
| 65.11 | 145 | 10–12 | 284 |
| | | 10.13 | 288 |
| **Jeremiah** | | 10.21 | 288 |
| 6.15 | 127 | 11.3 | 92n175 |
| 10.15 | 127n321 | 11.27 | 95 |
| 12.1–4 | 216n38 | 11.29 | 95 |
| 21.7–10 | 216 | 11.33 | 292n105 |
| 25.11–12 | 216, 297 | 11.35 | 95 |
| 31.33 | 216 | 12 | 97n194 |
| | | 12.1 | 91n172, 288 |
| **Ezekiel** | | 12.1–2 | 288n85 |
| 8.5–18 | 127 | 12.2 | 92 |
| | | 12.4 | 180, 180n207 |
| **Daniel** | | 12.7 | 95 |
| 1–6 | 332n251 | 12.9 | 292n105 |
| 2 | 39, 103, 104n231, 108–9, | | |
| | 112n263, 114, 133, 161, | **Joel** | |
| | 285–86 | 2 | 308n158 |
| 2.21 | 120n289, 121 | 2.28–32 | 190–91, 307–8 |
| 2.23 | 286n75 | 3.1–5 LXX | 307–8 |
| 2.24 | 286n75 | | |
| 2.28 | 161 | **Amos** | |
| 2.34–45 | 104 | 5.25–27 | 244 |
| 2.37–43 | 112n263 | | |

## Deuterocanonical Books

| **Wisdom** | | 16.11 | 90 |
|---|---|---|---|
| 4.19 | 246n154 | 16.28 | 159n115 |
| 12.19 | 159n115 | | |
| 16.4 | 161n126 | | |

## Sirach
| | |
|---|---|
| 34.1–5 | 177n196 |

## 2 Maccabees
| | |
|---|---|
| 1.5 | 93 |
| 1.7 | 93 |
| 1.11–17 | 173n178 |
| 1.21 | 173n178 |
| 1.22 | 93n181 |
| 2.4–7 | 173, 223n65 |
| 2.17–18 | 173n178 |
| 2.21 | 173 |
| 2.23 | 45 |
| 2.24–32 | 45n117 |
| 3.5 | 93n181 |
| 3.9 | 145n42 |
| 3.24–40 | 173 |
| 4.6 | 145n42, 149 |
| 4.14 | 296 |
| 4.16–17 | 173n179 |
| 4.17 | 91n173, 166n151, 218n44, 233 |
| 4.23 | 93n181 |
| 4.32 | 93n181, 145n42 |
| 4.38 | 173n179, 217, 233 |
| 5.1 | 93n181 |
| 5.2–4 | 173–74, 173n182 |
| 5.8–9 | 145n42 |
| 5.12–17 | 233 |
| 5.17 | 217 |
| 5.17–18 | 234 |
| 5.17–20 | 218n44 |
| 5.18 | 173n179 |
| 5.20 | 217 |
| 5.21 | 233–34 |
| 6–7 | 90, 218, 233, 233n104, 283, 296 |
| 6.2 | 145n42 |
| 6.10–11 | 90n165 |
| 6.12–14 | 217–18 |
| 6.12–15 | 90 |
| 6.12–16 | 92, 296 |
| 6.12–17 | 93, 217, 219, 223, 240, 266, 283 |
| 6.14 | 236n115 |
| 6.15 | 59n7 |
| 6.16 | 94, 285 |
| 6.20 | 159n115, 162n132 |
| 6.22 | 145, 145n42 |
| 6.26 | 91, 92n176 |
| 6.30 | 91 |
| 6.31 | 88n157 |
| 7 | 91–2 |
| 7.8 | 234 |
| 7.9 | 91–92, 131n337, 174, 218 |
| 7.14 | 91–92, 131n339, 218–19 |
| 7.15 | 92n175 |
| 7.17 | 218, 296 |
| 7.18 | 217 |
| 7.18–19 | 234 |
| 7.19 | 91n173, 218, 233 |
| 7.23 | 91–92, 131n337, 174, 218 |
| 7.28–29 | 92, 218 |
| 7.29 | 91, 131n337, 174 |
| 7.31 | 218 |
| 7.31–38 | 92 |
| 7.33 | 94, 217, 285 |
| 7.36 | 91, 131n337, 174 |
| 7.37 | 145n43 |
| 7.38 | 90, 217 |
| 8.5 | 173n179, 217, 296 |
| 8.11 | 91n173, 166n151, 173n179, 217, 296 |
| 8.18–20 | 173n178 |
| 8.19 | 284 |
| 8.20 | 218 |
| 8.24 | 173n179 |
| 8.36 | 173n178 |
| 9.1 | 93n181, 145n42 |
| 9.4 | 233 |
| 9.4–12 | 173n179 |
| 9.4–28 | 218, 233 |
| 9.9 | 246 |
| 9.11–12 | 233 |
| 9.18 | 173n179 |
| 9.25 | 93n181 |
| 10.3 | 93n181 |
| 10.4 | 94, 284–85, 334 |
| 10.29–30 | 173, 284 |
| 10.29–31 | 218 |
| 10.38 | 173n178, 218, 219n49, 284 |
| 10.11–19 | 174 |
| 10.2–12 | 174 |

| | | | |
|---|---|---|---|
| 11.3 | 218 | 14.3 | 93 |
| 11.8 | 218 | 14.5 | 93n181, 145n42 |
| 11.8–9 | 173 | 14.10 | 145n42 |
| 11.13 | 173n178 | 14.33 | 234 |
| 11.18 | 161n125 | 14.38 | 93 |
| 12.11 | 173n179, 218, 284 | 15.1–6 | 234 |
| 12.15 | 93 | 15.3–7 | 234 |
| 12.15–16 | 173n178, 217–18, 284 | 15.7 | 145n42 |
| 12.22 | 173, 283 | 15.7–16 | 174 |
| 12.22–23 | 219, 219n48 | 15.11 | 147n54, 174 |
| 12.28 | 173n178, 218, 284 | 15.12–16 | 284 |
| 12.39–45 | 88n157 | 15.21–24 | 173n179, 284 |
| 12.40 | 218 | 15.22 | 284 |
| 12.42–45 | 93 | 15.25–27 | 173n179, 219 |
| 12.43–45 | 92, 131n337, 174, 218–19, 283, 303n139 | 15.27 | 284 |
| | | 15.29 | 173n179 |
| 13.4 | 173n179, 284 | 15.32 | 234 |
| 13.7 | 145n42 | 15.34–35 | 173n179 |
| 13.13–14 | 284 | 15.35 | 219n47 |
| 13.13–17 | 218 | 15.37 | 284 |
| 13.17 | 173n179, 284 | 15.37–39 | 94, 285 |

## Pseudepigrapha

### 2 Baruch

| | | | |
|---|---|---|---|
| 2.1 | 222 | 20.1–2 | 294 |
| 5.3 | 223, 223n65 | 20.6 | 108, 136, 294 |
| 5.5 | 222 | 21.11 | 112 |
| 6.7–9 | 173n181, 223n65 | 21.17 | 107 |
| 6.8–9 | 224 | 22.2–4 | 108 |
| 7.1 | 234 | 23–30 | 107, 108n248, 112, 181n208, 228 |
| 9.1 | 222 | 23.3–5a | 223 |
| 9.1–2 | 223, 223n65 | 23.4–7 | 223 |
| 9.1–12.4 | 222 | 23.7 | 294 |
| 10.2–4 | 222 | 25.2–3 | 293 |
| 10.6–19 | 223, 223n65 | 25.4 | 112 |
| 12.4 | 224 | 26–28 | 110, 131n336, 291 |
| 12.5–20.4 | 222 | 27.1 | 223 |
| 13.5 | 224 | 27.15 | 110, 126, 291–92 |
| 13.8–11 | 223 | 28.1 | 112, 292n105 |
| 14.1 | 223 | 29–30 | 291 |
| 14.2 | 224 | 29.8 | 111, 294 |
| 15.2 | 110, 131n339, 291 | 30.1 | 110, 110n254 |
| 15.5–7 | 222 | 30.1–2 | 291 |
| 15.7–8 | 224 | 30.2 | 224 |
| 16.4 | 222 | 30.3 | 112, 131n337 |
| 19.1 | 222n61 | 31.5–32.2 | 226 |

| | | | |
|---|---|---|---|
| 32.1 | 224 | 55.2 | 181 |
| 32.2 | 224 | 55.3 | 181 |
| 33.1–2 | 222 | 56.2 | 181, 223 |
| 33.2 | 222–23 | 56.11 | 230 |
| 35–40 | 297 | 56.14–15 | 230 |
| 35.1–4 | 222 | 57.1–3 | 108 |
| 36.5–7 | 224 | 67.7–8 | 233n102, 299 |
| 36.9 | 294 | 69.2 | 223 |
| 37.1 | 224 | 70.7 | 110, 131n336, 291 |
| 39.1–8 | 108 | 73.1 | 110, 131n340 |
| 39.8–40.4 | 224 | 73.1–74.2 | 110, 291 |
| 40.2 | 223 | 73.1–74.21 | 131n339 |
| 42.1–2 | 224 | 74.2 | 110n257 |
| 42.6 | 107 | 74.2–4 | 81n121, 98, 111, 294 |
| 44.2–3 | 224 | 76.5 | 224 |
| 44.11 | 295 | 76.8–9 | 222n63 |
| 44.11–15 | 224 | 77.3–4 | 222 |
| 44.15 | 110, 131n338, 291 | 77.10 | 222n63 |
| 45.1–2 | 224 | 78.6 | 223 |
| 46.5 | 224 | 79.2–4 | 222 |
| 46.5–7 | 224 | 80.2 | 173n181, 223n65 |
| 48.3 | 110, 126, 291, 293 | 82.9 | 233n102 |
| 48.29 | 224 | 83.1–2 | 294 |
| 48.31 | 293 | 83.4 | 294 |
| 48.33 | 110, 126, 291, 293, 293n106 | 83.8 | 224 |
| | | 83.8–23 | 327 |
| 48.38 | 107 | 83.10–23 | 224, 253, 267 |
| 48.40–41 | 224 | 84.2 | 222 |
| 48.43 | 224 | 84.5–11 | 224 |
| 48.47 | 224 | 84.6 | 224 |
| 50.2–4 | 110n254 | 84.9 | 224 |
| 51.3 | 224 | 85.4 | 224, 327 |
| 51.11–13 | 110, 131n339, 291 | 85.9 | 224 |
| 52.1–7 | 224 | 85.10 | 108, 112 |
| 52.2–3 | 110n254 | 85.10–12 | 294 |
| 52.7 | 224 | 85.11 | 224 |
| 53–74 | 111n258 | | |
| 53–76 | 59, 68, 107–8, 111, 114, 181n208, 184n220, 230 | **1 Enoch** | |
| | | 85–90 | 59n9, 108n246 |
| 54.1 | 223 | 89.1–9 | 313n179 |
| 54.4–5 | 293 | 89.65–90.19 | 103n228, 107n244 |
| 54.5 | 181 | 90.6 | 126 |
| 54.14 | 222 | 90.9 | 126, 292n105 |
| 54.14–22 | 224 | 90.19 | 284 |
| 54.15 | 222 | 90.38 | 111n262 |
| 54.15–16 | 110, 131n339, 226, 291 | 90.39–42 | 181n210 |
| 54.19 | 222 | 91.12 | 284 |

Index of ancient sources — **385**

| | | | |
|---|---|---|---|
| 91.12–17 | 59n9, 107n244, 108n246 | 7.70 | 110, 131n338, 291 |
| 91.14 | 292n105 | 7.72 | 225 |
| 93.1–10 | 59n9, 107n244, 108n246 | 7.74 | 181 |
| 93.4 | 313n179 | 7.78–101 | 59n9 |
| 93.10 | 292n105 | 7.102–15 | 218n46 |
| 93.17 | 81n121, 98 | 7.116–19 | 222n63 |
| | | 8.2–3 | 225 |
| **4 Ezra** | | 8.3 | 229 |
| 3.4–27 | 227n76 | 8.15 | 226 |
| 3.19 | 226 | 8.34 | 226 |
| 3.25–36 | 225 | 8.34–35 | 225 |
| 3.27–28 | 227 | 8.41 | 226 |
| 4.4 | 300 | 8.43 | 226 |
| 4.22–23 | 180 | 8.44–45 | 226 |
| 4.26 | 292n104, 293 | 8.47 | 227 |
| 4.26–27 | 111n261 | 8.50 | 233n102 |
| 4.40 | 293 | 8.51–61 | 291 |
| 5.1–12 | 110, 131n336, 291 | 8.53 | 226 |
| 5.43 | 181 | 8.55 | 226 |
| 5.54–55 | 112 | 8.56–58 | 226, 327 |
| 6.6 | 181 | 8.56–61 | 227 |
| 6.7–28 | 107 | 8.57–58 | 227 |
| 6.18–28 | 110n254 | 8.59–60 | 227n75 |
| 6.20 | 110, 111n261, 126, 291, 292n105 | 8.62 | 226 |
| | | 8.63 | 180, 318 |
| 6.21–24 | 98n198, 110, 131n336, 291 | 9.1 | 291 |
| | | 9.1–2 | 269 |
| 6.25 | 111n261 | 9.11 | 226 |
| 6.34 | 227 | 9.13 | 226 |
| 6.35–9.25 | 291n100 | 9.14 | 225 |
| 6.55–59 | 225 | 9.18 | 110, 131n338, 291 |
| 7.10–44 | 108 | 9.21 | 225 |
| 7.12 | 226 | 9.21–22 | 226 |
| 7.16 | 227 | 10.21–22 | 300 |
| 7.19–25 | 225 | 10.25–38 | 300 |
| 7.26 | 110 | 10.27 | 300 |
| 7.26–44 | 291 | 10.45–46 | 300n125 |
| 7.28 | 110, 291 | 10.51–54 | 300 |
| 7.29 | 110n254 | 10.54 | 300 |
| 7.29–31 | 291 | 10.58–59 | 293 |
| 7.31 | 110n254 | 11–12 | 39, 103, 108, 109n253, 111, 113, 184n220, 288n85, 291, 297 |
| 7.32 | 291 | | |
| 7.42 | 227n75 | | |
| 7.46–48 | 225 | 11.39 | 228 |
| 7.48 | 226n71, 228 | 11.39–46 | 181 |
| 7.50 | 111n261 | 11.40 | 292 |
| 7.52–61 | 225 | 11.44 | 293 |

## Index of ancient sources

| | | | |
|---|---|---|---|
| 12.2–3 | 292 | 14.18 | 112, 293 |
| 12.9 | 293 | 14.20 | 293 |
| 12.11 | 107, 113n267, 292 | 14.22 | 229 |
| 12.11–12 | 182, 297 | 14.23 | 291 |
| 12.28 | 293 | 14.26 | 110, 126, 293 |
| 12.31–34 | 109 | 14.29 | 228n81 |
| 12.32 | 110, 291 | 14.34 | 260 |
| 12.34 | 110, 131n338, 291 | 14.34–35 | 228n80, 229, 291, 327 |
| 12.36–38 | 110, 126, 291, 293 | 14.44–48 | 292n105 |
| 13 | 291 | 14.45–47 | 110, 126, 291 |
| 13.26 | 110, 291 | 14.45–48 | 180, 180n207, 293 |
| 13.29 | 293 | 14.46 | 181 |
| 13.32 | 49n137 | | |
| 13.35–36 | 110 | **Testament of Job** | |
| 13.36 | 286n75 | 48–50 | 217n42 |
| 13.37 | 49n137 | | |
| 13.52 | 110, 291 | **Jubilees** | |
| 13.53–56 | 110, 126, 291, 293 | 50.4 | 98n200 |
| 13.58 | 110, 131n338, 291 | | |
| 14.1–6 | 292n105 | **3 Maccabees** | |
| 14.9 | 111n261 | 1.12 | 159n115 |
| 14.11 | 112 | | |
| 14.11–12 | 293 | **4 Maccabees** | 233n104 |
| 14.13 | 293 | 12.18 | 92n176, 219n51 |
| 14.13–15 | 229 | | |

## Dead Sea Scrolls

**1QM**

| | | | |
|---|---|---|---|
| | | 5–12 | 98 |
| 1.1 | 290 | 5.1 | 288n83 |
| 1.1–2 | 94 | 5.3–6.16 | 46n120 |
| 1.2 | 287n79, 290, 297 | 6.5 | 287 |
| 1.5 | 94–95, 97, 131n338 | 6.5–6 | 287 |
| 1.5–7 | 287 | 8 | 297 |
| 1.8 | 95, 98, 131n339 | 9.5–6 | 94, 97, 131n338, 287 |
| 1.8–9 | 94, 131n340, 287, 287n79 | 10.3 | 96 |
| 1.9 | 96, 98, 287n79 | 10.11–16 | 298 |
| 1.10 | 94 | 10.14–15 | 96 |
| 1.10–11 | 182–83, 229 | 10.15 | 123 |
| 1.11 | 229 | 11.1 | 298 |
| 1.12 | 97n194 | 11.1–9 | 298 |
| 1.13 | 97 | 11.2 | 298 |
| 2–14 | 47 | 11.3 | 299 |
| 2.1–4 | 46n120 | 11.4 | 298 |
| 2.5 | 287n79 | 11.6–8 | 182n212 |
| 2.10 | 290 | 11.9–10 | 299 |
| 3–4 | 46n120 | 11.11–12 | 182n212 |

| | | | |
|---|---|---|---|
| 11.13 | 299 | 18.1–4 | 287 |
| 11.13–17 | 287 | 18.7 | 299 |
| 11.17 | 183 | 18.7–9 | 291 |
| 12.1 | 287n79 | 18.8 | 290 |
| 12.2 | 97n194 | 18.10 | 94, 182 |
| 12.4 | 287 | 18.11 | 287n81 |
| 12.6 | 287n79 | 18.11–12 | 94, 131n340, 287n79 |
| 12.9 | 288n83 | 19.2–5 | 288n83 |
| 12.10–15 | 287 | 19.2–8 | 287, 287n79 |
| 13.2 | 183 | 19.5–7 | 97 |
| 13.4 | 98n202, 183 | 19.6–7 | 287 |
| 13.7–8 | 96 | 19.2b-8 | 94n184 |
| 13.7–10 | 291 | | |
| 13.10 | 288n83 | **1QpHab** | 60n16 |
| 13.11 | 183, 230 | 3.11 | 288n85 |
| 13.14 | 94, 182 | 7.1–4 | 289 |
| 13.18 | 94 | 7.9–10 | 289 |
| 14.2–4 | 96 | | |
| 14.4 | 97n195 | **1QS** | 288n83, 290n97 |
| 14.4–5 | 291 | 5.23–24 | 290 |
| 14.4–18 | 298 | 6.2 | 290 |
| 14.5–12 | 267 | | |
| 14.6 | 98, 146n51 | **1QSa** | 288n83, 290n97 |
| 14.7 | 290 | 2.5–7 | 290 |
| 14.8–9 | 96 | 2.7–8 | 98n197, 267 |
| 14.8–10 | 291 | | |
| 14.9 | 299 | **4Q246** | 46n119 |
| 14.10–11 | 98, 146n51 | | |
| 14.13 | 94 | **4Q285** | 288n83 |
| 14.13–14 | 96 | | |
| 14.16 | 287n81 | **4Q398** | |
| 14.17 | 287n79 | f11–13.4 | 289 |
| 15.1 | 94, 131n340, 287n79 | | |
| 15.2 | 94, 97, 131n338, 287 | **4Q426** | 287 |
| 15.7–18 | 298 | | |
| 15.12 | 94, 97, 287 | **4Q491–96** | 46 |
| 15–19 | 47 | | |
| 17.4–6 | 183, 183n218 | **4Q492** | 288n83 |
| 17.5 | 182 | | |
| 17.5–6 | 94 | **4QInstruction** | 50n138 |
| 17.6–7 | 288, 297 | | |
| 17.6–9 | 291 | **4QMMT** | 289n91 |
| 17.7 | 98, 126 | C21 | 289 |
| 17.7–8 | 287n79 | | |
| 17.8 | 97n194 | | |
| 17.9 | 98 | | |
| 18.1 | 94, 97, 131n338 | | |

| | | | |
|---|---|---|---|
| 11QMelch | 288n84 | | |
| CD | 288n86 | | |
| 16.3–4 | 98n200 | | |

## Ancient Jewish Writers

**Josephus**
*Against Apion*

| | | | |
|---|---|---|---|
| 1.37 | 177 | 6.210 | 233 |
| 1.156 | 101n215 | 6.316 | 194, 194n267 |
| 1.159 | 101n215 | 7.383 | 151n75 |
| 1.204 | 175n185 | 8.262 | 176 |
| 1.246 | 232n97 | 8.307 | 151n75 |
| 1.263 | 232n97 | 8.418–19 | 178n199 |
| 2.168 | 221n57 | 9.28 | 176n190 |
| 2.218 | 91, 101–2, 106 | 10 | 39 |

*Jewish Antiquities*

| | | | |
|---|---|---|---|
| 1–11 | 151n71 | 10.142 | 178 |
| 1.14 | 249 | 10.194 | 178 |
| 1.14–15 | 205, 220n54 | 10.200 | 178 |
| 1.41 | 105 | 10.203–10 | 285 |
| 1.46 | 105 | 10.205–10 | 297 |
| 1.108 | 176 | 10.206–7 | 286n75 |
| 1.113–21 | 232n99 | 10.207 | 286, 286n75 |
| 1.333 | 150n67 | 10.210 | 104, 106, 131n340, 143, 178, 221, 286 |
| 2.261 | 232 | 10.237 | 178 |
| 2.268 | 232 | 10.239–41 | 178 |
| 2.284–302 | 233n101 | 10.241 | 233 |
| 2.286 | 233 | 10.241–23 | 233 |
| 2.291–92 | 232 | 10.242 | 233 |
| 2.307 | 232n97, 233 | 10.242–22 | 286n78 |
| 2.330 | 233 | 10.244 | 105n237 |
| 2.344 | 233 | 10.266 | 177 |
| 3.81 | 176–77 | 10.266–81 | 285–86 |
| 3.268 | 176 | 10.267 | 285 |
| 3.322 | 176 | 10.272–76 | 297 |
| 4.3 | 232 | 10.276 | 105–6, 221, 285n73 |
| 4.100–31 | 285n72 | 10.276–81 | 152n79 |
| 4.114–17 | 178 | 10.277 | 221n57 |
| 4.158 | 176 | 10.277–80 | 105, 143, 148, 179 |
| 4.243 | 232 | 10.281 | 176, 286 |
| 6.89 | 232 | 11.237 | 165n147 |
| 6.181 | 233 | 12.322 | 105 |
| 6.183 | 233 | 13 | 152n78 |
| 6.186–91 | 233 | 13.171–73 | 151, 210 |
| 6.186–92 | 233 | 13.172 | 209n13 |
| | | 14.355 | 194–95 |
| | | 16.397–404 | 155 |

| | | | |
|---|---|---|---|
| 16.404 | 166n151 | 3.144 | 148n62, 165n148 |
| 17.354 | 176 | 3.171–75 | 177 |
| 18.12–22 | 151, 210 | 3.186–88 | 177 |
| 18.369 | 194, 194n267 | 3.271–75 | 177 |
| 19.4 | 233 | 3.352 | 177 |
| 19.108 | 176 | 3.352–54 | 177 |
| 19.155–56 | 233n103 | 3.354 | 102, 143, 167n153, 175 |
| 19.345–51 | 246 | 3.374 | 101–2, 106, 131n337 |
| *Life* | | 3.391 | 148n60, 148n62, 165n148 |
| 12 | 221n57 | 4.204–5 | 220 |
| 15 | 148n61 | 4.219 | 148n62 |
| 17–18 | 102, 286 | 4.287 | 175 |
| 425 | 148n61 | 4.289 | 175 |
| *Jewish War* | | 4.297 | 151n72, 175–76 |
| 1.19 | 101 | 4.323 | 220n56 |
| 1.29 | 101 | 4.366 | 148n62, 165n148 |
| 1.31 | 101 | 4.388 | 220n56 |
| 1.62 | 101 | 4.622 | 143n31, 148n62 |
| 1.82 | 148n62 | 4.622–25 | 151 |
| 1.117 | 101 | 4.623 | 177 |
| 1.127 | 101 | 5 | 103 |
| 1.218 | 101 | 5.2 | 143n31 |
| 1.328 | 175 | 5.18 | 220 |
| 1.331 | 175 | 5.19 | 220n56 |
| 1.377 | 176 | 5.257 | 176 |
| 1.593 | 165n148 | 5.362–419 | 102, 199n285, 286 |
| 1.662 | 151 | 5.363 | 220 |
| 2 | 152n78, 205n1 | 5.364 | 220 |
| 2.114 | 167n153, 175 | 5.365–67 | 234 |
| 2.119–66 | 151, 210 | 5.367 | 102–3, 106, 143, 143n31, 179, 221, 285–86 |
| 2.159 | 175 | | |
| 2.159–66 | 179 | 5.368 | 234 |
| 2.162 | 209n13 | 5.372 | 106, 178 |
| 2.162–63 | 211 | 5.372–73 | 106, 221 |
| 2.164–66 | 286n77 | 5.372–74 | 220 |
| 2.219 | 246n156 | 5.376–94 | 106 |
| 2.345–401 | 102n220, 199n285, 234, 286 | 5.377 | 177, 234 |
| | | 5.377–78 | 155, 220 |
| 2.352–55 | 99 | 5.377–400 | 220 |
| 2.390 | 103 | 5.378 | 205, 219, 234 |
| 2.390–31 | 99 | 5.390 | 220 |
| 2.457 | 148n62 | 5.395–96 | 219 |
| 2.650 | 176 | 5.401–2 | 220 |
| 3.6 | 143n31 | 5.401–3 | 155 |
| 3.28 | 148n62, 165n148 | 5.402 | 106 |
| 3.52–54 | 219 | 5.407 | 106, 155 |
| 3.142 | 177 | 5.412 | 106, 219, 234n105 |

| | | | |
|---|---|---|---|
| 5.415 | 177, 221 | 6.305 | 175 |
| 5.415–16 | 106 | 6.305–13 | 211, 221 |
| 5.416 | 178 | 6.308 | 175 |
| 5.416–18 | 220n56 | 6.310 | 179, 185n224, 205, 220n54 |
| 5.572 | 151 | | |
| 6.108 | 178n199 | 6.313 | 176 |
| 6.110 | 220 | 6.313–14 | 177 |
| 6.249–53 | 99 | 6.314–15 | 178 |
| 6.250 | 165n149, 177 | 7 | 233n103 |
| 6.252 | 165n148, 220–21 | 7.82 | 148n62 |
| 6.254–56 | 220 | 7.318 | 148n62 |
| 6.266 | 165n148, 220 | 7.319 | 165n149 |
| 6.285 | 106, 155 | 7.453 | 148n62, 233n103 |
| 6.285–88 | 175n185, 191n252 | | |

## New Testament

**Matthew**

| | | | |
|---|---|---|---|
| 2.1 | 350 | 12.38–42 | 302n131 |
| 2.6 | 131n340 | 12.40 | 350 |
| 2.7 | 347 | 12.41–42 | 131n337, 131n338 |
| 2.16 | 347 | 13.1 | 349 |
| 3.1 | 349 | 13.14–15 | 263n226 |
| 3.8 | 262 | 13.22 | 119, 345 |
| 4.2 | 350 | 13.30 | 346, 346n6, 346n7 |
| 6.33 | 132n345 | 13.39 | 345 |
| 6.34 | 350 | 13.40 | 345 |
| 7.22 | 351 | 13.49 | 345 |
| 8.13 | 349 | 14.1 | 346 |
| 8.29 | 346 | 14.15 | 348 |
| 9.15 | 351 | 15.28 | 349 |
| 9.22 | 349 | 15.32 | 350 |
| 10.6 | 131n340 | 16.2–3 | 347n11 |
| 10.15 | 131n338, 351 | 16.3 | 347 |
| 10.19 | 348 | 16.21 | 350 |
| 10.21–23 | 131n339 | 17.1 | 350 |
| 11.12 | 116n275, 350 | 17.18 | 349 |
| 11.12–13 | 117 | 17.23 | 350 |
| 11.19 | 193n260 | 18.1 | 349 |
| 11.22 | 351 | 18.7 | 156 |
| 11.22–24 | 131n338 | 19.28 | 131n338 |
| 11.24 | 351 | 19.28–29 | 131n339, 131n340, 302 |
| 11.25 | 346 | 20.2 | 350 |
| 12.1 | 346 | 20.3 | 348 |
| 12.32 | 119, 345 | 20.5 | 348 |
| 12.36 | 351 | 20.6 | 350 |
| 12.36–37 | 131n338 | 20.9 | 348 |
| | | 20.12 | 349–50 |

Index of ancient sources — **391**

| | | | |
|---|---|---|---|
| 20.19 | 350 | 28.15 | 351 |
| 21.19 | 345 | 28.20 | 345, 352 |
| 21.34 | 346 | | |
| 21.41 | 346 | **Mark** | |
| 22.23 | 349 | 1.3 | 350 |
| 22.23–46 | 119n287 | 1.9 | 349 |
| 22.29–33 | 131n337 | 1.15 | 346 |
| 22.46 | 351 | 2.1 | 349 |
| 23.30 | 350 | 2.19 | 347 |
| 23.37 | 251n178 | 2.20 | 351 |
| 23.37–39 | 163n141 | 3.29 | 345, 345n3, 345n4 |
| 24.1–35 | 318n199 | 4.12 | 263n226 |
| 24.3 | 345 | 4.19 | 119, 345 |
| 24.6 | 320n208 | 4.27 | 352 |
| 24.13–14 | 131n339 | 4.35 | 349 |
| 24.19 | 131n336, 351 | 5.5 | 352 |
| 24.21–22 | 131n336 | 6.21 | 351 |
| 24.22 | 351 | 6.35 | 348 |
| 24.23–27 | 313 | 6.37 | 35 |
| 24.29 | 302, 351 | 8.1 | 349 |
| 24.36 | 348, 351 | 8.2 | 350 |
| 24.37 | 350 | 8.11–12 | 302n131 |
| 24.37–39 | 313n179, 314 | 8.17–18 | 263n226 |
| 24.38 | 350–51 | 8.31 | 350 |
| 24.42 | 351 | 9.2 | 350 |
| 24.42–51 | 329 | 9.21 | 347 |
| 24.43–51 | 302 | 9.31 | 350 |
| 24.44 | 348 | 10.29–30 | 131n339, 131n340 |
| 24.45 | 346 | 10.30 | 119, 345, 345n4, 347 |
| 24.50 | 348, 351 | 10.34 | 350 |
| 25.1–13 | 329 | 11.11 | 348 |
| 25.13 | 302, 348, 351 | 11.13 | 346 |
| 25.14–30 | 315n184 | 11.14 | 345 |
| 25.19 | 347 | 12.2 | 346 |
| 26.2 | 350 | 12.18–34 | 119n287 |
| 26.18 | 346 | 12.24–27 | 131n337 |
| 26.29 | 351 | 13 | 81n120 |
| 26.40 | 349 | 13.5–31 | 318n199 |
| 26.45 | 348 | 13.7 | 320n208 |
| 26.55 | 349, 352 | 13.8 | 320 |
| 26.61 | 350 | 13.11 | 348 |
| 26.64 | 308n161 | 13.12–13 | 131n339 |
| 27 | 246 | 13.17 | 351 |
| 27.40 | 350 | 13.19–20 | 131n336, 351 |
| 27.45–46 | 348 | 13.24 | 131n336, 351 |
| 27.63 | 350 | 13.24–25 | 302 |
| 27.64 | 350 | | |

| | | | |
|---|---|---|---|
| 13.32 | 323n221, 326, 326n233, 348, 351 | 1.68–79 | 188n237 |
| | | 1.69 | 302 |
| 13.33 | 346 | 1.70 | 345 |
| 13.33–37 | 302, 315n184 | 1.75 | 352 |
| 14.1 | 350 | 1.80 | 351 |
| 14.12 | 351 | 2 | 253, 265 |
| 14.25 | 351 | 2.1 | 349 |
| 14.35 | 348 | 2.6 | 351 |
| 14.37 | 349 | 2.11 | 187n236, 302 |
| 14.41 | 348 | 2.14 | 254 |
| 14.49 | 352 | 2.21 | 350 |
| 14.58 | 350 | 2.22 | 351 |
| 14.62 | 308 | 2.25–27 | 187n235 |
| 15.16 | 35 | 2.26 | 302, 187–88 |
| 15.25 | 348 | 2.26–32 | 321n213 |
| 15.29 | 350 | 2.27 | 186 |
| 15.33–34 | 348 | 2.29–30 | 302 |
| | | 2.29–32 | 132n345 |
| **Luke** | | 2.32 | 251, 265 |
| 1–4 | 187n234, 263n228 | 2.34 | 251–52, 255, 265 |
| 1.2 | 124 | 2.34–35 | 130, 187, 307n154 |
| 1.4 | 200 | 2.36 | 352 |
| 1.5 | 125, 246n155, 350 | 2.36–38 | 187–88 |
| 1.7 | 352 | 2.37 | 352 |
| 1.8–22 | 188n238 | 2.38 | 188n237, 324n222, 349 |
| 1.10 | 348 | 2.43 | 351 |
| 1.17 | 130, 188 | 2.44 | 350 |
| 1.18 | 352 | 2.46 | 349n14, 350 |
| 1.18–20 | 249 | 2.49 | 158n108, 159n118 |
| 1.19 | 188n238 | 2.68–79 | 132n345 |
| 1.20 | 346, 351 | 3.1 | 246n155 |
| 1.23 | 351 | 3.4–6 | 252 |
| 1.24 | 349 | 3.7–9 | 246n151 |
| 1.25 | 349 | 3.8 | 262 |
| 1.32–33 | 322n215 | 3.15 | 302 |
| 1.33 | 130, 188, 345 | 3.16 | 190n246 |
| 1.37 | 257 | 3.18 | 164n142 |
| 1.38 | 257 | 3.38 | 129 |
| 1.39 | 349 | 4 | 249 |
| 1.46–55 | 98n197, 146n51, 253n186, 253n187 | 4.2 | 349–50 |
| | | 4.5 | 347 |
| 1.52–53 | 256 | 4.5–6 | 249n170 |
| 1.53–55 | 252, 254 | 4.13 | 249, 346 |
| 1.55 | 345 | 4.16 | 351 |
| 1.57 | 347 | 4.16–18 | 264 |
| 1.59 | 350 | 4.16–19 | 189 |
| 1.63–64 | 257 | | |

| | | | |
|---|---|---|---|
| 4.16–30 | 163, 202n294, 253, 253n186, 264n233 | 8.29 | 348 |
| | | 9.12 | 349 |
| 4.18–19 | 129 | 9.20 | 302 |
| 4.19 | 127, 196, 254 | 9.22 | 157n105, 158n108, 164, 196n272, 350 |
| 4.21 | 189 | | |
| 4.25 | 125, 350 | 9.23 | 352 |
| 4.27 | 190n245 | 9.24 | 252 |
| 4.28–30 | 253n186 | 9.26 | 255n194 |
| 4.41 | 186, 302 | 9.27 | 321n213 |
| 4.42 | 351 | 9.28 | 125, 350 |
| 4.43 | 158n108, 162, 202n294 | 9.36–37 | 349 |
| 5.17 | 349 | 9.51 | 259n214, 260, 316, 349 |
| 5.17–26 | 245n148 | 9.52–56 | 248n165 |
| 5.27–32 | 302n134, 327 | 10.12 | 125, 351 |
| 5.35 | 351 | 10.13 | 131 |
| 6.7 | 312n174 | 10.18 | 308n160 |
| 6.12 | 349 | 10.20 | 302 |
| 6.13 | 351 | 10.21 | 349 |
| 6.20–26 | 252, 254–55 | 10.25–37 | 162, 253, 302 |
| 6.23 | 351 | 10.31 | 146 |
| 6.43–45 | 246n151 | 10.31 D | 157 |
| 7.18–23 | 193 | 11.3 | 352 |
| 7.18–35 | 313 | 11.19 | 198n283, 262n221 |
| 7.18–50 | 327 | 11.20 | 185n224, 313, 316n192 |
| 7.21 | 349 | 11.31 | 131, 302n131 |
| 7.23 | 193n257 | 11.31–32 | 131 |
| 7.24–28 | 193 | 11.37–52 | 302n134 |
| 7.29–30 | 192–93 | 11.42 | 159 |
| 7.30 | 163, 202n297, 203 | 11.43 | 198n281 |
| 7.31–35 | 193 | 12 | 125, 246 |
| 7.36–50 | 193n260, 250n172, 252, 253n185, 255, 302n134 | 12.1–13.9 | 244–45, 245n147 |
| | | 12.4–6 | 245 |
| 7.41–43 | 262n221 | 12.7–8 | 245 |
| 7.44–46 | 327 | 12.8–10 | 245 |
| 7.44–50 | 327 | 12.11 | 132n345 |
| 7.50 | 327n236 | 12.11–12 | 245 |
| 7.50–8.1 | 162n136 | 12.12 | 159n118, 348 |
| 8.1–15 | 132 | 12.13–21 | 245 |
| 8.4–15 | 246n151 | 12.20–21 | 329 |
| 8.8 | 186n228 | 12.22–32 | 245 |
| 8.10 | 263n226 | 12.32 | 132n345 |
| 8.12 | 250 | 12.33–34 | 245 |
| 8.13 | 346 | 12.35–40 | 191n252, 302, 329 |
| 8.14 | 345n1 | 12.35–46 | 245 |
| 8.22 | 349 | 12.35–48 | 314, 323, 326, 326n233 |
| 8.27 | 347 | 12.39 | 348 |
| 8.28 | 186 | 12.39–40 | 125 |

| | | | |
|---|---|---|---|
| 12.40 | 348 | 16 | 117 |
| 12.42 | 346 | 16.1–13 | 117 |
| 12.43–46 | 329 | 16.8 | 345 |
| 12.46 | 125, 348, 351 | 16.8–9 | 119 |
| 12.47–53 | 245 | 16.10–13 | 119n286 |
| 12.54–49 | 245 | 16.13 | 118 |
| 12.54–56 | 319 | 16.14 | 117 |
| 12.56 | 127, 329, 347 | 16.16 | 6n23, 116–18, 307n156 |
| 13.1 | 245, 346 | 16.18 | 117 |
| 13.1–5 | 132, 207 | 16.19 | 352 |
| 13.1–9 | 244n146, 245n147, 246, 261n219, 327 | 16.19–31 | 117, 252, 253n186, 254–55, 302, 317n195 |
| 13.2 | 245 | 16.29 | 190 |
| 13.3 | 245 | 16.29–31 | 132 |
| 13.4 | 245, 266n243 | 16.31 | 190, 306 |
| 13.5 | 245 | 17 | 125n312 |
| 13.6–9 | 245 | 17.1 | 156 |
| 13.12–13 | 261 | 17.4 | 350 |
| 13.14 | 159n115, 350–51 | 17.20 | 311 |
| 13.16 | 159n115, 250, 261, 351 | 17.20–21 | 311n171, 312n173 |
| 13.22–30 | 191 | 17.20–37 | 317n197 |
| 13.30 | 252, 252n182 | 17.20–18.8 | 311–15 |
| 13.31 | 349 | 17.20a | 311 |
| 13.33–34 | 163 | 17.20b | 313n176 |
| 13.33–35 | 132 | 17.20b-21 | 312–13 |
| 13.34 | 251 | 17.21 | 311n171, 313, 315, 316n192 |
| 13.34–35 | 127n323 | | |
| 13.35 | 251 | 17.21–24 | 326 |
| 14.1 | 312n174 | 17.22 | 125–26, 351 |
| 14.1–24 | 327 | 17.22–37 | 191, 311n171, 312 |
| 14.5 | 351 | 17.23 | 311n171, 318n202 |
| 14.7–24 | 252n182, 302n134 | 17.24 | 125, 130, 313, 351 |
| 14.8–11 | 255n197 | 17.25 | 163, 319 |
| 14.11 | 252, 252n180, 252n182, 254–55 | 17.26 | 126n315, 350 |
| | | 17.26–27 | 313 |
| 14.12–13 | 327n236 | 17.26–29 | 125 |
| 14.12–14 | 255n197 | 17.26–37 | 130–31 |
| 14.14 | 131, 302 | 17.27 | 314, 351 |
| 14.15–35 | 255n197 | 17.28 | 314, 350 |
| 14.16–24 | 255–56 | 17.28–29 | 313 |
| 14.17 | 349 | 17.29 | 351 |
| 14.17–24 | 253 | 17.30 | 351 |
| 14.18 | 156 | 17.30–31 | 125 |
| 15.2 | 327 | 17.30–37 | 314 |
| 15.11–32 | 253, 253n185, 256 | 17.31 | 351 |
| 15.13 | 349 | 17.31–32 | 314 |
| 15.32 | 159n115 | 17.31–35 | 313 |

| | | | |
|---|---|---|---|
| 17.33 | 252, 315 | 20.41–44 | 307n154 |
| 17.37 | 314 | 20.42–44 | 130, 191 |
| 18.1 | 159, 314 | 21 | 125n312, 127n322, 128, |
| 18.1–8 | 311n171, 312, 315 | | 201n294, 321n213, |
| 18.1–18 | 13n51 | | 328n239 |
| 18.4 | 347 | 21.5–6 | 318, 323 |
| 18.7 | 352 | 21.5–33 | 185n224 |
| 18.7–8 | 314–15, 326, 329 | 21.5–36 | 313n178, 318–21, 326, |
| 18.8 | 314 | | 329 |
| 18.9 | 312n173 | 21.6 | 125, 132n345, 328, 351 |
| 18.9–14 | 252, 311n171 | 21.7 | 311, 311n169, 318, |
| 18.14 | 252, 252n180, 254–55 | | 318n200, 325, 325n232 |
| 18.15–17 | 312n173 | 21.8 | 326, 346 |
| 18.18–27 | 302, 312n173 | 21.8–9 | 191, 318 |
| 18.18–30 | 162, 252 | 21.8–36 | 318 |
| 18.28–30 | 302, 312n173 | 21.9 | 319, 319n207 |
| 18.29–30 | 131 | 21.9–10 | 320n209 |
| 18.30 | 119, 345, 345n4, 347 | 21.9–26 | 131 |
| 18.31–34 | 312n173, 316n193 | 21.10–11 | 319–20 |
| 18.33 | 350 | 21.12 | 319, 319n207 |
| 19.1 | 315n185 | 21.12–14 | 132n345 |
| 19.1–10 | 252n184, 327, 327n236 | 21.12–19 | 319–20 |
| 19.5 | 162 | 21.19 | 302 |
| 19.9 | 316 | 21.20 | 319–20 |
| 19.11 | 311, 313n175, 315–16, | 21.20–21 | 328 |
| | 316n191, 316n192 | 21.20–24 | 318n200, 319–20 |
| 19.11–27 | 315–17, 316–17n194, | 21.20–24a | 320n209 |
| | 317n197 | 21.20–36 | 191 |
| 19.12–27 | 315 | 21.22 | 127, 254n190, 351 |
| 19.28 | 315n185, 316 | 21.22–23 | 125 |
| 19.41–44 | 127n323, 207, 251 | 21.22–24 | 319 |
| 19.42 | 252, 349 | 21.23 | 156n99, 351 |
| 19.43 | 125, 351 | 21.24 | 127, 128, 346 |
| 19.43–44 | 191 | 21.25–26 | 301 |
| 19.44 | 127, 252, 346 | 21.25–27 | 318n200 |
| 19.47 | 352 | 21.25–28 | 130, 319 |
| 20.1 | 350 | 21.27 | 310 |
| 20.9 | 195, 347 | 21.27–28 | 132n345 |
| 20.9–19 | 132 | 21.28 | 131, 261, 302, 319–21 |
| 20.10 | 127, 346 | 21.29–33 | 319, 320 |
| 20.19 | 349 | 21.29–36 | 319 |
| 20.20 | 312n174 | 21.31 | 321 |
| 20.27–38 | 131, 302, 302n132 | 21.32 | 321, 321n213 |
| 20.34 | 345 | 21.34 | 319n204, 351 |
| 20.34–35 | 119 | 21.34–36 | 131, 185n224, 302, 320 |
| 20.35 | 345 | 21.36 | 347 |
| 20.37–38 | 306 | 21.37 | 352 |

| | | | |
|---|---|---|---|
| 22 | 116n275, 308 | 2.19 | 350 |
| 22.3 | 249 | 2.20 | 350 |
| 22.6 | 207 | 4.6 | 348 |
| 22.7 | 159, 351 | 4.14 | 345, 345n4 |
| 22.14 | 349 | 4.21 | 348 |
| 22.28–30 | 131 | 4.23 | 348 |
| 22.30 | 131, 302 | 4.40 | 349 |
| 22.37 | 160 | 4.43 | 350 |
| 22.39–46 | 259n214 | 4.52–53 | 348 |
| 22.53 | 125n311, 348, 352 | 5.6 | 347 |
| 22.59 | 349 | 5.9 | 351 |
| 22.66 | 351 | 5.25 | 348 |
| 22.66–71 | 308 | 5.28 | 348 |
| 22.67 | 302 | 5.35 | 349 |
| 22.69 | 130, 308, 310 | 6.39 | 351 |
| 23.7 | 350 | 6.40 | 351 |
| 23.8 | 347 | 6.44 | 351 |
| 23.12 | 197, 197n276, 207, 246–47n156, 351 | 6.51 | 345 |
| | | 6.54 | 351 |
| 23.27–31 | 127n323 | 6.58 | 345 |
| 23.28–31 | 131–32, 301 | 7.6 | 346 |
| 23.29 | 125, 351 | 7.8 | 346 |
| 23.43 | 328n241 | 7.30 | 125n311, 348 |
| 23.44 | 348 | 7.33 | 347 |
| 23.47 | 330–31n246 | 7.37 | 351 |
| 23.51 | 192, 192n256 | 8.20 | 125n311, 348 |
| 23.54 | 351 | 8.35 | 345 |
| 24.7 | 350 | 8.51 | 345 |
| 24.13 | 350 | 8.52 | 345 |
| 24.18 | 350 | 8.56 | 351 |
| 24.21 | 131, 350 | 9 | 244n146 |
| 24.26 | 157n108, 160–61, 302 | 9.4 | 351 |
| 24.26–27 | 190, 302 | 9.14 | 351 |
| 24.29 | 190n246, 350 | 9.32 | 345, 345n5 |
| 24.33 | 349 | 10.28 | 345, 345n4 |
| 24.44 | 160 | 11.6 | 350 |
| 24.44–47 | 190 | 11.9 | 349–51 |
| 24.46 | 302, 350 | 11.17 | 349n14, 350 |
| 24.49 | 325 | 11.24 | 351 |
| 24.50–53 | 310 | 11.26 | 345 |
| 26.22–23 | 302 | 11.53 | 351 |
| | | 12.1 | 350 |
| **John** | | 12.7 | 351 |
| 1.39 | 348–49 | 12.23 | 125n311, 348 |
| 2.1 | 350 | 12.27 | 125n311, 348 |
| 2.4 | 125n311, 348 | 12.34 | 345 |
| 2.12 | 349 | 12.35 | 347 |

Index of ancient sources — **397**

| | | | |
|---|---|---|---|
| 12.39–40 | 263n226 | 1.11 | 191, 302, 308–9n162, 310, 321, 322n215, 323 |
| 12.48 | 351 | | |
| 13.1 | 348 | 1.15 | 349 |
| 13.8 | 345 | 1.16 | 160, 263n225 |
| 13.31 | 125n311 | 1.16–20 | 207 |
| 14.9 | 347 | 1.21 | 347 |
| 14.16 | 345 | 1.22 | 304, 351 |
| 14.20 | 351 | 1.26 | 161n124 |
| 16.2 | 348 | 2 | 118n280, 128, 308n158, 323, 326 |
| 16.4 | 348 | | |
| 16.21 | 348 | 2.1 | 351 |
| 16.23 | 351 | 2.14–36 | 129, 190, 193 |
| 16.25 | 348 | 2.15 | 348, 350 |
| 16.26 | 351 | 2.17 | 10, 124, 191, 307, 324–25, 351 |
| 16.32 | 348 | | |
| 17.1 | 348 | 2.17–21 | 132n345, 191, 307 |
| 19.14 | 348 | 2.17–36 | 306–7 |
| 19.27 | 349 | 2.18 | 186n227, 351 |
| 19.31 | 351 | 2.20 | 351 |
| 20.19 | 349 | 2.22–23 | 309n165 |
| 20.26 | 350 | 2.22–24 | 193–96, 203 |
| | | 2.23 | 158n108, 160n121 |
| **Acts** | | 2.24 | 204, 304, 334 |
| 1 | 323n218 | 2.24–39 | 196 |
| 1.1 | 124 | 2.25–28 | 130, 306–7 |
| 1.2 | 258n209, 323n220, 351 | 2.28–32 | 307 |
| 1.3 | 202n294, 321n214, 350 | 2.29 | 351 |
| 1.3–11 | 321–24, 326 | 2.29–32 | 201, 304 |
| 1.4–5 | 323 | 2.31 | 130, 302, 306–7 |
| 1.4–8 | 190n246 | 2.32 | 196n272 |
| 1.5 | 321, 323n220, 325, 349 | 2.32–39 | 132n345 |
| 1.6 | 89n159, 311, 321, 321n214, 322n215, 323, 347 | 2.33 | 308 |
| | | 2.34–35 | 130, 306–7 |
| | | 2.36 | 131, 207, 302, 306–7, 328 |
| 1.6–7 | 120, 131 | | |
| 1.6–8 | 188n237, 324n222 | 2.37–39 | 261 |
| 1.6–10 | 310 | 2.38 | 126, 262, 327 |
| 1.6b | 118n282 | 2.41 | 327, 349 |
| 1.7 | 121–22, 122n303, 123, 302, 322n216, 323n220, 323n221, 324n222, 326, 346–47 | 2.46 | 352 |
| | | 2.47 | 352 |
| | | 3 | 128 |
| | | 3.1 | 348 |
| 1.7–8 | 322–23 | 3.1–10 | 191 |
| 1.8 | 8n33, 120n292, 246, 262n223, 322, 322n217 | 3.2 | 352 |
| | | 3.8 | 262 |
| 1.9 | 323n220 | 3.11–12 | 130 |
| | | 3.13–15 | 207, 328 |

| | | | |
|---|---|---|---|
| 3.13–26 | 189 | 5.36 | 350 |
| 3.15 | 196n272, 252, 304, 334 | 5.37 | 125, 350 |
| 3.17 | 126n316, 131, 131n342, 244, 261 | 5.38–39 | 167n156, 197–200, 203, 207, 247, 260 |
| 3.17–21 | 261 | 5.39 | 158n112, 247 |
| 3.18 | 302 | 5.41 | 132 |
| 3.19 | 126, 244n142, 262, 327 | 5.42 | 302, 307, 352 |
| 3.20 | 128, 302, 346 | 6.15 | 249 |
| 3.20–21 | 191 | 6.17–26 | 349 |
| 3.21 | 128, 130, 160–61, 310, 310n167, 311n168, 345, 347 | 7 | 118n280, 190, 266n242 |
| | | 7.2–53 | 102n220, 132, 243 |
| | | 7.8 | 350 |
| 3.21b-25 | 306 | 7.17 | 347 |
| 3.24 | 351 | 7.20 | 346 |
| 3.26 | 261 | 7.23 | 347 |
| 4.1–21 | 196–97 | 7.41 | 350 |
| 4.10 | 196n272 | 7.43 | 244, 266n242 |
| 4.12 | 160, 162 | 7.45 | 125, 350 |
| 4.16 | 191 | 7.46–47 | 243–44n141 |
| 4.19–20 | 198 | 7.48 | 243 |
| 4.22 | 191 | 7.51 | 216, 248 |
| 4.24 | 196 | 7.52 | 131 |
| 4.24–30 | 164, 196 | 7.54–60 | 308 |
| 4.25 | 258n209, 263n225 | 7.55–56 | 130n332, 191 |
| 4.26–27 | 196 | 7.56 | 310 |
| 4.27 | 246n155, 246–47n156 | 7.57 | 309 |
| 4.27–28 | 244, 196–97 | 8–28 | 322n217 |
| 4.28 | 158n108, 189n244, 203 | 8.1 | 196, 199, 309n165, 349 |
| 4.30 | 191 | 8.1–3 | 207 |
| 5 | 260n217 | 8.1–4 | 251 |
| 5.1–11 | 246 | 8.4 | 196, 199, 207 |
| 5.3 | 248–49 | 8.5 | 302 |
| 5.7 | 349 | 8.11 | 347 |
| 5.9 | 248 | 8.12 | 202n294 |
| 5.10–42 | 197 | 8.26 | 260 |
| 5.12 | 191 | 8.26–39 | 260 |
| 5.12–16 | 250 | 8.26–40 | 258n206 |
| 5.13 | 198, 198n281 | 9.1 | 249 |
| 5.17–26 | 199n285 | 9.3–7 | 191 |
| 5.21 | 197 | 9.6 | 163 |
| 5.26 | 198 | 9.8–9 | 249 |
| 5.29 | 198 | 9.9 | 350 |
| 5.29–32 | 304 | 9.10–19 | 260 |
| 5.30 | 196n272 | 9.11–12 | 130, 188, 188n239, 191 |
| 5.31 | 126, 261–62, 327 | 9.14–16 | 163 |
| 5.32 | 261 | 9.15–16 | 130, 188, 188n239, 191 |
| 5.35–39 | 199n285, 327 | 9.16 | 132 |

| | | | |
|---|---|---|---|
| 9.17 | 185 | 13.16–41 | 200 |
| 9.19 | 349 | 13.18 | 347 |
| 9.22 | 163, 302 | 13.26 | 118n280 |
| 9.23 | 349 | 13.26–27 | 200 |
| 9.24 | 312n174, 352 | 13.26–37 | 304 |
| 9.37 | 349 | 13.27 | 190, 252, 260 |
| 9.43 | 349 | 13.27–28 | 118n280 |
| 10.3 | 125, 348, 350 | 13.28–30 | 200 |
| 10.3–6 | 188, 188n239, 191 | 13.30 | 196n272 |
| 10.9 | 348 | 13.31 | 349 |
| 10.11–20 | 188, 188n239, 191 | 13.33–34 | 196n272 |
| 10.19–24 | 260 | 13.34–39 | 190 |
| 10.24 | 156n102, 302 | 13.36 | 204 |
| 10.30 | 350 | 13.36–37 | 200–201, 203 |
| 10.31 | 348 | 13.37 | 196n272 |
| 10.33 | 327 | 13.38 | 118n280 |
| 10.34–35 | 254, 264 | 13.39 | 117n279 |
| 10.38 | 250 | 13.41 | 350 |
| 10.39–41 | 304 | 13.45–47 | 265n235 |
| 10.40 | 350 | 13.46 | 156 |
| 10.40–41 | 196n272 | 14.3 | 347 |
| 10.42 | 131, 306n149, 311 | 14.15–17 | 245 |
| 10.43 | 255n193 | 14.16 | 244 |
| 10.44–48 | 327 | 14.17 | 120, 122n303, 123, 346 |
| 10.48 | 349 | 14.22 | 131–32, 132n345, 162, 202, 202n294, 302, 328 |
| 11.15 | 124 | | |
| 11.17 | 261n220 | 14.28 | 347 |
| 11.18 | 126, 254, 261, 265, 327 | 15.7 | 350 |
| 11.19–21 | 207 | 15.8 | 345 |
| 11.27 | 349 | 15.15 | 159n115 |
| 11.28 | 185, 185n225, 258 | 15.28 | 156n102 |
| 12 | 243–44, 246n155, 251 | 15.33 | 347 |
| 12.1 | 346 | 15.36 | 349 |
| 12.1–4 | 207 | 16.5 | 352 |
| 12.3 | 351 | 16.6–7 | 258–59 |
| 12.18 | 351 | 16.6–10 | 258 |
| 12.20 | 249 | 16.8–9 | 258 |
| 12.20–23 | 207, 246 | 16.9 | 259–60 |
| 12.21 | 351 | 16.9–10 | 260 |
| 12.24 | 251 | 16.10 | 165n145 |
| 13 | 117n280, 118n280 | 16.12 | 350 |
| 13.1–9 | 244 | 16.13 | 351 |
| 13.6–12 | 247n159 | 16.16–18 | 186 |
| 13.10 | 249 | 16.18 | 349–50 |
| 13.11 | 249, 346 | 16.30 | 159n115, 162 |
| 13.14 | 351 | 16.33 | 349 |
| 13.16 | 118n280 | 16.35 | 351 |

| | | | |
|---|---|---|---|
| 16.35–40 | 330 | 20.18–35 | 201–202 |
| 17.3 | 160, 302, 304n141 | 20.20 | 202n295 |
| 17.5–9 | 330 | 20.21 | 126, 327 |
| 17.6 | 253n187 | 20.23 | 258 |
| 17.11 | 352 | 20.25 | 202n294 |
| 17.17 | 352 | 20.26 | 350 |
| 17.18 | 304n141 | 20.26–27 | 202 |
| 17.22–31 | 122 | 20.27 | 201–203 |
| 17.24 | 123, 129, 196, 243 | 20.31 | 352 |
| 17.26 | 122–23, 307n155, 346 | 20.32 | 261 |
| 17.29–31 | 243 | 20.35 | 159 |
| 17.30 | 122n303, 126, 131–32, 244–45, 261–62, 327, 347 | 21.1–14 | 259 |
| | | 21.3–14 | 260 |
| | | 21.4 | 350 |
| 17.30–31 | 123, 304, 311, 324–25, 344 | 21.4b | 258–60, 259n212 |
| | | 21.5 | 350 |
| 17.31 | 125, 129–31, 185n224, 189, 191, 196n272, 204, 255n193, 265–66, 271, 302, 306n149, 307, 307n155, 309, 311, 325, 325n229, 329, 333, 351 | 21.6–10 | 117 |
| | | 21.7 | 350 |
| | | 21.9 | 185 |
| | | 21.10 | 350 |
| | | 21.10–11 | 185n225 |
| | | 21.12–13 | 259 |
| 17.32 | 304n141, 327 | 21.13–15 | 259 |
| 18.5 | 302 | 21.15 | 350 |
| 18.6 | 251n177, 265n235 | 21.17–22 | 264n233 |
| 18.12–17 | 330 | 21.20 | 264, 264n233 |
| 18.14 | 260 | 21.23–28 | 264n233 |
| 18.18 | 350 | 21.26 | 350–51 |
| 18.20 | 347 | 21.27 | 350 |
| 18.23 | 347 | 21.38 | 350 |
| 18.28 | 302 | 22.13 | 349 |
| 19.8 | 202n294 | 22.17–21 | 186n231 |
| 19.9 | 352 | 23.1 | 351 |
| 19.13–17 | 248n165 | 23.6 | 304 |
| 19.21 | 161n130 | 23.11 | 161–62 |
| 19.22 | 347 | 23.12 | 351 |
| 19.23 | 346 | 23.23 | 348 |
| 19.26 | 243 | 24.1 | 350 |
| 19.34 | 349 | 24.2 | 149 |
| 19.35 | 260 | 24.11 | 350 |
| 19.35–41 | 330 | 24.15 | 131, 302 |
| 19.36 | 159n115, 159n118 | 24.15–21 | 304 |
| 20 | 116n275 | 24.19 | 159n115 |
| 20.3 | 350 | 24.24 | 350 |
| 20.6 | 351 | 24.25 | 346 |
| 20.16 | 351 | 25.1 | 350 |
| 20.18 | 347, 351 | 25.6 | 350 |

Index of ancient sources — 401

| | | | |
|---|---|---|---|
| 25.10 | 161n130 | 28.23–28 | 253, 324n222 |
| 25.13 | 350 | 28.24 | 264 |
| 25.13–27 | 260 | 28.24–28 | 207 |
| 25.14 | 350 | 28.25–27 | 262–63 |
| 25.19 | 304n141 | 28.26–27 | 265 |
| 25.24 | 159n115 | 28.26–30 | 250n172 |
| 25.27 | 264 | 28.27 | 263, 264n231 |
| 26 | 246n155, 304 | 28.28 | 265 |
| 26.4–5 | 124n309 | 28.29 | 262n222 |
| 26.6–8 | 304 | 28.30 | 265, 327 |
| 26.7 | 352 | 28.30–31 | 263 |
| 26.8 | 304 | 28.31 | 89n159, 202n294 |
| 26.9 | 159n115 | | |
| 26.13 | 350 | **Romans** | |
| 26.14 | 249 | 2.15 | 216 |
| 26.18 | 250 | 2.29 | 216 |
| 26.20 | 126, 260, 262, 327 | 8.29 | 159n115 |
| 26.22 | 160n122, 351 | 12.3 | 159n115 |
| 26.22–23 | 190, 196n271, 302n130, 304–5, 306n149, 309 | 12.12 | 314n182 |
| | | 13.14 | 149 |
| 26.22b-23 | 305n144 | | |
| 26.23 | 131, 302, 304, 334 | **1 Corinthians** | |
| 26.28 | 306 | 7.37 | 156 |
| 26.28–32 | 327 | 11.19 | 161n126 |
| 26.30–32 | 260 | 15.12–24 | 304 |
| 26.31–32 | 330–31n246 | 15.25 | 161n126 |
| 27.7 | 350 | 15.53 | 161n126 |
| 27.9 | 347 | | |
| 27.12 | 192n256 | **2 Corinthians** | |
| 27.20 | 350 | 4.14 | 304 |
| 27.21 | 159n115 | 5.10 | 161n126 |
| 27.24 | 130, 161–62, 188, 188n239, 191, 258 | 9.7 | 156 |
| 27.26 | 161 | **Ephesians** | |
| 27.29 | 351 | 6.20 | 161n126 |
| 27.33 | 350–51 | | |
| 27.39 | 351 | **Colossians** | |
| 27.42 | 192n256 | 4.6 | 159n115 |
| 28 | 190, 263n228, 265, 265n239, 323n218 | **1 Thessalonians** | |
| 28.7 | 350 | 1.10 | 324n224 |
| 28.12 | 350 | 2.16 | 90 |
| 28.13 | 350 | 4.1 | 159n115 |
| 28.14 | 350 | 5.1 | 121–22 |
| 28.17 | 350 | 5.17 | 314n182 |
| 28.17–28 | 265, 262–63 | 5.21 | 128 |
| 28.23 | 190, 202n294, 351 | | |

## 2 Thessalonians
| | |
|---|---|
| 3.7 | 159n115 |

## 2 Timothy
| | |
|---|---|
| 2.6 | 159n115 |
| 2.24 | 159n115 |

## Philemon
| | |
|---|---|
| 14 | 156 |

## Hebrews
| | |
|---|---|
| 7.27 | 156 |
| 8.8–12 | 216 |
| 9.23 | 156n98 |
| 10.16–17 | 216 |

## Revelation
| | |
|---|---|
| 1.1 | 161n126 |
| 4 | 328n238 |
| 4.1 | 161n126 |
| 5 | 328n238 |
| 7 | 328n238 |
| 11.1–2 | 127 |
| 12 | 288n84 |
| 12.14 | 95n191 |
| 17.10 | 161n126 |
| 20–22 | 328n238 |
| 20.3 | 161n126 |
| 22.6 | 161n126 |

# Rabbinic Works

## Pirke Aboth
| | |
|---|---|
| 3.19 | 260n215 |

# Early Christian Writings

## Apocryphon of John
| | |
|---|---|
| 25.16–30.11 | 154n87 |

## Bede
*Commentary on the Acts of the Apostles*
| | |
|---|---|
| 5.34 | 199n284 |

## John Chrysostom
*Homilies on the Acts of the Apostles*
| | |
|---|---|
| 14 | 199n284 |

## Pseudo-Clementine literature
*Clementine Recognitions*
| | |
|---|---|
| 1.65.4 | 199n284 |

# Greco-Roman Literature

## Aristotle
*Metaphysics*
| | |
|---|---|
| 5.5.1015a 33f | 154n88 |

## Diodorus Siculus
*Library of History*
| | |
|---|---|
| 1.1.praef | 73 |
| 1.1.3 | 70, 73, 147–48, 204 |
| 1.1.4–5 | 71 |
| 1.1.5 | 73 |
| 1.2.3 | 73 |
| 1.3.3–6 | 70n63 |
| 1.3.5–8 | 41, 45n117 |
| 1.3.8 | 71n69 |
| 1.4.1 | 41 |
| 1.4.5 | 41 |
| 1.4.6–7 | 70 |
| 1.4.6–1.5.1 | 41n90, 70n60 |
| 1.5.1 | 70 |
| 1.6.1 | 70n65 |
| 1.6.2 | 70 |
| 1.6.3 | 72 |
| 1.8.1–4 | 72 |
| 1.8.1–9 | 72 |
| 1.73 | 148n57 |
| 2.55.1 | 73 |

| | | | |
|---|---|---|---|
| 3.53.4–5 | 73 | 19.42.5 | 143n30 |
| 5.28 | 148n57 | 19.108.2 | 143n30 |
| 5.41.4 | 73 | 20.99.1 | 143n30 |
| 5.42.4 | 73 | 21.11 | 143n30 |
| 5.45.3 | 73 | 22.13.6 | 143n30 |
| 5.46.1 | 73 | 26.24.2 | 143n30 |
| 9.2.2 | 143n30 | 30.8 | 72n74 |
| 9.20 | 148n57 | 31.10 | 142–43 |
| 10.9.5 | 63n29 | 31.10.2 | 67n49 |
| 10.9.7 | 158n114 | 31.12 | 143n30 |
| 11.1.1 | 70 | 31.15.1 | 274 |
| 11.38.1 | 70 | 31.26.2 | 71 |
| 11.48.1 | 70 | 32.10.5 | 143n30 |
| 11.49.4 | 70 | 34/35.28.2–3 | 143n30 |
| 11.91.1 | 162n132 | 34/35.28.30c | 143n30 |
| 12.1 | 274 | 36.5.3 | 143n30 |
| 12.1.2 | 143n30 | 36.7.2 | 143n30 |
| 12.1.2–4 | 142n26 | 37.1.1–6 | 71 |
| 12.10.2 | 70 | 37.2–8 | 274 |
| 12.26.1 | 70 | 37.2.12–14 | 71 |
| 13.1.2–3 | 70 | 37.3–8 | 72n74 |
| 13.24.6 | 70n62 | 37.3.1 | 71–72 |
| 14.45.5 | 70n62 | 37.3.1–4 | 71 |
| 14.46.4 | 143n30, 274 | 37.4 | 71–72 |
| 14.76.1 | 142 | 37.17 | 142 |
| 14.76.1–4 | 142 | 37.29.5–30.2 | 71 |
| 15.63.2 | 154 | 38.41.6 | 274 |
| 15.64 | 148n57 | 38.42.1 | 274 |
| 16 | 141n25 | | |
| 16.61–64 | 235 | **Dionysius of Halicarnassus** | |
| 16.63.3 | 235 | *Roman Antiquities* | |
| 16.64.1 | 235 | 1.6.5 | 71n68 |
| 16.64.2 | 235 | 6.54.2 | 150n69 |
| 16.64.3 | 235 | | |
| 16.91 | 176 | **Euripides** | |
| 16.91.3 | 168 | *Bacchae* | |
| 16.92.2–3 | 168 | 794.5 | 249 |
| 16.95.1 | 235n110 | | |
| 17.20.1 | 143n30 | **Herodotus** | |
| 17.38.4–6 | 274 | *Histories* | |
| 17.101.2 | 143n30 | 2.161 | 158n113 |
| 18.8.7 | 143n30 | 8.53 | 158n113 |
| 18.59.4–5 | 141 | | |
| 18.59.6 | 70n66 | **Hesiod** | |
| 18.60.1 | 274 | *Works and Days* | |
| 19.1.1–8 | 71 | 106–201 | 83n132, 109 |
| 19.1.10 | 70 | | |

# Index of ancient sources

**Homer**
*Iliad*
18     42, 82n126
20–21     84n136
    240, 240n131
*Odyssey*
11     42
19.562–67     82n126
    171n174

**Horace**
*Satires*
1.5.97–103     176n190

**Livy**
*History of Rome*
31–45     40n85

**Lucan**
*Civil War*     139n13

**Ovid**
*Metamorphoses*
1.89–150     83n132, 109
1.166     241
1.177–252     109n251
1.262–347     109n251
1.588–600     241
15.870–79     109n253
15.871–79     62n26, 164n145

**Plato**
*Poetics*
1447a     23
*Republic*
3     23

**Plutarch**
*Romulus*
7.4     165n146
8.7     141n22
*Theseus*
15.1–2     235n112
24.1     65n36
32.4     237n118, 259n213

**Polybius**
*Histories*
1–2     65

1.2.1     64
1.2.1–6     65, 67
1.2.7–8     64
1.2.8     69
1.3.1     64
1.3.3     65n38, 272n12
1.3.3–4     65, 272
1.3.4     66, 68
1.4.1     66
1.4.1–3     272
1.4.1–5     69, 141
1.4.2–3     68
1.4.3     57
1.4.4     65
1.4.6–10     68, 71n69
1.5.1     64
1.12.6–9     65
1.14.1     68
1.29.8     65
1.32.1     65
1.35.2     140n19
1.35.5     140n19
1.35.6     67
1.35.6–10     67, 273
1.45.5     65
1.57.1     140
1.58.1     140, 239
1.59.4–12     140
1.60.4–6     140
1.63.4     140
1.65.89     66
1.66.10     65n38
1.88.8     65
2.11.1     65
2.15.1     66
2.15.1     66n41
2.20.7     66n39
2.26.1     65
2.27.1     65
2.37.1     65
2.38.5     67n47
2.39.5     66
2.55.1     65
2.56.7–12     24
2.67.1     65
2.71.1–10     65–66
2.71.2     66

| | | | |
|---|---|---|---|
| 2.71.2–6 | 66n43 | 4.1 | 238 |
| 3.47.6–3.48.12 | 238n126 | 4.1–3 | 238, 238n124 |
| 8 | 57n1 | 4.32–33 | 78n109 |
| 8.2.1 | 57n2 | 4.64.1 | 169 |
| 8.2.2–3 | 57, 65, 68, 272 | 5.22 | 153 |
| 8.2.2–11 | 57 | 6.46.3 | 153n85 |
| 8.2.3 | 57 | 9.71 | 79n116 |
| 8.2.7 | 57 | 12.43.1 | 169 |
| 9.1.1 | 64 | 14.22.4 | 237n120 |
| 10.2.12 | 147, 147n53, 169 | *Histories* | |
| 10.2.6 | 67n47, 238 | 1.1 | 77n102, 79n114, 238 |
| 10.2.7 | 238 | 1.2.1 | 77, 274, 276 |
| 10.5.8–10 | 67n47, 238 | 1.2.2 | 77 |
| 10.5.9 | 238n126 | 1.3 | 237 |
| 10.7.4 | 147n54 | 1.12 | 77, 78n104 |
| 10.9.2–3 | 67n47, 238 | 1.12–13 | 274 |
| 10.11.8 | 147, 169 | 1.13 | 78 |
| 11.1.1 | 64 | 1.13–16 | 78n104 |
| 14.1.5 | 64 | 1.13.2 | 77 |
| 15.20.5 | 238n125 | 1.16 | 77 |
| 16.32 | 151 | 1.16.2 | 77 |
| 18.54 | 151 | 1.16.3 | 78, 274 |
| 23.17.10 | 147, 169 | 1.16.4 | 238 |
| 29.21 | 140, 142, 169 | 1.18 | 77, 78n104, 274 |
| 29.21.4 | 67 | 1.19 | 78n104 |
| 29.21.6–7 | 141 | 1.22 | 78 |
| 31.22 | 71 | 1.26 | 78n104 |
| 36.17 | 151 | 1.27.1 | 170n171 |
| 36.17.2–4 | 140 | 1.28 | 78n104 |
| 38.21–22 | 273 | 1.83–84 | 78 |
| 38.21.1–2 | 68 | 1.86 | 169, 169n164 |
| 38.21.2–3 | 273 | 2.1 | 144 |
| 38.22.2 | 68 | 2.4 | 170n166 |
| 39.8.4–6 | 65n37 | 2.4.2 | 170n171 |
| 39.8.6 | 64 | 2.78 | 169n163, 170, 170n168, 170n170, 176 |
| **Sallust** | | 2.80 | 144 |
| *Catiline War* | | 3.1 | 144 |
| 6.1 | 52n147 | 3.71 | 237 |
| | | 3.71–2 | 80n117 |
| **Tacitus** | | 3.72 | 237 |
| *Annals* | | 3.75 | 237n119 |
| 1.1.1 | 241 | 4.1 | 78 |
| 1.10 | 77n100, 274, 276 | 4.1.1 | 78 |
| 1.24 | 238 | 4.1.3 | 78 |
| 3 | 78n110, 80 | 4.4.3 | 238, 276 |
| 3.26–28 | 78–79, 83n132 | 4.26.1–2 | 169 |

| | | | |
|---|---|---|---|
| 4.27 | 144 | 4.196–278 | 240n132 |
| 4.54.2 | 80 | 6 | 82n126, 86–87, 277–79, 281n55 |
| 4.57 | 144 | 6.2 | 86n147 |
| 4.81 | 164n145, 170n168 | 6.235 | 82 |
| 5.13 | 165n149, 170, 170n168, 170n170, 176 | 6.343–46 | 172 |
| | | 6.745 | 84n135 |

**Thucydides**
*History of the Peloponnesian War*

| | | | |
|---|---|---|---|
| | | 6.752–892 | 83, 171 |
| 1.76.2 | 103n226 | 6.773 | 280 |
| 3.89.5 | 159n116 | 6.788–89 | 279n41 |
| 4 | 138n10 | 6.788–92 | 279n41 |
| | | 6.788–97 | 276, 278–79 |
| | | 6.791–92 | 281 |

**Virgil**
*Aeneid*

| | | | |
|---|---|---|---|
| | | 6.792 | 84 |
| 1 | 171, 277, 281, 281n55, 282n60 | 6.793 | 83, 239, 278 |
| | | 6.851–53 | 276 |
| | | 6.860–92 | 278n39 |
| 1.7 | 85 | 6.889–90 | 276, 277n31 |
| 1.20 | 240n132 | 6.896 | 171, 280n49 |
| 1.148–53 | 241 | 7.41 | 282n60 |
| 1.229–53 | 135 | 7.116 | 172 |
| 1.257–62 | 135 | 8 | 86, 171, 278–279 |
| 1.258 | 85n143 | 8.324–25 | 83 |
| 1.261–64 | 85 | 8.324–35 | 239 |
| 1.262 | 150 | 8.520–29 | 170n169 |
| 1.262–304 | 83, 171, 240n133 | 8.624–728 | 83, 171 |
| 1.264 | 276 | 8.678–79 | 84 |
| 1.276–90 | 85 | 8.714–28 | 84 |
| 1.278 | 276 | 8.730 | 84 |
| 1.279 | 123, 276, 278, 280 | 8.730–31 | 85 |
| 1.279–82 | 86n147 | 12.791–842 | 240n132, 277, 280 |
| 1.283 | 135, 150 | 12.826 | 82 |
| 1.287 | 276, 280 | 12.939–53 | 277n31, 281 |
| 1.290 | 277 | *Eclogues* | |
| 1.291 | 82, 276n29 | 4.4–10 | 83n129, 239 |
| 1.293–94 | 276n29, 278 | *Georgics* | |
| 1.299–300 | 86n147 | 1.121–28 | 83n131 |
| 1.321–411 | 171 | 4 | 239 |
| 1.445 | 82 | | |
| 1.450–90 | 171 | **Valerius Maximus** | |
| 1.606 | 82 | *Memorable Doings and Sayings* | |
| 2 | 277 | 1.praef | 43, 45n117, 75–76, 164n145 |
| 3.94–98 | 172 | | |
| 3.131 | 86n147 | 1.1.10 | 76 |
| 3.205 | 86n147 | 1.1.11 | 75 |
| 3.255 | 172 | 1.1.14 | 236 |
| 3.278 | 86n147 | 1.1.15 | 236, 240 |

| | | | |
|---|---|---|---|
| 1.1.16 | 236n113 | 1.7.ext8 | 167, 167n153, 168 |
| 1.1.16–21 | 236 | 2.1 | 43 |
| 1.1.ext1–4 | 236 | 2.1–6 | 74n85 |
| 1.2 | 165n148 | 2.2.1a | 75 |
| 1.4–8 | 166–67 | 2.2.6 | 75n89 |
| 1.4.praef | 75 | 2.4.6 | 75n89 |
| 1.4.2 | 168, 236, 259n213 | 2.5.2 | 75 |
| 1.4.3 | 76 | 3.2.praef | 75 |
| 1.5.praef | 165n148 | 3.2.3 | 75 |
| 1.5.4 | 167 | 3.2.11 | 75 |
| 1.5.ext1 | 165n149 | 3.4.praef | 75 |
| 1.6.1 | 165n148 | 3.5 | 43 |
| 1.6.4 | 167 | 3.7.praef | 75 |
| 1.6.6 | 165n149, 168, 236, 259n213 | 3.7.ext6 | 168, 168n158 |
| | | 3.8.6 | 75 |
| 1.6.7 | 167, 167n154, 275 | 5.3.ext3f | 148 |
| 1.6.8 | 168, 237, 259 | 6.9 | 144 |
| 1.6.10 | 167n154, 168 | 6.9.praef | 274 |
| 1.6.11 | 168, 236, 259n213 | 7.1 | 144 |
| 1.6.ext1a-b | 167n152 | 7.1.praef | 274 |
| 1.6.ext1b | 168, 236, 259n213 | 7.5 | 75 |
| 1.7.2 | 167n153, 168 | 7.6.3 | 148 |
| 1.7.6 | 167n153, 168 | 9.1.3 | 75 |
| 1.7.8 | 167 | 9.8 | 43 |
| 1.7.ext1 | 150 | | |
| 1.7.ext2 | 144 | **Xenophon** | |
| 1.7.ext4 | 168, 184n222, 237, 275 | frag. D8 (B11) | 240n136 |
| 1.7.ext5 | 154 | frag. D9 (B12) | 240n136 |

# Index of modern authors

Adams, Edward   81, 115, 128, 306, 319–21
Adams, Sean A.   15–16, 22, 52, 148
Ahl, Frederick   278–79, 281
Aitken, James   36–37
Alexander, Loveday   14–16, 39, 187, 262–63, 265
Alexander, Phillip S.   37, 46–47, 230, 290
Alter, Robert   21
Ashton, John   28
Attridge, Harold W.   45, 89, 99, 104, 143, 175, 220
Aune, David E.   22, 25–26
Austin, R. G.   84

Bachmann, Veronika   227
Balch, David L.   64
Ballard, Paul H.   255
Barchiesi, Alessandro   84
Barclay, John M. G.   11, 36, 50, 102, 143, 175, 208–210, 212, 214, 216, 219, 226–27, 229–231, 241–243, 251, 261, 266, 300, 338
Barr, James   59, 66, 95, 118–121, 123, 125, 213
Barreto, Eric D.   120, 262
Barrett, C. K.   4, 9, 121, 156–57, 194, 202, 264, 306–7, 322, 325
Barton, John   21,
Bauspieß, Martin   12, 137, 161, 308–9, 320, 328
Becker, Eve-Marie   16–17, 22, 25, 38
Begg, Christopher T.   104–106, 285
Ben Zeev, Miriam Pucci.   41
Bergren, Theodore A.   49
Berthelot, Katell   45, 99
Bilde, Per   99–100, 102–105, 143, 177–179, 285, 333
Bizzarro, Laura   108, 292, 297
Bloomer, W. Martin   43, 74–76, 274–75
Bobzien, Susanne   137, 149, 154, 208
Boccaccini, Gabriele   36, 137, 234
Bock, Darrell L.   8, 13, 121, 196, 207

Bockmuehl, Markus N. A.   54, 179, 230–31, 310
Bonz, Marianne Palmer   16–17, 43, 282, 330
Bovon, François   1, 4, 7, 13, 116, 126–27, 157–58, 162–164, 196, 313–14, 318–19, 328, 332, 342–43, 348
Brandenburger, Egon   50
Braun, Willi   255, 327
Braund, S. H.   138–39, 241
Braund, Susanna Morton   74, 83, 137, 240
Brett, Mark G.   214
Bruce, F. F.   90, 160, 194, 305–6, 324
Brueggemann, Walter   214, 216
Bultmann, Rudolf   3–5, 7–8, 10, 58, 313
Burke, Peter   33
Burridge, Richard   15, 22, 25–26, 52
Burton, Anne   69–70, 72, 147, 153–54
Busse, Ulrich   13
Byrne, Brendan   117, 127, 193, 253–54, 302

Cadbury, Henry J.   6, 14, 55, 184, 194
Campbell, Douglas A.   12, 231
Cancik, Hubert   15, 22, 60, 74, 88, 137, 186, 281–82
Carroll, John T.   4, 8, 13, 38, 116, 126, 193, 253–54, 311–314, 316–17
Carter, C. J.   43–44
Chandler, Daniel   24–27
Chartier, Roger   33
Childs, Brevard S.   145
Clark, Gillian   281
Clarke, Katherine   28, 41, 59, 63–64, 66, 68, 70, 72, 109
Cohen, Ralph   23, 25
Cohen, Shaye J. D.   41, 99, 143, 146, 177
Collins, Adela Yarbro   40
Collins, John J.   18, 26, 47, 60–61, 81, 88, 111, 113, 121, 161, 180, 227, 284, 287–89, 294–95, 297, 302, 331–33, 335
Conzelmann, Hans   1, 3–13, 55, 58, 60–61, 115–16, 118, 120, 122–124, 131–133,

136, 157, 159–60, 185–86, 191, 194, 197, 202–3, 207, 249, 258–59, 304–5, 307, 310–11, 313–315, 318, 320–322, 325, 328–330, 337, 339–40, 342
Cornford, Francis MacDonald   138, 140, 206
Cosgrove, Charles H.   157, 159–60, 162
Crabbe, Kylie   49, 103, 131–32, 146, 162, 190, 192–93, 198–99, 220, 234, 256, 258, 302, 327
Culler, Jonathan D.   25–26
Cullmann, Oscar   9–12, 19, 38, 59, 118, 207, 250, 266, 271, 306, 328, 334, 342–43
Cunningham, Scott   162, 302, 328

Darr, John A.   131, 137, 198–99
Davies, G. I.   18, 40, 61, 100, 180
Davies, J. P.   61
Davies, Philip R.   46–47, 97, 103, 213, 285, 287–89, 297–98, 306, 331–32
Dibelius, Martin   14, 122, 132
Dick, Bernard F.   138–39, 145, 153
Dicken, Frank   246, 249–50
Dimant, Devorah   107, 183
Dodds, E. R.   63, 67, 72, 113
Donahue, J. R.   248
Doran, Robert   45, 89–93, 174, 285
Doty, William G.   21
Dräger, Paul   154
Dreyer, Boris   40
Drury, John   3–4, 8, 130, 304–5, 330, 342
Dubrow, Heather   23–24.
Dunn, James D. G.   17, 208

Eckstein, Arthur M.   140, 238–39, 273, 308
Edelstein, Ludwig   59, 63, 72
Edwards, Mark   24–25, 27
Edwards, Mark W.   240
Ego, Beate   219
Eliade, Mircea   59
Elliott, Gregory   269
Ellis, E. Earle   8, 55, 120, 191, 262, 305, 323, 329
Elvers, Karl-Ludwig   52
Emmrich, Martin   245, 252, 255, 303, 327
Engberg-Pedersen, Troels   209
Errington, R. M.   65
Evans, Craig A.   262–264

Fairclough, H. R.   83, 171, 278, 280
Fantham, Elaine   42, 82, 86
Farahian, Edmond   188–89
Farrell, Hobert Kenneth   8, 322
Farrell, Joseph   22–23, 27, 29–30
Fascher, Erich   161
Febvre, Lucien   33
Fee, Gordon D.   90
Feeney, D. C.   42, 86, 137, 278–280
Feldman, Louis H   105, 165, 176–179, 232
Fishbane, Michael A.   130, 184, 189
Fisher, Mark   103, 159
Fitzmyer, Joseph A.   5–6, 8, 13, 116–118, 120–21, 127, 146, 156–57, 184, 188, 245–248, 258, 314–15, 317–319, 322, 328, 330
Flaig, Egon   44
Flannery Dailey, Frances   112
Flender, Helmut   8–9, 138, 250, 308, 310, 342
Foakes Jackson, F. J.   194
Fowler, Alastair   26–27
France, R. T.   320
Francis, Fred O.   10–11
Franke, Thomas   44
Franklin, Eric   9
Fukuyama, Francis   269
Fusco, Vittorio   191, 319

Galinsky, Karl   42, 74, 83, 85–86, 137, 276, 279, 281
García Martínez, Florentino   95, 180, 183
Gaventa, Beverly Roberts   8, 14, 61, 120, 122, 162–63, 188, 261, 322
Goldstein, Jonathan A.   89, 93, 283
Goold, G. P.   83, 171, 278, 280
Gottlieb, Gunther   33, 215–16, 277
Goulder, M. D.   115, 130
Gowler, David B.   193, 198
Grabbe, Lester L.   99, 213
Grässer, Erich   3, 7
Gray, Rebecca   48, 100, 105–6, 143, 155, 177–78, 220
Green, Anna   33–34
Green, Joel B.   4–5, 8, 12, 118–19, 156, 186–87, 193, 245–46, 259, 314, 316–17, 327

Gregory, Andrew  54–55
Grethlein, Jonas  22, 68–69, 166
Griffin, Miriam T.  44, 78–79, 153, 169, 235, 237, 275
Gruen, Erich S.  41, 48, 68, 99, 273
Guffey, Andrew R  217
Gundry, Robert H.  35
Gunkel, Heidrun  7–8, 115
Gunkel, Hermann  50
Gurtner, Daniel M.  110

Haaland, Gunnar  151
Habicht, Christian  40, 57, 64, 272
Haenchen, Ernst  3, 5, 120, 122, 129, 158, 194, 197, 200–1, 258, 261, 304–5, 322, 330
Hakola, Raimo  198–99
Hall, R. G.  99, 104
Hanks, William F.  26
Hanneken, Todd R.  18, 180
Hardie, Philip  42, 84, 279
Harnisch, Wolfgang  50, 225
Harrington, Daniel J.  45, 91, 94
Harrison, S. J.  23–27, 86, 279
Hau, Lisa Irene  42, 235, 274
Hays, Christopher M.  248, 317
Hegel, G. W. F.  269
Hejduk, Julia Dyson  62, 109, 241
Hengel, Martin  36, 143
Henten, Jan Willem van  91–93, 218
Henze, Matthias  49–50, 180–81, 222, 294
Hernadi, Paul  23, 27, 29, 34, 68
Hill, Charles E.  110
Hobbins, John F.  97
Hoekstra, Kinch  103, 159
Hogan, Karina Martin  50, 226–27, 292
Holladay, Carl R.  13–14, 159–60, 162, 184, 190, 196, 200–202, 207, 244, 247–48, 250, 263–64, 308, 322–23.
Hornik, Heidi J.  199, 306
Horsfall, Nicholas  86, 171, 277–279
Horst, Pieter W. van der  53

Jackson, John  238
Jeffrey, David Lyle  14, 254, 318
Jervell, Jacob  13, 194, 255, 264, 319
Johnson, Luke Timothy  13, 54, 122–23, 125, 127, 129, 157–58, 161–163, 186–87, 189, 194, 199, 245, 261–62, 264, 305, 316
Joyce, Paul.  234
Just, Arthur A., Jr.  302

Kamerbeek, J. C.  232, 240, 249
Karris, Robert J.  248
Käsemann, Ernst  3, 5, 7, 61, 206–7, 266, 331, 336, 342
Kearns, Emily  240
Keener, Craig S.  13, 15, 32, 38, 120, 161, 184, 322–23
Kenney, E. J.  62, 109
Ker, James  30
Kim, Young Ho  3, 6, 18, 116, 303
Kim-Rauchholz, Mihamm  302
Klawans, Jonathan  152, 178, 221
Klein, Günter  3, 7, 9
Klijn, A. F. J  49–51, 223
Knauer, G. N.  42, 82
Knibb, Michael  290
Knight, Jonathan  116, 191, 318
Kostopoulos, Zachary L.  16
Kovacs, Judith  128
Kraus, C. S.  52
Kraus, Hans-Joachim  31
Krauter, Stefan  16, 86, 282
Kümmel, Werner Georg  1, 7, 9, 116, 336

Lake, Kirsopp  194
Lamberton, Robert  240
Law, T. M.  37
Lee, DooHee  15, 100
Lemche, Niels Peter  213
Leoni, Tommaso  47
Lichtenberger, Hermann  300
Liebeschuetz, J. H. W. G.  169–70
Lincicum, David  217
Longenecker, Bruce W.  226, 300
Löwith, Karl  59, 342
Luce, T. J.  70–71
Luther, Susanne  15
Lyne, R. O. A. M.  43, 277
Lyons, William John  167, 199

MacDonald, Dennis R.  16, 43, 247
Maddox, Robert  4, 7, 13, 38, 55, 131, 191, 255, 302, 308, 317–18, 320–21, 323
Mallen, Peter  184, 264
Mannheim, Karl  282, 331–32, 338
Marguerat, Daniel  15–16, 29, 139
Marincola, John  38–39, 64, 67
Markschies, Christoph  36
Marshall, I. Howard  9, 121, 194
Martin, Ronald  150, 153
Martyn, J. Louis  12, 61, 210, 231
Marx, Karl  269
Mason, Steve  100–1, 151, 198, 256
Maston, Jason  11, 152, 208–211, 242
Matthews, Lydia  144–45, 152–53, 241
Mattila, Sharon Lea  46, 94, 287
Mattill, Andrew J.  10–12, 191, 318, 325
McConville, Gordon  214
McGing, Brian  140
Meister, Klaus  41
Mermelstein, Ari  11, 61, 107–8, 129, 270, 303
Metzger, Bruce M.  49, 262, 347, 351
Meyers, Eric M.  47
Millar, Fergus  44
Miller, Amanda C.  253
Miller, John B. F.  160, 177, 258
Minear, Paul S.  6, 55, 116
Moessner, David P.  12, 15, 17, 36, 41–42, 54–55, 124, 130, 184, 189, 262, 328
Molthagen, Joachim  17, 41
Momigliano, Arnaldo  59, 63, 67, 109, 112, 137
Moore, Clifford H.  238
Moore, Nicholas J.  98, 290
Morgan, Teresa  33–35, 74–75, 144, 239, 275
Mowery, Robert L  157
Mroczek, Eva  129–30, 189
Mueller, Hans-Friedrich  44, 74–76, 137, 168, 170, 274

Najman, Hindy  11, 23, 25, 49–50, 229, 270, 299
Nave, Guy D.  252, 260, 265, 327
Newsom, Carol A.  29, 180, 208

Nickelsburg, George W. E.  90, 92, 97, 111, 257, 284
Nicklas, Tobias  91
Nielsen, Anders E.  308–9
Nitzan, Bilhah  226
Nobbs, Alanna  332
Nolland, John  245, 312–13, 319
Noth, Martin  213

O'Hara, James J.  42, 84–86, 171–72, 277, 280, 282
Oldfather, C. H.  41, 72, 154
Olson, Daniel C.  103, 224, 297
Ooi, Vincent K. H.  243–44

Palmer, Darryl W.  15
Panagopoulos, Johannes  11
Parsons, Mikeal C.  14, 16, 54, 199, 306
Paton, W. R.  64, 272
Penner, Todd  17, 19, 22, 29, 55
Perlitt, Lothar  213
Pervo, Richard I.  13, 16, 22, 32, 54–55, 116, 156, 163, 194, 199–202, 246, 248, 258–59, 305–6, 329
Peterson, David  16, 120
Phillips, Thomas E.  16
Popovic', Mladen  135, 182
Puech, Emile  97

Quint, David  42, 77, 82, 85–86, 281

Rad, Gerhard von  12, 21, 213
Rajak, Tessa  39, 53, 81, 99–100, 102, 143, 146, 222, 233, 303, 333
Rapske, Brian  157
Rasco, Emilio  11
Read-Heimerdinger, Jenny  55, 120, 162, 186, 258, 323
Regev, Eyal  106, 220
Reynolds, Benjamin  18, 28, 180
Richardson, Peter  247
Ringe, Sharon  320
Rius-Camps, Josep  55, 120, 162, 186, 258, 323
Robinson, William Childs  8, 306
Ropes, James Hardy  194
Rosenmeyer, Thomas G.  30

Rosmarin, Adena   23–24, 27
Rosner, Brian S.   17
Rothschild, Clare K.   14, 16–17, 23, 28–29, 42, 100, 130, 137, 158, 160–61, 184, 187, 189, 232
Rowe, C. Kavin.   18, 54–55, 123, 129, 253, 327, 330–31
Rowland, Christopher   81, 110, 119, 128, 179–80, 228–230, 243

Sacks, Kenneth S.   24, 41–42, 70–73, 138–39, 141–143, 147–48, 235, 273–74
Sailor, Dylan   77–80, 170, 238, 274
Sallmann, Klaus   52
Salvesen, Alison G.   37
Sanders, E. P.   32, 36, 152, 184, 208, 213, 215, 220–21
Sanders, James A.   255
Satterthwaite, Philip E.   214
Scheffler, Eben   303, 328
Schlapbach, Karin   147
Schlaudraff, Karl-Heinz   10
Schultz, Brian   46–47, 290
Schulz, Siegfried   5, 7, 137, 161
Schwartz, Daniel R.   40, 45, 47, 60, 89, 94, 143, 148, 165, 174, 233, 284–85, 330
Schweitzer, Albert   4
Schweitzer, Steven   331
Schweizer, Eduard   14
Scott, James M.   111–12
Scott, Russell T.   78–79, 143–45, 274
Seitel, Peter   25–27, 29
Shackleton Bailey, D. R.   43
Shauf, Scott   4, 12, 16–17, 21, 100, 192
Shillington, V. George   13
Sievers, Joseph   100–1
Skidmore, Clive   43
Slater, D. A.   83
Sleeman, Matthew   309, 311
Smith, Daniel L.   16
Smith, Robert H.   11, 310, 323
Sparks, H. D. F.   7, 50
Spencer, F. Scott   186, 189
Speyer, Wolfgang   232
Spilsbury, Paul   104–106, 285

Squires, John T.   16–17, 21, 42, 49, 100, 136–37, 148–151, 154–55, 157–159, 162, 169, 185, 192, 198–99, 203–4
Stählin, G.   258
Stemberger, Günter   37
Sterling, Gregory E.   15, 22, 27, 36, 48–49, 99, 102–3, 115, 117–18, 120, 124, 130, 137, 184, 189, 199–200, 204, 231, 244, 252, 327
Stone, Michael E.   18, 49–50, 61, 110–11, 288, 291–293
Strazicich, John   307
Stuckenbruck, Loren T   11, 28, 60–61, 98, 179, 270–71, 283–84, 288–89, 295, 297–299, 301, 333, 335
Stylianou, P. J.   41–42, 72
Syme, Ronald   44, 76–79, 164, 238, 274

Talbert, Charles H.   5–7, 9, 15, 22, 52, 129, 245, 250
Talmon, Shemaryahu   288
Tannehill, Robert C.   8, 13, 17, 120, 122, 137, 157, 186–87, 196, 199, 251, 263–265, 302, 310, 322–23
Tanner, Kathryn   209
Taubes, Jacob   59
Thackeray, H. St. J.   101–2, 105, 175–177
Theissen, Gerd   247
Theodorakopoulos, Elena   30, 86, 281
Thomas, Richard F.   109
Thompson, Alan J.   157
Tiller, Patrick A.   224, 297
Todorov, Tzvetan   26
Tomson, P. J.   199
Tov, Emanuel   32, 47

Unnik, W. C. van   148, 152, 175
Uytanlet, Samson   16–17, 21, 51, 137, 139, 150, 165, 192

Van Seters, John   21
VanderKam, James C.   109, 113, 179, 230, 278, 289, 292
Vermes, Geza   46–47, 95, 98–99, 152, 183, 230, 288
Vielhauer, Philipp   3, 5, 340
Villalba i Varneda, Pere   177

Vogel, Manuel 100
Vovelle, Michel 34

Waanders, F. M. J. 58
Walaskay, Paul W. 330
Walbank, F. A. 64, 272
Walbank, Frank W. 24, 29, 65, 67–69, 138, 140–42, 146–47, 165, 169, 238–39, 272
Wallace, Daniel B. 195
Walters, Patricia 54
Walton, Steve 330
Wardle, D 43–44, 164–65, 236
Waterfield, Robin 140
Weinfeld, Moshe 214–15, 331
Wells, Kyle B. 12, 208–210, 215, 242
West, D. A. 85, 240, 281
White, Hayden 23

Wilckens, Ulrich 5, 7
Willett, Tom W. 229
Williams, Gordon 78
Williams, Howard 269
Williams, R. D. 42, 82, 84, 277, 279, 281
Wilson, S. G. 8
Witherington, Ben, III 35, 305, 307–8
Wolter, Michael 61–62, 188, 232, 247, 249, 302, 311, 315–317
Woude, Adam S. van der 46–47
Wright, N. T. 61, 81, 97, 116, 228, 254, 310, 318

York, John O. 252, 254, 256–57, 302
Young, Frances 231

Zerwick, Max 194, 305, 348

# Index of subjects

agency, models of divine and human agency   208–12, 215–16, 219, 229–30, 241–43, 251, 261n220, 266
Antiochus IV   48, 66n43, 89n161, 91–92, 100–1, 104–5, 145, 218, 220, 225n68, 232–34, 238, 247, 265n237, 266
apocalypse, genre   10–11, 18–19, 26, 28–29, 31, 39–40, 51–52, 59–62, 88, 99–100, 108–9, 111, 126, 180–182, 228n80, 244n142, 297n116, 331–333, 339–40
apocalypticism   18, 28n41, 40, 100, 103–4, 180n205, 209n12, 217n42, 332
– „Apocalyptic eschatology"   6n24, 8, 10, 13n51, 40, 61, 99, 100n210, 104n230
– apocalypticism and Paul   11–12, 61, 210n17, 230–31n91, 270–71, 298n121
– definitions of apocalypticism   18n74, 28n41, 39–40, 180
augury   166–67, 175n185
Augustus   42–43, 76–77, 79, 84–87, 109n253, 164n145, 278–281

Belial   98n202, 183, 229–231, 242, 290, 299
biography, genre   15–17, 22n7, 25n22, 38n77, 52–53

Chrysostom, John   105n233, 199n284, 285n73
covenant   61n19, 87, 96, 108, 114, 208, 215–16, 223, 225, 287n79, 289–90, 298, 303n138
creation   59, 61n19, 81, 87, 92, 94, 96, 105, 108, 111, 114, 123–24, 129, 133, 181, 218, 230–31n91, 291, 295n113, 298, 303n138
cyclical schemas of history   59–60, 82–83, 84n135, 89, 95n189, 284n68, 295n113, 330n246

Day of the Lord or judgement, the   121–22, 125–26, 188n238, 302, 313–14, 319n204, 324, 351
decline, historical   52, 58, 60n17, 62, 63n28, 72nn74&75, 76–80, 81n121, 83, 105, 107–14, 135n2, 180–81n207, 274, 293, 295, 333
– ageing of the world   63n29, 107, 112
– moral decline   63, 72n74, 76–77, 78–80, 235, 274–75
destruction of
– Carthage   40, 68, 273
– Jerusalem/Jerusalem temple   37, 47–50, 80n117, 105–7, 125n312, 127, 175–78, 205–6, 211, 221–22, 228n81, 248n165, 270n4, 299–300, 317n198, 318–21, 328
– Rome   67–69, 71–72, 80, 99, 103–6, 133, 221, 228, 273, 285–86, 292, 297
– Troy   42, 70, 82, 86, 277
determinism   19, 30–31, 43, 48, 50, 56, 59, 100, 135, 137, 139, 146n48, 149n66, 154, 166, 171–172, 178, 180–184, 196, 203–206, 211, 221, 223–24, 227n75, 228n80, 270, 295, 297n116, 325, 332n256, 337
Deuteronomistic theology   49–50, 90, 146n48, 197n277, 203, 212–29, 241, 243–44, 255n197, 266–67, 294n111
Dionysius of Halicarnassus   52, 64n35, 70n65, 71n68, 136n5, 150nn69&71, 176–77n191
divine plan/βουλή   1, 4n15, 5–6, 7n28, 16, 20, 98, 100n213, 131, 136–138, 149, 156n101, 157, 158nn108&112, 159–60, 162n134, 164, 173, 182–185, 189, 190–204, 206–7, 211n23, 230, 243, 247, 249n170, 250–51, 257–61, 266–67, 271, 302n129, 305n145, 309n165, 327n234, 328n240, 337, 339–41, 343
dreams   104–5, 121, 144, 147, 150, 154, 161–62, 165n145, 166–68, 171–175, 177, 183, 188, 191–92, 258, 260, 286

„early catholicism" 1, 7, 15n56, 343
*ekphrasis* 84, 172n176, 279
elites 44, 76, 79, 153, 252n181
epic 16–17, 19, 22n7, 23, 27, 29, 40, 42–43, 53, 82, 138–39, 189n243, 240–41, 330n245, 340
Epicurianism 32, 105n235, 148–49, 152–53, 179
eschatological war 46, 94–98, 114, 182–83, 229–30, 284, 287, 289–90, 297–99, 334
Eusebius of Caesarea 41n89, 332

fate, εἱμαρμένη/*fatum* 7n28, 16, 85, 135, 137–139, 144–45, 148–159, 161nn124&129, 164, 168–69, 171–72, 175, 178, 203–4, 210–11, 215n36, 221n57, 240n133, 259, 275, 280, 337
Flavians 44, 76–78, 108, 144, 292 (see also Titus and Vespasian)
fortune, τύχη/*fortuna* 16, 29n46, 34, 41, 44, 48n131, 64–67, 69–71, 74, 102–3, 137–148, 150–55, 157, 164–65, 168, 177, 204, 206nn2&4, 238–39, 241, 253–54, 267, 272–275, 337
four- (or five-) kingdom paradigm 93, 103–6, 108–9, 111n261, 112–14, 122n300, 181, 228, 285–6, 297, 332n255

genre 1–2, 14–31, 34n61, 36–40, 43n100, 50, 52, 56, 103, 167n157, 180n205, 182, 235n112
– ancient genre theory 23–24, 30n49
– contemporary genre theory 21–27, 34n61
– definitions of genre 24–27, 40n83
– importance of genre 16, 18, 21–23, 27–28, 31, 56, 100, 103n228, 134, 137, 339–40
– *see also Luke/Acts, genre of*
golden age 30n51, 72–73, 78–80, 82–84, 105–6, 110n254, 114, 239–40, 277–81
Graeco-Roman and Jewish cultural interaction 35–37, 143

Herod 246n155
– Herod the Great 125, 155, 175, 195, 350

– Antipas 197, 244
– Agrippa I 243, 246, 249
– Agrippa II 102n220, 160n122, 190, 205n1, 234, 246n155, 260, 286, 304–6
Herodotus 17n67, 69n58, 138, 139n16, 158n113, 176n191
Hesiod 51, 74n84, 83nn131&132, 109
historicity 5n20, 21–22, 55, 68n52, 89n163, 93n180, 116n276, 151–52n78, 211n19, 213n24, 246–7n156, 248n164, 293n107, 331n251
historiography, genre 2, 14–17, 22–25, 28–29, 38–39, 40n83, 52–53, 55, 76n96, 89, 100, 137–39, 158n110, 180n205
conventions or themes 14–15, 23–24, 28–29, 38–39, 124, 140–41, 187n235
– continuations 38–39, 64n32, 130
– moral focus 29n46, 42, 44–45, 52, 70–73, 76–77, 140n18, 156, 233n101, 235, 273n14
– political or military focus 41, 67, 71n67, 77, 140n18, 142n27, 272–73
– universal (or general) historiography 41–42, 65, 68–71, 80, 113, 141n23, 147–48, 272–73
history of *mentalité* 32–35
Homer 16n61, 42, 51, 82, 84, 138, 171n174, 189n243, 240

Ignatius of Antioch 305n147
individual eschatology 88–92, 100–2, 303
insight of a privileged group, eschatological moment 98, 101, 110, 126, 178, 180–81, 187n235, 191–92, 278, 291–93
irony 24, 44, 86–87, 91n173, 109n253, 112–13, 156n103, 164–65n145, 167–69, 171–72, 186n231, 190, 194, 196, 199–200, 203, 234, 237, 240, 247, 260, 306, 309n165, 313

Jerusalem 35, 80n117, 105n233, 111, 125, 127, 163n141, 175, 185n225, 188, 190, 194, 200, 202, 257–260, 315–320, 322–24
– destruction of *see Destruction*

- heavenly   see Zion
- Temple   36n68, 47n125, 48–49, 105n233, 106, 107n242, 173, 186, 205, 220–21, 223n65, 228n81, 229n82, 243–44, 270n4, 285n69, 299–300, 318, 349n14
judgement, final   88, 90n167, 92–94, 107n242, 109–10, 122, 123n304, 125–129, 131, 136–37n6, 181, 204, 218, 224–25, 229, 245, 266, 271, 287–88, 291–93, 295, 302–3, 306n149, 307, 309–311, 313–14, 317, 318n200, 320n209, 325, 327, 328n238, 339, 350
Justin Martyr   305n147

Kittim, the   46n121, 95, 105n234, 182, 287n79, 288n85, 290, 297n117

Livy   40n85, 52, 70n65, 76, 79n111, 150n68
Lucian of Samosata   23n11, 52, 76n96, 176n191
Luke/Acts
- audience of   35, 187n235, 199n287, 315–16
- authorship of   36–37, 54n152, 55
- date of   1n5, 55
- genre of   1–2, 14–18, 22, 28–31, 37–40, 43n100, 137, 339–41
- literary unity of   54–55, 263n228

martyrdom   88, 90–92, 94, 132, 162n132, 217–18, 233–34, 250–51, 283–84, 303n139, 308–9, 333
messianic woes   88, 110, 122, 125, 127–28, 283, 286, 289, 291, 293–95, 301–3, 328n238, 333, 338, 348, 350

necessity   4n15, 13n52, 72–73, 114, 149n66, 150nn67&71, 151, 153–164, 168, 194, 259n214, 305, 323n218, 332n256
- ἀνάγκη/necessitas   4n15, 139n11, 150–51n71, 153–57, 164, 168, 204
- δεῖ   28n42, 29n46, 139, 151n71, 157–65, 185, 189, 196n271, 198, 202, 305, 337
nostalgia   52, 62, 76, 83, 105–6, 274, 281, 294
novel (ancient), genre   16, 22n7

olympiads   64–66, 70, 80
opponents   20, 50n139, 88, 89n161, 92, 196n273, 197, 210–212, 216, 219, 221–227, 229, 235, 237–43, 246n155, 247n156, 265–267, 290n93, 296, 299, 338, 348
- of God, θεομάχοι   89n161, 198–99, 220, 231–34, 242–43, 246–51, 265n237, 266–67
Orosius   332

panegyric   164n145, 279
parousia, delay of   3–10, 13–14, 18n73, 58, 116n276, 136, 206, 308n162, 310n167, 311–16, 319–323, 326, 330n245, 332–33
periodisation of history   3–8, 19, 58–62, 64–67, 70, 73, 75–77, 80, 82–83, 88, 93, 95–96, 98–105, 107–9, 111–28, 133, 135n1, 180, 181n207, 182, 201, 207, 249n169, 270, 283, 286, 287n79, 289–91, 294–95, 297n116, 301, 307–10, 312n172, 320n208, 321n212, 322–24, 326, 329, 331–33, 335–39, 341, 343–51
Philo of Alexandria   36–37, 53, 89n159, 99n207, 119n286, 231n91
philosophy of history, post-war   7n30, 59–60, 138n9, 336, 342–43
Pliny   52, 176n191
politics, of Luke/Acts   2, 4, 136n3, 174n184, 196–97, 206–7, 253n187, 262n223, 322–24, 327n235, 330–35, 339, 342–43
portents   166–70, 173–75, 177–78, 183, 185n224, 191–92, 237, 319
post-mortem reward or punishment   73, 88–94, 96n194, 217–18, 254–55, 277, 296, 302, 333
progress, historical   60, 62–73, 82–87, 114, 132, 148, 272–73, 281n55, 282–83, 336
prophecy   39–40, 43, 46, 48, 67–69, 80, 81n120, 83, 85–87, 100–1, 105, 108–9, 117, 118n280, 124–30, 133, 137, 140–42, 144, 150, 152n79, 160–64, 166–92, 196n275, 200–1, 203–4, 237,

251–53, 257–60, 262n223, 263–65, 276–81, 285–86, 289, 292n105, 292–97, 304–8, 312n173, 318–21, 324–25, 337–38, 343, 345n2
providence, πρόνοια/*providentia* 16, 29, 42, 53, 70–71, 73, 99–100, 136–37, 141n24, 143nn31&33, 146–49, 151, 152n79, 154, 155n96, 157, 164–65, 169, 179, 185n224, 204, 206n4, 211, 215n36, 220n54, 233, 238, 244n145, 246, 341
punitive miracle 231–34, 246–51

Qumran community 47, 97n195, 230, 288–90

redaction criticism 4n16, 5, 13, 55, 302n133, 308n158, 319–20, 328n240, 340
repentance 48, 106, 123n306, 126, 128, 177–78, 185n224, 196, 201, 202n297, 220–22, 240, 244n142, 245–46, 248, 249n166, 254, 260–62, 265n236, 286, 293–94, 297, 309–10, 325–29, 333, 335, 338, 343–44
restoration within history 30–31, 45, 88–90, 94, 213–19, 224, 248, 284–85, 296, 333
resurrection
of Jesus 9–10, 20, 117–18, 122–23, 126, 129–132, 163–64, 190, 193, 196, 199–200, 203–4, 207n7, 250n172, 255n196, 261–62, 265–66, 298n121, 304–7, 309–10, 312n173, 324–25, 327–31, 333–35, 337–39, 343–44, 349n14, 350
general 87–89, 91–94, 97, 100n254, 111–12, 119, 131, 134, 187, 283, 286n77, 287n79, 291, 295, 302–6, 334, 338
reversal 79, 81n121, 97–98, 142n26, 144, 146, 163, 174, 224, 243, 251–257, 262n221, 264, 267, 275n24, 302
„rewritten Bible" 303n138
rhetoric 14, 17–18, 23n8, 28–29, 31–32, 34, 75–76, 100–1, 124n309, 137, 141, 152n78, 158, 160–61n123, 161n129, 180, 184n223, 187n235, 189n293, 204, 248n164, 261n220, 302, 305, 341

„rule of the stronger" 103, 141n22, 177, 199n285, 205, 234, 286

*saeculum* festival 73, 74n84, 102, 106
Sallust 17n68, 25n22, 52, 79n111
sealed books 180–81, 292n105
Second World War 3–4, 7n30, 10, 59–60, 86n148, 138n9, 279n45, 336, 341–43
Septuagint 36, 38–39, 45n114, 51, 95n191, 103, 105n234, 115, 118n283, 119n289, 120–21, 125, 127n321, 130, 149, 150n67, 158n110, 161nn125&127, 188n238, 194, 197nn276&278, 233, 263, 264n231, 307
Stoicism 30, 32, 52, 90, 113n268, 141n24, 146–47, 149n66, 150n71, 152–55, 162n137, 208n10, 217, 220n55, 221n57, 241, 259n211, 339
suffering 2, 4, 12, 20, 31, 86n148, 111, 130n333, 132, 135, 160–164, 171, 181, 184, 190, 196nn271&272, 201n294, 202, 206–7, 210n18, 216–217, 222n63, 223, 226n72, 227–28, 231–32, 234, 243–46, 251, 257–259, 271, 281–283, 285n72, 297, 303n136, 304–6, 309, 312n173, 313, 315–16, 326–329, 331–35, 339, 343
– as sign of the end 4, 62, 81n121, 109, 125, 128, 291
– suffering as discipline 83n131, 90–91, 162n137, 213–17, 219

teleology
– Literary technique 69n58, 166n151
– View of history 2, 19, 43, 50, 53, 58–63, 69n58, 74n84, 76, 79n115, 80–81, 85–88, 89n159, 93–94, 98–99, 106–7, 109n253, 111, 112n264, 114, 129–34, 138, 179–80, 203–4, 239, 269n1, 270, 272, 276, 282–83, 285, 296, 303, 332, 337, 341
temporal terminology
– αἰών 73, 101, 118–20, 128, 345–46
– ἡμέρα 125, 127, 349–51
– καιρός 65–67, 70, 93, 95n191, 101, 115n271, 118n283, 119–23, 127–28, 133, 145, 272, 307n155, 322–23, 346

– χρόνος  65n38, 67n49, 70, 93, 95n187, 115n271, 118n283, 119–23, 126, 128, 133, 322–23, 347
– ὥρα  125, 348
– *saeculum*  74n84, 75, 77, 82–83, 169n164, 276n29, 278, 293
– *tempus*  85, 293
theodicy  61n20, 110n255, 216n40, 217–39, 241–42, 229n84, 244–46
*theologia gloriae/theologia crucis*  4n15, 7, 163n138, 206, 266, 328, 331, 339, 343
Thucydides  17nn67&68, 25n22, 38–39, 51, 52n147, 103n226, 138n10, 140n19, 159n116, 176n191, 206n2
Titus  48, 100, 170nn170&171, 220
tragic themes  15n57, 24, 91n169
two-age framework  8, 10, 61, 111n261, 115n272, 119n286

universality  11n45, 20, 84, 129n328, 186n231, 212, 226n74, 260–61, 262n221, 265n236, 267, 287, 310–311, 324, 338
*Urzeit zu Endzeit*  59, 68, 81, 108, 111, 123, 129, 133, 181, 295n113, 297n116
utopia  72–73, 282, 331–32, 338

*vaticinium ex eventu*  31, 49, 58n6, 84, 86, 107, 114, 127n332, 150, 166, 171–72, 179, 182–84, 191, 214, 278, 280n51, 292, 318, 320, 326
Vespasian  48, 78, 101–2, 143n31, 144, 151, 164n145, 169n163, 170
vindication of the righteous  59, 62n26, 104, 107, 110, 113–14, 126, 131, 136, 188, 201, 225, 245, 250n172, 284, 287–88, 291, 295, 302–3, 317, 327–28, 333

Zion, glorious  88, 110, 111n261, 299–300, 309

www.ingramcontent.com/pod-product-compliance
Lightning Source LLC
Chambersburg PA
CBHW031410230426
43668CB00007B/267